GW00578343

THE FIRST
BATTLE
OF THE
FIRST WORLD
WAR

With the permission of the Bavarian Army Archive

Bayerisches Hauptstaatsarchiv
Abt. IV Kriegsarchiv
Leonrodstraße 57
80636 München
www.gda.bayern.de

THE FIRST BATTLE
OF THE
FIRST WORLD WAR

ALSACE-LORRAINE

KARL DEURINGER

TRANSLATED AND EDITED BY TERENCE ZUBER

Cover image: French infantrymen bayonet charge, 1914.

First published 2014

The History Press
The Mill, Brimscombe Port
Stroud, Gloucestershire, GL5 2QG
www.thehistorypress.co.uk

© Karl Deuringer, ed. Terence Zuber, 2014

British Library Cataloguing in Publication Data.
A catalogue record for this book is available from the British Library.

ISBN 978 0 7524 6086 4

Typesetting and origination by Thomas Bohm, User design
Printed in Great Britain

Contents

Preface

This book recounts not only the first battle of the First World War, but also the only battle in which the Bavarian Army, under Bavarian leadership, fought independently. Later it would be split up to fight as Bavarian corps, and even divisions, mixed with other formations of the German Army. All of the source material available in the Bavarian State archives in 1929, principally war diaries and after-action reports, was drawn upon. These were usually meagre, incomplete and inexact.[1] The Bavarian documents were supplemented with the 1st, 3rd and 4th volumes of the *Reichsarchiv* Official German History, *Der Weltkrieg*,[2] the available portion (to 5 September 1914) of the French General Staff Official History,[3] and two other French works.[4]

Every attempt was made to present the events accurately, even when this was sometimes not flattering. The only way that the purpose of all military history, which is to instruct future generations, can be accomplished and fostered is by an unvarnished presentation of the events. In particular, the German people have a serious need to investigate the reasons for its defeat, and to recognise and acknowledge the mistakes that were made. No criticism can be made of the troop units and their leaders. They were all motivated by the desire to do their best. Considering the enormous friction that accompanies everything in war, errors and mistakes cannot be avoided.

Names are mentioned only to the limited degree that the source document itself requires. In our present time, the cause is to be placed above the individual, the deed above the name. In the last analysis, every unit's accomplishments were a joint effort.

Various considerations have caused the Bavarian Army Archive to limit its description of the deeds of the non-Bavarian units. Nevertheless, their contribution is always recognised to the degree necessary to understand the continuity and form of the overall Battle of Lorraine. The Bavarian Army Archive thanks the *Reichsarchiv* in Potsdam for the assistance it provided in this matter.

Translator/Editor Preface

The first great battle of the First World War began with an offensive by the French First and Second Armies into German Lorraine on 14 August 1914. The first massive clash of arms in the Great War came when the Germans counter-attacked in Lorraine on 20 August, a stunning German tactical victory, followed by a disorderly French retreat back into France.

The battle in Lorraine, and not the later battles in the Ardennes or northern Belgium, had been anticipated by both sides since 1872. Indeed, until Joffre decided to conduct the main French offensive into Belgium on 2 August, he had always reserved the option of conducting the decisive offensive in Lorraine. As late as 15 August, Moltke believed that the main French offensive would be made in Lorraine. Nevertheless, the only references to this battle in French, English or German histories are short one- or two-page summaries in accounts of the Marne Campaign: most of these are uninformative (generally ascribing German success to 'heavy artillery') and some positively erroneous.

There has only been one serious monograph on this battle: Karl Deuringer's *Die Schlacht in Lothringen und in den Vogesen 1914* (*The Battle in Lorraine and the Vosges 1914*), published by the Bavarian Army Archive (*Bayerisches Kriegsarchiv*) in 1929. The challenge as translator and editor was to condense *Die Schlacht in Lothringen* into something that could be published today.[5]

Lorraine was defended by the German Sixth Army, almost all of whose major units were Bavarian, commanded by the Bavarian Crown Prince. This would also be the last time that the Bavarian Army, whose history went back to the early seventeenth century, would fight as a unit. After Lorraine, the Bavarian corps would be intermixed with those of Prussia and the other German states. The

Bavarian Army Archive wanted to record this last great battle in an appropriate manner, so Deuringer produced a two-volume, 893-page work with 74 maps (including a total of seven extra large map sheets in pockets at the back of both volumes). Deuringer chronicled the entire Bavarian battle in Alsace-Lorraine until it was broken off by both sides in mid-September.

The one-month timeframe meant that Deuringer had to focus on the decisions taken at the Sixth Army level and tactical operations at the battalion level. He was simply unable to describe small-unit tactics at the squad, platoon and company levels. In Deuringer's time, the Bavarian Army Archive was reputed to be a disguised continuation of the Bavarian General Staff, and the professional support Deuringer received is clearest in the quality of the maps. The war diaries and after-action reports held by the archive are the best of their kind. Given the destruction of the *Reichsarchiv* by British bombers on the night of 14 April 1945, the Bavarian Army Archive is rivalled only by the Baden-Württemberg Archives in Karlsruhe and Stuttgart.

Deuringer has little to say about the French Army. In fact, even today, there is practically no good information on the French Army in Alsace-Lorraine; the source material available at the French Army Archive at Vincennes is distressingly meagre, while most of the French regimental war diaries are practically worthless. There are no monographs. He gleaned what he could from the French Official History, which does not go below the corps level, and that is probably all anyone will be able to do. Deuringer also only discussed casualties in the most general terms, as 'light' or 'heavy' etc. The Bavarian Army was in serious contact for an entire month and determining the casualties on a specific day was generally difficult. Deuringer also clearly wanted to focus on tactics rather than body count, which would be meaningless anyway because there were no figures for French casualties.

The German Army realised that it was massively outnumbered in a two-front war and faced an immediate manpower crisis. The desperate measures this led the Germans to take are clearly revealed in Deuringer's description of the battle in the Vosges, where the Germans committed *Ersatz* (replacement) units, which only had basic weapons, no equipment or unit training, and *Landwehr* units, composed of family men 33–39 years old, into mountain warfare. No other army dared to take such steps; however, the German *Ersatz* and *Landwehr* units generally performed as well as the French active army units.

The German combined-arms team won a shattering tactical victory on 20 August, wrecking the French infantry, which thereafter was no longer capable of offensive action and frequently unable to hold its defensive positions. On the other hand, as of 24 August, the French artillery came into its own, pummelling the German infantry whether it was on the offensive or defensive. German counter-battery fire was generally ineffective. In the first week of September, the

German infantry began to adapt to avoid the French artillery by digging in more effectively and conducting night attacks. I intend to show in future works that this was not an isolated development. The German right wing was held at bay by French rearguard artillery. The decisive factors during the Battle of the Marne were not strategic or operational, but the fact that the French Army opened their artillery magazines and buried the German infantry in a hail of shells, leading to similar adaptations by the German infantry.

Anyone who wants to learn about German war planning and strategy during the Marne Campaign should consult *The Real German War Plan, 1904–1914* (The History Press, 2011). For German tactical doctrine and training, see the opening chapters of *The Battle of the Frontiers, Ardennes 1914* (Tempus, 2007) or *The Mons Myth* (The History Press, 2010).

A Note on the Maps

The First Battle of the First Word War includes, in the text, thirty-one map sketches (on scales from 1:25,000 to 1:75,000).

There is also a general map of the Franco-German border area (1:300,000), three large situation maps (I, II, and III; scale 1:100,000), nine situation maps (numbered a to i; scale 1:1,000,000) and thirty situation maps (scale 1:50,000). These were all very large (map 4, Mörchingen 20.8 II b. AK, is about 10in × 14in, or 250mm × 330mm) and in the German original were included in very large sheets located in a pocket at the back of each volume. It was not possible to reprint these maps by conventional means; therefore, we have made these large maps, and the maps already in the book, available online.

This has two additional advantages. First, the nine situation maps and some of the thirty large maps are in colour, which can be seen online. Second, the maps are all highly detailed and can be enlarged online.

German dates are day first, followed by the month – 24.8 is 24 August.

The German letter ß is a double s.

The maps are available at www.thehistorypress.co.uk/first-battle.

Glossary

AK	*Armeekorps* (Army Corps)
b.	*bayerisch* (Bavarian)
Bde	Brigade
Berg	Hill
Bhf	*Bahnhof* (Rail Station)
Bn	Battalion
Bty	Battery
Chevauleger	Light cavalry
Co.	Company
Cpl	Corporal
Div.	Division
ED	*Ersatz* Division
Eng.	Engineer
FA	Field Artillery
FO	Forward Observer
GR	Grenadier Regiment
GQG	*Grand Quartier Général* (French Senior HQ)
Jäger	Light Infantry Battalion
Jäger zu Pferde	Light Cavalry
HKK 3	*Heereskavalleriekorps 3* (Cavalry Corps 3)
ID	Infantry Division
IR	*Infanterie-Regiment* (Infantry Regiment)
KD	*Kavalleriedivision* (Cavalry Division)
L	*Landwehr*

LIR	*Landwehr* Infantry Regiment
LNO	Liaison Officer
MG	Machine Gun
MGK	Machine Gun Company
MP	Military Police
NCO	Non-Commissioned Officer
OHL	*Oberste Heeresleitung* (German Senior HQ)
OP	Observation Post
Pr.	*Preußisch* (Prussian)
POW	prisoner of war
R	Regiment
RD	Reserve Division
Res.	Reserve
RFAR	*Reserve Feldartillerie-Regiment* (Reserve FA Regiment)
RIR	*Reserve Infanterie-Regiment* (Reserve Regiment)
RK	*Reserve-Korps* (Reserve Corps)
Rücken	Ridge
Sec.	Section
sFH	*schwere Feldhaubitze* (Heavy Howitzer)
Sqn	Squadron
Wald	Forest
Weiher	Pond
Wü.	*Württemberg*

I/IR 3	1st Battalion, Infantry Regiment 3
II/RIR 6	2nd Battalion, Reserve Infantry Regiment 6
3/LIR 12	3rd Company, *Landwehr* Infantry Regiment 12
4/*Ersatz* Bde IV	4th Company, *Ersatz* Brigade IV
I/FAR 7	1st Section, Field Artillery Regiment 7
6/Foot Artillery R 1	6th Battery, Foot (Heavy) Artillery Regiment 1
2 *Ersatz*/FAR 8	2nd *Ersatz* Battery, Field Artillery Regiment 8
I/RFAR 2	1st Section, Reserve Field Artillery Regiment 2
3/Eng. Bn 2	3rd Company, Engineer Battalion 2
1 Res/Eng. Bn 4	1st Reserve Company, Engineer Battalion 4
2 *Ersatz*/Eng. Bn 1	2nd *Ersatz* Company, Engineer Battalion 1

The Bavarian Army
at the Outbreak of War

The Peacetime Army

The Bavarian Army at the outbreak of the war can be considered from two points of view. From the outside it appeared to be an integral part of the German Army, but from within it was a complete, separate and independent army. The titular commander of the army was the King of Bavaria; the War Minister exercised command in his name, as well as having administrative authority. The Bavarian General Staff was subordinate to the Bavarian War Ministry. This was in contrast to Prussia, where, in addition to the War Ministry, the Military Cabinet, Great General Staff, Corps Commanding Generals and General Inspectors of the various arms all had immediate access to the King.

The peacetime Bavarian Army consisted of three corps, each with two divisions:

24 infantry regiments (72 battalions)[6]
2 *Jäger* (light infantry) battalions
1 machine-gun section
12 cavalry regiments (57 squadrons)[7]
12 field artillery regiments (72 field artillery batteries, 3 horse artillery batteries)[8]
3 foot (heavy) artillery regiments (22 batteries and 4 draught horse sections)
4 engineer battalions (14 companies)
1 railroad battalion
2 telegraph battalions (5 companies and a draught horse section), plus a cavalry telegraph school
1 transportation battalion (1 airship and 1 truck company)

1 aviation battalion (aviation company and flight school)
3 supply battalions (12 companies)

The production, procurement and administration of military equipment was the responsibility of the Bavarian Quartermaster Office, which included a small-arms factory in Amberg, a gun foundry and munitions plant in Ingolstadt, an artillery maintenance plant in Munich, the central laboratory and a powder works in Ingolstadt, as well as seven artillery depots and three supply depots. Bavaria also administered a separate military educational system, with a General Staff college, artillery, engineer and infantry schools, and a corps of cadets, a school of military equitation and a non-commissioned officer (NCO) academy. Bavaria also possessed a separate army archive, topographic bureau, army museum and library.

Bavaria had three Major Training Areas at Grafenwöhr, Hammelburg and Lechfeld. Troop support was provided by civil servants: commissary officers, facilities managers, garrison administrators and finance officials, etc. There was a military hospital system, including a military medical school. Bavaria had its own military justice system and a military police (MP) corps, with a MP headquarters and a detachment in each of the eight regional governments. The personnel replacement system consisted of three *Landwehr* inspectorates and thirty-four county replacement commands. The Bavarian fortress at Germersheim had gained in importance and been equipped as a bridgehead over the Rhine. The fortress at Ingolstadt had been reduced to caretaker status.

The authorised peacetime strength of the Bavarian Army at the start of the war was 3,375 officers, 289 doctors, 102 veterinarians, 1,015 senior and mid-grade administrators, 11,830 NCOs, 71,295 enlisted men and 16,918 horses.

After the Franco-Prussian War of 1870–1 Bavaria adopted the Prussian military system in accordance with the alliance treaty of 23 November 1870.[9] This did not affect the independence of the Bavarian Army, however. Only with the declaration of war – at the beginning of mobilisation – did the Bavarian Army fall under the command authority of the German Emperor, but still remained an independent element of the German Army under the command and administration of the King of Bavaria. In peacetime, the German Emperor had the right and duty to inspect the Bavarian Army to insure that it was complete and combat effective. Initially, these inspections were entrusted to Prussian officers. In 1892 the Bavarian General of Cavalry, Prince Leopold of Bavaria, was named commander of the newly established Fourth Army Inspectorate in Munich,[10] with a Prussian officer as chief of staff. His successor (in 1912) was General of Infantry Crown Prince Rupprecht of Bavaria. Bavaria also maintained a military representative in Berlin.

The King of Bavaria enjoyed complete freedom in military personnel matters, and could determine the locations of garrisons.[11] All other units of the German Army received numbers according to the Prussian system, except the Bavarian units. To support the army, Bavaria annually received a portion of the German tax revenues, based on the authorised strength of the army. The internal financial administration was the responsibility of the Bavarian Army.

The Bavarian Army before the war had shortcomings, which it shared with the rest of the German Army. The important role that technology played in all aspects of modern war was recognised too slowly in training and equipping the army: vehicular mobility was underdeveloped; communications between aircraft and ground units was not thought through, tested and insured; and stocks of ammunition held in peacetime were not nearly adequate to feed the modern quick-firing weapons. Above all, the army was numerically weak. While France conscripted no fewer than 80 per cent of those eligible, which is to say anyone who could possibly serve, Germany did not exploit its numerical superiority. Even considering the far higher physical standards in the German Army, a considerable percentage of physically fit young German men were never conscripted; the size of the peacetime army, set by law, did not allow it. Those who were not conscripted were to have served for a short training period, but even this proved to be impossible. No preparations were made to train, equip and arm these men, and form them into units on the outbreak of war. The Great General Staff attempted to realise reforms several times before the war, but was continually prevented from doing so by false economy. This at a time (7 August 1913) when the French passed the Three Year Service law, laying the heaviest of burdens on its citizens.

In 1913 in Bavaria, 66,338 men were mustered for conscription. In total, 3,603 were removed as permanently unfit and 133 found ineligible to serve because of a criminal record, so that 3,736 men, or 5.6 per cent, were immediately found unsuitable. Consequently, 42,915 were found completely fit for service, or 64.7 per cent, but of these, including 5,139 volunteers, only 41,158 were inducted, or 62.1 per cent. No fewer than 1,757 (45,000 in all of Germany) completely fit men (2.6 per cent) were declared supernumerary or, due to family circumstances, sent to the *Landwehr* or the *Ersatz* (replacement) reserve, together with 19,687 limited duty or temporarily unavailable (27.9 per cent). Therefore, in Bavaria in one year alone 21,444 young men, almost a third (32.3 per cent), who in France for the most part certainly would have been conscripted, were free from service and remained without training whatsoever. If, as in France, 80 per cent were conscripted instead of 62.1 per cent – 11,912 more men in 1913 alone – Bavaria could have raised a seventh infantry division in peacetime and a second reserve corps in wartime.

The spirit and inner constitution of the Bavarian Army was sound. The army worked with feverish determination, year in and year out, but perhaps too much as, at the beginning of the war, many of the officers and NCOs were not fresh and well rested. To some degree this was due to the increasing workload heaped on the officers, with many units short of lieutenants. Many of the company commanders, who are the backbone of their units in peace and war, were too old – in the infantry even the youngest were 36 years old.

Strict discipline in peacetime did not undermine the trust between officers, NCOs and men, but rather reinforced it. In spite of its stiff formalities, the old army was characterised by fairness and comradeship. Promotion to the highest ranks was open to every man without regard to origin and birth. The Bavarian units in the last peacetime years could stand comparison with any other in the German Army.

Mobilisation

The mobilisation of the army was prepared in detail. In addition to the necessary quantities of clothing, equipment, tools, weapons and ammunition, the mobilisation calendar (written each winter and put into effect on 1 April) contained exact instructions for the sequence of mobilisation measures – nothing was forgotten. The short mobilisation order served to set the entire machine in motion. As well as the mobilisation of the regular army, there were also reserve, *Landwehr*, *Ersatz*, *Landsturm* and rear-echelon, units that had to be created outright.[12]

In the last years before the war, the mobilisation calendar had become more complex, as the possibility of a sudden enemy attack increased, especially after France introduced the three-year conscript duty, which in turn raised the number of troops present for duty in each French unit and reduced the length of time the French needed to mobilise. Special measures were taken to quickly recall reservists in the winter because that year's class of conscripts was still untrained. Further measures were introduced for a 'Period Preparatory to War'. As the situation became more serious at the end of July, a series of non-threatening measures were taken in order to insure the smooth functioning of a later mobilisation. As of 28 July, armed railwaymen guarded the most important installations against foreign or domestic sabotage. On 30 July I/Foot Artillery R (Regiment) 1 provided anti-aircraft gun protection for the Rhine bridge at Germersheim.

Because the fortress of Metz was exposed to surprise attack, on 26 July I/Foot Artillery R 2 occupied its wartime positions in the armoured gun positions of the west-facing Forts Lothringen, Leipzig and Kronprinz. On 29 July Infantry Regiment (IR) 4 and IR 8 conducted a field training exercise in blue peacetime uniforms in their wartime defensive positions on the Gravelotte–St Privat battlefield and occupied the armoured forts there with security detachments, and *Cheveauleger* (light cavalry) R 3 deployed security posts to the border. All Bavarian troops at the Major Training Areas and all troops on leave were ordered to return to garrison.

At 1400hrs on 31 July the order to institute the 'Period Preparatory to War' arrived from Berlin at the Bavarian War Ministry and was transmitted to the Bavarian Army. Between 120 and 410 reservists per infantry regiment (about ten to thirty-five per infantry company) were recalled to bring these units to the highest peacetime manning level. All rail installations were provided with security detachments, which were local home guardsmen, but in the Rhineland-Palatinate, close to the French border, they were reinforced by troops from 3 Infantry Division (ID). Four infantry regiments also secured Rhine bridges at Speyer and Germersheim, and another a bridge in Lorraine. The previously deployed border security units (IR 4, IR 8, plus all of *Chevauleger* R 3) occupied their defensive positions in earnest. All troops were given strict instructions not to initiate hostilities, open fire or enter French territory. On the other hand, French patrols crossed the border on 30 July at St Marie-aux-Chênes, northwest of Metz. A press blackout on military activities was instituted. The Rhineland-Palatinate was placed under martial law.

At 1740hrs on 1 August the order to mobilise the German Army was issued in Berlin, arriving in Munich at 1800hrs, with the first day of mobilisation set for 2 August.

The French Army, with three-year conscript service, enjoyed a higher state of readiness than the Germans, who only had a two-year service. In particular, the infantry companies of French border corps were kept at a peacetime strength of 150–200 men[13], which would allow early attacks into German territory. This required the German Army to immediately deploy a covering force to the border. At 2000hrs on 2 August, the first day of mobilisation, each of the three Bavarian corps deployed an infantry brigade, reinforced with one or two cavalry squadrons and an artillery section. All these units were at peacetime strength, the infantry battalions with 11 to 14 officers and 456 to 614 men on 14 horse-drawn vehicles (including ammunition wagons and field kitchens), the cavalry squadrons with 5 to 8 officers and 142 to 165 men, the artillery with 4 light howitzers, but with only the guns and ammunition caissons, and no light ammunition columns. These units then mobilised on the border on 5 and 6 August. The covering force was reinforced by the Bavarian Cavalry Division (b. KD) and the Bavarian *Jäger* Battalions (Bn) 1 and 2, whose reservists reported directly to their units on the first and second days, and were ready to move on the second and third days of mobilisation.

For the most part, the mobilisation proceeded smoothly and according to plan. The men reported to the district recruiting office and were then transported as a group by train to the troop units; the reservists travelled on the second, third and fourth mobilisation days; the *Landwehr* men on the fourth, fifth and sixth days, some earlier. For reasons of speed and simplicity it was not always possible to allow every man to return to the unit with which he had conducted his peacetime service. Only the reservists or *Landwehr* men who had served in the Household Infantry Regiment (*Infanterie-Leibregiment*, in effect the Bavarian Guard Regiment) were returned to the regiment. Many Bavarians who had moved to other parts of Germany were sent to non-Bavarian units.

The necessary riding and draft horses were requisitioned from the first to the seventh mobilisation days, though a high proportion of the horses found fit for duty were not used – only 61 per cent in the Bavarian III Corps (III b. AK) area, for example. The horses and their escorts were sent in groups, usually by road, to the troop units. The unequal distribution of horses made some rail movement necessary. At the same time, the necessary wagons and harnesses for the combat and rear-echelon supply units were requisitioned, as were motor vehicles.

In general, the units were given two days after the arrival of the last reservists and requisitioned horses to organise themselves. The active duty troops had to turn in peacetime blue uniforms and be issued with wartime field grey; the reservists had to be issued everything, including boots, field equipment and weapons. The harnesses had to be fitted to the horses, the unridden horses broken and the horse teams trained to pull together. So far as possible, the units established their inner cohesion during this time.

The active army infantry and divisional cavalry were ready to deploy on the fifth and sixth mobilisation days (6 and 7 August), the field artillery between the fifth and seventh days, the heavy artillery on the eighth day, engineers on the sixth day, signals on the fourth and fifth days, aviation on the fifth day, medical on the fifth, sixth and eighth days, ammunition and supply on the eighth, ninth and tenth days, and the field bakeries on the third and fifth days.

The reserve combat units were ready to deploy on the eighth, signal units already on the fourth day, ammunition and supply on the ninth and tenth days, and field bakeries on the sixth day. *Landwehr* units that were to be used in the field were in part ready on the ninth, in part on the twelfth day. The fortress garrisons were ready between the fifth and eighth days, and the labour units on the fourth day. Some of the lines-of-communication troops, lorry columns and railway units were available immediately or on the first day, and the mass of the rear-echelon units ready on the twelfth day.

The larger part of the professional officers remained with the manoeuvre units. Nevertheless, only a quarter of the infantry and field artillery platoon leaders were professional officers, half were reserve officers and a quarter were active army or reserve officer candidates. Conversely, professional officers predominated the cavalry units.

In reserve infantry and field artillery units the regimental, battalion and artillery section commanders were professional officers. Five-sixths of the infantry company commanders and three-quarters of the artillery battery commanders were professional officers, while the platoon leaders were either reserve officers or officer candidates, generally in the proportion of 2:1 or 1:1.

In the *Landwehr* infantry, only the regimental commanders and battalion commanders were professional officers. Company commanders were reserve officers or former professional officers, while platoon leaders were equal parts reserve and *Landwehr* officers, officer candidates and NCOs.

The *Ersatz* battalions of infantry regiments usually had four to eight (sometimes up to fourteen) professional officers, while the field artillery *Ersatz* detachments had two to four. All other replacement units had either former professional officers or reserve officers. Many positions were filled with officer candidates and NCOs.

Overall, the active army infantry units gave up 43 per cent, and the field artillery 29 per cent, of their professional officers to higher staffs, reserve units, *Landwehr* units, replacement detachments and so forth.

The capabilities of each unit were largely determined by the age of the enlisted personnel. After mobilisation, the active army units, which had the greatest combat power, were made up of equal parts serving conscripts and of the youngest classes of reservists. The reserve units consisted of a small cadre of active duty troops and equal parts of reservists and *Landwehr* Class I men (28–32 years old). The largest part of the *Landwehr* units was composed of *Landwehr* Class II men (33–39 years old). The artillery included *Landwehr* men, usually employed as drivers. The proportion of active army, reserve, *Landwehr* and *Ersatz* NCOs was the same in the various units as the enlisted personnel.

The percentage of reservists and *Landwehr* in the units varied according to the number of men locally available:

	Active army	Reserve	*Landwehr* Class I	*Landwehr* Class II
Infantry				
Active army	53–58	42–47		
Reserve	1–1.5	36–60	39–62	
Field *Landwehr*			17–48	52–83
Garrison *Landwehr*	2–14	86–98		
Cavalry				
Active army	56–91	9–44		
Reserve	2–20	52–64	16–46	
Landwehr	100			

Table continued on next page

	Active army	Reserve	*Landwehr* Class I	*Landwehr* Class II
Field Artillery				
Active army	46–48	42–52	2–10	
Reserve	10–23	11–47	34–66	
Foot Artillery				
Heavy Artillery	44	28–32	6–16	10–22
Reserve	1.5–3	36–49	18–43	13–35
Landwehr	1		22–40	59–77
Engineers				
Active army	53–57	43–47		
Fortress	39	43	18	
Reserve	9	41–82	9–50	
Landwehr	0.5	5	62–100	0–38

On 1 August each corps was ordered to assemble a brigade of *Ersatz* troops – to be employed in combat operations – out of unassigned NCOs and men of the reserve and *Landwehr*, the Bavarian 1, 5 and 9 *Ersatz* Brigades, which on the tenth mobilisation day were united as the Bavarian *Ersatz* Division (ED).[14]

The remaining reserve and *Landwehr* men were used to fill the *Ersatz* units. Each infantry and field artillery regiment formed a replacement battalion; each cavalry regiment a replacement squadron; and each engineer battalion a replacement company. The authorised strength by personnel category of these replacement units was:

	Total	Active army	Reserve	*Landwehr*	Class II	Untrained
Infantry						
Active army	1,961	104–172	454–508	469–504	0–40	800–820
Reserve	1,485		0–45	271–561	474–814	400
Landwehr	1,485		0–102	1,062–1,075		400
Cavalry						
Active army	262	29–70	46–175	0–95	49–71	
Reserve	153		76	79	7	

Table continued on next page

	Total	Active army	Reserve	*Landwehr*	Class II	Untrained
Field Artillery	386	16–37	19–55	90–121	10–31	180–192
Engineers	654–1,093	14–40	0–103	15–115	111–444	200–798

A wave of volunteers quickly filled the replacement units at the regimental home stations far beyond their authorised strength. There was not enough billeting space, uniforms and equipment for such masses: peacetime preparations in this area were particularly inadequate. The untrained volunteers were sent to recruit depots.

The garrison army remained in Bavaria and consisted of the various unit rear-area headquarters, replacement units and the fortress garrisons.

In total, Bavaria mobilised:

Headquarters

1 Army HQ (Sixth Army)
1 Fortress HQ (Germersheim)
3 Corps HQ (I, II, III)
6 Infantry Division (ID) HQ
1 Cavalry Division HQ
12 Infantry Brigade HQ
3 Cavalry Brigade HQ
6 Field Artillery (FA) Brigade HQ
1 Reserve Corps HQ
2 Reserve Division (RD) HQ
7 Reserve Infantry Brigade HQ
4 *Landwehr* Infantry Brigade HQ
1 Fortress Garrison Command (Ingolstadt)
1 *Landsturm* Inspectorate
1 *Ersatz* Division HQ
Liaison officers (LNO) to the Prussian War Minister and General Staff

Infantry

24 Infantry Regiments (IR) with a total of 72 Battalions and 24 Machine Gun Companies

2 *Jäger* Battalions

14 Reserve Infantry Regiments (RIR) with a total of 42 Battalions and 7 MG Companies

2 Reserve *Jäger* Battalions

8 Field *Landwehr* Infantry Regiments (LIR) with 24 Battalions

2 Garrison *Landwehr* Infantry Regiments with 8 Battalions

24 Infantry Regiment Replacement Battalions, each with a double-sized Recruit Depot[15]

12 Brigade *Ersatz* Battalions to form the *Ersatz* Brigades

2 Replacement Detachments for the *Jäger* Battalions (each with two Companies and a Recruit Depot)

6 *Ersatz* MG Companies, one Platoon (2 guns) of which were assigned to the *Ersatz* Brigades

14 Reserve Infantry Regiment Replacement Battalions, plus Recruit Depot

10 *Landwehr* Infantry Regiment Replacement Battalions, plus Recruit Depots

33 *Landsturm* Infantry Battalions

1 MG Section and Replacement Detachment

Cavalry

12 Cavalry Regiments, each with 4 Squadrons, with a total of 48 Squadrons

1 Signal Detachment for the Cavalry Division

2 Reserve Cavalry Regiments, each with 3 Squadrons, with a total of 6 Squadrons

4 *Landwehr* Squadrons

9 Replacement Squadrons

3 Replacement Depots

3 Cavalry *Ersatz* Detachments for the *Ersatz* Brigades

1 Reserve Replacement Squadron

11 dismounted *Landsturm* Squadrons

Field Artillery

12 Field Artillery (FA) Regiments with 24 Sections (including 6 Light Howitzer) with a total of 54 Gun Batteries, 18 Light Howitzer Batteries and 24 Light Munitions Columns

1 Horse Artillery Section with 3 Batteries and 1 Light Munitions Column

6 Munitions Sections with 12 Infantry Munitions Columns (wagons with 6 teams of horses), 24 Artillery Munitions Columns

2 Reserve Field Artillery Regiments (RFAR) with a total of 4 Reserve Field Artillery Sections, 12 Reserve Batteries and 4 Reserve Light Munitions Columns

2 Reserve Munitions Sections with a total of 4 Reserve Infantry Munitions Columns and 4 Reserve Artillery Munitions Columns

12 Reserve Field Artillery Replacement Sections with a total of 17 Gun Batteries, 6 Light Howitzer Batteries (each Battery with a double-sized or reinforced Recruit Depot) and one Horse Battery, of which 6 *Ersatz* Sections, with 9 Gun Batteries and 3 Light Howitzer Batteries, formed part of the *Ersatz* Brigades.

4 *Landsturm* batteries.

Foot (Heavy) Artillery

2 Foot Artillery Regiment HQ

4 Foot Artillery Battalions[16] with a total of 12×15cm Howitzer Batteries, 2×21cm Mortar Batteries, 4 Light Munitions Columns. In addition, 4 Foot Artillery Munitions Sections with 28 Foot Artillery Munitions Columns (24 for the 15cm howitzers, 4 for the 21cm mortars)

2 Foot Artillery Battalions (Metz garrison) with 8 Foot Artillery Batteries and 2 Depot Companies

3 Reserve Foot Artillery Regiment HQ

6 Reserve Foot Artillery Battalions with 16 horse-drawn 15cm Howitzer Batteries, 4 horse-drawn 10cm Gun Batteries, 4 static 21cm Mortar Batteries, 2 Light Reserve Munitions Columns and 6 Depot Companies

1 *Landwehr* Foot Artillery Regiment HQ

3 *Landwehr* Foot Artillery Battalions with 12 *Landwehr* Foot Artillery Batteries and 3 Depot Companies (equipped with excess 15cm howitzers from the fortresses)

3 Foot Artillery Replacement Battalions with 12 Batteries, 3 double-sized Recruit Depots and 3 Draught Horse Detachments

4 *Landsturm* Foot Artillery Battalions with 12 Batteries

Engineers

1 Engineer Regiment HQ

6 Engineer Battalion HQ

14 Engineer Companies, 4 Reserve Engineer Companies, 3 Field *Landwehr* Engineer Companies, 2 Garrison *Landwehr* Engineer Companies, 6 *Landsturm* Engineer Companies, 4 Engineer Replacement Battalions[17], of which 2 Companies formed part of the *Ersatz* Brigades

2 Searchlight Platoons

6 Division Bridge Trains, 3 Reserve Division Bridge Trains

3 Corps Bridge Trains each with an Engineer Detachment

1 Engineer Section for the Cavalry Division

Signal Troops

1 Army Telephone Section (Sixth Army HQ), 3 Telephone Sections (for Corps HQ), 1 Reserve Telephone Station (Reserve Corps HQ)
1 Army Telegraph Centre (Sixth Army HQ), 4 Long-Range Telegraph Stations (Corps and Reserve Corps HQ), 2 Short-Range Telegraph Stations
1 Telephone Replacement Company
1 Telegraph Replacement Company

Aviation

1 Non-Rigid Airship Section with gas column; 1 Replacement Section with Recruit Depot
Zeppelin '*Saxsen*' (Saxony)
3 Aviation Sections, each with 6 aircraft[18] (one per active army corps); 1 Recruit Section

Supply

6 Supply HQ; 2 Reserve Supply HQ
17 Heavy Ration Columns, 1 Light Ration Column, 3 Reserve Heavy Ration Columns
21 Supply Parks, 6 Reserve Supply Parks
6 Remount Depots, 3 Replacement Remount Depots
36 Field Hospitals, 1 Reserve Field Hospital
6 Field Bakeries, 1 Reserve Field Bakery, 1 Reserve Field Bakery with obsolete equipment
9 Medical Companies, 2 Reserve Medical Companies
3 Supply Replacement Companies, 3 Supply *Ersatz* Companies formed part of the *Ersatz* Brigades

Siege Train

1 Foot Artillery Brigade HQ with 1 Siege Park Column (initially in Germersheim) and 1 Park Battalion HQ
1 Engineer General Officer with Sixth Army HQ
1 Engineer Siege Train consisting of a HQ, 2 Park Companies and a Supply Column
1 Entrenching Equipment and Tool Depot (Germersheim)

Railway Units

1 Military Rail Section

3 Rail Construction Companies with 1 Supply Column, 2 Reserve Rail Construction Companies with 1 Supply Column, 1 Garrison *Landwehr* Rail Construction Company with Supply Column

3 Railroad Operating Companies

3 Rail Depot Operating Companies

1 Armoured Train (Number 9, initially in the XXI AK area)

3 Field Rail Line HQ

15 Field Rail Station HQ

33 Garrison Rail Station HQ

2 Garrison Port HQ

2 Garrison Bridge HQ

1 Rail Battalion Replacement Section with Recruit Depot

Motor Vehicle Units

1 Commander of Motor Vehicle Troops (Sixth Army)

2 Jäger Motor Vehicle Columns[19]

1 Cavalry Motor Vehicle Column (for Bavarian Cavalry Division)

7 Rear-Echelon (lines of communication) Motor Vehicle Columns

3 Rear-Echelon Motor Vehicle Munitions Columns

1 Rear-Echelon Motor Vehicle Park

1 Garrison Motor Vehicle Park

1 Garrison Motor Vehicle Auxiliary Depot

Rear-Echelon (Lines of Communication) Units

1 Rear Echelon HQ

1 Rear Echelon Ammunition HQ, 6 Rear-Echelon Ammunition Columns

1 Commander of Rear Echelon Supply

15 Rear-Echelon Supply Park Columns

18 Field Supply Companies

3 Rear-Echelon Auxiliary Bakery Columns, 1 Rear-Echelon Auxiliary Bakery Column with obsolete equipment

3 Military Hospital Sections, 1 Ambulance Section, 1 Ambulance Train, 1 Auxiliary Ambulance Train, 1 Rear-Echelon Medical Supply Depot

1 Rear-Echelon Telegraph HQ

1 Rear-Area Construction HQ

1 Post-Horse and Wagon Depot, 1 Army Clothing Depot

3 Military Police Sections

15 Field Rear-Area HQ, 9 Garrison Rear-Area HQ

1 Rear-Area Aircraft Park

2 Depot Wagon Columns (186 wagons each)

Fortress Units

8 Fortress Signal Troops, 2 Fortress Telephone Sections, 1 Fortress Telegraph Construction Section,

1 Fortress Non-Rigid Airship Troop

1 Fortress Aviation Section (Germersheim), with 6 Otto biplanes

1 Light, 2 Heavy Fortress Searchlight Platoons, 2 Fortress Searchlight Platoons with obsolete equipment

1 Fortress Rail Company

1 Fortress Motor Vehicle Park

1 Fortress MG Company with 4 guns, 5 Independent Fortress MG Platoons (2 guns each)

In addition, for Ulm:

11 Labour Companies

1 Telegraph Construction Troop

1 Munitions Labour Troop

1 Field Railroad (60cm gauge) Construction Troop

1 Troop for Interior Construction

3 Artillery, 2 Fortress Transport Park Columns

1 Fortress Meat-Slaughtering Section

In addition, for Germersheim:

13 Labour Battalions

1 Fortress Transport Park

2 Fortress Foot Artillery Munitions Columns

The fortress of Ingolstadt was not armed.[20] Bavaria was involved in arming Ulm.[21] At Germersheim, a bridgehead of field fortifications was established in a half circle, 6–8km west of the Rhine.

Rear Echelon Supply: Munitions, Equipment, Fuel, Food[22]

24 Infantry Munitions Railroad Trains

22 Artillery Munitions Railroad Trains

15 Ration Railroad Trains

2 Flour Railroad Trains
8 Oats Railroad Trains

As Mobile Reserve:
7 Ration Railroad Trains
1 Flour Railroad Train
1 Oats Railroad Train

The Bavarian Army, therefore, included all the combat arms, combat support, service support and administrative support necessary to an independent armed force. It comprised about one-eighth of the German Army. Never before had Bavaria established such a force.

Strength of the Bavarian Army on war footing:[23]

Army

	Officers	NCOs/ Enlisted men	Doctors	Veterin- arians	Admini- strators	Horses
Entire Army	9,667	406,247	1269	320	1267	90,032
Field Army[24]	5,953	227,158	949	266	828	76,346
Fortresses[25]	1,452	65,026	118	22	95	5,534
Garrison Army	2,262	114,063	202	32	344	8,152

Weapons[26]

	Machine gun	7.7cm Gun	10.5cm Howitzer	15cm sFH	21cm Mortar
Entire Army	314	538	144	112	24
Field Army	222	486	126	48	8
Fortresses	26	–	–	64	16
Garrison Army	66	52	18	–	–

Vehicles[27]

	Horse-drawn	Motor Passenger	Cargo	Ambulances	Aircraft
Entire Army	13,546	260	357	14	24
Field Army	12,184	189	254	10	18
Fortresses	975	23	52	4	6
Garrison Army	387	48	51	–	–

The civil administration had a large role in preparing and conducting the mobilisation, with the municipalities and rural districts particularly involved in requisitioning horses and wagons. The post office prepared to quickly and reliably disseminate the mobilisation order. In July and August there was an immense mass of information to be transmitted: the Munich telegraph office alone processed 47,000 telegrams. Other information had to be supervised and censored.

Even more impressive was the work of the rail system, which was aided by comprehensive and thorough peacetime preparations. The beginning of the war fell during the summer travel period, with innumerable guests in the Bavarian vacation spots and spas wanting to return home immediately. The number of travellers rose alarmingly, especially at the Munich rail station, though the Bavarian rail administration was equal to the task. On 3 August goods traffic was suspended and that evening the peacetime rail schedule was replaced by the military mobilisation plan, which reduced civil traffic to the absolute minimum. First, the reservists had to be brought to their mobilisation stations and covering force units dispatched immediately to Lorraine, then the rolling stock reconfigured and reallocated to begin deployment, which began on the sixth mobilisation day (7 August) and went smoothly and without stop until 16 August. The Bavarian rail network transported no fewer than 5,500 troop trains with about 285,000 wagons, and just as many empty trains. The deployment was complicated by the fact that about 70,000 Italians had to be transported home through Salzburg and Kufstein.

The rail move to the border was like a triumphal procession. Everywhere the populace not only gave the troops flowers and refreshments, but also sang patriotic songs together with the men. The troops crossed the Rhine cheering.

Initial Deployment

In the west, the German Army deployed five armies between Crefeld in the north and Metz in the south, with the Sixth Army between Metz and Saarburg, and the Seventh Army (XIV *Armeekorps* (AK), XV AK, XIV *Reserve-Korps* (RK)) at Strasbourg and on the Upper Rhine to the south.

The mass of the Bavarian Army was employed together as the Sixth Army.[28] The only other major Sixth Army unit was XXI AK, which was stationed in Lorraine. The Bavarian 5 *Landwehr* Brigade conducted rear-area security. The Cavalry Corps 3 (*Heereskavalleriekorps* (HKK) 3) was attached to Sixth Army, under the command of a Bavarian general, and consisted of the Bavarian, 7 and 8 KD and the Bavarian *Jäger* Battalions 1 and 2. The Sixth Army HQ and Rear-Area HQ were made up almost entirely of Bavarian officers. The Sixth Army chief of staff was the chief of the Bavarian General Staff, Krafft von Dellmensingen.[29]

The 3 and 10 Bavarian Reserve Infantry Brigades formed part of the garrison of Strasbourg; 8 Bavarian Infantry Brigade, along with three Bavarian foot artillery regiments and *Ersatz* units, were part of the garrison of Metz. The entire garrison of Germersheim, some 23,000 men, was Bavarian. Ulm was held only by *Ersatz* units. Two Bavarian *Landwehr* brigades manned bridgeheads on the Upper Rhine. The Bavarian *Ersatz* Division was later attached to Seventh Army.

2

Covering Force, Deployment and Combat to 19 August

The OHL (*Oberste Heeresleitung* – the senior German HQ) deployment directed the XV AK to the north-west of Strasbourg, with XIV AK and XIV RK side-by-side on the right bank of the Rhine in the area Lahr–Neu-Breisach–Lörrach.[30] Since the Seventh Army commander anticipated an early French attack from Belfort and across the Vosges to the north of Belfort, he decided to prepare to counter-attack by moving XIV AK north to Neuenburg–Burkheim and XIV RK north to Burkheim–Lahr, with covering force units in the Vosges.[31] In the Seventh Army area there were fortresses on the left bank of the Rhine at Strasbourg, Neu-Breisach, fortified bridgeheads at Neuenburg and Hüningen and the right-bank fortress at Istein. Three bridgeheads with field fortifications were also established.[32] Between Fortress Kaiser Wilhelm II (KW II), on the foothills of the Vosges, and Fortress Strasbourg, field fortifications were dug behind the Breusch River to form the 'Breusch position'.

Between the fifth and tenth mobilisation days, two Italian cavalry divisions were expected to arrive at Strasbourg; and as of the seventeenth mobilisation day, an entire Italian army of three corps was due on the Upper Rhine. These forces never appeared.

The first, albeit temporary, mission for Seventh Army was the protection of the Upper Alsace and Upper Rhine against a weak French attack during the German deployment. In the event of a major French attack, Seventh Army was to withdraw to Strasbourg and across the Rhine.

Until 6 August only weak French forces appeared on the border in the Vosges, and were not very active. The French XXI Corps was identified east of Rambervillers, south of the French VII Corps. Both units were stationed in this area in peacetime. On 7 August the German XV AK and XIV AK were still deploying when the French VII Corps of the French First Army attacked from Belfort towards Mühlhausen in southern Alsace, with the mission of destroying the Rhine bridges south of Neuf-Breisach, or blocking the crossings, then turning north towards Colmar–Schlettstadt. By the evening of 8 August the French 41 ID was reported in the area of Sennheim, 14 ID in Mühlhausen and 8 Cavalry Division (Div.) to the south at Altkirch. The German covering force units from XIV AK had conducted a fighting withdrawal to Neuenburg.

On 7 August the Seventh Army commander decided to attack in order to drive the French into Switzerland if possible. On 8 August XV AK was sent in motion towards Colmar, XIV AK to Neu-Breisach and Neuenburg, while the Strasbourg reserve, 30 RD, was sent to reinforce the covering forces in the Vosges passes and guard the XV AK right flank and rear. XXI AK, which was providing the covering force in Lorraine, was asked to advance towards Baccarat and Raon l'Étape to fix those French forces in place. By midday, after a 60km forced march in the burning sun, both corps were approaching Mühlhausen. By evening, XV AK took Sennheim, while XIV AK reached the area north and east of Mühlhausen in close proximity to the enemy. On 10 August XIV AK liberated Mühlhausen and the French withdrew, sometimes in panic, towards Belfort.[33] While the mass of XV AK and XIV AK held the positions they had taken, mixed detachments pursued the French, who had left German territory by 13 August. The commanders of the French VII Corps and 8 Cavalry Div. were immediately relieved of their duties. In the Vosges, the Germans fought off French attacks on the passes west of Schlettstadt.

In any war the first victory is important and the French would have made a great deal out of an unopposed march into Mühlhausen. It was understandable that the German Empire would not want to leave the Alsace, such an old bone of contention, in French hands. However, XIV AK and XV AK, which had been thrown into battle precipitately, required some time to recover from their exertions and the effect of their first day in combat, and were late redeploying to Lorraine. If the Germans had restricted themselves to the defence of the east bank of the Upper Rhine and the Strasbourg–KW II line, abandoning Alsace, then the Seventh Army would have been available on a timely basis for the main battle.

Deployment of the Sixth Army and First Combat to 13 August (map a)

Bavarian III Corps (III b. AK) deployed on the right to the south of Metz. Next left was II b. AK, then XXI AK, with I b. AK on the left at Saarburg. I b. RK was in reserve at Saargemünd. The Sixth Army Rear Area HQ was at Zweibrücken, with 5 *Landwehr* Brigade (Bde) providing security.

The army troops included:

II/Bavarian Foot Artillery R 3 (21cm mortars), 2 Batteries; HQ, II and III/Foot
   Artillery R 18 (21cm mortars) each Battalion with 2 Batteries
Heavy Coastal Artillery Mortar Battery 2 (30.5cm)
Naval Cannon Battery 1 (42cm)
Bavarian Engineer R, with 6 Companies; Engineer R 19, with 6 Companies
Bavarian Non-Rigid Airship Section
Aviation Section 5
The total strength of the Sixth Army was 131 battalions, 39 squadrons, 133 batter-
   ies (24 heavy) with 746 guns (92 heavy) and 27 engineer companies.
HKK 3 was attached to Sixth Army. It deployed the 8 *Kavalleriedivision* (KD)
   in the II b. AK sector, the Bavarian KD and *Jäger* Battalions 1 and 2 b. in the
   XXI AK sector and 7 KD in I b. AK sector. HKK 3 included *Jäger* battalions 2,
   72 squadrons and 9 horse artillery batteries (36 guns). Its initial mission was to
   reconnoitre towards Pont-à-Mousson–Lunéville–Blâmont–Baccarat.

Since the declaration of 'Period Preparatory to War', XXI AK and XIV AK, which
were stationed near the border, provided security with units in peacetime strength
and uniforms. These were relieved on 4 August by a covering force brigade (two
infantry regiments, a cavalry squadron and an artillery section) in each corps
area, which prepared defensive positions. The unit advance parties arrived in
the deployment areas on 3 August, followed in the next two days by the cavalry
divisions and, from 8–12 August, the active army corps. During the deployment,
the covering force brigade was spread thinly over a corps-wide sector, and had to
anticipate either a French attack in force or large-scale cavalry raids.

   The II b. AK and III b. AK were facing the French XX Corps, reinforced by
the French 2 Cavalry Div., heavy artillery and forestry officials, which limited
themselves to occupying the Selle bridges, although, on 6 August, two batteries of
Bavarian horse artillery conducted a forty-five-minute duel with French artillery.
On the heights, which rose 200m between the Selle and the Moselle, the French
had already constructed field fortifications in peacetime, which from 8–11 August
they reinforced. I b. AK was faced by the French XXI Corps. The covering force,
divisional cavalry and HKK 3 continually sent out reconnaissance patrols, which
were hindered by the Selle River, the Rhine–Marne Canal, and the French
cavalry and infantry security screen. The Bavarian KD had soon lost 200 horses,
though the cavalry took French prisoners and captured documents.

   On 8 August the HQ of the German XXI AK and HKK 3 received the request
from Seventh Army to attack in the direction of Baccarat–Raon l'Étape to
support Seventh Army's attack on Mühlhausen. At this time XXI AK had only
the covering force available, 3 Bavarian Infantry Bde in Saarburg, so it was the

first unit to cross the French border, occupying Blâmont; 3 Bde continued the advance on 9 August against light resistance, but the Bavarian KD and 7 KD were not able to support because pursuing the French cavalry in the intense heat had already exhausted the horses.

On 10 August the available units of I b. AK attacked towards Badonviller–Raon l'Étape to support the Seventh Army. The corps had only partially deployed, however, with many combat, munitions and supply units still on the rails or at home station. The troops had just been mobilised and completed their rail movement and were not marching fit, and along with the heat there were many march casualties. The Bavarians continually took fire from men in houses, often in civilian clothing, and responded by shooting the men and burning the houses down. The Bavarians lost 30 Killed in Action (KIA) and 120 Wounded in Action (WIA). On 11 August it was clear that the French had been defeated at Mühlhausen and I b. AK was ordered to halt in place. The last combat units of I b. AK arrived and the units rested.

Early in the morning of 9 August the Sixth Army HQ arrived in the sector. On the evening of 10 August Crown Prince Rupprecht was given the overall command in Alsace-Lorraine, including Sixth and Seventh Armies and HKK 3.

The Cavalry Charge at Gerden[34], 11 August (sketch 1)

On 10 August the French 59 Infantry Bde had driven the German outpost company, 8/IR 131, out of the town of Gerden, on the border in the middle of the German XXI AK sector. The Bavarian cavalry patrols had been unable to penetrate the French border covering force screen, so it was decided to conduct a reconnaissance in force at Gerden, in conjunction with the 42 ID. On the right, the 65 Infantry Bde of 42 ID, supported by Prussian (Pr.) Field Artillery Regiment (FAR) 8, would attack south from Ley and Ommery (off the map to the upper left), while in the centre the *Jäger* Battalion (Bn) 2 b. and 8/IR 131 attacked along the Bortenach–Gerden road, supported by 5/FAR 8. Meanwhile, 59 Bde would attack on the left on Remoncourt and Vaucourt (off the map to the left), supported by Pr. FAR 15 against the enemy flank and rear. The Bavarian KD would be held in reserve.

At 1000hrs 2 b. *Jäger* entered the Chantal-Holz (Chantal Wood), where it took bursts (*rafales*) of fire and casualties from French artillery located 500m north of Gerden. The French had placed hats and packs on the edge of Gerden to deceive the Germans, while in fact they had prepared the interior of the town for protracted defence. Machine guns (MG) were installed in the church tower. At about 1km from Gerden, the *Jäger* took up the firefight with 1, 4 and 3 Companies on line, and 2 and 8/IR 131 in reserve. 5/FAR 8 opened fire against

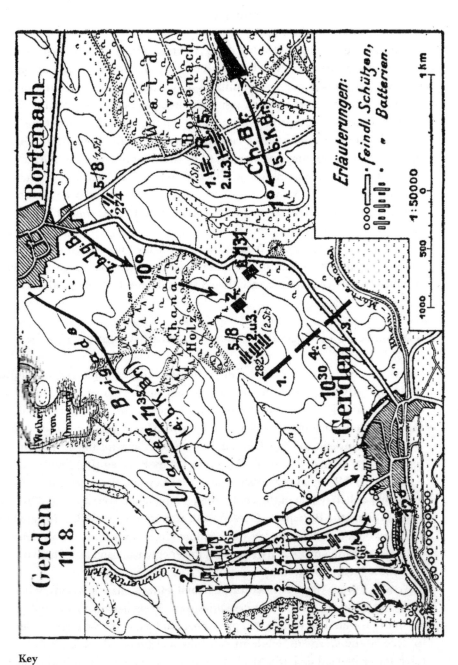

Key

Feindl. Schutzen – enemy infantry

 "   *Batterien* – enemy batteries

the French artillery from a position south of Bortenach, as did the Bavarian KD horse artillery battery (R/FAR 5) from a position west of Wald Bortenach.

While 65 Infantry Bde (not shown on map) advanced over Hill 265, north of Gerden, under the burning sun, *Jäger* 2 advanced slowly by bounds across the open ground in front of Gerden while taking casualties. At 1200hrs, when the French artillery north of Gerden was silenced, 5/FAR 8 and the 2 and 3/FAR 5 displaced forward to positions on Hill 282, only 1km from Gerden.

At 1115hrs the commander of the Bavarian KD ordered the 4 (*Uhlan*) Cavalry Bde to attack the French artillery, which had been suppressed and would probably attempt to withdraw. It would be followed in support by 1 Cavalry Bde, and MG Section (Sec.) 1 was also ordered forward. The *Uhlan* Bde used the low ground south-west of Bortenach as a covered and concealed avenue of approach to the attack position on Hill 265, passing to the left flank of the French infantry in Gerden. Movement was hindered by marshy meadows and barbed-wire fences which enclosed pastures. From Hill 265, looking across rolling terrain and fields of high grain, the brigade commander could discern the French artillery. *Uhlan* R 2 deployed to the right of the road to Gerden behind the north slope of Hill 265, *Uhlan* R 1 to the left of the road, each with two squadrons forward and one in the second line, with the brigade occupying a front of 500–800m. The squadrons advanced in open-order waves. Enemy fire and the press of time did not permit a careful reconnaissance of the terrain, however. High standing grain, as well as unexpected wet ditches and barbed-wire fences, sometimes slowed movement, but, nevertheless, the advance picked up speed. South of Hill 265 the *Uhlans* passed through a thin skirmisher line of IR 131. Soon the first groups of French appeared; they fled through the grain, hid in the bushes or played dead in order to shoot the *Uhlans* in the back. They were ridden down, taken prisoner or speared with lances. The *Uhlans* then reached the two shot-up French batteries; the surviving French gunners surrendered.

The advance continued to gather speed, but the brigade was still in good order when it encountered a 3m-high steep cut on the north side of the road leading west from Gerden. On the road itself, and in the small strip of land covered with hedges, trees, bushes and fences that separated the road from the Rhine–Marne Canal, were groups of withdrawing French troops. French troops at Gerden fired into the left flank of the *Uhlans*. All of these obstacles brought the wave of cavalry to a halt. Here and there *Uhlans* steered their horses down the steep slope, while others found easier ways down. In this manner, 4 and 5/*Uhlan* R 2 reached the road. The horses were by now out of control and the herd swung down the road to Gerden. 4/*Uhlan* R 1 followed them. French troops in the way were overrun or jumped in the canal. The *Uhlans* took fire from the town, the south side of the canal and MGs positioned in the church tower. Horseless *Uhlans* fought on foot with their carbines. Part of the stream of *Uhlans* broke into the town and dismounted to fight house-to-house, while other *Uhlans* followed the brigade commander to the orchards at the north-west edge of Gerden, where the road cut was no longer so steep and where they were joined by 1/*Uhlan* R 1.

3/*Uhlan* R 1 stopped at the top of the road cut and, under the leadership of the regimental commander, attacked French infantry on a small hill near the canal bridge 1km to the west of Gerden, capturing most of them. 2/*Uhlan* R 2 had been held up by terrain obstacles, swung to low ground south of the Kreuzberg Forest, attacked a third French battery and then took both ends of the bridge west of Gerden on foot, bringing in 120 prisoners of war (POWs).

The entire wild and bloody ride took place between 1135 and 1200hrs. Neither MG Sec. 1 nor 1 Cavalry Bde had the opportunity to become engaged. The fragments of the two *Uhlan* regiments were rallied by their commanders and withdrawn to Hill 265, the POWs turned over to the Prussian infantry. *Jäger* Bn 1 and a battalion from 65 Infantry Bde drove the French out of the Kreuzberg Forest and pushed on to the Rhine–Marne Canal.

In the meantime, *Jäger* Bn 2 had approached to within 200m of Gerden, bounding by half-platoons, squads or individuals, taking casualties from both enemy fire and the heat. 2/*Jäger* 2 reinforced 2/*Jäger* 1. At 1245hrs the *Jäger* assaulted the town at almost the same time that IR 131 did so from the north, pushing the French back from house to house, though defending themselves both bravely and cunningly. Fire fell on the *Jäger* from upper-story and attic windows, as well as the church tower. Many prisoners were taken. Corporal (Cpl) Drees from 1/*Jäger* 2 captured a French standard. 59 Infantry Bde drove into Gerden from the south, and the battle was over by 1500hrs. The enemy had withdrawn or fled in panic, for the most part during the charge of the *Uhlan* Bde. There was no pursuit. The Germans bivouacked in towns a short distance to the east.

The casualties were:

	KIA			WIA			MIA**		TOTAL		
	OFF	EM	H*	OFF	EM	H	EM	H	OFF	EM	H
Jäger 2	1	32	–	4	129	–	3	–	5	164	–
Uhlan 1	4	31	29	3	61	13	20	87	7	112	129

*Horses

**Probably KIA

Table continued on next page.

	KIA			WIA			MIA		TOTAL		
	OFF	EM	H	OFF	EM	H	EM	H	OFF	EM	H
Uhlan 2	3	34	20	4	27	11	14	135	7	75	166
Total	8	107	49	11	217	24	37	222	19	351	295

The commander of 4 Cavalry Bde was seriously wounded and his adjutant killed, and there were also a large number of heat casualties.

The *Uhlan's* losses were similarly heavy. A critic could certainly say that the attack had achieved its objective when it arrived at the canal in that dismounted troopers holding the heights west of Gerden would have cut off the French as well as, or better than, wild masses of cavalry storming into the town. But this does not consider that long peacetime training had inculcated the offensive spirit into the troops, nor does it reckon with the maddened horses. The arrival of the Bavarian *Uhlans* in and behind Gerden, with hurricane force, had undoubtedly spread fear and panic among the enemy, shaking his morale, and contributed to the quick capture of the town, which spared greater losses among the attacking Prussian and Bavarian infantry and increased the scope of the victory.

In addition to numerous dead and wounded, the enemy lost eight guns, six MG, a standard and 1,467 POWs. Important documents were captured, including a French Second Army operations order found on the body of a dead French brigade commander, which showed that at least six French corps were assembled between Toul and Épinal.

Reconnaissance aircraft from Bavarian Aviation Sec. 1 reported one to two French divisions opposite the I b. AK sector.[35] At 1800hrs 2/IR 3, which was on outpost duty, was attacked by superior French forces coming from Badonviller. The commander of I/IR 3 reinforced with 3 on the left and the 4 on the right. 4 took fire in the right flank from French forces in a wood, then attacked and drove the French from the wood in close combat. 1 attacked through 4 and engaged the retreating French with pursuit fire. The French were thrown back along the entire front, at the cost of a number of casualties.

By 11 August reports led Sixth Army HQ to believe that the enemy had assembled strong forces between Nancy and Épinal. Since the French might launch an offensive soon, the corps, which were still deploying, were instructed to hold their positions along the border.

The French fortress of Manonviller, 12km east of Lunéville, supported the French covering force and would disrupt any advance by the Sixth Army. The Sixth Army engineers were therefore ordered to begin measures to take the fort, and were given operational control over the Bavarian Foot Artillery Brigade HQ and the HQ of I b. Foot Artillery R 1 and Foot Artillery R 18, as well as the Bavarian Engineer Regiment (Eng. R) with the Engineer Siege Train. Bavarian Rail Construction Company (Co.) 1 was already at work on the rail lines for the 42cm mortars.

Badonviller, 12 August (sketch 2)

The Sixth Army order for 12 August instructed I b. AK to defend a line on the Vezouse River, between Blâmont and Cirey, and to begin the reconnaissance of Fort Manonviller. However, in order to spare the troops the march back to the Vezouse, the corps HQ ordered them to remain in position north of Badonviller and remain strictly on the defensive.

On the night of 11/12 August, 6/Household IR occupied an outpost position on the road from Les Carrières. At 0600hrs they were discovered and engaged by French infantry – the position was untenable. The tradition and training of the Household IR allowed only one course of action: attack. The company commander was reinforced in this decision by reports that night patrols had been able to traverse Badonviller, which was weakly held. Then II/Household IR followed 6/Household, as did I/Household R on the left. The regimental commander gave his approval and committed III/Household through the woods south of Bréménil with orders to take Badonviller from the east. II/FAR 7 opened fire at 0630hrs. The Household attack gathered steam quickly, particularly II/Household R, and 6/Household, deployed in very open order, took the heights north of Badonviller at 0620hrs, in spite of enemy fire in the left flank and serious casualties. 5/Household followed on the right, 8/Household on the left, while 7/Household, which had outpost duty at Battant Mill (on map, Battant-M.), moved in the direction of the Badonviller rail station. Aided by high grain and not bothering to return the enemy fire, by about 0800hrs the skirmisher line of II/Household had reached the edge of Badonviller and moved into the gardens and houses. The French must have been deeply asleep because it was not the initial troops, but rather the following platoons and companies that met resistance. I/Household bypassed the town centre to the east, delayed by underbrush, walls, fences and hedges, while III/Household swung even further east along the roads in the woods. 9/FAR 7 galloped forward to the heights on the north-west edge of Badonviller at 0900hrs, followed by 4/FAR 7, while 5/FAR 7 took up a position 1km south of Les Carrières. The Household regimental

Badonviller 12. 8.

Textskizze 2.

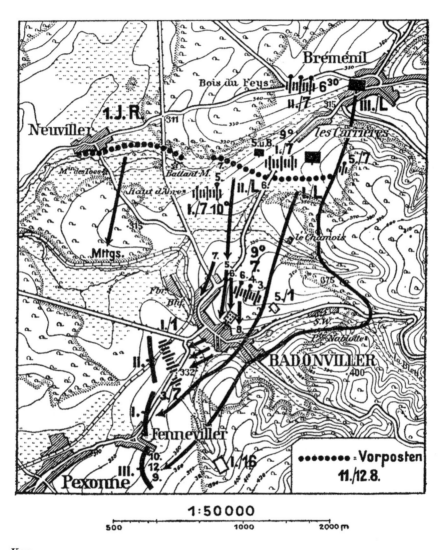

Key

Vorposten – outposts

L – *Leibregiment* (Household Regiment)

commander moved to Badonviller, while bringing the MG Company (MGK) to the north edge of the town. The commander of I b. AK moved forward to Blâmont, while specifying Badonviller as the limit of advance, in order to keep the fight from expanding.

Soon after 0800hrs the Household Regiment called for help: the fight inside Badonviller had escalated. II/Household had advanced to the end of the main street when it took fire from all sides, particularly from an MG in the cemetery or the church to its rear, opening a bitter house-to-house battle in which II/Household bored its way through the centre of Badonviller. Where French resistance was particularly strong, the Household infantry would bring up a platoon of MGs.

At 0900hrs I/FAR 7 unlimbered on the heights south of Les Carrières, while 3/FAR 7 was soon brought forward to the north side of Badonviller. At 1000hrs 1, 2 and 5 displaced forward to Haut d'Arbre and drove off French artillery that had been firing from south of Badonviller.

At around 0900hrs the French were fleeing Badonviller, which could be considered in the control of the Household IR, but was by no means cleared. French soldiers found all sorts of hiding places from which they fired on the Bavarian troops, even on stretcher-bearers and the wounded. There can be no doubt that civilians of both sexes took part in these underhand attacks, for there were gunshot wounds that could only have been caused by hunting rifles, shotguns and similar non-military weapons.

5/Household had quickly pushed through Badonviller to the south edge of the town, and the rest of II/Household followed. I/Household attacked on the left, suffering numerous casualties while taking Fenneviller. The remaining two platoons of the MGK were committed in these two battalions' sectors and engaged the French with pursuit fire. III/Household attacked across the hill to the south of Fenneviller against French infantry, who were well concealed in the standing grain and fields of potatoes. The battalion commander was killed. A French MG on the treeline north-west of Fenneviller and artillery south of Pexonne inflicted further casualties, destroying a platoon of 4 Co. III/IR 16 was brought forward to the hill south of Neuviller to cover the right flank. The order to halt the attack finally reached the front lines at 1200hrs and the firing died down.

5/IR 1 and 6/Household now began systematically clearing Badonviller. At 1600hrs it was discovered that a French MG had been firing from the church tower and it was set on fire by German artillery, which eventually consumed the entire town.

The Household IR held its positions at Fenneviller until relieved in place at 2000hrs by IR 2, then withdrew to Neuviller. IR 16 had been brought forward to Le Chamois (south of Brémenil). It unsuccessfully tried to extinguish the fires in Badonviller, hindered by a lack of equipment and the bad faith of the populace.

III/IR 2 took fire from houses while marching through the town, the combat trains of I/IR 16 was ambushed from the city hall, and troops and horses wounded by fire from small-calibre weapons. A search of the houses turned up an unusual number of young, fit men with papers that showed they had been mobilised then released from duty. It was obvious that their mission was to conduct guerrilla warfare in civilian clothes in areas near the border.

The Battle of Badonviller developed out of an outpost battle, against the intentions of the higher leadership. The casualties suffered by the Household IR − 8 officers and 90 enlisted men KIA, 14 officers and 300 enlisted men WIA − might appear at first glance to have been pointless. This was not the case. The French 25 Infantry Bde had been providing border security at Badonviller. In particular, the Household IR had been engaged with the French Light Infantry Battalions 17, 20, 21 and IR 17, and had taken 800 POWs. The first victory, even one fought without a higher purpose, reinforced the morale and confidence of the Bavarians, and reduced that of the French.

The tradition and training of the German Army emphasised the honourable offensive, which showed itself from the very beginning of this great test of arms to be superior to the cunning, underhand methods of the French. The Household IR had fought masterfully, worthy of its noble history.

The batteries of FAR 1 and FAR 7 had provided exemplary fire support. They moved right behind the skirmisher line and unlimbered in the open to provide close fire support. In peacetime this had been practised zealously, although criticised by many as out-dated. Now this technique had proven itself once again, even in the face of modern weapons. Above all, during the offensive battles at the end of the war, it would once again be used successfully.

Doubtless the offensive conducted by I b. AK ran considerable risk and could have had serious negative consequences. The corps could have been encircled and destroyed by superior forces. The cohesion of the newly mobilised unit, which was not yet marching fit, had been seriously tested, particularly since the logistics system had not yet been established. All of these dangers were clear to the commanders, particularly the Sixth Army command group, which ordered the offensive, and the I b. AK commander, who initially opposed it. In this case, the situation justified the risk. That it succeeded without any negative consequences was due to the morale of the troops and the character of the leaders.

Deployment Completed, 13 August

By 13 August the mass of the Sixth Army ammunition and supply units had deployed. The army was now fully prepared for combat. III b. AK on the right flank had been digging in since 11 August, with 6 ID on the right flank, nearest

Metz, and 5 ID on the left. The enemy was quiet. II b. AK deployed 4 ID in a strong position on the heights at Delm, and 3 ID on the dominating terrain on both sides of Château Salins. The security detachments on the Selle were engaged occasionally with French outposts and patrols. In one of these battles, 7/IR 16 fell into an ambush, took considerable casualties and its company commander was killed. XXI AK was assembled in the sector, with 31 ID on the right and 42 ID on the left. I b. RK completed deployment in Saargemünd.

I b. AK began to construct field fortifications. Since the left flank at Badonviller was far forward and exposed to an attack from the Vosges, 1 ID was pulled back to high ground 4km to the rear, leaving only a security detachment in Badonviller, with 2 ID on its right. As a precaution, the supply units were moved back over the Vezouse River, and the troops did not occupy their positions, but were dispersed to assembly areas to the rear. The corps was therefore positioned to withdraw in the face of an attack by superior French forces and, in fact, French strength in the corps area increased to the point that the security detachment in Badonviller was withdrawn.

HKK 3 cavalry reconnaissance patrols had great difficulty penetrating the screen established by the enemy covering force, reinforced by Fort Manonviller and the water obstacles of the Selle and Rhine–Marne Canal. HKK 3 decided not to conduct a reconnaissance in force, conscious of the fact that Lorraine was unsuited for the employment of large bodies of cavalry and large-scale offensives would only lead to high casualties, if not outright defeat. So far as possible, on 12 and 13 August, HKK 3 preserved the strength of its units.

On 13 August 2/Heavy Cavalry R 1, led by Rittmeister Prince Heinrich of Bavaria, was covering the reconnaissance of Manonviller by the staff of Foot Artillery R 18 when it encountered two French squadrons, one in front and one on the flank. Prince Heinrich charged one of these and both fled. The Bavarian cavalry chased after the French and slowly closed the gap, until the terrain forced the French to turn and fight. Prince Heinrich, far ahead of his squadron, reached the French first and was surrounded and lightly wounded, but was quickly supported by his troopers, who overwhelmed the French, some of whom dismounted and surrendered, then fired at the Bavarians' backs. Such underhandedness quickly received its just desserts: the French squadron was soon destroyed, the few survivors pursued until they reached the safety of their own infantry.

German and French War Plans

The concept of the German war plan, the foundation of which had been developed by Field Marshal von Schlieffen, was that the mass of the German Army would advance through Belgium and Luxembourg in order to go around the French fortress line at Belfort–Verdun. Five armies (first to fifth) would march from the area of Liège–Diedenhofen (Thionville) and swing in a great arc towards Paris. While the right wing, the First Army, would march towards Brussels and set the pace, the left wing, Fifth Army, would maintain contact with Diedenhofen and therefore move slowly, because this was the point at which the enemy could pry the attack off its hinges. The farther the Fifth Army moved west, the more dangerous the enemy attack originating from Verdun became. An even more serious danger would occur if the enemy succeeded in breaking through in Lorraine, between the fortresses of Metz and Strasbourg and to the Lower Moselle. Metz had been expanded to the north-east with a fortified line behind the Nied River (the 'Nied Position') to the Saar at Molsheim, garrisoned by seven Landwehr brigades and eight batteries of 10cm cannons, which would only delay a strong enemy for a limited time and not prevent him from crossing the Saar. The left flank of the forces advancing in Luxembourg and Belgium needed to be reliably protected in depth from Verdun to the Rhine.

This was the principal mission for Crown Prince Rupprecht and the Sixth and Seventh Armies. In addition, he was to fix strong enemy forces in place in Lorraine by advancing on the Moselle above Fort Frouard and on the Meurthe; this was no longer a consideration if the French attacked between Metz and the Vosges with superior forces. If Rupprecht's forces were forced to withdraw, they were to do so in the direction that would prevent the French from outflanking the Nied Position to the east, as well as reinforce the Nied Position itself. If Rupprecht's armies were not opposed by numerically superior French forces, then Rupprecht might attack to the west bank of the Moselle at and south of Metz. A French attack that included the Upper Alsace was favourable for the Germans, so long as it did not pass north of the line of KW II–Breusch Position–Strasbourg.

Rupprecht was therefore placed in a complex situation. A French attack into Alsace-Lorraine, the old bone of contention between France and Germany, had to be taken into consideration. On the other hand, this attack might either have limited objectives or be designed to penetrate to the Rhine and the Upper Moselle. The Chief of the German General Staff, Moltke, also expected that the French might commit the mass of their forces in Lorraine and that the decisive battle would be fought there.

Rupprecht could not allow his armies to be defeated by superior French forces, uncovering the left flank of the main body. Conversely, he could not allow himself to be deceived by equal French forces, or even inferior French forces acting aggressively. In the first case, he had to withdraw or meet the French in a prepared position. In the second, in order to fix the French forces in place, he had to attack, perhaps as far as Toul-Épinal. If the French attacked the left flank of the main body, Rupprecht might have to counter-attack from Metz. Until the German right wing began its advance, Rupprecht had to fix the greatest number of French forces in Lorraine. But if the French attacked with superior forces, then Rupprecht could expect no relief until the right wing began its advance.

The situation therefore contained many possibilities and dangers. It could change often and quickly, and there were many gradations in each possibility. To accomplish such a mission, leaders and troops had to possess a high degree of flexibility. The shifting mission might cause morale and aggressiveness to suffer unless they were supported by the discipline and enthusiasm of the troops and by the cool presence of mind of the leadership, which avoided precipitate action and overexertion of the troops. There would be no rapid victorious advances, such as those that beckoned the right wing. The danger of losing the initiative to the enemy was great.

The deployment of the Sixth Army prescribed by OHL did not correspond to the multiplicity of missions it gave to Rupprecht. The corps were deployed too close to the border and the enemy, and were distributed too evenly on line. There was insufficient space outside enemy range to manoeuvre and mass for a concentrated thrust against an enemy weak point. Against an early French offensive, the army would be forced to fight on the border in an over-extended position. In either case, in order to obtain room to manoeuvre freely, the army had to move to the rear, which at the beginning of the war was best avoided.

While still in Munich, Rupprecht sent a memorandum to OHL explaining his concept of the operation.[36] The principal mission was to guard the flank of the main body as it conducted its right wheel. The way to execute this mission was to gain time by conducting a feint attack, making Sixth Army appear stronger than was actually the case. Sixth Army would then advance in a broad and deep formation on Pont-à-Mousson–Baccarat, and Seventh Army from the Rhine Valley across the Vosges on St Dié–Gérardmer. Of course, there was some doubt that the French would be fooled. If the enemy attacked with superior forces, Rupprecht intended to withdraw to the Saar between Saarlouis, Saarburg and the Donon hill mass, supported on the right by the Nied Position and on the left by the Breusch Position. This line was a good 120km long, a considerable distance for the forces available. If the French succeeded in taking the Donon, they could roll up not only the Saar line but also the Breusch Position. The entire Seventh Army would therefore defend the Donon, while the Sixth Army defended the Saar. From here Rupprecht hoped, after a time, to be able to conduct a decisive offensive, in the best case in conjunction with other forces attacking from Metz. The memorandum also considered the possibility of a withdrawal to and over the Moselle, and requested that operational control of Metz be given to Sixth Army.

The premature attack by Seventh Army into the southernmost corner of the Alsace immediately compromised Rupprecht's plans. Sixth Army had to commit I b. AK, not fully deployed and isolated, to an attack to support Seventh Army, dislocating the Sixth Army's deployment in the process. Seventh Army was exhausted, weakened and far out of position. Thus the first requirement was to pull Seventh Army out of Mühlhausen and nearer to Sixth Army.

It was known only that the French had a considerable head start and could attack as of about 11 August. Since they did not attack by 13 August, it was possible that they intended to remain on the defensive, which meant that Rupprecht had to consider going on the offensive towards Nancy and Épinal.

It had originally been intended that, as the Sixth Army attacked in the direction of Lunéville, the Seventh Army would attack from Colmar–Barr to both sides of St Dié to take the French forces facing Sixth Army in the flank. However, it became apparent that the French VII Corps at Belfort was still capable of offensive operations and could threaten the Seventh Army left flank on either side of the Vosges. There was also doubt that Seventh Army could quickly take the mountain passes. Rupprecht decided on 13 August to pull Seventh Army all the way back to the Breusch Position, from where it would cover the left flank of the Sixth Army advance against Lunéville. XIV AK would move by rail to Saarburg, XV AK by rail to the south-west of Strasbourg and XIV RK by foot march to the Breusch Position. If XIV RK advanced over Schirmeck with XV AK south of it, they would be in a position to threaten the French left flank while guarding the right flank of Sixth Army. The general advance on the Meurthe River could only begin when the Seventh Army had completed movement and was fully assembled.

The French had also completed their deployment. The French First Army under General Dubail assembled on the west slope of the Vosges between Belfort and Baccarat. On the army right flank, VII Corps and 8 Cavalry Div., along with the Belfort garrison, had conducted the unsuccessful attack on Mühlhausen. VII Corps was now north of Belfort, and 8 Cavalry Div. was on the army right flank, south of the fortress. There was a considerable gap between VII Corps and the next unit to the north, XIV Corps, which was south of St Dié. XXI Corps, on the left of XIV Corps, north of St Dié, had already taken some of the Vosges passes. Alpine Battalions 12, 13, 22, 28 and 30, with their attached artillery, had arrived from the border with Italy and were attached to 41 ID on the XXI Corps right; Alpine Battalions 7, 11 and 14 reinforced XIV Corps. XIII Corps was north of Raon l'Étape, VIII Corps west of Gerbéviller, 6 Cavalry Div. in the area of Fort Manonviller. 57 RD was the mobile reserve for Belfort, 71 RD for Épinal. Reserve Division Group 1, consisting of 58, 63 and 66 RD, was at Vesoul. 2 Colonial Brigade was also attached to First Army.

The French Second Army under General de Castelnau deployed between Lunéville and Pont-à-Mousson with, from east to west, XVI, XV, XX, and IX Corps. XX Corps with 2 Cavalry Div. and, later, 10 Cavalry Div. provided the covering force. In the second line at Toul were XVIII Corps and the Reserve Division Group 2 (59, 63, 70 RD). Light Infantry Battalions 6, 23, 24 and 27 were also attached.[37] IX Corps, reinforced by 70 RD, began work on 12 August on digging field fortifications around the heights east of Frouard. 79 RD constituted the reserve for Toul.

The French Third and Fifth Armies completed their deployment along the Meuse, east of St Mihiel and Charleville, with a flank detachment at Vervins and Hirson. Behind them the Fourth Army assembled on the Upper Aisne, east of Châlons. The Italian border was watched by a few divisions, as the French were sure that no danger threatened from this direction.

The French General Staff was not certain that the German right wing would march through Belgium, but if it did, it would stay south of the Meuse and Sambre. The French may also have underestimated the combat power of the German RK and may not have expected them to be employed immediately with the active army corps. Strong German forces were expected in Alsace-Lorraine, particularly in the area of Metz–Diedenhofen.

General Joffre, the French commander in chief, intended to attack with all his forces as soon as possible – simultaneously with the Russians. There was, however, probably no firm plan for the conduct of the attack. An advance with the mass of the army on both sides of the Vosges and then along the Lower Moselle to the Rhine had been seriously considered. Joffre himself, and the generals Pau, de Castelnau and Foch, advocated such a course of action, and, in particular, an attack into Lorraine. To counter a German advance into Belgium, it was intended to attack from Verdun–Charleville to the north-east into the Ardennes, which was designed to produce a decisive victory by cutting off the German right wing and pushing it to the north. But Joffre made his final decision only when he had clarity concerning the form and direction of the German advance. Nevertheless, the French deployment allowed the main attack to be made in Lorraine, or on both sides of Metz, or in the Ardennes. In the event, the French attacked in both Lorraine and the Ardennes, with the main point of effort in the Ardennes, where on 20 August Third Army attacked north of Metz, with a heavily reinforced Fourth Army on its left. The Fifth Army moved into the angle between the Sambre and Meuse, in order to advance in conjunction with the British Army (two corps, one cavalry division) and the Belgian Army (six infantry divisions, one cavalry division), which was deployed between Antwerp and Brussels, to block the German right wing swinging around Namur.

The First and Second Armies were also given offensive missions, to advance to Saarburg and Saarbrücken. According to Barthelemy Edmonnd Palat (perhaps the most famous late nineteenth- and early twentieth-century French military historian, who also wrote under the pseudonym of Perre Lehautcourt), the purpose was not so much to gain a decisive victory as to fix the greatest number of German troops in Alsace and Lorraine, and protect the French right flank. They would therefore attack before the offensive into the Ardennes. Both armies soon gave up troops to the French left wing: the XIX Corps from Africa, which was originally to go to First Army, was diverted to the left wing; XVIII Corps from the Second Army was sent to Fifth Army on 16 August; and IX Corps was diverted to the Fourth Army on 18 August.

It is remarkable that, until 22 August, the French thought that the German XIII AK was on the right flank of Seventh Army,[38] while they failed to identify XIV RK. This may have been due to the fact that 26 RD, a XIV RK unit, had been established by XIII AK. Aside from this, the French had an accurate picture of the German order of battle in Alsace-Lorraine.

The French First and Second Armies had the same mission as the German Sixth and Seventh Armies. This was due to the fact that in Lorraine, the Vosges and Alsace there was only room for secondary operations. There was too little manoeuvre space between the Rhine and the Moselle for quick and decisive actions. A German attack quickly ran into the French border fortresses at Verdun–Toul–Épinal–Belfort. The gap in this line at Charmes was a trap. Even if the French got across the Saar, they would encounter the forested hills of the Hunsrück and the Haardt, which were significant barriers to movement and easy to defend. The French flanks would be threatened from the west by the fortresses of Metz and Diedenhofen, and from the east by Strasbourg and Germersheim. Blocking these and protecting the flanks would probably occupy so many forces that the main attack would lose momentum even before it encountered the Rhine, a serious obstacle itself. South of Strasbourg, the Rhine was reinforced by fortifications at Neu–Breisach, Neuenburg, Istein and Hüningen, while to the east of the river was the Black Forest, another significant obstacle. The French command saw these difficulties and eventually – though perhaps not initially – recognised that the decisive battle would be fought north of Verdun in the Ardennes or on the Belgian border.

It is necessary to examine the concept of the German war plan in Lorraine to determine if it was justified. The German left wing in Lorraine had to be protected, but the success of the German right-wing attack was not predicated on fixing strong French forces in Lorraine, helpful as that might be. The right-wing attack could succeed even if the French drew their troops out of Lorraine. The open terrain between Brussels, Paris and the English Channel coast permitted the quicker and more efficient employment of the numerically superior and more combat-effective German masses than Alsace-Lorraine with its mountains and fortresses. If the French made correct use of the Verdun–Toul–Épinal–Belfort fortifications, it was a certainty that the Germans could not fix significant French forces in Lorraine. It was a fundamental error to push Sixth and Seventh Armies towards the strong French fortifications on the Meurthe without an appropriate level of siege artillery and equipment. To accomplish the necessary mission of initially fixing a portion of the French forces between Toul and Belfort, it would probably have been necessary to merely deploy the two German armies in Alsace-Lorraine. Then they should have been moved as quickly and in the greatest strength as possible, either by rail or foot through Metz, to the west side of the Meuse and Moselle to take part in the decisive battle. Rupprecht wanted to do this from the beginning. The defence of Alsace-Lorraine, assisted by natural obstacles, the fortifications at Metz, Strasbourg and the Upper Rhine, could have been entrusted to a limited number of troops, with extensive use of *Landwehr* and *Landsturm* units. Of course, this would not prevent a French advance into Alsace-Lorraine, which was actually to be desired, and which would be ineffective so long as it did not extend to the Lower Moselle. As Frederick the Great said: 'He who defends all, defends nothing'. If the right-wing attack succeeded, Alsace and Lorraine would be regained.

Both the French and Germans therefore wanted to fix as many opposing forces in the secondary theatre of operations in Lorraine. The side that did so successfully would initially commit fewer forces there and not allow enemy actions to force it to send reinforcements to Lorraine. The mission of guarding each army's flank in Lorraine could be solved by standing on the defensive, while attempting to fix enemy forces in Lorraine required the offensive. Rupprecht was therefore correct in his initial intention to go on the offensive and, if the enemy attacked in strength, his armies would turn to the defensive. It would, however, be difficult to establish how strong the enemy actually was, and the enemy could also withdraw forces from Lorraine. Again, clarity could be established only by choosing the proper time to go from the defensive to the offensive.

In order to renew the attack on Mühlhausen, the French formed an army detachment under General Pau, the *armée d'Alsace*, on 10 August. To VII Corps, 8 Cavalry Div. and 57 RD (the Belfort reserve) were added the Reserve Division Group 1 (58, 63, 66 RD), 44 ID was brought from the Italian border and Alpine Battalions 12, 13, 22, 28 and 30, which were already in the Vosges, were also incorporated. Assembling these forces took time, and the detachment was not ready to move until 16 August, this time to make a 'decisive effort'. The French command, in view of the uncertain situation at Liège and in Belgium, obviously wanted to fix German forces in Alsace, as well as support the offensive into Lorraine. The mission of the *armée d'Alsace* was to attack through Mühlhausen to Colmar and Schlettstadt, blockade Neu-Breisach and destroy the Rhine bridges.

The attack into Lorraine began on 14 August. The French First Army, reduced to the XIV, XXI, XIII, and VIII Corps, had as its first objectives Saarburg, the Donon hill mass and the Breusch Valley. General Dubail, concerned for his right flank, ordered XIV and XXI Corps and 71 RD to attack over the Vosges passes between Diedolshausen and the Donon, though he hoped to be able to divert one corps towards Saarburg.

The French Second Army was to maintain contact with Nancy on the left flank, and with First Army on the right, while attacking through Duß–Château

Salins to Saarbrücken (off map, north of Saargemünd). At first the direction of
march was east, then north. XVIII Corps was kept at Toul under control of GQG
(*Grand Quartier Général* – the French senior HQ).

Diespach, 14 August (sketch 3)

In order to cover the movement of XIV and XV AK north, on 12 August Seventh
Army HQ ordered 30 RD to block the French attack at Urbeis, Bavarian 1 and
2 *Landwehr* Brigades and the 55 *Landwehr* Brigade, reinforced by the garrisons of
Neu-Breisach and Neuenburg, *Landwehr* IR 110 and 119 (on the map, 'Mathy',
the 55 *Landwehr* Brigade commander) to guard the other passes of the Vosges
from Strasbourg to the Swiss border.

Between 8 and 12 August the French had unsuccessfully attacked the passes at
Urbeis, Markirch and Diedolshausen. On 10 August the French XXI Corps had
taken the Col du Hantz (Hantz Pass) 12km south-west of Schirmeck and, on
14 August, XIV Corps finally took Urbeis.

The commander of 60 Bde was sent to Diespach on 13 August to stop the
French attack at Col du Hantz with a truly unusual mix of units: Bavarian RIR
15, RIR 99 (I/RIR 99, half of II/RIR 99, IV/RIR 99), Strasbourg Fortress MG
Sec. 1, 2/Mounted *Jäger* R 3, the *Ersatz* Sec./FAR 15 (a horse and a field artillery
battery), a platoon of 5/Foot Artillery R 10 (sFH), and one from 1 *Ersatz*/FAR 51.

On 14 August this force was prepared for battle on the high ground above
Diespach. III b. RIR 15, reinforced by Fortress MG Sec. 1, held the centre on an
800m front west of Diespach and oriented to the west. South of this position was
I/RIR 99 (with two platoons of the RIR 99 MGK) and then two companies
of II/RIR 99 (with one MG platoon), oriented south. On the far left was I b.
RIR 15. II b. RIR 15 and IV/RIR 99 were in reserve north of Hill 581. *Ersatz*
Sec./FAR 15 and the platoon of 1 *Ersatz*/FAR 51 were in the centre at Hill 558,
while 5/Res Foot Artillery R 10 (sFH) was behind Hill 581. The position was
extraordinarily unfavourable, for the ridge from Hill 581 to Hill 558 was small,
while the long slopes to the east and west could be swept by flanking fire from
the south. Most importantly, the position was dominated by wooded hills, which
offered the enemy concealed avenues of approach and superior firing positions.

At 0730hrs French artillery opened accurate fire from a dominating hill 2.5km
to the south-west. French infantry advancing in close formation were destroyed
by the MG attached to II/RIR 99. The French artillery fire increased in intensity,
wounding the 60 Bde commander and killing the commander of III b. RIR 15.
At 1100hrs French artillery appeared 6km south-east of Breusch-Urbach. The
Diespach detachment was now being hit by artillery – probably eight batteries –
firing from two directions. The French infantry began to manoeuvre along the

Diespach 14. 8.

Textskizze 3.

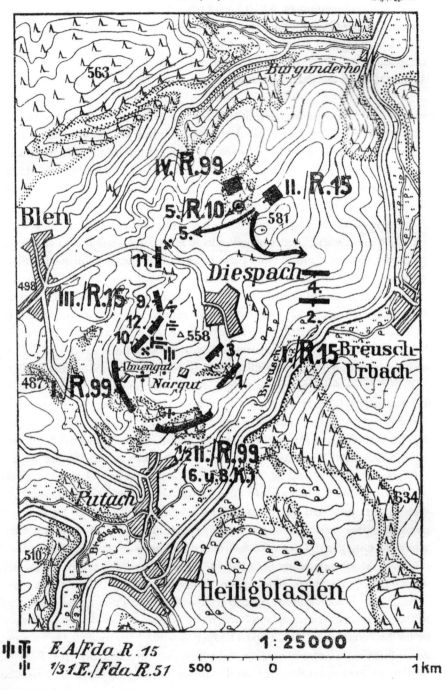

1 : 25000

E.A./Fda.R.15
1/31 E./Fda.R.51

500   0   1 km

treeline north-west of Blen and over the hills east of Heiligenblasien to take the Diespach detachment in both flanks. By 1100hrs they had approached to within 600m. II b. RIR 15 extended the left flank, 5/RIR 99 the right. In the middle the MGs with I/RIR 99 had brought the French infantry to a halt at a range of 700–900m. However, the French artillery gained fire superiority and, by 1400hrs, the German artillery had been silenced. 5/Res Foot Artillery R 10 (sFH) was able to save the guns, but the rest of the artillery was lost. Around 1600hrs the German commanders ordered a withdrawal. I b. RIR 15 provided the rearguard while II b. RIR 15 covered its movement from Hill 581 and the high ground north-east of Breusch-Urbach. Both units broke contact with relatively little difficulty. III b. RIR 15 apparently did not receive the order and pulled back with great difficulty and heavy losses, leaving their packs and moving up the hillside individually in complete view of the enemy. Some of the battalion could not vacate the position until 2000hrs. All the MGs of Fortress MG Sec. 1 were lost. IV/RIR 99 began to withdraw between 1500hrs and 1600hrs. I/RIR 99 and the two companies of II/RIR 99 withdrew at 1800hrs, taking considerable casualties. The four MGs in their sector held on until dusk, by which time they were practically encircled; the MGs were lost and the crews took heavy casualties. The disorganised remnants of the Diespach force withdrew by foot and rail that night to Lutzelhouse (not on map, 20km to the east of Diespach, only 12km west of Fort Kaiser Wilhelm II ('KW II') at Molsheim) to reorganise. The enemy did not pursue.

The border security at Schirmeck and b. RIR 15 had suffered a serious defeat. This was due to the poorly chosen position and superior enemy forces. In addition to strong artillery, the French committed at least an infantry brigade from the XXI Corps, which also took the Donon on 15 August. Nevertheless, the Diespach detachment had held its position until late afternoon. RIR 15 lost 1 officer and 61 enlisted men KIA, 5 officers and 105 enlisted men WIA, 2 officers and 231 enlisted men MIA. The French claimed to have taken a standard, 12 guns, 8 MG and 537 POWs.

On 15 August III/RIR 15 was brought to Lutzelhouse. The French had advanced to Schirmeck and were feeling towards Lutzelhouse, as well as 7km east of the Breusch and south of Lutzelhouse, and were capable of outflanking Lutzelhouse through the mountains. The troops at Lutzelhouse therefore fell back to KW II at Molsheim.

Seventh Army to 17 August (map b)

On the night of 14–15 August 13 b. RIR 4 was driven out of Sennheim, but retook the town on 15 August with the assistance of armoured train No. 9. By 1200hrs reports and rumours made it likely that the French were close to Thann,

Sennheim and Gebweiler, and the commander of the 55 *Landwehr* Bde ordered an evacuation of Mühlhausen and a withdrawal over the Rhine at Neuenburg. The German population of Mühlhausen fled.

The order to rail-march XV AK to the south-west of Strasbourg and XIV AK to Saarburg on 14 August was issued on 13 August at 2120hrs. Contrary to orders XV AK, positioned at Sennheim, foot marched all but one brigade; the situation in the Vosges seemed so threatening to the corps commander that he did not think a rail movement west of the Rhine to be safe. By the end of 14 August the mass of the corps had reached Colmar.

The withdrawal of the covering force to KW II caused considerable concern at Seventh Army HQ. Fortress Strasbourg and KW II were not 'armed'; that is, the field fortifications between the permanent fortifications had not been completed, and a great part of the fortress reserve, 30 RD, was no longer in the fort. As a precaution, 56 Infantry Bde (XIV AK), which was moving by rail, was diverted to KW II along with a cavalry squadron and three artillery batteries on 14 August. The sole brigade of XV AK that was moving by rail, 60 Bde, had reached Obernai (not on map, 6km north of Barr). XIV RK at Schlettstadt, which was to have foot marched to Wasselnheim, north-west of Strasbourg, was turned west towards the Vosges and spread out from Epfig (not on map, 5km south of Barr) in the north to Colmar in the south.

The 30 RD, 8km north-west of Schlettstadt, was ordered to march north-west to relieve the pressure on KW II. However, the heat forced a long halt after only 3km. The division was then placed under the operational control of XIV RK, which returned it to its start point with orders to defend in place and to allow the French to come to them. 2 *Landwehr* Bde was moved by rail to the north-east of Markirch on 14 August. 1 *Landwehr* Bde reached Colmar by narrow-gauge rail that evening.

Although the Seventh Army was moving north, considerable forces swung west towards the Vosges on 14 August and, as units were being broken up and intermixed, the chain of command was becoming confused. There was a danger that the corps would disappear into the mountains. Rupprecht was forced to intervene sharply in order to get operations back on track and unite both armies at Saarburg. It was becoming apparent that this goal, and the advance on the Moselle and Meurthe, could hardly be achieved before 17 August.

In the meantime, OHL had gained the impression from intelligence reports that the French had gathered extraordinarily strong forces from Pont-à-Mousson to Raon l'Étape, perhaps the mass of their army. In the first wave were twelve corps and five cavalry divisions; in the second, west of Charmes, another three corps; and behind each wing at Toul and Épinal, a group of reserve divisions (each with four to six divisions), with VII AK and 8 KD at the minimum (there could have been more than VII Corps (not AK) and the French 8 Cavalry Division) at

Klein=Rumbach 13. 8.

Textskizze 4.

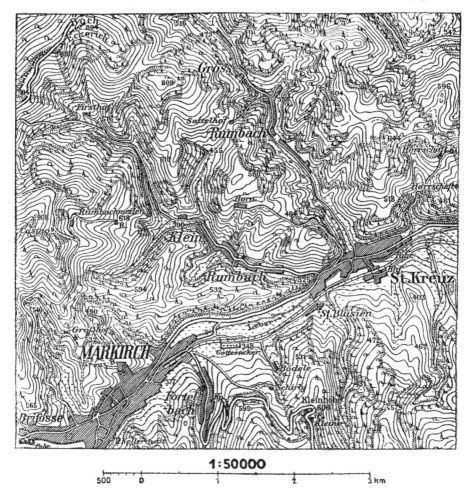

1:50000

500   0   1   2   3 km

Belfort. The main French attack between Metz and Strasbourg that Moltke had expected seemed to be coming to pass.

Rupprecht received this OHL estimate on the morning of 14 August. It now appeared that the situation and mission had been clarified. Previously it seemed necessary to attack a tentative enemy who was at most of equal strength; against this massively superior enemy the only course of action was to withdraw. The enemy would be first confronted on the Saar at Saarlouis–Saargemünd, in the Vosges between Pfalzburg and Molsheim, and on the Breusch Position. The Sixth Army would maintain contact on its right flank with the Nied Position and extend left as far as Metting (not on map, 6km north-west of Pfalzburg). The Seventh Army had the mission of holding the Breusch Position and, above all, to prevent a breakthrough on the middle Vosges at Pfalzburg and Molsheim. The entire Seventh Army would be assembled north of the Breusch; Alsace was to be left to the enemy. On 15 August XIV RK reached Barr–Schlettstadt and XV AK arrived at Colmar. XIV AK was in rail movement. 56 Bde, at KW II, was sent to Wasselnheim (not on map, north 14km north of KW II) and was replaced by 42 *Landwehr* Infantry Bde at KW II on 16 August. The units in the Vosges continued to provide security for the Seventh Army movement north.

The French positioned in the Vosges hardly moved in the following days. Rather, the commander of the French First Army intended to reinforce the advance of his left wing, where he expected the strongest resistance or, indeed, a German counter-attack. Therefore, on 16 August, he ordered the XXI Corps to hold the Donon and the Breusch Valley at Wisches (not on map, 13km west of KW II) with 13 ID, but move 43 ID north towards St Quirin. The French XIV Corps was to extend its left flank north and limit its activities to the defence of the Vosges passes. These northward movements occupied the two corps for the following days. The only forward movement was made by XIV Corps, which occupied Markirch on 16 August and Weiler the next day.

Thanks to French inactivity, the rearguard of the Diespach detachment was able to maintain itself in the Breusch Valley immediately south of KW II on 15 August. 3 Res. Bde dug in on the Breusch Position. 30 RD shifted its defensive position north, to a location just south of Barr, which allowed the French to occupy Weiler.

On 15 August 2 *Landwehr* Brigade, which had neither MGs nor artillery, blocked the Leber Valley, 2km east of Markirch. At 1600hrs II/ b. *Landwehr* IR 12, while defending a hilltop devoid of cover, was attacked by a battalion of French Alpine troops supported by MGs and artillery. Nevertheless, the *Landwehr* men delivered well-aimed fire, which kept the French Alpine infantry at the respectful distance of 1,200m until dark, when the firing ceased. The brigade commander decided to withdraw from the valley. During the day it had begun to rain, and the night withdrawal was conducted in a downpour, with mist and fog filling the valleys illuminated by lightning. By morning on 16 August the brigade had taken up position at the mouth of the valley, 6km west of Schlettstadt, to cover the last rail movement out of Schlettstadt, and remained there on 17 August. The French approached to within 5km, but did not attack. At Colmar, between 15 and 17 August, 1 *Landwehr* Bde marched and counter-marched, but did not make contact.

By noon on 17 August the redeployment of Seventh Army had practically been completed, undisturbed by the enemy. XIV AK was at Pfalzburg. The mass of XV AK did finally rail-march from Colmar and Schlettstadt to Wasselnheim, while XIV RK had arrived at the area between the Breusch, Barr and Erstein.

Sixth Army Withdrawal, 14–17 August

In Lorraine, the French began their attack on 14 August. On the left flank of the French First Army, XIII Corps advanced on Cirey and VIII Corps on Blâmont. This was the French main point of effort, aiming for a breakthrough at Saarburg. The Second Army was in an echelon left formation: XVI Corps advanced from Lunéville towards Elfringen, XV Corps on Duß, and XX Corps from Nancy on Château Salins. IX Corps and 70 RD held the high ground east and south of Pont-à-Mousson and protected the left flank. 59 RD and 68 RD were south of Nancy.

The two French armies formed a wedge aimed at Saarburg and the left flank of the German Sixth Army, particularly I b. AK, which was far forward. It had been ordered on 13 August to withdraw if seriously attacked, in preparation for which it had moved its supply units to the north side of the Vezouse and deployed in depth. At 0800hrs on 14 August French infantry was sighted, and at 0900hrs I b. AK was attacked unsuccessfully by the lead elements of the French VIII and XIII Corps, supported by artillery. At 0930hrs I b. AK ordered a withdrawal across the Vezouse to Cirey–Elfringen, which, thanks to the prior preparation, was conducted smoothly, and by 1600hrs was in its new position, with 1 ID on the left and 2 ID on the right. The French followed cautiously and did not make contact with infantry; their artillery often bombarded empty positions, and in the resulting artillery duel the German 15cm howitzers gave first proof of their effectiveness, quickly silencing the opposing guns.

Superior French forces, XV and XX Corps, also attacked the German XXI AK on 14 August. The only significant combat occurred when the French 29 ID (XV Corps) was caught in march column and handled so severely that it did not advance the next day. In the II b. AK and III b. AK sectors the day passed in complete quiet.

When OHL informed Sixth Army HQ that the French main attack was going to be made in Lorraine, Sixth Army decided to withdraw over the Saar. During the course of 14 August, Sixth Army made its concept known in general terms to the subordinate commands, as well as the intended routes of withdrawal, rearguard positions and defensive sectors on the Saar. The supply trains were to be moved across the Saar early. There were to be no rail demolitions in the area formed by Metz, Saarlouis and Saarburg. Firm orders were not issued. Planning for the attack on Fort Manonviller was suspended

Since the enemy had kept his distance from II b. and III b. AK, Sixth Army saw no need to order them to move on 15 August. XXI AK and I b. AK, which were already in contact with strong enemy forces, were to withdraw. I b. AK, which was to cover the disembarkation of XIV AK, was required to gain as much time as possible, and therefore had to conduct a delay on successive positions without becoming decisively engaged. 7 KD was attached and given the mission of guarding the corps' left flank.

Cirey, 14 August (sketch 5)[39]

On the afternoon of 14 August, 2 Bde, on the left flank of I b. AK, had occupied a position at Cirey, reinforced by 1/FAR 1 and II/FAR 7, with 1 Bde on its right. I/IR 2, with II/FAR 2 immediately behind it, was near the churchyard on the north side of the Vezouse, while II/IR 16 and two platoons of the MGK and III/IR 2 with a MG platoon were dug in on the south side of Cirey; houses and trees restricted the fields of fire. In reserve were II/IR 2, 600m north of the cemetery, and I and III/IR 16, in a wood 1km north-east of Cirey. 2/IR 16 was later positioned in the cemetery while 10/IR 16, in the castle park, covered two batteries of I/FAR 1. II/IR 2 was corps reserve.

An artillery duel was already in progress when, at about 1700hrs, enemy skirmishers, supported by artillery, began a firefight with III/IR 2, and at 1900hrs launched a more serious attack on II/IR 16. Initially the French attack gained little ground, particularly due to the fire support of 2/FAR 1 and 3/FAR 1 in the castle park. By dark, however, the French had approached to within 500m. Since the French were also attacking the Bavarian left flank from Chatillon, at 1900hrs III/IR 2 extended the line left, while 3/IR 16 was inserted in the centre. After dark I and III/IR 16 were ordered to extend the left flank further. This did not proceed smoothly: there were considerable delays in transmitting orders and the direct route crossed a hillside totally devoid of cover and concealment, so the two battalions moved east to descend a path through a wood, which soon disappeared into dense bushes. The combat trains and MG vehicles stuck fast. There was heavy firing to the front and, as the battalions finally arrived, they too opened fire, causing the French to withdraw, leaving equipment and weapons on the field and in the villages of Chatillon and Petitmont (1km south). II/IR 16 withdrew to its

Cirey 14. 8.

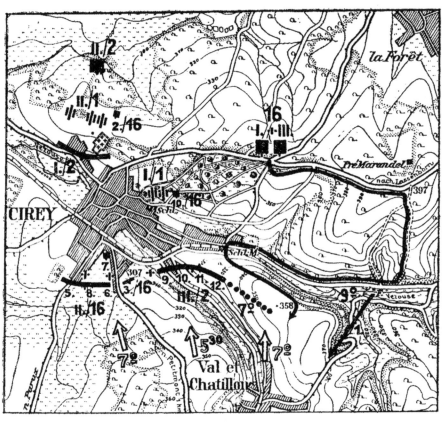

1:50000

500   0   1000   2000 m

original position by marching through Cirey and was apparently fired upon from the houses, which led to a confusing, noisy firefight.

The French also continued to advance after dark in the 2 ID sector. Due to its exposed position in the valley, Blâmont was evacuated. The French occupied the town and, at 0300hrs on 15 August, heavy firing broke out north of the town. It appeared that the French were attempting to break through between 4 and 3 Bde. On the left flank of 4 Bde the French hit II/IR 15, and 6/IR 15 in particular, which threw back the French attack. At daybreak three French officers and numerous men were found dead in front of the company position. IR 20, on the right flank of 3 Bde, was also threatened. II/IR 20, which was in reserve, moved forward in column, which drew heavy French fire, resulting in considerable confusion and mixing of the units (the chain of events here was never clarified). In any case, the advance guards of the French VIII and XIII Corps did not break through at Blâmont or Cirey.

However, the commander of I b. AK could expect renewed French attacks at both towns on 15 August, along with a manoeuvre to turn his right flank, and consonant with his mission he decided to avoid combat and conduct a withdrawal. Preparations were made during the night, and the supply trains sent to the rear. Only the most important points were to be held, and those with weak forces. Artillery rearguards would delay the French, particularly the long-range mortars of II and III/Pr. Foot Artillery R 18. 7 KD guarded the left flank. At 0500hrs the corps HQ ordered each division to form two marching columns, with movement to begin between 0600hrs and 0700hrs, and a rearguard position located halfway to Saarburg. Preparations were made to cross the Rhine–Marne Canal, and the dominating heights south of Saarburg were fortified by a battalion from each division and the Eng. R. The music of the regimental bands sweetened the bitter taste occasioned by the withdrawal, and the French did not disturb or follow the movement. There was a traffic jam where five roads connected at St Georges (10km north-east of Blâmont), but by noon the rearguard position had been occupied (primarily by artillery) while the troops were ready to march along the Rhine–Marne Canal. 7 KD patrols found no enemy forces on the roads to the Donon. Sixth Army HQ, which was in telephonic contact with I b. AK, directed that serious resistance be offered only behind the Saar. Although the French were still nowhere in evidence, the corps HQ ordered the withdrawal to continue over the Rhine–Marne Canal at 1430hrs, with rearguards to remain on the canal. The troops continued their movement until they bivouacked at Saarburg and to the west. The main bodies of the French VIII and XIII Corps reached Blâmont and Cirey.

On the I b. AK left, the b. KD and 8 KD fell back about 22km from the border at Elfringen. The French XVI Corps, tired out and restricted by the lack of progress of XV Corps on its left, only reached the border at Elfringen. The

French XV Corps had evidently not overcome the damage suffered by 29 ID the previous day, for it hardly budged, nor did XX Corps on its left. The German XXI AK was therefore able to stand fast. The same was true in the II and III b. AK sectors, which also did not move. I b. RK took position behind I b. AK.

The *Generalquartiermeister* (executive officer) at OHL, General von Stein, advanced the idea, which reached Sixth Army on 15 August, that the French should be lured into a sack between Metz, the Nied and the Saar and destroyed there: the Sixth and Seventh Armies would then counter-attack from the east, and the Fifth Army would move through Metz to attack from the west. Even the participation of Fourth Army was considered. Moltke had favoured such an operation from the beginning, and in the last few days it had taken on firmer contours. Such an operation might even decide the campaign. But there was no guarantee when, or if, the French would enter the sack. The French advance had been conducted cautiously. On 15 August the French Second Army commander prescribed that his troops advance carefully, step by step, from one piece of terrain to the next, similar to siege warfare. If the post-war statements by French officers are correct, the French recognised before the war the dangers and difficulties awaiting them in Lorraine. The French would have to be very self-confident or very careless to fall into the German trap. In any case, this plan granted the French the initiative and they could advance where and when they wished, which was not consonant with Rupprecht's mission to fix the greatest number of French forces in Lorraine. The mission also stated that, if the French were inactive in Lorraine, then by the time the German right wing began to advance, Rupprecht had to attack. For the immediate future, Rupprecht's only justifiable course of action was to withdraw behind the Saar.

General von Stein also relieved Sixth Army from the requirement to maintain contact on the right with the Nied Position at Saarlouis. He recommended that the right wing should extend only to Saarbrücken. On 15 August OHL decided to fill the gap between the Nied Position and Sixth Army with *Ersatz* troops. OHL communicated directly with Seventh Army to emphasise the need to quickly assemble strong forces at Pfalzburg. That evening Rupprecht repeated to Seventh Army the requirement to evacuate the Upper Alsace, not engage in secondary operations, and to assemble the mass of its forces as soon as possible between Molsheim and Zabern.

To conduct the decisive battle in Lorraine, Moltke ordered the six and a half uncommitted *Ersatz* divisions there on 15 August. It had originally been intended to send these units to the right wing.[40] 4, 8 and 10 *Ersatz* Divisions (ED) were assigned to Sixth Army and would arrive at Saarlouis and Saarbrücken on 17 August to fill the gap between the Nied Position and the right flank of Sixth Army. The Guard ED, Bavarian ED and 19 ED were assigned to Seventh Army and would move to Strasbourg, while 55 *Ersatz* Bde assembled at Mühlheim.

At noon on 15 August, Sixth Army HQ thought that the enemy was advancing all along the front, maintaining contact on the left with his fortifications at Nancy while pushing forward his right, doubtless with the intention of breaking through at the Donon and outflanking both the Saar and Breusch Positions. Although at no point was the Sixth Army involved in close combat, Rupprecht decided to withdraw Sixth Army to the Saarbrücken–Saarburg Position on 16 August. The right flank of Seventh Army, XIV AK, would maintain contact with the left flank of Sixth Army. HKK 3 would withdraw to the area between the Nied Position and Saarbrücken to prevent penetration there by enemy cavalry, while 7 KD would continue to protect the left flank of I b. AK.

The Sixth Army order of 16 August covered the entire period required to withdraw to the Saar and establish a defensive position there. To maintain morale, the troops were to be informed of the purpose of the withdrawal. The units had to be prepared to go over to the attack if enemy actions required it. The degree of resistance during the delaying movement had to provide enough time to adequately fortify the Saar Position; advance parties would begin the defensive work. Phase lines for the rearguards were specified. For 16 August this was the French Nied–Finstingen. All units were to be on the Saar Position by 18 August. 5 RD would constitute the army reserve.

On 16 August I b. RK (minus 5 RD) began to fortify its sector north of Finstingen. The rearguard of I b. AK on the Rhine–Marne Canal was weak in infantry but contained most of the artillery. The mass of the infantry was south of Saarburg, prepared to withdraw or occupy a position on the canal. The first steps had been taken the previous evening to fortify the Saar. During the morning, strong enemy columns appeared and an artillery duel developed in which II/FAR 4 suffered from the fire of enemy heavy artillery, until the 21cm mortars of II/Pr. Foot Artillery R 18 arrived and silenced it. After dark 2 ID, the right-flank division, was withdrawn over the Saar to the north of Saarburg. In spite of all the preparation, there were considerable march delays in the pitch-black night and pouring rain, so that some troops did not reach their positions until morning. An infantry regimental combat team and 1 Bde were left west of the river as rearguards. 2 ID bivouacked around Saarburg. Work began on the I b. AK position north of Saarburg, principally clearing fields of fire. The Engineer Regiment supported the 2 ID, three companies of corps engineers supported the 1 ID. Three days of withdrawal had severely fatigued the troops, particularly the artillery, which had continually moved from one rearguard position to the next. Jammed roads, conflicting routes for marching columns and rain added to the difficulties. The staffs had many problems to solve and spent sleepless nights. 7 KD guarded the left flank, but was unable to penetrate the French counter-reconnaissance screen. The French XIV Corps had contact with the I b. AK left at a point 3km south-east of Saarburg. The

French XIII and VIII Corps were 15km to the south, and had barely crossed the border.

The two cavalry divisions of HKK 3 were on the I b. AK right flank, about 11km north of the border and the Rhine–Marne Canal. The French XVI Corps had carefully pushed elements across the canal, but had gone no further. The German XXI AK had pulled back about 25km from the border, with its right flank at Bensdorf, and begun digging in, but had left a rearguard at Duß, only 14km from the border. The French XV and XX Corps also advanced carefully and penetrated only 3km across the border at Wich, and to the south. II b. AK began its withdrawal to the area south-east of Falkenberg, with rearguards about 6km south of the main body. III b. AK withdrew over the German Nied at and northwest of Falkenberg, with rearguards on the French Nied. The French IX Corps remained on French territory and did not cross the Selle.

The Bavarian air reconnaissance was suffering from a lack of aircraft. Aviation Sec. 1, from I b. AK, had already lost two aircraft by 15 August. The II b. AK aviation element, Aviation Sec. 2, had lost enough aircraft by 16 August that its effectiveness was severely restricted.

The French had advanced timidly and only a short distance. While the French First Army moved towards Saarburg, for the last two days Second Army had moved in echelon left on the First Army left flank. Second Army now began to swing north-east. The Second Army right flank had three corps on an 18km front, while on the left flank, which had hardly budged, it positioned two corps on a 21km front; one of these, XX Corps, was obviously deployed in depth.

Early on the morning of 16 August OHL informed Sixth Army by telephone that further intelligence reports had shaken its conviction that the French were going to make their main effort towards Saarbrücken. Enemy strength in Lorraine had been seriously overestimated. OHL now had doubts that the French would enter the trap between the Nied and Saar. At the very least the Sixth Army withdrawal had to slow down. The French were now thought to have ten to twelve corps in Lorraine, which was still too strong for Sixth and Seventh Armies to attack. However, Rupprecht and his chief of staff, Krafft, thought that nothing to this point prevented the French from deploying fewer forces in Lorraine; the character of the French advance did not allow the Germans to say whether the French were in earnest or just conducting a feint. There were reports of French forces withdrawing from the Moselle. In addition to covering the left wing, Rupprecht's mission was to fix strong enemy forces in Lorraine, which now moved into the foreground, and could only be accomplished by attacking. The Germans were numerically inferior and Rupprecht recognised that the offensive involved risk: a defeat at the beginning of the war would be especially damaging. But a favourable opportunity presented itself to attack the French in front of their fortress line and fix them in place. The German superiority in tactics and morale, which had been demonstrated in the initial engagements, gave favourable prospects if the offensive were conducted against equal or even superior numbers. Therefore, on the morning of 16 August, Rupprecht decided to attack.

A decisive envelopment was not possible. The French had anchored their left flank on the field fortifications at Nancy, and the Vosges protected their right against a surprise attack in strength. Rupprecht was therefore forced to attack frontally; the force of the attack and surprise would replace envelopment. The French corps did not advance in a continuous front, but in numerous small columns deployed in depth; the Germans could hope to overrun the lead elements before support arrived. If the French continued to advance in the Vosges, a shallow envelopment might be feasible there.

It was advantageous to attack as soon as possible, while the French would be surprised and restricted by the ponds, watercourses and forests in the Duß−Saarburg area. The overall situation required the attack in Lorraine be conducted before that in Belgium, to prevent the French from reinforcing their left. Due to excellent prior planning, the Sixth Army was well positioned to go over to the offensive. On the morning of 16 August the corps had been instructed to suspend rearward movements and halt in place. The rearward movement had given the army enough distance from the enemy to allow it to mass at the decisive point. This also argued for immediate action, before the enemy closed in. Rupprecht initially intended to attack on 18 August. However, the cooperation of the Seventh Army was essential, and Seventh Army reported that it would be ready on 20 August at the earliest. There was no choice but to delay the attack.

The Sixth Army order for 17 August therefore said that the army would remain in its 16 August positions. I b. AK and XIV AK were to continue to dig in; XXI AK was to begin digging in. The remaining corps would hold themselves ready to march. The 16 August rearguard positions were to be held if attacked.

On the Saarburg−Pfalzburg road flowed a stream of civilians moving east who had been driven by fear of the impending great battle to load their moveable possessions on wagons and abandon their homes and farms.

(Map c) On 17 August the French once again approached the I b. AK sector slowly and cautiously with the lead elements, about 5km to the west and south of the Bavarian position. Indeed, the commander of the French First Army thought the troops required rest and made only a short day's march, so that at the end of the day the divisional main bodies were only 2−3km across the border. General Dubail viewed the withdrawal of the I b. AK as a trap, and feared that it would turn around south of Saarburg and attack, in conjunction with two corps that he thought just arrived in the Bavarian rear. He held VIII and XIII Corps back and considered reinforcing them with elements of XXI Corps and, if necessary, XIV Corps. Joffre gave his assent, for he was also of the opinion that the withdrawal of Seventh Army from Mühlhausen was merely the prelude to an attack from Zabern. This removed the basis for any hope that the French could be drawn into the well-known trap between Metz, the Nied Position and the Saar.

I b. AK continued work on the Saar Position. Sixth Army HQ sent I b. AK barbed wire, pioneer tools and sandbags by rail from the depot at Germersheim. The Bavarian Siege Train was divided between I b. AK and 1 RD.

There was no change on the Sixth Army front. 7 KD reported that its horses were completely exhausted and, except for one brigade, remained in place. 1 RD dug in behind the Saar, while XXI AK, II and III b. AK prepared the rearguard positions for a determined defence and reconnoitred positions behind the Saar. During the withdrawal a gap had formed between II b. AK and XXI AK, which was filled by HKK 3.

In front of III b. AK the enemy only crossed the Selle with patrols. The advance guard of the French 17 ID had moved to the border due west of Château Salins. Otherwise the French IX Corps and 70 RD on the heights of Nancy had not budged. On the other hand, the French XX Corps had reached Château Salins, XV Corps Duß and XVI Corps had advanced to the Saar–Kohlenkanal (Saar–Coal Canal) just south of Mittersheim. The French Second Army swing to the north was even more pronounced than on the previous day. It was led by the XVI Corps, with the left flank of the First Army, XIII and VIII Corps, considerably to the rear south-west of Saarbrücken. The French were moving in wedge formation, aimed at the gap between XXI and XIV AK. In fact, the French commanders judged that they had already broken through the German line, and wanted to widen this supposed breach. On the basis of statements from the local inhabitants, they assumed that the German withdrawal was at least in part disorderly.

Rupprecht reported his decision to attack to OHL on the morning of 17 August. Late in the evening, Lieutenant Colonel von Dommes arrived from OHL and reiterated that the principal mission of the Sixth and Seventh Armies was to cover the left flank. OHL was concerned at the consequences of a defeat in Lorraine for the decisive right-wing attack. OHL thought that the French were numerically superior and displayed a tendency to dig in, so that even a successful attack would be costly and did not promise decisive results; if the French followed their doctrine, they would bring forwards units held in depth to counter-attack and a German defeat might still be a possibility. In addition, the enemy could not be enveloped and, if attacked too soon, would be in position to withdraw. OHL had not entirely given up the idea of trapping the French between the Nied and the Saar, even though the right-wing advance would begin the next day. In order to protect the right wing, OHL now desired the right wing of the Sixth Army to withdraw to the Nied Position, as originally intended, not to the Saar. Nevertheless, Dommes was only expressing OHL's point of view; he did not bring binding orders.

Rupprecht and Krafft carefully considered OHL's arguments, but their determination to attack remained unshaken. The troops of Sixth Army were burning to fight. Nevertheless. Rupprecht had unhesitatingly ordered them to withdraw in order to gain significant advantages. Now withdrawal was a sin against the morale of the troops, and he was absolutely convinced that the attack would be completely successful. He did not hide his opinion from Dommes, who was in agreement. OHL left the decision to attack up to Rupprecht.

Thanks to the training and morale of the troops, and thorough planning, the withdrawal had led to no discernible reduction in combat power. However, it did have some negative consequences. Some immobile vehicles and stockpiled ammunition had to be abandoned, while stragglers and immoveable wounded and sick, and the attending medical personnel, fell into enemy hands. This also provided the enemy with valuable intelligence information.

Frequent traffic jams had characterised the initial movements and the withdrawal. Traffic control had been a subject of careful peacetime training, but it was impossible to prepare for the masses of vehicles which only appeared after mobilisation, many of them difficult to move and turn. Traffic was often completely gridlocked. Officers carrying important orders had to leave their vehicles and mount horses. The solution was to require all stationary vehicles to leave the road. The initial marches, despite these difficulties, did acclimatise the troops to operations under wartime conditions.

Initial Advance: Combat in the Vosges, 18–19 August (map c)

By 17 August the Seventh Army had completed its redeployment. XV AK and XIV RK were on the right flank in the Rhine Valley west of Strasbourg, with 30 RD and 1 and 2 *Landwehr* Brigades between Barr and Colmar. Three brigade task forces, named after their commanders (Mathy, Dame and Bodungen) guarded the Upper Rhine; they consisted of between four and nine *Landwehr* battalions. The three *Ersatz* Divisions had also arrived by rail in the Rhine Valley.

Rupprecht had informed Seventh Army on the morning of 17 August of his decision to attack. Since the troops, above all XV AK, had been tired out by the battles and marches of the last ten days, and the *Ersatz* Divisions would not be ready for operations until 19 August, the Seventh Army commander proposed to delay the attack until then, while pushing all available forces into the Vosges. On 17 August Rupprecht agreed to this plan.

Seventh Army issued its operations order on the morning of 18 August. XIV AK, reinforced by Strasbourg's heavy artillery, would initially defend in place east of Saarburg. XV AK was ordered to secure the Vosges passes north-west of Dagsburg and, on 19 August, attack to turn the enemy flank just north of St Quirin. XIV RK, reinforced by the 19 ED and 30 RD, was to attack up the Breusch Valley on 18 August and cross the Donon. The Guard ED was to assemble at Zabern and the Bavarian ED 12km south-west of Strasbourg, under Seventh Army control. The two *Landwehr* brigades and the three detachments on the Upper Rhine were placed under XIV RK control and would support by advancing towards the border.

Weiler, 18 August (map 1)

At midnight on 17 August 30 RD was ordered to advance into the Vosges to Triembach, just east of Weiler, and on the next day advance east to the border. Including the attached 5 *Ersatz* Bde, 30 RD had nine battalions, six 7.7cm batteries and one battery of 10cm canons. 10 Res. Bde was to advance before dawn to Triembach and organise it for defence, followed by 5 *Ersatz* Bde. The division commander then decided to attack the French forces reported at Weiler before noon. This required that 30 RD conduct a difficult night march. 2 *Landwehr* Bde on the left was asked to support 30 RD by advancing.

By 0400hrs 10 Res. Bde had marched over muddy roads to Triembach, with RIR 11 on the right, north and east of Triembach, two battalions of RIR 14 on the left at St Petersholz and Thannweiler, and III/RIR 14 and Fortress MG Sec. 2 in reserve in Hohwart. 3/Foot Artillery R 14 (10cm cannons), 1 and 2 *Ersatz*/ FAR 80, and 1 *Ersatz*/FAR 84 were in support, covered by the Bicycle Co./RIR 60 (all Prussian units). 5 *Ersatz* Bde arrived at 0900hrs. The rain stopped and the day became humid.

The 30 RD commander thought that the French were deployed in loose groups on the hill north of Weiler, in the town itself and on the west side of the Gießen Valley as far as Gereuth. He intended to turn the French left flank with 5 *Ersatz* Bde, and he counted on 2 *Landwehr* Brigade to attack the French right, while RIR 11 fixed the French frontally. He issued his order at 0940hrs.

Steep terrain, a traffic jam caused by supply units, the need to sweep the woods for enemy troops and, finally, 600m of roads blocked by fallen trees delayed 5 *Ersatz* Bde's movement, so that the advance guard did not reach open terrain until 1330hrs. It was then discovered that the main body was far behind.

The firefight in the 10 Res. Bde sector had started at 0730hrs when French artillery shelled the outposts of RIR 11, and the German artillery replied. At 1100hrs the brigade commander ordered III/RIR 14 to attack towards Triembach, while I and II/RIR 14 attacked Neukirch, and 5 and 6/RIR 11 would support by fire from their trenches. The attack was only to begin when 5 *Ersatz* Bde was in position.

Between 1300hrs and 1400hrs the French guns, deployed in depth and directed by forward observers (and largely immune to counter-battery fire), began to win the artillery duel; particularly effective was the French fire from the south of Gereuth into the German flank. The crews of both batteries south of the Hohwart–Triembach road (1 *Ersatz*/FAR 84 and 1 *Ersatz*/FAR 80) were forced to take cover several times, while 2 *Ersatz*/FAR 80 had to move 1km and 3/Res. Foot Artillery R 14 (10cm cannons) lost three guns to direct hits and was reduced to one gun, which continued to fire. The limbers and the town of Hohwart, which was packed with supply vehicles, were also hit and some of the horse teams panicked.

Under these circumstances, the commander of 10 Res. Bde saw that the only possibility was to attack, even without 5 *Ersatz* Bde, and he ordered the attack telephonically at 1400hrs. Reserve MG Sec. 3 was attached to III/RIR 14, Fortress MG Sec. 2 to I and II/RIR 14, and RIR 11 was to join the attack. 2 *Landwehr* Bde reported that it could not assist 30 RD. The 30 RD commander decided that he could delay no longer; he had to attack before the French did. The attack he conducted was contrary to all the rules of German doctrine: due to the late hour, there would be no envelopment of either French flank; it would be conducted on a 6km front with no coordination; and, far from enjoying artillery support, the attack was made in order to save the artillery from destruction.

III/RIR 14 attacked by bounds immediately after receiving the order at 1400hrs, with 11/RIR 14 on the right, 12/RIR 14 in the middle, 9/RIR 14 left and 10/RIR 14 following. Although it was advancing in a valley under fire, it took Weiler by 1800hrs, with fire support from a platoon of Res. MG Sec. 3 south-east of Triembach and two in the vineyards to the north. 9/RIR 14 took fire from the high ground west of Neukirch and swung in that direction, joined by 5 and 6/RIR 11, took this ground and engaged in a firefight with French troops to the north of Breitenau.

RIR 11 attacked immediately, with 1 and 2/RIR 11 on line, 3/RIR 11 following and 4/RIR 11 echeloned left, 7/RIR 11 and 8/RIR 11 in the second wave. RIR 11 soon took artillery fire, as well as rifle and MG fire from the high ground east and north of Weiler. 3 and 7/RIR 11 were committed to the firing line, while 4/RIR 11 extended the line on the left. At 1515hrs the high ground was assaulted, and RIR 11 pushed into Weiler, where it became intermixed with RIR 14.

5 *Ersatz* Bde advanced at 1500hrs with *Ersatz* Battalions V and VI, supported by *Ersatz* MGK 5. 2 *Ersatz*/FAR 2 got stuck in the woods and had to hack a path to the treeline, where it set up. With this fire support, the infantry climbed the hill south of Erlenbach at 1700hrs and took up the firefight with well-hidden infantry and MGs on the opposite treeline. French artillery deployed here was driven off. The 30 RD commander had decided that the main effort was to be on the left flank, so there was no assault.

1 and 4/RIR 14, supported by 9/RIR 14 and 5 and 6/RIR 11, assaulted Neukirch and then Hill 370 to the west of the town, taking six abandoned French guns, an observation wagon, thirty-six horses and seventy POWs.

By 1700hrs II/RIR 14 had reached the cover of the slope 500m south-west of Thannweiler, with 5/RIR 14 on the right, 7/RIR 14 in the middle, 8/RIR 14 on the left and 6/RIR 14 behind the left wing. It was not strong enough to attack the French forces by Gereuth, which consisted of Alpine troops and riflemen from two infantry regiments. At 1810hrs Fortress MG Sec. 2, which had been moving forward since 1400hrs, arrived at the firing line. Since 1300hrs 1 *Ersatz/ FAR* 2 had been engaged in an artillery duel from east of St Petersholz against French guns south of Gereuth. In order to engage French infantry, it moved first to the Scheiben-Berg (Scheiben Hill) south of the town, then to an open position directly behind II/RIR 14.

In order to bring a decision, between 1600hrs and 1700hrs the commander of 30 RD committed *Ersatz* Bn VIII on Diefenbach, with 1 and 2/*Ersatz* Bn VIII on line, 4/*Ersatz* Bn VIII behind the centre and 3/*Ersatz* Bn VIII echeloned left. As it reached the same level as II/RIR 14, it extended that battalion's right flank. The infantry attack provided relief for the German artillery, which, reinforced by the *Ersatz* batteries, resumed the artillery duel, reduced the French artillery fire and put fire on the French infantry.

2 *Landwehr* Bde was watching the exits from the Vosges at Rappoltsweiler and 4km west of Schlettstadt. On 17 August the French, estimated at division strength, had advanced to within 6km of the forward German units. However, on 18 August the French did not budge. The commander of 2 *Landwehr* therefore did not decide until 1600hrs to send II and III/*Landwehr* IR 3 and I/LIR 12 to take the enemy artillery at Gereuth, which was only 4km north-west of his forward elements, and he did not actually receive permission to do so until 1700hrs.

III/LIR 3 crossed the 3–4m wide and ½m deep Glessen stream and the wet valley at a run at 1800hrs, under late and weak artillery fire, and drove off a few French infantry from the woods south of Gereuth. 4/LIR 12, on outpost duty, attacked on the left flank. I/LIR 12 moved north on the Gereuth road at 1740hrs, 2/LIR 12 in the lead, followed by 10/LIR 12 and 3/LIR 12. Led by a local *Gendarme*, in order to avoid the open valley it turned left towards the sound of French artillery firing through the woods, where the thick undergrowth slowed movement. The packs were dropped, bayonets fixed and the *Landwehr* men moved in groups up the last 200m of the steep, heavily wooded hill. 2/LIR 12 on the left and 10/LIR 12 on the right charged straight into the French battery, which had set up on a forest road in the middle of the woods. Two guns were able to limber up and get away, but the crews of the other two were shot or bayoneted and the guns taken. It took considerable effort for the leaders to get the elated *Landwehr* men under control and lead them north through the woods, taking a few prisoners as they went. 3 and 4/LIR 12 came up and linked up with III/LIR 3 on the right. Both battalions made contact with French infantry, which had failed to protect their guns and were apparently trying to take them back. Some French appeared in the flank and rear. A wild firefight began at point-blank range, becoming hand-to-hand in places. As dusk fell, there were surely incidents of friendly fire. The battle swung back and forth and, in order to keep the French from retaking a gun, it was rolled downhill into the woods. Finally, the French were beaten and retreated. The two *Landwehr* battalions were completely intermixed and it took every means available – shouts, whistles and signals – to cease the firing and re-establish control. The enemy left a large number of dead, wounded and about 100 prisoners. It was now dark. As though it were a peacetime manoeuvre, the *Landwehr* men left the woods, taking the wounded with them, and formed up on the valley road. There they met II/LIR 3, which had moved straight north on the road and taken artillery fire; the battalion deployed and fired on the guns at 1.5km range and they quickly withdrew. Elements of 6 and 7/LIR 3 had joined in the I/LIR 12 fight.

The attack of the *Landwehr* battalions, which took the French by surprise, added impetus to the attack on Gereuth. In addition, 1 Ersatz/FAR 12 went into battery on the high ground south-west of St Petersholz and engaged French infantry and MGs in front of Gereuth. At about 2000hrs II/RIR 14 and Ersatz Bn VIII and VI, supported by Fortress MG Sec. 2, drove the French back into the woods.

The troops were now out of control, and although the division ordered them to defend in place, they streamed back into the towns looking for food and shelter. The enemy did not use this opportunity, but contact with him was lost, as well as some of the captured enemy equipment. After dark in St Moritz, troops on the streets received fire from, as it was later determined, French stragglers in the houses, doubtless aided by the inhabitants. The troops evacuated the town, which was then burned to the ground.

The combat trains moved nearer or further from the battlefield, according to the rumours that circulated, some of which reached Strasbourg, saying that the entire 30 RD staff had been captured. In fact, the enemy had lost 400 prisoners and eleven guns. Often they had been unable to stand against the fire, bayonets or shouts of 'Hurrah' of the Bavarian troops. From an order found on the body of a French officer, it was learned that the entire French XIV Corps was advancing, with 27 ID on Markirch and 28 ID on Weiler. The French corps was swinging left and soldiers from both divisions were captured. The French had apparently been deployed in assembly areas on a broad front and in groups between Weiler and Gereuth, and were surprised by the 10 Res. Bde attack, for nowhere had they prepared defensive positions, although they had time to do so.

The Germans had also apparently defeated superior enemy forces. Second-rate German units, which had been formed during mobilisation and had limited unit cohesion, had defeated elements of the active army French XIV Corps and Alpine battalions. 30 RD had actually been formed on the battlefield and had only received operational control of 10 Res. Bde the previous evening. The division commander did not know the names of the 5 *Ersatz* Bde leaders, or even the unit designations. This significantly increased the difficulties of command and control. 10 Res. Bde had been moved hither and thither for the last ten days, 5 *Ersatz* Bde had just completed a two-day rail-march, and before the fight both units conducted a night march in the hills and humidity. Nevertheless, the troops found the strength to conduct an attack that the enemy could not withstand. Outstanding training and morale overcame physical exhaustion. According to the testimony of the 30 RD commander, who was from Württemberg, in spite of the difficult terrain, the Bavarian attack was conducted 'just like in training', in successive loose skirmisher lines that coalesced to form a firing line behind cover, which minimised casualties.

1 *Landwehr* Bde was to relieve the covering force, 82 Bde (XV AK). The front was so wide that the Bavarians were reinforced by the Württemberg (Wü) *Landwehr* IR 121 (still in blue peacetime uniforms), II/Wü Landwehr IR 123, a MGK and three 9cm cannon batteries. The artillery was of questionable value, as it consisted of the completely obsolete Model 1873 gun, which lacked a recoil brake and armoured shield. It could only be fired from open positions and few of the gunners had actually trained on the gun. Each battery had four guns and four rickety open wagons, which had no brakes, to carry 140 shells per gun, plus fourteen wagons per battery as a light munitions column. In Colmar it was possible to requisition six horses per gun, but the wagons were pulled by two old, tired, often broken-down farm horses with plough harness and led by farmers, sometimes boys. The gunners and citizens of Colmar regarded the batteries as a bad joke.

Sending the *Landwehr* to combat in the Vosges was practically an act of desperation. Their *Landsturm* artillery batteries and engineer companies had not arrived. They had no MGs, field kitchens, field telephones, pack animals or supply units of any kind. They had not been trained for mountain warfare. These units, organised on mobilisation out of older married men, were to fight against French Alpine troops: crafty, resourceful, superbly trained and equipped for mountain warfare.

1 *Landwehr* Bde was not ready to move out until 19 August. The French were at Diedolshausen and Münster. The brigade was to enter the mountains in three groups. In the north, *Landwehr* IR 1, with two MGs, was to occupy Urbach and Urbeis (6km east and south-east, respectively, of Diedolshausen) The centre column, I/LIR 2, 5 and 6/LIR 2, two MGs and 9 Battery (Bty) 8 was about 2km south of Urbeis. The southern group, III/LIR 2, LIR 121 (minus II) II/LIR 123, three MGs, 9cm Batteries 9 and 10 and 6/Pr. Foot Artillery R 18 (sFH), had already moved to halfway between Colmar and Münster on 18 August. 1/*Landwehr* Squadron (Sqn)/I b. AK and II/LIR 121 were brigade reserve. The covering force, 82 Bde, returned to XV AK.

On 18 August the detachments of the Generals Mathy, Dame and von Bodungen crossed the Rhine at Neuenburg, Istein and Hüningen and advanced to the area of Mühlhausen to attack the right flank of the *armée d'Alsace*, which was also advancing, leading to a series of meeting engagements. The French were massively superior (VII Corps, 44 ID, 66 RD – forty-eight French battalions versus seventeen German), so by evening the Germans were forced to withdraw back over the Rhine. The French reoccupied Mühlhausen, but did not continue the advance north towards Colmar.

The Bavarian ED consisted of three infantry brigades, each with a MGK of four MGs, and four artillery sections of three batteries each, one with light howitzers. Like the *Landwehr*, it was poorly suited for field operations. The division HQ was established only on 14 August and inadequately staffed. On 8 August the Bavarian War Ministry began organising a medical company, two field hospitals, three infantry ammunition columns, three artillery ammunition columns and three supply columns, plus three more light munitions columns on 13 August, but they did not arrive until 25 August–1 September; one supply column never arrived at all.[41] Until then, as far as supply was concerned, the division was on its own. It used the time to 18 August to requisition vehicles from the towns in which it was billeted, which proved to be poorly suited to mountain operations, being too heavy and with a large turning radius. For a considerable period in the future, it would also lack a field telephone section, bridging, a field bakery, remount section and MP section. The absence of field telephones was felt keenly, for transmitting reports and orders by mounted and bicycle messenger in mountainous terrain was time consuming and difficult. The troop units lacked the regimental pioneer tool wagon, company field kitchens, range estimators and signal lamps, binoculars and individual entrenching tools. There were few artillery aiming circles which were necessary for firing from covered positions. The division did not get tactical maps until 26 August. During the night of 18/19 August OHL attached the Bavarian ED to XIV RK and ordered it to Schlettstadt, where it would assume operational control over 2 *Landwehr* Bde.

On 17 August Rupprecht and the commander of the Seventh Army, Heeringen, had agreed to attack on 19 August. On 18 August, however, the French had become more aggressive against Sixth Army than previously. The hope that they would concentrate there and leave a weak flank facing Seventh Army could not be disregarded. Heeringen therefore recommended delaying the Seventh Army attack, and Rupprecht agreed.

Weier im Thal and Giragoutte, 19 August (sketch 6)

On the far left flank of the *armée d'Alsace* the French 81 Bde and Alpine Infantry Battalions 13 and 30 had advanced from Diedolshausen and Münster across the

Vosges, where they encountered 1 *Landwehr* Bde, which was awaiting the arrival of reinforcements before resuming movement that afternoon. The leftmost *Landwehr* column had deployed III/LIR 121 on the west edge of Weier im Thal (Weier in the Valley), I/LIR 121 and 9cm Bty 10 on the spur north-west of Weier, 6/FAR 13 (sFH) on the east side of Weier, and III/LIR 2 and 9cm Bty 9 about 4km to the rear. II/LIR 123 was expected to arrive soon. At 1000hrs four French companies attacked north of Günsbach, but were halted 500m east of the town by German infantry and artillery fire. At about 1050hrs the *Landwehr* detachment commander received the order from the brigade commander to prevent the French, estimated at a division, from withdrawing to the north. The detachment commander therefore attacked with III/LIR 121 on the right and 5 and 7/LIR 123 on the left, which initially made good progress, pushing into and north of Günsbach. French resistance stiffened on the east edge of Münster (2km west of Günsbach), and a standing firefight developed, the Landwehr men receiving support from the heavy howitzers and 9cm cannon. Then French Alpine troops were reported advancing on Sulzbach from the south, and III/LIR 2, which had just arrived 500m east of Weier, moved to block the threat. At the same time, French infantry advanced through the woods north of Günsbach and threatened the right flank of III/LIR 121. Every available *Landwehr* man was thrown against them and they were pushed back, sometimes only after close combat with the bayonet. I/LIR 121, guarding the 9cm cannons north of Günsbach, was attacked by French Alpine troops, while the guns came under artillery fire. The farmers driving the ammunition wagons immediately fled. Two wagons were found in pieces down the hill behind the gun position. 6 and 8/LIR 123 went to the aid of I/LIR 121, helped drive back the French and move off the guns. In view of the danger to both flanks, at 1430hrs the detachment commander, with the approval of the brigade commander, decided to withdraw 6km to Türkhiem, which proceeded in perfect order, undisturbed by the enemy. At 1700hrs a detachment of French Alpine troops, accompanied by mountain artillery, appeared in Sulzbach – the *Landwehr* detachment had left just in time.

(Sketch 7) The middle *Landwehr* group was cooking lunch when it received a request for assistance from the column on the left. With empty stomachs, the detachment set out, with 3/LIR 2 as the advance guard and the main body made up of I/RIR 2, the MGs, 9cm Bty 8 and 5, and 6/LIR 2. The point had just reached the Weier Kreuz (Weier Cross) when it took fire from the woods on all sides, principally from snipers in the trees. 3/LIR 2 deployed immediately, followed by 1/LIR 2. On the right, 2/LIR 2 was sent into the woods, while 4/LIR 2 climbed the hill to the left to outflank the French. The companies had had no time to train, and these movements were conducted with a good deal of confusion. A disorganised, heavy and loud firefight ensued. At the same time, the fire from hidden French artillery (presumably only 2km to the west) blocked

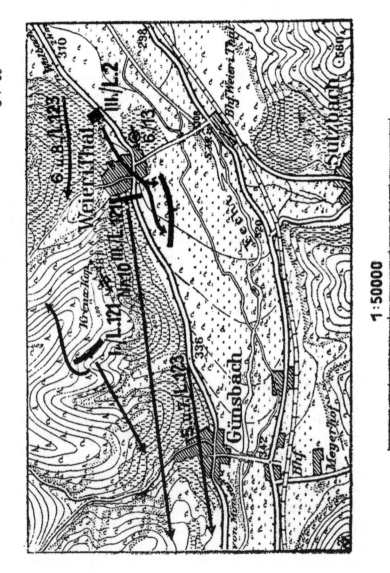

Weier im Thal 19. 8.   Textskizze 6.

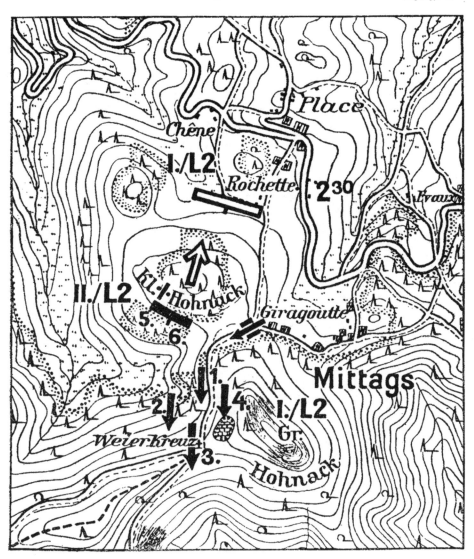

Giragoutte 19. 8. Textskizze 7.

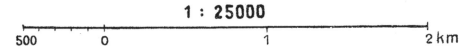

1 : 25000

500 0 1 2 km

Key

Mittags – Noon

St. Martin 19. 8.   Textskizze 8.

the saddle at Giragoutte. Nevertheless, this was the only position where the 9cm battery could go into action. Since he did not have a mounted messenger, the detachment commander had to personally order the battery to set up there. The battery had no aiming circle to lay the guns for indirect fire, so it was forced to fire from the open. It was possible, with the assistance of the infantry, to bring one gun into position, which was able to fire only three shells before being smothered by rifle, MG and artillery fire and rendered inoperative. Several shells landed near the rest of the guns in the rear and some of the horses bolted, along with the civilian drivers. Nevertheless, another gun was brought into action behind the hill, which fired a few shells and at least drew the enemy's attention away from the infantry. The French were well concealed and practically invisible. I/LIR 2 had nearly expended its basic load of ammunition and had to be resupplied from II/LIR 2 ammunition vehicles. Individuals and groups of I/LIR 2 began moving to the rear, so the detachment commander withdrew I/LIR 2 through 5 and 6/ LIR 2 and the MGs, which had deployed on the Klein-Hohenack Hill, to a new position at Rochette. The French did not pursue. The detachment commander decided that the French were trying to move through the woods to the south in order cut the road about 2km to his rear (which turned out to be true), so he withdrew to the edge of the Vosges about 4km north-west of Colmar.

St Martin, 19 August (sketch 8)

30 RD was completely exhausted by the previous day's fighting and the units were thoroughly intermixed. Command and control in a division that had been formed on the battlefield was rudimentary. The officers summoned on the evening of 18 August to receive the division order arrived the next morning, poorly or completely uninformed and concerned about the condition and location of their units. The division commander therefore delayed the continuation of the attack until 1530hrs. The French had obviously been badly handled on 18 August and left weak rearguards at St Martin, with stronger forces digging in 2.5km to the west of Weiler at Meisengott.

During the day 5 *Ersatz* Bde deployed *Ersatz* Bn V at Breitenbach, VII at St Martin, and at 1800hrs attacked towards Meisengott–Weiden-Berg, with VI and VIII following. *Ersatz* MGK 5 opened fire from St Martin at 1815hrs and drove the French from Meisengott. At the same time, 2 *Ersatz*/FAR 2, which had moved over small, rocky paths to the high ground between Erlenbach and Breitenbach, opened fire on trenches at Weiden-Berg. It also suppressed French artillery there, which had just opened fire on 5 *Ersatz* Bde infantry. By 2200hrs the brigade took Meisengott and Weiden-Berg without making contact. Most of the brigade bivouacked in Meisengott.

10 Res. Bde attacked at 1530hrs with RIR 11, moving west from Weiler towards the woods. II/RIR 11 pushed the French back and took Hill 613 south of Meisengott. I/LIR 11 moved in the heat up and down steep slopes covered in thick underbrush. The rations could not be brought forward and the battalion bivouacked in the open on a cold and damp night. The French held the spur of the hill immediately to the front.

A task force made up of I/RIR 14, 6/RIR 14, an understrength 8/RIR 14 and Res. MG Sec. 3 attacked at 1700hrs from Hill 370 west of Neukirch, supported by 1 *Ersatz*/FAR 2, 1 *Ersatz*/FAR 12 and 1 *Ersatz*/FAR 84 on Hill 370. By 1900hrs it had driven the French from Grube and Lach. The rest of RIR 14 was in reserve in Neukirch.

The Bavarian ED defended the area around Schlettstadt, while 19 ED marched to Barr after suffering from the heat. The Guard ED arrived in Pfalzburg.

XIV RK attacked along the Breusch Valley, driving the French before them and taking 1,000 POWs and eleven guns. 28 RD occupied Schirmeck and advanced towards the Donon. XV AK established itself on the west side of the Vosges.

The flank corps of the French First Army, XXI Corps and XIV Corps, were inactive on 19 August. XIV Corps was reinforced by 115 Bde (half of the 58 RD) and the Épinal reserve, 71 RD, at St Dié. XIV Corps was now ready to concentrate on the Breusch Valley, leaving the Vosges passes to the 71 RD and 115 Bde.

18 and 19 August in Lorraine

The rain of the past few days gave way to sun on 18 August. XIV AK and I b. AK (minus 1 Bde, corps reserve) continued to dig in. A regiment of French cavalry appeared that morning, in the 1 ID sector, on the corps left, followed by large bodies of cavalry south of Saarburg that moved so carelessly that they were initially taken to be the German 7 KD. They could not be reached by the field artillery, but were engaged by the 21cm mortars of II/Foot Artillery R 3, whose shells landed in the middle of their formation, scattering them. The mortars also silenced or drove off the French horse artillery. In the 2 ID sector, on the corps right, 3/FAR 4, which was deployed with the outpost line, pushing the guns right up to the German infantry positions, also successfully engaged French cavalry and artillery. Before noon numerous French all-arms columns marched towards the Saar and the German security screen was forced to withdraw. By evening I b. AK had gained the impression that the French were strong south of Saarburg, but weak to the west.

In fact, only the French VIII Corps on the First Army left had reached Saarburg, with XIII Corps on its right. On the other hand, the right wing of the French Second Army, XVI Corps, was pushing into the gap between I b. AK and

XXI AK. The Second Army commander was convinced that the Germans were in full retreat and did not restrain his troops as he had previously done. Indeed, pursuit was now the watchword, which was, however, not transformed by the troops into action.

Sixth Army HQ ordered 7 KD from the left flank of I b. AK to fill the gap. Sixth Army HQ also ordered 1 RD to send a regimental task force to Mittersheim with the mission of holding the town to prevent a breakthrough between the two corps.

Mittersheim, 18 August (sketch 9)

1 RD formed this task force from RIR 2, 1/Res. Cavalry R 1 and 1 and 2/RFAR 1 under the commander of 1 Res. Bde. Shortly after 1200hrs the task force reached the open ground east of the town, which was held by Dragoon R 7. It deployed and oriented south-west, with III/RIR 2 on the high ground north of the town, II/RIR 2 and the MGK on the high ground to the north-east, with the cavalry on its right, the artillery behind it and I/RIR 2 in reserve. Security detachments were sent to the north and west of the town, and on the rail bridge south of it. At 1500hrs combat noise was heard from the direction of XXI AK and the Bavarians began to dig in. The noise increased, and at 1600hrs the brigade commander sent an officer to 42 ID on the XXI AK left to ask if they needed help. This officer did not return until 1825hrs to report that the French had taken Lautersingen (4km south-west), were attacking the 42 ID left flank, and 42 ID wanted RIR 2 to drive the French out of Lautersingen. The regiment was preparing to do so when it was reported that several French battalions were advancing from Lautersingen to Mittersheim. The Saar–Kohlencanal was a significant obstacle, and the rail bridge directly west of Mittersheim was being held by only a half-platoon of infantry. Given the changed situation, the commander of RIR 2 immediately sent forward 12/RIR 2 and MGK/RIR 2 to hold the west side of the bridge. While they were deploying there, they took fire from the woods 700m to the front. 12/RIR 2 and MGK/RIR 2 took up the fight, with express orders not to attack in isolation. I/RIR 2 was already moving forward, deployed down Hill 248 to Mittersheim. The streets of Mittersheim were blocked with supply vehicles, so the battalion commander led most of 2 and 3/RIR 2 around the south side of the town and over the footbridge next to the rail line to the west side of the canal, picking up 5/RIR 2 on the way, and they deployed to the left of 12/RIR 2 and attacked, with 4/RIR 2 covering the left flank. In the middle of the firefight the day's burning heat was replaced by pouring rain, thunder and lightning. I/RIR 2, with elements of 2 and 3/RIR 2, arrived and was committed on the right of 12/RIR 2, north of the road, to turn the French left. I/RIR 2 attacked by bounds,

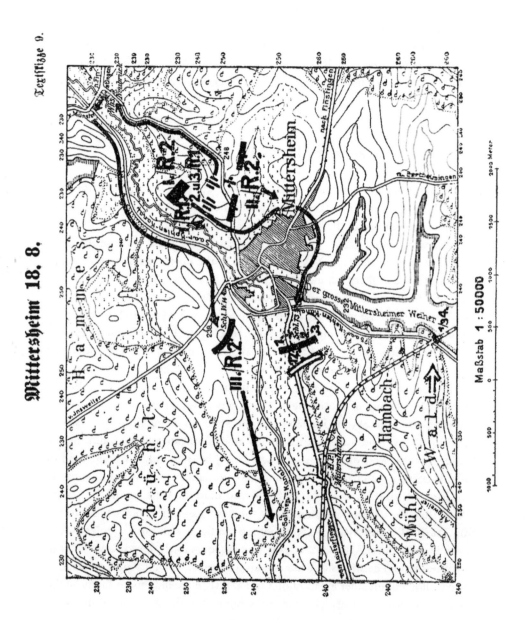

led by the battalion commander, and quickly closed on the right flank to within 200m, although casualties mounted. The French tried to extend their left flank, but in doing so left the cover of the woods and took heavy losses, in particular from MG fire. II/RIR 2 began to arrive, and 8/RIR 2 crossed the bridge and reinforced the firing line. With difficulty the brigade commander kept 6 and 7/ RIR 2 in reserve on the east side of the canal.

The Bavarian artillery could not support from the position on Hill 248 and Mittersheim lay under French artillery fire, so the artillery went back north to the bridge to cross the canal and then turned south-west, sometimes at a gallop, along the north bank to set up in open positions on the high ground north of the town and engage the French at close range at 1900hrs. As RIR 2 closed on the French position the unit, and 12/RIR 2 in particular, was in danger of friendly fire from the German artillery. This was averted by the actions of determined infantrymen, who informed the artillery, which lifted its fires into the wood, then ceased fire altogether, at which point the infantry assaulted the French position. The French ran, leaving dead and wounded behind. The pursuit began immediately and some detachments may have advanced as far as Lautersingen, but the darkness forced the Germans to stop 500m west of the Mittersheim rail station (HP Mittersheim).

From the beginning of the fight a platoon of 4/RIR 2, at the rail bridge 1.5km south of Mittersheim, held off superior forces before being forced to withdraw across the pond (Weiher). III/RIR 2 was supported by fire and advanced with the rest of the regiment. XXI AK had retaken Lautersingen. Late in the afternoon, 7 KD horse artillery, MGK and the bicycle company of *Jäger* Bn 1 were able to engage thick enemy columns with concentrated fire as they emerged from the woods south of Lautersingen. RIR 2 returned to Mittersheim.

RIR 2 had lost 50 KIA and 123 WIA, including 6 officers. About 70 French KIA (including a lieutenant colonel and three other officers) were found outside the woods, which could only be swept the next afternoon, the wounded evacuated and the dead buried. Captured documents showed that the enemy had been two battalions of the French 31 ID, which had the mission of taking Mittersheim. The French appeared at the treeline, already deployed, 700m to the German front, while RIR 2 had to cross the bridge and deploy. That RIR 2 was able to do so was a real accomplishment, in particular because the unit had just been formed a few days previously and, in addition to reservists, contained a significant proportion of *Landwehr* men. RIR 2 was aided by the MGK, which was in position at the start of the fight and suppressed the French fire. The assault was conducted an hour and a half after the beginning of the firefight. The men of 12/RIR 2, which had lost almost all its officers, were permitted to nominate the awardees of the first Iron Crosses.

II b. AK continued to dig in. Strong French marching columns were seen advancing, but they stayed out of range. The Bavarian KD covered the corps left flank, 8 KD the right, whose commander decided to conduct a reconnaissance in force. III b. AK continued to dig in south of the Saar; only weak French detachments appeared in the sector. 8 ED had arrived north of St Avold, 10 ED at Saarlouis and 4 ED 15km south-west of Saarlouis.

Krafft, the Sixth Army chief of staff, called OHL at midday to make Sixth Army's determination to attack clear. He spoke with Moltke's number two, Stein, who repeated the reservations that Dommes had presented the previous day, but also made clear that Rupprecht had freedom of action and OHL would not interfere.

In the French Second Army, only XVI Corps had collided with the Germans, at Mittersheim—Lautersingen. XV and XX Corps hardly advanced. The army commander recognised that the Germans to his front had stopped, but still believed that the Germans were conducting a delay. The line of advance for 19 August was set just short of the Metz—Saarburg rail line. On the left flank of Second Army, 17 ID of IX Corps was ordered to pull out of line to be sent to Fourth Army on 19 August. It would be replaced by 68 RD. 64 RD and 74 RD would replace 18 ID, but they were still at Lunéville.

The French First Army commander still felt that his right flank was threatened. On 19 August only half of VIII Corps (16 ID) on his left flank, supported by Conneau's Cavalry Corps, would attack north of Saarburg. The other half of VIII Corps (15 ID), plus XIII and XXI Corps, would remain on the defensive.

The French may have supposed that they were only going to encounter rearguards on 19 August. Instead, they met an opponent who was determined to hold his positions. Nevertheless, the French maintained their slow and careful advance, so that there was only limited and local combat. The skies on 19 August were cloudless and sunny.

In the I b. AK sector French skirmisher lines appeared south of Saarburg, in front of 1 ID, at 0900hrs and again at 1600hrs, but did not attempt to cross the Saar and were engaged by FAR 1. French batteries that went into action were engaged by the 21cm mortars of II/Foot Artillery 3 and the heavy howitzers of 5 and 8/Foot Artillery R 1 and were silenced or forced to withdraw. In the 2 ID sector to the north, French infantry drove the Bavarian outposts back across the Saar, but were stopped by the fire of 2 FA Bde. French artillery that appeared was put out of action by the heavy artillery of both Bavarian divisions; the French crews abandoned their guns. The accuracy of the German artillery was due, above all, to the observation balloons of the Non-Rigid Airship Sec. With this help, II/Pr. Foot Artillery R 18 (21cm mortars) was able to beat down a French artillery section, forcing them to pull the guns back to a wood or abandon them outright. The artillery duel reached great intensity by noon. The French shelled the German trenches (or FAR 1) without being able to disrupt their work. The night was spent combat ready in the position. Reconnaissance by Aviation Sec. 1 revealed strong enemy forces directly in front of the corps. The weak attack, which 2 ID had easily beaten off, had been made by the French 16 ID. Conneau's cavalry failed to come anywhere near its objective of Saar–Buckenheim.

In the German XIV AK sector, left of I b. AK, the day passed quietly as the French XIII Corps was largely inactive. So too was the French XVI Corps in the German XXI AK sector to the right of I b. AK. Sixth Army used the pause to completely fill the gap between I b. AK and XXI AK with I b. RK, reinforced with units from Germersheim: *Landwehr* IR 8 and 10 and Res. Foot Artillery R 1 (I with four batteries of heavy howitzers, II with four batteries of 10cm guns) and 1/*Landwehr* Eng. R. Both *Landwehr* IR were fortress units and unequipped for mobile warfare.

Liedersingen, 19 August (sketch 10)

The inactivity of the French XVI Corps on 19 August may have been due to the fact that it was waiting for the assistance of the XV Corps, but the attack of that corps' 29 ID was stopped by the effective fire of the German XXI AK artillery.

The other division of the French XV Corps, 30 ID, was directed at the Bavarian KD and *Jäger* Bn 1, which held the gap between XXI AK and II b. AK. XXI AK was concerned for the security of its right flank and, at 0700hrs, asked II b. AK for support. The commander of II b. AK sent a regimental task force composed of RIR 5 and III/IR 23, 3/*Cheveauleger* R, I/FAR 12 and a medical platoon, under the 5 Bde commander, in march to defend the Fuchs Holz (Fox Wood) north of Liedersingen (Lidrezing, 3km south-west of Bensdorf). The march in the heat, cross-country and up and down hill, tired the troops considerably. At 1100hrs the troops were in position and digging in, with I/RIR 5 on the right and III/RIR 5 and the MGK on the left along the road heading south-east from Liedersingen, a reserve consisting of III/IR 23 in the centre and II/RIR 5 distributed behind the front, along with the gun positions of I/FAR 12. *Jäger* Bn 1 was on the left. When the Bavarian KD commander learned that the task force had moved south, he sent 1 Cavalry Bde, reinforced with MG Sec. 1, the Bicycle Co./*Jäger* Bn 2 and Horse Artillery Bty/FAR 5 to guard the right. In spite of reports of strong approaching French forces, patrols from the forward battalions found nothing.

At 1430hrs the staff on Hill 337 drew fire, which did not cause casualties but bolted the horses. The task force commander immediately ordered an attack on the high ground to the front. I/FAR 12 opened fire on the treeline 700m in length and only 650m away. The two forward battalions opened the firefight from thick skirmisher lines with some intermixing of units. The horses of the *Cheveauleger* had also bolted, so the cavalrymen joined the firefight on foot. In long bounds

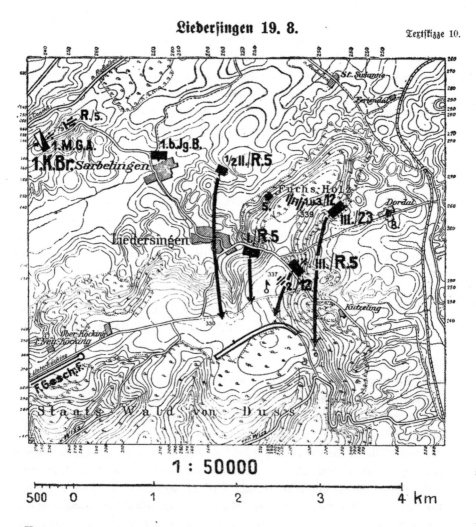

Liedersingen 19. 8.   Textskizze 10.

1 : 50000

500 0   1   2   3   4 km

Key

Fr. Geschützfeuer – French artillery fire

they soon reached the farm road in the middle of the hill. The troops were so enthusiastic that they neglected to take cover and fired too fast, so that ammunition began to run short, and the ammunition wagon and 5/RIR 5 had considerable difficulty coming up the steep hill. The II/RIR 5 commander led the half of his battalion (6 and 7) forward on his own initiative, with battle standards waving (and with extra ammunition), to the right flank of I/RIR 5; at 1530hrs his personal example drove the attack forwards. The enemy also received reinforcements and, between 1530hrs and 1600hrs, they repeatedly advanced against the left flank of III/RIR 5, where the woods offered an avenue of approach, but the MGK stopped them. At 1630hrs hidden French artillery south-west of RIR 5 fired straight into the right flank, causing considerable loss. German counter-battery fire suppressed the French guns. As the fire died down at 1800hrs, the task force commander committed III/IR 23 to envelop the French right flank. In places the battalion met with resistance, which it broke with cold steel, while RIR 5 assaulted frontally. The French dead and wounded lay in heaps, the Bavarians took about 400 POWs and the French withdrew. The Bavarians had been opposed by the French 59 Bde, which had already suffered a reverse at Gerden.

The exposed position of the task force did not permit pursuit. The troops were not even given the satisfaction of remaining on the terrain they had won, for at 2145hrs the Bavarian KD ordered the task force to withdraw to its assigned position: the Bavarian KD commander was not aware until 2000hrs, after the withdrawal order had already been sent out, of Sixth Army's intention to attack the next day. The enemy used the opportunity to reoccupy the heights south-east of Liedersingen during the night.

RIR 5 lost 5 officers and 105 enlisted men KIA, 10 officers and 314 enlisted men WIA, 40 MIA and 8 POWs. The regimental commander and the commanders of I and III Battalions were wounded, the commander of I Battalion later dying of his wounds.

The Battle of Liedersingen was unnecessary and warned the enemy of the blow that was to be struck the next day. The casualties were unfortunate, but the French had suffered significantly greater casualties and, once again, had been made painfully aware of their tactical inferiority, even when faced by reservists and *Landwehr* men, this time factory workers from the Palatinate: Ludwigshafen, Kaiserslautern and Pirmasens. The military tasks placed upon the reservists and *Landwehr* men had not been great, but being unaccustomed, had worn the troops down considerably. Numerous footsore men had been sent to the supply units for transport. However, as it became known that there would be a fight on 19 August, not a man fell out, in spite of the heat.

During the fight at Liedersingen the French also advanced against the reinforced 1 Cavalry Bde on the right. The bicyclists of *Jäger* Bn 2, a platoon of MG Sec. 1 and the division horse artillery section were able to engage marching columns and thick skirmisher lines and clearly inflict heavy losses. But the enemy committed even stronger forces and his artillery fire became troublesome, so that in the evening the 1 Cavalry Bde was withdrawn 3–4km.

In the II b. AK sector there were no enemy forces in front of 4 ID on the corps left, but the entire French XX Corps deployed in front of 3 ID on the right. The only attack occurred at 1400hrs, in a 700m section of line located behind the little Rotte River and held by I and II/IR 2, reinforced by the MGK and supported by II/FAR 12. German fire soon forced the French to break off the attack. A few French squads and platoons that continued to press forward suffered heavy losses or were destroyed. In the rest of the division sector there was only artillery fire.

8 KD reported that its horses were exhausted and practically immobile, and occupied an assembly area far to the rear, at Lixingen, 8km south of St Avold. III b. AK continued work on its positions, and the enemy, presumably the advance guard of the French 68 RD, appeared only that evening. The *Ersatz* Divisions were united into the *Ersatz* Corps.

3

The Battle in Lorraine
and the Vosges, 20–22 August

On 18 August the German right-wing First, Second, Third, Fourth and Fifth Armies began their advance through Belgium: the time for the Sixth and Seventh Armies to attack had come. The enemy estimate that Rupprecht had formed in the least few days served as the basis for his battle plan. Doubtless the enemy was attempting to make his main point of attack between Mörchingen and Saarburg and break through there, at the west end of the Vosges. Both enemy wings were clearly weak and held back.

It appeared that the German XV AK at Dagsburg would encounter only weak resistance: a shallow envelopment was possible there. The enemy in front of the Sixth Army right was also not thought to be strong behind the outposts on the Delm Heights, 12km north-west of Château Salins. Since the French positioned here were marching east, they were creating a long, thinly held left flank and were leaving the fortifications of Nancy behind – a weakness that invited attack. Granted, Fort Nancy restricted the manoeuvre space to some degree, but if it were possible to break through west of the line Château Salins–Falkenberg and penetrate quickly, an envelopment might be possible here too; the more so because the mass of the French First and Second Armies were concentrated in a mass and fixed between Mörchingen and Saarburg. 4 ID and III b. AK stood uncommitted at exactly the right point to exploit this opportunity; indeed they had been held back in order to remain hidden and be in position to attack the enemy flank.

Rupprecht therefore placed his main points of effort on the Sixth and Seventh Army flanks; on the right in the direction of Delm and on the left towards St Quirin (French 43 ID). The troops moved to their attack positions on

19 August so that they could rest that night and attack fresh in the morning of 20 August. Fifth Army made the Metz reserve available, but the fortress reserve artillery was already employed elsewhere; it could have materially increased the pressure on the French left at Delm. Seventh Army was given operational control over I b. AK.

On 19 August the corps were given warning orders for the attack. The operations order, issued at 1930hrs, set the time of attack at 0500hrs, with the intent of taking the enemy by surprise. III b. AK was to attack towards Delm. II b. AK and XXI AK were to attack straight ahead, shoulder-to-shoulder, with I b. RK guarding the left flank, while 33 RD guarded the right against Pont-à-Mousson–Nancy. HKK 3 was behind the army right flank. In reserve were 7 RD and 8 ED, while 10 ED was to move to Han on the Nied. 4 ED was attached to II b. AK, and the troops from Germersheim to I b. RK. The Sixth Army HQ planned to move closer to the front line at 0600hrs, at the price of degraded telephone communications.

Seventh Army would attack at 1100hrs, because it was expected that XV AK would have difficulties moving in the mountains. The mission for I b. AK, XIV and XV AK was to turn the French right flank. 10 ED was positioned 10km east of Saarburg. XIV RK, 19 ED, 30 RD and Bavarian ED were to attack across the Vosges, while 1 and 2 *Landwehr* Bde guarded the left flank.

On 20 August a serious French plan of attack was not evident. The French First Army was still concerned about the threat from the Vosges and, on 19 August, attacked only with the 16 ID against I b. AK. On 20 August the French would only commit 15 ID left of 16 ID. Their mission was to take two bridges over the Saar, about 6km north of Saarburg, allowing Conneau's cavalry to cross. They would be reinforced with the entire army heavy artillery, while the rest of the army would defend in place.

The commander of the French Second Army was unsure whether the II b. AK and XXI AK intended to conduct a determined defence, or if he faced rearguards. On 20 August he therefore ordered only XV and XVI Corps to attack. XX Corps, which on 19 August moved considerably in advance of XV Corps, would stand fast. 59, 70 and 68 RD would protect the army left flank against Metz. However, the XX Corps commander, Foch, had already given the order to continue the attack towards Mörchingen, and the army order arrived too late to stop it.

On 20 August the German and French corps fought a meeting engagement. The broad deployment and the extensive forests and lakes led to a series of isolated battles. The French attacks were piecemeal and weak, while the German attacks were powerful and determined. On 20 August the sun rose blood red in a cloudless sky.

The Battle of Lorraine, 20 August (map 2)

33 RD[42], the Metz reserve, assembled behind the south side of the fortifications on the evening of 19 August to support the Sixth Army offensive by attacking south-east towards Delm. It was reinforced by the Metz garrison in this sector, the 31 Pr. *Landwehr* Bde (Task Force Hoffmeister), consisting of Pr. *Landwehr* IR 30 (four companies) and Pr. LIR 68 (nine companies), supported by I/b. Res. Foot Artillery R 3 (sFH), II/Pr. Foot Artillery R 16 (sFH) and a *Landwehr* engineer company. Lorries from the Metz garrison were to provide supply and medical evacuation. The enemy was thought to weakly hold the Selle, with stronger forces at Nomeny and heavy artillery at three points behind it.

The advance guard, under the 8 b. Bde commander, composed of Bavarian IR 4, 1/Pr. Res. Hussar R 2, *Ersatz* Sec./Pr. FAR 34 and a telephone platoon, moved out at 0530hrs. The right flank was covered by a task force composed of Pr. RIR 130, some cavalry, Pr. Fortress MG Sec. 12 and *Ersatz* Sec./Pr. FAR 69, which moved out at 0400hrs. When the enemy was reported at Mailly at 0745hrs, 33 RD turned south-west towards them and away from Delm. At 0915hrs IR 4 deployed from the Waldhofen Wald to attack Mailly, supported by *Ersatz*/FAR 34. Mailly was found to be unoccupied and the advance guard continued the attack towards Nomeny, with I/IR 4 on the left of the road (3/IR 4 on the right and 4/IR 4 on the left, 2 behind 3/IR 4, 1 behind 4/IR 4), and III/IR 4 to the right (11/IR 4 on the right, 10/IR 4 on the left, 9 behind 10/IR 4).[43] II/IR 4 and the MGK followed. I/Foot Artillery R 2 (sFH) reinforced the fire support. By 1100hrs I/IR 4, in advance guard, had reached the north edge of Nomeny without a shot being fired; when it entered the town, it took heavy fire from the houses. 1/IR 4 returned fire, supported by 4/IR 4, the units becoming thoroughly intermixed, while 3 and 2/IR 4 manoeuvred right around the north-west side of the town. The other two IR 4 battalions received infantry fire, then artillery fire from high ground 3km to the south-west. They took cover and returned fire against enemy troops behind hedges and fences, and in houses and attics. The mass of the French forces had long since gone, but, as the French commonly did, had left infantry squads as stay-behind forces to ambush the Germans. It was established for a certainty that civilians participated in the battle. The commander of 8/IR 4, who had good visibility since he was still mounted, saw a fleeing civilian throw a rifle away. Even if they were soldiers, they were fighting in civilian clothing. The measures IR 4 took in self-defence were fully justified: civilians taken while under arms were shot, and houses from which the troops took fire were set alight. The regiment pushed through the town to the opposite side by 1300hrs. Nevertheless, fire from the houses continued. To avoid further German casualties, 33 RD ordered the light artillery and 5/Foot Artillery R 2 (sFH) to burn the town to the ground. 6 and 11/IR 4 crossed the Selle and continued the attack to the south, with 5 and 10/IR 4 on their left, while 8/IR 4 and a platoon from 4/IR 4 moved south-west. These companies met advancing French forces and brought them to a halt. However, the isolated movement south of the Selle by a few companies was not the intent of the senior leaders. Most of the 4 Bde units took up positions between Nomeny and the Selle and were shelled by French artillery, which disturbed the digging in.

Since there were reports of strong French forces approaching from Pont-à-Mousson, and dust clouds were observed in that direction, at 1100hrs the commander of 33 RD turned the main body west. Bavarian IR 8 advanced on Rouves, which had been reported to be weakly held, and enemy artillery fire was expected. I/IR 8 led, and attacked the town at 1130hrs: 3/IR 8 took the cemetery north of the town and began a firefight with infantry on the slopes on the opposite side of the Selle. 1/IR 8 entered the town under fire and captured an armed civilian. 4/IR 8 was ordered to search the town, breaking down the doors if necessary, and burn all houses from which fire was received. In the early afternoon hours the French positioned west of Rouves withdrew. At 1330hrs RIR 130 was ordered to occupy Eply, which it did without a shot fired; RIR 67 moved south of RIR 130. II and III/IR 8 remained division reserve.

I/Res. Foot Artillery R 2 (sFH) had displaced forward at 1300hrs and unlimbered on the high ground south of Mailly in an excellent, dispersed and covered position, and engaged French artillery and trenches, eliminating enemy Observation Posts (OPs). At 1600hrs its direct support fire against enemy infantry significantly helped IR 4. French artillery was located in dominating positions on Mt Toulon (375m), about 5km to the south-west, and Mt St Jean (376–406m), 6km to the south. Smoke from the burning town of Nomeny hindered observation. II/b. Res. Foot Artillery 2 (sFH) went into position behind RIR 67. This concentration of troops, plus smoke from the field kitchens, drew fire from enemy artillery that was out of range of howitzer counter-battery fire, so that the section displaced to the low ground south of Raucourt at 1500hrs.[44] *Ersatz* Sec./FAR 33 was forced by counter-battery fire to shift from Nomeny back to the Selle Valley south of Mailly. Only *Ersatz* Sec./FAR 70 remained north of Nomeny.

At 1630hrs III/b. IR 8 was ordered to drive the inhabitants of Nomeny towards enemy lines and burn the rest of the town to the ground. The companies that had pursued south of the Selle were ordered back north of the river at 1700hrs. This must have encouraged the French, for they attacked, with artillery support, from the south at 1800hrs. However, they made no progress at the Brionne Mill and were unable to cross the Selle; IR 4 was supported by the MGK and MGK/IR 8, which was firing from the walled cemetery. On the road from the south, the position of 5 and 10/IR 4 was more serious, as the French used the streambed 1.4km south of the edge of town for cover and were supported with artillery fire from Mt St Jean. IR 4 had to resupply ammunition several times. The fire of I/Res. Foot Artillery R 2 (sFH) proved decisive in breaking up the thick French skirmisher lines in the streambed. Five times the French infantry attempted unsuccessfully to pass through the heavy howitzer barrage, until finally they fled. An attack from the south-east was beaten back by 6, 8 and 11/IR 4 and 11 and 12/IR 8. By dark the French attack, which had been conducted in brigade strength by elements of 59 RD and 70 RD, had been defeated

33 RD dug in, with 66 Res. Bde between Eply–Rouves and 8 b. Brigade the heights around Nomeny. Task Force Hoffmeister occupied the terrain northwest of Eply. 53 Landwehr brigade arrived from the Nied Position at Raucourt. The day's casualties were light to moderate.

33 RD, in particular 8 b. Brigade, received its baptism of fire, tough house-to-house combat, and was immediately confronted with the cunning French combat methods, as well as the hostility of the French civil population, which had undoubtedly been stirred up by the French government. But the troops adapted quickly and did not lose their aggressiveness. The troop leaders immediately adopted the sole effective course of action when the enemy defends a large town: they evacuated Nomeny, sealed it off and shelled it. Guilt for the subsequent destruction of the town lay solely on the French leaders, who chose to defend in the town rather than in the open field.

Delm (map 3)

III b. AK had dug in on a 15km-long line behind the French Nied and its eastward extension, the Rotte; 6 ID on the right, 5 ID on the left. The corps was given Delm as the objective to attack on the corps left flank, only 5km wide. The corps was to have concentrated on the left, but a report that the French were advancing south of Hahn (which turned out to be false) put an end to this movement in the 5 ID sector, while causing 6 ID, 11 Bde and FAR 3 in particular, difficult night marches.

The corps had initially set the 20 August objectives at Lixingen–Badenhofen, only 2km from the start line, but when the French offered no resistance on the Rotte, the objectives were set much further south: 5 ID was to take Neuheim, 6 ID Weiher, in an advance of about 7km.

In the 6 ID sector, IR 13, supported by FAR 3, occupied an assembly area in the woods north of Tranach with the initial mission of attacking Hill 328, west of Badenhofen, at 0500hrs, but was delayed by the movements of the preceding night and did not advance until 0545hrs. 12 Bde jumped off on time at 0500hrs, supported by FAR 8, from its assembly area at Baldershofen and to the west, with objectives at Badenhofen and the high ground 2½km to the east. IR 10 and the two engineer companies were in division reserve.

6 ID advanced deployed and covered by the artillery, which advanced by bounds. By 0900hrs, IR 13 had reached the saddle between Badenhofen and Dinkirch, with II/IR 13 on the right, III/IR 13 left and I/IR 13 as brigade reserve echeloned left, without making contact. FAR 3 shelled the weakly held town of Dinkirch and French troops north-east of Neuheim.

12 Bde did not meet resistance until it reached Handorf. I/IR 6 on the left chased withdrawing French troops back to the east to the Wald von Serres (Serres Forest) before being called back. Their movement was hindered by French snipers in the trees: 4/IR 6 was pinned down until afternoon and took casualties from MG and artillery fire. IR 11 had reached Probsthofen by 0930hrs. FAR 8 followed 12 Bde by bounds. At 0700hrs it had been able to support 5 ID with fire; at 0930hrs 1 and 2/FAR 8 engaged French forces at Handorf; and at 0850hrs a platoon of 6/FAR 8 shelled Weiher. *Cheveauleger* R 2 covered the division right flank. Corps HQ took I and II/IR 10 and the regimental HQ for its own reserve, leaving 6 ID with only III/IR 10 and the MGK.

Chevauleger R 7, riding in front of 5 ID, took fire from Lixingen. 10 Bde crossed the Rotte at 0500hrs, IR 7 on the left and IR 19 on the right, and occupied the high ground north of Lixingen to wait for the artillery, I/FAR 6 on the right and I/FAR 10 on the left. The rest of the 5 FA Bde and I/Foot Artillery 3 (sFH) provided support from the north side of the Rotte. 9 Bde also crossed, with IR 21 coming up on the left of IR 19, while IR 14 was division reserve. Reserve *Jäger* Bn 2 was 9 Bde reserve. At 1030hrs 10 Bde attacked Hill 241 north-west of Fremerchen, with the two forward artillery sections firing support.

Leading the regiment, II/IR 7 moved quickly to take up a position west of Lixingen, where it engaged in a firefight with French troops in the woods south-west of Lixingen. I/IR 7 was deployed on the right and the woods taken. 10 and 12/IR 7 (9 and 11/IR 7 were regimental reserve, along with the MGK) were committed on the left and, when the regiment approached at 0845hrs to within 800m, the French retreated off Hill 241. I/FAR 10 set up on Hill 270, north of Lixingen, between 0725hrs and 0750hrs and soon bounded forward, being thereafter replaced by II/FAR 10. They engaged retreating French skirmisher lines near Orn and shelled Fremerchen, which began to burn. The reserves of 10 Bde came under artillery fire, which caused casualties, but the lead elements easily took the first objective, Hill 241, north-west of Fremerchen, and then continued the attack. The commander of II/IR 7 was wounded in the engagement.

In the 9 Bde sector, I/IR 21 reached the south side of the wood by Lixingen at 0730hrs and began a firefight with enemy troops in trenches on the Gal-Berg (Gal Hill). Between 0800hrs and 0900hrs, II/IR 21 was committed on the left, initially swinging south-east. In spite of artillery fire from the direction of Château Salins, the two battalions took the hill at 1000hrs. The division commander moved up to Lixingen. The brigade commander immediately ordered the advance to continue to the next objective, the hills south-west and east of Fax.

At 1030hrs I/FAR 10 opened fire on French trenches that could be seen south-east of Orn, at the edge of the Staatswald (Municipal Forest) of Château Salins, as well as artillery in covered positions near Fonteningen. Soon it was joined by II/FAR 10 on Hill 241, north-west of Fremerchen, and, at noon, by FAR 6 on the Gal-Berg, while I/Foot Artillery R 3 moved north of the Wald von Lixingen, all with the mission of preparing the 10 Bde attack.

Even before it had received the brigade order, IR 21 crossed over the Gal-Berg, with the two forward battalions and troops from IR 19 becoming intermixed. They took heavy rifle, MG and artillery fire from the high ground to their front, where the French clearly had decided to make a stand. IR 21 returned fire, advanced by bounds and took Orn.

South of Niedhof, the skirmisher line of II/IR 7, and in particular 5 and 8/IR 7, took lively fire from the north treeline of the Wald von Serres, which was returned. These two companies, and elements of 6 and 7/IR 7, then assaulted with the bayonet and penetrated into the wood, but were forced out again by artillery fire and the loss of several leaders. The fight in the wood had cost II/IR 7 significant casualties. Snipers in the trees had even fired on stretcher-bearers, and many wounded could not be saved. I/IR 7 deployed against Hill 242, south-west of Fremerchen, and took heavy artillery fire.

6 ID designated the wood south-west of Weiher as the next objective for 11 Bde, and the high ground south-west of Fax for 12 Bde. 11 Bde would also guard the right flank by attacking Dinkirch at 1000hrs with IR 13. The French evacuated the town and were engaged by the MGK, which was on the Hochberg. French infantry and artillery could be seen between Delm, Neuheim and Weiher, either in position or withdrawing to the south and west. 4/FAR 3 had taken up an excellent firing position on the south treeline of the wood on the Hochberg and engaged the withdrawing French, soon joined by 2/FAR 3. The damage their shells inflicted on the thick groups of French infantry was clearly visible. 4/FAR 3 also forced French batteries positioned south-east of Weiher to limber up, one gun at a time, and withdraw. II/IR 13 reached the wood south-east of Dinkirch by 1030hrs and began a firefight with French infantry and MGs along the road and in the wood south-west of Weiher. A MG platoon immediately came to their aid, and soon thereafter III/IR 13 moved up on the right. 5 and 6/FAR 3, which had been delayed by the columns of 8 KD, were ordered to support IR 13 and opened fire at 1130hrs from a covered position behind Hill 269, just south of Dinkirch. 6/FAR 3 joined to the right and engaged the enemy near Delm. 1 and 3/FAR 3 fired from the saddle west of the Hochberg against troops on Hill 260, south of Delm and by Orhofen. At 1100hrs the enemy

south-west of Weiher withdrew, leaving a considerable number of dead and wounded, and several POWs. The commander of 11 Bde immediately ordered IR 13 to pursue. At 1330hrs II/IR 13, reinforced by a second MG platoon, captured two French field pieces at the wood south-west of Weiher and began a firefight with French troops at Neuheim. III/IR 13 was held up by fire from Delm, where the enemy seemed to be growing in strength. I/IR 13, the brigade reserve, had reached the slope 200m south-west of Dinkirch, where it received flanking fire from the direction of Delm.

Shortly after 1000hrs in the 12 Bde sector, the regiments were given a prominent tree on the high ground south-west of Fax as their objective. Meanwhile, the troops had closed in on the enemy at Handorf. II/IR 6 was taking fire in the left flank from the Wald von Serres, so that 6/IR 6 attacked into the forest. As I and III/IR 11 descended the high ground to Handorf, they took artillery fire and significant casualties. 2/FAR 8 had already set Handorf ablaze; the enemy withdrew and IR 6 occupied the town at 1015hrs, and soon thereafter, in conjunction with IR 11, the high ground north of Weiher, with the regiments becoming intermixed. As this was the objective, the brigade halted. Fire from 4 and 5/FAR 8, located 500m north of Handorf, also chased the French out of Weiher. The French columns marching towards Neuheim were also engaged, and then trenches 1km north of Neuheim. At 1100hrs the brigade resumed the attack towards Fax. IR 11 utilised the low ground north-east of Weiher to provide cover against French artillery fire and quickly took the high ground south-west of Fax. IR 6 moved through the concealed approach provided by the Wald von Serres. 2 and 3/FAR 8 supported the advance and engaged long enemy columns marching from Fonteningen to Orhofen, forcing some of them to scatter. At 1100hrs the batteries moved forward to a difficult open position on a steep slope west of Probsthofen, from where, under fire, they engaged enemy batteries and infantry south-west of Fax. At noon 3/FAR 8 moved from Hill 241 north-west of Fremerchen to Hill 260 south-west of Handorf.

8 KD, guarding the army right, was also in contact. The division assembled 2km west of Hahn and moved west towards the Delmer Rücken (Delm Ridge), crossing the march routes of the 6 ID and 33 RD. Supported by the divisional horse artillery, the cavalrymen dismounted to attack Delm. *Jäger* Bn 2, covering the right flank with 1 and 3/*Jäger* Bn 2 in the first line, and 2 and 4/*Jäger* Bn 2 in the second, took heavy rifle fire from the edge of Püschingen and took up the firefight, soon supported by MG Sec. 8. In platoon-sized bounds, it gradually closed to within 200m, aided by the fact that the enemy generally fired too high. It was now noon. The 8 KD commander decided not to assault the town because the *Jäger* did not have bayonets and considerable enemy artillery fire began to land: the Jäger were therefore withdrawn to the south-west slope of the hill. The Bavarian KD reached the area of Badenhofen around 1400hrs.

II b. AK HQ gave 6 ID the area between Delm and the small wood 1km south of Weiher as its next objective. At 1120hrs 6 ID ordered 11 Bde to take Hill 260 south of Delm and 12 Bde the slope between Weitblick Farm and the wood south-west of Weiher. The commander of 11 Bde could only commit his reserve, I/IR 13, to the attack, but the unit was very effectively supported by the fire of 6/FAR 3. At 1310hrs 5/FAR 3 moved into an open position to their right. The inhabitants of Delm said later that there had been two battalions of the French 68 RD in the town, most of whom fled the artillery fire in panic. The infantry of I/IR 13 therefore gained ground quickly, and had to open fire only when they had approached to within 100m of the town. At 1345hrs, 1, 2 and 4/IR 13 broke into the north-east side of the town, while 3/IR 13 swung to the north-west side. A hundred POWs were hauled out of the trenches and houses. The German artillery fire had inflicted heavy casualties: French dead and wounded lay in masses.

Shortly after noon in the 12 Bde sector, I/IR 11 advanced with 3 and 4/IR 11 in the first line, followed by 6 and 9/IR 11, which had become detached from their battalions. It reached the top of the hill west of Fax without taking fire, but then suddenly saw French troops 100m to the front. A ferocious firefight ensued, in which the French immediately suffered murderous losses, broke and ran. The German pursuit fire cut them down in masses. The Bavarians took fire in the rear from French troops that had hidden in the oat fields and shocks of grain and been bypassed. The colour bearer was killed by such underhand methods. About 200 French POWs were taken. II/IR 6 and III/IR 6 occupied an attack position in the south side of the Wald von Serres, while I/IR 6 attacked over open terrain against the high ground south-west of the town, with MGK following III/IR 6. By 1230hrs, 6, 8 and 5/IR 6 were 300m from Fax when IR 6 and a MG platoon advanced from the wood. The skirmisher lines of both battalions became intermixed and rapid bounds brought them near to the edge of the town, from which they received moderate fire. 3/FAR 8 set up on Hill 260, south-west of Handorf, and provided fire support. At 1300hrs IR 6 entered the town and was met by heavy fire, especially from two houses, which was suppressed by a MG platoon on the north end of town firing at 150m range. Volunteers set the houses on fire, which ended French resistance. 10 and 12/IR 6 moved on the high ground north of Fax, swept the field for French stragglers and pursued the retreating enemy with fire. Many prisoners were taken, as well as all kinds of military equipment. Large numbers of enemy dead and wounded lay in front of and inside Fax. About 160 French, who had hidden in the Wald von Serres, surrendered to IR 6. The batteries of FAR 8 bounded forward to Fax at 1430hrs so quickly that the horses were exhausted. 2, 3 and 6/FAR 8 were able to shoot groups of withdrawing French skirmishers to pieces. 12 Bde took a breather in place.

The 6 ID order prescribed an attack south-west, but, even before this order reached the forward regiments, the fight at Fax had pulled the division to the south-east. However, the fight at the Wald von Serres had slowed 5 ID, so III b AK ordered 6 ID to attack towards Fax—Fonteningen with a brigade in order to cut off the French forces opposing 5 ID, while screening the right flank at Delm and Weiher. This order was superfluous, for by the time it reached 6 ID at 1240hrs, the division was already moving in that direction. At 1430hrs 6 ID was exactly where III b. AK wanted it to be.

The loss of Fax seems to have had the desired effect on the French, for at 1400hrs they retreated from their positions on the heights south of Orn and on the north edge of the Staatswald von Château Salins. The fire of 5 FA Bde and I/Foot Artillery R 3 (sFH) contributed to the French retreat. They engaged French infantry, MG and trenches at the edge of the two forests, as well as enemy batteries on Hill 272, south-east of Orn, and at Fonteningen. They also may have shelled Fax after IR 12 had occupied it. Their pursuit fire caused the French forces withdrawing from Fax, Fonteningen and the high ground south-east of Orn considerable casualties. The troops of IR 21 on the Orn—Niederweiler road did not limit themselves to pursuit by fire, but immediately advanced across the French Nied, and at 1430hrs 9 Bde received a report that IR 21 was on the heights south-east of Orn. Masses of French dead and wounded were found there, and several abandoned MGs and artillery pieces were taken. On the other hand, the commander of 10 Bde did not give the pursuit order until after he had committed IR 7 to advance on both sides of the Wald von Serres, in which some French troops were hiding. At about 1600hrs IR 19 reached the high ground on both sides of Fax and, a bit later, IR 7 was positioned on the Fax—Weiher road. The right flank of 5 ID had fallen behind the left of 6 ID.

At 1230hrs the commander of 5 ID had received instructions that it was important to take Château Salins that day. Initially, the division commander only ordered IR 21 to occupy the ridge north-east of Fonteningen, with IR 14 following through Orn; he would issue his pursuit order when the status of the left wing of 6 ID, which was in front of his 10 Bde, had been determined.

Between 1600hrs and 1700hrs Sixth Army HQ repeatedly emphasised the importance of taking '*Auf der Telegraph*' (Telegraph Hill), which was 4km north-west of Château Salins and dominated the city. III b. AK HQ passed this mission down to 5 ID. The commander of 6 ID reported to the III b. AK commander that his troops were very tired, and at 1530hrs received permission to give them a short rest. Only when 5 ID reported at 1645hrs that it intended to take Telegraph Hill, freeing up the terrain, did 6 ID order an advance to a line 2km to the south of Delm. Even before the order arrived, heavy enemy artillery fire, which came from the direction of Telegraph Hill and also from the south-west, hit the rest areas: II/IR 13 and the MGK in the woods north-west of Neuheim took serious casualties. 3 FA Bde was unable to locate the enemy artillery; it did find enemy guns far to the south, but these were out of range. Only I/IR 13 fully executed the 6 ID order to advance, occupying its assigned positions at 2100hrs.

Once Fax had been taken, the commander of 12 Bde was determined to pursue in the direction of Neuheim and Hill 321 south of the town, but at 1600hrs received instructions from 6 ID to allow the troops to rest. At 1800hrs an order arrived directing the brigade to move south-west to the area between Lehmhofen and the high ground south-west of Ohrhofen. By this time enemy artillery fire had forced the troops to disperse, in part seeking cover along the Fax—Weiher road. There were few casualties in IR 6 and IR 11, but II/FAR 8, which had moved at 1730hrs to the western slope of Hill 305, west of Fonteningen, to engage infantry south of Orhofen, suffered severely from exceptionally effective high-explosive flanking fire, 6/FAR 8 in particular. Once again, the location of the enemy guns could not be determined. I/FAR 8 withdrew in time to the Wald von Serres. 12 Bde had to delay the move south-west until after the fall of darkness. When IR 6 moved out at 1900hrs, it was soon blocked at Fonteningen by the marching columns of 5 ID, which were also moving south and had priority, so it returned to the Wald von Serres.

Reports from the troops and its own observations had led III b. AK HQ to conclude that, in view of the French artillery fire, which continued until it was dark, further advance was impossible. In particular, the heat had tired the troops to such a degree that further exertions were unjustified; a point made repeatedly by the 6 ID commander. The divisions were directed to deploy their outposts along a line from Delm to the woods south-west of Weiher to Fonteningen, and bivouac the troops on the reverse slope, which required 6 ID to make small but aggravating shifts of bivouac areas in the dark.

The commander of 5 ID had ordered an advance to the high ground at Menival at 1710hrs. IR 21, which had reached the area south of Fax at 1730hrs, resumed the march an hour later. In spite of the fact that they still met no resistance, they were halted in the area of Fonteningen at 1900hrs because 10 Bde was still back at Fax, where heavy enemy artillery fire had restricted movement, and broken down command and control. At 2000hrs III b. AK ordered 5 ID to hold in place at Neuheim—Menival, and at 2050hrs the order to march to Telegraph Hill was cancelled.

However, IR 21 had already resumed the march to Telegraph Hill at 2030hrs. It advanced deployed to Menival, then formed marching column (III, I, II, MGK) near Hill 321. By the time the order to halt arrived, the regiment had reached the Staatswald von Château Salins, so the 9 Bde commander allowed it to continue the advance. Aided by two local guides, the regiment arrived at the treeline north of Telegraph Hill at midnight. Since patrols to the hill took fire, IR 21 withdrew 1km into the wood and bivouacked. It was joined by *Jäger* Bn 2 at 0215hrs.

IR 19 (10 Bde) marched (minus I/IR 19) in column (II, III (minus 10), MGK) from the area east of Fax at 1945hrs on the paths from Fonteningen–Hill 321 to the Delm–Château Salins road. In silence and without light they reached Telegraph Hill. The point element, with the regimental commander, took fire, and the regiment began preparations to attack when it was discovered that the fire came from IR 21. Singing 'The Watch on the Rhine' as a recognition signal, IR 19, in spite of all fatigue, resumed the advance and took Telegraph Hill at 0130hrs. The enemy had left. In the rear, a traffic jam developed, especially near Orn and Fax, as marching columns converged. Several artillery units were not able to move forward to Fonteningen as ordered.

To the right of III b. AK, 10 ED arrived east of the Delm ridge as ordered. The heat and the 30km march from Bolchen, which started at 0400hrs, caused numerous march casualties; the division's combat power could not be rated very highly. Nevertheless, it was enough to hold the strong Delm ridge position and guard the army right flank.

HKK 3 had intended to advance 7km south-west to the border at Fossieux (off the map), but III b. AK did not make much progress on the right flank that afternoon, and considering the strong French forces on the high ground between the Selle and the Moselle, it was not possible for the cavalry corps to conduct a pursuit, and it bivouacked north-west of Delm.

6 ID had attacked the French 68 RD between Delm and Weiher while it was in bivouac; it was probably reinforced by elements of 70 RD. Between Orn and the Château Salins Forest, 5 ID had attacked 39 ID on the left wing of the French XXI Corps while it was advancing towards Mörchingen. Apparently the French were caught unprepared. The uncoordinated French resistance appeared to III b AK as a withdrawal. This was reinforced by the standing grain, which hid French movements and casualties and produced an empty battlefield. Nevertheless, the French had suffered a serious defeat. III b. AK took a considerable number of POWs and the 6 ID engineer company buried 1,200 French dead in the area Delm–Dinkirch–Handorf–Fonteningen. Everywhere, but especially along the route of IR 19 and IR 21 to Telegraph Hill, signs of French panic flight were evident: discarded weapons, equipment, packs, chests and abandoned vehicles. As early as midday, Aviation Sec. 1 reported a French general withdrawal. The Bavarian troops advanced so aggressively that they took their objectives even before the orders to do so reached them: the corps HQ may have failed to exploit several favourable opportunities. But the unclear situation that morning justified a certain caution and tight control: when the corps crossed the start line on the Rotte, it was impossible to see where and when it would meet the enemy, or if he would fight or withdraw. It appeared necessary to restrain the troops in order to prevent piecemeal engagement or intermixture of units. The troops advanced in the burning sun, fully deployed, cross-country, for long distances, over hill and

dale, through woods, scrub and standing grain. The artillery hastened behind by bounds to provide support. For the most part the troops had little rest the previous night and during a long approach march. By afternoon they were tired, hungry and thirsty, but their aggressiveness was unimpaired: when, in the gathering dark, the leaders of the two regiments ordered them to take the dominating Telegraph Hill, they accomplished their mission.

Mörchingen (map 4)

In the early morning of 20 August, II b.AK was poorly positioned to attack: while 3 ID was in contact with the enemy, 4 ID was echeloned to the right rear and could not attack much before 0500hrs. 4 ID had the mission of attacking across the Rotte (off map, to the north) towards Bruch-Kastel and Marthil, and then on to the Rote-Berg (Red Hill, Hill 326, south of Merthil). 3 ID was to attack as soon as possible with the left wing in the direction of Reich. The detachment at Liedersingen was to attack with 3 ID towards Neu–Köding Farm. On the morning of 20 August, it was ordered to orient on the 31 ID (XXI AK) to its left. 4 ED was ordered to the rail station at Landrorff (off map, on the Rotte, 6.5km north of Baronweiler).

The battle began in the 3 ID sector at 0500hrs, with a French attack on I/IR 22 (5 Bde) on Hill 316, 1km south-west of Baronweiler and the Kanonen-Berg (Cannon Hill) to the east. II/IR 22 was not engaged. Although the enemy fire rose to a disturbing intensity, I/IR 22 stood fast, supported by II/FAR 12 in defilade directly to their rear. 6 Bde had deployed south of Mörchingen the previous day, and the preparations for the attack could be made undisturbed by the enemy. The 3 ID commander retained I/Foot Artillery 1 (sFH) under his control, with III and MGK/IR 17 as divisional reserve.

4 ID, echeloned right, had the opportunity to take the French troops attacking 3 ID in the left flank. The 4 ID commander recognised this opportunity at midday on 19 August and communicated it to the corps HQ, which agreed. Reconnaissance began immediately, which revealed that the Schmiede-Holz (Blacksmith Wood) the Gemeidewald von Lesch (Lech Community Forest) and the Herren-Wald (Noble's Wood), in the high ground north of Marthil, were difficult or downright impossible to traverse. As a result of this reconnaissance, the troops were moved up to the Rotte (off map to the north) during the night and, on the morning of 20 August, 4 ID advanced on a broad front. As the advance guard of RIR 8 reached the high ground on the east end of the Herren-Wald, at least six enemy batteries became visible between Marthil and Eschen, firing against the right flank of 3 ID, but offering their left flank to 4 ID. In addition, there was a massed infantry battalion and two individual guns, apparently heavy

artillery. The division commander, who was with the lead infantry, instructed 4 FA Bde to engage them immediately. In spite of the steep terrain, by 0630hrs II/FAR 2 was able to go into an open position, with only hedges and bushes for concealment, on the east end of the Herren-Wald, and opened fire. The infantry battalion fled, leaving a mass of weapons and equipment behind. The French gunners panicked, abandoning their guns. Only one French battery returned fire, causing II/FAR 2 some casualties, but it lost the artillery duel. Only a few guns were able to limber up and escape at a gallop. The rest of the gun teams bolted or were mown down. Four or five French batteries fell as booty to the infantry.

In the meantime, on the orders of the division commander, RIR 8 occupied an attack position on a narrow front on the east tip of the Herren-Wald, with II/RIR 8 leading, I/RIR 8 and the MGK following, and the objective being the Rote-Berg. IR 9 appeared to the right. It had moved through the Herren-Wald on poor, swampy paths and occupied an attack position, with I/IR 9 on the right of the road to Marthil, II/IR 9 to the left and III/IR 9 echeloned behind the right flank. The MGK had left the swampy path and moved to the east of the Herren-Wald, but was delayed by steep slopes and had not yet caught up.

IR 5 reached the south treeline of the Gemeindewald von Lesch and began a firefight with weak enemy forces north of the Neuscher Kapell (Neusch Chapel, at crossroads 1km to the south). Trenches could be seen west of Bruch-Kastel. I/IR 5 deployed right of the road to Bruch-Kastel, III/IR 5 (minus 11/IR 5) to the left, with II/IR 5 echeloned to the right of I/IR 5. I/FAR 11 was able to slowly ascend the steep, slick path, dotted with swampy holes, through the Schmiede-Holz and the Gemeindewald von Lesch, although only with the help of the engineer company and 11/IR 5. As of 0900hrs, the batteries finally began to arrive one after the other, sometimes as individual guns, on Hill 337, north-west of Diexingen.

When the 4 ID had reached the south treeline of the Gemeindewald von Lesch and the Herren-Wald, RIR 8 attacked at 0715hrs on the division left to take the Rote-Berg (Hill 326), with IR 9 on the right to take the Gerichts-Berg (Hill 314), both about 2km away, followed echeloned right by IR 5 and I/FAR 11. The attack made rapid progress, faster than in a peacetime exercise, sometimes at a run, at other times pushing through high-standing grain or crossing the swampy French Nied. The firefight began at a mere 800m range. Overzealous leaders committed all their troops to the firing line: soon they lay shoulder-to-shoulder and one behind the other. Every French bullet had to find a mark: there were painfully heavy casualties. Farmer's barbed-wire fences disrupted movement. Nevertheless, by 0800hrs the high ground had been taken and the French were running away, to be cut down by the pursuit fire of IR 9. III/IR 9 had taken flanking fire from Niedweiler, deployed in that direction and took the town.

To the left, IR 22 (3 ID) attacked in a thin, 5km-long line. I/IR 22 deployed on Hill 316, south-west of Baronweiler, and the Kanonen-Berg, and attacked between Eschen and Rode. II/IR 22, reinforced by 10 and 11/IR 22, attacked from Destrich towards Marthil, but soon turned towards Eschen. 9 and 12/IR 22 were soon committed to fill a gap between the two battalions. II/IR 22 advanced quickly and encountered superior enemy forces when it reached the main road at 0900hrs. After a tough fight with the bayonet, 6, 10 and 12/IR 22 threw the enemy back in the direction of Böllingen. Later that morning some troops panicked under French artillery fire, but were halted by the regimental commander.

Elements of III/RIR 8 had moved up behind the right wing of II/IR 22, entered the fight at the crossroads south-east of Marthil and were pinned down in a shallow hollow by MG fire. The French attempted to attack, but were forced to retreat. II/FAR 12 had supported the attack from the beginning, and at 0900hrs moved right up to Hill 330.

In the 4 ID sector, at 0800hrs the commander of 4 FA Bde ordered his regiments to follow the infantry by bounds to the Rote-Berg. The II/FAR 2 commander was killed by a rifle bullet while far forward on Hill 330 on reconnaissance. Nevertheless, at 0900hrs first 4/IR 22, then 5/IR 22 occupied open positions at the crossroads west of the hilltop to engage French troops retreating to Böllingen. 6/IR 22 and I/IR 22 were kept in the position at the Herren-Wald as insurance against a French counter-attack. The commander of 4/FAR 11 moved his battery forward to the high ground north-east of Bruchheim on his own initiative, in order to support the infantry, which had reached Marthil. His howitzers arrived just in time to aid the IR 9 attack on the Gerichts-Berg. Initially, the hill appeared to the IR 9 commander to be an unusually strong, practically impregnable position, and he wanted to allow his battalions to close up and give the troops a breather before attacking. 2/IR 9 on the right flank detected a mass of French supply wagons on the road to Bruch-Kastel and engaged them effectively with the company's fire concentrated at the extreme range of 1,500m. But as II/IR 9 came up on the left and attacked, I/IR 9 (with only 2 and 4/IR 9) attacked too. In spite of flanking fire from the Staatswald von Château Salins, I/IR 9 quickly seized the weakly held Gerichts-Berg, in the same moment that French reinforcements climbed the other side of the hill: a bitter, deadly, close-range firefight broke out, in which, thanks in good part to the leadership from the I/IR 9 commander, the two companies held their position. Nevertheless, strong enemy forces were still on their right flank and practically in their rear in the Staatswald. The IR 9 commander had dispatched 1 and 3 companies in that direction and called III/IR 9 forward, but they were slowed down by the heat and flanking fire from Bruchheim and the Staatswald. 4/FAR 9, firing from open positions, paved the way for IR 9, and III/IR 9 in particular. After twenty long minutes the first reinforcements reached I/IR 9, and the MGK set up in the ranks. III/IR 9, with half of 2/Eng. Bn 2, extended the line to the right. The battle continued into the afternoon and the units became badly intermixed. But IR 9 had boldly seized the hill, which formed a key part of the corps position, and was not about to give it up. In particular, the rapid movement of I/IR 9 brought it in possession of the terrain first and spared the regiment a difficult and bloody attack. Counter-battery fire forced 4/FAR 9 to move to a covered position, but it was still able to suppress the fire into the IR 9 right flank, and finally swept the enemy infantry out of the Staatswald.

Weak enemy fire met the attack of RIR 8; there were only a few French infantrymen on the Rote-Berg. Then strong enemy forces were reported marching from the south; the II/RIR 8 commander threw all his companies into the first line and reached the crest before the French. The firefight began at 0900hrs at 100−150m range, and the overwhelming fire of the thick Bavarian skirmisher lines put the enemy to flight. Platoons and companies of I/RIR 8 either joined the firing line or extended it to the crossroads on the left. Two platoons of the MGK came forward under heavy enemy fire and put pursuit fire on the fleeing French. Heavy artillery fire caused casualties and forced a withdrawal to the reverse slope, but the Rote-Berg remained firmly in the hands of RIR 8. On the road south of Marthil, the sixteen guns that the French had abandoned under the fire of II/FAR 2 that morning were taken.

At 0930hrs I and 6/FAR 2 were ordered to displace forward. French artillery fire halted them in Marthil, but the division commander personally got them moving again. At 1100hrs they occupied covered positions between the Gerichts-Berg and the Rote-Berg, followed by 4 and 5/FAR 2. At the same time, II/FAR 11 displaced forward to the Gerichts-Berg.

At 0745hrs IR 5 moved out from the south treeline of the Gemeindewald von Lesch to attack Bruch-Kastel. By 0900hrs I/IR 5 and III/IR 5 had cleared out French outposts on the high ground north of the crossroads. As II/IR 5 came into the open it received flanking fire from Diexingen and sent 8/IR 5 in that direction. The 7 Bde commander held up IR 5 until 1000hrs, when IR 21 on the left flank of III b. AK had taken the Gal-Berg. About this time, strong French skirmisher swarms fled from Diexingen, pursued by 8/IR 5, which took thirty POWs, and by the fire of I/FAR 11. As IR 5 crossed the road, the MGK took up position on the heights west of the crossroads to sweep the French trenches west of Bruch-Kastel. Around 1300hrs the French withdrew. IR 5 pushed through Bruch-Kastel and took the high ground north-west of Warnhofen and Dalheim, level with IR 9, at 1500hrs. I/FAR 11 bounded forward.

Bavarian 4 ID had taken the dominating ground on the Gerichts-Berg and Rote-Berg early in the morning and at little cost. The Sixth Army decision to hold 4 ID in echelon behind the Rotte had justified itself: the enemy had been surprised and struck in the flank. 4 ID, although temporarily exhausted by the effects of these meeting engagements, stood on the flank of the enemy forces engaged with 3 ID.

The left flank of the 3 ID, 6 Bde, was to attack in conjunction with 6 ID to the right. When 6 ID did not appear, at 0600hrs the 6 Bde commander gave the order to attack anyway. The commander of IR 18, which had operational control over II/IR 17 and I/IR 18 (with 9/IR 18), had the decisive and most difficult mission, to take the heavily fortified and strongly held Hill 250, south-east of Pewingen. First, I/IR 18 moved out of its trenches on Hill 261, south of Mörchingen, to come closer to II/IR 17, but instead pushed forward and came under heavy rifle fire as it advanced on the strongly fortified town of Pewingen; with an open right flank it only made slow progress. The job of taking Hill 250 thus fell to I/IR 18 alone, which also took flanking fire from Pewingen. 1/IR 18 and 4/IR 18 initially formed the firing line, and were reinforced by 3/IR 18 on the left (2/IR 18 was regimental reserve at the south-west corner of Mörchingen). At 0800hrs the MGK was brought forward from Mörchingen, and II/IR 18 returned to IR 18 control. At 0730hrs III/IR 18 moved along the south edge of Mörchingen to the south-west corner under heavy artillery fire. By 1000hrs the I/IR 18 attack had stalled. 9/IR 18 was committed on the right, 8/IR 18 on the left, and II/IR 18 pushed onto Hill 250, where they were hit by a counter-attack against the left flank by superior forces. I/IR 18, weakened by casualties and the loss of almost all its leaders, began to waver. 2/IR 18 was committed to the right flank. Fortunately, the IR 18 commander brought II/IR 18 west of Mörchingen, for a French artillery barrage now completely blocked the west exit from the town, which inflicted casualties on III/IR 18 and delayed it considerably. The IR 18 commander pushed 5, 6 and 7/IR 18 into the firing line, which stabilised the situation. But the crisis was not yet passed: the left was still in danger of being flanked by superior French forces. From its positions south-east of Mörchingen, I/FAR 5 directed its fire onto Hill 250. At 1000hrs II/FAR 5 (minus 5/FAR 5) moved to the south-west corner of Mörchingen to provide close support. At the height of the crisis, 6/FAR 5 arrived and, at the direction of the IR 18 commander, galloped straight into the crumbling skirmisher line, losing almost all of the horses in the process; however, their fire broke apart the thick French masses on Hill 250 and raised the sinking courage and stiffened the backs of the IR 18 men. III/IR 18 appeared on the left flank, having moved through the artillery barrage in a succession of very open-order lines, with large intervals between each line. The lead element, 12/IR 18, with elements of 11/IR 18, immediately entered the fight, while the following companies arrived much later. The lead element of I/IR 23, 2/IR 23, was committed on the left of I/IR 18. At 1300hrs the enemy was finally thrown back, and at 1400hrs II/IR 17 took Pewingen. Battery by battery, 5 FA Bde moved to Hill 250.

The attack by the left wing of 6 Bde on Conthil involved a certain element of danger because of the high and wooded ridge of Ober-Köding on the left flank.

At 0630hrs II/IR 23 moved from Hill 274 and, with 7 and 5/IR 23 leading, soon took heavy rifle fire in the front from the hill north-east of Metzig and in the flank from Conthil. However, effective fire support from 5/FAR 5 suppressed the enemy on the rail embankment west of Conthil to such a degree that II/IR 23 was able to cross the Mörchingen–Conthil road before it formed a firing line. But now artillery fire began to land, apparently from the Wald von Habudingen (Habudingen Forest). 5/IR 5, well hidden in a fold in the terrain, took no losses, but at 0900hrs II/IR 23 retreated: 5/IR 23 did not stop until it reached Rakringen. On the other hand, the battalion adjutant succeeded in rallying elements of 7 and 8/IR 23 at the mill south of the pond, resupply them with ammunition and lead them back into the firing line. At noon II/IR 23 established contact with IR 18 and 2/IR 23 about halfway between the road and Metzing.

Jäger Bn 1 advanced towards Conthil at 0600hrs, with 1 and 3 on line, 2 in echelon left, 4 behind the centre. It opened fire on the weak enemy forces in Conthil at 600m range, and at 0800hrs pushed into the town and then to the west side. *Jäger* Bn 2 forced back enemy forces in the open fields to the south of the town. *Jäger* that had gathered in the streets were fired upon from windows and cellars. The *Jäger* also received overwhelming fire from a free-standing house surrounded by a 3m iron fence and 100m west of the town. All attempts to take this strongpoint failed with heavy losses. The battalion commander forbade further attacks and assembled fragments of 1 and 3 to mop up the houses in the centre of the town. 4 /*Jäger* 2 had arrived on the north side and their fire at 1km range forced enemy troops approaching from the west to retreat. By 1000hrs 1 and 3 prepared the west side for defence. Enemy artillery from the area of Ober–Köding began to shell the town. The battalion commander requested artillery support, and at noon a platoon of 5/FAR 5 arrived, which shelled the isolated house: ninety French surrendered after twenty minutes. An attempt to advance on the high ground to the west was unsuccessful due to a French artillery barrage.

By the early afternoon II b. AK had defeated the French along its entire front. At 0850hrs the commanding general had already assigned further objectives: 4 ID was to advance to Telegraph Hill, and 3 ID to the high ground between Püttingen and Dedlingen. However, the fight for the initial objective at Reich had cost the 3 ID the entire morning. IR 9 and RIR 8 seemed to have been tired out and to have suffered serious casualties from artillery fire taking the Gerichts-Berg and the Rote-Berg, so the 4 ID commander decided to stop. IR 5, guarding the right flank, was far behind. Bringing up the artillery required time. The proximity of the large and mysterious Staatswald von Château Salins, on the west side of which the III b. AK battle proceeded slowly, argued for caution on the right flank. So there arose all sorts of delays that prevented a determined pursuit.

Around noon the II b. AK commander received telephonic instructions from Sixth Army HQ to swing the corps sharply to the left front, and in conjunction with XXI AK attacking from the east, and which had already taken Duß, cut off the French forces that were south of Liedersingen. The corps commander therefore renewed the order at 1215hrs to continue the attack, and reinforced 4 ID by attaching I/Foot Artillery 1 (sFH) and three battalions and five batteries of 4 ED.

The 4 ID commander, who had been on the Gerichts-Berg since 1330hrs, had, like the corps commander, come to the conclusion that it was no longer a question of continuing the attack but of beginning a pursuit. As IR 5 and the battalions of 4 ED came forward, at 1500hrs he ordered IR 5 (with I/IR 14) to advance through Warnhofen to Wastingen, and IR 8 through Dalheim to Püttingen. IR 9 would follow, advancing as far as Dalheim, along with the elements of 4 ED.

IR 5 and I/IR 14 formed a marching column on the road to Château Salins on Hill 308, north-west of Warnhofen, at 1545hrs, and by 1700hrs had reached the low ground west of Wastingen. I/FAR 11 occupied an open position on the heights 500m north of Wastingen and east of the road, fired on French marching columns moving from Habudingen to Orbeck and broke them up. In turn, French heavy artillery, whose location could not be detected, inflicted considerable casualties on I/FAR 11.

At 1600hrs, after RIR 8 had reorganised and recovered the numerous wounded at the crossroads south-east of Marthil, it moved deployed towards Dalheim, I/RIR 8 leading, III/RIR 8 echeloned right, II/RIR 8 and the MGK left. 3/*Cheveauleger* R 5 attacked trenches on Hill 269 south of Dalheim, first mounted, then on foot, and hauled out prisoners. Both *Cheveauleger* R 3 and 5 then took fire from Dalheim. IR 9 had moved to the north of Dalheim. When the field kitchens attempted to get water in the town, they were fired upon. Since the regiment was also taking artillery fire, it moved to the low ground north-east of Warnhofen after dark. At about 1800hrs I/RIR 8 reached Hill 269, south-east of Warnhofen, but came under artillery fire. II and III/RIR 8 moved through Dalheim, and had been given water by the inhabitants, but once passed the town took lively fire from the attics and church tower, apparently from hidden French infantry and MGs. The town was surrounded by RIR 8 and then set ablaze with artillery fire. If civilians lost their goods and lives thereby, they had the underhand conduct of the French troops to thank.

FAR 2 moved forward by bounds, sometimes in front of the infantry, and at 1600hrs occupied an open position on the slopes north and northwest of Warnhofen, and engaged withdrawing enemy columns in the area of Burlingshofen. Soon heavy enemy artillery fire forced them to shift to a covered position; the regimental commander, who had been standing between the batteries, was severely wounded.

At 1530hrs the commander of 3 ID once again encouraged his troops to pursue the enemy. 5 Bde sent I/IR 17 and 3/Eng. Bn 2 through Eschen to Burlingshofen, with IR 22 following at 1700hrs. II/FAR 12 followed by bounds and was able to shell French detachments as they left the Wald von Habudingen. Even the engineers, on the left of I/IR 17, were able to engage with long-range pursuit fire. At and after dark, IR 22 reached Burlingshofen and I/IR 17 was positioned on Hill 268, south-west of the town.

In taking Hill 250 south-east of Pewingen, IR 18 had lost 26 officers and 900 enlisted men, and became division reserve. The commander of 6 Bde continued the attack with his remaining units to Habudingen–Reich–Linderchen. Soon thereafter he received orders from division to pursue, and at 1800hrs the area of Dürkastel was designated the brigade objective. Movement did not get under way until 1700hrs. By evening IR 17 (minus I/IR 17) had reached the area between Burlingshofen and Moutelotte. IR 23 (minus III/IR 23) reached Dürkastel–Dedlingen–Götzeling. The French had long since disappeared. FAR 5 pursued with fire from Hill 250, then moved forward to the south of Reich where it again engaged the French moving out of the Wald von Habudingen and through Dürkastel.

II b. AK HQ asked Sixth Army HQ if it was absolutely necessary to reach that day's objective, the plateau of Morsheim (3km east of Château Salins). It was told that it was not absolutely necessary, but very desirable. Since the troops had been tired out by marching, fighting and the heat, it did not seem prudent to climb and attack strong heights apparently defended by considerable enemy artillery. 3 ID therefore satisfied itself with the occupation of Burlingshofen and Dürkastel. At 1920hrs the commander of 4 ID ordered his troops to bivouac in the area of Wastingen–Püttingen–Warnhofen–Dalheim–Böllingen, but, since this was within range of the French heavy artillery at Morsheim, to bivouac in the open.

Complete peace by no means descended on the battlefield. French infantry, which had hidden in stooks of grain and other such places, frequently fired on German troops, including stretcher-bearers, even if they were themselves wounded. Merciless retaliation was, under such circumstances, fully justified.

On the far left flank of II b. AK, 5 Res. Bde occupied an attack position north-east of Liedersingen, and as the sound of combat in the XXI AK sector to the left became louder, the brigade attacked at 0600hrs. II/RIR 5 on the high ground north of Liedersingen had already gradually committed all of its companies into a close-range firefight against strong French forces on the edge of the town. French rifle and MG fire caused serious casualties and led the troops to recklessly fire off their ammunition, until an NCO moved down the ranks yelling 'Cease Fire!', which brought the men back to their senses. The French fire also stopped III/RIR 5 and III/IR 23 south-east of the town. The church tower was identified as the source of the trouble, but fire from an MG platoon could not suppress it. A platoon of 2/FAR 12 was brought forward at a gallop to the skirmisher line, losing most of the horses to MG fire; the first gun unlimbered 400m from the north side of the town and the entire gun crew became casualties. With the second gun the platoon leader silenced the MG in the tower and then turned its fire on the edge and interior of the town; nests of infantry, occupied buildings and incautious infantry were immediately engaged. A replacement crew was sent forward for the first gun. Bold infantrymen helped bring forward an immobilised ammunition wagon. The German fire made the French stay in Liedersingen unpleasant and caused them heavy casualties; first individuals, then smaller and, finally, larger groups fled the town, pursued by German fire. II/RIR 5 entered the town around noon against little resistance, and pulled numerous wounded and unwounded French troops out of bushes, cellars, barn and beds.

III/RIR 5 and III/IR 23 had crossed the open hill south of Liedersingen and were about 2km from the Conthil road when sporadic artillery fire brought the advance to a halt. The rest of RIR 5 (I/RIR 5, two companies of II/RIR 5 and the MGK) were brought forward on the left, but this only resulted in an overfilled skirmisher line. Both the brigade and regimental commanders moved forward, but the troops would not follow them: all aggressiveness had disappeared, the effect of the combat of the preceding day. Successive widely spaced waves of skirmishers lay unmoving in the fields of grain. At about 1400hrs the artillery fire intensified – most likely presaging an attack. Even though it did not do serious damage, the troops began to waver: the brigade commander called to II b. AK and XXI AK for help.

News of the unsatisfactory state of affairs at Liedersingen reached Sixth Army HQ, and in wildly exaggerated form. 8 ED was attached to II b. AK and sent to reinforce the corps left wing. It reached the crossroads south of Conthil after dark and bivouacked there without making contact.

II b. AK had thrown back the French 11 ID (XX Corps) on the left flank of German XXI AK. 4 ID had succeeded in attacking the left flank of the careless enemy and, in short order, had taken the Gerichts-Berg and the Rote-Berg, which dominated the Klein- (Little) Selle River Valley and the enemy lines of communication to Château Salins. But the troops had been exhausted by the exceptionally difficult approach march, the hilly terrain and the impact of being in combat for the first time. The division commander did not think that he could immediately ask the troops to conduct another difficult mission. He was also concerned about his right-hand neighbour: 4 ID was clearly in position to cut off the retreat of the enemy troops south of Mörchingen, who had been fixed in place by the sharp attack of 3 ID, or push them to the east and into the arms of XXI AK, but the opportunity was not used. When 4 ID did advance that afternoon, the French had already pulled their neck from the noose, gained a head start and prepared a blocking position on the dominating high ground at Morsheim. The chance for a great success had passed.

In the XXI AK sector, the French had approached during the night of 19–20 August to within 1.5km of the German position. On the morning of

20 August the initial German attack drove the French back in disorder. The morning fog assisted the attack, but prevented artillery support, which led to serious casualties. By 0900hrs the French position was in German hands, but now the resistance stiffened. The French blocked 31 ID at Vergaville (5km north-east of Duß) until that afternoon, while 42 ID met stiff resistance at Lindre-Haute (2km east of Duß) that lasted until evening. XXI AK took serious casualties, but finally the French were thrown out of Duß and back to the high ground 7km to the south and south-west, where they were able to securely establish themselves. This was the French XIV Corps, which had also been attacking when the German XXI AK hit and defeated it; the French retreat blocked the streets of Duß and caused a panic.

Lautersingen—St Johann (map 5)

The Sixth Army order for 20 August did not arrive at I b. RK until 2200hrs on 19 August. The corps mission was to guard the left flank of XXI AK and prevent a breakthrough at Mittersheim. The corps commander decided to do so by taking the offensive; the threat of enemy forces on the left flank of XXI AK in the woods to both sides of the Mittersheimer Weiher (Mittersheim Pond) could only be removed if I b. RK pushed into the woods, keeping pace with the advance of the XXI AK left flank. It was known that there was a French division 4–6km south-west of Lautersingen and a marching column had reached Bisping. Given the lack of time, I b. RK HQ issued a short fragmentary order at 2335hrs telling the divisions to attack at 0500hrs, with a written order to follow.

5 RD was to attack through Bisping to Freiburg. This order arrived very late – at 0015hrs – so that the troops had to be awakened early and moved with oral fragmentary orders. The division commander decided to initially enter the extensive Forst Albesdorf (Albesdorf Forest) with the advance guard, which was at Lautersingen (RIR 7, Res. Cavalry R 5, I/RFAR 5, 4/Eng. Bn 2, Res. Div. Bridge Train 5 and MGK/RIR 6) under the commander of 9 Res. Bde, but to keep the mass of his forces (11 Res. Bde) in the open terrain at Rohrbach. RIR 6 was division reserve behind Hill 251, north-east of Lautersingen, with the division HQ. The enemy was reported dug in near Rohrbach, Angweiler, Bisping and the north edge of Forst Albesdorf.

11 Res. Bde first made a night approach march of 3km through Insviller (off map to the north) to an assembly area north of the rail line and Lautersingen, which caused a traffic jam, the loss of an hour and led to units becoming separated and intermixed. The units could not cross the rail line and did not begin the attack on Rohrbach until 0600hrs. Morning fog reduced visibility, but also cloaked the units against enemy fire and favoured quick movement. RIR 10

crossed the rail line with I/RIR 10 and II/RIR 10 in the first line, and advanced in the direction of the strongly held Hill 255, north of Rohrbach. III/RIR 10 followed behind the right flank. The Salinenkanal (Salt Canal) on the right flank was unfinished and nearly dry, but nevertheless restricted movement. In order to cross it as quickly as possible, the units pressed together to the left. They also took fire in the left flank from the treeline west of the Niederstein Weiher (Niederstein Pond), so some elements swung in that direction and took position behind the banks of the canal. The batteries of 42 ID on the Grosser-Berg (Big Hill, Hill 289, north-west of Losdorf) supported the attack. The approach march of I/Res. Foot Artillery R 1 (sFH) from Fort Germersheim had been so delayed by 7 KD and supply units that it was continually brought to a complete halt. This was exacerbated by French interdiction artillery fire, but fortunately their shrapnel burst so high that it had no effect. A bit before 0900hrs 1/Foot Artillery R 1 (sFH) opened fire on the Grosser-Berg and immediately took counter-battery fire, which caused casualties and forced the battery to shift position. Thus warned, 5/Res. Foot Artillery R 1 (10cm cannons) set up behind the rail embankment, and was joined by 6/Res. Foot Artillery R 1 (10cm) and 4/Foot Artillery R 1 (sFH). II/RFAR 5 set up 1km north of Dommenheim.

Elements of RIR 10 pushed into the wood west of the pond at 0800hrs, but soon became disorganised by the fluid battle and both enemy and friendly fire. II/RIR 10 pushed on towards Hill 255 and became involved in a firefight, reinforced by two companies of III/RIR 10 on the right and 1 and 2/RIR 10; Hill 255 was taken by assault at 1000hrs. The enemy had disappeared into the wood at the last minute; numerous prisoners were taken. Hill 255 had cost several casualties, principally the result of flanking fire from the wood near the pond; many officers were killed or wounded.

RIR 13 had crossed the canal directly north of Lautersingen and deployed in the direction of Rohrbach, I and II/RIR 13 in the first line, and quickly entered the woods on both sides of the pond. III/RIR 13, echeloned left, moved forward to fill a gap between I and II/R13. In the thick underbrush of the woods, the forward troops mistook III/RIR 13 for French troops and a wild firefight began, in which unit cohesion collapsed. The regiment was assembled in open terrain on the Lautersingen road and led forward again, without enemy contact.

On 19 August the commander of 9 Res. Bde pushed his troops up to and over the canal; at midnight two companies were even sent into Lautersingen. On the morning of 20 August, I/RFAR 5 fired from positions occupied on the previous day on Hill 251, north-east Lautersingen, against enemy forces on the treeline on both sides of the road to Angweiler. At 0500hrs RIR 7 crossed the canal under the protection of the morning fog, pleasantly surprised by the lack of opposition. It deployed at 0600hrs with II/RIR 7 west of the road, III/RIR 7 east and advanced on the treeline, with I behind III/RIR 7. Enemy artillery, MG and rifle fire was not able to slow the regiment for long; it was as though the enemy were firing blank ammunition at the training area. At about 0800hrs the lead battalions had broken the enemy resistance and pushed into the treeline. The troops had been instructed to reorganise there, but artillery shells, apparently friendly fire, began to land, with the echoes in the wood magnifying their effect, and they pushed further into the wood. The enemy had left snipers in trees and infantry with MGs in the bushes, protected by all kinds of obstacles. The troops became confused, and not only were the RIR 7 units intermixed, but RIR 7 troops strayed into the RIR 13 area and vice versa. There were frequent incidents of friendly fire. Two French companies that had shown a willingness to surrender escaped in the confusion. I and II/RIR 7 were finally pulled out of the wood to reorganise south of Lautersingen, except for 2 and 4/RIR 7 and elements of other companies, which pushed all the way to the south treeline. III/RIR 7 got disoriented and moved to the south-east side of the wood. By 0800hrs 4/Eng. Bn 2 and Res. Div. Bridge Train 5 had put two bridges over the 18m-broad canal, east of Lautersingen, which were used by various units.

11 Res. Bde had assembled on the road to Lautersingen, and the 5 RD commander ordered it to move through Rohrbach to the south, and RIR 6, reinforced with two batteries of RFAR 5, to move on Angweiler to assist RIR 7. He thus anticipated the corps order, which arrived later instructing 5 ID to take Freiburg if possible.

Reserve Cavalry R 5, with two batteries of RFAR 5, was to pursue to the south-west. When it entered Das Grosse-Holz (The Big Wood) south of Rohrbach, it took heavy but badly aimed fire, and fell back to the crossroads between Kuttingen and Rohrbach. On the order of a senior officer of XXI AK, the two batteries moved west and fired in support of 42 ID.

11 Res. Bde moved on Rohrbach at 1230hrs, while Res. Foot Artillery R 1 and II/FAR 8 shelled the town. It found that the enemy had left both Rohrbach and the Das Grosse-Holz. Getting water at Rohrbach caused a delay, and numerous unwounded French soldiers were hauled out of the houses. Although the town was in German territory, the inhabitants, with a few exceptions, were unhelpful, even when it concerned aiding the Bavarian wounded. The brigade did not continue the march to Germingen until 1330hrs.

The commander of 7 Res. Bde instructed the elements of RIR 7 at Lautersingen to reorganise and eat. He then led them in march column on the road to Angweiler and into the Forst Albesdorf, preceded only by a weak advance guard 400m to the front. The troops were ordered to fix bayonets, and only the left and right files were allowed to load their weapons. At every east–west forest road the column was halted until patrols could confirm that the crossroad was clear. There was always a danger of artillery fire or ambush, but the thick column could put overwhelming return fire into the woods. The southern treeline was reached at 1500hrs without incident. A strong enemy position, 800m wide at Angweiler and to the east, was clearly visible, and an attack prior to the arrival of RIR 6 did not seem advisable. II/RIR 7 took up position to the west of the road, with I/RIR 7 to the right, and began a slow firefight.

RIR 6 reached Rohrbach at 1300hrs, although III/RIR 6 became separated in a traffic jam at the Lautersingen road. As the regiment left the wood it took considerable close-range artillery and rifle fire. The attached artillery, 2/RFAR 5 and 6/FAR 8, could not enter the wood because the road was blocked by the RIR 6 combat trains, so it set up east of Rohrbach to provide fire support. 2/RFAR 5 and infantry drove off an enemy battery 1.2km north-west of Angweiler and moved up to occupy that position. One after the other, all three batteries of II/FAR 8 appeared. Nevertheless, RIR 6 felt threatened by such strong enemy forces in close proximity and called RIR 10, which had moved through Rohrbach at 1500hrs, for help. I and II/RIR 10 swung east into the wood and reinforced the RIR 6 left, along with III/RIR 6, which had caught up. At 1600hrs they began the assault on Angweiler, which cost several casualties: the commander of II/RIR 6 was killed. RIR 7 attacked, with III/RIR 7 approaching from the south-east of the town. The enemy was thrown back and the town soon taken. A French battalion, which had been cut off in the west side of the Forst Albesdorf, attacked the limbers of 2/RFAR 5, but was taken prisoner by elements of 6, 7 and 10/RIR 6.

South of Rohrbach, the point element of RIR 13, which was advancing in closed-up column on the road, reached the southern treeline of the Das Grosse-Holz at 1430hrs when it took close-range rifle and artillery fire from the high ground immediately to the left front. There may also have been French troops in the woods, while French artillery fired into the woods. The RIR 13 men deployed left and right of the road into the thick undergrowth or took cover. The brigade commander ordered the MGK pulled back to Rohrbach, while some troops did so on their own. The brigade commander also committed Res. *Jäger* Bn 1 west of the road with instructions to reach the southern treeline. The battalion moved out at 1530hrs, but, as the increasing disorder in the woods became apparent, the *Jäger* battalion commander, Major Düwell, moved all of his troops back to the road to get them under control, and elements of RIR 13 coalesced around the *Jäger*. Düwell's cold-blooded composure, and his order to sing 'The Watch on the Rhine', steadied the troops in spite of the chaos going on around them, and he led them forward to the treeline. At 1600hrs the brigade commander ordered his last reserve, II/RIR 10, to unload their weapons and fix bayonets, and, mounted on his horse and with his sword drawn, personally led them forward. The roadside ditches left and right were filled with wounded, the combat noise deafening. The brigade commander also ordered the troops to sing 'The Watch on the Rhine', which smothered every tendency to weakness or hesitation.

The *Jäger* and II/RIR 10 reached the treeline at about the same time, and all hell broke loose in the form of French rifle and MG fire at 400m range. The brigade commander attempted to lead his men forward, but was severely wounded by a French shell. That was the end of the II/RIR 10 attack. Seeing this, and the absence of RIR 13 troops, Düwell decided to take the French strongpoint, a farm directly to the Jäger front. He deployed his men east of the Rohrbach road and then sprang forward out of the thicket and into the open field, yelling 'Jäger! Follow me!' The *Jäger* called out, 'Look at our major charging forward! Don't let him down!' and the entire skirmisher line (principally 3 and 4/Res. *Jäger* 1) rose to attack the farm. In spite of increased French fire and *Jäger* casualties, the field was crossed in a few rapid bounds and practically in one movement. Some of the French got away at the last moment; those who continued to resist were cut down as the *Jäger* and some RIR 13 and RIR 10 men took the farm at 1715hrs. 1 and 2/Res. *Jäger* 1 took the high ground to the east. The Bavarians pursued the French through enemy artillery fire into the woods to the south. In the assault on the farm, Res. *Jäger* 1 had lost one-quarter of its strength; in the course of the day, RIR 13 had lost one-third. The 5 RD artillery had not been able to support the fighting in the forest.

1 RD had the mission of attacking Disselingen and Rodt at 0500hrs, with a combat team built around 1 Res. Bde on the right, start line on the rail line, and a 2 Res. Bde combat team on the left, setting off from St Basel. Enemy troops were reported the previous day at Bisping and Alberschhofen, as well as Forst Finstingen and Alzing, so early contact could be expected, as well as combat in woods.

III/RIR 12 (minus 11) was sent during the night of 19/20 August west along the Bisping–St Johann road to seize the bridge on the west side of the Saar–Kohlenkanal for 1 Res. Bde. 12/RIR 12 was north of the road, with 9/RIR 12 following and 10/RIR 12 to the south. When they reached the treeline near the canal, they suddenly received murderous rifle and MG fire from an enemy who was invisible in the fog that lay thickly over the canal. Nevertheless, the skirmishers, and even the support troops, immediately began to return fire. Thinking that an assault was being prepared, 9/RIR 12 came forward, but the enemy was too strong and alert to be overrun, and the bridge was mined and barricaded. The battalion stayed on the treeline, while 10 Co. moved left to try to seize the canal lock to the south.

2 Res. Bde assembled on the road north of Rommelfingen, moved out at 0330hrs and reached St Johann at 0445hrs, when it was reported that two enemy bicycle companies had occupied the treeline south-west of St Johann and that an enemy battalion was approaching from the south-east. As the advance guard, 9/RIR 3, left the south-west side of St Johann at 0500hrs, it took fire. It was being followed by two cavalry squadrons, several staffs with their horses, a number of

provisions wagons, field kitchens and engineer equipment wagons, all of which were pushed together and blocked the exit from the town. Two heavy howitzer batteries, which by mistake had entered the column behind the advance guard, were only able to turn around with difficulty and set up on the north side of town, from where they had no observation to fire. III/RIR 3 succeeded in deploying on both sides of the road to Gosselmingen and advanced by bounds to the nearby Hill 275. To the left, I and II/RIR 3 moved through the woods directly east of the town, while 3/RIR 3 and the MGK were held in reserve. Initially the troops fired too fast, but it was gradually possible to identify the enemy 1km away in trenches and fields of grain and re-establish fire discipline. II/RFAR 1 was able to set up in an open position on Hill 275, directly behind the infantry, and engage the enemy infantry at and west of Gosselmingen, who was being reinforced and going over to the attack. RIR 12 reinforced RIR 3 and extended the skirmisher line to the right, with some intermixing of the units.

As soon as RIR 3 had been sorted out, the commander ordered it to attack. The French near Gosselmingen gradually withdrew. Elements of II/RIR 3 entered and swept the town between 0800hrs and 0900hrs. The French had also been motivated to retreat by effective flanking fire from 2 ID on the 1 RD left. On the other hand, RIR 12 had taken strong fire from the Gabel-Wald (Fork Woods) to the right, which for a time even threatened its right flank. 3/RIR 3 and 4/RFAR 1 were sent to reinforce the right flank, while 2 and 3/Res. Cav R 1 screened the extreme right. RIR 12 also began to take strong fire from the woods to the front. Numerous snipers in the trees inflicted more casualties on troops in the rear than were taken on the skirmisher line. The enemy was invisible, and the firefight consumed a large quantity of ammunition.

Concern for the right flank was amplified by rumours brought by numerous stragglers and wounded from 1 Res. Bde on the right that it had been defeated. Gosselmingen had been taken, so II/RIR 3 was brought back to Berthelmingen as a reserve, available to reinforce the right if necessary. In addition, since the troops on the left would not advance until 1100hrs, the commander of 1 RD held 2 Res. Bde in place.

On the right the 1 Res. Bde assembled on the Finstingen–Mittersheim road and turned onto the Bambach Schneuse (Bambach Forest road) at 0330hrs. As the column crossed the rail line, 1/Res. Cavalry R 1 moved forward to provide security towards Bisperg and found the enemy along the Saar–Kohlenkanal, though there was no trace of III/RIR 12. The 1 Res. Bde commander halted the main body and attacked the canal with 4 and 2/RIR 1 and a platoon of MG, which deployed on the treeline 30m from the canal. The French occupied the west bank of the canal for 1–1½km in both directions, which was higher than the east bank and dominated it, and put snipers in the trees, barricaded all the crossing points and fortified the canal lock house. The strength of the French fire was estimated at two to three battalions. The firefight soon lost intensity. The Bavarian riflemen found little cover behind the canal bank or in a wet ditch in front of it, while the French would show their heads only to fire. Shortly before 0600hrs 1 and 3/RIR 1 were committed on the left and the right, and the MGK had placed its guns south of the road. Casualties mounted. Volunteers from the 1 Res./Eng. Bn 2 attempted unsuccessfully to blow up the barricades. III/RIR 1 was sent north, while 6/RIR 1 headed south to cross the canal at the next available point. A platoon of I/RFAR 1 was brought into position on the Bisping road, 500m from the canal, with great difficulty. The French artillery now began firing onto the Bisping road and the Bambach Schneuse. The staff horses, the MG and artillery horse teams, as well as some field kitchens and other vehicles on both roads, stampeded north on the Bambach Schneuse. Two artillery munitions wagons caught fire and exploded. In the Forst Instingen (Instingen Forest) RIR 2 began firing wildly, and the brigade commander brought the regiment back under control by moving it forward to the Bisping road and appearing in person. A stronger frontal attack was not going to alter the situation, especially because the woods prohibited artillery support, so there was nothing to do but await the success of the flanking movements.

Two platoons of MGK/RIR 2 reinforced RIR 1 on the canal north of the road. In spite of time-consuming preparations, a second attempt by the engineer company to destroy the barricades failed. Gradually all of II/RIR 1, except 5 Co., was committed to the firing line to replace casualties and maintain the firefight. 9 and 11/RIR 1 thoroughly prepared the final assault with fire and the barricaded crossing was taken with the bayonet at 1100hrs. III/RIR 1, along with elements of 1 and 4/RIR 1 and fragments of III/RIR 12, had also crossed the west side of the canal 1.5km north of the lock and turned south, rolling up the French position. At 1300hrs III/RIR 1 took the canal lock house, whose desperate defenders were almost all cut down. RIR 1, with 5/RIR 1 in the lead, immediately took up the pursuit towards Bisping. Without making contact, they reached the treeline east of Bisping and saw thick masses of French and skirmisher lines north and north-west of the town fleeing south, unfortunately out of range. After a short firefight with a French detachment that had been cut off, Bisping was occupied at 1600hrs.

Since the French positioned south-west of St Johann had successfully broken contact, at 1100hrs the commander of RIR 2 decided to pursue south to Alzing (on southern road to Bisping, 2½km south-west of St Johann), which it reached by 1200hrs. The enemy had left behind numerous dead, an aid station and a number of stragglers. To round these up, and to cut off the enemy route of retreat, RIR 2 continued the attack to the south-east; I/RIR 2 on the right and II/RIR 2 on the left. On leaving the treeline about 700m from the St Johann road, enemy infantry and MGs were seen on Hill 275 at Bromsenhof. 3/RIR 2 was detached to the *Ziegelhutte* (brickyards) on the right, while the rest of the two battalions attacked straight ahead. The enemy quickly fled. Elements of II/RIR 2 even chased the French north-east towards Gosselmingen, but the mass of the regiment swung right in the direction of 3/RIR 2 and the Langd road. Fire from Hill 273, west of Langd, put an end to the pursuit. Since strong enemy forces were also seen withdrawing south-west, the regimental commander moved his troops back to Alzing at 1400hrs. At 1500hrs RIR 2 was ordered to march west and cross the canal at Alberschhofen, and at 2200hrs it linked up with RIR 1 at Bisping.

At 1500hrs 2 Res. Bde began the pursuit down the southern road to Bisping, RIR 12 north of the road and RIR 3 to the south, with the initial objective, the canal, at Alberschhofen. Since contact was expected, both regiments were fully deployed and movement was slow. RIR 12 traversed the Gabel-Wald and did not reach the canal until 1900hrs. At Alzing RIR 3 expected an enemy attack and occupied defensive positions. The enemy never appeared, and a report arrived that 1 Res. Bde had crossed the canal. RIR 3 formed march columns on the road, intermixed with I/RFAR 1 and half of I/Res. Foot Artillery R 1 (sFH) to protect the artillery during the march through the woods, which also took time, so that it was dusk before the column moved off. RIR 3 crossed the canal at Alberschhofen and turned south towards Rodt. There was no enemy contact. Withdrawing enemy infantry regiments were visible 3km away from the treeline north-east of Rodt, but the artillery was not able to engage them. At 2200hrs RIR 3 entered Freiburg and RIR 12 marched into Rodt.

The troops of I b. RK bivouacked on the battlefield, but the night was unquiet. Now and again shots fell in the woods and there were friendly fire casualties. French stragglers came in to surrender and French wounded sought medical attention.

Unquestionably, I b. RK had a difficult day. Sixth Army HQ had not ordered I b. RK to attack, as it was justifiably concerned about involving newly established reserve units in combat in woods. It would have welcomed an enemy attack on I b. RK, which could have been taken on both flanks by XXI AK and I b. AK. I b. RK could have easily remained on the defensive, but the I b. RK commander had so much confidence in his troops that he decided to attack through the forested area 12km broad and deep between Lautersingen and the Saar. The risks involved in this attack were made greater by the fact that the right-hand neighbour would attack at 0500hrs, while the left-hand neighbour would attack six hours later.

Regular troops have failed while fighting in woods, which is one of the most difficult operations in war. For reserve units, which have just been formed and lack cohesion (in addition to which 5 RD consisted of older year groups), it is a far more difficult test, particularly in a wooded area – as here – which was unbroken and large, filled with impenetrable underbrush and large ponds. Nevertheless, the troops of I b. RK went into battle full of enthusiasm and aggressiveness. They overran the enemy and conducted their attacks as if they were in the training area. Even the unexpected meeting engagement at St Johann did not seriously shake their morale and discipline. Only occasionally were the reservists at first not equal to the confusion and disorganisation that comes with combat in wooded areas, which the troops need not be ashamed of. Without exception, they rallied around their leaders and drove off the enemy.

I b. RK had completed its mission and reached the south side of the woods; in places the troops had advanced 15km. The troops felt that they had won a complete victory, even if at the cost of considerable casualties, and this impression was reinforced by the great number of prisoners taken. If there were any doubts concerning the combat power and cohesion of reserve units at OHL or elsewhere, they were completely removed, indeed reversed, by the accomplishments of I b. RK on 20 August.

I b. RK had been opposed by the French XIV Corps; the whole weight of the Bavarian attack had hit the French 32 ID, which formed the corps first line in the woods south of Rohrbach, while 31 ID was in the second line and did not advance past Bisping. The left column of 1 RD may have encountered troops from the French VIII Corps at St Johann. The German 7 KD had been in Sixth Army reserve behind I b. RK.

Saarburg (map 6)

The I b. AK order for 19 August, issued at 1030hrs, prescribed a continuation of the defence in place. When the Sixth Army attack order arrived at 0100hrs on 20 August, the corps did not immediately issue its own order, for the corps was in close contact with the enemy and the attack would be dependent on the enemy actions: the army attack order called for the corps to shift its 10km defensive sector to the left to an attack zone on a 5km front at Zittersdorf–Saarburg. If the enemy attacked that morning with full force, as was to be expected, the corps could not reposition for its own attack. There were significant advantages to be gained from allowing the enemy to attack and then counter-attacking. The corps therefore gave the divisions only a general overview of the planned attack.

The French 15 ID did advance against 2 ID. At 0430hrs the outpost at St Johann, 2 and 4/IR 3 with a MG platoon, were attacked by the French 29 Bde, and thus became involved in 2 Res. Bde's fight on the right, as did 12/IR 3 in front of Gosselmingen; a platoon of 2/IR 3 in Gosselmingen was overrun. The French 30 Bde attacked IR 12, which was holding a 3km front at Oberstinzel–Saaraltdorf, with all three battalions dug in on line. IR 12 received the French, whose attack was obviously directed at Saaraltdorf, with well-directed fire, particularly from the MG on the flanks, which either pinned the French to the treeline west of the Saar or mowed them down to the last man if they attempted to advance. 2 FA Bde and elements of 4 FA Bde soon supported IR 12. 4 FA Bde also supported 2 Res. Bde at St Johann: it was not always easy to distinguish friend from foe, but their fire was effective. The balloon of the Bavarian Non-Rigid Airship Sec. went up east of Kirberg.

During the morning the enemy infantry grew stronger in the 1 ID sector: on the southern section of the Saar-Wald (Saar Forest), the Unter-Wald (Lower Forest) and the north side of Saarburg, at Gross-Eich and Bahnhof (on map, Bhf. – rail station) Rieding. This was the French 16 ID preparing to attack with 13 Bde on the right and 32 Bde on the left. A sharp artillery duel began, but nowhere in the I b. AK sector did the French conduct a determined and coordinated attack.

I b. AK HQ could therefore issue the attack order at 0710hrs. Since the *Schwerpunkt* (focal point) was on the left flank, the corps reserve, 1 Bde and II/FAR 7, were returned to 1 ID, and 6 and 7/Foot Artillery 1 (sFH) were attached. 2 ID had to give up IR 3 and all of IR 20, except 1 and 4/IR 20 and an artillery section, to the corps reserve at Helleringen. 2 ID would occupy an attack position between Oberstinzel and Kastelwalderhof (west of Hilbesheim), and 1 ID from the latter Rieding: although 1 ID was twice as strong as 2 ID, it had a smaller sector. To assist in crossing the Saar, considered to be a significant obstacle, Eng. Bn 1, with three companies, was attached to 1 ID, while 4 and 2 Res./Eng. Bn 4 joined 2 ID. Instructions were given to commit a minimum of troops to combat in towns and woods, and to wait for the effect of supporting artillery fire. The attack was to begin at 1100hrs.

Reports received at I b. AK HQ led to the conclusion that the enemy in front of 2 ID was withdrawing, which was reinforced during the morning when the artillery duel gradually died down. On the other hand, 1 RD on the right had been engaged since 0500hrs at St Johann and could surely use help: rumours were circulating that 1 RD had suffered a serious reverse. In addition, Rupprecht had passed a request through Seventh Army HQ to move up the I b. AK attack time. I b. AK HQ did try to order the attack to commence at 1000hrs, but it could not be conducted before 1100hrs. Shortly after the order was issued, air reconnaissance reported that there were no signs of an enemy withdrawal: strong enemy forces were observed at Bisping (I b. RK sector), St Georges (13km south-west of Saarburg), Laneuveville (10km south-west of Saarburg) and Hesse (5km south of Saarburg). The French were not withdrawing, but, as per French military doctrine, had deployed their forces in depth. I b. AK completed the redeployment to the attack formation quickly, smoothly and unobserved by the enemy.

The 1 ID attack position was on the reverse slope of the Tinkel-Berg, with I and II/IR 16 and III/IR 2 in dug-in positions on the forward slope. 1/Eng. Bn 1 had cleared the obstacles to the front and laid footbridges over the stream at the west side of the Tinkel-Berg. The artillery preparation began before 1100hrs. The field artillery shelled the treeline and interior of the Saar-Wald and Unter-Wald, and the edges of Hof, Saarburg, Gross-Eich and Klein-Eich; the heavy artillery conducted counter-battery fire and drove off French artillery on Hill 321, south-west of Hof, which at the beginning of the attack seriously hindered the infantry. The French may have recognised what was coming, for shortly before 1100hrs their artillery switched from counter-battery fire to area fire behind the Tinkel-Berg. At 1050hrs the 1 Bde commander therefore gave the order to attack. The infantry passed through the 1 FA Bde positions and then descended the forward slopes, crossed the fully occupied IR 2 trenches, and took artillery fire, which caused the infantry to speed up and disperse, but order was maintained. Serious casualties were taken only when the troops reached the streambed at the foot of the hill, which the enemy covered with area fire from heavy artillery; the brigade commander was wounded here. Nevertheless, the Household IR entered Gross-Eich at 1200hrs, the Bavarian artillery having apparently driven off the French infantry. The lead elements, 5 and 7/Household, pushed on to the rail embankment, where they received lively fire from the buildings of Saarburg; 6 and 8/Household, after a detour to Hof, came up on the right; and 12 and 10/Household were positioned on the left. A MG platoon joined II/Household. I/IR 1 met determined resistance in Klein-Eich, from whose church flew the Red Cross flag. II/IR 1 came up on the left. At 1330hrs both battalions were stopped by French infantry and MGs in the Kasernen (barracks) at the east end of Saarburg. The MGK, to this point in reserve, was brought forward between 1400hrs and 1500hrs, which helped significantly. Both the Household IR and IR 1 had taken casualties in Gross-Eich and Klein-Eisch, and enemy artillery continued to hammer both towns. Numerous prisoners had already been pulled out of cellars, houses, barns and other hiding places. The adjutant of the Household IR surprised thirty French troops in a stall, who surrendered without offering any resistance.

In the 2 Bde sector the lead elements advanced from trenches at 1100hrs. On the left III/IR 2 took heavy artillery fire, but crossed the rail line and the small Biber (Beaver) stream with moderate losses. Here they had to stop due to the situation to the right, where IR 16, with the mission of taking Hof, attacked with only six companies: 8 and 7/IR 16 in the first line, 5 and 6/IR 16 in the second, and 2 and 4/IR 16 to the right. III/IR 16 was brigade reserve and 1 and 3/IR 16 had to hold the trenches south of Saaraltdorf. They initially made good progress, covered by overwatching MG fire, as far as the rail embankment in the Saar Valley, where they took effective fire in the front and right flank from well-concealed French troops in Hof and on the edges of the Unter-Wald and Saar-Wald, losing many leaders. Fortunately, between 1300hrs and 1400hrs, II/FAR 7 set up on Hill 325 and their close-range fire against the French infantry in and in front of the Unter-Wald was so effective that they tried to surrender or fled. Fire from II/FAR 7 also forced the French out of Hof. However, without special equipment there could be no thought of crossing the 20m broad and 2m deep Saar, although individual troops crossed using tree trunks, boards, doors and garden gates. 11 and 12/IR 16 reinforced III/IR 2, which had committed all its troops. When the force which was to relieve him in place had still not arrived at 1300hrs, the commander of I/IR 16, with 1 and 3/IR 16 and a MG platoon, moved down to Saaraltdorf to force a crossing. Here he met elements of IR 12. Between 1300hrs and 1400hrs the 1 ID attack had stalled everywhere.

2 ID commanded only 4 Bde, which was insufficient to evenly fill the entire 5km division sector. The division commander decided to conduct a concentrated breakthrough attack at Hill 304, north-east of Dolvingen (the 'Saareck', Saar Corner), which was easy to ascend and envelop. He deployed IR 15 (minus II/IR 15, division reserve) in and south of Oberstinzel to take Hill 304; once that had been done, IR 12 (minus I/IR 12, brigade reserve) would attack from behind and south of IR 15 to take the Saar-Wald west of Saaraltdorf. To better provide fire support, at 1100hrs 2 and 3/FAR 4 and 6/FAR 9 occupied open positions on Hill 293 north of Saaraltdorf. Their preparatory fire on the Saar-Wald soon had the French fleeing south in entire groups; when the French reached the open west side of the Saar-Wald at Hill 309, they were for the most part destroyed by artillery fire. I/IR 12 was committed at 1100hrs, soon reached the rail embankment south-east of Oberstinzel and, with 2/IR 12 and the MGK in Oberstinzel, directed their fire on the Hill 304 woodline. IR 15 attacked immediately and met minimal resistance. I/IR 15 (minus 3/IR 15 in Saaraltdorf) deployed on the south side of Oberstinzel. The enemy in the woods at the Saareck was well hidden, but could not escape the fire of MGK/IR 15 set up in the houses of Oberstinzel. After a short firefight, I/IR 15 was able to cross the bridge at the north end of the Saareck. To the left, III/IR 15 pushed 10/IR 15 to a wood on the rail embankment, which provided covering fire for 11/IR 15 to seize the bridge on the south end of the Saareck. But well-hidden French infantry in the Saar-Wald stalled the III/IR 15 attack, until 10/IR 15 could cross too and force the French resistance to slacken. While advancing, I and III/IR 15 passed piles of dead and wounded French who had been hit by German artillery fire; behind a hedge lay a complete row, scythed down by the MGs. The mass of the enemy had chosen to leave the woods soon after 1100hrs, but here and there individuals and groups on the steep slopes had to be eliminated; prisoners were also taken. Shortly after 1200hrs I/IR 15 reached the top, with III/IR 15 soon after, and I/IR 12 crossed the bridge. IR 15 casualties were light, probably because French artillery could not fire into the deep Saar Valley.

At 1230hrs IR 12 attacked. Beginning at 1000hrs the German artillery had thoroughly swept the Saar-Wald in this sector. II/IR 12, on the right, had driven off French infantry with fire. At 1230hrs it crossed the Saar at Saareck and at a chest-high ford to the south. It quickly moved through the Saar-Wald, taking 120 POWs. In the III/IR 12 sector on the left, at and north of Saaraltdorf, MGK/IR 12 set up on a rail bridge at the west end of town and completely cleared the opposite bank. 10 and 11/IR 12 crossed the Saar at the ford, while 9, 12 and MGK/IR 12, with the attached 3/IR 15, crossed at Saaraltdorf. This group met resistance at Saar-Wald (north of the road, 1.8km west of Saaraltdorf); 3/FAR 4 set up immediately behind the cheering infantry and eliminated it. By 1330hrs IR 12 had reached the top of Hill 309.

When there could no longer be a question that the attack had proceeded well, at 1445hrs the corps commander extended the division objectives, which initially had been only at Zittersdorf–Saarburg to Kirchberg–Rintingen–Hill 328, south-east of Imlingen.

In the 2 ID sector, at 1400hrs II/FAR 9 began moving onto Hill 304, which was strewn with French wounded. 4 and 5/FAR 9 were able to break up crowds of French retreating to Zittersdorf. FAR 4 also displaced across the Saar. I/FAR 4 tried to move to Hill 309, but was delayed by fire from snipers in trees, as well as treacherous fire from French wounded. II/FAR 4 was delayed for two hours by a traffic jam in Saaraltdorf. II and III/Foot Artillery 3 (21cm mortars) were brought up to the Saar.

As soon as IR 12 reached Hill 309, the 4 Bde commander ordered the attack to continue. Between 1400hrs and 1500hrs IR 15 moved through Dolvingen, full of French wounded, with the inhabitants openly expressing their joy at being freed from enemy occupation, to Zittersdorf. It then took heavy artillery fire from the area of Misselhof. II/FAR 9 and I/FAR 4 were able to suppress or drive off these guns, but other French batteries, with a greater range than the German guns, were able to inflict serious damage on II/FAR 9. IR 15 continued to advance, reaching the high ground north-east of Zittersdorf, but there became involved in a firefight with French infantry that held a 200m-long position on the road north-west of Zittersdorf. French infantry also set up on the road from Zittersdorf south to Saarburg, but were quickly driven off by FAR 9 and MGK/IR 15. III/IR 15 and II/IR 12 swung south and stormed St Ulrich. IR 12 encountered considerable resistance from French infantry in the west part of the Unter-Wald. Finally the French left the field of battle completely. At 1800hrs IR 15 was on both sides of Zittersdorf, with IR 12 south of St Ulrich and at the Mittel-Wald (Middle Wood). The 4 Bde commander brought his reserve, I/IR 12, forward to Saar-Wald; the 2 ID commander arrived there at 1600hrs, while moving his reserve, II/IR 15, to Saaraltdorf. The I b. AK commander arrived at 1700hrs and brought the corps reserve forward from Saaraltdorf. At 1710hrs the Seventh Army order reached I b. AK, giving Gunderchingen and Lörchingen as the day's objectives.

In the 2 ID sector, I/IR 16 had crossed at the Saaraltdorf bridges between 1300hrs and 1400hrs and turned south to the Unter-Wald, which the enemy no longer defended, driven out by the crushing Bavarian rifle, MG and artillery fire.

The battalion commander avoided the undergrowth of the forest and led his troops quickly along the treeline to Hof, gathering up 100 POWs along the way without a fight. Hof was bypassed to the north and west. I/IR 16 reached the west end of Saarburg at 1530hrs and was able to fire on French columns as they left the town: intelligent, determined action had reaped rich rewards.

Division Bridge Train 1 and 2/Eng. Bn 1 bridged the Saar shortly after 1500hrs, about 1.6km south of Saaraltdorf; the mass of IR 16 crossed and headed for Hof, which had been swept clean by Bavarian artillery fire and was taken shortly after 1600hrs without resistance. As the regiment left the south-west side of the town, heavy enemy artillery fire was falling in front, but the companies made intelligent use of the steep slopes and therefore avoided casualties. II/IR 16 also used the houses on the north-west edge of the town for cover. There was a momentary shock when a shell noisily collapsed the glass ceiling of the rail station. By 1700hrs the regiment had reached Hill 321, north-west of Saarburg. On the far side of the hilltop was an abandoned enemy artillery section – twelve guns and fifteen caissons – that had been shot to pieces by the division heavy artillery. Behind the abandoned artillery was a French skirmisher line, which 9/IR 16 drove off. 9 and 10/IR 16 then pushed forward 600m, but were forced to turn back due to artillery fire. On Hill 321 IR 16 took fire from Saarburg, while French troops withdrawing from the town provided excellent targets. III/IR 2 joined IR 16, avoiding street fighting in Saarburg by moving north of the town and crossing the Saar above the rail station (Bhf). 2 Bde had taken the first objective.

In the 1 Bde sector, the heavy artillery, principally II/Foot Artillery R 1 (sFH) and III/Foot Artillery R 3 (21cm mortars), shelled the barracks and other buildings on the east side of Saarburg, where strong French forces slowed the attack. 4/Foot Artillery R 1 displaced forward into the area of Rieding by 1400hrs. The Household IR and IR 1 used the pause in combat to thin out the thick skirmisher lines. Between 1500hrs and 1600hrs the artillery preparation allowed a renewal of the attack. The 1 Bde commander ordered the Household IR to avoid Saarburg as much as possible and to cordon it off to the north and east, while IR 1 was to move along the south side and take the high ground on the south-east side of the town.

II/Household moved along the rail line, while III/Household attacked into the city down the main street, where serious fighting developed against French troops in the houses. I/Household followed, behind the regimental band, and was hailed by the inhabitants with flowers and gifts as victors and liberators. II and III/Household took 600–700 POWs and, by 1800hrs, had pushed to the western end of the city.

IR 1 attacked at 1700hrs. Once again, the artillery had severely shaken the will of the defenders. The long walls of the churchyard on the south-east side were now rubble. By 1800hrs the high ground on the south-west side were in Bavarian hands, with many POWs taken in the quarries and outermost houses. Otherwise, the enemy had left the battlefield in wild flight, leaving great quantities of ammunition, weapons, bicycles and other equipment. IR 1 pursued with fire. The regiment linked up with Pr. IR 142 from XIV AK. Units throughout the brigade area were severely intermixed.

As the infantry of 1 ID quickly gained ground around 1700hrs, 1 FA Bde followed immediately, covered by the heavy guns behind the Tinkel-Berg. The lead elements of I/FAR 7 were stopped in Hof by fire from a French battery, probably on the high ground south-west of Saarburg. 1/FAR 7, the tail battery, went into firing position and drew the enemy fire, so that 2 and 3/FAR 7 could move through the town, passing the jubilant occupants, turn towards Saarburg and set up between Hill 321 and the city at 1800hrs. At 1845hrs II/FAR 7 moved through the town to high ground on the south-west side, led by 5/FAR 7, which was commanded by Captain Prince Adalbert of Bavaria. The exhausted horses climbed the last hill at the end of their strength.

At 1515hrs the 1 ID commander moved to Klein-Eisch and, thirty minutes later, ordered 1 Bde to take Hill 328, south-east of Imlingen, and 2 Bde to advance on Rintingen to the north-west. The corps commander arrived at Klein-Eisch at 1800hrs. Everyone was aware that the corps had won a victory and needed to pursue.

1 Bde soon had other concerns, for between 1800hrs and 1900hrs a French brigade was approaching from the south-west towards high ground south-east of Saarburg. French artillery appeared on Hill 328, south-east of Imlingen, and Hill 303, north-east of Bebing, and began shelling the high ground and the city. German counter-battery fire from II/FAR 1, I/FAR 7 and II/Foot Artillery 3 (21cm mortars) was immediate, catching some French batteries while they were moving up, and destroying them or forcing them to retreat.

The hot and exhausted troops of 1 Bde were resting on the streets and at the edge of Saarburg, enjoying the well water and the gifts offered by the inhabitants: the high ground to the south-west was unoccupied. The adjutant of the Household IR went there just in time to see that an entire French brigade was advancing on the high ground on a front of 1.5km, just 400m away. In frantic haste he and the commanders of the Household IR and II/Household indiscriminately threw all the platoons and companies of the Household IR and IR 1 they could find up the steep hill. The infantrymen and MG of the Household IR, IR 1 and IR 142, and the batteries of II/FAR 1 and II/Foot Artillery 3, which occupied open firing positions, gave the enemy a bloody rebuff, sometimes at 200m range.[45] 2 and 3/FAR 7 on Hill 321, north-west of Saarburg, turned their guns and fired straight down the French flank. The French attack soon became a rout; their withdrawal was initially protected by folds in the terrain, but when it led over the high ground at Hill 328 it ran directly into the massed fire of the Bavarian batteries.

While this was going on, the firefight in Saarburg was renewed. French troops, cut off and hidden in the houses, may have sensed that rescue was coming and renewed the fight, encouraged by the fact that, since all the local roads led to Saarburg, masses of German troops and supply units flowed into the city seeking billets, water and other essentials. Rifle fire continued on the high ground and in Saarburg until the peacetime training signal 'General Halt!' brought quiet at 2200hrs. The troops of 1 Bde were put in the best order possible and slept under arms in place. The enemy had disappeared.

1 ID therefore did not reach its objective at Rintingen. It had, however, inflicted unusually heavy casualties on a French brigade and prepared the way for the next day's advance. Traffic jams in Saarburg were a major hindrance, but not just for the Bavarians: Saarburg was a trap for retreating French units, who got stopped, were cut off and eventually taken prisoner.

On the other hand, in the open terrain near Zittersdorf, 2 ID had been able to conduct a vigorous pursuit. After 1800hrs the artillery in the Saar-Wald had been able to drive off the last French infantry and artillery east of Kirchberg and at Misselhof. II/Foot Artillery R 18 (21cm mortars) went into battery and opened fire north of Oberstinzel, while 2 FA Bde bounded forward to follow the infantry, but by 1850hrs it was becoming too dark to fire.

At 1715hrs the commander of 4 Bde ordered his regiments to advance to the high ground north-east of Kirchberg and to Rintingen. IR 15 took a short rest and moved out at 1900hrs, I/IR 15 moving through Langd, with III/IR 15 to the south. The MGK was able to engage groups of fleeing French at Misselhof and break them up. Otherwise, the regiment encountered only dead and wounded French and abandoned equipment. IR 12 began movement at 1800hrs and encountered bushy terrain at the Fudenhof, from which French stragglers opened fire. II and III/IR 12 pushed easily through the weak and scattered French, though the MGK, which was following, was ambushed in the open and had no small arms to defend itself with. The MGK were saved by the increasing darkness and the arrival of some stragglers. Between 1900hrs and 1930hrs the regiment reached Misselhof, formed march column and reached Rintingen at 2100hrs. IR 20, positioned south-west of Saaraltdorf, was ordered at 1830hrs to move to fill the gap between 4 Bde and 1 ID, and reached Rintingen at 2100hrs. Between 2000hrs and 2100hrs orders were issued that extended the pursuit to Gunderchingen and Herzing (bridgeheads on the Rhine–Marne Canal, off map, 3km south-west of Barchingen). IR 15 continued to roadmarch through the night. I/IR 15 took a crossing point over the Saar–Kohlenkanal, 4km west of Barchingen, with an advanced force and bivouacked on high ground 2km north of Gunderchingen. The field kitchens of III/IR 15 and the MGK came up and fed the men, who had not eaten all day, warm food and they reached the high ground north-east of Gunderchingen between 0300hrs and 0400hrs. IR 12 left Rintingen at 2330hrs and arrived at 0200hrs at the high ground west of Herzing. II/IR 12 was ordered to take the bridges at Gunderchingen and Herzing. 5/IR 12 found the bridge at Gunderchingen strongly held and, in view of the unfavourable terrain and lack of artillery support, did not attack. 7/IR 12 encountered heavy resistance from the rail embankment at Herzing, lost its commander, took heavy casualties and withdrew. The 2 ID artillery bivouacked between Kirchberg–Lagd–Zittesdorf.

I b. AK had won a complete victory. The attack had not, as was commonly believed, hit the advance guards or only the rearguards of the French VIII Corps, but rather the completely deployed main body, which was preparing to attack. The many dead found in the Saar-Wald and the Unter-Wald, and the great number of prisoners taken in Saarburg, prove that I b. AK had been opposed by strong forces, but the corps artillery was so effective that it forced the enemy to flee. It should not pass unnoticed that of all the corps in Sixth and Seventh Armies, I b. AK had the most heavy artillery, including three 21cm mortar battalions. The infantry often had an easy time, but, especially in the 1 ID sector where the infantry had to climb the long open slopes of the valley by Saarburg, took painful losses and in places had tough fights. 2 ID crowned its victory with an energetic pursuit; 1 ID by capturing the town of Saarburg. 1 ID took more prisoners and equipment; 2 ID more terrain.[46] That evening 1 ID also defeated an attack, probably by the French 49 Bde.

Left of I b. AK, XIV AK attacked at 1100hrs. It had to first cross a 4km wooded area, which also hindered artillery support. As it emerged from the south side of the wood it encountered an enemy position, dug the previous day. On the right flank the 29 ID took Bühl, south-east of Saarburg, and that evening took Schneckenbusch, 2km further south (on the Rhine–Marne Canal), in a tough fight, but was unable to hold it in the face of overwhelming French artillery fire. 28 ID on the left attacked almost without artillery support and took Niederviller, 2km south-east of Bühl, by noon. Plaine de Walsch, 2km south of Niederweiler, fell only that evening, and at the cost of heavy German casualties. The offensive power of XIV AK had been used up and the corps was exhausted. Further advance was not possible until the artillery had transited the wooded area. The enemy – the French XXI Corps – had fought bravely and well.

Next left, XV AK also had to exit the wooded terrain at Haareberg, 5km north-west of Dagsburg. First 30 ID had to beat off an early morning French attack south of the town. The 30 ID attack began at 1100hrs. In addition to enemy resistance, 30 ID had to contend with deep, wooded valleys, which made artillery support impossible. All troops were soon committed. The right flank was able to advance step by step and cut its way to open terrain, but the left flank was hung up. 39 ID was committed on the left and made initial gains, but was then brought to a halt. XV AK had been opposed by the French 43 ID (XXI Corps) and 3 Colonial Bde.

Rupprecht had fulfilled most of his responsibilities by forming his concept of the operation and translating it into orders for both armies. During the battle he attempted to push the wings forward quickly to envelop the enemy centre. The reserves, 4, 8 and 10 ED, were committed as the situation demanded, but there was little more that he could do that day. Hasty and detailed orders would have led only to confusion and uncertainty. It did not prove possible to envelop the enemy, but a complete victory had been won.

This was the first great battle of the war between the French and the Germans. In Germany, a trace of uncertainty may have been present, but this nightmare had now been banished; the superiority of German arms was clear. Concern for the security of the German left flank had been removed for good. It was the enemy who now had every reason to be concerned for the outcome in Lorraine, though, under the circumstances, the French could hardly withdraw forces from the region. OHL could concentrate its attention on the decisive right-wing battle. In this sense, the victory in Lorraine was a significant accomplishment, won principally by Bavaria.

The number of prisoners and guns taken, the usual measure of victory, was below expectations. On the evening of 20 August the troops and leaders often did not have the feeling that they had won a great victory. They sometimes suspected that they had engaged only enemy rearguards.

In fact, the blow had a deep and serious effect on the French. Their corps had been pushed back or routed everywhere. By 1000hrs the Second Army commander ordered a withdrawal to a line on the high ground 5km from the French border and centred on Château Salins–Marsal. At 1200hrs it was clear that they could not even hold this line, and the army was ordered to withdraw some 13km into French territory: XVI Corps to Lunéville, XV Corps to Dombasale (13km north-west), and XX Corps to the south-east of Nancy. The First Army commander ordered VII and XIII Corps to withdraw that afternoon; VIII Corps had to pull back immediately to the Rhine–Marne Canal. Only XXI Corps in the foothills of the Vosges had been able to maintain its position, but since Second Army had pulled back to Lunéville, the First Army left flank was hanging in the air. The First Army commander therefore decided during the night to pull back to the Vezouse River and dig in there. General Joffre suspended the movement of the second half of IX Corps north; three brigades of this corps remained attached to Second Army. The French troops used the night of 20 August to put as much distance between themselves and the Germans as possible.

The French admitted that the cause of their defeat lay in the piecemeal commitment of their forces, in the superiority of German heavy artillery and air reconnaissance, and simply in the concentrated force of the German attack. The enemy withdrawal was in part voluntary, but based on defeat in the field, the effect of which on the troops was not far to seek. In the Second Army units began to disintegrate.

The French defeat in Lorraine did not affect Joffre's overall plan, for the defeated armies could fall back on the fortress line. The centre two French armies, Third and Fourth, advanced to conduct the attack in the Ardennes, while Fifth Army on the left wing moved into the corner formed by the Sambre and Meuse, to link up with the British and Belgians.

The Pursuit on 21 August

Neither the troops nor Crown Prince Rupprecht could estimate the extent of the victory, nor could they detect that the enemy had begun a rapid withdrawal. The reports to Sixth Army HQ arrived sporadically, particularly since the victorious, exhausted troops had other priorities besides submitting extensive situation reports. At 2115hrs Rupprecht therefore ordered a continuation of the attack in the sector on 21 August. III b. AK was to advance on the high ground west of Château Salins, II b. AK against Château Salins itself and the high ground to the east, with XXI AK supporting, while I b. RK was to advance on the XXI AK left. 10 ED at Delm would guard the right flank, with 33 RD to the north. HKK 3, with 8 KD and Bavarian KD, was to operate against the flank and rear of the enemy forces on the high ground at Château Salins. As soon as the infantry had opened a path, 7 KD was to advance on the rear of the forces opposing Seventh Army. The Seventh Army commander also ordered a continuation of the attack. 21 August brought a complete clarification of the situation: by 0930hrs Sixth Army HQ recognised that the enemy was withdrawing as fast as possible and immediately instructed the troops to stay on his heels.

(Map 2) At Nomeny, 33 RD held the Sixth Army right flank. The enemy did not budge on 21 August, but held the high ground north-east of Frouard. The signs of panic flight were found all along the road from Nomeny: numerous discarded packs and weapons. 33 RD dug in, occasionally disturbed by French artillery fire. I/Foot Artillery R 2 (sFH) continually attempted to strike the enemy artillery on Mt Toulon, chasing off the OPs, and detachments that were careless enough to show themselves were dispersed and a battery put out of action. 10 ED dug in on the Delm Heights.

HKK 3 marched to the area of Château Salins that morning. It soon became clear that the French artillery on Mt St Jean and Mt Toulon, south-west of the city, prohibited large-scale cavalry manoeuvre. The Bavarian KD reported that the horses were exhausted and needed complete rest: since the start of the campaign the division had been moved back and forth, first to the Sixth Army left flank, then to the right. The cavalry patrols had expended a great deal of energy, but had not

2. Nomeny 20.8. — 33. R.D.—

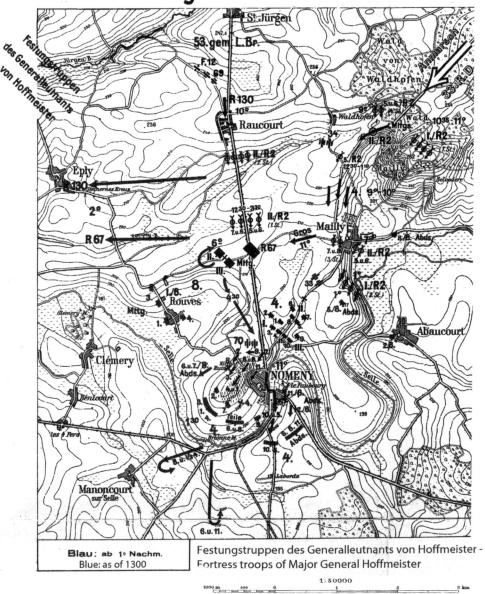

Blau: ab 1º Nachm.
Blue: as of 1300

Festungstruppen des Generalleutnants von Hoffmeister -
Fortress troops of Major General Hoffmeister

1 : 50000

been able to penetrate the enemy counter-reconnaissance screen. The roads were good, but glass-hard, which took a toll on the horses' legs and completely wore out the horseshoes. Cross-country movement was strenuous due to the loamy Lorraine soil: heavy and sticky when wet, crusty when dry. The division's only real fight had been at Gerden, but it was in the field ready for combat almost every day from dawn to dusk, either in burning sun or pouring rain. Often it was not possible to feed and water the horses or even feed the riders. At night there was little rest, as the billets were occupied after dark and were often overcrowded. By 18 August the division had lost 200 horses, and was therefore granted a rest day on 21 August.[47]

III b. AK had lost contact with the enemy. 6 ID was ordered to guard the right flank in conjunction with 10 ED. 5 ID was to advance to the high ground 4km south of Château Salins to pursue the enemy with artillery fire and support the 4 ID attack on the high ground 4km east of Château Salins. The troops had to break camp early, sometimes in the dark, after inadequate rest, and march deployed and cross-country in the heat. In the 6 ID sector II/IR 10 took artillery fire. *Chevauleger* R 7, riding in front of 5 ID, was able to engage withdrawing French troops with carbine fire. 10 Bde took the undamaged Selle bridge at Chambrey (on the border, 4km south-east of Château Salins). The division bivouacked south and south-west of Château Salins.

II b. AK attacked with 4 ID to take Château Salins and the high ground at Morville, 4km to the east, with 3 ID echeloned left and 4 ED following. The 4 ID commander had his troops ready to go in their bivouac areas at 0500hrs, but since heavy enemy artillery had been located on the high ground at Morville the previous evening, he wanted to approach it with great care. Early in the morning I/Foot Artillery R 1 (sFH) moved right up to the outpost line to cover the 4 ID advance, which began at 0820hrs. RIR 8 discovered signs of a hasty enemy retreat: discarded weapons, equipment and pieces of uniforms. The French had clearly evacuated Château Salins and the north bank of the Selle, and it was not necessary to deploy. At 1100hrs the division reached the high ground at Morville. 3 ID deployed and moved out at 0500hrs, and soon discovered that there was no enemy to the front. The division formed a march column at 0800hrs and the lead elements of the infantry reached Moyenvic (off map, 2km east of Wich, on the Selle) at 1100hrs. The inhabitants said that the French had left an hour before. The French sent some ineffective long-range shells in the Bavarian's direction. The mass of the division stopped at Burlingshofen and Hampont (off map, 2km south). 3/Eng. Bn 2 quickly replaced the destroyed Moyenvic bridge with a new one. The advance posts of 4 ID came up on the left and drove weak enemy detachments away from the south bank. 2/Eng. Bn 2 replaced two destroyed road bridges in the course of that evening and night.

At 0900hrs II b. AK was ordered to cross the Selle and advance 4km to the small Loutre Noire stream (off map), but only if this could be accomplished without serious combat. An over-hasty attack on a fortified position was also to be avoided. II b. AK decided to conduct reconnaissance before advancing. At 1414hrs Sixth Army HQ informed the corps that the enemy was withdrawing to the Meurthe; the corps commander ordered the division advance guards to cross the Selle, with the main bodies to follow. The 3 ID advanced guard moved out at 1800hrs from Moyenvic and reached the stream at dark; the main body closed up on Moyenvic. The mass of 4 ID bivouacked north of the Selle, between Morville and Wich. On the left, XXI AK advanced to the border without making contact.

7 KD moved through the I b. RK positions at 0730hrs, intending to penetrate into the rear of the forces engaged with I b. AK and Seventh Army. Reports indicated that the area in front of I b. RK was free of enemy forces and the way open for 7 KD. I b. RK also concluded at about 0800hrs that rapid pursuit was called for. Since the right wing of Seventh Army was hanging back, it appeared that 7 KD and I b. RK could cut off the French retreat in the area south of Saarburg. Speed was essential. 11 Res. Bde, accompanied by the division and corps commanders, moved out in march column at 0900hrs on the road to Assoncourt (off map, 8km south-west of Rohrbach), while 9 Res. Bde marched through Bisping to Disselingen. 11 Res. Bde was considerably delayed by columns from 7 KD and XXI AK using the same road, and only reached Assoncourt at 1300hrs, where the tired troops were fed and given a long rest. 9 Res. Bde stopped at Disselingen and fed the troops while the engineers repaired the road.

At 1000hrs it was clear to 1 RD that the enemy had withdrawn. RIR 12 became the advance guard, and moved from Rodt to Languimberg (off map, 3km south-west of Rodt) and Azoudange (3km further south-west). I b. RK instructed 1 RD to continue the march, without concern for the progress of its neighbours left and right, and cross the Rhine–Marne Canal to Elfringen. The poor condition of the road beyond Azoudange, the trampled fields to both sides of the road and the masses of clothing and equipment lying about were testimony to the enemy's panic flight. At 1400hrs RIR 3, now advance guard, encountered 7 KD in the woods south of Maizières-le-Vic (off map, 5km north-west of Elfringen). The cavalry had encountered French rearguards on the Rhine–Marne Canal about 2km south-east and taken the bridge, but did not feel strong enough to attack the French position. Half of I/Res. Foot Artillery 1 (sFH) silenced the French artillery while 5 and 6/Res. FAR 1 engaged the infantry. The woods south of Maizières-le-Vic began to fill up with troops from 7 KD, 2 Res. Bde and XXI AK, which blocked the roads and paths. The 1 RD commander decided to create some space by pushing the French off the canal. At 1800hrs 2 Res. Bde, with RIR 12 leading and RIR 3 following, crossed the canal unopposed at a mill; the enemy had left. It found the next town so full of Prussian troops that it could not bivouac, so it continued the march to Elfringen, which it reached at midnight; it did not make contact, but did encounter IR 15, which had been sent by I b. AK to seize a bridge over the canal. 1 Res. Bde pushed on to the canal and bivouacked in the open, with many battalions arriving long after midnight for a short night's rest. At 1500hrs Sixth Army HQ informed I b. RK that 1 RD had to be prepared to move early on 22 August to link up with XIV AK near Badonviller, so that jointly they could cut off the French forces south of Saarburg.

5 RD got no further forward than Maizières−Azoudange, 5km from the canal, where it bivouacked, the march there being made exceptionally difficult by roads overloaded with 7 KD and XXI AK columns. 7 KD also bivouacked at Maizières−Azoudange. On 21 August *Landwehr* Div. Wenig was formed in the I b. RK rear area, which would later become 1 Bavarian *Landwehr* Div.

During the night of 20 August, Seventh Army HQ told I b. AK to wait on 21 August for XIV AK on the left to catch up and assist its advance. Seventh Army HQ was as unaware of the extent of the victory on 20 August as Sixth Army. Even I b. AK HQ did not know that the right wing of 2 ID had reached the high ground north of Gondrexange (off map, on Rhine−Marne canal, 4km south-east of Kirchberg) and that the enemy had fled the battlefield as quickly as possible. Rather, both I b. AK HQ and even the commander of 2 ID thought that, at the most, 2 ID had reached the area south of Kirchberg. The French counter-attack at Saarburg on the evening of 20 August justified the conclusion that the enemy would renew his resistance on 21 August, and the German leadership did not recognise that the situation was ripe for a pursuit. The I b. AK order issued at 0115hrs called for a resumption of the attack at daybreak; XIV AK was to be assisted with artillery support.

The commander of 2 ID received a report at 0315hrs that 4 Bde (IR 15, IR 12) was already on the high ground north of Gondrexange, the objective for 21 August. 2 FA Bde, which had the foresight to form up on the road to Barchingen in march column, was immediately moved forward. IR 20 was at Barchingen and IR 3 at Zittersdorf. FAR 4 and II/Foot Artillery R 18 (21cm mortars) engaged infantry on the south side of the Rhine−Marne Canal and artillery 4km to the south of it. The commander of 4 Bde had instructed his troops to only deploy outposts on the high ground and keep the rest of the troops under cover.

IR 12 was digging in 1km north of the canal, initially taking only artillery fire, but at 0900hrs II/IR 12 on the left flank was attacked by superior forces and soon had all of its companies committed. 2/IR 12 reinforced on the left, 10/IR 12 on the right, while 5/FAR 4 and 5/FAR 9 provided fire support. II/IR 20 swung 6 and 8/IR 20 against the enemy right flank. 10/IR 20 and the MGK were also committed. The French could not stand such fire and, at 1100hrs, fled the battle. The commander of 4 Bde used the opportunity to pursue. IR 15 took the canal bridge at Gondrexange and the town itself without a fight. IR 12 moved on Hertzing (off map, 4km south of Kirchberg), took fire from the church tower, but suppressed it with MG fire. 3/FAR 4 set up just north of Herzing and provided close-fire support. IR 12 crossed the canal, where the remaining French were mostly taken prisoner. The artillery moved up.

1 ID delayed its planned attack at 0600hrs because XIV AK on the left would not be ready until 0900hrs. The French were reported to be in Imlingen and to the right. The first objectives were therefore Hill 303, north-east of Bebig, and Imlingen and Hill 328 to the south-east. Artillery preparation was provided by 6 and 7/Foot Artillery 1 (sFH) on the north edge of Hof, and 5 and 8/Foot Artillery 1 on the north-east side of Saarburg. When the fog lifted at 0800hrs the artillery shelled French trenches on Hill 328. A French artillery detachment on the hill was completely suppressed; the crews abandoned the guns. At 0800hrs 2 Bde advanced deployed from the area north-west of Saarburg to both sides of the road to Bebing. At 1000hrs 1 Bde advanced from the high ground south-west of Saarburg on Hill 328; the enemy had disappeared. The French left stay-behind parties well hidden in hedges, copses, bushes and elsewhere, who let the Bavarians pass in order to shoot them in the back and spread confusion. Once they had done so, they surrendered. By noon 2 Bde had reached Bebing and made contact with 2 ID, while 1 Bde gained the top of Hill 328, where the French artillery section suppressed by II/Foot Artillery R 1 that morning stood abandoned. III/Household took sixty prisoners, while II/IR 1 found three destroyed guns. The staff of Foot Artillery R 1 discovered a limbered-up but abandoned battery south of Imlingen. The first objectives had been taken and the artillery was displacing forward; the commander of 1 ID authorised the advance to the final objectives at 1125hrs – Heming and Lorquin (off map, major crossroads 8km south-west of Saarburg).

The corps commander arrived at Saar-Wald town on Hill 309, south of Dolvingen, at 0515hrs and, at 0800hrs, moved up to Zittersdorf. At the Misselhof Farm, 2km south of Zittersdorf, two MPs of the HQ guard captured 2 officers and 110 enlisted men. At 1300hrs the HQ moved forward again, to the high ground north of Barchingen, and the I b. AK commander was now convinced that the French had abandoned the field in front of 1 ID. A reconnaissance aircraft reported long march columns in retreat through Blâmont and Cirey. He therefore ordered the pursuit at 1430hrs. Yet care was still justified, for air reconnaissance also detected strong troop concentrations at Hattigny (off map, 6km north-east of Blâmont) and rearguards at Gondrexange and Landage (off map, 2km south of canal at Heming). Counter-attacks, as against 2 ID the previous day, were possible. The 2 ID objective was a bridgehead over the canal on the high ground south of Gondrexange, which the division already held, and the 1 ID objective was a bridgehead 2km deep on the high ground at St Georges and Lorquin.

1 ID expected a French attack against its left from the direction of Lorquin; 2 Bde occupied a defensive position behind the canal, but no attack came. I/FAR

1 detected withdrawing French columns. At 1730hrs 2 Bde crossed the canal to occupy the objective. Discarded French weapons and equipment littered the road. As the advance guard, I/IR 2, topped the high ground north of St Georges (2km south of the canal), the last enemy elements were going down the other side. 3/IR 2 and a platoon of MGs pursued with fire, resulting in a French panic. II/FAR 7 added its fire. 4/FAR 9 was attached to 1 ID and had already fired on withdrawing French troops. It was displacing forward on the road to St Georges when thick masses of French troops appeared on its left flank. In an instant the guns unlimbered and went into battery: together with the MGK/IR 2 there was a horrifying bloodbath and the surviving French were put to wild flight. 2 Bde closed up at St Georges. 1 Bde took artillery fire as it crossed the Saar. 1 FA Bde engaged the last withdrawing French detachments at ranges between 1–1.5km. III/Foot Artillery R 18 (21cm mortars) was able to engage French artillery at Hattigny and infantry south of St Georges. At dusk 1 Bde secured the bridgehead at Lorquin. 1 ID had hit the rearguards of the French 26 ID (XIII Corps), which was only able to break contact at the expense of heavy losses, including part of its artillery. At 1730hrs 1 b. AK ordered its units to bivouac in the bridgehead; 2 ID at Gondrexange-Hertzing (off map, on canal 1km south of Barchingen), 1 ID at St Georges–Lorquin (5km south-west and 4km south-east of Barchingen, respectively), and the corps reserve (IR 3, I/FAR 9, II and III/Foot Artillery 18 (21cm mortars), Eng. R) still north of the canal west of Zittersdorf. IR 15 moved west, south of the canal, to assist 1 RD in establishing a bridgehead at Moussey (off map, 6km east of Gerden), which it accomplished without making contact.

In the XIV AK area, 29 ID on the right had to first resupply the artillery and could not attack until 0900hrs, while 28 ID on the left was already in heavy contact at Hartzviller (off map, 6km south of Saarburg), where it captured a large number of French guns. By evening 29 ID had reached Hermelange (5km slightly south-west of Saarburg).

In the XV AK sector, by mid-morning 30 ID took high ground on the west side of the Vosges and overran several French batteries. 39 ID to the left was delayed by artillery fire and the hilly terrain, but nevertheless had reached Abreschviller (4km north-east of St Quirin) by evening.

It is hardly surprising that the troops were unable to reach the Seventh Army objectives, issued at 1800hrs, before dark. I b. AK had assisted the advance of XIV and XV AK, even if it had been unable to cut the French lines of retreat. That evening Sixth Army HQ moved to Duß.

The commander of the French Second Army had considered retreating over the Moselle, but General Joffre said that it was essential to hold on the east side of the river. The left flank of Second Army – 59 and 70 RD – defended the high ground east of the Moselle, opposite Pont-á-Mousson–Nancy, considerably reinforced by the three brigades of IX Corps. By that evening 68 RD was just east of Nancy, while XX Corps had reached the area between Nancy and St Nicholas du Port, with XV Corps on its right at Lunéville. XIV Corps saved itself by retreating behind the Vezouse at Lunéville, with the exception of a rearguard east of the river. 64 and 74 RD moved up behind XX and XVI Corps. On the left flank of First Army, VIII and XIII Corps reached both sides of Blâmont, their rearguards considerably worse for wear. XIII Corps had received the withdrawal order too late; its rearguard was isolated in front of its neighbours and had suffered severely. XXI Corps had withdrawn to Badonviller and to the south. The gap between the two armies, whose lines of retreat diverged, was covered by Fort Manonviller and 2, 6 and 10 KD.

The German pursuit lacked speed and force, and the extent of the victory was not recognised on 20 August. The leaders made concessions due to the troops' exhaustion, and concern for enemy counter-attacks led to excessive caution. Contact with the enemy was lost; the beaten French troops moved away more quickly than the victor dared to.

The Pursuit on 22 August (map e)

The full extent of the victory was finally recognised during the course of the day on 21 August. The Sixth Army order for 22 August – issued at 2145hrs on 21 August – was for a pure pursuit. II b. AK, with 4 ED attached, was to move with 3 ID on Réméréville (15km due east of Nancy) and 4 ID on Anthelupt (6km north-west of Lunéville). XXI AK, with 8 ED attached, would advance to the high ground north of Lunéville and to Croismare (6km east of Lunéville). I b. RK and 7 KD were to attack in the direction of Baccarat against the flank and rear of the enemy forces opposing I b. AK. The army right flank would not participate in the pursuit, but remain north of the Selle and swing west towards Nancy. This immobilised strong forces – 10 ED, III b. AK and the Bavarian KD. 8 KD moved towards St Nicholas du Port–Lunéville. Two Z (dirigible) airships were to follow the enemy.

To maintain close control over the corps and prevent XV AK from being pressed against the Vosges, the Seventh Army HQ pursuit order to the army right flank set short initial objectives: I b. AK to Blâmont; XIV AK to Frémonville (3km east of Blâmont); and XV AK to Cirey.

On the morning of 22 August it appeared to 33 RD at Nomeny, on the right flank of Sixth Army, that the enemy had withdrawn. RIR 67 was therefore ordered to conduct a reconnaissance in force from Port-sur-Selle (halfway between Nomeny and Pont-à-Mousson) to St Geneviève (5km south-west of Port-sur-Selle, almost to the Moselle). To provide fire support, 5/Res. Foot Artillery 2 (sFH) set up 2km north of Port-sur-Selle and fired on the high ground near St Geneviève. When the enemy artillery on Mt Toulon opened fire, it was silenced by 2/Res. Foot Artillery 2 on the north edge of Nomeny. This battery also found the opportunity to shell French infantry 6km south of Nomeny. At 1600hrs the Governor of Metz ordered 33 RD to return to the fortress; Sixth Army had only been given temporary use of the division, which was now needed on the left flank of Fifth Army. The troops broke off the action and withdrew, but were delayed by traffic jams and did not arrive until midnight. 10 ED continued to hold its positions on the Delm Heights undisturbed. The Bavarian KD rested in billets near Delm.

Given the III b. AK stationary defensive mission for 22 August, the corps commander granted the troops a rest day. On the corps right, 6 ID had the mission of feigning preparations for an attack, so it pushed outposts up to the Selle and conducted reconnaissance patrols. The mass of the division rested. 8 KD arrived on the 5 ID left and billeted early near Moncel (10km west of Wich).

Maixe (map 7)

At 1730hrs on 21 August II b. AK had already received a telephonic warning order from Sixth Army HQ for the advance on the following day, and had issued its own warning orders to the divisions. At 0500hrs on 22 August 4 ID moved out in march column from Wich, on the road to Réméréville, but not without difficulties, with *Chevauleger* R 5 leading. When the division reached Hoéville it was ordered to occupy billets, which was later changed to maintaining combat readiness in the area of the billets because enemy troops were reported at Haraucourt. 3 ID also moved out at 0500hrs from Arracourt, but the late arrival of orders and a hurried march from the billeting areas led to considerable friction.

Cheveauleger R 3 approached Maixe at 0715hrs and took fire. Since it was essential to seize a crossing over the Rhine–Marne Canal, the regimental commander attacked with 4/*Cheveauleger* R 3 on foot, which cleared out the town edge, but, as it entered the town, it received fire from the south side, where the canal bridge was located, as well as from civilian weapons in houses, attics and the church tower. 2 and 3/*Cheveauleger* R 3 were committed on each side, but they could not make any progress. As the point company, 6/IR 23, reached the north side of the town, the cavalrymen retired so that the advance guard artillery, a platoon from 3/FAR 12, could set fire to the town. 6/IR 23 then took Maixe. II/IR 23 then arrived and thoroughly searched the town, accompanied by 1/ Eng. Bn 2 men with hand grenades, then proceeded to Petite Maixe on the south side of the canal. At 0830hrs II b. AK ordered 4 ID to occupy an attack position north of Maixe; it moved off the road while IR 23 held the bridgehead south of the town.

Shortly before noon, artillery, some heavy calibre, was heard firing from the area of Deuxville. Enemy trenches were also seen there. The corps HQ thought that there were only French rearguards north and north-west of Lunéville and ordered 3 ID to attack the enemy between Hill 316, west of Anthelupt, and the high ground south of Deuxville. 4 ID would guard the 3 ID left and also detached I/Foot Artillery R 1 (sFH) to join 3 ID in the attack. 4 ED would be brought up to Athieville, while XXI AK was asked to put pressure on the enemy right.

Before 3 ID could attack, enemy skirmishers were seen approaching Petite Maixe from Deuxville, but were stopped by fire from I/IR 23 and the artillery. In order to support the attack across gently rising ground to the hill 100m higher than the canal, 1 and 3/FAR 5 were brought into battery at Hill 316, north-west of Maixe, and were later joined by I/Foot Artillery 1 (sFH). 5 Bde would attack Anthelupt–Deuxville; IR 18 would attack through Crévic and Flainval to the high ground west of Anthelupt; and IR 17 was division reserve behind the right flank.

The MGK/IR 23 moved left into the wood by Hill 247, as did III/IR 23, which the brigade commander kept under his own control. IR 23 was to await the arrival of IR 22 on the right, but when it did not appear at 1730hrs, and the regiment received a call for help from 31 ID on the left, IR 23 attacked on its own. In spite of heavy artillery fire, I/IR 23 gained ground quickly and took the trenches on Hill 285, which the French had left. II/IR 23, echeloned left, did not even take small arms fire, and the MGK had not needed to fire at all.

IR 22 was delayed avoiding French artillery interdiction fire north of Maixe, but few casualties were taken. The lead battalion, III/IR 22, received a call for help from 31 ID, whose right flank had been turned and was under considerable pressure. The battalion commander swung through the wood at Hill 247, joined by most of III/IR 23, hit the enemy left flank and, in conjunction with the Prussian troops pursuing in the direction of Lunéville, forced the enemy to retreat. The rest of IR 23, I/IR 23 leading, II/IR 23 in second line followed by III/IR 17, attacked right of IR 22 towards Anthelupt, taking only artillery fire.

IR 18 moved at 1500hrs over Hill 316, north-west of Maixe, against Crévic; II and III/IR 17 leading, IR 18 and MGK behind. The attack was supported by II/FAR 5. 5/FAR 5 moved at 1530hrs to the north-east corner of the village to break the last resistance. Between 1800hrs and 1900hrs IR 18 pushed into the burning town, taking many prisoners in the ensuing street fighting.

While IR 23 was moving south of Maixe, 5 and 6/FAR 5 continued to shell Crévic, while I/FAR 5 and 4/FAR 5 limbered up and, at 1800hrs, the batteries galloped one after the other down the serpentine road to Maixe. Without stopping, the batteries wound through the burning town, the streets full of obstacles, under fire from heavy enemy artillery, but also cheered by the infantry. They then crossed the Rhine–Marne Canal and the stream behind it on two small, high bridges, galloped 1km further and went into an open position; the speed of the regiment's movement had protected it from serious loss. Fire was immediately opened on the withdrawing enemy on Hill 337 between Anthelupt and Deuxville, where French artillery still stood.

At dusk IR 22 and IR 23 reached the Crévic–Vitremont road. The enemy no longer defended the steep hill, which provided a superb field of fire over the ground the two regiments had just crossed.

Due to a reverse suffered by 31 ID that evening, the commander of 3 ID ordered IR 17 to Maixe. At 2000hrs it moved out and gained the high ground between Anthelupt and Deuxville at midnight, having marched beyond IR 23 in the dark. IR 22 reached the Lunéville road early the next morning.

After taking Crévic, IR 18 deployed again to attack Flainval, but was fixed in place by heavy artillery fire. At 2000hrs it again moved out towards Flainval, this time in the dark and in march column, but found the town prepared for defence and strongly held, so it pulled back to Grandvezin. At dawn the next morning it took the town without a fight; the enemy had withdrawn.

In the late evening of 22 August 3 ID had driven the rearguards of the French XV and XX Corps from the dominating terrain north-west of Lunéville. The troops were tired out by the approach march and fight, and became so intermixed in the dark that it was not possible to bring the field kitchens forward to them. *Cheveauleger* R 3 billeted at Drouville. IR 9, detached from 4 ID, moved forward in the dark from Drouville to Crévic, which was burning, to assist IR 18, but the IR 18 troops opened fire on them, resulting in a blue-on-blue firefight and considerable confusion.

XXI AK moved out at 0500hrs towards Lunéville. 31 ID, on the right, took Einville at 1000hrs and pushed the French off the high ground at Bonviller at noon. The enemy then counter-attacked, but, with the assistance of 3 ID, was driven back. 42 ID came up on the left and pushed the French off the high ground south-east of Bonviller. The rearguards of the French XVI Corps retreated to the south side of the Meurthe, while taking heavy casualties. By evening XXI AK stood before the gates of Lunéville, which was occupied during the night by outposts.

Autrepierre (map 8)

The I b. RK HQ had received a Sixth Army warning order at 1800hrs on 21 August to be prepared to move as early as possible on the next morning towards Baccarat and into the flank and rear of the forces opposing I b. AK. Unaware that

8. Autrepierre 22.8. –I.b.R.K.–

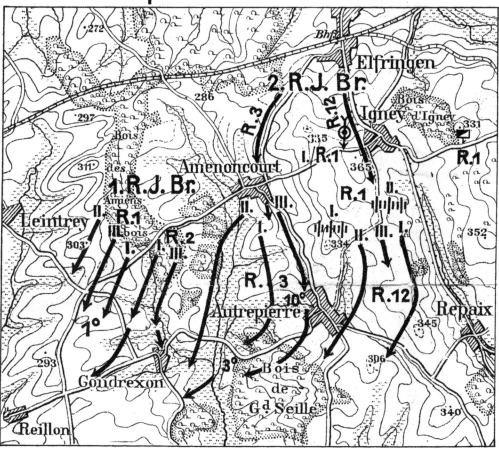

the enemy had gone, the corps issued an order at 2245hrs for 1 RD to attack Elfringen (4km south of the canal) and Rixingen (2km to the north-east, and 2km from the canal) at 0600hrs. When no enemy resistance was encountered, the corps commander ordered the advance on Blâmont.

The advance guard, an all-arms team built around RIR 12, left Elfringen at 0730hrs and crossed the German–French border cheering. 1 Res. Bde, which had deployed at dawn to attack Elfringen, formed march column in the main body. Numerous French cavalry had been reported near the next towns, Amenoncourt and Igney, which might indicate the presence of a cavalry division, so RIR 12 advanced on Igney with I and II/RIR 12 deployed, while RIR 3, reinforced by 3/RFAR 1, moved as a flank detachment on Amenoncourt; Res. Cavalry R 2 covered the left flank. 1 RD was advancing on Autrepierre when it took rifle and MG fire from Bois de la Gd. Seille. RIR 12 attacked, supported at once by II/RFAR 1, which was already in battery 2km north of Autrepierre. RIR 3 was leaving Amenoncourt when it received a report that Autrepierre was occupied, and it deployed III/RIR 3 on the left and I/RIR 3 on the right, with II/RIR 3 echeloned right. 3/RFAR 1 unlimbered on Hill 334, 1.2km south-east of Amenoncourt, and was soon joined by the rest of I/RFAR 1. I/Res. Foot Artillery 1 brought its heavy howitzers into the fight near Igney; an artillery duel soon developed, while the German artillery drove the French infantry from the wood and took out a MG in the Autrepierre church tower. By 1000hrs the two infantry regiments had taken the woods, the town and the high ground south of it. RIR 3 then took rifle, MG and artillery fire in the right flank from the area of Gondrexon and, by 1200hrs, the entire regiment was oriented west to engage.

At 0900hrs 1 RD was uncertain as to whether the French were still north of Blâmont and stopped. Having established that they were, at 1020hrs 1 RD ordered 1 Res. Bde forward through Amenoncourt to support 2 Res. Bde at Gondrexon; the brigade was already prepared to march, executed the movement quickly and deployed in the Bois de Amiens (Amiens Wood) north of Gondrexon, with RIR 1 on the right (III and I/RIR 1 on line, II/RIR 1 echeloned behind the right flank, MGK/RIR 1 behind the left), and RIR 2 on the left (I and III/RIR 2 on line, MGK/RIR 2 behind the right, though II/RIR 2 had lost contact avoiding artillery fire). On the southern treeline, 1 Res. Bde took steadily increasing fire from groups of trenches that extended north-west from Gondrexon. Nevertheless, it attacked as it would have at the training area. The brigade had almost reached the Gondrexon–Leintrey track when an uncommonly heavy thunderstorm brought down hail and torrential rain: low ground became rushing streams and lakes, but the attack continued. RIR 1 enveloped the French left flank and took the position by 1300hrs. RIR 2 took heavy artillery fire at the last minute and began to waver; presumably the shells came from 1/Res. Foot Artillery 1 (sFH), which was firing on the French trenches at Gondrexon and had not noticed the approach of RIR 2 because of the storm. It could also have come from Fort Manonviller, which was also firing on RIR 1. Fortunately, the regimental commander, assisted by the cold-blooded actions of the officers, the I/RIR 2 commander in particular, who was often up to his chest in water, were able to rally the troops around the unfurled colours by singing 'The Watch on the Rhine' and other methods. They then took Gondrexon and pushed on to Reillon. The heavy shells, friendly or enemy, also hindered RIR 1 from exploiting its victory and forced some troops to retreat.

At 1330hrs the commander of 1 RD ordered 1 Res. Bde not to advance onto the high ground at Gondrexon, which lay in range of Fort Manonviller's artillery. At the same time, he apparently ordered the signal 'General Halt!' sounded. The 1 Res. Bde commander pulled RIR 1 behind the Bois de Amiens, while RIR 2, whose pursuit to Reillon had got out of the control of the officers, assembled at Gondrexon. The French had not defended the trenches south of Gondrexon, which were occupied by RIR 3.

Around 1200hrs the commander of I b. RK recognised that I b. AK was approaching Blâmont and that the advance of 1 RD was not leading anywhere. He told 1 RD it could bivouac north of Elfringen, with 5 RD behind it north of the canal. 7 KD reported that its horses were totally exhausted and also bivouacked north of Elfringen. The *Landwehr* Division bivouacked north of 5 RD.

I b. AK, positioned on the right wing of Seventh Army, was being squeezed out by its neighbours, I b. RK to the right and XIV AK to the left. The corps had only one supply road and the divisions were forced to use small, winding secondary roads. The corps was to begin its advance at 0600hrs, but, since the army order did not arrive until 0245hrs, a delay was necessary. 2 ID moved out from its bridgehead at Gondrexange and across the canal at 0700hrs. *Cheveauleger* R 4 reported the high ground south of Gogney, on the French side of border 10km to the south of Gondrexange, to be occupied by the French, but by the time the advance guard, IR 12, arrived the French had left. I and II/IR 12 were held up by French artillery fire, but III/IR 12 pushed straight on, quickly breaking weak resistance. The MGK/IR 12 trotted out front and annihilated half a French company. III/IR 12 took Blâmont by noon, while I and II/IR 12, using a rail embankment and road cuttings as cover, moved through artillery fire and gradually caught up. IR 15 on the right pushed back weak enemy forces, established contact with 1 RD and, at noon, was on the high ground west of Blâmont. 2 FA Bde followed by bounds, but had only one opportunity to engage French artillery.

1 ID assembled in march column on the road south from the canal bridgehead at Heming, but, although the road was quite wide, the units became so jammed up that movement ceased at times. At 0800hrs the advance guard moved through St Georges (4km south-west of Heming). 3/*Cheveauleger* R 8 drove off French cavalry on the border in a dismounted action. The regiment reported the high

ground just south of the border to be occupied and took fire from heavy artillery. When the point element of the advance guard, II/Household, reached the area it found the enemy gone, but also took casualties from artillery fire. At 1000hrs I/ FAR 1 arrived and shelled withdrawing French columns and was itself engaged by French counter-battery fire. I/Foot Artillery 1 (sFH), which had originally been last in the division order of march, came forward at a trot and went into battery at 1100hrs. The enemy guns were difficult to locate, and it took an hour to drive them off.

At 0830hrs I b. AK received an order from Seventh Army to temporarily halt on the Vezouse; the corps told both divisions to remain on the high ground west and north of Blâmont. The corps HQ arrived west of Blâmont at 1100hrs. There was no further combat at Blâmont; the enemy had disappeared. Seventh Army definitively ordered the corps not to cross the Vezouse, and for the most part it bivouacked in place. 1 and 3/b. Eng. Bn had been left at Saarburg to police up the battlefield and repair roads damaged by artillery fire. The attached army siege units (HQ, II and III/Foot Artillery R 18 (21cm mortars), HQ/Foot Artillery R 1, II/Foot Artillery R 3 (21cm mortars), b. Eng. R and b. Airship Sec.) joined the forces that were to attack Fort Manonviller.

XIV AK was also forced by enemy rearguards to deploy on the Vezouse. 28 ID was stopped at Cirey, while 29 ID on its right pushed the advance guard 3km over the Vezouse. XV AK marched on only one road, but did not encounter resistance, although it did capture forty-eight abandoned French artillery pieces. The corps' lead elements reached the Vezouse 4km east of Cirey.

On 22 August the French Second Army crossed back to the west side of the Meurthe: XX Corps assembled by St Nicholas du Port; XV Corps in the Moselle Valley, north of Bayon. Its rearguard at Flainval−Anthelupt had been attacked by II b. AK and relieved during the fight by 22 Bde from XX Corps. XVI Corps had been instructed to fall back from the high ground north-east of Lunéville when strong German forces approached, and to withdraw its divisions by bounds to the area north of Bayon. As the German XXI AK approached, the French 31 ID defended the high ground 4km north-east of Lunéville, but became too heavily engaged and was forced to conduct a hasty withdrawal under pressure. The march through Lunéville led to traffic jams and disorganisation, and the division arrived 4km north-east of Bayon badly shaken. 32 ID had earlier arrived east and south-east of Bayon. Left of XVI Corps, and in front of XV Corps, 64 and 72 RD held the high ground south of St Nicholas du Port and west of the Meurthe. 2 and 10 Cavalry Divs were south of Gerbéviller, totally exhausted.

The commander of the French First Army had determined it was necessary to hold the high ground at Blâmont on 22 August to gain time and allow the supply units to withdraw in an orderly manner; he would only withdraw over the Meurthe when the enemy attacked. However, the rapid withdrawal of Second Army exposed the First Army left flank. Citing the First Army commander's authorisation, VIII Corps withdrew during the morning to within 6km of the Meurthe; both corps to the right conformed, with XIII Corps falling back to the west of Badonviller and XXI Corps to Badonviller. In the evening VIII Corps withdrew over the Meurthe. The deteriorating state of discipline and morale became significant in both French armies. The roads were filled with stragglers, VIII Corps had lost half of its infantry and XIII Corps many of its guns. Numerous senior officers in First Army were relieved of their posts.

The German pursuit on 22 August had progressed a considerable distance, with II b. AK and XXI AK in particular advancing ruthlessly and quickly. The right flank of Seventh Army had also gained ground. Only I b. RK, its route forward blocked by Fort Manonviller, had been unable to advance.

The Battle in the Middle Vosges

In the open fields of Lorraine between 20 and 22 August there was, for the most part, a unified battle resulting in a decisive German victory and pursuit, while the left flank of the Seventh Army clawed its way forwards in the Vosges. This was mountain warfare: isolated units moved forward uphill and through valleys in endless forests, their routes designated by the major valleys, roads and passes. Attacks could not be coordinated. Unexpected encounters and surprise played a dominating role. The enemy's Alpine battalions were elite units specifically trained for such warfare; the terrain also favoured use of traps and tricks, which were the natural characteristics of the French soldier. The German troops were composed of reserve divisions, *Landwehr* and *Ersatz* units: second and third-line formations. The German strength was in combat in the open field and the German Army had made no peacetime preparations for mountain warfare; in particular, there was no mountain artillery, and the troops' tutorial in the Vosges was paid in blood. They advanced, but only slowly and with heavy casualties. The head start that their attack had been given was insufficient, and Crown Prince Rupprecht's hope that the right flank of the French armies in Lorraine could be turned by an advance through the Vosges was not realised.

XIV RK, 20–22 August

The XIV RK mission was to take the massive Mt Donon. 28 RD, with a brigade from 26 RD, attacked on 20 August from Schirmeck, but by late evening had only been able to take the lower slope on the east side. 26 RD, attacking from Schirmeck south along the Breusch Valley, met advancing French forces and was forced to turn back. 19 ED, attached to XIV RK, moved to assist 26 RD, but the march on 20 and 21 August in the mountains and heat caused numerous casualties and split up the division. On 21 August 28 RD attacked around the Donon, but was not able to take the mountain. The battle in the mountain forests was difficult, costly and nearly impossible to control. 26 RD, south of Schirmeck, fended of a few weak attacks. A quick thrust to Badonviller–Raon l'Étape into the flank and rear of the French forces at Saarburg was clearly out of the question. On 22 August the Donon was found free of enemy forces, but the 28 RD advance on the first French town, Raon-sur-Plaine, 4km from the Donon, was held up by an attack against the right flank; it was taken by noon, but a battle developed just west of the town which lasted until dark. 26 RD pushed the enemy slowly back at the cost of heavy casualties. 19 ED was still so exhausted that it could only conduct a weak firefight. There were also incidents of friendly fire.

The French 13 ID defended the Donon and Raon-sur-Plaine. On 22 August it fell back on XXI Corps at Badonviller. 26 RD and 19 ED had fought the left wing of the French XIV Corps, which had concentrated on the Breusch Valley, leaving the defence of the southern passes to 71 RD, reinforced by a regiment from the French 28 ID. The French XIV Corps was to delay back to the crest of the Vosges, which was then to be defended.

30 RD at Steige, 20 August (sketch 8, map 9)

At Weiler 30 RD continued the attack at 0430hrs on 20 August. 5 *Ersatz* Bde moved out with *Ersatz* Bn V and VIII in the first line, VII and VI following echeloned on the flanks, covered by the fire of 2 *Ersatz*/FAR 2. *Ersatz* Bn V on the right was initially held up by friendly artillery fire on abandoned trenches north-east of Steige, but this objective was taken at 0530hrs, and at 0630hrs 3, 2 and 4/*Ersatz* Bn V were in a firefight with enemy forces on Hill 763 (La Guiche). When the French tried to turn the right flank at 0745hrs, 1/*Ersatz* Bn V was committed there, while 1/*Ersatz* Bn VIII reinforced the firing line. On the left flank, 3/*Ersatz* Bn VII had pushed forward the previous day to the east end of Steige; it was instructed to await the rest of the battalion. At 0800hrs the other three companies were advancing down the road when rifle fire forced them to deploy 1km west of Meisengott. 2/*Ersatz* Bn VII and a MG platoon turned left against the steep, almost inaccessible ridge south-east of Steige, while 1/*Ersatz* Bn VII moved north of the road. The enemy was exceptionally well hidden and the attack made slow progress. Most of 3/*Ersatz* Bn VII was forced to withdraw from Steige to the slope 300m east of the town by French rifle fire, supported by a platoon of Ersatz MGK 5; only a half-platoon remained in the town. *Ersatz* Bn VI had bivouacked in Meisengott; 3 and 4/*Ersatz* VI went forward with the brigade left flank, stalking by bounds through bushes and steep slopes on the south side of the road. In error, 1 and 2/*Ersatz* Bn VI returned to the previous day's position on the hills north of Meisengott.

The attack stalled principally because the terrain made artillery support nearly impossible. Using all the battery's horses and crews, 2 *Ersatz*/FAR 2 managed to bring one gun up the steep slope north of Meisengott so that it could fire on French trenches – but not without casualties. The best results were obtained by the 10cm guns of 3/Res. Foot Artillery 14, which shelled the French on Hill 763.

The situation facing 10 Res. Bde was even more difficult. The troops were spread far and wide and difficult to contact; in particular, parts of RIR 11 had got lost in the woods on the ridge and north slopes of Hill 613, north of Lach. The brigade also had the mission of guarding the left flank, so I/RIR 11 spent a cold night there, with 1/RIR 11 to the west end of Lach and 4/RIR 11 halfway down the hill. 2/RIR 11 advanced at 0500hrs against the next hill to the west; on its right 5/RIR 11 led II/RIR 11 through the wooded slopes south of Meisengott. At 0730hrs the regimental commander designated Hill 623, south of Wagenbach, as the next objective; given the delay required transmitting orders in the hilly and wooded terrain, the start time was set for 1000hrs.

RIR 14 was employed piecemeal: II/RIR 14 was division reserve at Weiler, III/RIR 14 was to follow RIR 11, while I/RIR 14, which was already at Lach, moved with 1 and 4/RIR 11 down the road to Mittelscher. The march down the narrow, steep-sided valley was not without delays, particularly since it was fired on by French stragglers on the hillsides. Fortress MG Sec. 2 followed 10 Res. Bde, Res. MG Sec. 3 followed III/RIR 14, but lost contact and returned to Weiler. Nevertheless, by 1200hrs all of 10 Res. Bde was making progress.

The advance of 10 Res. Bde forced the enemy in front of 5 *Ersatz* Bde to withdraw from the hillside west of Wagenbach at 1200hrs, and *Ersatz* Bn VII was able to enter Steige, but encountered an enemy position in the middle of the town that extended up both hillsides. At 1400hrs 1 and 3/*Ersatz* Bn VII were deployed north of the road, 2/*Ersatz* Bn VII south of it, 4/*Ersatz* Bn VII moved along the south side of the town, and a platoon of *Ersatz* MGK 5 went into position north of the church. On the 5 *Ersatz* Bde right flank, the attack on Hill 763 made no progress due to enemy fire.

In the 10 Res. Bde sector, 1 and 4/RIR 11 reached the top of Hill 668, south of Steige (1km west of Hill 709), at 1300hrs, gaining visibility to the west of Steige, 300m north-west of which a French battalion was digging in: the two companies deployed and engaged them at very long range (1.6km). On the left, 1 and 4/RIR 14 joined the fight, along with the rest of RIR 11. The enemy had been surprised and took heavy losses, but defended his half-completed trenches. I/RIR 11 and I/RIR 14 advanced by bounds, and the French fled at 1500hrs; pursuit fire cut down entire groups before they could reach the protection of the woods to the rear.

3/Res. Foot Artillery 14 (10cm cannons) succeeded in suppressing the artillery fire coming from Hill 763, north of Steige, and engaged a French battery on the high ground north of Salzheim, forcing the French crews to abandon the guns. This enabled 5 *Ersatz* Bde to enter Steige, taking many prisoners, and reach the west end by 1800hrs. 1 and 4/*Ersatz* Bn V were able to advance north of Steige at 1630hrs, while 2 and 3/*Ersatz* Bn V took Hill 763 at 1730hrs, though French troops were able to maintain themselves between the two halves of the battalion for some time.

The commander of 10 Res. Bde arrived on Hill 668 and, at 1500hrs, gave RIR 14 permission to pursue to the west, reinforced by 1 and 2/RIR 11. 9/RIR 14 had already been sent through the woods to Salzheim, and it was able to put long-range fire on withdrawing French columns in the area of Roggensbach. 11 and 12/RIR 14 deployed left of I/R 14 and together they drove off French troops, which were already wavering, from the treeline north-west of Steige. The descent into the valley was made under lively French rifle fire, but many prisoners were taken in the hedges and sunken roads, and between 1600hrs and 1700hrs the French trenches were reached. It was now absolutely necessary to reorder the intermixed units and give the troops a short rest. The III/RIR 14 commander and several squads moved 300m down the road and found the four French guns abandoned under the fire from 3/Res. Foot Artillery 14. When they reached the treeline east of the fork in the road, they saw strong enemy skirmisher lines advancing from Salzheim–Roggensbach. 11 and 12/RIR 14 were brought up to the road fork, then I/RIR 14 came up on the right and deployed as well as time and the situation allowed; RIR 14 opened fire. The French were reinforced and began to turn the right flank; the French artillery revived and took the regiment in an uncomfortable crossfire. At 1930hrs the RIR 14 commander ordered a withdrawal to the hills to the south-east. The exertions of the day, the heat, the march over the hills and the gathering dark had prepared the ground for all sorts of illusions and mistakes. A wild firefight broke out in the woods, which led to a panic; while some of the troops ran back to Hill 688, most streamed back to Steige, pulling II/RIR 11, which had come up on the left, along with them. In the dark, wooded and hilly terrain, the troops of RIR 11 and RIR 14 became ever more confused and intermixed. Nevertheless, in the first half of the night the officers succeeded in assembling and separating the two regiments

At 1800hrs *Ersatz* Bn VII had been ordered by the 10 Res. Bde commander to move, with *Ersatz* MGK 5, west to the fork in the road. It was dusk as the lead companies, 1 and 2, climbed the slope to the north-west of the town, and as the RIR 14 troops fled towards the town, *Ersatz* VII took up a position after dark at the fork in the road; the enemy had clearly not pursued. I/RIR 11 moved forward in the dark wooded hills to assist, but had to cease movement 1km west of Steige. III/RIR 14 recovered the abandoned French artillery. 5 *Ersatz* Bde had several firefights with French troops in the woods to the north. On 21 and 22 August the division left flank at Urbeis was guarded by the Bicycle Co./RIR 60.

Roggensbach–Salzheim, 21–22 August (sketch 11 and 12)

Salzern (5km north-west of Roggensbach) was the 30 RD objective for 21 August; the division commander ordered the attack to resume at 0430hrs. 5 *Ersatz* Bde would attack with a strong right wing towards Roggensbach, while 10 Res. Bde would advance on Salzheim.

2 *Ersatz*/FAR 2 began climbing the Weiden-Berg (Meadow Hill) on an extremely steep and difficult path, covered with large and small stones, and sometimes marshy. The horses had hardly been unsaddled since leaving garrison at Würzburg, and had been so exhausted by the exertions of the preceding days that it was necessary to use two teams for each gun; the battery was not in position until 0500hrs. 1 *Ersatz*/FAR 12, which had mistakenly left Weiden-Berg the previous day, would reappear later. *Ersatz*/FAR 80 went into battery on Hill 763, north of Steige, and would engage enemy infantry at Salzheim and, later, artillery on the Wein-Berg (Wine Hill) to the south. 3/Res. Foot Artillery 14 (10cm cannons) was in firing position at 0430hrs east of Meisengott.

Ersatz Bn VIII and V attacked towards Roggensbach at 0500hrs; 3 and 4/*Ersatz* Bn VI followed. V was composed of 2/*Ersatz* Bn V and 7 and 8/RIR 14 in the first line, while 3/*Ersatz* Bn V followed (1 and 4/*Ersatz* Bn V were still in Steige and only arrived later in the day). At 0600hrs a French bivouac west of Roggensbach was sighted and engaged. The French offered serious resistance from rifle and MG fire, supported by batteries at Kolrein, Stamberg and on the Wein-Berg, so at 0800hrs 3/*Ersatz* Bn V was committed, and it was possible to advance to the west side of Roggensbach and the folds in the terrain there. However, further progress was blocked by artillery barrages. *Ersatz* Bn VIII initially moved west, then swung half-left and deployed 1 and 3/*Ersatz* Bn VIII, while 4/*Ersatz* Bn VIII followed echeloned behind the right flank. Strong rifle fire from a sunken path topped by a hedge north of Roggensbach slowed the attack, and, at noon, 4/*Ersatz* Bn VIII was committed in the centre. At 1300hrs the sunken path and the north tip of Roggensbach were taken. 3 and 4/*Ersatz* Bn VI seem to have joined the firing line.

In the 10 Res. Bde sector, RIR 11 attacked from Steige at 0300hrs, with RIR 14 following an hour later. RIR 11 occupied the treeline 500m south-west of the road fork by 0600hrs and opened a firefight at 700m with enemy infantry, which was nearly invisible on the slopes north-east and south-west of Salzheim. II/RIR 11 arrived first and deployed 5 and 6/RIR 11, with I/RIR 11 coming up on the left and engaging 3 and 4/RIR 11. Some of the guns of Res. MG Sec. 3 and

Fortress MG Sec. 2 were employed left and right of II/RIR 11. 9/RIR 14 was once again sent through the woods to find the enemy left flank while 10/RIR 11 was sent to help *Ersatz* Bn VII. I/RIR 11 was continually annoyed by enemy patrols that obviously originated from an enemy detachment on the Wein-Berg to the south. On their own initiative, a platoon from 3/RIR 11 and one from 4/RIR 11 climbed the north slope of the hill, but in the thick woods suddenly encountered strongly held trenches at 300m, took heavy losses and were forced to turn back. Protection of the left flank was taken over by 11 and 12/RIR 14.

The 30 RD attack suffered from a lack of artillery support. The flat trajectory field artillery batteries could not find suitable firing positions, and the division did not have howitzers. The long-range 10cm guns of 3/Res. Foot Artillery R 14 were able to engage only French artillery at Stamberg, Fonbach and Wein-Berg. Therefore, in the course of the morning, a platoon of 1 *Ersatz*/FAR 2 was brought forward to the fork in the road and shelled the fortifications at Salzheim, but was itself suppressed by concentric enemy rifle and artillery fire. At noon the 10 Res. Bde commander ordered the remnants of the crews to fall back from the guns. The rest of 1 *Ersatz*/FAR 2 had brought the French guns captured the day before back to Weiler, then climbed back up to Hill 763 and successfully engaged the now-visible French trenches at Salzheim and Wein-Berg.

At noon the enemy fire in the 10 Res. Bde area ceased completely; it appeared that the brigade had won fire superiority and that an assault was possible. But when RIR 11 broke out of the treeline at 1400hrs, the enemy resumed fire. Nevertheless, the regiment made progress bound by bound, although at the cost of considerable casualties; the fire from the riflemen and MGs cleared the way and, by evening, the enemy had been defeated. II/RIR 11 cleared Salzheim and the high ground to the south-west. On the left, I/R11 had driven along the north slope of the Wein-Berg, somewhat held up by wet ground and long-range enemy fire. Elements of III/RIR 14 pushed even farther west along the hillside.

The enemy had been thrown out of Roggensbach and Salzheim, but still held Kolrein, Stamberg and the top of the Wein-Berg: 30 RD was now stuck fast, with both flanks threatened. To the right, 19 ED had withdrawn to the Rhine Valley. The troops were exhausted, the units shrunken in size. Between 1700hrs and 1800hrs the 30 RD commander ordered the division to defend in place. Bringing forward rations for the troops was difficult: French artillery dominated the road to Steige by day and RIR 11 and 14 were only fed late that night, with some of the food having gone cold. 5 *Ersatz* Bde was in a worse position, having no field kitchens in the first place; carrying parties would have to bring food from the reserve infantry regiments kitchens, a long haul through the woods in the dark; the emergency iron rations had long since been eaten or thrown away. Most of the 5 *Ersatz* men preferred to make do with whatever they could find in Roggensbach.

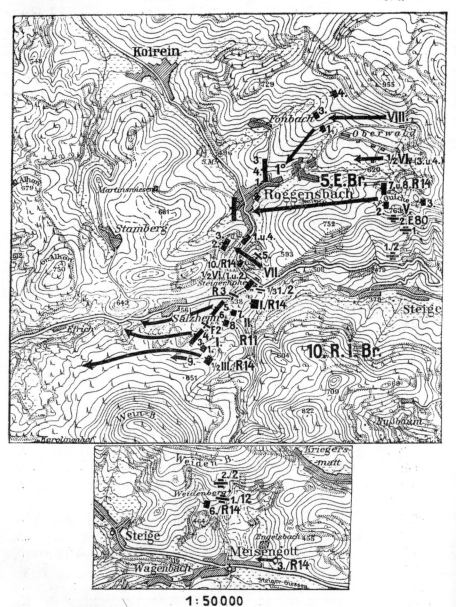

Roggensbach—Salzheim 21. 8. Textſkizze 11.

1 : 50 000

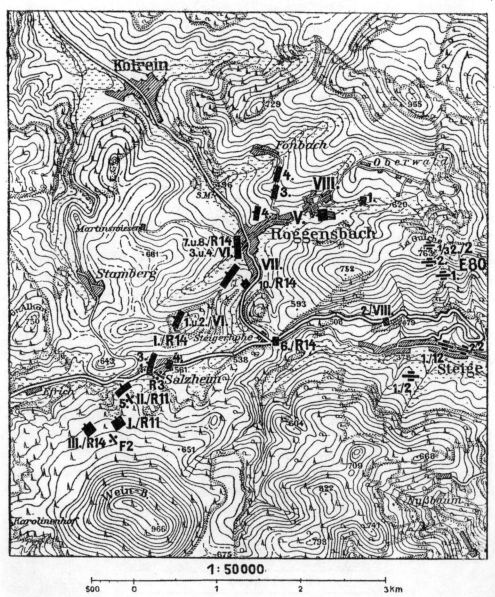

Roggensbach—Salzheim 22. 8.

1:50000

(Sketch 12) However, in spite of all these difficulties, the enemy appeared shaken and needed just one more push to be completely defeated. The 30 RD commander ordered a resumption of the attack on 22 August. The most important task was to win enough ground to allow the artillery to come forward to the high ground near the road fork. To provide the infantry fire support, 1 *Ersatz*/FAR 2 was brought into a shallow depression on the north side of Hill 668, south of Steige. Forty men pulled two guns of 2 *Ersatz*/FAR 2 with ropes to Hill 763 and opened fire, only to be discovered by the enemy artillery and suppressed. *Ersatz* Sec./FAR 80, on the south slope of Hill 763 engaged the enemy artillery, but was unable to prevent the French guns from gaining the upper hand. Only 3/Foot Artillery 14 (10cm cannons) was once again able to suppress the French artillery on Hill 750, north-west of Salzheim and the Wein-Berg. Given the insufficient fire support, an infantry attack on the strong enemy positions on Hill 681, west of Roggenbach, and Hill 750, north-west of Salzheim, was out of the question; it would be a success if the gains of the preceding day could be held under the French shelling, which increased through the morning. *Ersatz* Bn VIII, on the high ground north of Roggensbach, engaged in a daylong firefight with French infantry to the west.

There was a continual threat from the Wein-Berg, but the French only sent patrols forward. They also sent patrols from the north-west against Salzheim; at 1500hrs stronger groups of skirmishers appeared, but were forced back with losses by a platoon of Fortress MG Sec. 2 located on the treeline south of the town. At 1900hrs French shells fell like hail against the woods south-west of Salzheim, where RIR 11 and III/RIR 14 were located, followed shortly by French infantry attacking II/RIR 11 from the west. They were met by fire from *Ersatz* MGK 5. The II/RIR 11 commander had anticipated such an attack and committed 5/RIR 11 on the threatened left flank. When the French approached, II/RIR 11 counter-charged. The noise of battle drew I/RIR 11 (minus 3/RIR 11) and III/RIR 14, who also assaulted with the bayonet. The French fled, pursued westwards through the wood until dark; III/RIR 14 chased them for 2km. The battalions then returned to their positions.

The commander of 30 RD waited all day in vain for the promised assistance from 19 ED, but at 1700hrs it was learned that this division would continue the attack west, not south-west towards 30 RD; even in the best scenario, no help would arrive from this side until the next day. The commanders of 5 *Ersatz* Bde and 10 Res. Bde reported that the troops had just enough energy to hold out under the enemy artillery fire until that evening. Seventh Army HQ wanted 30 RD to hold Weiler. The 30 RD commander therefore decided to withdraw to Weiler, which would pull his division out of a dangerous situation and allow him to give the tired troops a rest.

The orders to withdraw reached the troops between 2200hrs and 2400hrs. Only the Steige road was available to withdraw the entire division. The artillery moved first. The two guns of 2 *Ersatz*/FAR 2 had to be lowered down from

Hill 763. At 2400hrs 5 *Ersatz* Bde began to move, first 1 and 2/*Ersatz* Bn VI on Hill 763, then from Roggensbach, right flank first, *Ersatz* Bn VIII, V, VII and attached or intermixed elements. Last was 10 Res. Bde; RIR 11 left Salzheim at 0100hrs and I/RIR 14 at 0200hrs. The enemy did not pursue. The march was conducted in complete quiet and order; all the equipment was retrieved. Only a few dead and any wounded that were not found in the woods around Salzheim were left behind. 30 RD took quarters in Weiler. III/RIR 14 did not get the order and stayed in place until 0900hrs when it heard a rumour that strong French columns had already marched through Steige. It withdrew – undisturbed – along difficult mountain paths and through thick underbrush to Steige.

From 20–22 August 30 RD had been engaged with the right flank of the French XIV Corps and pushed it slowly back through the mountains. The troops of the French 27 ID had been gradually replaced by a regiment of the French 58 RD.

Bavarian *Ersatz* Division and 2 *Landwehr* Brigade, 20–22 August

The commander of the Bavarian ED had come to the conclusion on the evening of 19 August that there was no danger from the south. On the other hand, there were enemy forces in the Leber Tal (Leber Valley), which led to Markirch, but so far had not moved, though they were in position to strike the flank of 30 RD. He received permission from the commander of Strasbourg, his superior, on 20 August to attack up the valley and, if possible, take Markirch town and the pass. 2 *Landwehr* Bde would hold Schlettstadt.

St Kreuz, 20 August (sketch 13)

Ersatz Bn II moved out at 0030hrs up the Leber Tal to secure Leberau, about halfway from Schlettstadt and Markirch; it reached Hurst, about 3km east of Leberau, at 0200hrs, and the commander decided to halt and conduct a reconnaissance. Shots were suddenly fired from close range, which were returned. 1 and 2/*Ersatz* Bn II deployed, but immediately began wild firing, until the battalion commander was able to re-establish order. *Ersatz* Bn II moved out deployed with the dawn at 0500hrs, but the enemy, whose strength had doubtlessly been overestimated in the dark, had left. At 0700hrs Leberau was reached without resistance. 3 and 4/*Ersatz* Bn I also arrived, having marched on the high ground south of the road. The first exaggerated reports of the Hurst fight reached the 1 *Ersatz* Bde commander at 0600hrs, just as the brigade began movement. He decided to immediately go to the aid of *Ersatz* Bn II, but found the road to Hurst free.

St. Kreuz 20. 8.   Textskizze 13.

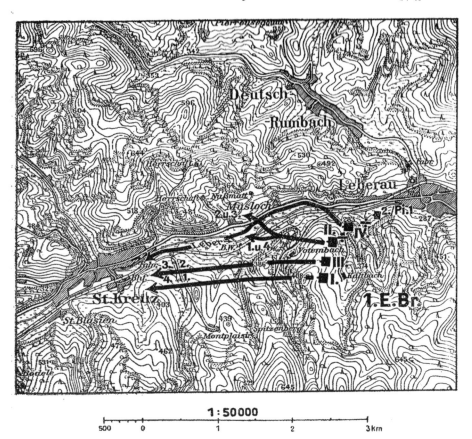

The Bavarian ED commander expected resistance, if not at Hurst then at St Kreuz. It would be necessary to deploy the division out of the valley and, on 19 August, patrols had been sent out to reconnoitre possible routes, though their reports had not yet arrived. The division commander therefore decided to move the mass of his unit south to Rappoltsweiler, which would put them on a good road which led deep into the rear of the enemy at Markirch. 1 *Ersatz* Bde was instructed to advance no farther than Leberau and to send excess forces back to rejoin the main body. Due to a series of errors, *Ersatz* FA Sec. 1, which was supposed to support 1 *Ersatz* Bde, did not march down the Leber Tal.

The inhabitants of Leberau reported that French troops of all arms had been in the town on 18 August, but had left, and only bicycle troops had been seen on 19 August. French troops were supposed to be at Musloch and St Kreuz, about 1.5km and 2.5km further up the valley. The French had dug in on the slopes north and south of Musloch and south of St Kreuz. The 1 *Ersatz* Bde commander either received the division commander's order late or not at all. At 1500hrs he decided to attack, in spite of the fact that he had only four battalions, the troops had been tired out by the exertions of the preceding days, there was no artillery, and no help far and wide. The terrain was exceptionally unfavourable, compartmented by hills and valleys, and it was hot. This decision was justified by the situation: his attack would relieve the threat to the 30 RD flank, and even if the enemy at St Kreuz were not defeated, he could be fixed in place, which would facilitate the envelopment by the main body.

The 1 *Ersatz* Bde commander avoided an advance down the Leber Tal in favour of a cross-country march south of it, on steep and bad paths, sometimes through thick woods, which often required single-file movement. The brigade deployed behind the ridge south-west of Leberau, with *Ersatz* Bn II and III in the centre, IV and the Ersatz MGK 1 echeloned right, and *Ersatz* Bn I echeloned left. 2 *Ersatz*/Eng. Bn 1 probably remained at the west end of Leberau. All battalions would use *Ersatz* Bn III as a guide, which headed for the St Kreuz church tower. As the troops crossed the crest and left the cover of the woods at about 1700hrs, they took rifle fire from Musloch and St Kreuz, and artillery fire from the south-west, but continued to advance. II swung right back down into the Leber Tal towards Musloch; 1 and 4/*Ersatz* Bn II deployed behind the rail line while 2 and 3 attacked from the east, accompanied by a platoon of *Ersatz* MGK 1. *Ersatz* Bn III, with 3 and 4/*Ersatz* Bn III in the first line, turned towards St Kreuz, followed on the left by Ersatz Bn I. With great difficulty the battalion crossed the wooded fingers of the ridge that descended to the Leber Tal. The skirmishers gradually approached by bounds to within 600m from the south-east side of St Kreuz with moderate losses. It was hardly possible to reply to the weak enemy rifle fire, because the French could not be seen. Only when 2 and 4 reached Hill 403 south of St Kreuz did they take casualties from French shrapnel. *Ersatz* Bn IV was ordered by the brigade HQ to move back into the Leber Tal and attack west on St Kreuz, along with a platoon of *Ersatz* MGK 1. 2/*Ersatz* Bn IV in the lead took fire 200m from Musloch, but bypassed the town to the south and began a firefight with St Kreuz. 1/*Ersatz* Bn IV came up on the left and the attack rolled forward quickly. 3 and 4/*Ersatz* Bn IV reached the west end of Musloch in march column when they took fire from houses on both sides and the rear. This unexpected baptism of fire initially caused confusion, particularly since there were casualties. Detachments from 3/*Ersatz* Bn IV took up overwatch positions south of the town, with the MG platoon to the east, and fired on windows. 4/*Ersatz* Bn IV broke down doors, stormed and searched houses. Elements of *Ersatz* I, II, and III and 2 *Ersatz*/Eng. Bn 1 became involved. The village finally caught fire, dooming the defenders. The ambush was probably the work of French stragglers, aided by the inhabitants. 3 and 4/*Ersatz* IV and the MG were assembled south of Musloch and advanced on the right echelon of 1 and 2/*Ersatz* IV. Farms and barns on the east end of St Kreuz were watched or searched and, if fire was taken from them, burned down. In addition to the heights south of the town, the factory on the west end fell into German hands, while the French still held the town centre, at which point darkness ended the fight. The troops bivouacked in place and the officers strove to reorganise the units.

The mass of the Bavarian ED reached Rappoltsweiler at noon. The heat and humidity, unrelieved by a breath of air, caused numerous march casualties and cases of heat stroke. The division commander called an hour-long rest north of Rappoltsweiler. In the town, the commander learned that the enemy in Wasserbourg (not on map, 3km south of Markirch) had withdrawn into the mountains. The post office in Colmar reported that the French had advanced to the immediate west of the city and that 1 *Landwehr* Bde had withdrawn to Neu-Breisach. At the same time, a loud noise could be heard from the south; as it was later established, the Germans had blown the rail bridge. To clarify the situation, the division commander sent all available cavalry south in two patrols to Colmar. These confirmed that the *Landwehr* had withdrawn and that the French were approaching in force.

The Bavarian ED commander cancelled the advance on Markirch; guarding the left flank of Seventh Army in the Rhine Valley had now become paramount, and the division oriented south at Rappoltsweiler. Since *Ersatz* divisions had no combat support or service support units, the city government of Rappoltsweiler was tasked with providing sixty wagons to transport rations, ammunition and the wounded, which produced thirty wagons pulled by broken-down horses and driven by old men, boys and women. There was no contact with 1 *Landwehr* Bde, which had in fact withdrawn over the Ill River, directly east of Colmar. The enemy did not even dare to enter Colmar. But since there was a threat to the Seventh Army left, the Bavarian ED would be reinforced with troops sent from Fort Strasbourg by rail to Schlettstadt.

Markirch, 21 August (sketch 14)

At 1900hrs hours on 20 August the Seventh Army HQ informed the Bavarian ED, via the commander of Strasbourg, of the victory in Lorraine, as well as the fact that the enemy was standing fast in the south. Seventh Army estimated the enemy forces in the Rhine Valley at Colmar as cavalry, reinforced by light infantry and MGs. In view of this, the Bavarian ED commander decided to guard the army left flank against Markirch and Colmar by concentrating his troops at Schlettstadt. Withdrawal was out of the question due to the effect it would have on morale. The artillery at Neu-Breisach would make a French attack over the Ill River east of Colmar difficult. He requested permission from XIV RK to attack south. Instead, at 0940hrs he was given the two-fold mission of blocking the Rhine Valley and covering the left flank of 30 RD. The Bavarian ED was subordinated directly to Seventh Army HQ. In light of the German victory in Lorraine, the Bavarian ED commander did not think the French would make a serious effort in the Rhine Valley, but was capable of attacking the 30 RD left flank; protecting it would be best accomplished by clearing the French completely out the Leber Tal. The troops arriving from Strasbourg would guard the German Army left at Rappoltsweiler, while the Bavarian ED would conduct the attack on Markirch planned for the previous day.

The forces sent by Fort Strasbourg, under the commander of 52 *Landwehr* Bde (a Württemberger), included the Bavarian RIR 4 (four battalions) and RIR 15 (four battalions) and the Prussian II/RIR 60, RIR 70 (two battalions), Fortress MG Sec. 1, 1 *Landwehr* Sqn/XIV AK, 2 *Ersatz*/FAR 15 and, under the command of *Ersatz* Sec./FAR 84, 1 *Ersatz*/FAR 51 and 2 *Ersatz*/FAR 84, plus 5/Res. Foot Artillery R 10 (sFH), HQ I and 4/Res. Foot Artillery R 14 (10cm cannons) and 4 Res./Eng. Bn 15. There was considerable friction in the rail move on the night of 20/21 August. The Bavarian ED commander asked 52 Bde that an artillery battery be sent from Schlettstadt to 1 *Ersatz* Bde; in addition, the 52 Bde commander provided 2 *Ersatz*/FAR 15 and III/RIR 4.

Rumours of French troop movements in the Rhine Valley circulated all day, including one of a French cavalry division approaching Schlettstadt, which caused 2 *Landwehr* Bde to go on alert, and one at 1900hrs of an impending French attack on Rappoltsweiler that caused the forces from Fortress Strasbourg to assume defensive positions and lose a night's sleep. In fact, the French only advanced with security detachments.

Until the Strasbourg forces arrived, the Bavarian ED commander felt he had to guard the Rhine Valley and Rappoltsweiler. He therefore only sent a brigade task force from Schlettstadt to Markirch under the command of 9 *Ersatz* Bde: *Ersatz* Bn X and XI, 1st Platoon/*Ersatz* MG Sec. 9, half of *Ersatz* Cavalry Sec./III b. AK and 1 *Ersatz*/FAR 10. The marchng order was issued at 0515hrs.

Gefechte vor Martirch 21. 8.   Textskizze 34.

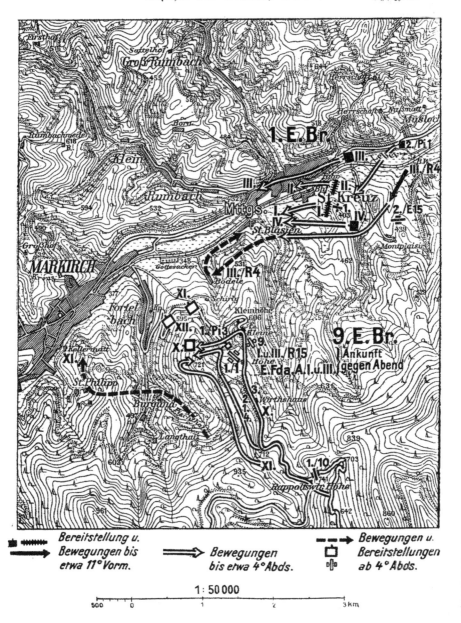

Bereitstellung u. Bewegungen bis etwa 11° Vorm.

Bewegungen bis etwa 4° Abds.

Bewegungen u. Bereitstellungen ab 4° Abds.

1 : 50 000

Key

Bereitstellung und Bewegung bis etwa 11 Vorm – assembly area and movement to about 1100

Bewegung bis etwa 4 Abends – movement to about 1600

Bewegungen und Beretistellungen ab 4 Abds. – movement and assembly area after 1600

Ankuft gegen Abend – arrived during the evening

The 1 *Ersatz* Bde mission at St Kreuz was to fix the enemy in the Leber Tal in place. *Ersatz* Bn I and II had dug trenches or were doing so. *Ersatz* Bn III and IV were entirely untangled and organised. III/RIR 4 arrived at 0500hrs and was moved behind the left flank. 2 *Ersatz*/FAR 15 unlimbered on Hill 439, protected by a platoon of 2 *Ersatz*/Eng. Bn. At daybreak a firefight began between the French on the edges of St Kreuz and *Ersatz* Bn II, which 2 *Ersatz*/FAR 15 and French artillery west of St Kreuz joined. *Ersatz* MGK 1 set up in the *Ersatz* Bn I position at 0700hrs to engage French infantry at the south-west end of St Kreuz. Two platoons of 2 *Ersatz*/Eng. Bn also joined *Ersatz* Bn I, while *Ersatz* Bn IV extended the line left. Enemy infantry on the east end of St Kreuz were able to fire into the right flank of *Ersatz* Bn II, so, between 0700hrs and 0800hrs, *Ersatz* Bn III was brought forward and attacked; in the next two and a half hours it succeeded, in a tough firefight, in advancing to within 500m from the town. At 1100hrs the brigade commander ordered it to assault, which cost numerous casualties, particularly in officers, including the battalion commander, who was killed. Nevertheless, the battalion broke into the town, pushed through to the west end and pursued the retreating enemy with fire. Following the example of *Ersatz* Bn III, the other battalions also assaulted. *Ersatz* Bn II pushed into the south side of St Kreuz, while *Ersatz* Bn I and IV took the hills south of the town. III/RIR 4 came up on the left at a run, with 10/RIR 4 leading. By noon the battle had died down, with the French still blocking the valley at the west end of the town.

1 *Ersatz* Bde had to await the arrival of 9 *Ersatz* Bde, which could not march until 0700hrs because the artillery battery, 1 *Ersatz*/FAR 10, was an hour late. As the advance guard, 1 and 2/Ersatz X, with the brigade commander, approached Point 642 (bottom of map), the cavalry reported from the pass (741m) at Rappoltsweiler Höhe (Rappoltsweiler Heights) that enemy artillery was visible west of St Kreuz and firing on 1 *Ersatz* Bde. The 9 Bde commander galloped forward with 1 *Ersatz*/FAR 10 and chose a firing position for the battery that was concealed by the trees, but from which the enemy artillery, 400m lower, could clearly be seen. 1 *Ersatz*/FAR 10's fire immediately suppressed the French artillery, which did not reply for a quarter hour, and then tentatively and without effect. *Ersatz* Bn X moved past the guns behind a hilltop and was soon in contact with the enemy at Wirtshaus (public house) at 1030hrs, deployed 800m north of the pass with 3/*Ersatz* Bn X (minus a platoon) east of the road, 2/*Ersatz* Bn X (and a platoon from 1 and 4/Ersatz Bn X) on the road and the steep slope to the west; 1/*Ersatz* Bn X (minus a platoon, but with one from 3/*Ersatz* Bn X) moved along the crest 400m west of the road in close column. 4/*Ersatz* Bn X got lost and ended up on the *Ersatz* Bn X right flank. *Ersatz* Bn XI followed behind on the right. The attack proceeded slowly; the enemy had skilfully established himself in the Wirtshaus and the houses and treelines of Hill 606 to the north,

and was practically invisible. The brigade commander ordered an artillery piece to be manhandled down the road until it could shell the Wirtshaus at close range; the building was soon in flames and taken. However, this was obviously only an outpost. The enemy seemed determined to defend the farm and trenches 700m further north. *Ersatz* Bn X stalked forward on both sides of the road, occasionally taking artillery fire until, at 1100hrs, it reached the treeline south of the farm and began the firefight. The artillery piece caught up and blasted the way forward at a range of 300m; the farm burned, the fire from the trenches died out. At 1300hrs the right flank of *Ersatz* Bn X assaulted, which succeeded at small loss; the battalion took the treelines, Forester's House (F on map) and other buildings on Hill 606. The left wing took a farmhouse at the bend in the road south-west of Hill 606 at 1500hrs; the crew and horse team of a French gun that was trying to escape were shot down. The brigade attempted to pursue to the north, but the French had disappeared, leaving behind weapons, equipment and a few prisoners, and general exhaustion also called for a rest. The commander of *Ersatz* Bn X had suffered from heat stroke, and the commanders of 1 and 3/*Ersatz* Bn X were killed.

At 1500hrs the commander of *Ersatz* FA Sec. I reported to the 9 Bde commander at Hill 606. His unit was followed by *Ersatz* Bn XII and IX, with 2nd Platoon/*Ersatz* MGK 9 and 1 *Ersatz*/Eng. Bn 3. They marched through a narrow and deep valley, which went continually uphill, gaining 500m elevation. The heat was oppressive. Surely packs were left by the side of the road, which were usually lost, and with them the shelter halves, iron rations and some of the ammunition. Gradually the road was lined with exhausted men who displayed the symptoms of oncoming heat stroke. Some of the companies melted down to eighty or ninety men. *Ersatz* Bn XII reached the pass at 1515hrs.

The commander of 1 *Ersatz* Bde informed the 9 *Ersatz* Bde commander of his situation at St Kreuz. In spite of the late hour, the 9 Bde commander decided to continue the attack on Markirch, for which reconnaissance of the difficult terrain was essential. There were no covered avenues of approach or positions for artillery. Only 1 *Ersatz*/FAR 1 was able to set up on the ridge between the Wirtshaus and Hill 606, engaging enemy staffs and closed-up units at Klein-Rumbach. Field fortifications could also be seen on the high ground immediately north of Markirch. At 1600hrs *Ersatz* Bn XII attacked towards Fortelbach, with *Ersatz* Bn XI on its right; *Ersatz* Bn X remained west of Hill 606 with *Ersatz* MGK 9. IX (which on the map is incorrectly labelled 'XI') and was to support the attack from the high ground south of Markirch. Ignoring its fatigue, the battalion climbed the steep ridge to St Phillip, took several prisoners there and, at 2100hrs, stood on the assigned objective. The other battalions also took stragglers prisoner during their approach march. The commander of 9 *Ersatz* Bde was forced to postpone the attack on Markirch until the next morning; the day was too far advanced, the

troops too exhausted and the artillery not yet ready. At 1845hrs he informed the
1 *Ersatz* Bde commander of his decision. I and III/RIR 15 arrived at Hill 606
between 1900hrs and 2000hrs, with 2 *Ersatz*/FAR Sec. III joinging then later.

1 *Ersatz* Bde had ordered III/RIR 4 to establish contact with 9 *Ersatz* Bde
by moving south of the Leber Tal towards Markirch. It marched through steep
terrain in pathless woods and great heat, driving the enemy before it, and linked
up with 9 *Ersatz* Bde. That evening it returned to St Kreuz.

20 and 21 August had brought the Bavarian ED its first battles, and the gaps
in its organisation became painfully apparent, particularly the lack of medical
support and supply units. Ammunition resupply caused considerable difficulty.
The wagons requisitioned in Schlettstadt did good service, bringing forward
rations and evacuating wounded on the return trip. Fortress Strasbourg helped
out by providing lorries. In general the division had to fight under far less
favourable conditions than those enjoyed by well-equipped active army units; it
fought well nonetheless.

First Conquest of the Col de Ste Marie, 22 August (sketch 15)

The Bavarian ED received neither a situation report nor orders from Seventh
Army HQ for 22 August. Since liaison had been established with 30 RD, the
situation there was known. Strong enemy forces were suspected to be south of
Rappoltsweiler and in the valleys of Markirch and Kaysersberg (5km north-west
of Colmar). The Bavarian ED commander saw no reason to change the already
planned operation: the attack on Markirch would continue while the Fortress
Strasbourg troops held Rappoltsweiler. On his own initiative, the commander of
9 Bde had decided on the evening of 21 August to attack Markirch and informed
the 1 *Ersatz* Bde commander.

That morning the Bavarian ED was once again subordinated to the governor of
Fort Strasbourg, who was convinced that strong French forces, the *armée d'Alsace*,
was going to attack north. He expressly ordered the Fortress Strasbourg troops to
remain near Rappoltsweiler and forbade any movement to the south. He did not
approve of the Bavarian ED advance up the Leber Tal, but did not interfere. That
evening he arrived personally at Colmar and put the Fortress Strasbourg troops
directly under his control, so that the Bavarian ED commander could concentrate
on his own operations. The French in the Rhine Valley hardly budged the entire
day, but the uncertainty (and the lack of pioneer equipment) hindered digging in.

On the night of 21/22 August, from its position on the high ground south of
Markirch, *Ersatz* Bn IX sent patrols into the city, which met no resistance; friendly
inhabitants reported that the French had left on the afternoon of 21 August. At
dawn 1 *Ersatz* Bde also found the way clear and began to advance into Markirch.

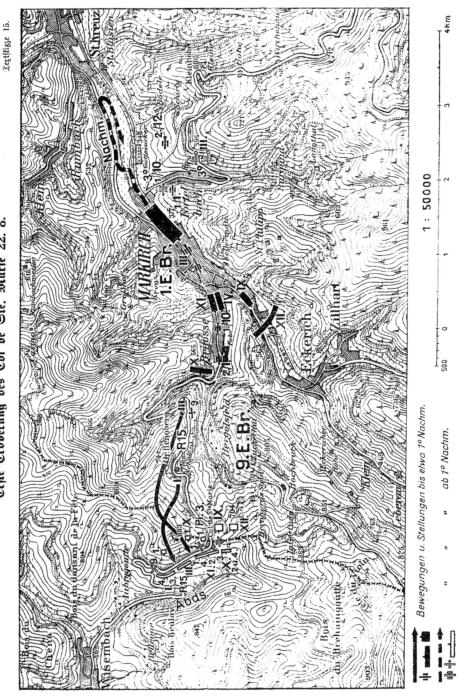

Key

Bewegungen und Stellungen bis etwa 1 Nachm – movement and positions until about 1300
" *ab 1 Nachm* – after 1300

The *Ersatz* Bn IX report reached the 9 Bde commander at 0600hrs on 22 August, and he decided to march at once on the Col (Pass) de St Marie; the order was issued at 0635hrs and the brigade moved out, with RIR 15 (minus II/ RIR 15) in the lead. At Markirch it met 1 *Ersatz* Bde, which halted to allow them to pass by. 2/RIR 15 (minus a platoon) provided reconnaissance and security in the woods north and northeast of Markirch, and 1 *Ersatz*/FAR 10 and 2 *Ersatz*/ FAR 12 provided artillery overwatch from the high ground west of Fortelbach.

Shortly before 0900hrs, and as 1/RIR 15 approached the last bend in the road about 1km from the pass, it received heavy rifle fire; numerous small trenches and obstacles were terraced in a half-circle on both sides of the pass road, though this was not obvious at first glance. The battalion deployed 1/RIR 15, soon followed on the right by 3/RIR 15, to attack and clarify the situation. The slope, which began at the road, was steep (there were several cliffs) and covered with large trees. There were obstacles everywhere: fallen trees, abates (fallen trees positioned as an obstacle), barbed wire and trip-wires. Fog created a gloomy half-darkness which hindered visibility. The enemy riflemen were in trees, behind bushes, boulders and stone walls, in holes and trenches. The fights began at point-blank range, with furious rapid fire, and ended with bitter hand-to-hand combat. Each trench had to be torn from the enemy by storm. There was no place for 1 *Ersatz*/FAR 10 to set up and it was sent back to the west end of Markirch. For the same reason, the MGs could not be brought into action. 1 *Ersatz*/Eng. Bn 3 and 4/RIR 15 were committed on the left, while the enemy resistance drew 1 and 3/RIR 15 to the ridge crest on the right. When it appeared the attack had stalled, the commander of RIR 15 committed his last reserve, III/RIR 15. To the left of the road the terrain was open and exposed to flanking fire from the south, so the battalion was committed on the right. It moved up a long finger of the main ridge, once again meeting a virtually invisible enemy defending behind rocks and obstacles and in trenches. Position after position was taken with cold steel. The units became intermixed. The fight became even more intense near the German–French border on the crest, which the enemy would not give up and which he defended furiously. The sound of combat roared through the forest. French snipers in trees shot at the backs of the thick groups of Bavarian riflemen. Bavarian troops suffered setbacks, but these were made good. The wounded streamed downhill. Rumours circulated that entire battalions were surrounded and companies had been wiped out, which led the RIR 15 commander to think that the enemy was far stronger; he gave permission for the battalions to retreat to Markirch. However, the commander of I/RIR 15 soon heard shouts of 'Hurrah!' and beating drums: the RIR 15 men and the engineers had stormed the crest and the French fled down the wooded west slope. I/RIR 15, which was advancing west, crossed paths with III/RIR 15, which was going south-west, and organisation now largely consisted of men from various units following individual officers and moving towards the road that led to Wisembach. The commander of III/RIR 15 captured the staff of a French regiment in houses at the pass. Everywhere there were signs that the enemy had been completely surprised, such as pots full of prepared but untouched food and tables set for a meal. German artillery fire began to land on the pass and the RIR 15 men had to take cover; it was undoubtedly not easy for the gunners to distinguish friend from foe at a wooded pass 300m higher in elevation and at 5km range, and the batteries, which had not been able to take part in the combat in the woods, were eager to engage the enemy. 1 *Ersatz*/FAR 1 discovered a French battery at the pass, and this was the principal target. As it attempted to withdraw down the road to Wisembach, the lead French gun ran directly into the engineers, who cut down gunners, drivers and teams. The rest of the guns fell to RIR 15. *Ersatz* MGK 9 arrived just in time to pursue the French infantry with fire. The artillery fire was stopped with horn signals at 1400hrs.

The rest of 9 *Ersatz* Bde was resting in Markirch; some troops had been fed by the RIR 15 field kitchens or the inhabitants of Markirch, and 1 *Ersatz* Bde had taken billets in the town. At noon it was reported that the enemy was at Diedolshausen and moving to Markirch; his outposts were detected at Klein-Leberau (left corner of map, 3km south-west of Markirch). *Ersatz* Bn XII was deployed at the south-west end of Markirch on the high ground on both sides of the road, backed up by *Ersatz* Bn IX. *Ersatz* Bn X took up a position on the high ground north of Brifosse, while *Ersatz* Bn XI remained in the town.

At the same time, unfavourable reports of the situation at the pass reached the 9 *Ersatz* Bde commander, who decided to send reinforcements and take the pass under all circumstances; the threat to the left flank had to be accepted. For lack of a suitable firing position 1 and 3/*Ersatz* FA Sec. III went into battery on the road east of Fortelbach, and 1 *Ersatz*/FAR 10 probably in the same area. *Ersatz* Bn XI was sent up the road to the pass to back up the advance guard, its movement harassed by friendly artillery fire. It found RIR 15 on the pass and occupied the houses and treeline north of the pass on a 500m front. *Ersatz* Bn X (minus 3/ *Ersatz* Bn X) followed at 1400hrs and took up a position on the right flank of RIR 15. *Ersatz* Bn IX, uncertain of the situation, moved by bounds, did not get to the top until 1500hrs and moved behind the left flank of *Ersatz* Bn XI. *Ersatz* Bn XII left 3/*Ersatz* Bn XII at the south-west end of Markirch and arrived left of *Ersatz* Bn IX at 1730hrs. *Ersatz* MGK 1 set up on Hill 883. Two guns from 2 *Ersatz*/FAR 1 went into position in the houses on both sides of the pass road. That evening it began to rain; the troops that had dropped their packs on the march from Rappoltsweiler now felt the loss of their coats, tents and iron rations. The French held Wisembach.

The losses in RIR 15 were considerable, but enemy casualties were also heavy, including a battery and thirty-five POWs. On the next morning a stretcher-bearer found the standard of the French RIR 309. The Bavarian ED had taken the first Vosges pass. On 20 and 21 August it had engaged the French XIV Corps, which was in the process of moving to the Breusch Pass, being replaced on the crest of the Vosges on 22 August by the Fortress Épinal reserve, 71 RD.

Colmar and Mühlhausen, 20–22 August (sketch 16)

On the morning of 20 August the 1 *Landwehr* Bde commander saw that his position west of Colmar was indefensible, and he evacuated the city and occupied a position to the west behind the Ill River. At midnight he was informed by his higher HQ, the deputy commander of XIV RK, that a French cavalry division was approaching from Mühlhausen, so he moved his brigade to a defensive position west of Colmar, facing south-west and west. By noon on 21 August the French cavalry had not materialised, so he moved his brigade back to the east side of the Ill. The French between Colmar and Mühlhausen hardly moved on 20–21 August.

On the evening of 21 August the deputy commander of XIV RK told the 1 *Landwehr* Bde commander that the mission of the troops in Alsace was to keep the French *armée d'Alsace* from moving elsewhere; this meant that the brigade had to attack. The French were known to be in Ingersheim, but had only sent patrols to Colmar. At 0300hrs *Landwehr* R 2 moved towards Colmar and, by 0900hrs, had reached the rail line in town; fire from I/LIR 2 forced a French company approaching the rail station to make a hasty retreat. By 0945hrs LIR 1 had reached the rail line north of the city. The LIR 1 commander went to Colmar twice to coordinate the attack with LIR 2. With the approval of the brigade commander, it was agreed that LIR 2 would attack through Logelbach and Ingersheim, while LIR 1 attacked to the north. While the LIR 1 commander was returning to his unit after the second conference, the commander of *Landwehr* District Colmar (in charge of replacements, with no command authority) set LIR 1 in motion towards Logelbach; the battalions disappeared in the vineyards and became disorganised, and III/LIR 1 became disoriented and swung half-left. The LIR 1 commander succeeded in turning III/LIR 1 back north-west, but it got lost again and ended up behind I/LIR 1, which itself had split into two groups. 1 and 4/LIR 1, with a half-platoon of 2 and 3/LIR 1, crossed the River Fecht and entered into a standing firefight with enemy infantry in Ingersheim, on the road north of the town and on Hill 308, north-west of the town; every man was committed, and the battalion commander himself took up a rifle. 2 and 3/LIR 1 continued in a south-westerly direction and were the first to reach the houses on the near side of the bridge at Ingersheim, where they also took heavy fire. The houses were strongly held, the street barricaded and the enemy defence desperate. They also took fire from Logelbach into their flank. Two groups of houses were taken

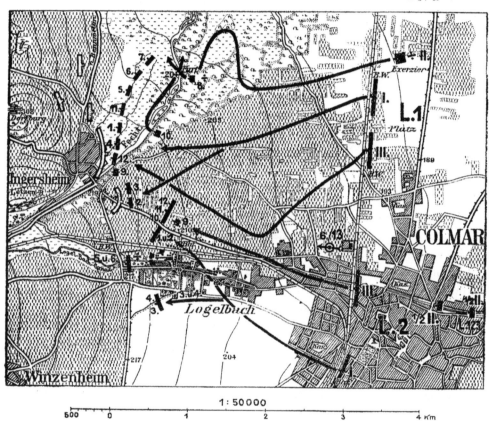

Jngersheim 22. 8.

Textskizze 16.

1 : 50000

500   0   1   2   3   4 Km

by storm and lost again. 9 and 12/LIR 1 attacked to the right of 3/LIR 1. As they approached the Fecht, they were met by close-range rifle fire. The battalion commander ordered bayonets fixed and the bushes were cleared out. Flanking fire from the bridge 200–300m away swept the riverbed, making a crossing impossible. Only 12/LIR 1 on the right succeeded in crossing and joining 1 and 4/LIR 1, while 9/LIR 1 took cover behind the flood-control levee. 12/LIR 1 sought several times to take the bridge, but without success. 11/LIR 1 joined 1 and 4/LIR 1; the battalion commander retained 10/LIR 1 as reserve. It was noon. II/LIR 1 moved too far to the right, but was put back on track by the regimental commander, and it crossed at a ford 1.2km north of Ingersheim. By 1400hrs, 5, 6, and 7/LIR 1 were engaged on the right flank.

LIR 2 attacked when LIR 1 crossed the rail line. 6/Foot Artillery R 13 (sFH) cleared the way by setting a factory on the west end of Logelbach on fire, then displacing to the north-west of Colmar, where it engaged Hill 308, Ingersheim and the woods east of the town at noon. The enemy was invisible. The left flank of I/LIR 2 was slowed by flanking fire from Winzenheim; 3 and 4/LIR 2, reinforced by platoons from 1 and 2/LIR 2, swung south, while 1 and 2/LIR 2 attached themselves to III/LIR 2, which was moving along the road to Ingersheim. 5 and 6/LIR 2 filled the gap between them; they were approaching the park at the west end of Logelbach in march column when they suddenly took heavy fire from an unknown source. The leaders, the commander of 6/LIR 2 in particular, sort to quell the panic. By coincidence, the battalion had prepared the park for defence several days previously and cut firing ports in the park wall, and this position was quickly occupied. A firefight developed with an enemy that was just 400m distant and who had themselves occupied field fortifications prepared by German engineers. 2 *Ersatz*/MGK XV AK also set up in the park. III/LIR 2, with 12, 11 and 10/LIR 2 forward and 9/LIR 2 following, slowly worked its way through the vineyards north of the road towards Ingersheim, searching the buildings it passed. 1 and 2/LIR 2 moved south of the road and all joined in the firefight against the town. 9/LIR 2 was committed and, later, 5 and 6/LIR 2. The battle swayed back and forth until, at 1830hrs, the *Landwehr* men succeeded in taking one house after the other up to the bank of the Fecht. The prisoners were Alpine troops. LIR 2 was no longer strong enough to take Ingersheim. Heavy rifle and MG fire prevented further advance. The French brought up artillery on the high ground both to the north and the west. They were suppressed by 6/Foot Artillery R 13 (sFH), which was running out of shells. The French reinforced their infantry and the artillery resumed firing. The LIR 2 skirmisher line began to move back through the vineyards. 6/Foot Artillery R 13 had to shift position to avoid counter-battery fire.

LIR 1 conducted a standing firefight the entire afternoon. 6/Foot Artillery R 13 succeeded in flushing enemy infantry out of their positions on Hill 308 and the vineyards on the Ingersheim–Bennweier road, to be shot down by the *Landwehr* men. Towards evening, the French Alpine infantry at Sigolsheim (off map, 5km north of Colmar), which until now had been inactive, threatened the open right flank; it was necessary to commit first 8/LIR 1, then 10/LIR 1, in this direction. The intensity of the French fire increased, and the French brought mountain guns up to Sigolsheim. This crossfire hit 6/LIR 1 hard, and it retreated to the meadows by the Fecht. The units farther to the left also began to withdraw, in particular because a hidden MG opened fire at 300m range. Only 10/LIR 1 and a platoon of 8/LIR 1 held the right, a few groups of 11/LIR 1 in the centre stood fast. The II/LIR 1 commander set up a rally position on the floodwall on the east side of the river, 500m north of the ford. In the twilight LIR 1 retreated from the battlefield.

The enemy only pursued with unaimed artillery fire into the vineyards and did little damage. On the other hand, the park wall and the west end of Logelbach were reduced to rubble; 5 and 6/LIR 2 were forced to withdraw, which initially did not proceed in good order, particularly since there was only one narrow gate to pass through, and two weapons from 2 *Ersatz*/MGK XV AK were lost, though the enemy infantry did not pursue. LIR 1 reorganised on the Exerzierplatz (training area), as did LIR 2 and 5 and 6/LIR 123 in Colmar, and then withdrew behind the Ill River.

The mission given to the two *Landwehr* regiments would have been difficult for active army units to execute: in combat formation, cross an extensive, flat area of vineyards that restricted visibility and provided all manner of surprises and obstacles. The vines were ripe and fully grown, and supported by horizontal knee- and chest-high wires, an entanglement that the troops could only overcome with great difficulty, particularly since they had no wire cutters. On the other side of the vineyards the enemy waited invisible and in a dominating position: the *Landwehr* men even had the sun in their eyes. Bad French marksmanship worked against the *Landwehr* men: most of the French fire was too high, but hit troops coming up in the rear, leading to undirected return fire, and the front-line troops to think they were being fired on from the rear. In spite of all this, the *Landwehr* men bravely answered (in all but a few exceptions) with aimed fire. The men were on their own, for the vineyards isolated them and cut off the men from their leaders. When they could get at the enemy, as on the bridge south-east of Ingersheim, he was beaten. The troops and leaders were determined and had high morale; all that was lacking was equipment and training. The brigade was completely unsupported on both the left and right, and there was only one heavy howitzer battery for artillery support. When the enemy attacked, the brigade withdrew; but they fulfilled their mission, which was to prevent the enemy from marching north. Each regiment lost 150–200 men; the dead and many wounded remained in the vineyards.

The French units were probably the leftmost detachment of the *armée d'Alsace*, 81 Bde reinforced by the Alpine Bn 13 and 30. The *armée d'Alsace* had been made cautious by the defeat of the First and Second Armies and had no interest in advancing in the Rhine Valley.

Officially, on 22 August, as the Battle in Lorraine and the middle Vosges ended, the Battle of Nancy–Épinal began. In fact, there was no sharp difference and one flowed into the other. Nevertheless, on 22 August the Sixth and Seventh Armies more than accomplished their initial mission: the German main attack, the centre and right-wing armies had begun their advance on 18 August, undisturbed by the French forces between Toul and Belfort, which had not only been fixed in place but been defeated, unable either to attack north of Metz or move forces to Belgium.

OHL had expected a more far-reaching result – a decisive envelopment of the French between Metz and the Saar – but not a syllable of this was mentioned or even hinted at in the deployment orders given to Crown Prince Rupprecht. The principal, indeed only, mission was to protect the left flank of the army and fix the French forces in place. In case of attack by a superior enemy, he was to withdraw; when this appeared to be the case on 16 August, Rupprecht did so. But a plan to lure the French into a trap between Metz and the Saar to prepare a decisive battle seemed to him to be risky and uncertain. On the same day this idea was stillborn; the French advance was so careful and hesitant that it appeared very unlikely that he would take the badly concealed bait. If the Sixth and Seventh Armies continued to withdraw, there was nothing to prevent French forces from being transferred to Belgium; what sort of reproaches would have been made against Rupprecht then! That a LNO from OHL had verbally made a recommendation to draw the French into a trap did not relieve Rupprecht of the responsibilities stated in his written orders. Had OHL wished, it could have made its intent clear with an express order; it did not do so, nor did it prohibit Rupprecht from his stated intent of immediately going over to the attack. Rupprecht chose the path that would surely lead to the accomplishment of his mission and avoided the one that might have brought greater glory, but only if the enemy made a serious mistake.

The Bavarian Army had preformed brilliantly in its baptism of fire and, with whirlwind force, had blown the enemy from the field of battle. On the evening of 22 August it saw the way before it open, and it was eager to accomplish further great deeds.

4

The Battle at Nancy–Épinal, 23 August – 14 September

On 22 August the commander of the French Second Army decided to withdraw to the fortified heights east of Nancy and the corner formed by the Meurthe, Mortagne and Moselle south of the city; he would accept battle there and, in the best case, go over to the attack. The troops occupied this position on 23 August, south to north: 2 and 10 Cavalry Divs east of Charmes, XVI Corps and 74 RD east of Bayon, then XV Corps and 64 RD, XX Corps at St Nicholas du Port (which would, with 70 RD, reinforced by a brigade from IX Corps, conduct the attack), while 59 and 68 RD and the remaining two brigades of IX Corps would hold the high ground east of Nancy.

Joffre agreed with this decision. He ordered First Army to maintain its position on the Vosges with the right wing while echeloning its left flank so that it could attack the German troops pursuing the Second Army on the left flank. On the right, XIV Corps, reinforced by 71 RD and half of 58 RD, would hold the Vosges in a bow east of St Dié; XXI AK, reinforced by 2 Colonial Bde east of Raon l'Étape; XIII Corps north of Rambervillers with VIII Corps on its left: the last three corps would be oriented north-west. 6 Cavalry Div. would close the gap with Second Army. These positions were assumed almost undisturbed on 23 August. The *armée d'Alsace* was to release 44 ID and twelve Alpine Groups (Alpine battalions reinforced with artillery batteries) to Second Army: they would move to the east of Épinal.

On 23 August Joffre ordered the *armée d'Alsace* to cover the right flank of First Army by occupying a position on the crest of the Vosges, while standing fast in the Upper Alsace. VII Corps (minus 41 ID, which was to withdraw to Münster) was to assemble for redeployment north by rail. The *armée d'Alsace* began movement north on the night of 24/25 August; 68 RD was withdrawn to replace 41 ID in VII Corps. Joffre no longer had any interest in the Upper Alsace and, on 25 August, decided to dissolve the *armée d'Alsace*.

On 23 August the French retreat in Lorraine ended; the French were determined to show the enemy their teeth. If the Germans continued their pursuit, a serious battle was unavoidable. Crown Prince Rupprecht recognised that, on 22 August, the time had come to decide whether to break off the pursuit or attack the enemy in front of the Nancy–Épinal fortress line. II b. AK and XXI AK had almost reached the Meurthe, which Rupprecht regarded as the limit of advance for the Lorraine offensive. Sixth and Seventh Armies had fulfilled their mission: they had given the attacking French such a sound thrashing that the German right wing need not be concerned for its left flank, while the second element of the mission – fix strong French forces in Lorraine – had also been accomplished. In Belgium, Brussels had fallen, the attack on the Sambre–Meuse had begun and an enormous meeting engagement was being fought in the Ardennes: fixing French forces in Lorraine was no longer necessary and, because of the Nancy–Épinal fortress line, not even possible.

Rupprecht and his chief of staff, Krafft, decided to continue the pursuit as far as the Meurthe and transfer a large part of the German forces in Lorraine by rail to Belgium,[48] or by foot march through Metz to the left wing of the Fifth Army, as provided in the deployment orders. The situation on the evening of 22 August favoured breaking contact with the enemy; the Sixth Army and the right wing of the Seventh Army had complete freedom of movement. Contact with the enemy had been lost in places, which was an error, but in the present circumstances could perhaps be seen as an advantage. In particular, I b. RK was available since its forward movement was blocked by Manonviller.

Rupprecht had been waiting since 21 August for such orders from OHL, but when none arrived by noon on 22 August, Krafft called the OHL operations officer, Lieutenant Colonel Tappen, and let him know he expected the order to march through Metz. Tappen relayed Moltke's decision that the Sixth and Seventh Armies' next mission was to pursue in the direction of Épinal, in order to cut off the French forces in the Vosges.

Until now, the concept of Schlieffen's plan of operations had not been completely lost. It would have been possible to rescue it at the last moment through redeployment of strong elements of the Sixth and Seventh Armies. However, this decision by OHL pronounced its death sentence irrevocably.

Crown Prince Rupprecht could not comprehend this inconsistency and, perhaps having a presentment of the disaster to come, called personally at 2115hrs to demand a formal order from OHL, which was given first telephonically and then in writing. Seventh Army thought that XIV RK in the mountains was facing two full corps, an estimate that OHL accepted. The thought of cutting off such a strong force was tempting. The Seventh Army commander, Heeringen, recommended that I b. AK, XIV and XV AK attack directly south to Badonviller. OHL also ordered Rupprecht to adequately protect the right flank against any threat from Nancy.

Continuation of the Pursuit, 23–26 August

23 August

At 2230hrs on 22 August Rupprecht issued the order for the following day. The first mission was to reach the Meurthe all along the line. Seventh Army was a day's march away; Sixth Army was already there and would initially remain in place; it occasionally took French artillery fire and conducted local reconnaissance. Manonviller, between Sixth and Seventh Armies, was to be enveloped; the Sixth Army chief of engineers was tasked with immediately reducing the fortress. I b. RK would provide a brigade for the siege, while the rest of the corps would remain in the bivouac areas, as would the cavalry divisions, which were still in need of rest.

Seventh Army directed I b. AK, XIV and XV AK to attack on a very narrow 6km front towards Badonviller. That morning the enemy evacuated the south bank of the Vezouse at Blâmont and Cirey; air reconnaissance reported masses of French marching through Baccarat and St Dié towards Épinal. On the other hand, XIV RK in the Vosges still thought it was opposed by two corps.

Montigny (map 10)

The Seventh Army order for I b. AK to march at 0800hrs through Blâmont to the Meurthe was only issued only at 0350hrs and arrived at 0515hrs; in the resulting confusion and haste the corps was not able to march until 1000hrs, and even then not in good order. Almost immediately, *Chevauleger* R 4 took fire as it left the Bois le Comte, deployed the point element, but then pulled back to give the infantry a free field of fire and to screen the division right flank. I/IR 12 occupied the treeline under fire from infantry on Hill 318, north of Montigny, which was covered in hedges and bushes. 4/IR 12 straddled the road, with 2 and 3/IR 12 to the left, while 1/IR 12 was sweeping the Bois de Banal to the right rear. The advance guard commander received a report that enemy columns were marching on the road from Montigny to the north-west and decided to attack. II/IR 15 moved west of the Montigny road through the Bois le Comte, but was slowed by thick underbrush and enemy artillery fire, which caused serious casualties, but the southern treeline was reached in good order and 8, 6 and 5/IR 15 lengthened the

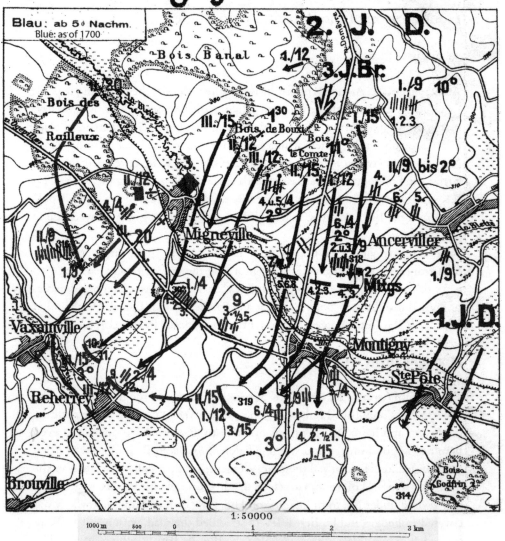

10. Montigny 23.8.– I. b. A K.–

Blatt 2 Ruckseite

1:50000

right flank of I/IR 12, while 7/IR 15 remained in reserve. The MGK also moved by platoons to the southern treeline. It was not possible to find the positions of the enemy artillery firing into the Bois le Comte to put counter-battery fire on it. Nevertheless, the attack of II/IR 15 and I/IR 12 gained momentum, supported by I/FAR 9 on the high ground 1.5km north-west of Ancerviller. The commander of 2 ID wanted to support the attack with the entire 2 FA Bde, but so long as the infantry occupied the treeline, there were no firing positions

At around 1200hrs the French were driven from Hill 318. II/FAR 9 swung east of the woods and set up in an open position north-east of Ancerviller, while I/FAR 9 bounded forward under heavy artillery fire, 1/FAR 9 to the south of Ancerviller, and 2 and 3/FAR 9 onto Hill 318. The French batteries could still not be located. I/IR 15 came up on the left of I/IR 12 (3 and 4/IR 12 in the first line, 2/IR 12 following), while 1/IR 15 guarded I/FAR 9. The IR 15 mission was to take the high ground south of Montigny.

The capture of Hill 318 got the attack moving. In spite of the continued French artillery fire, IR 15 could not be stopped. The regiment conducted a short firefight with French infantry in Montigny, then stormed down Hill 318, covered by the fire of FAR 9. The MGK on the south treeline of the Bois le Comte loaded its guns back onto the vehicles and, followed by French artillery fire, trotted and galloped to the valley of the Blette stream, dismounted the guns and carried them at the run up the road to Montigny until they could see the town. For the next half an hour they were able to place effective fire on French troops withdrawing from the town. The Bavarian infantry pushed through Montigny and up the slope to the south. About 1km from the town they reached open ground and took French artillery fire, as well as small arms fire from trenches on Hill 314, south of St Pôle, 1.2km to the front. I/IR 15 was under fire on the left flank, due south of Montigny, with 4, 2 and half of 1/IR 15, while 3/IR 15 was 800m to the west. The MGK bounded forward by platoons under fire from hedge to hedge and joined the firing line east of the road, where they found concealment but not cover against enemy fire. To the west, I/IR 15 and I/IR 12 gained the high ground, while II/IR 15 turned towards enemy infantry at Reherrey.

Since the advance guard alone was not strong enough, control over all four brigade units in reserve was returned to the brigade commander at 1135hrs. When it was reported that the French troops withdrawing to the north-west had turned around, he sent IR 12 (minus I/IR 12, but with III/IR 15 attached) through the Bois de Bouxi to take the high ground west of Montigny. Moving through the thick undergrowth in the Bois de Bouxi considerably delayed IR 12. The MG vehicles sank to the axles in mud, the horses to their bellies, so that the guns had to be off-loaded and carried for the rest of the day, an exhausting process for the crews. By 1400hrs the regiment (left to right: III/IR 12, II/IR 12, III/IR 15) deployed on the southern treeline and attacked the high ground 1.5km north-west of Montigny.

They were received by artillery fire, which followed them the entire way forward, but could not stop their aggressive advance. The regimental commander had intended to advance only as far as Mignéville, but III/IR 12 continued the attack across the Ogéviller road and then took small arms fire from an enemy position on the high ground north of Reherrey. 9 and 12/IR 12 were deployed in this direction and, finally able to see the enemy, began the assault 800m from the position and quickly took it, with III/IR 15 coming up on the right. II/IR 12 and the MGK were halted in the wood west of Mignéville.

It was now 1500hrs and the pressure on the troops south and south-west of Montigny increased: some were out of ammunition. Casualties mounted, morale dropped and the impression of being cut off was reinforced by enemy artillery fire falling in Montigny. Artillery support was absolutely necessary. Since 1100hrs II/FAR 4 had been trying without success to find a way through or east of the Bois le Comte, but the ground was too swampy. Finally, it moved straight through enemy fire on the main road and, between 1300hrs and 1400hrs, unlimbered with 4 and 5/FAR 4 south-west of the woods, and 6/FAR 4 north of Hill 318, but it still was not possible to directly support IR 15 or to locate the French artillery. The commanders of I b. AK and 2 ID ordered 2 FA Bde to move south of the Blette stream, which some units had already done on their own initiative, in particular FAR 9, whose commander had moved early through Montigny. The 2 and 4 FA Bde commanders issued sometimes contradictory orders that led to much to-and-fro movement, but eventually batteries and staffs appeared in and around Montigny, where enemy artillery fire caused casualties and restricted movement. French soldiers hidden in the houses and supported by the inhabitants ambushed the German troops, but were not able to stop them, and elements of IR 12 and IR 15 cleaned them out. At 1600hrs 6/FAR 4 deployed on the south end of Montigny and moved forward, but the slope was so steep that the horses could only go at a walk. Once on the high ground they were hit by fire of all kinds, and some of the teams bolted and took off back downhill, so that only two guns could be unlimbered close behind I/IR 15. At this moment the enemy attacked in masses and were blasted back by the fire of these two guns. The infantry brought shells forward from immobilised caissons, as well as a third gun. At 1620hrs 2/FAR 9 approached from Montigny at a gallop; the battery commander was immediately wounded, but the senior lieutenant brought the guns into battery behind MGK/IR 15. It soon shot off the basic load of ammunition, but with the result that the enemy infantry no longer dared expose their heads from cover. 3/FAR 9 and a platoon of 5/FAR 9 set up along the road 1km west of Montigny. 5/FAR 4 occupied a covered position immediately east of Montigny, while 4/FAR 4 answered a call for help from the infantry and unlimbered in front of the south-west corner of Mignéville. I/FAR 4 was delayed by farmer's barbed-wire fences, but found a concealed position on the road south of Mignéville. These four FAR 4 batteries were able to silence the

French artillery at Brouville. II/FAR 9 was forced off the road north of Montigny and it occupied a position behind Hill 318. The appearance of the Bavarian artillery on the high ground south of Montigny reduced both the rate of French artillery fire as well as its accuracy; the French infantry abandoned its trenches south of Montigny, and the combat died away.

During the fight the 2 ID commander gradually moved 3 Bde to the south edge of the Bois le Comte, then to Mignéville. At 1530hrs IR 20 was ordered to extend the corps right by occupying the high ground north of Vaxainville. With III/IR 20 on the left, I/IR 20 on the right, and the MGK following, the regiment crossed the low ground east of Mignéville under heavy artillery fire, but did not encounter enemy infantry. II/IR 20, which had been detached to the west side of the Bois de Banal, was brought back. II/FAR 9 (plus 1/FAR 9) moved to Hill 316 north of Vaxainville to support. That evening IR 20 reached Vaxainville, Reherrey and Brouville. Apparently the enemy troops, who were coming from the east, wanted to push past I b. AK. The retreating French 2 Colonial Bde, attached to XXI Corps, had been forced by 2 ID to fight.

1 ID, marching south from Blâmont, did not encounter serious resistance. On the La Blette stream, 8km south of Blâmont, *Chevauleger* R 8 discovered an enemy position south of St Pôle. The advance guard stopped at Ancerviller to allow the entire artillery to deploy near Ancerviller. During the afternoon, as enemy artillery appeared south of St Pôle, and stronger enemy resistance appeared likely, 1 Bde deployed alongside the advance guard (Household IR on the right, IR 1 on the left) under harassing fire from the French guns. The German artillery began preparatory firing against French trenches and likely gun positions, taking effective return fire in the left flank. Since a serious fight at Montigny had begun, the corps commander moved 2 Bde, II/FAR 7 and his HQ to the north edge of the Bois le Comte.

1 Bde began the attack on the high ground south of St Pôle at 1600hrs. The Household IR took uncomfortable but ineffective artillery fire, but IR 1 also received small arms fire from the Bois Godfrin, 800m south-east of St Pôle, which was taken after a sharp fight. IR 1 also took casualties from enemy artillery 4km to the south-east. FAR 1 and II/FAR 7 moved onto the high ground the infantry had won and conducted pursuit fire on the withdrawing enemy. Some of the troops of 1 ID were pulled back to Ancerviller, but their march routes conflicted with those of XIV AK and they were only able to bivouac late into the night.

According to reports, the French were loading troops onto trains at Raon l'Étape, Baccarat and Rambervillers. In order to disrupt this rail movement, I b. AK sent cavalry patrols to destroy the rail lines that night. Two lieutenants and thirty troopers from *Chevauleger* R 4 succeeded in reaching the Meurthe Valley, about 9km west of Reherrey, and blow up the rail line. II/Foot Artillery

1 (sFH), south-west of Ancerviller, shelled the rail stations near Baccarat at long range.

Aviation Sec. 1 returned to the airfield that it had been forced to abandon on 15 August and found 2,500l of aviation fuel that it had been forced to leave behind. Masses of French dead and abandoned equipment lay everywhere.

Since enemy resistance at Montigny and St Pôle prevented I b. AK from reaching the Meurthe in order to shift right, XIV AK was squeezed out of the front line. The XV AK objective was Raon l'Étape, but French rearguards contested every step of the advance and, by evening, the advance guards had only reached Badonviller.

24 August (map f)

Crown Prince Rupprecht never had any great hopes for the success of the pursuit towards Épinal and warned the OHL in this sense. The troops had already accomplished too much to have the strength left for a long-distance pursuit. The cavalry divisions were exhausted and, in any case, did not have the firepower to break the French rearguards. The terrain in Lorraine and the fortifications at Épinal, Nancy and Manonviller further restricted manoeuvre. On 24 August Rupprecht therefore intended that the left wing of Sixth Army, II b. AK and XXI AK, which were the only forces available for the pursuit, would advance south over the Meurthe, but even then only a short distance, at most to the Bayon–Baccarat road.

I b. RK at Elfringen was to be prepared to march south to Lunéville to reinforce III b. AK, but was dependent on the situation at Manonviller, where 1 and 2 Res. Bde were already committed: I b. RK was reduced to 5 RD and the *Landwehr* Div. The 7 KD objective was Rambervillers; HKK 3 had been broken up and the HQ retired to Arracourt.

Nevertheless, on the evening of 23 August OHL demanded ruthless pursuit. It assumed that there were still 100,000–120,000 French troops in the Vosges and was afraid that they would get away. At the same time, the first great battles in Belgium had resulted in complete German victories, and OHL calculated that an immediate French withdrawal in Lorraine would leave an open road for rapid pursuit by Sixth and Seventh Armies.

Rupprecht's order of 23 August was therefore changed to conform to OHL's intentions. The objective for II b. AK and XXI AK was pushed another 10km south to the Charmes–Rambervillers road. The Seventh Army objective was the Rambervillers–St Dié road. The intent was clearly to conduct a deep penetration to block the French withdrawal to Épinal and push them to the south-east.

This would extend the exposed Sixth Army right flank even further and require a continual increase in forces to defend it. North of the Meurthe, 10 ED was at Delm; to its left was 4 ED and then 8 ED, with III b. AK and b. KD in reserve, all under the commander of III b. AK. Any counter-attack here had to avoid the artillery of the French field fortifications east of Nancy: where these were located, the strength and range of the artillery was unknown. South of the Meurthe the defence was the responsibility of II b. AK (reinforced by 8 KD). Sixth Army offensive combat power and room for manoeuvre were considerably reduced.

At 1200hrs the III b. AK commander was informed that 4 ID (II b. AK) was heavily engaged south-west of Lunéville. Air reconnaissance reported an enemy corps on the right flank of 4 ID. The III b. AK commander received telephonic permission from Sixth Army to move his corps south towards Lunéville, to assist 4 ID, which he ordered at 1650hrs. 8 ED was also ordered to shift south to the high ground 3km north of Lunéville.

At 1900hrs 8 ED was beginning its move when it was attacked. The division ordered the movement halted, which was later approved by the commanders of the *Ersatz* Corps and III b. AK. In the dark it was not entirely possible to turn the troops around; there was considerable friction and confusion in 8 ED and a gap appeared with 4 ED on the right. Enemy troops appeared in front of the 4 ED left flank, but the division attacked and chased them off.

6 ID had difficulty forming march column because the road was packed with the supply units of II b. AK and XXI AK. Crossing the Selle on a temporary bridge cost time; it was soon dark and movement became stop-and-go over hill and dale. The troops reached their bivouacs at Arracourt and Einville (north of Lunéville) at and after midnight: I and II/IR 11 and 3/FAR 8 arrived at 0500hrs after a 40km forced march. However, the march could not dampen the troops' enthusiasm on crossing the border.

The order to march to Lunéville caught some 5 ID units on the way to Château Salins; it was not easy to turn them around. Again, many units did not reach their objectives until after midnight. I/IR 7, which was to provide security at Hoéville (14km north-west of Lunéville), was blocked by roads full of 8 ED units and did not arrive until 0430hrs. The enemy was reported in a fortified position 8–10km east of Nancy; 5 ID had closed to within artillery range.

Bavarian Aviation Sec. 3 noted in its war diary that its aircraft were too heavy and were therefore continually being chased by French aircraft.

II b. AK Attack Over the Meurthe: Blainville–Remenoville (map 11)

II b. AK HQ issued its order for 24 August at 2310hrs on 23 August. Movement was to begin early, with 3 ID holding the crossing at Blaineville and clearing the road for 4 ID by 0500hrs. The lead elements of the main body were to be at Mont by 0700hrs and then march Lamath already issued Franconville–Moriviller to Rozelieures. 4 ID was to march through Maixe, the advance guard reaching Blainville at 0800hrs and then continuing the march 6km to the south, with the mission of covering the army right flank.

At 0130hrs on 24 August, a Sixth Army message (sent 2200hrs on 23 August) arrived at II b. AK HQ, expressing concern that the enemy forces in the Vosges might succeed in withdrawing. In accordance with orders from OHL, the corps was to move as soon as possible with all troops capable of marching and reach the objective (Charmes–Rambervillers road) by 1200hrs. It was, however, too late to change the orders that had already been issued.

The commander of 3 ID assigned 5 Bde the mission of taking the crossings at Blainville and Mont, and attached a cavalry platoon, FAR 12, 1 and 3/Eng. Bn 2 and Division Bridge Train 3. In the morning fog II/IR 23 crossed the Meurthe on the completely undamaged bridge next to the rail line, took the weakly defended town after a short fight, in which the inhabitants were apparently involved, and occupied the high ground south-west of the town. At 0700hrs IR 22 occupied the east side of Hill 276, south-west of Mont; its left flank encountered weak resistance from a French light infantry battalion. MGK/IR 23 and I/FAR 12 crossed next, with II/FAR 12 occupying I/FAR 12's position on Hill 251, north of Blaineville.

The order to continue the attack to Lamath–Franconville now reached the 3 ID commander. Since 5 Bde was completely deployed and would take too long to form marching column, he ordered the main body – IR 17, FAR 5 and IR 18 – to continue the march; IR 17 became the advance guard, while the rest of the troops merged into the column as best they could. I/FAR 12 moved by bounds to cover the march. When the advance guard reached Lamath at 1000hrs, a one-hour rest halt was called. *Chevauleger* R 3 screened the left flank at Lunéville–Hériménil.

Early on the morning of 24 August, I and III/IR 23 and 3/Eng. Bn 2 occupied an assembly area on the woodline opposite the destroyed Blaineville bridge. Since it had not been possible to construct a new crossing over the rapidly flowing river, at 0700hrs the troops climbed across on the partially collapsed bridge frame in the fog and occupied the hills south of Damelevières and Blaineville. Weak enemy resistance in Blainville was broken with the aid of 1/Eng. Bn 2 troops using hand grenades.

4 ID formed march column at 0500hrs, somewhat hindered by 3 ID supply units that had not cleared the road. *Chevauleger* R 5 (minus 2/*Chevauleger* R 5) rode in front of the advance guard, which consisted of IR 9, half of 2/*Chevauleger* 5, FAR 2, 2/Eng. Bn 2 and Division Bridge Train 4 under the 7 Bde commander. The main body followed with half of 2/*Chevauleger* 5, IR 5, 11 FA Bde and 5 Res. Bde. When it was learned that the Blaineville bridge was down, the engineers and bridge train were sent on ahead.

By 0900hrs all three engineer corps companies and Bridge Train 4, which had come forward at a trot, were assembled at Blainville. While one worked on improving the trafficability of the rail bridge at Damelevières, the rest built a pontoon bridge west of the destroyed road bridge at Blaineville. Bridge Train 3 arrived just in time to provide material assistance.

The advance guard of 4 ID soon arrived. The march through the Forêt de Vitrimont, in the humidity of a late-summer day, tired the troops. The division commander and *Chevauleger R 5* crossed at a ford west of the rail bridge: the cavalry moved forward to Bois de Clairlieu. IR 9 began to cross over the collapsed rail bridge – all vehicles and horses had to be left on the north bank. 2 FA Bde could not find firing positions, as they had all been occupied by 12 FA Bde.

IR 9 had hardly begun to climb across the bridge, one man behind the other, when enemy artillery fire from the west landed. Nevertheless, all three battalions crossed without serious casualties or loss of time, though some acrobatic climbing was necessary. Even the dismounted MGs were brought across. 3/Eng. Bn 2 brought some sections across on small boats.

The point element of the 3 ID advance guard, 4/IR 17, encountered weak resistance at 1200hrs south of the Bois de Broth and threw the French back into Franconville. Since an attack on the town required artillery, I/FAR 12 was brought forward. When the lead battery, 1/FAR 12, left the woods it was hit by MG fire at a range of 1km. The first team was shot down and blocked the road. It was possible to unlimber four guns at the spots where their teams had been mown down. The battery and section commanders and the adjutant manned a gun themselves and fired on the MG, which after a short time fell silent. Now several French batteries north of the Bois de Rouatant opened fire, but the exit from the woods had been cleared of bodies and shot-up vehicles, so that 2 and 3/FAR 12 could move forward and take positions on both sides of the road in front of 1/FAR 12. The enemy artillery was silenced and driven off. IR 17 had deployed with I/IR 17 astride the road, II/IR 17 right and III/IR 17 left, and quickly and easily gained ground, swept through Franconville at 1300hrs and occupied the high ground to the south. The French, apparently light infantry and dismounted cavalry, withdrew.

During the morning the II b. AK HQ moved forward to Mont. Reports, particularly from Aviation Sec. 2, showed that the heights east of Bayon were fortified and that strong French forces were assembled behind them on both sides of the Meuse. II b. AK would be taking a serious risk if it tried to march past such strong enemy forces; it was prudent to push the French to the west bank of the Meuse first. Therefore, at 1130hrs 3 ID was ordered to attack from Einvaux and Moriviller against the French position, while 4 ID defended between Blainville–Méhoncourt and provided a regiment as the corps reserve.

The pontoon bridge at Blainville was ready shortly before noon: the enemy artillery apparently had been waiting for this as, from this time until dark and at regular intervals, volleys of shells landed on the bridge and the roads leading to it. The bridge units assembled behind the road embankment between Blainville and the rail station were scattered. The engineer companies took casualties and those not needed on the bridge withdrew to the cover of the woods. One of the first shells destroyed a bridge element, but in spite of enemy fire the engineers soon had it repaired, and at 1200hrs 4 ID could begin crossing. By 1700hrs IR 5 crossed, generally running at double-time, intermixed with the guns of I/FAR 2 and II/FAR 11, which by 1500hrs took up position in a clearing in the woods south-west of Le Rendez-vous and attempted to suppress the enemy artillery fire. There were few casualties during the crossing, thanks to the cold-blooded calculations of the engineer officers, who sent units across during pauses in the artillery fire. The bridge itself was continually in motion and the engineers had to remain in place under fire to push loose floorboards back into position and cover them with gravel, taking many casualties.

By the early afternoon IR 9 had occupied Damelevières and the high ground to the east, supported by I/FAR 2 and FAR 11. RIR 5 assembled south of Blainville. Troops that had to occupy exposed positions suffered from the fire of enemy artillery, whose location was almost impossible to determine. Only a single French battery at the copse south-west of Barbonville could be discovered and successfully engaged.

On the basis of the corps order of 1130hrs, 4 ID gave 5 Res. Bde the mission of assigning one regiment to corps reserve while occupying the line Bois de Grimont–Méhoncourt, supported by II/FAR 2. The brigade was located on the trail from St Richard to Le Rendez-vous, with RIR 5 leading and RIR 8 following. They had to turn around and make their way through the combat trains, as the thick underbrush prohibited movement through the woods. III and half of II/RIR 5 lost contact and rejoined much later. At St Richard the movement continued cross-country, straight through the woods, to Mont. RIR 8 moved to the woods north of Lamath to become corps reserve. RIR 5 moved from Mont through the Bois de Vacquenat to reach the Lamath–Méhoncourt road. Enemy shells landing in the area, including tree-bursts, created some confusion and even panic, but the brigade staff, moving down the road, was able to stop the retreating companies and combat trains and turn them around. The corps commander gave an oral order for the brigade to stop at the rail line. The last elements of the brigade did not arrive until dark. I/RIR 5 established an outpost line in the woods west of the rail line; 3/RIR 5 was the corps HQ guard at Mont. II/FAR 2 also encountered blocked and wet paths in the Forêt de Vitrimont, and bivouacked on the east side of the Bois de Clairlieu. In the late afternoon *Chevauleger* R 5 conducted a reconnaissance-in-force at the gallop from Bois de Clairlieu, but was forced to turn back by artillery fire just short of Landécourt. 4/FAR 1 (15cm howitzer) went into position between Mont and Lamath.

At 1305hrs the commander of 3 ID received the corps order to occupy an assembly area at Einvaux–Moriviller. Since the enemy had been reported in that area (probably a security position), 3 ID ordered an attack at 1330hrs. In marching order south of Mont, IR 17, IR 22, IR 18 and IR 23 were instructed to move through Landécourt and Franconville and deploy to the south-west. This caused the brigades to be intermixed. The artillery had already occupied suitable firing positions. Around 1400hrs IR 17, with III/IR 22 following behind the left flank, approached Moriviller from the north-west, while to the north the rest of IR 22, with II/IR 23 and MGK/IR 23 to its right, moved through the thick underbrush of the Grand Bois and then into open country. IR 18 was probably on the Lamath–Franconville road north of the Bois de Rayeux, followed by I and III/IR 23 and I/Foot Artillery R 1 (minus 4/FAR 1).

At 1430hrs Major von Xylander from Sixth Army HQ arrived at 3 ID HQ with a report that the enemy at Einvaux–Moriviller was weak, but that French march columns were withdrawing towards Épinal and the Moselle, and was most emphatic that quick action might prevent their further movement and put the French in a dangerous situation. XXI AK reported serious resistance at Gerbéviller, but nevertheless intended to attack at Giriviller and Mattexey. The corps HQ supported the 3 ID commander's decision to continue the attack towards Essey-la-Côte.

Strong enemy forces could be hidden on the right flank behind the high ground between Einvaux and Moriviller, which was defended by only I and II/IR 22, II and MGK/IR 23 and I/FAR 12: three battalions and three batteries under the 5 Bde commander, joined later by II/IR 17. As soon as these troops left the cover of the Grand Bois, they took artillery fire in the flank and rear from the west and north-west, but encountered no serious resistance and reached the high ground north of Moriviller between 1800hrs and 1900hrs.

IR 17, which was already north-east of Moriviller, turned sharply left and reached Remenoville at 1800hrs, which was very weakly defended, then occupied the high ground north of Vennezey. III/IR 22, attached to IR 17, occupied the Bois du Haut du Mont. IR 18 came up. I and III/IR 23 moved along the north treeline of the Bois de Broth and then deployed and moved cross-country to the south. IR 23 then received a ridiculous message to the effect that 150,000 French could be captured if it moved quickly and dropped the packs, which could only be recovered late in the night, with considerable mix-ups and losses.

In position north of Franconville, II/FAR 5 took casualties from French artillery fire, which were especially severe in 5/FAR 5. By 1745hrs I/FAR 5 was on the road to Vennezey and reached the high ground south of Remenoville when it put French march columns leaving Essey to flight; it drew fire from French artillery that was apparently on the east slope of the Essey-la-Côte, causing heavy casualties in 2/FAR 5. French infantry was only seen at St Voigt. It was growing dark and the situation in the XXI AK sector at Gerbéviller was unclear, so I and III/IR 23 defended the division rear north-east of Remenoville and the continuation of the attack was postponed until the next day. *Chevauleger* R 3 had ridden west of Seranville, taken artillery fire, but had seen no French on the roads.

At noon in the XXI AK sector on 24 August, the enemy had engaged 31 ID at Gerbéviller and 42 ID at Moyen. The Germans were victorious, but the enemy had gained time. XXI AK had also received reports that pointed towards a general enemy withdrawal across the Moselle. 31 ID advanced as far as Mattexey, while 42 ID encountered an enemy position at Xaffévillers (8km south-east), which could not be attacked in the darkness. 7 KD, 8KD and 2 *Jäger* Bn followed XXI AK, taking occasional artillery fire. 2 *Jäger* marched 50km.

A gap appeared at Lunéville between III b. AK and II b. AK on the south side of the Meurthe, which at noon Sixth Army ordered I b. RK (with only 5 RD) to fill. 5 RD did not arrive until late at night, after a 30km march in the dust and heat, which, in spite of a long rest halt, caused many casualties. Along the road the signs of the recent combat and hasty French withdrawal were visible. Combat and field trains and munitions units of II b. AK and XXI AK passed through Lunéville in an unbroken stream. The *Landwehr* Div. conducted training and continued to police the battlefield of 20 August. At 1400hrs it began to march, reaching the area north of Gerden. Half of the 1 RD (1 Res. Bde) was attached to I b. AK, while 2 Res. Bde surrounded Fort Manonviller.

Seventh Army had given its corps the following objectives on 24 August: I b. AK north of Baccarat; XIV AK south of Baccarat; XV AK Raon l'Étape; XIV RK Senones.

I b. AK at Baccarat (map 12)

The mission for I b. AK on 24 August was to seize the crossings over the Meurthe at Azerailles and Baccarat, and then turn south towards Rambervillers. 2 ID on the corps right marched from Hablainville to Azerailles, followed by 1 RD (1 Res. Bde), with 1 ID on the left from Reherrey to Baccarat.

The army order did not arrive until 0100hrs. Montigny had to be kept free until 0630hrs to allow XIV AK to march through, and assembling the troops, which involved a shift to the right and changing the march order, took considerable time: I b. AK could not begin movement until 0900hrs.

Chevauleger R 4 was forced to turn west, 2km south-west of Hablainville, by artillery fire. Between 0900hrs and 1000hrs the advance guard, IR 20, covered by 1 and 2/FAR 4, drove weak groups of enemy infantry from the Hauts Bois and the high ground west of Brouville. As it descended into the Meurthe Valley

12. Baccarat 24.8. — I. b. A. K. —

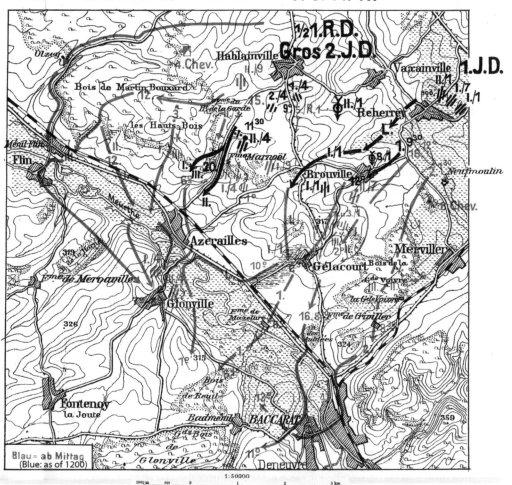

Blau = ab Mittag
(Blue: as of 1200)

1:50000

at Ferme Marnoël, it came under fire from enemy artillery apparently located south-east of Glonville. FAR 4 displaced forward to Marnoël and opened fire on Azerailles and trenches on the south side of the Meurthe; it also took artillery and small arms fire from nearby copses and from the Hauts Bois. 2/FAR 4, which unlimbered in the open, and 3/FAR 4 took heavy losses. The division main body closed up on Hablainville. I/FAR 9 set up on the high ground 1km west of Brouville and took heavy artillery fire. Nevertheless, 1/FAR 9 was able to shoot up an enemy battery near Glonville. II/FAR 9 set up 1km west of Hablainville. 2/Eng. Bn 1 and Division Bridge Train 2 were brought forward to Marnoël and prepared for an assault crossing of the Meurthe.

To cover the 1 ID advance, I/FAR 1 set up east of Reherrey, with II/FAR 1 and I/FAR 7 to the north. Scouting ahead, east of Brouville, *Chevauleger* R 8 had to manoeuvre to avoid artillery fire. The advance guard, IR 1, accompanied by 1/Eng. Bn 1, deployed south of Reherrey at 0900hrs and had taken Brouville by 1000hrs. I/FAR 1 then displaced to a position west of Brouville, with II/Foot Artillery 7 (sFH) to the north.

In the meantime, XIV AK reported that it had made contact at Merviller (5km north-east of Baccarat). At 1000hrs XV AK reported that it had to give up Baccarat.

Since the enemy showed no signs of leaving his trenches on the high ground 1.2km south-west of Brouville, the commander of 1 Bde deployed the Household IR (minus III/Household) from Reherrey through the low ground north of Brouville, behind IR 1, while 2 Bde occupied an attack position between Reherrey and Neufmoulin: IR 16 on the right and IR 2 on the left.

IR 1 did not wait for the general attack. Around noon III/IR 1 advanced towards the enemy trenches north-east of Gélacourt, supported by artillery fire and the MGK, and followed by II/IR 1 and 1/Eng. Bn 1. 9/IR 1 and the MGK began the firefight, joined by 10/IR 1 on the left and 12/IR 1 on the right, and the battalion advanced steadily. 11/IR 1 guarded the right flank and 6/IR 1 also came forward to help. 12/IR 1 gained the enemy flank, the trench was taken and, after a short pause, the attack continued towards Gélacourt. By this time the battalion had taken significant casualties, including the III/IR 1 standard bearer, who was killed. At 1400hrs III/IR 1 broke into Gélacourt and drove the French out, some of whom had been preparing lunch, which the Bavarians did not let go to waste. II/Foot Artillery 1 (sFH) (minus 8/Foot Artillery 1) had supported the attack and engaged a French battery east of Ferme de Griviller, forcing the French to abandon three guns and their caissons, which were captured that evening. I/IR 1, following the Household IR, crossed the high ground north-west of Gélacourt and moved quickly through French light and heavy (10cm cannon) artillery fire, taking some casualties. They were stopped by a knee-deep marsh in the low ground west of the town. The enemy had disappeared.

2 Bde attacked from south-east of Reherrey with IR 16 at noon and IR 2 at 1300hrs. IR 16 deployed III and II/IR 16 in the first line, I/IR 16 behind the left flank, and took fire from invisible infantry and MG in the Bois de la Grande Voivre and the woods on the north bank of the Meurthe. A standing firefight developed, but was later broken by the fire of the German artillery. 3/FAR 1 displaced forward at the gallop at 1510hrs to the high ground immediately north-east of Gélacourt and put a French battery on the Grande Voivre to flight. Shortly thereafter, 6 and 7/FAR 7 unlimbered in the IR 16 skirmisher line, the MGK opened fire from the III/IR 16 sector and 3/IR 16 was committed on the left against the enemy flank. The enemy fled at 1600hrs. The advance was halted by higher HQ at the Gélacourt–Baccarat road. IR 2 had advanced with III and II/IR 2 in front (I/IR 2 was division reserve) and, by 1600hrs, had passed through the Bois de la Grande Voivre. On the far left flank, 6/IR 2 attacked the south-west side of Merviller to assist the XIV AK.

During the course of the morning the I b. AK HQ, on the high ground 1km north-east of Vaxainville, had gained the impression that the enemy had strongly occupied the south side of the Meurthe and, at 1145hrs, ordered the corps to occupy attack positions between the Haut Bois and the Bois de la Grande Voivre. 1 RD moved to occupy the woods at Olzey, 2km north of Flin.

Therefore, during the afternoon, 2 ID deployed II/FAR 9, 6/FAR 4 and 3 Bde west of the Hablainville–Azerailles road on the south side of Les Hauts Bois, with IR 3 on the right and IR 20 on the left. From 4 Bde, IR 15 remained in Hablainville while IR 12 moved through the Bois de Martin Bouxard at 1500hrs with the mission of supporting the 3 Bde attack from the treelines north-east of Flin. III/IR 12 in the lead, found the Meurthe bridge at Flin undamaged, crossed immediately and occupied the high ground north-west of Glonville at 1900hrs. The enemy had disappeared. This was also reported by 3 Bde, which was not given permission to take independent action. Only at 1500hrs did the corps HQ authorise the attack at 1600hrs. 3 Bde took Azerailles without a shot fired and crossed the Meurthe over the undamaged bridges. Between 1900hrs and 2000hrs, IR 3, 12 and 20 entered Glonville. 3/IR 20, which had moved to Flin that morning as flank guard, crossed the Meurthe on its own initiative and occupied the Ferme de Mervaville by 1300hrs; it then advanced to the high ground north of Fontenoy and took a withdrawing French company and battery under fire. 2/Eng. Bn 1 and Division Bridge Train 2 built a pontoon bridge over the Meurthe north-west of Azerailles to assist the 3 ID crossing. The Meurthe had been crossed with unexpected ease, although the troops were now massed in Glonville.

In front of 1 ID the enemy had also withdrawn to the south bank of the Meurthe, pursued by fire from German batteries at Gélacourt. At 1800hrs IR 1 crossed over a half-destroyed footbridge near the Ferme de Mazelure and had already reached the Bois de Reuil by 1845hrs. With the aid of III/Household,

1/Eng. Bn 1 began building a bridge here. Since Division Bridge Train 1 did not arrive until 2030hrs, the work was not completed until 0245hrs. The Household IR marched at 2200hrs and took the route through Azerailles and Glonville, filtered through the march columns and bivouac areas of 2 ID and arrived at the high ground north-west of Bois de Reuil at 0100hrs. At 1800hrs III/IR 2 searched through Baccarat, but found it empty of enemy troops. The mass of 2 Bde began the march at 2000hrs. IR 16 marched cross-country, sometimes single file, to cross the Meurthe on a temporary bridge south of the Bois des Aulnées, then through the north-west corner of Baccarat to bivouac on the high ground south-east of Badménil at 0100hrs. IR 2 moved through several traffic jams in Baccarat (a barricade on the bridge was removed by the inhabitants) to put up its tents north-west of the town. Pursuant to higher orders, the town was not occupied. 1 RD bivouacked between Flin and Ménil Flin. The morale of I b. AK on the evening of 24 August was high, due to the wonderful weather and the news of victories on other fronts.

Since I b. AK had curved to the west, XIV AK was able to move back into the front lines. In spite of considerable French resistance, it reached the Meurthe south of Baccarat. On 23 August XV AK had bivouacked in a deep column between Badonviller and Cirey. Even before the lead unit, 30 ID, positioned north of Badonviller, could begin movement it was attacked, which forced the outposts to withdraw. With the assistance of 39 ID, the initial position was regained. The ruins of Badonviller were again the scene of bloody street fighting, but XV AK was finally in control of the town by 1200hrs. The French withdrew, leaving two batteries in German hands. 30 ID conducted the pursuit as far as Raon l'Étape, while the mass of 39 ID and the Guard ED remained in their bivouac areas of the previous night between Badonviller and Cirey.

On 24 August II b. AK and XXI AK had crossed the Meurthe in the gap between the French First and Second Armies: the French 12 and 10 Cavalry Divs and Light Infantry Bn 2 had attempted to oppose II b. AK, while the French 6 Cavalry Div. engaged XXI AK. The commander of the French Second Army had come to the conclusion that it was time to attack the Germans in the right flank. Nevertheless, the order given at 1130hrs only provided for an attack by 11 ID of the French XX Corps from St Nicholas du Port to Serres, supported by 70 RD (plus a brigade of IX Corps) advancing from Lenoncourt (east of Nancy). The mass of the army would remain on the defensive. In the course of the day, elements of 11 ID and the entire French 39 ID were in position to penetrate into the gap between II b. AK and III b. AK and take the dominant terrain north-west of Lunéville. On the left flank the French 70 RD threatened the German 8 ED. On the right flank of the French Second Army, the French XV and XVI Corps had not budged and opposed the advance of II b. AK with artillery fire.

On the left flank of the French First Army, the French VIII Corps had moved on its own initiative to strike the German forces advancing against the French Second Army in the left flank, but its deep formation and concern over its own right flank delayed the march, so that the 15 ID had only reached St Boingt and Essey-la-Côte (map 11) by evening. II b. AK was faced to the east and south by forces three times as strong. The French XIII Corps, north of Rambervillers, was ready to either move left to support VIII Corps or right to defend the Meurthe below Baccarat. In the evening it was attacked by the German XXI AK, and by 42 ID in particular. On the morning of 24 August the French XXI Corps was near Baccarat. A mixed brigade from VIII Corps opposed I b. AK north of Baccarat, while the French 43 ID and part of the 13 ID engaged the German XIV and XV AK. Since the French 13 ID was forced by the right flank of the German XIV AK to withdraw to Raon l'Étape, at noon the commander of the French XXI Corps decided to withdraw 6–7km west of the Meurthe. The French First Army commander demanded that the Meurthe be held, along with the Col de St Marie and the Col du Bonhomme in the Vosges. The French 44 ID detrained at St Dié.

The End of the Pursuit: The Front Stabilises, 25 and 26 August

25 August

The French First and Second Army commanders decided to continue and expand the attack on 25 August. The First Army commander ordered 'Forward at any price!' The French VIII Corps, with 6 Cavalry Div. attached, was to attack Vennezey (bottom of map 11), and XIII Corps to advance on Domptail (9km east). XXI and XIV Corps were to attack on both sides of Raon l'Étape. The Second Army objective was the Wich–Lunéville road, as it was the main supply route of the German troops that had crossed the Meurthe. Second Army was deterred from making an all-out attack here by concern for the Nancy–Bayon position. Therefore only XX Corps, reinforced by two brigades of IX Corps and 70 RD, were to conduct the attack, while the troops at Nancy were to hold their position at all costs: 70 RD was to break off its attack rather than risk a defeat. South of Lunéville, only XVI Corps, reinforced by 29 ID from XV Corps, was to attack in support of VIII Corps. Only later that morning, as the battle expanded and intensified, was all of XV Corps committed. Since the Germans also planned to continue the attack, the opposing sides collided full-force.

The events of 24 August had not satisfied Crown Prince Rupprecht and justified his warning to OHL. The French troops withdrawing from the Vosges had not been cut off and French resistance was tough everywhere. Strong French forces were undoubtedly opposite the lengthening Sixth Army right flank.

OHL had asked if it were possible to send elements of III b. AK and 10 ED
through Metz to assist Fifth Army. Two days previously, nothing stood in the way
of moving the mass of Sixth Army in this direction, but now the exposed position
opposite Nancy required every man. Nevertheless, Rupprecht said that he was
ready to send 10 ED. In spite of all this, Rupprecht attempted to accomplish his
mission of attacking to the south. OHL no longer hoped to cut off the French in
the Vosges, but aimed at fixing French forces in Lorraine.

Rupprecht ordered XXI AK to advance on Rambervillers and to the west,
with II b. AK right of XXI and Seventh Army marching towards Épinal. The
right flank, from Delm, would be 75km long. 4 ID was added to the flank
guard force, opposite Bayon. I b. RK (actually only 5 RD) was army reserve at
Lunéville, with the *Landwehr* Division 7km to the north-west. 7 KD was attached
to Seventh Army, and 8 KD to XXI AK. The attack on Manonviller was to begin
on 25 August.

Hoéville—Maixe—Léomont (map 13)

Almost all of 8 ED had abandoned its position between Hoéville and Serres the
previous evening and now was in assembly areas prepared to retake it: 51 and 41
Ersatz Bde on Hill 288, east of the Bois St Libaire and at Serres; and 29 *Ersatz* Bde
scattered between Serres and Eineville. 10 ED assembled on the Sixth Army far
right flank to march to Fifth Army. The III b. AK commander issued telephonic
orders between 0130hrs and 0200hrs for the *Ersatz* Corps (4 and 8 ED) to hold
the sector from the Selle (off the map to the north) to the high ground at Hoéville
and Serres.

On the morning of 25 August the left flank of 4 ED (not displayed on map),
with 13 *Ersatz* Bde between Bois Morel and the Bois de Faulx, was attacked
from Erbéviller and to the south. When the enemy was completely engaged, the
brigade counter-attacked against his left flank and threw him back into the woods
west of Erbéviller. The French extended left to Champenoux, which brought
33 *Ersatz* Bde at Mazerulles into the fight. 9 *Ersatz* Bde, which now consisted of
only two battalions, had spent the night behind Hill 328, north of Hoéville.

The entire III b. AK was initially to move to Lunéville, but due to the retreat by
8 ED, 5 ID was ordered at the last minute to move its advance guard to Serres, and
the main body to Athienville by 0600hrs. 6 ID was to move the advance guard to
Anthelupt, and its main body to Deuxville—Vitrimont. The corps would thus be
able to assist II b. AK, on the south side of the Meurthe, or advance against the
right flank of a French attack on the *Ersatz* Corps.

In the course of the night, 5 ID had taken over the protection of the 8 ED
assembly areas. I/IR 14 was in Hoéville, with 1/IR 14 forward in the Bois de la

Fourasse. The battalion received reports of enemy movements at Réméréville, and at dawn was digging in on the edge of town, with a platoon of 3/IR 14 on the west side of the Bois St Libaire. III/IR 21 was 1km south-west of Serres on the road to Drouville and had 9/IR 21 in the Ferme St Libaire, and 11/IR 21 as security on the Drouville road at the north end of the Bois d'Einville. The main body of 5 ID moved out at 0500hrs to occupy the forward assembly area at Serres.

At 0530hrs broad French skirmisher lines moved from Réméréville against 1/IR 14, which withdrew, but the fire of I/IR 14 at Hoéville stopped the French at 800m range: they got no further than the east edge of the Bois de la Fourasse. In the IR 21 sector, the security companies, 9 and 11/IR 21, under attack by a brigade-sized force from Courbesseaux–Drouville at 0500hrs, were unable to withdraw and were reinforced by two platoons from both 10 and 12/IR 21. II/IR 14 occupied the high ground east of the Ferme St Libaire on the right of III/IR 21 at 0800hrs. The French maintained a respectable distance from the two Bavarian battalions – about 1km – and made no more than tentative attempts at attacking, so that a standing firefight developed. III/IR 14 and the attached MGK were instructed to engage in the firefight from the high ground south of Serres if possible.

The commander of 8 ED decided to counter-attack. 51 *Ersatz* Bde moved forward through the Bois St Libaire, and 41 *Ersatz* Bde into the open ground south of the wood. 29 *Ersatz* Bde was kept by III b. AK order at Valhey. The artillery deployed on the high ground around Serres and their fire probably helped IR 14 and 21.

At 0700hrs to the north of Hoéville, 9 *Ersatz* Bde extended the right flank of I/IR 14 and counter-attacked against the French forces approaching from Réméréville, entering the woods west of Hoéville and carrying 1/IR 14 with it. When the I/IR 14 commander received a report that II/IR 14 had also moved forward, he followed their example. Since I/IR 14 was spread out in a 900m-long defensive position, the attack broke up into company sized engagements. On the right flank, 2/IR 14, with two Prussian companies, advanced quickly north of the Bois de la Fourasse, in spite of flanking fire coming from the trees, and put the enemy to flight. Heavy shrapnel fire shook the company's morale, but due to the company commander's energy and determination, 2/IR 14 held its position. 1/IR 14 fought its way through the Bois de la Fourasse in unconnected small unit actions. 4/IR 14 advanced south of the wood. 3/IR 14, left of 4/IR 14, closed to within 400m of the French and had fixed bayonets for the assault when the French fled.

5 FA Bde arrived relatively late. Heavy enemy artillery fire after 0800hrs made the occupation of gun positions slow and difficult. It was rarely possible to find and engage the enemy batteries: the German guns did not have sufficient range. I/Foot Artillery 3 (sFH), which was under corps control, moved forward on its own initiative into position at Foucray la Haute at 0730hrs and engaged enemy

artillery south of Drouville, a dug-in position on Hill 285 north of the town, as well as advancing enemy infantry in the same area.

The III b. AK commander arrived on the high ground on the road halfway between Valhey and Serres at 0600hrs, and, half an hour later, ordered the 5 ID commander, who was at the road cut 1.5km north of Serres, to meet the enemy attack at the position of the advance guard, between Serres and Valhey. By 0730hrs there could be no doubt of the seriousness of the enemy attack, and the corps commander ordered 6 ID to attack with its right flank through Maixe to Drouville and envelop the enemy.

The commander of 5 ID ordered 9 Bde to defend between Valhey and Serres, and 10 Bde from Athienville to the road junction 6km to the south, with the exception of III/IR 19, which was attached to 8 ED. 10 Bde gradually moved to the area of Valhey. The corps HQ was moved to Einville to be closer to 6 ID.

The commander of 9 Bde moved IR 21 (minus III/IR 21) back to Serres, with I/IR 21 in the depression 400m north of the town, and II/IR 21 in the churchyard and later on the west side. The MGs were distributed by platoons in the skirmisher line at 0930hrs and effectively engaged the enemy, sometimes with flanking fire. *Jäger* Bn 2 moved to the left flank of III/IR 21 at 0930hrs and its fire drove the enemy infantry north of the Drouville road. 3/IR 21 had been sent to take an enemy battery reported west of the Bois d'Einville, but was only able to engage the battery's covering force, which was withdrawing.

Between 0900hrs and 1000hrs the battle was proceeding well. 8 ED had gained ground and, in conjunction with I/IR 14, had put the enemy infantry to flight. II/IR 14 reported that it intended to pursue, and the commander of IR 14 ordered III/IR 14 to support them. But the enemy heavy artillery gained accuracy and effectiveness, and the German artillery was unable to silence it. It is not surprising that, as of 1000hrs, 8 ED in the Bois St Libaire, which lacked unit cohesion, began to crumble. 9 *Ersatz* Bde, postioned on Hill 328 north of Hoéville, fled to the rear, intermixed with numerous wounded. I/IR 7, which was in an assembly area north of the hill, deployed and stopped the withdrawal. But the other two brigades of 4 ED retreated north to Sornéville, where they were relieved by 10 ED units. 10 ED had been moving to the railheads for transportation to Fifth Army when it received word of the difficulties 4 ED was experiencing. On his own initiative, the 10 ED commander marched his division in the direction of Mazerulles and Sornéville. By evening the lead elements of 10 ED had reached Moncel and 4 ED withdrew to Bezange-la-Grande and Kambrich.

To the west of Hoéville the retreat of the *Ersatz* troops pulled I/IR 14 with it. The heavy artillery fire had dispersed the battalion and caused eight officer and 200 enlisted casualties. The companies appear to have initially assembled on the north edge of the Bois St Libaire and withdrawn by bounds to Serres, but only found cover in folds in the terrain east of the town. Hearing a rumour of a general withdrawal, it moved to Château Salins, where it arrived at midnight.

On the south side of the Bois St Libaire, two platoons of 7/IR 14, on the right flank of II/IR 14, were pulled along by the withdrawal of 41 *Ersatz* Bde. At Athienville, 150 stragglers from all four 5 ID regiments assembled and reached Château Salins shortly before I/IR 14.

The mass of 8 ED withdrew towards Athienville and assembled near Arracourt, while 29 *Ersatz* Bde assembled at Bezange-la-Grande. The enemy did not pursue 4 and 8 ED. By noon the battle near Hoéville had died down, the town not occupied by either side.

The Bois St Libaire remained in German hands. At 0900hrs 51 *Ersatz* Bde, on the west side of the wood, began to waver under the French artillery fire. III/IR 19 was under the operational control of 51 *Ersatz* Bde and located north of Serres; the battalion commander threw his men into the fight. The commander of 10/IR 19 went forward, only accompanied by another officer, found a Prussian skirmisher line 300m in front of the south-west side of the wood and brought it forward, allowing the rest of the battalion to deploy. The arrival of III/IR 19 stabilised the situation, but the enemy artillery fire eventually forced III/IR 19 back into the woods. The commander of 10/IR 19, using 'drastic methods', kept thirty-five Prussians and Bavarians around him in the open ground, then attacked a French trench 600m to his front and captured three officers and fifty-six men.

South of the Bois St Libaire III/IR 21 and II/IR 14, with the exception of 7/IR 14, held their position in spite of the French artillery fire. III/IR 14 was hidden by high grain and took few casualties. The commander of 9 Bde refused to allow IR 14 to attack, which would have been pointless

In spite of the overwhelming French artillery fire and the defeat of 8 ED, the situation gave no cause for concern. The enemy had obviously given up any idea of advancing, and apparently intended to withdraw his infantry back under the protection of his artillery. But the effect of the heavy fire and the events at Hoéville led to the instant circulation of wild rumours, which caused panic. The importance of a tactical reverse was exaggerated. There was even a wild rumour of an attack by Russian cavalry squadrons. Some rear-echelon units fled at a trot or even gallop. Château Salins was prepared for defence. Order was re-established, but only very slowly.

Simultaneous with the 5 ID fight, 6 ID and the Bavarian KD and 5 RD were moving towards the high ground north-west of Lunéville. 5 RD and the cavalry were in their assembly areas by 0700hrs. By 0830hrs the horse artillery was in action, while French artillery searched the terrain occupied by the cavalry with area fire. *Uhlan* R 2 had dismounted, heavy shells landing near the lead horses spooked them and they took off for Lunéville and the Forêt de Vitrimont. 5 RD was also shelled by invisible French batteries. 9/IR 6, which was securing Maixe until 6 ID arrived, found itself faced by superior enemy forces which seemed to be preparing to attack. The advance of 6 ID was accompanied by the sound of combat at Hoéville and Serres. The commander of 6 ID decided to attack the French in the right flank. At 0800hrs the advance guard was north of Vitrimont. Since the heights at Flainval on the left flank of the line of march were strongly held by the enemy, the advance guard (IR 6) turned in that direction. 11 Bde, 2km south-east of Maixe, was ordered to attack from Maixe to Drouville, supported by 6 FA Brigade (minus II/FAR 8). IR 11 was division reserve. At 0810hrs the corps order of 0730hrs arrived, instructing the 6 ID commander to take the action that he had already ordered.

IR 6 kept the mass of the regiment under cover on the east (reverse) slope of a hill, with only MGs and skirmishers on the forward slope, supported by II/FAR 8, which set up behind IR 6 and engaged enemy artillery limbers west of the Bois de Crévic, then artillery OPs on the high ground west of Flainval. As of 0900hrs enemy artillery fire began to fall near the advance guard, without causing casualties, though *Chevauleger* R 2 and the division commander were forced to move.

IR 13 attacked towards Maixe and IR 11 towards Crévic. FAR 3 went into position south-west of Maixe and opened fire at 0815hrs against French artillery on Hill 316, north-west of Maixe, and on trenches and skirmishers visible on the south slope of Hill 316. Repeated enemy attempts to cross over the hill were stopped. The Bois de Crévic was also shelled. II/FAR 3 received unpleasant area fire into the left flank from light and heavy French batteries evidently located in the area of Flainval and the ridge south-east of the Varengeville–Haraucourt road; at times the section was forced to cease fire and take cover. Some of the limber teams of 5/FAR 3 bolted.

Between 0700hrs and 0730hrs I/FAR 8 was brought into a position south-east of Maixe to overwatch the advance of the division advance guard. At 0810hrs it limbered up to move behind FAR 3, at the crossroads south-east of Maixe, and came under fire from the French artillery on Hill 316, before occupying its firing position and engaging the French guns. At 0900hrs it moved north of Vitrimont, behind IR 6. It was then ordered to Hill 285, west of Deuxville, to support the 6 ID attack, but did not arrive until 1230hrs. I/FAR 8 got stuck in soft ground east of Deuxville.

At 0800hrs IR 13 began its advance on Maixe, with I/IR 13 north of the Lunéville road and II/IR 13 to the south, which took enemy artillery fire but reached the town, already held by 9/IR 6 and 9 and 11/IR 13, at 0900hrs. They occupied the north-west side of the town, facing Drouville, under artillery fire. 9 and 11/IR 13 withdrew to the south side of the canal. 10 and 12/IR 13 had been sent by 11 Bde to Crévic to hold the canal crossings, which they found destroyed, so the two companies marched back to Maixe. The IR 13 commander wanted to delay his attack on the steep Hill 316 until IR 10 had come up on his left. At 1000hrs he ordered I and II/IR 13 to advance only far enough to put fire on the upper part of the hill; however, when they left the town they immediately took rifle fire in the left flank from the ridge 1km north-east of Crévic. Elements of 3, 1, 2, 8, and 7/IR 13 swung west and, in conjunction with 9/IR 6, drove the French back to Crévic and the Bois de Crévic. Some pushed as far as Crévic, but were forced back by French artillery fire.

At 0800hrs IR 10 was given the objective of taking Crévic. III/IR 10 was made brigade reserve. II/IR 10 moved through Deuxville and deployed 6 and 8/IR 10 west of the town on both sides of the road to Crévic. 7/IR 10 followed behind the left flank; 5/IR 10 had lost contact with the battalion in Deuxville. As soon as the battalion crossed Hill 285 it took not only artillery fire, but MG and rifle fire from Flainval. 6, elements of 8 and, finally, elements of 7/IR 10 turned left against an enemy invisible in the fields of hops and the woods at the south-east corner of the town. They then began to receive MG and rifle fire on the right, apparently from Crévic, as well as artillery fire from Sommerviller. This was IR 10's baptism of fire, and II/IR 10, forgetting Crévic was the objective, launched itself at Flainval, the closest enemy, which had the additional advantage that the bed of the Moulinot stream provided cover from the artillery fire. 2/IR 10, which was following, took a direct artillery hit and scattered. It reassembled, but drifted too far to the left and joined the forward elements of IR 6. 1 and 4/IR 10 took too long drawing water at Deuxville and fell behind. They received artillery fire crossing south-east of Hill 285 and, in spite of the efforts of the regimental commander to direct them to Crévic, 1/IR 10 was drawn into the fight for Flainval left of II/IR 10, and they were able to close to 450m of the town. Elements of 4/IR 10 also appear to have moved in this direction. The commander of IR 10 finally succeeded in getting individual platoons from 4, 7 and 8/IR 10 moving together towards Crévic along the ridge east of the road, with 3 and the MGK/IR 10 following far behind.

It was clear to the 6 ID commander that IR 10 was not going to be much help in taking Drouville. The key terrain for the entire III b. AK area of operations was Hill 316. The 6 ID commander recognised that French artillery standing at Flainval and Haraucourt were able to effectively take any attack on Hill 316 in the flank. On the other hand, the hill seemed to be weakly held. He ordered the 11 Bde commander to attack Hill 316 immediately, and gave him the division reserve, IR 11, which was already in movement towards Maixe, and 2/Eng. Bn 3.

At 1015hrs III b. AK ordered 5 ID to attack from Serres and the Bois d'Einville east of the Drouville–Courbesseaux road to Réméréville. At the same time, Sixth Army HQ attached 5 RD to III b. AK, which ordered 5 RD to attack the enemy at Flainval–Hudiviller and free up the corps' left flank.

The 11 Bde commander committed IR 11 to the right of IR 13. On the north-west edge of Maixe, IR 11 deployed I/IR 11 east of the road to Drouville, with

II/IR 11 on its left, III and MGK/IR 11 behind the right flank. At least half of the companies of I and II/IR 13 had moved towards the high ground north-east of Crévic, and could only be turned later, if at all, towards Hill 316. Only III, 4, 5 and 6 and a platoon from 1/IR 11 were available to attack Hill 316. Two MG platoons were set up in the churchyard to support the attack, while one platoon was attached to IR 11. The 11 Bde commander moved to Maixe at 1130hrs, bringing with him III/IR 10 (minus 10/IR 10, which was covering 3 Artillery Bde) and 2/Eng. Bn 3, which built footbridges over the canal and the Sanon stream.

11 Bde attacked just before noon. IR 11 moved through the Etang Valley and the Bois d'Einville against the east side of the hill while enveloping it from the north; IR 13 attacked straight uphill. The exact conduct of the attack will probably never be known. IR 13 took the top by 1300hrs, but in uncoordinated groups, and stormed the French trenches 150m behind the crest. The enemy withdrew to Drouville and the Bois de Crévic, pursued by German fire. IR 13 climbed the hill from the east. There was considerable intermixing both within and between the regiments. The French artillery fire, which had followed the regiments up the hill, became more accurate: the top of the hill attracted intense fire. The troops drifted down the steep south-east side into the Etang Valley and sought dead ground there. When the French fire slackened, the top was reoccupied, but it was impossible to remain there long. At 1200hrs the enemy had attempted to attack from the Bois de Crévic, but two companies of III/IR 13 and the MGK pushed them back. Later III/IR 13 and the MGK were thrown into the cauldron at Hill 316.

III/IR 10 (minus 10/IR 10) was ordered by the 11 Bde commander to cover the left flank, west of Maixe, against an enemy attack from the Bois de Crévic, and arrived at the churchyard at 1300hrs. At this time the troops between Maixe and Crévic (3, 1, 2, 8, 7/IR 13 and 9/IR 6) began to retreat towards Maixe, but were stopped by the officers of III/IR 10 and added to the defensive position. 9/IR 10 and most of 12/IR 10 reinforced the disorganised troops of IR 11 and IR 13.

The troops exposed to the enemy guns on Hill 316 felt they were being fired on by their own artillery, but this was not the case. Hill 316 was such a clear target that mistakes by the German artillery was out of the question. The French artillery was, however, able to fire at the German flanks and even halfway into the German rear, which may have deceived the infantry. The German artillery was unable at any time to find the French batteries. A message from an air observer at 1800hrs, which gave the location of the French guns, fell into the light munitions column of II/FAR 3 too late to be of use. The heavy French artillery fire prevented the attachment of close-support batteries to IR 10 for its attack on Crévic. 1/FAR 3 brought a platoon into position on the north side of Maixe, which for a short time engaged enemy infantry on the edge of the Bois de Crévic, but it was soon forced to cease fire. 5/FAR 3 and the two remaining batteries of 1/FAR 3 moved through the Etang Valley, sometimes under heavy artillery fire, to set up on the north-east side of Hill 316, driving off a French counter-attack and the accompanying French battery. At 1145hrs I/Foot Artillery 3 (sFH) set up on the south edge of the wood south of Maixe and engaged enemy infantry on Hill 316, in the Bois de Crévic and north of Sommerviller.

At noon III b. AK again ordered the 5 and 6 ID to attack aggressively. At 1230hrs a Sixth Army order arrived, directing the Bavarian KD to fill a gap between II b. AK and III b. AK. In place of the cavalry, the *Landwehr* Div. and all of I RK, except the elements at Manonviller, were assigned to III b. AK.

In order to use IR 6 against Hill 316, the commander of 6 ID asked the commander of 5 RD to take over the IR 6 sector: the 5 RD commander agreed. He also attached RIR 7 to 6 ID. The enemy artillery fire had grown stronger and the 5 RD troops moving forward were forced to exercise extreme caution, using covered approaches and wide dispersal. Given the superiority and invulnerability of the French artillery, the 5 RD commander received permission from III b. AK at 1345hrs to call off the attack on Flainval–Hudiviller. French artillery fire, attracted by the staffs and mounted leaders that moved openly on the hills, and directed by aircraft, increased in intensity: the gates of hell opened. Direct hits were scored on infantry companies hugging the ground and into vehicles in the open.

At 1045hrs the 5 ID commander ordered 10 Bde to be prepared to attack from the Bois d'Einville and 9 Bde from Serres, with division objective located at Réméréville. The 9 Bde commander ordered I and II/IR 21 and 1 and 3/ Eng. Bn 3 into the Bois St Libaire, which was under continuous artillery fire and through which streamed back soldiers from IR 14, 19, 21 and 8 ED. The 9 Bde commander personally stopped them and brought order to the troops in the woods. At 1600hrs MGK/IR 21 moved to the wood to avoid the artillery fire south-west of Serres. Although there was no enemy to be seen far and wide, the 9 Bde commander did not think it wise to expose his troops in the open in daylight; even the smallest detachment that did so was met with overwhelming enemy artillery fire. The IR 14 situation at Serres was no better. 2/FAR 6 and II/ FAR 10 were told by the commander of IR 14 not to come too far forward for fear of drawing artillery fire. II/FAR 10 went into position on the high ground north of Serres, but took heavy artillery fire, while the infantry left the Bois St Libaire in groups: II/FAR 10 withdrew to Athienville. Per division order, 9 Bde was not to attack until 10 Bde came up on the left. This never occurred.

When 10 Bde received the order to attack, IR 7 (minus I/IR 7) was in low ground east of Valhey and under French area artillery fire, while IR 19 (minus III/ IR 19) was on the north-east extension of the Bois d'Einville. IR 7 swung south of Valhey, detaching III/IR 7 as division reserve. By 1320hrs II/IR 7 reached the north-west corner of the Bois d'Einville, joining IR 19, which had arrived shortly before. Individuals and small groups from units that were west of the wood were picked up. The 10 Bde commander had intended to move from the north half of the wood over the high ground to the west, but this was already occupied by Res. *Jäger* Bn 2, which was taking heavy flanking artillery fire. He decided to shift further south to attack from the middle of the wood to Courbesseaux or Drouville, but only after the friendly artillery had engaged the enemy artillery, which was incorrectly thought to be on Hill 316. IR 19, in the lead, reached the treeline at 1500hrs, which was under heavy enemy artillery fire, so the regiment occupied an assembly area further to the rear. There was no contact with 6 ID on the left. Disorganised groups of infantry could be seen in ever-greater numbers moving across the Etang stream and into the Bois d'Einville. In order to prevent a serious reverse, the IR 19 commander ordered the advance to Drouville on his own initiative. The MGK had already taken up a position on the high ground forward and put effective fire on the enemy trenches visible on both sides of Drouville. The two battalions, along with numerous stragglers from other units, were able to quickly gain ground, in spite of the enemy artillery fire. The regimental commander and other officers standing in the open formed a chain behind the troops and nipped unsteadiness in the bud: the troops passed through the artillery fire with a rush. II/IR 7 and the MGK were committed on the right, with Res. *Jäger* Bn 2 on their right. This was too much for the enemy infantry: when the Bavarians had approached to within 700m they abandoned their trenches, filled with dead. By 1800hrs IR 19 and 7 occupied Drouville. Res. *Jäger* Bn 2 had been forced north-east by enemy artillery fire and pinned down 150m from the town by small arms and MG fire.

The only 6 ID artillery to support the 10 Bde was I/FAR 6 in low ground 1.2km south of Serres. II/FAR 6 had tried to move through the Bois d'Einville, but was stopped by the steepness of the trail. At 1700hrs it set up behind the forest and shelled Courbesseaux. In 5 ID, 1 and 5/FAR 3 had almost run out of shells and had to leave their positions on the north-east slope of Hill 316 between 1600hrs and 1700hrs. 4/FAR 3 moved through the jammed streets in the burning town of Maixe, then advanced by platoons – sometimes at a trot or a gallop, sometimes in laborious slow pace down the steep hillside – under heavy enemy fire, down the road to Serres and past Hill 316 to set up in the IR 19 skirmisher line at 1630hrs. Standing grain and haze from the fields made target identification difficult: the battery opened fire on the Bois de Crévic, and followed IR 19 as it advanced.

At 1600hrs IR 6 and RIR 7 had arrived at Maixe and the commander of 11 Bde committed them to the attack. A corps General Staff officer told the IR 6 commander that the success of the day lay in holding Hill 316. On the north edge of Maixe he deployed I/IR 6 on the right of the road to Drouville, with III/IR 6, reinforced by 6/IR 6 and two MG platoons, on the left. II/IR 6, reduced to 7 and 8/IR 6, and a MG platoon remained as regimental reserve in Maixe. 5 and 6/IR

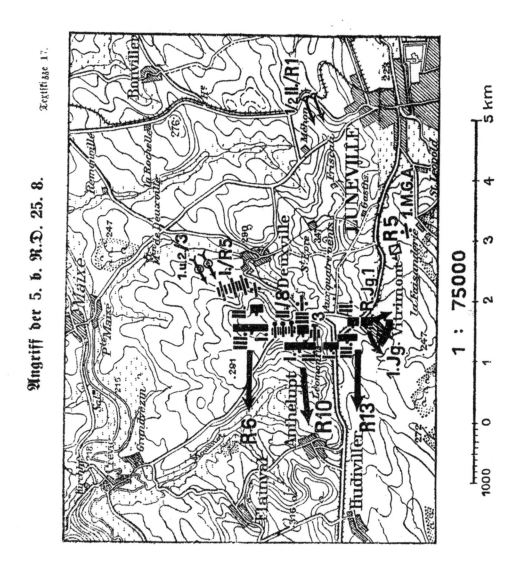

Angriff der 5. b. R.D. 25. 8.

Textskizze 17.

1 : 75000

6 were 11 Bde reserve. I and III/IR 6 advanced in waves of loose skirmisher lines, with large intervals between the waves. They too were followed in their climb up Hill 316 by murderous flanking artillery fire, but they continued their advance, pulling soldiers from IR 10, 11 and 13 with them. The regimental commander soon recognised that the attack was pointless, but his order to break it off did not always come through to the troops.

I/RIR 7 was held back as 6 ID reserve. III/RIR 7 was attached to IR 13 and moved in dispersed waves to the top of Hill 316 and stayed there, mixed in with troops of other units, in heavy artillery fire. II/RIR 7 was ordered by the commander of 11 Bde to the east of Hill 316 and moved there in open formation, followed by artillery fire. Here it found only the weak remnants of *Ersatz* Bn 35.

The arrival of IR 6 and RIR 7 on Hill 316 at 1700hrs encouraged the elements of IR 10, 11 13 and *Ersatz* Bn 35 there. The east side of the Bois de Crévic was taken, but the enemy heavy artillery fell with renewed rage on the wood, and the troops were at the end of their strength.

The commander of I/RIR 10 pulled together the elements of 4, 7 and 8/ IR 10 which had not moved towards Flainval, followed by 3 and MGK/IR 10, then took Crévic from the east and established themselves north-east of the town opposite the Bois de Crévic. The MGK crossed the Rhine–Marne Canal on a cargo barge and reinforced III/IR 10. North of the Maixe–Crévic road, troops from IR 6, 10, 13 and 11 were intermixed. Groups from these had also entered the Bois de Crévic from the east. The elements of IR 10 in front of Flainval (1 and 6/IR 10, parts of 4, 7 and 8/IR 10) were forced by overwhelming MG fire to crawl back across the Crévic–Vitrimont road, taking heavy casualties. The enemy attempted to follow, but was thrown back.

The III b.AK commander quickly recognised the cause of the difficult situation on Hill 316 and, at 1600hrs, ordered 5 RD to attack towards the high ground at Flainval–Hudiviller to divert the artillery that was firing into the 6 ID flank. 4 and 8 ED reported that they had been forced to retreat; at 1610hrs he ordered 5 ID to hold in place at Hoéville, Bois St Libaire and the high ground north-east of Drouville. No order was given to halt the 6 ID attack on Hill 316.

5 RD attacked with RIR 6 on the right, west of Deuxville, with I and III/RIR 6 in the first line, II/RIR 6 behind the centre and MGK/RIR 6 on the west end of the town. It appears that some companies of IRIR 6 tried to avoid the artillery fire by moving right, down the steep slope west of Deuxville, and came behind III/RIR 6. Under heavy artillery fire they reached the Crévic–Vitrimont road, just in time to throw back French troops from Flainval that were attacking the few remaining groups from IR 10. French fire and darkness brought the RIR 6 advance to a halt on the Moulinot stream.

Behind the ridge north of Léomont, RIR 10 deployed I and II/RIR 10, each on 400m fronts, followed by III and MGK/RIR 10. Even before the regiment could advance, however, enemy artillery fire forced it to retreat. The troops were halted and reorganised. The subsequent enemy attack from Anthelupt was welcomed as a relief: RIR 6 attacked with cold steel, threw the French back and, by dark, had gained the ridge east of the town, but the units were completely intermixed and losses had been serious. The commander of III/RIR 10 was killed.

On the Vitrimont–Hudiviller road, RIR 13 deployed to attack Hudiviller after 1200hrs, with I/RIR 13 north of the road, III/RIR 13 echeloned to the left rear and II/RIR 13 at the bend in the road north of Vitrimont. The enemy artillery fire had somewhat less effect than on RIR 10, though I/RIR 13 withdrew towards Aux Quatre Vents. The French attacked RIR 13 at 1800hrs, but were thrown back at close range and RIR 13 counter-attacked. II/RIR 13 deployed on the left of III/RIR 13 on its own initiative and RIR 13 gained the ridge north-west of Vitrimont. A new French attack from the wood south of Vitrimont prevented further advance and seriously threatened the 5 RD left flank. The Bavarian KD MG Sec. and the Bicycle Co./*Jäger* Bn 2 were pulled out of the line and moved 1.5km east of the village, while the *Jäger* Bn continued to defend in place for the entire day: an enemy infantry attack was a respite from the continual artillery fire. The support troops threw themselves enthusiastically into the firing line on the west edge of the town held by 2, 4 and 3, while 1, in reserve, extended the left flank. Reserve *Jäger* Bn 1, which had found a steep road cut north of Vitrimont that protected it from the artillery fire, moved west and east of the village. The Bavarian KD MG Sec. once again took up a position at La Faisanderie. The fire of the two *Jäger* battalions stopped the French attack – probably in regimental strength – at 500m range, and put the attackers into a disorganised and costly retreat.

I/FAR 5 had suffered severely under the enemy artillery fire and at times had been forced to leave the guns. Although it tried to support the infantry, it had never been possible to find the enemy artillery. Half of II/Res. Foot Artillery 1 (10cm cannons) was also unable to find the French guns, but it did assist in defeating the attack on Vitrimont that evening. It was no better for the 6 ID and Bavarian KD batteries in the 5 RD sector. In particular, at 1630hrs 3/FAR 5 took heavy casualties from artillery fire and the crews had to take cover behind the gun shields or in Léomont. The caissons were hit and the gun teams cut down or bolted. The same happened to the Bavarian KD MG Sec. vehicles. The fire lasted until dark, but 3/FAR 5 stood fast and assisted in throwing back the French evening attack. II/FAR 8 was also hit early and hard, lost all the horses and could only be moved with the help of the light munitions column: the caissons and wagons had to be left behind. Later it fired off all of its shells supporting the 5 RD attack.

At 1800hrs the commander of 6 ID recognised that, given the overwhelming enemy artillery fire, Hill 316 could not be held and ordered IR 11 to hold in place. His intention was to withdraw his troops from the zone of enemy artillery fire under cover of darkness. The III b. AK commander expanded this order to include the entire corps area. Above all, this was due to the fact that the 5 RD attack on Flainval–Hudiviller had failed in the face of the enemy artillery fire superiority. 5 ID was also to fall back behind the protection of the ridge east of Hoéville to the north-east end of the Bois d'Einville; 6 ID from Einville to Bonviller; 5 RD from there to the north edge of Lunéville. The *Landwehr* Div. was to move between 5 ID and 6 ID.

As of 1900hrs, before the withdrawal order arrived, the skirmisher line from Drouville into the Bois de Crévic had already begun escaping the artillery fire by moving to the Etang Valley and the Bois d'Einville. There was no possibility of an organised withdrawal. Leaders of all grades gathered the nearby troops of whatever regiment and moved east in a calm and orderly fashion, with unshaken discipline. Most of the wounded were evacuated on limbers, wagons and shelter halves. FAR 3 and 8 covered the movement, which proceeded on the road to Serres and along the Marne Canal. The withdrawal order did not reach 9 Bde until 2225hrs, as the troops were moving into or preparing position on the line Hoéville–Bois St Libaire, and they did not begin movement back until the next morning. 11 Bde was ordered not to withdraw, but to hold the west edge of the Bois d'Einville at and north of Maixe. The guns of 3/Horse Artillery 5 could only be recovered with the help of Res. Cavalry R 5, after the enemy had already occupied Léomont. The other vehicles had to be left behind. The battery lost half of its personnel and 80 per cent of the horses.

The mass of III b. AK occupied bivouacs dead tired. The leaders had often lost contact with their units and were only able to re-establish it that night or the next day. The enemy had not disturbed the withdrawal and had not pursued.

The mission assigned to III b. AK – defend the right flank against Nancy – was defensive. But as the enemy attacked on the morning of 25 August, the commanding general of III b. AK was forced to push the enemy far enough back to prevent him from putting artillery fire on the Arracourt–Lunéville road, which was the supply line for II b. AK and XXI AK: since the enemy still held Fort Manonviller, this supply line could not be moved to the east. It was clear to the III b. AK commander that his troops at St Libaire, Maixe and Léomont occupied terrain near Fort Manonviller and that the French would know every fold of the ground and could dominate it with its heavy artillery. But he calculated that this fire could be adequately suppressed: unfortunately, he was wrong. The German artillery did not have the means to ascertain the well-concealed enemy batteries. Counter-battery equipment, such as sound detectors, and the employment of aerial reconnaissance, were in the developmental stages. On 25 August this cost the III b. AK infantry streams of blood.

In retrospect, it would have perhaps been better to have broken off the battle for Hill 316 somewhat earlier and pulled the infantry in a timely fashion out of range of the enemy heavy artillery. But at this stage in the war, such a painful decision could not be made until the last prospect of success had disappeared.

The difficulty in carrying out the OHL concept of a deep pursuit in Lorraine was put into sharp relief. Six divisions had to guard the right flank, the defence of which brought actions that produced significant casualties. The troops held out bravely under overwhelming artillery fire, and the regimental and brigade commanders were to be found in the foremost ranks. The artillery set up close behind the infantry under heavy fire.

The French infantry, on the other hand, felt its way carefully forward, and when it could be engaged, it retreated in haste behind the protection of the heavy artillery at Nancy. It never attempted to pursue, so that a considerable distance separated the two sides on the morning of 26 August. The French troops were from 34 and 35 Bde of IX Corps, which attacked Erbéviller and Réméréville, and 70 RD, which struck towards Hoéville and the Bois St Libaire. They were not able to advance; instead they withdrew to within 3–6km from the Moselle. The French XX Corps had committed 39 ID with the mission of taking the Bois d'Einville and continuing the attack on the Einville–Lunéville road. Instead, 39 ID was stopped at Drouville and Hill 316, and, by evening, had withdrawn to the west side of the Meurthe, leaving only rearguards at Haraucourt. South of the canal the French 11 ID was unable to take the high ground at Léomont–Friscati, but held on at Sommerviller–Flainval–Anthelupt–Hudiviller. French XX Corps lost between 3,000 and 4,000 men.

Withdrawal of II b. AK behind the Mortagne

Lamath, 25 August (map 15)

The Sixth Army order for 25 August arrived at 0320hrs. At 0100hrs the 3 ID commander had ordered the troops to be combat-ready in their positions by 0500hrs. At 0530hrs, before the corps order arrived, he directed 6 Bde to attack over Vennezey to Haillainville, while 5 Bde followed echeloned right over Rozelieures to Damas-aux-Bois.

3 FA Bde, attached to 6 Bde, opened fire on French artillery at Côte d'Essey. IR 17, with I, II and MGK/IR 17 on the high ground south of Remenoville, quickly became involved in a firefight with French infantry between Vennezey and Rozelieures. FAR 5 unlimbered on the high ground north of Vennezey to provide fire support. IR 22 (minus III/IR 22) moved out at 0715hrs from

Moriviller, but immediately ran into serious resistance in the Bois de Filière. II/IR 22 moved through the wood in heavy artillery fire, took Hill 341 and advanced on Rozelieures, while I/IR 22 drifted to the west side of the Bois de Réthimont. I/FAR 12 moved at a gallop through the Bois de Filière and unlimbered in heavy artillery fire on the south edge to support IR 22.

The 3 ID attack had already begun when, at 0800hrs, it ploughed into the French attack from the south over Vennezey and Giriviller, but principally from the west against the 3 ID right flank. The commander of 6 Bde decided to stand on the defensive between the Bois de Réthimont and the Bois du Haut du Mont. The battle quickly rose in intensity, and ammunition had to be sent forward for both infantry and artillery. III/IR 17 extended the right flank of I/IR 17 on the south-west side of the Bois de Réthimont. In part to carry out the attack order, but also to escape the enemy artillery fire, IR 17 attacked and threw back the French infantry. Around noon II/17, with 1 and 4/IR 17 and supported by the MGK, took Vennezey and pushed on to the hill 500m to the south. III/IR 17, with 2 and 3/IR 17, turned towards Rozelieures, with III/IR 22 attaching itself on the right, and IR 22 (-) on the south edge of the Bois de Filière and on Hill 341, headed for Rozelieures. II/IR 22 and the MGK opened the fight, while I/IR 22 was held back at the south-west corner of the Bois de Réthimont. The right flank of IR 17 approached to within 400m of Rozelieures when I/IR 23 provided a welcome reinforcement, joining the firing line and bringing additional ammunition with them. By noon Rozelieures was in German hands, with IR 17, 22 and 23 completely intermixed. The enemy repeatedly sought to attack from Borville and the Bois de Lalau, but was always thrown back. Bavarian troops even appear to have penetrated into the Bois de Lalau. A mixed platoon-sized force from III/23 took Hill 305, south-east of Rozelieures. I/IR 22 was brought forward to Rozelieures and committed to the fight: the battalion commander was killed. At 1400hrs III/IR 18 and the MGK were relieved by 31 ID in the Bois du Haut du Mont and moved towards the fight at Vennezey, by companies and even platoons, resulting in more intermixing of troops. I/Foot Artillery 1 (sFH) was reinforced by 7/Res. Foot Artillery 1 (10cm cannons).

At 0800hrs II/IR 23 and the MGK at Relécourt were ordered to advance into the valley of the Broulliot stream, south of Clayeures. They had just begun to move when French infantry appeared on Hill 337, east of Einvaux, and at the Bois de Jontois. The MGK was in overwatch at Relécourt and its fire drove the French back over Hill 337. II/IR 23 deployed 7 and 5/IR 23 to attack the Bois de Jontois frontally, with 6/IR 23 enveloping the enemy on the right and 8/IR 23 on the left. At 0900hrs 5 and 7/IR 23 stormed the wood with flying colours, while 6 and MGK/IR 23 occupied Hill 337 and pursued the enemy with fire. The battalion now held a strongpoint in the gap between 3 ID and 4 ID. In the course of the morning the MGK repeatedly threw back strong attacks from Einvaux, even though it took artillery fire.

3 ID had suffered from the enemy artillery fire and the units were intermixed. Nevertheless, the situation at noon gave no grounds for concern. The right flank was secure, while I/IR 18 was still in reserve. All reports sent to corps since 1000hrs were positive. 4 ID defended the right flank. The enemy artillery fire resumed during the morning. Although the troops were dispersed and used the terrain for cover, casualties were serious, especially in the 5 Bde sector after noon and in II/IR 9. The bridge at Blainville could not be rebuilt. 4 FA Bde was unable to locate the French guns.

I/RIR 5 occupied a position on the treeline east of Méhoncourt. The MGK was divided up amongst the battalions. Early in the day the I/RIR 5 began to take French artillery fire, and a standing firefight at 900m range began with French infantry in and to both sides of Méhoncourt. II/RIR 5 moved up on the right of I/RIR 5 to occupy the entire treeline. Though the French remained in their trenches north of the town, they attacked south of it quite early with considerable force, threatening the regiment's left. 1 and 6/RIR 5 and two companies of III/RIR 5 were committed in this direction. The enemy seemed to reinforce his attack. The intensity of the French artillery fire increased. The Bavarian infantry began to run out of ammunition and the ammunition wagons brought renewed supplies to the treeline under enemy fire. II/FAR 2 was forced to bring its guns by platoon directly behind the firing line, where they would engage the enemy until forced by counter-battery fire to change position, which was extremely difficult in the thick woods: 5/FAR 2 moved eight times. RIR 5 was forced to pull the left flank from the rail line and back to the woods.

At 0900hrs this situation forced the corps commander to commit the reserve, RIR 8, which was at Lamath. I/RIR 8, with two MG platoons, was sent to the Grande Bois. II/RIR 8, with a MG platoon, was sent to Landécourt, immediately took artillery fire as it left Bois Bouxat, and occupied the town and the heights to the south-west. It suffered continually from the enemy artillery fire and withdrew between 1400hrs and 1500hrs to the Bois de la Haye, west of Franconville, where it joined I/RIR 8. III/RIR 8 was sent to reinforce RIR 5. One kilometre west of the rail line the battalion commander deployed 10/RIR 8 north of the road, 12/RIR 8 to the south, followed later by 9 and 11/RIR 8. Artillery fire echoed through the thick undergrowth and retreating troops told of what they had endured. Several III/RiR 8 men surely hid in the undergrowth. By noon half the battalion succeeded in reaching RIR 5. The commander of 10/RIR 8 reached the open ground west of Bois Grimont with a handful of men and reported that the enemy had withdrawn. The French in and south of Méhoncourt seemed weak and had lost interest in attacking. But after 1400hrs the enemy artillery fire increased, and finally the nerves of the reservists and *Landwehr* men of RIR 5 and 8 cracked. Some skirmisher lines crumbled into the woods, but others stood fast. Since the enemy did not push into the woods, deceived by the remaining squads on the treeline, they were probably unaware of the situation there.

Both the 4 ID and II b. AK commanders, under the influence of grim reports from the front, evaluated the situation to be more serious than it actually was. Had the enemy been energetic and determined, then there were grounds for concern. The corps was split into two parts on a 20km front on a sector that, under the prevailing doctrine, could not be defended. The corps commander requested support from Sixth Army and was told that it would arrive at Lunéville at 1900hrs. Sixth Army also said that the corps had to stop the enemy attack, with the final defensive line on the River Mortagne. At 1430hrs the corps commander ordered a withdrawal behind the Mortagne. The situation had fundamentally changed: it was no longer a question of cutting off the enemy retreat, but of defeating an attack by superior forces. This mission would be easier to accomplish behind the Mortagne and out of range of the enemy heavy artillery. 4 ID would defend between the town of Mortagne and Xermamaénil, with 3 ID on the high ground north-east of Gerbéviller.

The 4 ID commander ordered that the rearward movement not begin until the wounded had been evacuated. I/FAR 2 was positioned to overwatch from the woods 500m north-east of St Antoine, with FAR 11 south of Mont. As I/FAR 11 moved into firing position, it received such effective artillery fire that the teams of the 1/FAR 11 limbers bolted. The four immobilised guns were later recovered. The elements of 7 Bde at Blainville withdrew between 1600hrs and 1700hrs in complete order; the enemy did not follow. 1/Eng. Bn 2 began building footbridges over the river south of Mortagne town.

The last 7 Bde troops were approaching the division commander's position west of Mont when an officer from Sixth Army arrived and reported that I b. AK and XXI AK were winning and that the withdrawal of II b. AK would transform the battle into a defeat. He ordered, in the name of the Sixth Army commander, that the positions west of the Mortagne be held. Sixth Army officers told the commanders of the withdrawing units the same thing. The II b. AK officers replied that the withdrawal was already underway and that a countermarch would only lead to confusion, unnecessarily tire the troops and reduce the troops' confidence in the leadership, without accomplishing anything positive. The commander of 4 ID said that he would hold the towns of Mont and Lamath on the west bank with IR 9. Eventually the enemy recognised that 7 Bde was withdrawing and shelled Mont, which was packed with troops, but without doing any damage. The French infantry probed towards Mont, but were blocked by III/IR 9. Nevertheless, the defensive situation appeared so unfavourable that the 4 ID commander ordered the evacuation of the west bank of the Mortagne during the evening. At midnight the enemy occupied Mont.

In the 5 Res. Bde sector the withdrawal order had already been overtaken by events. Although II/IR 5 held the west side of Lamath, the remnants of RIR 5 and III/RIR 8 streaming out of the Bois de Clairlieu and Bois de Vacquenat were ordered to the Mortagne bridges, assembled and brought to the Bois St Mansuy, north-east of Xermaménil. 4/RIR 5, reinforced by two MGs, held out on the treeline north-east of Méhoncourt, as did the 10/RIR 8 commander and his small group north of the Bois Grimont, but at 1800hrs they retreated in the face of superior forces advancing from Romain. Numerous wounded probably remained and died in the woods between Méhoncourt and Lamath. Stragglers arrived in the Bois St Mansuy during the entire night. A stream of lightly wounded moved down the Xermaménil–Rehainviller road. RIR 8 (minus III/RIR 8) at Franconville had been ordered to withdraw to Mont at 1630hrs, but was halted at Lamath and, together with II/IR 5, ordered to hold the town. Enemy infantry and, presumably, cavalry appeared around midnight, and were sent back with a bloody nose. Nevertheless, the commander of RIR 8 thought it prudent to withdraw during the night over the Mortagne to Xermaménil. The Bavarian KD reached Rehainviller at 1600hrs; at 1800hrs it marched east to cross the Meurthe and bivouacked near Lunéville. The bridging equipment at Blainville, which was as good as destroyed, was lost.

Lunéville exercised a great power of attraction to units in the area, the supply units of II b. AK and XXI AK especially. The roads were blocked by two or three units next to each other; columns of wounded and prisoners also arrived. During the day order was preserved. The approaching dusk brought out hidden French stragglers and hate-filled residents who fired on German troops, columns, wounded and hospitals, which led to panic. The vehicles fled in all directions, while their escorts fired at random. The aircraft of Bavarian Aviation Sec. 2, at the parade ground on the east side of the city, were flown off. The Aviation Sec. leader collected a handful of men and swept through the town to re-establish order, as did other groups of troops. During the fighting an Aviation Sec. officer took a banner of the local militia from one of the inhabitants. In and around Lunéville numerous buildings were soon in flames.

The commander of 3 ID immediately objected to the corps' withdrawal order, but without effect. Since the right wing of the 3 ID was facing south, the withdrawal was far more difficult than that of 4 ID. Many of the troops were flushed with victory and some had begun pursuit: the order to retreat was most unwelcome. The artillery covered the withdrawal moving rearwards by bounds. Due to the intermixing of the infantry units, a doctrinal withdrawal using a clearly defined rearguard was impossible. At Vennezey it was easy to break contact and some kind of rearguard was quickly formed from elements of IR 17 and 18. Groups of discouraged or angry men made their own way to the rear and were hastily organised on the road to Gerbéviller. The situation at Rozelieures was far less favourable. The Bavarian and French infantry were in close contact; Bavarian attacks from the town were thrown back by superior French forces, while the French tried unsuccessfully to break into the town. The town was destroyed by the continual French shelling, and also cut off the Bavarian infantry, which began to run out of ammunition. The losses mounted and the wounded could not be properly treated. The withdrawal order saved the defenders from being surrounded. The town was not evacuated until 1800hrs, with the troops marching to Remenoville and Gerbéviller. MGK/IR 23 held out on the hill east of Einvaux and followed II/IR 23 towards Franconville, where *Chevauleger* R 3 covered the division right flank. The French infantry did not pursue either at Vennezey or Rozelieures, but the French artillery fire caused significant casualties.

The Sixth Army order to stop the withdrawal was received by 3 ID with a sense of self-justification. The division commander at Fraimbois immediately tried to stop the troops at Moriviller and Remenoville, but it was too late. It was possible to stop them on the high ground south-west of Haudonville and Gerbéviller, but this position, with the burning town of Gerbéviller and the Mortagne directly to the rear, seemed too dangerous for the tired and disorganised troops to hold. That evening 3 ID, which had suffered heavy casualties, pulled back over the Mortagne.

II b. AK had not been defeated: it had withdrawn in accordance with Sixth Army orders. It is an open question whether it was necessary to break the battle off so quickly and accept the disadvantages that went with it. II b. AK had been attacked by considerably superior enemy forces. During the early morning the French VIII Corps attacked from the south, with 15 ID moving on Remenoville and 16 ID on Mattexey. 15 ID succeeded in advancing as far as Rozelieures, but was defeated by 3 ID and streamed back to St Voigt–Essey-de-Côte and then 4km further south. In the meantime, the French XVI Corps attacked from the west, led initially by only a brigade of the 74 RD and one of 32 ID moving on Méhoncourt–Clayeures, but followed by 29 ID with a brigade of 31 ID on each flank, with the remaining brigades of 74 RD and 32 ID in reserve. By mid-morning the lead elements of this mass reached Méhoncourt–Einvaux–Bois de Jontois. The open right flank of 3 ID was seriously threatened, the more so because the cries for help from French VIII Corps caused the French Second Army commander to urge XVI Corps forward. It was fortunate that the XVI Corps halted at Méhoncourt–Einvaux to wait for XV Corps, which in the meantime had also been ordered to attack. Initially, the XV Corps commander committed only 30 ID towards Blainville, while he held 64 RD 5km to the west. 30 ID did not reach the woods south-west of Charmois until afternoon. The French XV Corps was now ready to advance, but II b. AK had already begun to withdraw. This caused the Second Army commander to urge his troops to pursue, but by evening the French troops had only advanced to St Voigt (15 ID), Rozelieures (a brigade each from 74 RD, 32 ID, 31 ID), Moriviller (brigade,

32 ID), Landécourt (brigade, 74 RD), Méhoncourt (brigade, 31 ID), Charmois (64 RD) and Blainville (30 ID). II b. AK, thanks to French caution, had avoided the danger of being enveloped the next day by overwhelming French forces.

When XXI AK attacked on 25 August, it also ran into advancing French forces: the right flank of French 16 ID (VIII Corps) at Giriviller–Mattexey and the French XIII Corps, 5–7km east of Mattexey. The XXI AK quickly won the upper hand and took Mattexey and Domptail (7km east). Further advance was stopped by the situation in the II b. AK sector. The XXI AK commander left only weak forces in contact with the enemy and assembled 31 ID at Seranville, plus 42 ID at Mattexey–Magnières, in order to be able to assist II b. AK. The French 16 ID retreated to a position 6km south of Mattexey, and XIII Corps 7km to the south-east.

The German 8 KD, attached to XXI AK, was ordered on 25 August to advance on Rambervillers (11km south-east of Mattexey), but was soon stopped by superior French forces and assembled at Domptail on the XXI AK left flank. The horse artillery went into action there and suffered severely from counter-battery fire. 7 KD attempted to advance from a position 3km on the 8 KD left, immediately ran into resistance and dismounted, but ultimately made no progress.

Bazien (map 16, sketch 18)

The Seventh Army gave the mass of I b. AK a rest day on 25 August. At 0500hrs the sound of combat was heard in the direction of Baccarat, which was occupied by XIV AK. The commander of 2 Bde, west of the town, did not send his troops to the town, but deployed IR 2 on the high ground west of it and held IR 16 in its bivouac area on Hill 341. At 0530hrs IR 16 was attacked on both flanks by French infantry from the west side of Baccarat, as well as the north-west corner of the Forêt de la Rappe. II/IR 16 on the right swung immediately to the south-west, while III/IR 16 on the left moved to the south-east. I/IR 16, which was already deployed towards Baccarat, stood fast. II/IR 16 quickly deployed 5 and 8/IR 16 on a small ridge south-west of the bivouac, just in time to give French skirmisher lines emerging from the Forêt de la Rappe and the Grands Bois de Glonville a bloody reception at 600m range. The French stopped and then pulled back into the woods, but opened up a murderous fire and manoeuvred to the north. 7/IR 16 had to be committed on the right, 6/IR 16 in a gap between 5 and 8/IR 16. Well-aimed fire stopped every enemy advance, which was estimated to be in regimental strength and supported by a MGK. III/IR 16 was ordered to clean out the north-east finger of the Forêt de la Rappe. With fixed bayonets, 10/IR 16 drove easily into the wood, joined by 11/IR 16 to the left and right, but at once took fire from an invisible enemy in the undergrowth and was forced to take cover. The Bavarians continued their attack with cold steel and the signal

16. Bazien 25.8. — I. b. A. K. —

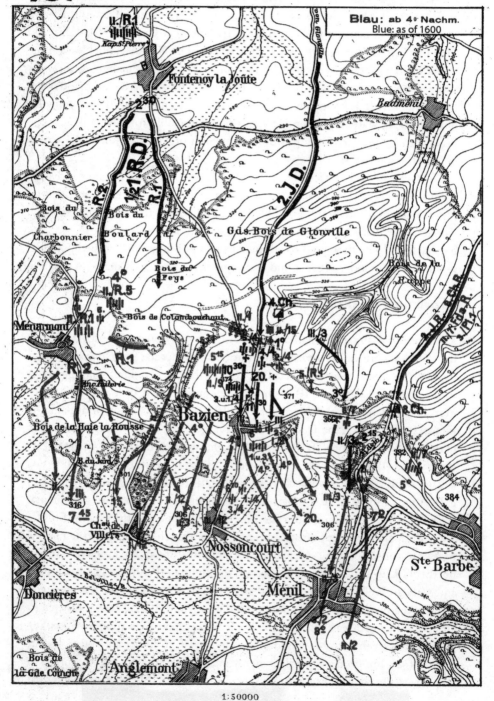

Blau: ab 4⁰ Nachm.
Blue: as of 1600

1:50000

1000 m   500   0   1   2   3 km

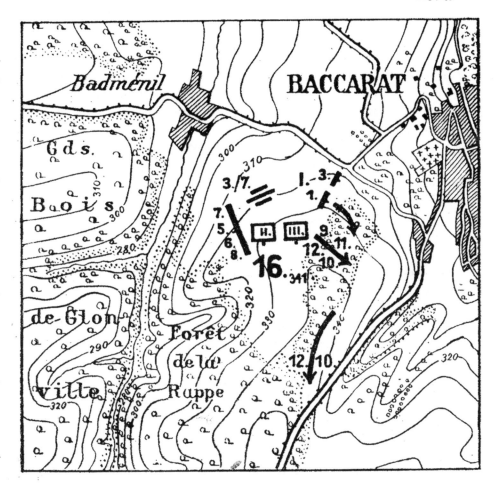

Baccarat 25. 8.   Textskizze 18.

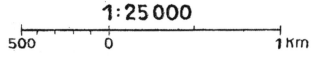

1:25 000

'Charge!', but the French took to their heels before the Bavarians could close. The Bavarians pushed to the south-east treeline and engaged the retreating French infantry in the open with pursuit fire. French stragglers in the woods were swept up by a second wave composed of 9 and 12/IR 16. 10 and 11/IR 16 attempted an advance into the open ground, but were stopped by a French MG in the left flank, which mowed down nearly an entire platoon of 11/IR 16. While the battalion caught its breath and reorganised, a lieutenant and five men were sent out on reconnaissance in the Forêt de la Rappe and encountered a withdrawing French company in march column, took them under fire and scattered them to the four winds. 10 and 12/IR 16 attempted once again to advance from the woods to the south-east and took fire from the right. 10/IR 16 turned south beyond the woods, 12/IR 16 inside it, and pushed the French out of the Forêt de la Rappe and captured four full artillery caissons. Once II/IR 16 had thrown back the enemy attack, it pushed into the Grands Bois de Glonville and came in close contact with the French. 3/FAR 7 provided effective support from 0600hrs onwards, unlimbering on the high ground south-east of Badménil, directly behind the II/IR 16 skirmisher line. II/FAR 7 also went early to its position on the heights north-west of Baccarat. 5/FAR 7 provided II/IR 16 excellent support in the fight against French infantry in the Grands Bois de Glonville. On the other hand, enemy artillery and, most likely, the artillery of German XIV AK engaged both IR 2 and 16. At 0800hrs a gun from I/FAR7 on the north-east entrance of Baccarat took a direct hit. By noon Baccarat was quiet; the enemy had withdrawn. IR 16 and elements of IR 2 had taken serious casualties.

2 ID was ordered to send a brigade battle group – 3 Bde (minus I/IR 3), *Chevauleger* R 4, FAR 4 and 2/Eng. Bn 1 – to Nossoncourt. The advance guard (II/IR 20, the cavalry and engineers) moved out from Glonville at 0900hrs, followed at a 400m interval by the main body – I/IR 20, I/FAR 4, III/IR 20, MGK/IR 20, II/FAR 4 and IR 3 (minus I/IR 3). The point company, 7/IR 20, cleared out weak enemy infantry from the north treeline of the Grands Bois de Glonville. *Chevauleger* R 4 then boldly rode forward into the 3km-deep wood. At 1000hrs the point sighted enemy infantry at the south treeline. The squadron commander dismounted half his troopers (two squads, sixteen men). The left squad got stuck in the underbrush, but the right squad reached open ground and found a French company in mass formation at 50m range: the eight *Chevaulegers* and their lieutenant could hardly miss and the French ran off in panic. They had probably encountered an entire French battalion, for the *Chevaulegers* took overwhelming fire from the right. They were joined by the left squad, then 2 and 3/*Chevauleger* R 4, but since the regiment could only engage with sixty dismounts, the fight was unequal. Then 7/IR 20 came down the road at the run, with 5/IR 20 arriving on the right, while 6/IR 20 remained echeloned on the right rear; *Chevauleger* R 4 could pull its troopers out of the firefight.

The II/IR 20 colours were unfurled, the drums beat the charge and the battalion fixed bayonets; 5 and 7/IR 20 fell on the enemy at the south treeline and swept him away. The French that had not fallen or fled were bayoneted or surrendered. As soon as the Bavarian infantry came into the open, it was met by heavy artillery fire from Anglemont. Bazien was also held by the enemy. 6/IR 20 was engaged at close range by French infantry firing standing, but 2/Eng. Bn 1 came up on the left and the French were driven off with heavy losses.

At 1030hrs I/FAR 4 (minus 2/FAR 4) occupied a spectacular firing position on Hill 374 north of Bazien that dominated the entire countryside, and engaged French march columns in the Belville Valley. 3/FAR 4 suppressed a French battery at the west exit of Nossoncourt. The commander of IR 20 brought the MGK forward at a trot and deployed I and III/IR 20 to the left of II/IR 20. Two MG platoons were attached to II/IR 20, and one to I/IR 20. Disregarding the heavy artillery fire, at 1130hrs II/IR 20 stormed the north-west side of Bazien, while I/IR 20 attacked the east side and III/IR 20 attacked French troops on the slopes east of the town that were moving to the west. One platoon of 2/Eng. Bn 1 took part in the fight for Bazien, while the other two engaged the enemy east of the town. Driven out of Bazien, the French continued tough resistance at Nossoncourt.

3 Bde was now isolated and far in front of the rest of I b. AK, but this was not a concern for the brigade commander. In order to take Ménil and cut off the French at Baccarat, at 1100hrs II/IR 3 and the MGK were sent from the crossroads 2km north of Bazien in the direction of the Bois de la Pêche and Hill 366, east of Bazien, while III/IR 3 moved behind II/IR 3 to the south treeline of the Grands Bois de Glonville. Unfortunately, II/IR 3 got lost in the woods.

IR 20 spent some tense hours. French area artillery fire covered the open ground around Bazien, the treeline north of the town and the road north from Bazien. The regiment had run out of ammunition. The adjutant of I/IR 20 assembled stragglers and collected ammunition, sometimes from other units, and carried it forward to the firing line. Above all, around noon the French launched a strong attack from the Bois de la Pêche at the regimental left flank, especially III/IR 20, which had 9, 11 and 12/IR 20 under fire in the open ground east of Bazien, with only 10/IR 20 in reserve on the south treeline of the Grands Bois de Glonville. The enemy succeeded in stealthily reaching a small wood 400m east of Bazien, close to the III/IR 20 left flank. A French MG fired directly into the battalion flank and French infantry began advancing, but the skirmisher lines of 11 and 12/IR 20 charged the enemy, who was only 100m away. Some of the French ran back to the woods, some played dead. Any who resisted were cut down. The small wood was soon in the hands of IR 20. A platoon of the MGK found a firing position on a spur and broke up a number of closed French columns approaching from the south. FAR 4 on the high ground north of Bazien provided effective fire support when IR 20 ran low on ammunition. The enemy attacks were defeated, but at the cost of heavy IR 20 casualties. 2/Eng. Bn 1, which also ran out of ammunition, lost 14 KIA and 52 WIA.

At the crossroads north of Bazien, the commander of 3 Bde received numerous worrying reports and expected to be attacked from the woods to the east at any minute. His reports to 2 ID resulted in I/IR 3, II/Foot Artillery R 1 (15cm) and 5/Res. Foot Artillery R 1 (10cm cannons) being dispatched as reinforcements at noon. At 1400hrs the 2 ID commander sent the rest of the division in motion and moved his HQ to the south side of the Grands Bois de Glonville. About the same time, 1 ID sent a regimental battle group – IR 2, *Chevauleger* R 8, II/FAR 7 and 3/Eng. Bn 1 – in march from Baccarat to Ménil. The first of the reinforcements to arrive was 4/FAR 4 at 1300hrs, which set up on the high ground north-east of Bazien, behind the threatened IR 20 left flank. At 1415hrs II/IR 3 and the MGK finally arrived on Hill 366 east of Bazien and at once pushed 8 and 5/IR 3 to the south side of the Bois de la Pêche and then to Ménil. III/IR 3 arrived at the treeline north of Hill 366, with I/IR 3 at the treeline north of Bazien.

The road in the woods north of Glonville was now blocked with field kitchens and ammunition wagons, while wounded and empty wagons streamed to the rear. The French shelled the exit from the wood, while the undergrowth prevented all off-road movement. At 1400hrs II/Foot Artillery 1 (15cm) and 5/Res. Foot Artillery 1 (10cm cannons) began to displace forward to the open ground north of Bazien. Pushing through the soft ground took the combined efforts of the horse teams, gun crews and assistance from the infantry. With FAR 4 they then won the duel with the French artillery. IR 20 had made no progress since noon due to casualties and shortage of ammunition. II/IR 3 had succeeded in advancing 400–500m south of the Bois de la Pêche. By 1600hrs 4 Bde units began to gradually arrive, having slowly made their way through the woods.

The intent at all levels was to push the French east into the Vosges and the German right wing. The first 4 Bde unit, III/IR 12, attacked towards Nossoncourt with I/IR 3 on the right. IR 12 (minus III/IR 12), followed by IR 15, moved through the woods 1km west of Bazien on the Château de Villers. IR 20 advanced towards the north-west side on Ménil while III/IR 3 attacked from the north, with II/IR 3 and the MGK following. The artillery fired in support. II/FAR 9 arrived north-west of Bazien at 1715hrs and immediately took counter-battery fire in the right flank, which caused casualties in 4/FAR 9. I/FAR 9 was pulled to and fro by countervailing orders, but the commander of 5/Foot Artillery 1 (sFH) moved his four guns on his own initiative to the right of II/FAR 9 and engaged three groups of French artillery that had occupied open positions to support their infantry and shot them to pieces; this relieved the pressure on II/FAR 9.

At some time after 1700hrs the 3 Bde attack began to gather steam and the French withdrew. By dusk II/IR 3 was directly in front of Ménil, with III/IR 3 and IR 20 on the high ground north-west of the town, while III/IR 12 had taken Nossoncourt. To the west I/IR 3 had taken heavy artillery fire, but was supported in a timely manner by II/IR 12. I/IR 12 and the MGK had taken Château de Villers, although they were temporarily forced to take cover in the castle park by artillery fire. The MGK, in position south of the château, engaged French infantry emerging from the woods at Anglemont and chased them back. IR 12 reached the wood north of the château, with IR 15 behind it to the west of Bazien. II/IR 15 was the sole division reserve, and brought ammunition forward to IR 20 just before the final attack. As the infantry gained ground, 1 and 3/FAR 4 advanced to the north of Nossoncourt and I/FAR 9 moved to the area of Bazien. During the afternoon the corps HQ moved to the south side of the Grands Bois de Glonville. The IR 2 battle group from 1 ID reached the Bois de la Pêche at 1700hrs, slowed by advancing columns of XIV AK, and bivouacked north of Ménil, which had been set on fire by XIV AK artillery.

Separated by extensive woods from the right flank of 2 ID, 1 Res. Bde reached Fontenoy by 1400hrs, where the 7 KD horse artillery was engaged. The 1 RD commander instructed the brigade to wait until the artillery arrived before advancing on Ménarmont. But at 1430hrs the 1 Res. Bde commander received a call for help from 3 Bde at Bazien, and the French had left the treeline south of Fontenoy, so he sent RIR 2 directly to Ménarmont, while RIR 1 advanced on the left through the Bois de Boulard. Initially, RIR 2 advanced deployed, but formed march column to traverse the woods, and was held up by fallen trees on the road. Nevertheless, the brigade reached the treeline north of Ménarmont shortly after 1600hrs. II/RFAR 1 overwatched the movement of the infantry from a position north-west of Fontenoy and then displaced to a covered position in a clearing in the Bois de Colombouchaut in front of Ménarmont, with 6/RFAR 1 in the open to the right front. Far to the south, a long enemy column was visible, which had stopped to cook. At Xaffévillers (off map, 2km south-west of Ménarmont) several enemy batteries were visible, as well as a number of infantry columns moving south-east to Doncières. Initially, these were taken to be XXI Corps troops, but at 1830hrs II/RFAR 1 moved forward to an open position north-east of Ménarmont and opened fire: the crews of the French batteries abandoned their guns and several ammunition caissons exploded. At 1715hrs the chief of staff of I b. RK ordered 1 Res. Bde to attack the high ground north of Doncières, while also notifying it that Sixth Army HQ would order it to move to Lunéville the next day. Therefore, the brigade attacked with only RIR 2, while RIR 1 remained at the Bois de Colombouchaut. RIR 2 led with II/RIR 2, while III and I/RIR 2 followed echeloned right and left, with the MGK following on the road in the middle. II/RIR 2 drifted to the west and took fire from the French artillery at Xaffévillers, and III/RIR 2 had to move left and down both sides of the road to Doncières. On the south side of the Bois de la Haie la Rousse, both battalions got into a firefight with French infantry on the high ground north of Doncières and, in a steady advance, drove the French from the field by 1945hrs. 1 Res. Bde then had to make a fatiguing 9km night march with frequent stops and starts to its bivouac site, which it found already occupied by 7 and 8 KD, forcing it to bivouac in the open. The day's operations had also prevented the troops from being properly fed.

The attack on the morning of 25 August against IR 16 on the high ground south-west of Baccarat had probably been conducted by the brigade of the French XIII Corps that was attached to XXI Corps. It was defeated and withdrew to Ménil, but then the troops of XXI Corps proper appeared. The lead elements of I b. AK hit four battalions of French 43 ID (the mass of the division was guarding the XIII Corps right flank) and a regiment from XIII Corps at Bazien and pushed them out of the town; it also drove Light Infantry Bn 31 diagonally across the north-west side of the Bois de Glonville. Elements of the French 2 Colonial Bde at St Barbe and the reassembled XIII Corps brigade at Ménil attempted unsuccessfully to rescue the situation. The defeated left flank of XXI Corps (2 Colonial Brigade) withdrew to Rambervillers, as did 43 ID to a position 4–8km to the east. The advance of I b. AK also hit the right flank of the French XIII Corps; in particular, 1 Res. Bde struck deep into the flank of the French 26 ID, broke it up and caused it to flee to Rambervillers (off map, 4km south of Doncières). The French First Army commander committed the newly arrived 44 ID east of Rambervillers (4–5km south of Nossoncourt–St Barbe) to close the gap between XXI and XIII Corps and prevent I b. AK from taking the high ground there. The troops of I b. AK were subjected to the fire of heavy guns brought from Épinal. IR 20, which was most heavily engaged, lost 900 men.

The Otto biplanes of Aviation Sec. 1 had maintenance problems, which also caused many forced landings. They also had a low ceiling. Nevertheless, the section overcame all difficulties and energetic reconnaissance kept the command well informed of the situation.

On 25 August the German XIV AK, to the left of I b. AK, was pulled into two parts. On the right flank, 29 ID was attacked early in the morning by French troops from Baccarat, but drove them off and, in the course of the day, advanced as far as Ménil and St Barbe. On the left flank, 28 ID, plus a brigade from 29 ID, encountered resistance and swung south-east to assist XV AK south of Raon l'Étape. At the end of the day, the two divisions were separated by the woods at St Barbe, which was still held by the enemy.

The XV AK mission on 25 August was to take Étival (4km south of Raon l'Étape). However, even before 30 ID could leave Raon l'Étape, bitter house-to-house fighting broke out in the town with French infantry hidden there. The division finally succeeded in breaking through, but the enemy occupied the heights and woods to the south and could not be driven off them. 39 ID remained largely in reserve.

XIV and XV AK had been engaged on the west side of the Meurthe with the right flank of the French XXI Corps, with 13 ID reinforced by elements of 43 ID. The French here had also attempted to attack, but by the end of the day withdrew to the woods near St Barbe. On the east side of the Meurthe, the left wing of the French XIV Corps, 27 ID, had tried unsuccessfully to take Raon l'Étape.

26 August

25 August was a tense day for Crown Prince Rupprecht. The corps submitted disturbing reports. At noon OHL sent a message that General Joffre was in Verdun and probably intended to attack on both sides of Metz. Two hours later it reported that the left flank of Fifth Army had been heavily attacked from Verdun. OHL wanted Sixth Army to detach forces towards Metz as soon as possible. Considering the tense situation at Lunéville, this was impossible. It was becoming increasingly clear that the pursuit in Lorraine should have been broken off on 22 August. The French attacks had now fixed Sixth Army in place. II b. AK and XXI AK, which on the morning of 25 August were attacking south, were now forced to orient west, with their lines of communication restricted by Fort Manonviller to the Einville–Lunéville road. Defending the exposed right flank could be considered a success. All available forces had to be concentrated at the most sensitive point, between Château Salins and Delm – the three cavalry divisions reunited under HKK 3, the Guard ED and all available troops from the fortifications at Strasbourg and the Upper Rhine. 1 Res. Bde was already underway from I b. AK to Lunéville. 2 Res. Bde was to leave only two battalions at Manonviller and move to Lunéville, along with two 15cm howitzer battalions.

At 2100hrs a liaison from OHL arrived at Sixth Army HQ at Duß with a new mission. Sixth Army was now to break through the French fortress line between Toul and Épinal and link up with Fifth Army approaching behind this line from the north. If this operation were successful, the results would be decisive: it might be possible to encircle a French army. Sixth Army, however, lacked the resources for such an operation. It would continue to engage the enemy: II b. AK and XXI AK would continue the attack, but avoid the heavily fortified French position at Bayon. Seventh Army required no new instructions.

On the French side, 25 August awakened justifiable hopes. The First Army commander intended to continue the attack on 26 August, while the Second Army commander thought that the Germans in his sector had been defeated and ordered the pursuit. He soon recognised that the Germans were not continuing to retreat, and revised his objectives downward. The French troops did not maintain their enthusiasm for the attack, with morale also reduced by fatigue and wet weather.

Events North of Lunéville (map 13, sketch 19)

In the III b. AK group area the French hardly budged. The *Ersatz* Corps was able to push its positions forward. On the morning of 26 August the III b. AK could reorganise, remunition and feed the troops undisturbed. Stragglers found their units and it became clear that casualties on the previous day were not so severe as feared. 5 ID used the high ground on Hill 301, east of Hoéville, and south to the Bois d'Einville for artillery firing positions. The infantry occupied this high ground with outposts, but kept the mass of the troops on the reverse slope. During the afternoon the enemy artillery began firing at extreme range without doing any damage. French infantry felt their way forwards, but received an appropriate reception from the German artillery. 6 ID held a line from Einville and the crossroads south-west of Bonviller. The division artillery engaged enemy infantry that appeared at noon between Maixe and Deuxville. The enemy artillery had apparently moved forward, and its fire was becoming problematic. It was suppressed somewhat by I/Foot Artillery R 3 (sFH), although the battery positions and the OP at La Rochelle, 700m west of Bonviller, took heavy counter-battery fire. Clearly the enemy was advancing with more resolution towards the 6 ID positions south of the Rhine–Marne Canal than on 5 ID and the *Ersatz* Corps north of it.

At noon the Bavarian KD at Hénaménil (off map, 2km west of Bauzemont) was ordered to move to the area north-west of Château Salins to cover the right flank of the III b. AK group. It appeared that the enemy was sending reinforcements by rail to Nancy. A long, difficult march followed. 3/Horse Artillery 5 had to replace its losses with obsolete caissons and ammunition wagons.

I b. RK was still under the operational control of III b. AK. 5 RD was to hold between La Rochelle and Friscati (between Lunéville and Deuxville). Under the cover of I/Foot Artillery 5 (15cm howitzer) and half of II/Res. Foot Artillery 1 (10cm cannons), which immediately began to engage enemy detachments near Deuxville, the infantry dug in. Reorganising the intermixed units, feeding the troops and replacing ammunition took considerable time. On the right, 9 Res. Bde had only a 400m sector on the west slope of a hill, which it held with II/RIR 6, while the rest of the brigade was deployed in depth to the rear. 4/Eng. Bn 2 aided in preparing the positions. RIR 7 assembled at Charmois and the troops were fed. Left of RIR 6 was RIR 10 (11 Res. Bde), which held a 600m-long position with I and II/RIR 10 in battle positions forward and III/RIR 10 in reserve. On its left, II/RIR 13 occupied positions begun by 1 Res./Eng. Bn 2. I and III/RIR 13 covered the flank at Friscati, with Res. *Jäger* Bn 1 in a deep sunken road 600m east of the farm. Around noon, 1/RFAR 5 also appeared here. III/*Landwehr* IR 8 took position on the high ground west of Jolivet, with IV/LIR 8 east of the town to guard against an attack from the south-west.

Friscati 26. 8.

Tertskizze 19.

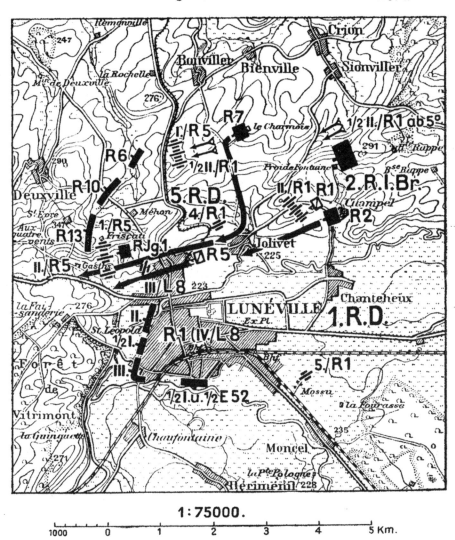

1 : 75000.

The morning was quiet. In the afternoon, enemy artillery began to shell the newly dug positions. Enemy infantry appeared to be preparing to attack from Hill 347, south-east of Deuxville, and the Forêt de Vitrimont. 1 RD sent II/RFAR 5 at exactly the right time. They went into position north-west of Lunéville and began firing to the south-west. RIR 13 had been forced to commit all its troops to line, along with 2 and 4/Res. *Jäger* Bn 1. These troops went over to the attack at 1800hrs and the French infantry fell back, but the French artillery engaged the thick RIR 13 skirmisher lines with such intensity that the regiment began to fall back and seek cover in the terrain along the road north from Lunéville. The commander of Res. *Jäger* Bn 1 brought 1 and 3/ Res. *Jäger* Bn 1 forward and sought to rally the troops: he succeeded in holding the gardens at Friscati. The commanders of 6 and 9/RIR 13 and 2 and 4/ *Jäger* Bn 1 held their men on Hill 347 south-east of Deuxville and threw back the enemy attacks, supported by RFAR 5 and half of II/Res. Foot Artillery 1 (10cm cannons) that displaced forward to low ground 1km south of Sionviller. The division commander sent III/LIR 8 and II and III/RIR 7 to help 11 Res. Bde. II/RIR 7 deployed on the right, III/RIR 7 on the left and moved towards Friscati, where an enemy breakthrough threatened. They climbed the hill under heavy artillery fire: some of the troops were swept back by retreating RIR 13 men, while others aided in holding Hill 347. At 1700hrs III/LIR 8 was also committed at Friscati. 13/LIR 8 was absorbed by RIR 7 and 13. The remaining companies followed the left wing of RIR 7, moving with great difficulty through the gardens, hedges and fences of the steep and close terrain on the south slope of Hill 347. 14/LIR 8 drifted right and joined RIR 7, while 15 and 16/LIR 8 covered the left flank. The situation was stabilised. The elements of RIR 13 and 7 on the road north of Lunéville were reorganised and brought forward to Hill 347.

1 Res. Bde had orders to move to Lunéville on 26 August. The brigade commander did not consider it prudent to conduct a hasty movement with tired troops in an uncertain situation, and began the march at a relatively late hour, stopping when the tactical situation to the west required it. At about 1300hrs the I b. AK commander ordered 1 Res. Bde to support 5 RD at Lunéville. II/ RFAR 5 returned to 5 RD control and moved to Friscati. RIR 1 moved to Lunéville, along a path of destruction and horror. The city was dead, and burning in several places. Doors and windows were barricaded. Many wounded French soldiers lay on the streets, while French stragglers were surely hiding in the town in large numbers. 1 Res. Bde was ordered to clear and defend Lunéville. II/RIR 1 occupied the west edge, with III/RIR 1 to the south-west on both sides of the rail line to Nancy. I and 1 Res./Eng. Bn 1 arrived later: half-deployed between II and III/RIR 1, the other half, along with *Ersatz* Bn 52 (8 ED), which was already in the city, went to the south side. IV/LIR 8 also arrived and was broken up. The

enemy did not attack. Panicked German stragglers spread wild rumours. RIR 2 had numerous troops drop out due to the heat; it bivouacked at Méhon (north of Lunéville) without tents, in a field full of corpses: the smell of decomposing bodies was nearly intolerable.

2 Res. Bde, which was to leave only two battalions in front of Fort Manonviller, spent the night turning over its positions to the engineers, assembling the troops and moving to Sionviller (4.5km north-east of Lunéville). The troops began marching at midnight and covered 4.5km in the heat: there were many stragglers. The troops' nerves had been tested by the appearance of the destroyed villages, the endless streams of wounded, and rumours of the seriousness of the situation forward and of the murderous effectiveness of the enemy artillery fire.

Stabilisation of the II b. AK Position, South-east of Lunéville

Xermaménil (map 17)

When the II b. AK commander received the Sixth Army order between 0400hrs and 0500hrs on 26 August, he immediately informed Sixth Army and XXI AK that he was unable to conduct the attack as ordered. The troops had been completely exhausted by the continual marching and combat of the preceding days, and had not had adequate sleep or food. 3 ID had suffered especially heavy casualties, particularly in officers. The situation north of Lunéville had separated the corps from its combat trains and part of the munitions columns and field trains. The right flank was threatened from the Forêt de Vitrimont. The commander of 3 ID also informed XXI AK that he could not attack. At dawn the II b. AK troops began occupying positions behind the Mortagne, from the town of Mortagne to Gerbéviller, often merely with the remnants of units on an over-extended front.

In the 3 ID sector, II/FAR 12 engaged French infantry appearing at Franconville and the woods west of Gerbéviller. Weak skirmisher lines, which remained at a respectful distance, also appeared at 1000hrs in front of IR 22 and 17: the French were clearly not attacking in earnest. The French artillery soon reopened fire.

Soon after dawn in the 4 ID sector, French troops in Mont, at the rail embankment to both sides of the town, and in the trees on the edge of the Bois de Vitrimont, opened fire on IR 9, located in and near Mortagne, in part into the regiment's flank. III and I/IR 5 and the MGK were deployed between Mortagne and Hill 273 to the south. The troops began to dig in, but were hampered by small arms fire from the high ground south of Mont. French artillery began to fall on 4 ID positions: the French guns had obviously moved forward behind the high ground south of Blainville. 4 FA Bde was unable to effectively engage the well-concealed French, whose guns were sometimes out of the Germans' range, but the German artillery was able to block the approach of the French infantry and keep it in the woods west of the Mortagne. Initially, the enemy had only brought light batteries into play, but as of 1000hrs began to employ heavy, long-range guns. At times the German gun crews had to take cover in the woods or take the guns out of their firing positions. Munitions wagons were shot to pieces, caught fire or exploded. The caissons and supply vehicles were hard hit, took casualties in horses and drivers and often had to change position, some moving into the Bois St Mansuy, where they got lost, blocked the few forest trails and became stuck in the undergrowth. Others moved far to the rear and became separated from their batteries. Fire control collapsed, as the telephone lines were continually cut and the section and regimental commanders were forced to change positions. The worst damage was inflicted on II/FAR 2, positioned on the west slope of the hill below the Bois St Mansuy, which was betrayed by the muzzle flashes. Gradually the French heavy artillery began to engage the 4 ID infantry. Xermaménil was set on fire. The enemy infantry gathered up their courage and attacked on Mont–Lamath at noon. They gained little ground, stopped by Bavarian small arms fire. The left flank of RIR 5, in particular 7/RIR 5 on the edge of the Bois de la Pte Frenoux, was attacked by two French battalions, which were easily pushed back, some immediately and some after a thirty-minute firefight. The average soldier in IR 9 fired off 400 rounds of 8mm Mauser ammunition. Lieutenant Kaufmann personally brought ammunition forward and took over command when the battalion commander was killed. Although the troops took casualties, they held out bravely under the artillery fire. Nevertheless, some individuals, even groups, slipped to the rear along with the wounded, where they spread rumours, incorrect information and false orders. Between 1400hrs and 1500hrs one such order for a general withdrawal to Hériménil circulated in 4 FA Brigade, and between 1400hrs and 1500hrs the already shaken batteries began to limber up. In many cases the drivers ignored the enemy fire and drove the limbers up to get the guns away. In other cases energetic and ruthless officers had to force the drivers forward. In its open position II/FAR 2 was immobilised by the enemy fire: 4/FAR 2 had to be abandoned. Slowly the morale of RIR 5, on an open forward slope facing the Mortagne and completely exposed to the French artillery fire, began to crumble. According to the 5 Res. Bde commander, the regiment stood up as one man and proceeded to the rear at a walk and in complete order. They occupied a position on the edge of the Bois St Mansuy without difficulty. But their example, and that of the withdrawing artillery, was the signal for a general withdrawal.

At 0900hrs II b. AK ordered 4 ID to hold the position, but if pressed to withdraw with the front facing to the north, and, if necessary, over the Meurthe using the Moncel bridge. When the division commander saw troops retreating without orders, he sent *Chevauleger* R 8 to the Bois St Mansuy with orders to stop them, using their lances if necessary. At 1100hrs both he and his General Staff officer were wounded by shell splinters. The 5 Res. Bde commander took command of the division. Although II b. AK again directed that the 4 ID position be held, it was necessary to order a retreat to a rallying position on the high ground immediately south of Hériménil: 7 Bde and 11 FA Bde on the right, 5 Res. Bde and 2 FA Bde on the left, making contact with 3 ID in the Bois de la Haye.

11 FA Bde and I/FAR 2 moved intermixed on the Rehainviller–Lunéville road. Many of the gun crews had removed the breech blocks when they left the firing positions. Several ammunition caissons remained behind, some shot-up. They halted and reorganised as best as possible at Chaudfontaine and moved to new firing positions.

At 1600hrs in the 5 Res. Bde sector, the commander of RIR 8 gave the order to evacuate Xermaménil, where the artillery fire had become insupportable and the troops had begun to leave their positions. RIR 5 and 8 became thoroughly intermixed. Troops dropped their packs. RIR 5 assembled at Beaupré and occupied the ridge south-west of the farm with a few companies, while part of RIR 8 assembled at Hériménil and covered the artillery, and part moved back to Moncel.

At 1700hrs 7 Bde broke contact. To cover the withdrawal the brigade commander sent a company of IR 9 from Hériménil to the north side of the Meurthe at Rehainviller. Due to complete exhaustion, the company lost three-quarters of its strength during the march. The III/IR 9 commander stopped the group, now only seventy strong, at Rehainviller in order cover to evacuation of the wounded. They pushed back French infantry approaching from the Forêt de Vitrimont. 2/IR 9 held Rehainviller until the last men passed. IR 5 had used a pause in the French artillery fire from 1300hrs to 1530hrs to prepare the withdrawal. IR 5 and 9 became intermixed in the open ground north of the Bois St Mansuy, where there was no cover and very heavy casualties were taken. Severely reduced companies of IR 5 took up positions in a rise at Hériménil and in the north part of the Bois du Fréhaut, while the disorganised remainder bivouacked at Hériménil or crossed the Meurthe on a XXI AK bridge at Moncel. IR 9 was assembled at Hériménil and Moncel, and led south of IR 5 where it established outposts.

The events of the day, compounded by the wet weather, lowered morale everywhere. Exhaustion had reached a dangerous level, and together with darkness hindered digging in at the new position. Nevertheless, discipline, which had been made second nature through peacetime training, gained the upper hand. The enemy did not pursue, and felt his way forward carefully. The 7 Bde commander (formerly the commander of IR 5) was wounded and replaced by the commander of IR 9.

The withdrawal of the 4 ID left caused 5 Bde to withdraw also, which caused 6 Bde to pull back in turn. The movements were accomplished in complete order and undisturbed. The troops dug in, although the work was made difficult by the clay soil and some enemy artillery fire. 3 ID, which had suffered more severely the previous day than 4 ID, used the respite on 26 August to complete its reorganisation. The extent of the 3 ID losses can be seen in IR 22, which could only form six companies (II/IR 22 with two companies, III/IR 22 with four).

Aviation Sec. 2 moved its airfield 20km to the north-east, but the aircraft flown off on 25 August were scattered in Mörchingen, Saarbrücken and elsewhere, and did not reassemble until 27 August.

II b. AK had ordered both divisions to stand fast, but their withdrawal presented the corps with a *fait accompli*. That evening it asked both I b. RK and I b. AK for assistance and ordered the corps bridge train to put two bridges over the Meurthe. The corps ordered the troops to hold their positions west of the Meurthe, but made preparations for a withdrawal over the river. It reported to Sixth Army that, weakened by exhaustion and heavy casualties, it would not be able to prevent an enemy breakthrough.

The French had also suffered heavy casualties. The French XV Corps had attacked the German 4 ID right wing with 30 ID at Mont and 64 RD south of Mont. The reinforced French XVI Corps had advanced against Lamath–Gerbéviller. The exhaustion of the troops, intermixed units and concern for French VIII Corps on the right, led the corps commander to be satisfied with possession of the Mortagne. The French 29 ID, reinforced with a brigade from 31 ID and one from 74 RD, had attacked at Lamath, 32 ID attacked south of it at Bois de Broth, while brigades of 31 and 74 RD at Gerbéviller were stopped by German artillery fire from advancing beyond the treelines west and south of the town.

On the morning of 26 August, German XXI AK renewed the attack against the French XIII Corps, which was also attacking. On the German XXI AK right, 31 ID soon encountered advancing French forces, saw its right flank threatened and was forced to withdraw to the high ground on the south-west side of the Mortagne, near Vallois (off map, 4km south-east of Gerbéviller). 31 ID had encountered 15 ID of the French XIII Corps. On the left, 42 ID had taken Deinvillers and the high ground south of Xaffévillers by noon. 42 ID was able to defeat the right wing of the French XIII Corps, 25 ID, before it could launch its own attack. The French First Army commander instructed VIII Corps to attack the German XXI AK in the left flank, which put 42 ID in a very serious situation, but it was assisted by the neighbour on the left, I b. AK.

8 KD was once again ordered to advance to Rambervillers and reached to within 4km of the town, before withdrawing 2km and supporting XXI AK with artillery fire. Only the artillery of 7 KD was in action supporting XXI AK.

At 1400hrs 7 KD moved to the right wing of Sixth Army on bad roads, packed with other units, and reached the area of Manonviller at midnight. 8 KD received the movement order late and only made it to the area north-east of Lunéville. Both divisions bivouacked in the open.

In the Seventh Army sector, the French still held the Forêt de St Barbe, which split XIV AK in half and put all of Seventh Army in an unfavourable position. The troops west of XIV AK – 7 KD, I b. AK and 29 ID – therefore could do no more than be ready to assist XXI AK if necessary. Only 28 ID and XV AK east of the woods were available to attack towards Étival (4km south of Raon l'Étape).

Doncières (map 18)

On the morning of 26 August I b. AK released 1 Res. Bde and assembled 1 ID near Baccarat in order to be able to move in the direction of Lunéville. 2 ID and the IR 2 battle group at Ménil were to defend in place and be prepared to support XXI AK moving south from Domptail. The gap left by 1 Res. Bde would initially be filled by 7 and 8 KD. Shortly after 0645hrs, Seventh Army regained complete operational control over I b. AK and the entire corps was prepared to attack on both sides of Nossoncourt by noon.

Early in the morning IR 16 searched through Baccarat and hauled out a number of French troops hidden in cellars and elsewhere, as well as numerous French soldiers' packs that contained civilian clothing. The main body of 1 ID moved under strong enemy artillery fire down the road to Ménil, but there was insufficient room to deploy between 2 ID and XIV AK. 1 Bde found the road completely packed with supply units of XIV AK. FAR 1 had to stop on the road in the woods. I/Res. Foot Artillery 13 (sFH) managed to find a firing position north-west of St Barbe. II/FAR 7, in place the previous day, engaged French infantry south-west of Ménil and at Doncières. French artillery at Anglemont shelled the Bavarian batteries and spread area fire over the slopes and treelines occupied by the infantry, as well as the approach roads and assembly areas in the Bavarian rear.

On the morning of 26 August 2 ID began to dig in, taking casualties from artillery fire. From positions occupied on the previous day, 2 FA Bde drove back enemy skirmisher lines that advanced from the woods by Anglemont, but was unable to suppress the French artillery. I/FAR 4 and I/FAR 9 had displaced somewhat from their unfavourable forward positions at Bazien and Nossoncourt, but were too closely packed together and suffered serious casualties. The caissons and vehicles took direct hits and were in part destroyed or dispersed. II/Foot Artillery R1 (sFH), north of Bazien, engaged enemy artillery at the north-west side of the Bois de Roville.

I b. AK HQ arrived at the treeline north of Bazien at noon. Reports received during the morning from XXI AK on the right said that 42 ID had reached

Xaffévillers and that the attack on the high ground south of the town was proceeding well: the enemy seemed to be falling back. A French division was reported marching west (away from I b. AK) from Rambervillers (5km southwest of Nossoncourt). 42 ID intended to continue the attack in the direction of St Maurice. I b. AK was concerned by the intensity of the French artillery fire and renewed French attempts to advance from the woods south of Anglemont. Shortly after 1500hrs, Aviation Sec. 1 reported that strong enemy forces, probably a corps, had been seen east of Rambervillers around noon and were being reinforced from Épinal.

At the same time, 4 Bde received an urgent call for help from 65 Bde (IR 17 and 131) on the left flank of 42 ID, which was hard pressed in its fight south of Xaffévillers. 4 Bde could see that French artillery fire had been landing there for hours. The 4 Bde commander decided to attack to assist 65 Bde. Only 5/FAR 9 was available to provide fire support, but it enjoyed magnificent observation from Hill 316, north-east of Doncières. When the infantry attack stalled, a few salvoes from 5/FAR 9 sufficed to break the French resistance on the Belleville stream and suppress their fire. In a single rush, 4 Bde climbed the hills on both sides of Doncières.

IR 15 advanced north on Doncières, with I/IR 15 in the lead, deploying 1 and 2/IR 15 in the first line, followed by 3 and 4/IR 15, then turned towards the woods 1km west of the town to assist 65 Bde, while under continual artillery fire. The battalion was stopped by fire into its left flank from the north side of the Bois de la Grande Coinche. I/IR 15 could not hold the wood. The withdrawal to the low ground on the south-west side of Doncières had the effect of thinning out the dense skirmisher lines. Some stragglers ended up at the Château de Villers. Later the battalion regained the high ground west of Doncières and held it until dark. III/IR 15 passed through Doncières, which was already occupied by Prussian troops. Soon the entire battalion was deployed against the high ground south-west of the town, along with troops of IR 17 and 131. Small arms fire from the north side of the Bois de la Grande Coinche drew the troops in that direction. The MGK/IR 15 followed but took such heavy fire from artillery and small arms that it had to move slowly and carefully by bounds to reach a firing position south-west of Doncières.

IR 12 was ordered to attack the north-east side of the Bois de la Grande Coinche. II/IR 12 crossed over Hill 316 and descended into the Belville stream, accompanied by French artillery fire, and followed by the MGK, which forded the stream, carrying the guns with water up to their hips. I/IR 12, with 1, 2 and 4/IR 12 in the first line, 3/IR 12 following, joined the attack from Château de Villers. II/IR 15 (minus 6/IR 15) was released from division reserve, arrived at Château de Villers at 1630hrs and followed I/IR 12. III/IR 12 was 4 Bde reserve east of Doncières. 4 and 6/FAR 9 arrived on Hill 316; they, as well as

5/Res. Foot Artillery 1 (10cm cannons) had lost considerable time waiting for 8 KD to pass by.

IR 12 took heavy fire, but the attack gained ground quickly. Wave after wave of skirmishers ascended the hill. Practically no time was lost returning the enemy fire; the troops fired standing behind stooks of grain. Confronted by the advancing waves, the unfurled colours and the glistening bayonets, the enemy lost heart. His fire became so unsteady that it hardly caused casualties; finally he fled. At 1715hrs I/IR 12 stood on the north-east edge of the wood. The commander of 2/IR 15, which was in the lead, pressed into the wood and encountered strong French detachments; he was killed in hand-to-hand combat. By 1800hrs II/IR 12, led by 6 and 7/IR 12, had approached to within 100m of the wood. The battalion commander, his staff and the two remaining companies joined the firing line and the woodline was taken by storm; the French fled into the undergrowth. 8/IR 12 was tasked with clearing snipers out of the trees. It pushed to the west edge of the forest and took fire from the south and turned in that direction. The platoon leaders raced far in front of their heavily laden troops and were forced to take cover and defend themselves with their pistols. The company captured two abandoned guns. To the right of II/IR 12, skirmisher lines from III/IR 15, IR 17 and IR 131 also entered the north side of the Bois de la Grande Coinche. The way for them was cleared by MGK/IR 12, which had set up on the high ground south-west of Doncières and swept the hedges in front of the wood with fire. Together with MGK/IR 15 they mowed down the fleeing French in rows.

The 4 Bde attack had suffered casualties, in particular in I/IR 15. But not only was the pressure on the left flank of XXI AK relieved, it was also pulled forward towards the Bois de la Grande Coinche. Nevertheless, the I b. AK and XXI AK commanders agreed to withdraw behind the Belville stream, while I b. AK extended its right flank to the Bois de la Horne, north-east of Xaffévillers. At 1900hrs IR 15 moved to the area east of Xaffévillers, and IR 12 to the wood south of Ménarmont. But both regiments felt they had won a complete victory. A heavy rain began that evening, which continued until the next morning.

Even though I b. AK had attacked that afternoon with only 4 Bde to assist XXI AK, this had sufficed to put paid to the attack by the reinforced French XIII Corps. The French 25 ID succeeded in holding St Maurice and Roville, but 26 ID, which had advanced against Doncières, was hit by 4 Bde and fled in disorder to Rambervillers. The French 44 ID attack on Ménarmont was turned back by I b. AK artillery fire. The French division thought its right flank threatened and withdrew to the east of Rambervillers.

On 26 August, 29 ID, on the right flank of XIV AK, remained largely inactive at St Barbe. 58 Bde attempted unsuccessfully to break through the Forêt de St Barbe, but only became involved in costly combat in the woods. On the corps left, 28 ID was to envelop the enemy forces facing XV AK and push its advance guard over the Rambervillers–St Benoit road. During the morning XV AK threw back several enemy attacks, but its own attack became bogged down in the woods. Both corps were opposed by the French XXI Corps. The left flank of XV AK was attacked by 27 ID of the French XIV Corps, which failed, and the French withdrew to Moyenmoutier (5km south-east of Raon l'Étape).

The only German corps in Lorraine that attacked with full force on 26 August, XXI AK, was now completely blocked and had to withdraw in the face of enemy attacks and artillery fire. The tip of the wedge that OHL intended would separate the French forces in the Vosges from Épinal was now dull and stuck tight. Everything had come to a standstill, including the French attack launched on 24 August, which also had not reached its objectives.

Conquest of Fort Manonviller

Fort Manonviller lay in the gap between Nancy and Épinal, close to the German border, 12km east of Lunéville. It blocked the Strasbourg–Nancy rail line and the roads from Badonviller and Blâmont to Lunéville. Its guns could interdict the Rhine–Marne Canal and ranged east 3km, in the south to the Meurthe and west to the gates of Lunéville: during its advance Sixth Army had to make extensive detours to avoid Manonviller.

Manonviller was France's strongest *Sperrfort* (forts built between the major fortresses of Verdun, Toul, Épinal and Belfort). The French had reinforced it against high-explosive shells. It had bombproof shelters for the entire garrison – two companies of infantry, one and a half batteries of foot artillery, a third of an engineer company and a platoon of foresters. The artillery consisted of four armoured turrets, each with two 155mm canons, with a range of 8km, twenty-three other long-range guns, twelve flanking guns to cover the fortress front, three depressing armoured towers (two with 57mm fast-firing canon, one with two MGs) and several MGs in open positions. There were six armoured observation towers and three watchtowers. The fort stood on a 318m-high hill that dominated the surrounding terrain. Three kilometres to the north was the Forêt de Parroy and to the south was the Forêt de Mondon, both thick and extensive wooded areas.

As early as 7 August OHL ordered Sixth Army to take the fort and attached siege units for that purpose. The siege was to be under the leadership of the Sixth Army engineer. It was clear that it would be conducted from the east. Between 10 and 14 August Bavarian Railway Co. 1 had laid 1.2km of track from Avricourt, the last German rail station on the Sarrebourg–Lunéville rail line, to bring up the 42cm mortar batteries. Reconnaissance began on 13 August. Then the withdrawal of Sixth Army put the operation in abeyance, to be resumed on 23 August. For the siege, the Sixth Army engineer was given operational control over (♦ denotes mobile gun (with horse teams and vehicles); other units had no organic mobility):

2 Res. Bde

Res. Cavalry R 1

2 Foot Artillery Bde HQ; Foot Artillery R 1 HQ; Foot Artillery R 18 HQ

I/Res. FAR 1

Three 15cm howitzer sections, each with sixteen guns: I/Res. Foot Artillery R 1; I/Res. Foot Artillery R 13; II/Res. Foot Artillery R 14

Three 21cm mortar sections, each with eight guns: II/Foot Artillery R 3; II; III/ Foot Artillery R 18♦

Heavy Coastal Mortar Bty β (30.5cm), two guns♦

Short Naval Canon Bty γ (42cm), two guns♦

Bavarian Eng. R; Eng. R 19★; Bavarian Siege Train

Fortress MGK Strasbourg♦

Bavarian Airship Sec.

Fortress Aviation Sec. Germersheim♦

Heavy Fortress Searchlight Sec. Strasbourg♦

Half of Railroad Co. 2

Fortress Light Railroad Co. 12 Strasbourg♦

Steam Tractor Park Strasbourg♦

On 23 August 2 Res. Bde began to invest Manonviller, with the RIR 3 main body 9km to the east and the outposts 4km from the fort; RIR 12 was south of RIR 3. On 24 August RIR 3 moved its outpost line into the Forêt de Parroy in the north, while RIR 12 occupied the Forêt de Mondon to the south. The remaining siege forces were assembled at Avricourt (10km north-east of Manonviller) and Blâmont, 13km east. The enemy had not touched the rail line constructed between 10 and 14 August for the 42cm mortars. I/Res. Foot Artillery 13 (sFH) had to be detached to assist I b. AK. On the night of 24/25 August the siege artillery moved into position. The roads were packed with both siege artillery and the supply units of the corps, and there was all kinds of friction, but Manonviller's artillery did not disturb the operation: preparations, reconnaissance and approach march and been successfully hidden from the enemy, who seemed to have been focused on the noise of combat at Lunéville. To maintain operational security, the inhabitants of the surrounding villages were sequestered in the churches. Engineers assisted the artillery in moving into and digging in the positions and bringing up shells.

Under the command of Foot Artillery R 18, I/Res. Foot Artillery 14 (sFH) and II/Foot Artillery 18 (21cm mortars) were 8km to the east of the fort; Foot Artillery R 1 was given control over II/Res. Foot Artillery R 14 (sFH), III/Foot Artillery

R 18 (21cm mortars) and II/Foot Artillery R 3 (21cm mortars), 5–7.5km south-east. The 42cm mortars were going into position north of Avricourt at a range of 13km, and the 30.5cm mortars were at Chazelles, due east of the fort at a range of 9.5km. The captive balloon of Airship Sec. 1 went up at 0800hrs east of Chazelles, 10km from the fort, where the artillery commander established his HQ.

At 1030hrs the artillery, with the exception of the 30.5cm and 42cm mortars, opened fire, completely surprising the garrison. Massive pieces of concrete and earth were thrown into the air and the fort was covered by smoke and dust, which blinded its observers and hindered counter-battery fire.

Under cover of the artillery fire, the infantry began to move forward. But in the middle of this movement Sixth Army ordered all available forces withdrawn to meet the crisis at Lunéville: this meant RIR 3 and III/RIR 4 moved to Parroy, while I/Res. Foot Artillery 1 (sFH) reinforced III b. AK and II/Res. Foot Artillery 14 reinforced I b. RK. These troops moved out during the night of 25/26 August.

Engineer R 19, which had been occupied with reconnoitring approach routes and bridges, and searching for mines and underground communications lines, now took over the RIR 3 sector. I/Eng. R 19 on the right approached to 1.2km from the north side of the fort. In the II/Eng. R 19 sector, on the left, 3/Eng. R 19 approached to within 500m of the fort, which appeared to be dead and perhaps even evacuated, but it then took fire and had to withdraw east to a safe 3.5km distance. The Bavarian Eng. R was fully occupied assisting the artillery.

Since the enemy guns were completely silent, during the evening I/Res. FAR 1 displaced forward, 1 and /Res. FAR 1 to a position 5.5km south-east of the fortress, and were able to register their guns before dark, while 2/Res. FAR 1 moved to a position 5km north-east of the fort the next morning. During the night of 25/26 August the artillery continued to bombard Manonviller.

Steam tractors brought up the 30.5cm guns; the heavy Lorraine clay made the work difficult. After the track had been laid for the 42cm guns, it took thirty-six hours of constant work to prepare the positions. The heavy batteries opened fire on the morning of 26 August in conjunction with the 21cm mortars. Fire was also directed against the wire obstacles and suspected minefields in the glacis. The OPs were pushed forwards. During the morning the French artillery returned fire for a short time.

It was intended that the engineers conduct the assault early on 27 August. On the night of 26/27 August their positions were moved forward, along with assault equipment. But the garrison used each interruption during the bombardment, which might signal a ground assault, to cover the front with searchlights, flares and defensive fires. I/Eng. R 19 and 8/RIR 12 on the right could only approach to within 800m, while 3 and 4/Eng. R 19 on the left approached to within 200m of the defensive obstacles. I/b. Eng R took the town of Manonviller, 1.7km south of the fort, while II/b. Eng R took Domjevin 4.4km south-east, and I and

II/RIR 12 approached in the south and south-east to within 600–700m of the fort. This was not close enough for an assault, and patrols reported that the fort was not *sturmreif* (sufficiently softened up for an assault).

The artillery continued the bombardment on 27 August. The captive balloon displaced forward at 0500hrs to 9.5km from the fort. At 0800hrs Sixth Army attached II/Foot Artillery R 3 (21cm mortars) to II b. AK and the battalion formed march column. II b. AK said it didn't need the guns, but their firepower had been lost. Between 1100hrs and 1300hrs equipment failure forced the 42cm battery to partially or completely cease fire. The German bombardment nevertheless kept the garrison in its bombproof bunkers. During the morning 1 and 2/Eng. R 19, followed by 2/RIR 12, advanced by bounds to within 300m. The b. Eng. R assisted RIR 12 digging in. A platoon of b. Eng. Bn 4 moved 250m forward from Manonviller town, while 2 Res./b. Eng. Bn 4 established itself on a hill opposite the fortress gate. Of the original seventy-six siege guns, all but twenty had been removed, but, as of 1400hrs, all were firing on the fort. The garrison, 20 officers and 759 enlisted men, surrendered at 1630hrs. It had suffered only 2 officers and 21 enlisted men as casualties, but the bombardment had crushed their morale. Two and a half days' bombardment had caused massive damage. All the artillery had been destroyed, the armoured turrets penetrated or immobile, the bunkers for the most part broken up or exposed, and the passages collapsed. The wire obstacles and barrier fence had large gaps. The wall had been turned into rubble. The flanking positions in the ditch had wide cracks. The artillery had fired 979 15cm, 4,596 21cm, 134 30.5cm and 159 42cm shells. The engineers destroyed the remaining bunkers, flanking positions and obstacles.

The Breakthrough Over the Vosges to the Meurthe, South of St Dié

23–27 August (situation map f)

The German forces in the Vosges – XIV RK, 19 ED, 30 RD, Bavarian ED, under the operational control of the commanding general of XIV RK – were not able to fix the French forces opposite them in place until they could be surrounded by Sixth Army attacking from the north. It had even been hoped that the French would be further cut off by an attack west from Markirch to St Dié. Nevertheless, the attack in the Vosges made steady progress. Initially the divisions attacked independently, separated by the mountains, but as they advanced out of the Vosges they were able to form a more continuous front. They were opposed principally by the French XIV Corps, Alpine battalions and the Épinal reserve (71 RD).

The XIV RK commander intended to renew the attack on 23 August, but the troops were exhausted. However, during the afternoon it appeared that the enemy was withdrawing, so offensive action was called for. 28 RD made slow progress against French rearguards in the mountains, while 26 RD had it easier. 19 ED, attached to XIV RK, remained in place. All three divisions made a slow and costly advance in the mountains on 24 August. On the night of 24/25 August the French withdrew and XIV RK took Senones on 25 August.

30 RD Advance Over the Col d'Urbeis, 23–25 August (sketch 20)

On 23 August 30 RD, which had withdrawn from Steige, rested at Weiler, then reorganised, maintained its equipment and fed the troops, some of whom had not had hot food for three days, and found local guides for the advance on 24 August. The French made no effort whatsoever to pursue. Also on 23 August 30 RD was informed that the French were withdrawing and, on 24 August, moved back up the valley towards Urbeis

At 0330hrs a task force composed of II/RIR 14, two platoons from 1 *Ersatz/* FAR 84 and a platoon of Res. MGK 3 was sent as a flank guard towards the Wein-Berg. When it was east of Weinberg town at 0900hrs, it took small arms fire from the town and the slope to the north-east. Initially, 5/RIR 14 took up the firefight, with 7 and 8/RIR 14 quickly coming up on the right and 6/RIR 14 on the left. An immediate attempt to advance was stopped by enemy fire.

The 30 RD advance guard – RIR 14 (minus II/RIR 14), Fortress MG Sec. 2, *Ersatz* Cavalry Sec./II b.AK, Bicycle Co./RIR 60 and one platoon 1 *Ersatz*/FAR 84 – reached Urbeis at 0630hrs and stopped for a two-hour rest in preparation for ascending the pass. The advance guard battalion, I/RIR 14, sent 1/RIR 14 through the hills to the north and 3/RIR 14 to the south as flank detachments. Nevertheless, III/RIR 14, which was following, continually took fire and had to comb out the hills itself. The main body consisted of I/RIR 11, Res. MGK 3 (minus a platoon), II/RIR 11, *Ersatz* Sec./FAR 80, *Ersatz* Bn VI, *Ersatz* FA Sec. IV, *Ersatz* Bn VII, *Ersatz* MGK 5, *Ersatz* Bn V and VIII.

The advance guard again moved towards the Col d'Urbeis at 0900hrs, sending flanking squads and platoons to chase off French skirmishers. 4/RIR 14 joined 3/RIR 14 to the south. 2 and 1/RIR 14, which had rejoined the column, set off straight up the pass, clearing the woods on both sides of the road. The two companies continually took small arms fire, but near the top they were shelled by a gun located on the pass itself, so 2 deployed north and 1 south of the road. In spite of the efforts of RIR 14, just beyond Urbeis RIR 11 continually took fire from the west and north-west. The division staff had to take cover. Word arrived that the battle at the Wein-Berg was not going well and the division commander

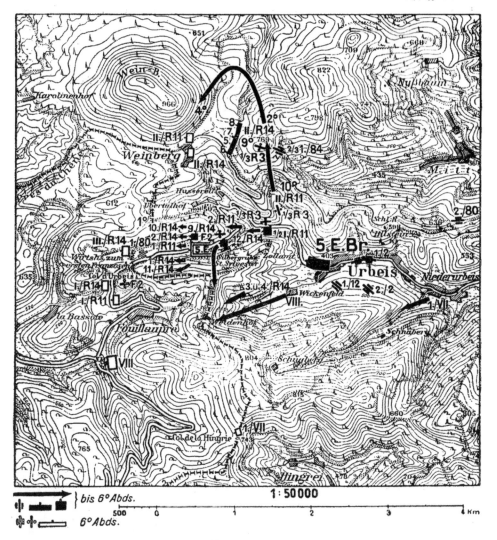

Col d'Urbeis. 24. 8.

Textskizze 20.

1 : 50 000

Key

bis 6 Abds – until 1800

6 Abds – 1800

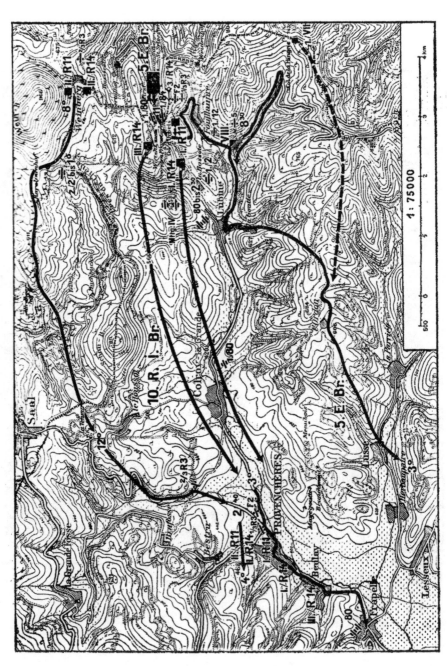

Loss of the Col [Pass] of Ste. Marie

Verluſt des Col de Ste. Marie. 23. 8.   Textſkizze 22.

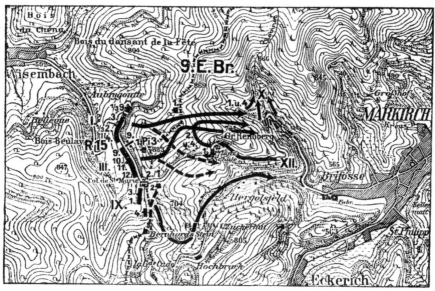

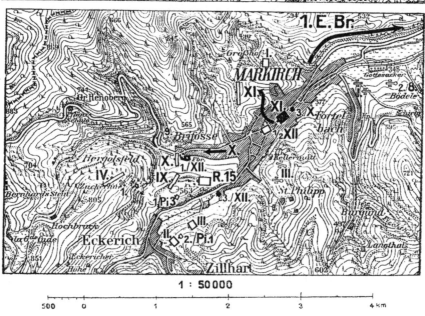

1 : 50000

500   0   1   2   3   4 km

➡ bis etwa 3°-4° Nachm.

⇨ nach 4° Nachm.

Key

bis etwa 3–4 Nachm – until about 1500–1600

nach 4 Nachm – after 1600

sent II/RIR 11 with a platoon of Res. MGK 3 in that direction. 10/RIR 14 was in the woods north of the road and engaged with a dug-in French position covered by barbed wire, but in spite of heavy losses had advanced to within 100m. When a platoon of 9/RIR 14 turned the French left flank, they fled.

1/RIR 11 had reached the open ground east of the pass. Although it received small arms and MG fire from the high ground north and west of the pass, it succeeded in taking the French gun. By 1300hrs the pass was securely in German hands; RIR 11 and 14 dug in. The next town 2km down the French side of the pass, Lubine, appeared strongly held. French troops could also be seen on the west side of the pass. That afternoon 1 *Ersatz*/FAR 80 set up under enemy artillery fire immediately east of the pass and chased them off. The German infantry on the pass came under occasional French artillery fire.

At 1000hrs II/RIR 11, under the regimental commander, set off towards Wein-Berg, climbing steep switchbacks in the heat. It was necessary to halt frequently. At 1400hrs contact was made with II/RIR 14, whose situation had materially improved when *Ersatz* FA Sec. IV, 2 *Ersatz*/FAR 2 and 1 *Ersatz*/FAR 12 went into position on the slopes south of Urbeis and suppressed the fire from the Wein-Berg. On the recommendation of the II/RIR 14 commander, II/RIR 11 enveloped the French left. Once again the troops set out in blazing heat across deep valleys and up steep hills. When the battalion appeared on the French left, the French fled, but not without leaving masses of weapons and ammunition, boxes of canned meat and a sack of bread. Both battalions bivouacked on the Wein-Berg. By evening *Ersatz* Bn VIII had reached the sawmill (*Sägemühle*) 1km east of Lubine. The mass of 5 *Ersatz* Bde was east of the pass. The troops had quickly taken the pass against weak resistance, but were tired out by combat in the heat and steep terrain.

(Sketch 21) On 25 August the 30 RD commander intended to continue the attack to Colroy-la-Grande and ordered the troops to be ready to move at 0500hrs, but general exhaustion and intermixing of units from the previous day caused a two-hour delay. The enemy was assumed to be on the high ground west of Lubine. The attack would be conducted by 10 Res. Bde, which would conduct a deep double-envelopment: on the right with II/RIR 11, II/RIR 14 and Res. MGK 3 (minus a platoon); on the left with *Ersatz* Bn VIII, while RIR 14 (minus II/RIR 14) attacked the high ground north of the road in the middle, followed by the rest of the division. The artillery was in position on the pass.

The troops had just begun movement when strong French forces were reported at Colroy-la-Grande–Provenchères heading north to Saal. It appeared possible to hit this force in the flank, so the right wing chose a route farther to the north, with I/RIR 11 and a MG platoon attached. The column moved out at 0800hrs. In the centre RIR 14 made its way through thick undergrowth, but the French withdrew. The artillery displaced forward and was able to engage the French columns. At 0830hrs *Ersatz* Bn VIII began moving south-east to conduct its deep envelopment, but when the French evacuated Lubine it counter-marched in that direction. By noon 30 RD was conducting a general pursuit, with the artillery moving by bounds to engage the French, who fled in disorder to Colroy-la-Grande. RIR 14 advanced fully deployed across the open ground north of Lubine. Given the mountainous terrain and heat, progress was slow. Between 1000hrs and 1100hrs the Governor of Strasbourg informed 30 RD – in part incorrectly – that XIV RK had taken Saal and the Germans had occupied St Dié. The 30 RD commander therefore turned his forces in a more southerly direction, with 10 Res. Bde aiming for Colroy-la-Grande and 5 *Ersatz* Bde for Lusse. 10 Res. Bde linked up with 26 RD at Saal and, at noon, it could see into the valley between Colroy-la-Grande and Provenchères, where French troops were in panic flight and being shelled by 30 RD artillery. By 1500hrs the Bicycle Co./RIR 60 had entered Provenchères. RIR 14 approached from the east, having rounded up numerous prisoners, while 5 *Ersatz* Bde reached Lusse after an exhausting march in the mountains.

Nothing prevented 30 RD from continuing the pursuit to the south-east. At 1300hrs a XIV AK order directed 30 RD to take Colroy-la-Grande and Provenchères, which now was overtaken by events. The same order directed 26 RD to Provenchères. The 30 RD commander therefore instructed his troops to bivouac at Frapelle and Lusse. III/RIR 14 moved 1km down the road, but took fire from French stragglers and stopped.

XIV RK and 30 RD had been opposed by the French 28 ID, which was positioned on the right flank of the French XIV Corps. The French troops that were moving north in front of 30 RD were probably elements of 44 ID repositioning to attack Raon l'Étape, and had not anticipated being attacked in the flank.

Advance of the Bavarian *Ersatz* Division over the Col de St Marie to Wisembach, 23–25 August

Setback on the Col de St Marie, 23 August (sketch 22)

On 22 August the Bavarian ED had taken its objective, the Col de St Marie. The commander of 9 *Ersatz* Bde, who was in charge at Markirch, anticipated a French advance against his right flank and, in this event, planned to withdraw east. Between 0700hrs and 0800hrs he ordered 1 *Ersatz* Bde and the artillery to assemble 4km east of St Marie, with 9 *Ersatz* Bde just east of St Marie. The north half of the pass would be held by I and II/RIR 15, the south half by *Ersatz* Bn IX, with *Ersatz* MGK 9 and 1 *Ersatz*/Eng. Bn 3 in reserve. One platoon of 2 *Ersatz*/FAR 1 was in the houses it had occupied the previous day, and the other two were positioned on the reverse slope of the pass. Digging in proceeded slowly due to the stony ground and lack of pioneer tools. The troops had instructions to fall back through the woods to Markirch if attacked by superior forces. Where this order originated is unknown.

Early in the day, activity was seen in the enemy trenches south of Wisembach. Artillery was detected on the high ground north of the town. At 1100hrs thick French skirmisher lines on the east side of the Bois Beulay opened fire and tried to advance over the valley of the Cude stream. However, III/RIR 15 threw them back into the wood, in conjunction with *Ersatz* MGK 9, which moved into the front line, and 2 *Ersatz*/FAR 1, which with great difficulty hauled four guns up to the open area near the houses on the pass, where they deployed wheelhub-to-wheelhub; at point-blank range the German gunners could not miss. The French were also able to use the woods south-west of the houses to get close to the guns and inflict painful casualties; the battery commander was badly wounded, but the French could make no progress against *Ersatz* Bn IX. By noon the French were enveloping I/RIR 15 on the regimental right flank; the battalion commander ordered a withdrawal. Platoon and squad cohesion collapsed in the woods. The RIR 15 commander directed 2 *Ersatz*/FAR 1, which in any case had fired off its ammunition, to limber up. About the same time panic broke out in the combat trains of RIR 15 east of the pass; the vehicles moved down the road to the valley at speed, with the artillery following. III/RIR 15 managed to hold onto the treeline north of the pass, covering the withdrawal, until it too was flanked on the right and forced to retreat. French skirmishers climbed the Gr. Henoberg and were descending towards Markirch; III/RIR 15 and 1 *Ersatz*/Eng. Bn 3 attacked them in the rear, succeeded in pushing them back up the Gr. Henoberg and clearing a route to Markirch, although III/RIR 15 also lost cohesion. On the left flank of III/RIR 15, *Ersatz* MGK 9 held the enemy in check at the saddle of the pass and then withdrew to Markirch. *Ersatz* Bn IX stayed the longest; the battalion commander did not give the order to withdraw until 1300hrs, when the situation was clearly hopeless. By a stroke of luck, 4/*Ersatz* Bn IX and a platoon of 2/*Ersatz* Bn IX on the left flank, with no knowledge of the situation, attacked the enemy and forced the French to withdraw. The 4/*Ersatz* Bn IX commander was killed, but his action allowed the battalion to break contact and withdraw to the south unhindered and in marching column. The Bavarian ED trains had withdrawn early, followed by 1 *Ersatz* Bde and *Ersatz* FA Sec. III. An aviator saw French columns withdrawing from Urbeis to the north.

At Markirch, the commanders of the Bavarian ED and 9 *Ersatz* Bde had no idea of the seriousness of the situation forward; around 1100hrs the sound of a few cannons firing was heard, and later the noise of combat was swept west by the wind or swallowed in the woods. At noon, but before the pass had been lost, a bicyclist brought a message from the RIR 15 commander, asking that *Ersatz* Bn X, XI and

XII be sent to reinforce. *Ersatz* Bn XII was stopped at Brifosse, immediately turned around and headed up the pass. 1/*Ersatz* Bn XII apparently reached the pass, but was swept downhill by the general retreat. 2 and 4/*Ersatz* Bn XII deployed right of the road and attacked the pursuing French, throwing them back over the ridge on the border. This probably cured the French of any ideas of conducting a serious pursuit. The two companies were able to withdraw undisturbed to Markirch. *Ersatz* Bn X was stopped in Markirch and turned around. At the same time, word of the fight on the pass reached the Bavarian ED and 9 *Ersatz* Bde commanders, though they were unaware of the outcome. The division commander decided to hold the pass; at about 1300hrs he sent orders to 1 *Ersatz* Bde and *Ersatz* FA Sec. III to return to Markirch. The 9 *Ersatz* Bde commander drove towards the pass, but came under fire at the bridge 1.5km west of Brifosse and bailed out of the vehicle just in time. Fortunately, the lead elements of *Ersatz* Bn X arrived: 1, 2 and 4/*Ersatz* Bn X deployed and disappeared to the north into the wood, joined by elements of the retreating RIR 15, while *Ersatz* Bn XII moved west.

Now the RIR 15 combat trains appeared from the west at the hairpin bend in the road, west of Brifosse, followed by the vehicles of 2 *Ersatz*/FAR 1 and *Ersatz* MGK 9, which both took French MG fire. The orderly columns dissolved in panic, the drivers fleeing south towards the valley at Brifosse. The horses bolted, vehicles crashed into each other, were pushed into the ditch or turned over. At Brifosse the fleeing troops were met by the 9 *Ersatz* Bde, artillery commanders and other officers who, using threats, admonishments and warning shots in the air, stopped the fleeing men and established some sort of order.

The mass of RIR 15 was assembled in the woods on the hill south of Brifosse, while a thoroughly mixed detachment and *Ersatz* MGK 9 held the spur north-west of the houses. *Ersatz* Bn XII pulled its companies back from RIR 15. *Ersatz* Bn IX reached Brifosse in good order at 1500hrs and occupied an assembly area on a hill south of the town, while *Ersatz* Bn XI took a position north of Markirch. 1 *Ersatz*/Eng. Bn 3 joined *Ersatz* Bn IX. *Ersatz* FA Sec I and III found positions south and south-east of Markirch. Between 1600hrs and 1700hrs *Ersatz* Bn X, having been unable to silence the French MG north of the road, returned and occupied the factory and slopes on the west side of Brifosse.

The leader of the Bicycle Sec./RIR 15 and some ten or twelve volunteers from RIR 15 and 1 *Ersatz*/Eng. Bn 3 went back up the road to try to recover the vehicles. On the way they encountered numerous retreating troops, most of whom refused to help and continued moving to the rear. When they reached the bend in the road the French MG again opened fire. Nevertheless, the dead and wounded horses were cut out of the traces, wagons hitched up and driven off at a canter; thirty to thirty-five pieces of equipment – guns, caissons, MG vehicles, ambulances, field kitchens, pack wagons, ration wagons, rucksack wagons – were brought back to Markirch.

Around 1400hrs the commander of the Bavarian ED decided to use 1 *Ersatz* Bde to attack south of Brifosse to take back the pass. Then at about 1600–1700hrs he was considering withdrawing back 5km to Lièpvre (off map); the division General Staff officer delayed executing the order until the division commander returned to his initial intent to attack. The late hour and general exhaustion of the troops made this impossible. 1 *Ersatz* Bde moved up steep hills to defend at Eckerich, south of Markirch. The enemy did not disturb these movements, but continually probed the Bavarian ED positions on both sides of Brifosse: the troops received little rest. The Governor of Strasbourg sent RIR 4 (minus IV/RIR 4) as reinforcements; it arrived at St Kreuz at midnight. *Ersatz* FA Sec. II was attached to the Bavarian ED and reached St Kreuz at 2100hrs.

Col de St Marie Finally Taken, 24 August (sketch 23)

The French counter-reconnaissance screen prevented the Bavarian ED from establishing the French locations, although the French were assumed to be in the same strength as the Germans. It was known that the crest of the Vosges was held by dug-in troops 500m to either side of the Col de St Marie and that numerous small positions and obstacles were on the slope to the east. The Bavarian ED commander was nevertheless still determined to take the Col de St Marie. This was reinforced by the XIV RK order which arrived at 2200hrs on 23 August, setting St Dié as the division objective.

The division was ready to issue the attack order when several captured French documents shed some light on the situation. On 20 August the Épinal reserve, 71 RD, had been split up: 141 Res. Bde had been sent to Urbeis, 142 Res. Bde to the Col de St Marie and Col du Bonhomme to the south. On 22 August 142 Res. Bde at the Col de St Marie was reinforced with three battalions and two batteries from 141 Res. Bde. These arrived too late to prevent the Germans from taking the pass, but surely participated in taking it back. The French were too exhausted to continue the attack to Markirch. The French planned to attack at 0800hrs on 24 August from the north through the Bois du Chéna, the Bois de Menaupré and l'Enclos du Vaches.

Deciphering these documents took time, but they showed that the concept of the Bavarian ED operation on 24 August was correct, and the division order was issued at 0015hrs on 24 August. The Col de St Marie would be enveloped from the north and the south, with the *Schwerpunkt* in the north. RIR 4 would advance through Klein-Rumbach against the enemy left rear. In order to allow the French to move into the trap, the start time for RIR 4 was delayed two hours until 0615hrs. The remaining troops of the Bavarian ED at Brifosse were to attack when RIR 4 was level with them. *Ersatz* Bn I, XI and XII, with *Ersatz* MGK 9, under the 9 *Ersatz* Bde commander, would advance north in conjunction with

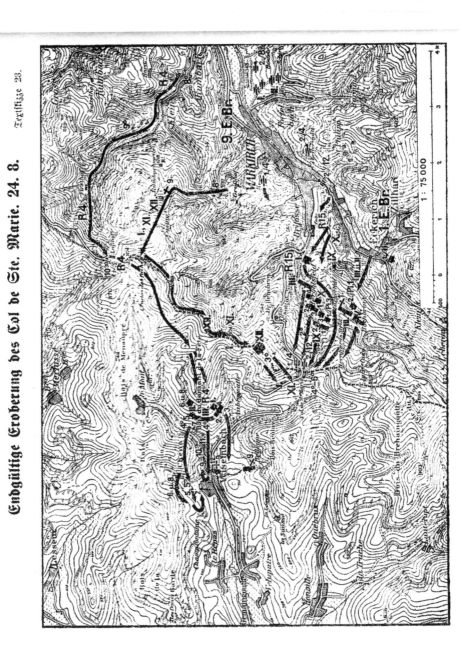

Final Capture of Col de Ste Marie

Endgültige Eroberung des Col de Ste. Marie. 24. 8.   Textskizze 23.

RIR 4. RIR 15, with *Ersatz* Bn IX and X, would advance in the division centre from Brifosse directly on the Col de St Marie, while 1 *Ersatz* Bde attacked on the left. Local *gendarmes* (civilian police), foresters and customs officers were assigned as guides. The artillery would support the attack, in part from positions at or east of Markirch occupied on the afternoon of 23 August. The woods around St Marie prevented observed fire; the artillery could only cover the crest with area fire at the time of the French attack at 0800hrs. On the pass itself there was a 300m open area where trenches were visible, and these were shelled with good results. French units in bivouac or cooking were also shelled and, as was later established, severely damaged. 1 *Ersatz*/FAR 1 detected French artillery trying to set up on the pass and chased them off.

RIR 4's route was up a difficult stony path that narrowed in the wood so that the men could only march two abreast: the column grew steadily longer. The combat trains were left behind. 1/RIR 4 was the point company, accompanied by the battalion and regimental commanders. By 1000hrs it was nearing the crest, and left the treeline 150m from Lußhof when it took fire from the front and both flanks: the company took cover. The company commander and the lead platoon then ran forwards without either taking casualties or sighting the enemy, but they heard artillery firing; they reached the crest and found an enemy battery on the other side. An enemy gun and four munitions wagons were overrun; a second gun made it 50m and then was stopped by German fire. The forty to fifty French troops that tried to rescue the artillery were shot to pieces. The battalion and regimental commanders appeared with the rest of the lead company and, at 300m range, they succeeded in shooting down the horse teams and crews of the last two guns and four caissons of the fleeing battery.

The French battery had evidently been firing on 9 *Ersatz* Bde, which was at Casino. It had moved out at 0800hrs from the north of Markirch, with *Ersatz* Bn I in the lead. The path was steep, stony, narrow and rutted. *Ersatz* MGK 9 had to dismount the guns from the vehicles and fell behind as the crews carried them uphill and down. The enemy battery at Lußhof was detected early, as were 300m of trenches on the crest. At Casino the brigade therefore deployed *Ersatz* Bn I and XI to its left, and RIR 4 took the crest at noon. The commander of 9 *Ersatz* Bde ordered RIR 4 to advance on Wisembach while 9 *Ersatz* Bde, with *Ersatz* Bn XI leading, moved down the crest to Col de St Marie. *Ersatz* Bn XI soon ploughed into a strong and well-hidden position astride the crest, so that *Ersatz* Bn I had to be committed on the right. The battalions became intermixed and formed thick packs crashing through the undergrowth; the fight was hot and costly, but the enemy was crushed and the brigade approached Col de St Marie at 1500hrs.

West of Brifosse, *Ersatz* Bn X attacked in the centre, with *Ersatz* Bn IX on its left and III/RIR 15 on its right, with I/RIR 15 echeloned right. The approach march and deployment in the steeply wooded terrain had cost considerable time and effort, and more time was needed to reorganise the intermixed units. At noon the skirmisher lines attempted to advance from the treeline and they took fire from well-concealed French infantry in the pass and the high ground to the south. *Ersatz* Bn X and III/RIR 15 had nearly reached the pass at 1400hrs when 9 *Ersatz* Bde approached from the right; the French fled. On the left, *Ersatz* Bn IX, with 1 and 2/*Ersatz* Bn IX in the first line, took flanking fire from the crest on the left. 3/*Ersatz* Bn IX and 1/*Ersatz* Bn X were committed in this direction. I/RIR 15 was brought from the opposite flank and began to turn the French right at 1500hrs.

1 *Ersatz* Bde deployed *Ersatz* Bn IV and *Ersatz* MGK 1 left of Ersatz Bn IX. *Ersatz* Bn IV moved left to make more room for its neighbour, which drew fire from the pass and the high ground to the south. Steep slopes and thick undergrowth made deploying difficult. The battalion began the fight at 1400hrs from the high ground 1.5km south-east of the pass, supported by *Ersatz* MGK 1. As the Bavarian infantry closed in at 1600hrs, the enemy retreated. The ascent through the woods dotted with obstacles, in which some enemy squads still offered resistance, was difficult, but 1 *Ersatz* Bde reached the Col de St Marie at 1800hrs, which was already occupied by 9 *Ersatz* Bde. The enemy retreat had all the characteristics of panic flight, with many pieces of abandoned equipment. Dead lay in masses, both in the open and in trenches, where the artillery fire had been especially effective.

At noon RIR 4 moved out towards Wisembach. It was soon clear that the enemy was digging in on both sides of Wisembach. At 1500hrs the 9 Bde commander ordered RIR 4 to attack. I/RIR 4 deployed on the treeline opposite Aubrygoutte, with 2 and 3/RIR 4 in the front line, 4/RIR 4 behind the centre (1/RIR 4 had followed *Ersatz* Bn I). On their right, III/RIR 4 deployed opposite Wisembach, with II/RIR 4 on the right wing. The regiment attacked at 1600hrs. I/RIR 4 found that the enemy had left and occupied the high ground south of Wisembach. By 1700hrs 12/RIR 4 quickly occupied the barricaded but weakly held Wisembach. To their right 9/RIR 4 encountered trenches and two MGs north-east of the town, but 10/RIR 4 entered the fight, swept the French away and took numerous prisoners. II/RIR 4 made a swing to the left with 5 and 7/RIR 4 in the first line, 6 and 8/RIR 4 in close column echeloned behind the right. It encountered an equally strong enemy, partially dug in on the high ground north-west of Wisembach, and a violent firefight developed. 6 and 8/RIR 4 crept through the wood to the enemy left flank, which decided the fight. In fifteen minutes the battalion was on the enemy position and took twenty-six POWs. Wisembach, the western gate to the Col de St Marie, was in the hands of RIR 4. Between 1900hrs and 2000hrs the regiment took heavy artillery fire and II and III/RIR 4 were withdrawn to a covered position north of Aubrygoutte.

I/RIR 4 remained on the high ground south of Wisembach and was joined by *Ersatz* MGK 9, which had caught up after a difficult climb to the crest. 2 *Ersatz/* FAR 12 at the Col de St Marie engaged enemy artillery at Gemaingoutte. The Bavarian ED bivouacked in place.

At 2030hrs the commander of the Bavarian ED received a report from Fortress Strasbourg that enemy columns were approaching from the south and could reach Markirch at any moment. Bavarian *Ersatz* FA Sec. I was already moving east; the Bavarian ED commander also ordered the three remaining batteries of *Ersatz* FA Sec. II and III to the east, and then scraped together all available forces to defend Markirch, including 4/*Ersatz* Bn XII, 1/*Ersatz* Bn II, bicyclists, the wounded and unit staffs. *Ersatz* Bn IV was called back from Col de St Marie, but did not arrive until midnight.

There was also a threat from the north. At noon *Ersatz* Cavalry Sec./I b. AK was riding north from Lubine to make contact with 30 RD when it reached the crest of the Vosges, encountered dug-in enemy infantry and lost half of its men and horses. This was only significant in that it lent credibility to a report that reached Markirch at 2300hrs saying that the artillery withdrawing to Leberau had been attacked by a brigade of French infantry.

What had in fact happened was that the artillery, moving east, had encountered the Bavarian ED field trains in Leberau moving west to join the division. At the same time, a rumour made the rounds that the French were approaching from the south. The field trains' vehicles attempted to turn around and jammed the road. Chaos ensued: vehicles became tangled together, wagon shafts broke and horses bolted. Men shouted curses in the dark. A gun rolled into the stream next to the road. Shots were fired, which led to general uncontrolled firing. Eventually discipline was re-established. The field trains moved back east, and the division waited in vain for its rations. Three artillery batteries returned to Markirch. The French forces advancing on Markirch from both the north and south proved to be imaginary.

The Bavarian ED took only 250 casualties. However, many dead and wounded still lay in the woods and would be only found on the following days. The enemy had far more severe casualties, including a number of POWs. The French 71 RD fell back to Laveline and the commander of the French XIV Corps was forced to move a brigade of 58 RD in support.

Advance Through Wisembach, 25 August (sketch 24)

In the afternoon of 24 August Fortress Strasbourg ordered the Bavarian ED to pursue in the direction of St Dié. RIR 15 was detached from the Bavarian ED and would remain on the Col de St Marie. The Bavarian ED commander thought that the enemy had fled in panic and would offer no serious resistance east of Laveline. Start time for the pursuit was set at 0630hrs. 9 *Ersatz* Bde, with

Wisembach 25. 8.

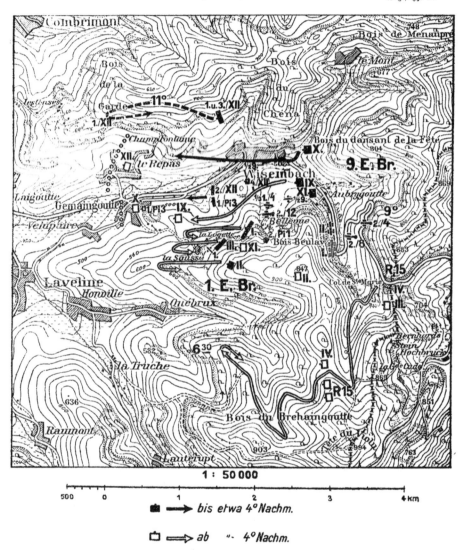

1 : 50 000

bis etwa 4° Nachm.

ab "- 4° Nachm.

Key

bis etwa 4 Nachm – until about 1600

ab " 4 Nachm – after 1600

1 *Ersatz*/FAR 4 and *Ersatz* FA Sec. III, were to advance on the main road west from Wisembach; 1 *Ersatz* Bde, with *Ersatz* FA Sec. II and III would turn towards Laveline. *Ersatz* Bn IV would hold Markirch and secure the rail line to the east. RIR 4 was called back to the Col de St Marie and, with RIR 15, would police up the battlefield and search the woods.

9 *Ersatz* Bde immediately took artillery fire east of Wisembach. The lead companies, 3 and 1/*Ersatz* Bn XII, crossed north-east through the valley, bounding by individuals or squads and moved into the Bois de la Garde, north of le Repas. This took so long that 2/*Ersatz* Bn XII pushed forward south of the road at 0830hrs. 4/*Ersatz* Bn XII and 1 *Ersatz*/Eng. Bn 3 remained in Markirch under cover against the artillery fire, with *Ersatz* Bn X to the north-east of the town, while *Ersatz* Bn IX and XI were to the south-east.

1 *Ersatz* Bde (minus *Ersatz* Bn IV) left the road at the turn south of Aubrygoutte, climbed the hill to the west, crossed over the crest and deployed with *Ersatz* Bn I and III forward, and *Ersatz* Bn II echeloned left. 2 *Ersatz*/Eng. Bn 1 followed *Ersatz* Bn I. *Ersatz* MGK 1 took up position at 0900hrs near La Logette and fired at enemy infantry that was moving down the valley to Gemaingoutte. I/RIR 4 pulled back into the Col de St Marie; *Ersatz* MGK 9 remained on the high ground south of Aubrygoutte. The French were to both sides of Gemaingoutte and did not seem inclined to leave. They were supported by very alert artillery on the high ground west of Le Repas and at Laveline.

Under these circumstances, the Bavarian ED waited for the arrival of their own artillery. Only 1 *Ersatz*/FAR 4 and 2 *Ersatz*/FAR 12, which had spent the night on the Col de St Marie, were immediately available; the rest had to climb the pass. They found the road blocked with supply vehicles, which had received the order to move forward late due to the confusion generated by the events that evening at Leberau. *Ersatz* FA Sec. III was able to attach itself to the end of the division supply column. 2 *Ersatz*/FAR 4 went into position at 0900hrs on the road east of Aubrygoutte and drove enemy infantry from trenches at Gemaingoutte. To the left, 2 *Ersatz*/FAR 8 unlimbered at noon and 2 *Ersatz*/FAR 12 moved to the high ground west of Aubrygoutte. 1 *Ersatz*/FAR 4 was completely blocked by supply vehicles. Only one platoon joined 2 *Ersatz*/FAR 12 by 1330hrs. *Ersatz* FA Sec. II (two batteries) was also brought to a halt by traffic west of the Col de St Marie. The few batteries that the Bavarian ED could bring into action were unable to deal with the French artillery. Only 2 *Ersatz*/FAR 4 was able to score a direct hit on a caisson and chase off a French battery.

1 and 9 *Ersatz* Bde were met by overwhelming artillery fire and forced to take cover. At 1100hrs 1/*Ersatz* Bn XII attempted to sneak through the woods on the west side of Le Repas to get at the French artillery, but 700m west of Champ Fontaine encountered French infantry and could do no more than hold Champ Fontaine. The 2/*Ersatz* Bn XII advance south of the road was also stopped 700m

east of Gemaingoutte by artillery fire, even though 1 *Ersatz*/Eng. Bn 3 was committed on the left. The gap between the two groups was filled with *Ersatz* Bn X, which moved through heavy artillery fire in Wisembach and the valley to the west to reach the wood east of Le Repas.

XIV RK informed the Bavarian ED that the French had withdrawn from Saal and Lubine in front of 30 RD to the north, and that these forces were also threatened with being cut off by a German cavalry division advancing from the north-west. The Bavarian ED was to take Raves (3km west of Gemaingoutte) and cut off their last line of retreat. The Bavarian ED commander ordered 1 and 9 *Ersatz* Bde to launch an immediate attack. The commander of RIR 15 made his troops available, although they were scattered around the Col de St Marie and had to be assembled. He was told to move through the woods to the south to Québrux, along with *Ersatz* Bn IV, who were marching from Markirch, and *Ersatz* FA Sec. I (two batteries).

1 *Ersatz* Bde had already attempted to advance in the direction of Laveline in order to take the enemy artillery east of the town. *Ersatz* Bn II moved on line left of *Ersatz* Bn III, but both were immediately stopped by artillery fire, as were troops that attempted to advance from the treeline on both sides of La Logette. In mid-afternoon four French battalions were observed advancing from Laveline to Québrux, while the artillery fire intensified, and any hope of advancing disappeared. *Ersatz* Bn I moved into the wood at La Sausse, *Ersatz* Bn II back to Hill 847, and *Ersatz* Bn III all the way to the area south of Col de St Marie, probably with the intention of stopping the enemy advance from Québrux. *Ersatz* Bn XI remained in the woods south-west of Bellvue.

On the other hand, 9 *Ersatz* Bde had made progress by evening. There was only weak and scattered opposition from enemy infantry. In spite of the artillery fire, *Ersatz* Bn XI moved in very open order to the high ground east of Gemaingoutte. During the evening the enemy withdrew and *Ersatz* Bn XII took Le Repas; after dark *Ersatz* Bn X occupied Gemaingoutte.

RIR 15 left Col de St Marie at 1600hrs, followed by *Ersatz* Bn IV, which had just arrived. By 1830hrs the lead element was 1km south-west of Québrux and the muzzle flashes of French artillery, as well as trenches, west of Laveline could be seen; the enemy was out of reach, it was growing dark and the troops were tired, so RIR 15 bivouacked in the woods. *Ersatz* FA Sec. II and I reached Aubrygoutte. The ration vehicles failed to make their way through the traffic jams.

The French First Army commander had ordered 71 RD back to Épinal, so on 25 August the Bavarian ED had engaged elements of 71 RD that had not been able to break contact. A brigade of the French 58 RD had reached Hill 517, 3km west of Gemaingoutte.

General Advance to the Meurthe and the Capture of St Dié, 26–27 August

Coinches, 26 August (map 19)

On 25 August XIV RK, 30 RD and the Bavarian ED, which had been pushing independently through the Vosges, linked up on the west side of the mountains. The commander of XIV RK planned to attack the flank and rear of the enemy forces south of Raon l'Étape opposing XV AK. XIV RK was stopped 8km south-east of Raon l'Étape and 4km north-east of St Dié by the French 28 ID, the right flank of the French XIV Corps.

30 RD had been ordered to attack from Frapelle through Neuviller to St Marguerite. The division commander thought that the river valley was too narrow an avenue of approach and ordered 10 Res. Bde to attack through the high ground to the north, with 5 *Ersatz* Bde to the south. This would put 5 *Ersatz* Bde in the Bavarian ED area of operations, but it seemed to be hanging behind. The 30 RD commander ordered his units to pursue without consideration for the troops on the right or left.

From 10 Res. Bde, II/RIR 11, Res. MGK 3 and III/RIR 14 were in division reserve. RIR 14 (minus III/RIR 14) moved through the concealment provided by the Bois d'Ormont to Charémont. The enemy was reported in Neuviller and Remomeix, so RIR 14 swung south-west to engage at 0930hrs. II/RIR 14 moved through the strips of woods south-west of Petit Charémont, with 7 and 8/RIR 14 leading, when they took small arms fire from le Paire and the woods to the north-west at 1100hrs. 6/RIR 14 deployed on the right. *Ersatz* FA Sec.VI had moved forward to the high ground south of Lusse and opened fire on Neuviller and le Paire. 1 *Ersatz*/FAR 80 set up on the high ground north-west of Frapelle at 1130hrs. I/RIR 11, which had been following echeloned right, committed 1/RIR 11 to the right of 6/RIR 14, while 4/RIR 11 directly reinforced the RIR 14 firing line. The attack stalled nevertheless. Only when 2 and 3/RIR 11 enveloped la Paire from the north did the French retreat, leaving a number of POWs in Bavarian hands. I/RIR 11 and II/RIR 14 stood fast at la Paire, but I/RIR 14 continued on to take Grandrupt, stopping there because Basses Fosses was strongly held by the enemy. Fortress MG Sec. 2 moved to the high ground north of Remomeix and fired into the town.

5 *Ersatz* Bde moved out from Lesseux at 0630hrs, with *Ersatz* Bn VIII as the advance guard. It reached Bertrimoutier at 0715hrs and found the wood south-west of Raves held by the enemy, with artillery on Hill 517. *Ersatz* Bn VIII deployed 1, 4 and 3/*Ersatz* Bn VIII on the south-west side of Bertrimoutier, with 2/*Ersatz* Bn VIII following behind the middle. The commander of 5 *Ersatz* Bde committed *Ersatz* Bn VII and VI left of *Ersatz* Bn VIII. *Ersatz* Bn VII deployed

3 and 1/*Ersatz* Bn VII in the first line, 4 and 2/*Ersatz* Bn VII echeloned left; *Ersatz* Bn VI, with *Ersatz* MGK 5 attached, marched on Bonipaire. *Ersatz* Bn V was in reserve behind the left flank. 2 *Ersatz*/FAR 80 went into battery west of Herbaupaire. It was soon clear that 5 *Ersatz* Bde, holding a 1–1.5km front, had met strong resistance. In particular, the right flank of *Ersatz* Bn VIII was taking artillery fire from the high ground north of Remomeix and MG fire from the woods east of Faing Thierry. Fire was also coming from the high ground south of Ginfosse on the left. *Ersatz* Bn V was therefore committed on the right. Before it could make itself felt, the other three battalions crossed the stream and took the treeline south-west of Raves at 0900hrs. Only the right flank of *Ersatz* Bn VIII was unable to advance; 4/*Ersatz* Bn VIII lost all its officers. *Ersatz* Bn VII and VI met tough resistance in the wood. 2 *Ersatz*/FAR 80 moved forward to a position east of Combrimont, while 3/Res. FAR 14 (10cm cannons) moved to the west of Lesseux at 1100hrs, and two batteries of *Ersatz* FA Sec. IV advanced to the south-west. At noon Hill 517 was stormed. *Ersatz* Bn VII, accompanied by *Ersatz* MGK 5, advanced to the north-east of Coinches. The commander of 4/*Ersatz* Bn V collected some men and pushed south to capture two French MGs south of Ginfosse. He then saw two French guns in Coinchimont 400m further south, chased off their crews and captured them. Penetrating into the town he took a gun that was trying to drive off, plus two more horse teams. French troops tried to retreat south of the town, but were engaged and scattered. *Ersatz* Bn V reached Coinches at 1800hrs.

The XIV RK order reached the Bavarian ED at 0700hrs, directing it to advance on Coinches. RIR 4 (minus IV/RIR 4) and RIR 15 (minus II/RIR 15) were reattached; both moved early towards Verpellière. At Le Repas and Gemaingoutte, whenever the 9 *Ersatz* Bde troops showed themselves, they took artillery fire from Hill 577 south of Ginfosse and Algoutte. Enemy infantry and MGs were at Laveline.

The enemy artillery was to some degree suppressed by German counter-battery fire. *Ersatz* FA Sec. II unlimbered on the high ground south of Wisembach. 2 *Ersatz*/FAR 10 engaged enemy artillery moving into position at Coinchimont. *Ersatz* FA Sec. I followed RIR 15. At a bend in the road south-east of Québrux, 1 *Ersatz*/FAR 4 brought three guns into action against enemy artillery at Laveline. 2 *Ersatz*/FAR 4 from *Ersatz* FA Sec. III covered 2 *Ersatz*/FAR 8 and 2 *Ersatz*/ FAR 12 as they displaced forward from Aubrygoutte at 0900hrs. In Wisembach the two batteries took such heavy artillery fire that they unlimbered on their own initiative south of the town. At 1000hrs the division staff reached Wisembach and were also shelled.

At 1100hrs the attack gathered steam, assisted by the pressure exerted by 30 RD. The French evacuated the west side of the valley. Withdrawing French troops were shelled as they became visible; *Ersatz* FA Sec. II moved forward to the high ground south of Gemaingoutte, with *Ersatz* FA Sec. I south of Québrux. The

French artillery fire died down. A French battery on Hill 577, south of Ginfosse, was silenced by a direct hit, and then engaged again as it tried to withdraw.

On the right flank of 9 *Ersatz* Bde, *Ersatz* Bn XII was engaged by artillery fire, but by 1100hrs had closed on Laigoutte and had the opportunity to pursue withdrawing French troops with fire. It crossed the valley in conjunction with 30 RD. At 1600hrs it was assembled in low ground 1km east of Coinches. On the brigade left, *Ersatz* Bn IX had moved in waves of open-order skirmishers through the low ground by Gemaingoutte under artillery and MG fire as it reached Laveline, to the high ground east of Velupaire. At noon it climbed the valley at Raves and pushed forward in open order, so that it reached the high ground west of Ginfosse at 1300hrs and advanced by companies almost unopposed to Coinches. By 1600hrs 9 *Ersatz* Bde was assembled in the low ground east of Coinches, behind 5 *Ersatz* Bde on the left flank of the Bavarian ED.

Once 1 *Ersatz* Bde crossed the open terrain east of Laveline under artillery fire, it encountered no further resistance. *Ersatz* Bn I reached Laveline in march column at noon, took a two-hour rest, and then continued the march to Fouchifol. The advance guard, 1/*Ersatz* Bn I, drove off isolated enemy patrols. Just before La Planchette, however, artillery fire forced a return to Fouchifol. *Ersatz* Bn IV moved in march column to Coinches, then Coinchimont, while *Ersatz* Bn III advanced to Ginfosse.

1, 5 and 9 *Ersatz* Bde were packed together and became intermixed near Coinches. The enemy occupied the high ground to the west and north-west, and *Ersatz* FA Sec. III set up on Hill 517 and began to bombard them. 5 *Ersatz* Bde, north-west of Coinches, could not attack because of flanking fire from the south-west. *Ersatz* Bn IV, which had just passed through Coinches, was ordered to attack in this direction. It deployed 1, 2 and 3/*Ersatz* Bn IV on line, with 4/*Ersatz* Bn IV following behind the centre, supported by *Ersatz* MGK 1 south of the town. The enemy was invisible and his fire on target, but as the left flank of 5 *Ersatz* Bde also advanced the enemy disappeared into the woods behind his position. *Ersatz* Bn IV occupied the high ground south-west of Remémont, and *Ersatz* Bn VI the village itself. *Ersatz* Bn II became disoriented and separated into three groups in the woods.

RIR 15 reached Les Grands Contaux at 1800hrs with little contact, and halted when it received artillery fire from the west side of the Meurthe. From Verpellière, I and II/RIR 4 had a difficult cross-country march to the high ground south-west of Coinchimont. III/RIR 4 reached La Croix at 1630hrs. *Ersatz* FA Sec. II moved to Hill 577 and *Ersatz* FA Sec. I to the south-west of Coinchimont.

At 1100hrs the XIV RK commander reached Frapelle and decided that the attack over the Meurthe would have to be postponed until the following day; at noon 30 RD was ordered to bivouac in the towns of Bertrimoutier—Le Paire—Coinches. 2/Res. Hussar R 9, which had arrived that morning, Bicycle Co./

RIR 60 and a platoon of Res. MG Sec. 3 were ordered to take the Meurthe bridge west of St Marguerite, but after a three-hour firefight with French infantry in the town the bicyclists returned to Lusse. The cavalry was forced to turn back by artillery fire, but found an abandoned French battery on Hill 400, south-east of St Marguerite, and brought it back.

At 1400hrs the commander of the Bavarian ED received the order to bivouac at Coinches–Entre-deux-Eaux. Much of the division had concentrated around Coinches and Coinchimont along with 30 RD; the Bavarian ED had to shift left. It was not easy to bring back the troops which had energetically pursued the enemy as far as Remémont and Les Grands Contaux. Some units could not be found; others had bivouacked and had requisitioned livestock, slaughtered it and begun cooking. They now had to move in the dark and leave the food behind. It then began to pour with rain. The battalions arrived tired, soaking wet and hungry (final positions the dark squares west of the Raves–La Croix road).

30 RD and the Bavarian ED had been opposed by a brigade of the French 58 RD, which withdrew across the Meurthe behind Les Cours. The French 8 Dragoon Bde was sent as reinforcement and arrived at Corcieux, 10km south-west of St Dié.

St Dié–Saulcy, 27 August (map 20)

For 27 August the XIV RK commander ordered an attack on both sides of St Dié. XIV RK would attack halfway between Raon l'Étape and St Dié, with 28 RD towards Étival (off map, 10km north of St Dié), and 26 RD on La Voivre (5km north of St Dié). The French artillery put a barrage in front of 28 RD. 51 Res. Bde of 26 RD took La Culotte and Dijon, but the division was unable to take La Voivre. The gap between 26 and 28 RD was filled by 19 ED. XV AK attacked south on both sides of the Meurthe and was able to take Étival by the evening. The French XIV Corps north of St Dié was pressed on its right flank by 30 RD and the Bavarian ED and forced to move to the west side of the Meurthe

The 30 RD mission was attack at 0500hrs and cross the Meurthe at St Dié to cut the enemy line of retreat. The division commander did not judge it prudent to advance up the open Meurthe Valley directly on St Dié without taking the hills and woods surrounding St Dié first, even if that meant entering the 26 RD area of operations. He instructed 10 Res. Bde to advance through the high ground north-east of St Dié with the right flank on Dijon, while 5 *Ersatz* Bde advanced through St Marguerite and La Paire. The mass of the artillery was to deploy immediately behind the outpost line. 1 *Ersatz*/FAR 80 was attached to 10 Res. Bde, 2 *Ersatz*/FAR 80 to 5 *Ersatz* Bde. II/RIR 11, III/RIR 14, Res. MG Sec. 3, 2/Res. Hussar R 9 and Bicycle Co./RIR 60 were division reserve at Faing Thierry.

While 3/Res. Foot Artillery R 14 (10cm cannons) and 1 *Ersatz*/FAR 80 engaged French artillery at Gratin, 10 Res. Bde deployed at 0800hrs at Hautes Fossés with I/RIR 11 on the right, II/RIR 14 on the left, and I/RIR 14 and Fortress MG Sec. 2 in reserve at Grandrupt. Along with troops of 51 Res. Bde, the enemy was quickly swept aside and the high ground at Gratin taken. There the French resistance stiffened, and their artillery north-west of St Dié shelled the hill; although it was somewhat suppressed by 3/Res. Foot Artillery R 14 (10cm cannons), it prevented movement in open terrain. So the troops on the left flank of 10 Res. Bde turned towards St Dié. Between 1000hrs and 1100hrs 2/RIR 11 was ordered to seize the eastern Meurthe bridge. When it approached to 400m, however, it was hit by exceptionally effective small arms and MG fire, which caused serious casualties; nevertheless, the bridge was taken. 8, 6, 1 and 2/RIR 14 advanced along the Gratin road and attacked the east side of St Dié, breaking determined enemy resistance by noon. As it entered the city it took overwhelming fire that never seemed to stop. 1 *Ersatz*/FAR 80 apparently fired in support of 5 *Ersatz* Bde.

At dawn 5 *Ersatz* Bde deployed *Ersatz* Bn V on the right and *Ersatz* Bn VIII on the left, plus *Ersatz* MGK 5, at the fork in the road 1km south of Remomeix, with orders to attack St Marguerite at 0700hrs. *Ersatz* Bn VI and VII were to wade through the Meurthe at Le Paire and advance on the south-west side of St Dié. 2 *Ersatz*/FAR 80 and *Ersatz* FA Sec. IV were to provide fire support from Hill 517 north of Ginfosse. Enemy resistance was weak and the attack quickly gained ground without loss. *Ersatz* Bn V entered St Marguerite at 0900hrs, but took fire from the houses and it needed thirty minutes to sweep the town and take the Meurthe bridge, and then smoothly continued the attack to reach St Dié by 1100hrs. *Ersatz* Bn VIII crossed the Meurthe over a footbridge at a mill south of St Marguerite and reached the road leading south from the town. 2/*Ersatz* Bn VIII occupied the churchyard on the south side of the city, but took small arms fire from the city and the woods to the west. *Ersatz* FA Sec. IV moved forward to the south of St Marguerite, with *Ersatz*/FAR 80 to the west side.

Ersatz Bn VII and VI moved out from Remémont at 0900hrs, but were considerably delayed on the east side of the river by artillery fire. 4/*Ersatz* Bn VII, which had outpost duty at Saulcy, applied pressure on the enemy right and eased the situation. Construction of a footbridge cost time and the crossing could not be made until noon. The advance was continued without interruption to Foucharupt. The division reserve moved to St Marguerite.

5 *Ersatz* Bde ordered *Ersatz* Bn V to move through St Dié. The enemy seemed to have left, the more so because the inhabitants appeared at their doors and windows and waved to the troops to show their good will. With 4/*Ersatz* Bn V in the lead, the battalion approached to within 200m of the city hall when it took fire from both sides, causing casualties. The column took cover, with the 4/*Ersatz*

Bn V commander and forty men occupying a pub, which they fortified, bringing in as many wounded as possible, and engaging the French Alpine troops in the adjacent buildings, who tried to approach using dead ground. The 4/*Ersatz* Bn V commander ordered the house opposite occupied, which allowed a crossfire and held the French in check. It took determined leadership to keep up the troops' morale in the face of the serious situation. Help was practically out of the question, as the rest of the battalion was similarly pinned down. At noon *Ersatz* Bn V was ordered to move back to a position 600m south of the city to allow it to be softened up with artillery fire. The companies of RIR 14 that had entered the city were also withdrawn. The 4/*Ersatz* Bn V detachment was pinned in the city centre. The division artillery shelled the city for about an hour, and it began to burn in several places. At 1700hrs the attack was renewed by I and II/RIR 14, I and II/RIR 11 and *Ersatz* Bn V. The enemy had withdrawn, and after an hour the city was in German hands and the 4/*Ersatz* Bn V detachment relieved.

By 1600hrs *Ersatz* Bn VI and VII were almost opposite the north-west side of St Dié, without meeting organised resistance and picking up French stragglers. A mistake by a reconnaissance patrol alerted French troops in company strength at Les Tignes, but 1 and 3/*Ersatz* Bn VII put them to flight, while 1/*Ersatz* Bn VII took prisoners. That evening they had a firefight with French troops and three guns withdrawing north-east. 30 RD was instructed to evacuate the town so that 26 RD could move in. It bivouacked – sometimes late at night – in the area St Marguerite–Raves–Coinches–La Paire.

The Bavarian ED was to take the bridge at Saulcy by 0430hrs and continue the attack towards Anozel and St Dié. Since there had been enemy forces on the west bank of the Meurthe at Saulcy the previous day, the division commander decided to send part of his forces to St Léonard. The division order at 0245hrs directed 9 *Ersatz* Bde, with RIR 15 (minus II/RIR 15) and *Ersatz* FA Sec. II and III, to attack from Entre-deux-Eaux at 0300hrs towards Saulcy and Anozel to St Dié. 1 *Ersatz* Bde, with RIR 14 (minus IV/RIR 14) and *Ersatz* FA Sec. I would assemble at Mandray at 0400hrs, cross the Meurthe at St Léonard and turn north to link up with 9 *Ersatz* Bde. *Landwehr* IR 71 and 2 *Ersatz*/FAR 51, which had just joined the division, would move to Saulcy.

When he issued these orders, the division commander assumed that 1 *Ersatz* Bde was positioned south of 9 *Ersatz* Bde, when in fact they were intermixed. Transmission of the orders took too much time, because the division had no telephones, and the lack of maps and movement in the dark over steep, poor, rain-soaked paths led to delays and wrong turns. The attack proceeded sporadically and out of sequence.

The units of 9 *Ersatz* Bde reached Entre-deux-Eaux late and at irregular intervals, with *Ersatz* Bn XI first at 0500hrs. When it approached Saulcy at 0700hrs it took small arms fire from Les Cours. 3/*Ersatz* Bn XI crossed the

Meurthe bridge and deployed south of the road, while 2 and 4/*Ersatz* Bn IX on the right waded through the Meurthe, and 1/*Ersatz* Bn IX remained in the village as reserve. 2 *Ersatz*/Eng. Bn 1 and 1 *Ersatz*/Eng. Bn 3 began building footbridges. *Ersatz* MGK 1 joined the firefight.

At 0700hrs RIR 15 began descending into the Meurthe Valley, when it took fire from the opposite side of the river. I/RIR 15 deployed right, III/RIR 15 left, but they were soon pinned down. As the fog lifted the enemy artillery began to fire. Initially, *Ersatz* Bn XI and RIR 15 had no fire support: *Ersatz* FA Sec. III had become separated, set up 1km north-west of Coinches and fired in support of 30 RD. *Ersatz* FA Sec. II was delayed by the chaotic and slow movement and did not reach Entre-deux-Eaux until 0900hrs, though its fire on Les Cours immediately eased the situation for the infantry. At 1000hrs RIR 15 bounded forward to Saulcy, with I/RIR 15 north of the bridge and III/RIR 15 to the south, and crossed the Meurthe, drawing *Ersatz* Bn XI with them. The attack over the river meadow stalled as the German infantry was unable to break into the town against the well-concealed enemy, and a standing firefight developed. It was not prudent to renew the attack until the rest of the 9 *Ersatz* Bde arrived or *Ersatz* Bn I approached from the south, so the troops were pulled back to the Meurthe.

Ersatz Bn IX reached Entre-deux-Eaux at 0800hrs, but was stopped by the brigade commander at Hill 450 east of Saulcy, with *Ersatz* Bn X and XII to the south-east. *Ersatz* MGK 9 arrived late and was set up on the bridge at Saulcy. At noon, *Ersatz* FA Sec. III finally arrived and set up in open positions tightly packed together north of Entre-deux-Eaux, with 2 *Ersatz*/FAR 51 to the right.

1 *Ersatz* Bde was even less concentrated than 9 *Ersatz* Bde. The four battalions marched separately to Mandray and arrived at wide intervals. Therefore, RIR 4, which had bivouacked at La Croix and begun to march at 0530hrs, led the brigade, and by 0800hrs had already reached St Léonard and the west side of the Meurthe; at 1000hrs it turned north, with II/RIR 4 on both sides of the road deploying 5 and 8/RIR 4, and engaged in a firefight with enemy troops on the south side of Les Cours. III/RIR 4, with 10 and 11/RIR 4 forward, attempted to take the high ground west of the road and was stopped by dug-in French troops. I/RIR 4 deployed left of III/RIR 4, so that only 3/RIR 4 was in reserve.

At 1100hrs 1 *Ersatz* Bde began to arrive. *Ersatz* Bn III was committed left of RIR 4. *Ersatz* Bn II and IV took up positions facing west against what were clearly strong enemy forces in the woods north of Sarupt, followed by *Ersatz* I. *Ersatz* FA Sec. I, which bivouacked south-west of Coinchimont, had great difficulty moving in the deep mud. It lost contact with the infantry and advanced without protection to the south-west of Mandray and appears to have supported 1 *Ersatz* Bde with fire.

Around noon, 6 and 7/RIR 4 took Les Cours and captured prisoners, but were forced to move 200m south of the town by friendly fire from Saulcy. At 1300hrs the enemy also withdrew in front of III/RIR 4. *Landwehr* IR 71 arrived (minus 5, 10 and 12/LIR 71, pulling artillery guard) and 6 and 7/LIR 71 pursued the enemy north-west into the wood. Now utterly exhausted, 1 *Ersatz* Bde rested and cooked lunch.

As 1 *Ersatz* Bde approached Les Cours around noon, the commander of 9 *Ersatz* Bde ordered *Ersatz* Bn IX to attack south of Saulcy, with *Ersatz* Bn X on its left. They moved out between 1300hrs and 1400hrs across the Meurthe and the broad meadow to the west, met no resistance and were in Moncel and the high ground to the south by 1500hrs. The rest of the brigade moved up.

At 1600hrs the commander of the Bavarian ED ordered 9 *Ersatz* Bde to move cross-country through Azonel to Foucharupt, while 1 *Ersatz* Bde took the valley road to St Dié. To secure his left flank, the 9 *Ersatz* Bde commander decided to take the pass west of Azonel with *Ersatz* Bn IX and X. The rest of the brigade and RIR 15 concentrated at Les Cours. As *Ersatz* Bn IX left Azonel it surprised enemy outposts, which left behind freshly slaughtered meat, potatoes and cooking utensils. When it took the pass it surprised more enemy troops, who had made themselves comfortable in the farms. However, *Ersatz* Bn IX soon took small arms, MG and artillery fire from the south-west; quickly dug holes provided some cover. *Ersatz* Bn X arrived and deployed on the treeline left of *Ersatz* Bn IX and it too took fire.

Initially, the enemy had stayed on the defensive, but he soon began to turn both open flanks. A platoon of 2/*Ersatz* Bn IX soon ended the threat to the right flank, while *Ersatz* Bn IX sent the rest of 2 and 1/*Ersatz* Bn IX to the left flank of *Ersatz* Bn X. An advance by 9 *Ersatz* Bde north on St Dié no longer seemed advisable and it remained behind 1 *Ersatz* Bde. 9 *Ersatz* Bde, joined by LIR 71, engaged in close-quarter combat with the French in the dark. There was considerable confusion and incidents of friendly fire. *Ersatz* Bn XI was committed south of the road, while *Ersatz* Bn XII on the right of it reinforced the firing line. In spite of local reverses, there was no cause for serious concern, and the enemy withdrew at 2100hrs. It seemed too risky to the 9 *Ersatz* Bde commander to leave the disorganised troops in the woods, so between 2200hrs and 2300hrs he withdrew them to Saulcy. The night march was characterised by stops, missed turns and intersecting marching columns, so that the troops arrived late, tired, wet and cold. *Ersatz* Bn IX and 1 *Ersatz*/Eng. Bn 3 provided security west of the Meuse, and stragglers and lost units from LIR 71 also spent the night west of the Meuse.

In the night the Bavarian ED lost its only ammunition supply column (Artillery Munitions Columns 1 and 3, Infantry Munitions Column 1 and Field Hospital 1). At 1900hrs it had halted at the west end of Mandray. The vehicles of the division staff and of 1 *Ersatz* Bde joined them. French Alpine troops were seen west of Mandray and the column commander had just turned the vehicles around when they took fire from the slopes south of Mandray; horses were killed or bolted, vehicles crashed together. Some of the drivers fled, others returned fire.

Darkness fell and the French Alpine troops used it to move between the vehicles. The remaining drivers, who had fired off their small supply of ammunition, fled or were captured. The German stragglers assembled in a house near the church of Basse Mandray, while the French collected 300 POWs in the school and other buildings of Haute Mandray. The senior doctor began recovering and treating the wounded, but was soon locked up with the other prisoners.

30 RD and the Bavarian ED had cut off the withdrawal of the brigade of the French 58 RD, which the French XIV Corps then ordered to turn around. The French 8 Dragoon Bde had found the open left flank of the Bavarian ED and its attached Light Infantry Battalion 13 had carried out the raid at Mandray.

XIV RK had drawn a difficult mission: break through the Vosges. These second-line units had insufficient cohesion and were inadequately trained and equipped. Their performance of duty must be measured with this consideration in mind. The capture of the Col de St Marie by the Bavarian ED, although the left flank was completely unprotected, was a signal accomplishment.

The Rhine Valley South of Schlettstadt, 23–26 August

The Governor of Strasbourg had to defend against a possible advance by the French *armée d'Alsace* north down the Rhine Valley. To prevent this, from 23 to 26 August a detachment held a position north-west, west and south of Bergheim, 6km south of Schlettstadt. On 24 August a French column was reported moving on Markirch against the rear of the Bavarian ED; to block this, II/RIR 60 was sent through Ruppoltsweiler into the mountains, encountering French Alpine troops on 25 August and throwing them back.

The XIV AK Rear HQ was in charge of the security of the Upper Rhine between Marckolsheim and Hüningen. 1 *Landwehr* Bde, with III/LIR 121, II/LIR 123 and 10cm Bty 10, was dug in on the east side of the Ill River, east of Colmar. 2 *Landwehr* Bde, with III/LIR 3 attached, was 10km north of Colmar at Illhausen. On the night of 23/24 August, XIV AK Rear HQ received reports that the enemy at Mühlhausen was being reinforced and was advancing 10km north of Mühlhausen and on Neu-Breisach, and ordered a withdrawal to the east side of the Rhine. 1 *Landwehr* Bde moved to the north of Neu-Breisach, joined by 1 *Landwehr* Bn/I b. AK and 1 *Landwehr* Eng. Co./I b. AK. III/*Landwehr* IR 121 and II/*Landwehr* IR 123 returned to Fort Neu-Breisach. 2 *Landwehr* Bde stayed on the west bank of the Rhine, 19km north of Neu-Breisach. 5 and 6/Foot Artillery R 13 (sFH) and 9cm Bty 10 returned to Neu-Breisach. On 25 August 1 *Landsturm* Bde moved back to the east of Colmar. The French were on the foothills of the Vosges opposite Colmar. 2 *Landwehr* Bde used 25 August to conduct field training. From 22 to 25 August the situation at the Upper Rhine garrisons of

Neuenburg, Istein and Hüningen was unchanged. On 26 August 55 *Ersatz* Bde was transferred to Lorraine.

In the *armée d'Alsace* 8 Cavalry Div. was at Remiremont, 41 ID in the Munster Valley, 63 RD north-west of Belfort, 57 RD (Belfort reserve), 66 RD and 14 Dragoon Bde (8 Cavalry Div.) at Belfort, 116 Res. Bde (58 RD) at Thann.

Deadlock and New Missions, End of August to Beginning of September

End of August to Beginning of September (situation map g)

On 26 August it was clear that the pursuit in Lorraine had failed; it was, however, unclear if the force of the French counter-offensive had been broken. The situation was serious and tense. It might have been prudent to reinforce the threatened right flank of the Sixth Army between Metz and Lunéville with troops drawn from the middle and left, but the morale of the troops forbade any movement that appeared like a withdrawal unless absolutely necessary. Then there was the order of the previous day to break through between Toul and Épinal, plus an order received that afternoon to bombard the fortified positions at Nancy, although these operations could not be conducted immediately. It therefore seemed best to defend in place, even though the units had come dangerously close to the French fortress line, with its heavy artillery, which Sixth and Seventh Armies had no means to counter. The first priority was to restore the troop units' combat effectiveness. Rupprecht reported this decision to OHL, with the recommendation to break off the pursuit. Late that evening this was approved, and the appropriate orders issued.

The German troops were in terrain that the French artillery doubtlessly knew intimately and had carefully surveyed, and was also directed by aircraft, a procedure unknown to the Germans due to the lack of aircraft, experience and practice.

Crown Prince Rupprecht directed the troops to adopt the procedures of German fortress warfare doctrine: dig concealed, dispersed positions; institute personnel rotation in three shifts – outpost, reaction force and reserve. Trench warfare began in Lorraine at the end of August.

First priority was to support II b. AK. The neighbouring corps, I b. RK and XXI AK, were ordered to assist, and 8 KD and 7 KD to act as backup. 28 ID was moved from Seventh Army to Sixth Army. On 27 August, only the left wing of the French First Army continued the attack, and even this attack had little force, particularly since rain and overcast skies diminished the effectiveness of the French artillery. Concern for II b. AK was reduced, and the reinforcement of the Sixth Army right was no longer necessary. The three cavalry divisions were united under HKK 3 at Delm. The Guard ED, reinforced by the arriving 55 *Ersatz* Bde and troops from Strasbourg, were to hold the high ground north-west of Château Salins. The three mortar battalions freed up by the fall of Manonviller were divided among II b. AK, XXI AK and I b. AK, with strict instructions to save their ammunition for engaging clearly identified enemy artillery. The situation on 27 August was far less tense. The positive situation on the German right wing would lead to further easing.

OHL maintained the pursuit with the German right wing, believing that the French would fight for time but not surrender Paris; it was unnecessary to transfer forces from the Sixth and Seventh Armies to the right flank. These two armies were to engage the enemy, whether he should attack again or withdraw; both were possible. OHL was inclined to think that the enemy in front of Sixth and Seventh Armies would withdraw and open the route for them to pursue on both sides of Charmes. This was the precondition for the 25 August order to Rupprecht to conduct the breakthrough here, even though it was not expressly stated in the order. This mission was repeated in writing on 27 August, in the order 'General Instructions to First through Seventh Armies for the Continuation of the Operation', which arrived on 28 August:

> The Sixth and Seventh Armies and HKK 3 are to prevent the enemy from penetrating into Lorraine or Alsace. Sixth Army has operational control over Metz. If the enemy withdraws, Sixth Army and HKK 3 will cross the Moselle between Toul and Épinal in the general direction of Neufchâteau. In this case Sixth Army is responsible for the protection of the army left flank. Nancy–Toul is to be encircled, with adequate security against Épinal. Sixth Army will be reinforced by XIV AK, XV AK and an *Ersatz* division from Seventh Army; 10 and 8 ED are to be transferred to Fifth Army. The Seventh Army will then be independent.
>
> Seventh Army initially remains under the operational control of Sixth Army. It continues to have operational control over Fortress Strasbourg and the upper Rhine fortifications. In the case above, Seventh Army prevents an enemy penetration between Épinal and the Swiss border. It is recommended that field fortifications be constructed opposite Épinal, and from there to the border, as well as in the Rhine valley in conjunction with Neu Breisach, and that the main body be deployed behind the right wing. XIV AK, XV AK and an *Ersatz* division will be detached to Sixth Army.

The commanders of both the Sixth and Seventh Armies had severe reservations concerning the breakthrough between Toul and Épinal, recognising the difficulty of this operation, which would be siege warfare, and that they did not have the necessary heavy artillery. The exhausted troops needed several days' rest, and the supply situation had to be improved. Both Rupprecht and his chief of staff thought that the gap at Charmes would be opened by the advance of the right wing. In contrast, OHL became increasingly impatient, contrasting the fluid advance of the right wing with the deadlock on the left.

The difference in outlook first became clear in a telephone conversation between Krafft and Tappen at noon on 29 August, with Krafft maintaining that the enemy had not weakened his forces in front of the Sixth and Seventh Armies, and that the situation was not ripe for a penetration between Toul and Épinal. OHL did not issue a formal order to attack. Instead, an LNO from OHL (Major Bauer) reported at Sixth Army HQ on 30 August that OHL expected serious resistance in front of the right wing between Paris and the French border fortifications, and it wanted the Sixth Army to launch the decisive attack through the gap between Toul and Épinal, striking the enemy in the right flank; the mission for Sixth and Seventh Armies were reversed, from being secondary to decisive. The OHL LNO emphasised that the breakthrough operation had to begin by taking the advanced position at Nancy. He characterised the operation as an easy one and placed the heavy artillery at Metz and Strasbourg at the disposal of Sixth Army.

Rupprecht recognised that he had been given an entirely new mission, whose importance was clear. The gap at Charmes between the fields of fire of the fortress artillery at Toul and Épinal was only 40km wide. The Nancy Position, which extended 20km east of Toul, restricted this gap further and gave the fortifications in the north depth, and had to be taken first. There was also a considerable French bridgehead over the Moselle at Charmes. It was essential to bring forward the artillery of Metz and Strasbourg, but these had neither horse teams nor ammunition columns and were nearly immobile. They would have to be transported by rail and the guns and ammunition could be moved forward from the railheads by using horse teams from other units. In the presence of the LNO, Rupprecht gave the initial orders for the attack on the Nancy Position.

Whether Major Bauer had the authority to give such a clear-cut order to Rupprecht is debateable. He seemed to be confused concerning the exact nature of his mission. When Rupprecht reported later on 30 August concerning the measures he had taken to begin the attack, OHL thought he meant the attack against Toul–Épinal, while Rupprecht meant Nancy. The confusion grew when Sixth Army sent an LNO (Major Xylander) to OHL on 31 August, who returned with the following written instructions:

1. Metz fortress reserve [33 RD] and foot artillery are not under operational control of Sixth Army
2. Sixth Army retains the [6 and 8] *Ersatz* Divisions

3. A 10cm battalion and half a 15cm battalion, with horse teams, will arrive from Mainz

4. The Sixth Army must maintain contact with Metz under all circumstances

5. Sixth and Seventh Armies must fix in place enemy forces of at least equal strength

6. A prior or simultaneous attack on Nancy is not necessary. Sixth Army must only be so strong opposite Nancy as to prevent an enemy breakthrough threatening contact with Metz

7. If the Sixth Army does not think it can in a short time conduct a successful attack over the Moselle [at Charmes], it should consider if it is not better to disengage a part of the army and send it through Metz to the Fifth Army. The remaining elements of Sixth and Seventh Armies must then pull back later. Addendum: In this case, the possible severe negative effect on troop morale must be seriously considered

OHL was not so hopeful that the enemy would soon withdraw, followed by a breakthrough between the fortresses. The mission for Sixth and Seventh Armies was reduced to fixing equal enemy forces in place, which was also Krafft's reading of the situation. But OHL could not completely bury its desire for a breakthrough at Charmes and expressed it again verbally.

Rupprecht had been given a completely free hand and saw no reason to revise his decision to attack the Nancy Position. Since the enemy had not budged, there was no reason to attack to fix him in place. Rupprecht intended to rest his troops and begin the advance on the Upper Moselle and the attack on Nancy at the earliest on 2 September. A breakthrough between Toul and Épinal would be very difficult, but not impossible. The option of redeploying the Sixth and Seventh Armies elsewhere was rejected. Since OHL thought that the enemy had actually withdrawn forces from Lorraine, on 1 September Rupprecht ordered the advance to begin the next day, but countermanded the order because the army was not ready.

On the morning of 2 September, Rupprecht went personally to OHL. Moltke acknowledged that the breakthrough at Charmes needed planning and could not be rushed. In any case, OHL estimated that thirteen enemy corps were in Lorraine. Sixth and Seventh Armies could count it a real success if they fixed such superior forces in place and pressure from the German right wing forced them to retreat between Toul and Épinal. Only when this occurred would it be possible to attack over the Moselle. Recognising when that had occurred would be difficult. Even when the enemy withdrew, it would be a work of art to push through the gap quickly enough to appear on the other side of the Moselle in time to deliver a decisive attack. It would be irresponsible to attempt such a step without strong heavy artillery. But the immobile fortress artillery, lacking horse teams (the use of motor vehicles to move artillery was still in its infancy) was like a ball and chain on Sixth Army operations.

Moltke thought that the gate between Toul and Épinal would soon be open. Krafft made no secret of his opinion that it would not be possible to fix equal forces in Lorraine, for the French could withdraw to their border fortresses and hold off far superior German forces, while transferring the mass of their troops elsewhere.

Rupprecht had recently rejected redeploying the mass of Sixth and Seventh Armies elsewhere in favour of attacking the Nancy Position. On 2 September Krafft went to OHL to say that there was no longer time to move Sixth and Seventh Armies from Lorraine, for then they would arrive too late to take part in the decisive battle. OHL regarded the attack on Nancy as a method of preventing the transfer of French forces to Northern France.

From 27 August to 2 September it had not been possible to discern the enemy's intentions, which he concealed well. At times he appeared to withdraw in places, in other places to mass for an attack, and II b. AK in particular was struck frequently. But it was not possible to establish whether these attacks merely served to screen the enemy's withdrawal.

Joffre had decided to withdraw in front of the German right wing with the intention of reinforcing his left and forming a counter-attack force there. On the night of 25/26 August he issued a general operations order: Third, Fourth and Fifth Armies and the BEF in his centre and left were to withdraw if necessary and form a line, from the Somme opposite Peronne to Verdun. A new army was to form on the far left flank at Amiens to counter-attack against the German right. First and Second Armies were to fix the German forces in Lorraine, which could only be accomplished by taking the offensive, which Second Army conducted on 28 August. However, Second Army was cautious; only XV and XVI Corps carefully put feelers across the Meurthe at and south of Lunéville, covered on the left by XX Corps. The six battalions of 73 RD were returned to Toul. First Army was more determined: the offensive missions of VIII, XIII and XXI Corps were unchanged, while a brigade from 58 RD and 8 Dragoon Bde were to hold the Meurthe at St Dié. 41 ID was to assemble at Gérardmer to attack the German left flank.

The enemy in Lorraine was far from thinking of withdrawing. To be sure, his attack lacked determination and unity. Joffre's instructions to Second Army emphasised holding on (*durer*) more than holding the enemy in place (*fixer*). The German troops were subjected to repeated and heavy, but uncoordinated, attacks.

Quiet North of Lunéville[49]

On 27 August the Bavarian KD was bivouacked on the Sixth Army right at the far north corner of the Delm Ridge. Elements of the division began to dig in, assisted by civilian labour. It was joined by 8 KD and *Jäger* Bn 1 and 2. 7 KD moved to Château Salins. On 28 August HKK 3 was united at Delm and given responsibility for the security of the Sixth Army right flank, with 8 KD digging in on the Delm Ridge. On 30 August 8 KD was relieved in place by 7 KD and sent to East Prussia. After 28 August the Bavarian KD conducted training, local security and practised occupying its defensive positions. On 30 August a reconnaissance in force with three squadrons was conducted to capture prisoners, but the target village was found to be empty.

Left of HKK 3 was the Guard ED, which had arrived at Château Salins on 27 August and then dug in to the north-west, together with 55 *Ersatz* Bde. On 30 August concern for II b. AK caused Sixth Army to move the Guard ED as army reserve to east of Lunéville, leaving the defensive sector to 55 *Ersatz* Bde, plus RIR 60, LIR 82 and a 10cm battery, which had just arrived from Strasbourg. To their left the *Ersatz* Corps dug in, with 10 ED on the right, 4 ED on the left and 8 ED in reserve.

III b. AK was on their left with 5 ID on the right, *Landwehr* Div. Wenning in the centre taking considerable artillery fire, and 6 ID on the left. The III/IR 10 position was very broad, and on the night of 26/27 August a French battalion penetrated it, but were thrown out in close combat. 3/IR 10 on their right also beat off an attack. The situation more and more approximated siege warfare, with regular reliefs of troops on the front line. The heavy artillery took up the fight with well-hidden long-range enemy guns, whose continual fire was obviously directed from aircraft. On 1 September a captive balloon from Fortress Airship Sec. 1 was set on fire by an enemy aircraft and the observer was killed. The troops dug trenches and underground shelters. On 29 August the *Landwehr* Div. was pulled out of the line to conduct training. Between the German and French outposts was a broad no-man's-land contested only by patrols. Wounded were recovered from the battles of 25 August at Serres and St Libaire. The French position consisted of seemingly random groups of trenches. On 1 September the French occupied Hoéville, the Bois St Libaire and the east side of the Bois d'Einville and pushed forward artillery. The Bavarian artillery in the Bois Saussi, particularly I/FAR 6, at times suffered serious casualties from enemy artillery fire, especially in the evening when the setting sun illuminated the forest. Foot Artillery R 3 (sFH) reinforced 6 ID on 29 and 30 August.

HKK 3 and the *Ersatz* Corps were opposed, as before, by the French 59 and 63 RD and three brigades of IX Corps, which were now designated 18 ID. In front of III b. AK was 70 RD in St Libaire and 39 ID (XX Corps) in the Bois d'Einville.

I b. RK dug in north of Lunéville. RIR 13 and Res. *Jäger* Bn1 were reinforced by close support platoons of 1 and 6/FAR 5. On 26 August II/Res. Foot Artillery 14 (sFH) was attached and took up positions east of Lunéville; the town was fortified. At 0600hrs on 27 August 2 Res. Bde was ordered to relieve 4 ID, which, according to rumours, had been half destroyed, and whose troops, still under the influence of the stress of the preceding days, described the situation as extremely serious. A 2 Res. Bde staff officer asked a group of about 100 4 ID men, 'Where is II b. AK?' and was told, 'This is all that is left of II b. AK! The enemy is following close behind us!' In fact, 2 Res. Bde spent 27 August digging in undisturbed; the reports of 4ID's destruction had been exaggerated. Although 27 August was quiet, French artillery fire cost I b. RK 300 casualties.

I b. RK dug in. Decomposing or partially buried bodies were a health concern, as were the civilian latrines common to the area, which drew innumerable flies. Cases of diarrhoea appeared everywhere. The enemy crept generally closer and dug in. His well-concealed artillery fired particularly in the afternoon, when it had the sun at its back, and engaged every target that its aviators identified with flares. The German artillery was helpless. The German infantry, thanks to its deep trenches and the numerous French duds, suffered only moderate casualties, but the effect on morale was serious. On 28 August the corps lost 400 men. The corps HQ ordered the units to adopt reverse-slope defences, only occupying the crest with OPs, which surely reduced casualties significantly.

In the 5 RD sector, the high ground at Friscati, which was held by RIR 13 and Res. *Jäger* Bn 1, was shelled heavily: the troops' exhaustion reached such a degree that some became indifferent. 11 Res. Bde established a rotation whereby RIR 10 and Res. *Jäger* Bn 1 relieved RIR 13 at two-day intervals. On the morning of 1 September, well-aimed fire from I/RIR 13 at Friscati drove off an enemy attack with heavy losses. In the 9 Res. Bde area, RIR 7 relieved RIR 6 on the night of 30/31 August. The forward platoons of RFAR 5 on the high ground at Friscati supported the infantry, but suffered from enemy artillery fire. I/Res. Foot Artillery 10 (13cm cannons) was attached to I/b. RK on 28 August, but was forced by counter-battery fire to change position on 30 August. II/Res. Foot Artillery 14 (sFH) frequently changed position, from the Lunéville barracks to gardens to parks and sometimes inside buildings, firing through the windows. The Bavarian Field Airship Sec. was also attached, and was also forced several times to shift position a short distance due to enemy fire.

1 Res. Bde continued to hold Lunéville, directly subordinate to I b. RK. II/ RFAR 1, 1 Res./Eng. Bn 1 and a number of MGs from Fortress Germersheim were attached. From 29 August RIR 2 defended the south half of the city, with RIR 1 positioned in the north. On 1 September 1/RFAR 1 was attached and took up a position in the courtyard of the Dragoon barracks. Enemy activity was limited to snipers in the trees on the east side of the Forêt de Vitrimont. The only French attack was on 1 September against the right flank of II/RIR 2, but this was thrown back; the French then shelled the town.

The Bavarian *Landwehr* Div., with Fortress MG Sec. 4 and 5, 1 *Landsturm* Eng. Co./II b. AK and the Fortress Searchlight Platoon attached, moved to the woods east of Lunéville and, in the course of the next days, relieved 1 Res. Bde in Lunéville and dug in.

I b. RK was opposed by 11 ID of the French XX Corps, which had occupied the Forêt de Vitrimont and the heights north of Vitrimont town. It did not attempt to attack.

On 1 September the army group under III b. AK was dissolved and the major units returned to direct Sixth Army control. 55 *Ersatz* Bde and HKK 3 were placed under the operational control of the *Ersatz* Corps.

II b. AK, the Sixth Army Problem Child (map 17, sketch 25)

On 27 August the enemy occupied the terrain east of the Mortagne, south of Rehainviller, so slowly and carefully that 4 ID was afforded time to re-establish its units. 3 ID took artillery fire and dug in. 28 ID arrived at St Clement, behind II b. AK, with nine battalions, twelve field artillery and four heavy howitzer batteries. II and III/Baden Household Grenadier Regiment (GR) 109 were attached to 6 Bde (3 ID) at 1800hrs. It became apparent that casualties on 25 and 26 August were far fewer than had appeared and the troops re-established cohesion more quickly than expected. Many stragglers came in. By 28 August 7 Bde in Lunéville was combat-ready with good morale and had an infantry strength of 3,000 men.

On the morning of 28 August the approach of strong enemy forces on Gerbéviller and in the woods west of Fraimbois was detected. At 1000hrs the enemy began to bombard the 3 ID positions, in particular the left flank, with light and heavy artillery, and attacked at 1000hrs with infantry from Gerbéviller and the Bois de la Reine against IR 17. While I/IR 17 on the right flank and II/IR 17 in the centre, supported by MGs and I/FAR 5 (particularly 1/FAR 5 1km north-east of Gerbéviller) stopped the French quickly, III/IR 17, under fire from heavy artillery, was forced off Hill 288. Although themselves under heavy and effective artillery fire, II/FAR 5 on the south-west side of the Bois des Rappes, and 3/FAR 5 far forward on the south side of the Bois du Fey, stopped the French infantry with rapid fire. II and III/GR 109, in an assembly area in the Bois des Rappes, counter-attacked, pulling IR 17 with them, pushed the French off Hill 288 and pursued them into Gerbéviller, where the French took significant casualties in street fighting, and threw the French back over the Meurthe. This terrain could not be held, and the IR 17 right flank was pinned down by flanking fire from the Bois de la Reine, so the 6 Bde commander ordered the troops to return to their old positions that evening. Due to a misunderstanding, II and III/GR 109 returned directly to the Bois de la Rappe and the enemy retook Hill 288. But two companies (11 and 12) of the recently attached III/IR 23 pushed the French back off it again. During the night GR 109 reoccupied the hill. Gruppe Weiss (made up of five companies of IR 18, two from IR 17 and the MGK IR 17), on the left of IR 17, was not attacked and engaged the enemy with flanking fire, while I/IR 18 was only attacked by weak enemy forces.

Gerbéviller 28. 8. Textskizze 25.

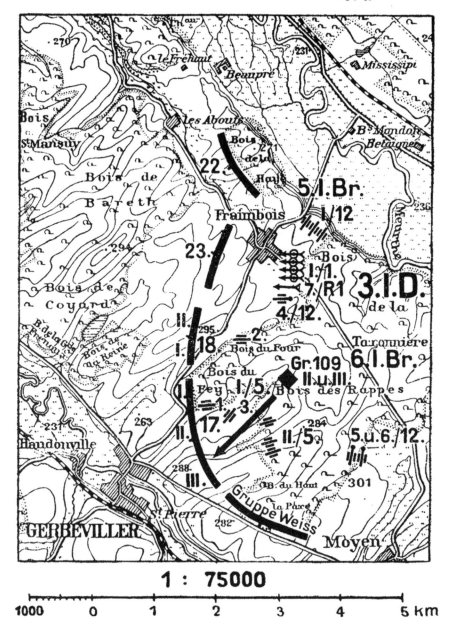

1 : 75000

1000   0   1   2   3   4   5 km

The French XV Corps had crossed the Mortagne between Mont and Xermaménil, and XVI Corps (reinforced by 74 RD) between Xermaménil and Gerbéviller. According to French sources, the German artillery severely hindered the attack. 74 RD was stopped by 6 Bde, but eventually held onto Gerbéviller, while 31 and 32 ID, in front of 5 Bde, withdrew to the south side of the Mortagne. In front of 4 ID the French XV Corps had occupied the Bois de St Mansuy with 29 ID, Rehainviller and the Forêt de Vitrimont with 30 ID.

4 ID had a generally quiet day on 28 August. Hériménil was shelled heavily, which set the town on fire and caused serious casualties among the supply columns that filled the streets. French infantry sneaking forward were thrown back by III/RIR 3. 7 Bde, resting in Lunéville, was alerted to assist 3 ID, but marched no further than Moncel when it received word that the attack on Gerbéviller had been defeated. In the meantime, French artillery fire was falling on Lunéville, so that 7 Bde had to bivouac in the farms to the east. 28 ID returned to XIV AK control.

7 Bde relieved the left wing of 2 Bde on 29 August, with IR 9 on the right and IR 5 on the left. The staff of 4 ID retook control of the division, under the former 2 Res. Bde commander. 5 Res. Bde remained division reserve and dug in south of Moncel. III/RIR 3 and II/RIR 12 from 2 Res. Bde remained southwest of Hériménil. Entrenching was significantly disrupted by French artillery fire; Hériménil was severely shelled. Although the enemy infantry did not launch a serious attack, it threatened to do so and continually pushed forward. On the previous day it had occupied Chaudfontaine and threatened the far right flank of 4 ID with envelopment. This was averted by the determination of 10/RIR 3 and 3/FAR 11, reinforced by I/RIR 3, MGK/RIR 3 and 10 and 11/RIR 12, which by evening extended the right flank.

As soon as the fog lifted, 3 ID was also shelled. The indicators of an enemy attack multiplied, and by evening the corps moved RIR 8 to Fraimbois, RIR 5 to Beaupré and III/IR 23 (probably also I/IR 23) to 6 Bde. 28 ID was called back by night march and arrived 5km south-east of St Clement at 0700hrs on 30 August. The commander of 3 ID suspected that the enemy was conducting a deception and, at 2300hrs, conducted a reconnaissance in force with two companies of IR 17, which did not make contact until they reached the north side of Gerbéviller.

The II b. AK position grew steadily stronger as the troops, assisted by the engineers, continued to dig in, but here were still difficulties to be overcome. Under cover of the morning fog, strong enemy forces attacked from the Bois de la Reine and the Mortagne Valley on both sides of Gerbéviller against the left flank of 3 ID. I/IR 18, I and II/IR 17, and the attached companies of I/RIR 8, stopped the enemy attack, but GR 109 was in great difficulty on Hill 288. At 0530hrs 6/IR 17 was relieving 8/IR 17 in place in the south-west corner of the Bois du Haut de la Paix when the enemy suddenly appeared out of the fog and broke into the position. However, together with 7/IR 18, the two companies attacked the equally astounded French with the bayonet and threw them back to the Mortagne. MGK/IR 18 appeared just in time to cover the enemy with fire at point-blank range. The French approached to with 300m of the south side of the wood, but were just as quickly thrown back by an attack conducted principally by 10/IR 17. 500 to 600 French dead covered the battlefield. The situation had been quickly stabilised, but disquieting reports were received. The 6 Bde commander even issued a withdrawal order at 0900hrs, but quickly countermanded it as these reports were shown to be false. The I/IR 17 commander simply ignored the order, as the enemy was only 300m to his front. II/IR 17 reoccupied its old positions and was reinforced by III/IR 17. As the fog lifted, GR 109 received intolerable enemy artillery fire, but was supported by II/RIR 8. The commander of 3 ID sent strong elements of IR 23 into the Bois du Four and Bois des Rappes and assembled all available elements of IR 22 from the position at the Bois de la Haye to support 6 Bde. The corps moved 28 ID to Moyen to flank attack the enemy in front of 6 Bde and XXI AK was asked to send forces in the direction of Gerbéviller. However, 3 ID defeated the enemy attack by noon, before these measures became effective. The 28 ID movement was stopped about 4km northeast of Moyen.

Near dawn on 31 August, and on 1 and 2 September, heavy firing broke out in the 5 Bde sector: the enemy appeared to prefer to conduct a wild firefight from the edge of the Bois de Bareth and Bois de Coyard rather than attack. The enemy artillery continually shelled the open high ground west and south of Fraimbois. In spite of being in good dug-in positions, 3 FA Bde took serious casualties, but with the aid of aerial observers conducted counter-battery fire. Forward observers provided with telephone lines and other means of communication moved into the front-line trenches. Thanks to excellent visibility, on 2 September MGK/IR 22 observed strong enemy forces far in the distance, moving west. On 31 August 28 ID was again released and replaced by the Guard ED at Laronxe. Two *Ersatz* battalions relieved GR 109, while the Guard *Ersatz* Bde relieved 2 Res. Bde (4 ID).

The 4 ID position was poorly suited for the defence. There were extensive, thick forests directly to the front, which concealed the enemy, while the Meurthe, a serious obstacle, was directly to the rear. The position had no depth: infantry and artillery were practically collocated so that the enemy bombardment could engage them simultaneously. Nevertheless, after the effects of the previous battle had been overcome, the entire division was confident it could hold the position; the infantry and artillery encouraged each other.

7 Bde, primarily IR 9, was attacked weakly in the early morning on 31 August, and on 1 and 2 September; these were easily and bloodily repulsed with the support of the artillery. The enemy limited himself to attacks by fire in front of IR 5 and did not appear at all in front of 2 Res. Bde. Scheduled reliefs of the

front-line troops were conducted; an attack on Hériménil during a relief was easily beaten off.

The French artillery thoroughly exploited its superiority, continually shelling the newly constructed trenches as well as roads and towns. It engaged 4 FA Bde from positions that were masterfully hidden, impossible to locate and unreachable. Fire from Forêt de Vitrimont flanked the entire Meurthe position, forcing the artillery to move to the east side of the Meurthe to escape it. On 31 August II/ Foot Artillery R 18 (21cm mortars) was attached to 4 ID, and on 1 September 4/ Foot Artillery R 1 (sFH) also joined them; they were sorely needed.

After 30 August the situation in the II b. AK sector became quieter, though the troops still had to accommodate themselves to the difficulties of positional warfare, principally the continual artillery fire and the little-loved trench digging. Only the regularity of the shelling and the poor quality of French shells, which were often duds or burned rather than exploded, kept the casualty rate low. There was a shortage of water on the Fraimbois highlands and elsewhere. Dysentery was widespread. Unburied bodies of men and animals fouled the air, especially in front of 6 Bde, where German MG fire had mown down the French in rows; attempts to bury them were prevented by French artillery fire. The corps commander declared II b. AK combat-ready on 30 August, but at half-strength; considerably more than half the officers were casualties, although replacements began to arrive.

The concern expressed after 26 August by Sixth Army for II b. AK was justified. The French XV and XVI Corps, reinforced by 64 and 74 RD, had repeatedly attempted to push to the Meurthe. Opposed by such superior numbers, II b. AK, reduced in strength and standing directly in front of the river, prevented the French from doing so.

On the night of 26/27 August XXI AK had evacuated the west bank of the Mortagne and dug in south of Moyen. Opposed by the French VIII Corps in the north and XIII Corps in the south, XXI AK had to continually expect an attack by superior enemy forces. On 27 August, 42 ID on the corps left wing came under heavy artillery fire and strong enemy forces were reported approaching Rambervillers, so XXI AK asked its neighbour on the left, I b. AK, to assist by launching an attack.

I b. AK at Xaffévillers–Anglemont, 27–28 August (maps 18 and 21, sketch 26)

While the left wing of Seventh Army continued the attack at St Dié on 27 August, I b. AK, with operational control over 29 ID, was instructed to defend in place. On the night of 26/27 August, I b. AK had shifted far enough to the right that it established contact with XXI AK in the Bois de la Horne, north-east of Xaffévillers. This march was conducted in pitch darkness and pouring rain;

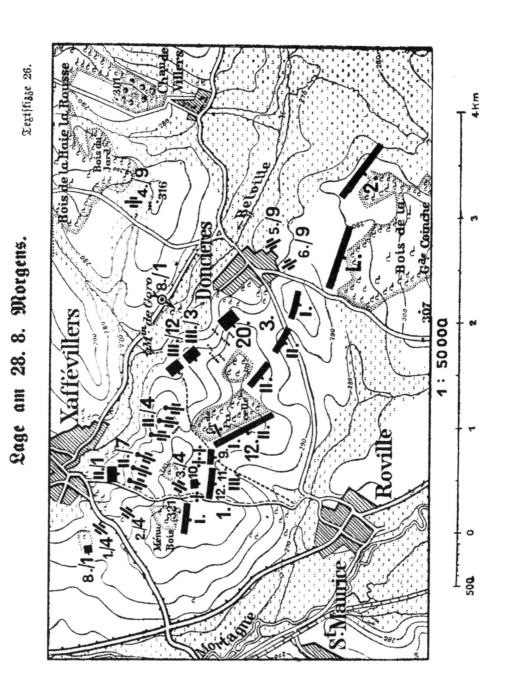

Lage am 28. 8. Morgens.

Textfigur 26.

many vehicles became stuck in the mud marching through the Grands Bois de Glonville and blocked the already narrow road. In Bazien, which was still burning and being shelled, march columns crossed and traffic came to a halt. Some units took a detour through Fontenoy. The troops arrived wet and tired, and many had to bivouac in marching column in the open.

On the morning of 27 August only weak enemy skirmisher lines moved carefully towards 2 ID, but enemy artillery, directed by aircraft and two captive balloons, reopened fire. The infantry of I b. AK had already constructed some cover and had learned how to avoid the fire. Nevertheless, there were casualties. With Sixth Army permission, at 1230hrs I b. AK ordered an attack over the Belville stream in order to assist XXI AK, which the troops greeted it as a means of avoiding the enemy artillery fire. The rain stopped around noon and the troops were in motion at 1500hrs. 29 ID, attached to I b. AK, slowly gained ground in the direction of Ménil.

In the 1 ID sector the artillery conducted preparatory firing against Anglemont and the woods west of the town. The infantry jumped off somewhat late at 1600hrs. On the 2 ID left, III/IR 16 turned hard right from the high ground north of Ménil towards Anglemont with 11 and 12/IR 16 in front, 10 and 9/IR 16 behind the left flank. They were received by lively artillery fire as they rose from the trenches and moved towards the Belville Valley, west of Ménil. There they took rifle fire from the village into the left flank, which forced them to engage in that direction, along with the attached MG platoon. The enemy fire was silenced and the battalion resumed the march, pushed away weak enemy infantry lying north-east of Anglemont and reached to within 200m of the village by 1730hrs. But the 2 ID artillery continued to hammer the village, and all means of communication were unable to stop the fire, which ceased only at dusk. Finally III/IR 16 could approach the west side of Anglemont, which was burning at several places, but did not enter, bypassing it to the left and right.

IR 12 attacked on the right of IR 16, with I and III/IR 12 forming the first line and II/IR 12 the second, but the units became intermixed and dispersed: the skirmisher line advanced, right to left, 3, 1, 9, 11 and 12/IR 12. Fire from Ménil seems to have drawn off 2/IR 2 to the left and 10/IR 12 joined the right. 7/IR 12 was attached to I/IR 12 as a reserve. The regiment avoided the artillery fire on the trenches north-west of Ménil and reached the bottom of the slope north-east of the Bois de la Grande Coinche, but took fire from the woods, while the German artillery did not lift its fire there. Nevertheless, the treeline was stormed at 1900hrs, which led to a furious close-range firefight and heavy losses; 7/IR 12 was committed. The enemy moved off, but it did not seem prudent to follow him into the dark wood, so the regiment bivouacked in the open 200m from the treeline.

To the right of IR 12 was the Household IR (minus I/Household), which moved out from Nossoncourt, II/Household on the right and III/Household on the left. Followed by enemy fire, the skirmisher lines crossed the broad Belville Valley as if they were on a training exercise. The fight began on the north-east side of the Bois de la Grande Coinche. As the last rays of the sun set, the Household IR assaulted the enemy and took the treeline; the commander of III/Household was killed and prisoners taken. But the fight went on in the wood against a crafty enemy. He fired close-range salvoes, which usually went high, and slipped through the woods to fire into the Bavarians from the rear. It was finally dark, the companies had pushed deep into the woods and, to assemble them in the open south of Doncières, the regimental commander ordered 'The Watch on the Rhine' be sung. The French responded by singing the 'Marseillaise'.

In the 2 ID sector the artillery also prepared the way for the infantry, particularly by engaging the French artillery at Deinvillers, south of Xaffévillers, and the Bois de Roville, as well as infantry on the ridge between Xaffévillers and Doncières. The commander of 9 FA Bde was badly wounded near Château de Villers, his adjutant killed.

The 3 Bde objectives were the middle of the Grande Pucelle wood and the high ground south of Doncières. Initially, only II/IR 3 and I/IR 20 were committed in this direction. From Hill 316, north-east of Doncières and Château de Villers, they moved in waves to the Belville Valley, covered by overhead fire from MGK/IR 3, which remained in the trenches, against Doncières and the trenches to both sides. To begin with, II/IR 3 had an easy time of it, particularly because the enemy artillery was little active. Then enemy resistance stiffened and artillery fire began to fall, so that, at 1800hrs, I and II/IR 20 moved forward from the Bois de la Haie la Rousse to assist, through Doncières and onto the small copse on high ground beyond, which could not be held due to artillery fire. I/IR 20 deployed 3, 1, and 4/IR 20 and, moving past the east side of Doncières, was so severely hindered by flanking fire from Bois de la Grande Coinche that 2 and 3/IR 3, in reserve east of the Château de Villers, had to reinforce the firing line at 1600hrs. The enemy fire still could not be suppressed, and 4 and 1/IR 3 were committed at 1800hrs. At 1930hrs they stormed the high ground and treeline south of Doncières. The objective had been taken, although IR 3 and 20 were completely intermixed. The leaders had begun reorganising when, at 2000hrs, the French launched a counter-attack, accompanied by bugle calls. I/IR 3, which had just assembled on the north side of the Bois de la Grande Coinche and was marching to the high ground south of Doncières, quickly deployed on the left flank, received the French with fire at 20m range and blasted them back.

The 4 ID objective was Menu Bois, south of Xaffévillers (I/Household) and the north half of the Grande Pucelle wood (IR 12), with IR 15 in reserve in the Bois de la Horne.

I/Household advanced slowly against alert enemy artillery, but reached the Menu Bois at 1800hrs. The French did not defend Xaffévillers, but a number of prisoners were taken there. At 1500hrs IR 12 advanced from the south treeline of the Bois de la Haie la Rousse with I/IR 12 on the right, II/IR 12 on the left at, III and MGK/IR 12 following behind the centre. It was much less hindered by artillery fire and quickly reached the Belville streambed and climbed the steep slope against weak resistance. I/IR 12, with 4, 2, and 3/IR 12 deployed, reached the high ground south of Menu Bois, and II/IR 12 the west side of the Grande Pucelle wood, when they became involved in a firefight with French infantry in ditches, bushes and hedges at Roville. At 1700hrs masses of French light and heavy shells began to land on I/Household and IR 12. I/Household also took fire directly into the right flank from the high ground north-west of Xaffévillers. The French were reported bringing up reinforcements and IR 12 committed 10, 12 and the MG along the firing line. The MGs were able to engage thick groups at Roville. Nevertheless, the troops felt more and more isolated, for not only did artillery fire fall on them, but it also formed a barrage to cut them off from the rear. At 1900hrs, under cover of darkness, the shaken survivors were withdrawn, I/Household to the Bois de la Horne, IR 12 to the Bois de la Haie la Rousse, covered by 1 and 3/FAR 4, which had moved up to the Bois de la Horne at 1900hrs.

In the course of the afternoon IR 15 moved up to the Bois du Grande Bras. I/IR 15 then moved to the west side of the Bois de la Horne, but was forced back by artillery fire. It deployed skirmishers and began a firefight with French troops on the high ground north-west of Xaffévillers that were firing into the flank of I/Household. When I/Household urgently asked for help, IR 15 was committed at dusk to the attack. I/IR 15 climbed the hill north-west of Xaffévillers, but ran into serious resistance as well as took fire from the Bois des Aulnes into the right flank. II and then III/IR 15 were committed on the right. There was a short delay crossing the Belville stream, which was stomach-deep, and units became intermixed, but in continual movement they reached the ridge north-west of Xaffévillers, while the MGK supported from the treeline of the Bois du Grande Bras. At 1745hrs the corps released IR 1 to 2 ID, which ordered it to relieve I/Household in place on the high ground south of Xaffévillers. It marched through Ménarmont and the burning Xaffévillers, and conducted the relief late at night, facing Roville.

It is difficult to determine whether the I b. AK attack was necessary. When 2 ID began movement at 1400hrs there was not a trace of an attack on XXI AK. The troops had once again demonstrated their aggressive spirit. But I b. AK was now 3km in front of XXI AK, which was on the high ground south-east of Domptail on the right, and 4km in front of 29 ID on the left, which had not reached Ménil. At 2045hrs IR 16 in the Bois de la Pêche was ordered to cover the corps left by moving through Ménil to Anglemont. 3/IR 16 had been sent to clear the town at 1930hrs; first it blocked the exits, and then searched house to house. The company was approaching the south side of the town when a French unit in marching column entered from the south, while shots were fired from the houses near the church on the south side. The company concentrated near the church and blocked all French attempts to penetrate into the town. The firefight lasted for hours and caused several casualties. II/IR 16 reached the north side of the town and sent 5/IR 16 towards the church. The brigade commander forbade the commitment of more troops into the town. I/IR 16 sealed off the town on the north, east and west. Volunteers from 1 and 2/IR 16, along with doctors from II/IR 16, reached the church; the Bavarians held out there until dawn. III/IR 16 was now completely in the air, as contact with IR 2 and 29 ID had been lost. From the Bois de la Grande Coinche on the right were heard cries of 'Hurrah!', signals, rifle fire, salvoes, 'The Watch on the Rhine', the 'Marseillaise' and combat in Ménil. An officer and two squads searching for food in Anglemont encountered a half-platoon of French Alpine troops. It was later determined that IR 2 was only 800m north-west of Anglemont and that the treeline south of the town was unoccupied. But as the fog began to lift at 0630hrs on 28 August, French troops could be seen 1km east of the road to Ménil; 10/IR 16 and the attached MG platoon engaged them in the flank and cut them down nearly to the last man. But the battalion had also revealed their own position and took fire from invisible riflemen in all directions, including the houses of Anglemont, which was suppressed by spraying the roofs with MG fire. Enemy detachments began to penetrate from the south-east into the open ground between Ménil and Anglemont; the battalion was threatened with encirclement. The battalion standard was sent to IR 2 with twelve men, only four of which made it through. III/IR 16 decided to break out to the north at 0800hrs. The companies moved by squads through low ground west of Anglemont. It was possible to suppress the fire from the town so that it could not disturb the movement. The battalion – now only six officers and 270 men strong – assembled between Château de Villers and Nossoncourt.

The commander of IR 16 gained the impression that the enemy planned to attack Ménil with new forces. He pulled I and II/IR 16 back to the old position on the treeline of the Bois de la Pêche astride the road. The attack never materialised. The German artillery set the town on fire and it was occupied by 29 ID.

1 ID intended to continue the attack on 28 August, but the open left flank put an end to that idea. After Anglemont was evacuated, IR 2 could not hold the north-east side of the Bois de la Grande Coinche, particularly since it took artillery fire in the left flank. It withdrew, dispersed in waves of skirmishers, to Château de Villers and Nossoncourt. The Household IR conducted a firefight with French infantry in the Bois de la Grande Coinche, then withdrew that morning to the Bois du Jard, followed by artillery fire, but in perfect order.

The enemy did not pursue, but once again squandered masses of shells on the 1 ID positions.

On 28 August 2 ID was determined to hold the positions south of the Belville stream. During the night and morning the units reorganised and dug in. IR 20 assembled on the slopes north-west of Doncières and pushed II/IR 20 to the small wood 1km west of the town. The regiment was split up and understrength: I/IR 20 counted six officers and 400 men. IR 3 held the high ground south-west of Doncières; 9 FA Bde was brought up to Doncières to support 3 Bde.

In the 4 Bde sector, IR 12 occupied its positions on the high ground south of Xaffévillers at 0400hrs. IR 1 and IR 15 were south and north-west of the town in the positions they had held the night before. 4 Bde subordinated itself to 65 Bde (XXI AK) in the Bois des Aulnes on its right. 4 FA Bde took position south of the town. II/Foot Artillery R 1 (sFH) was blocked by artillery fire from moving south of the town (except for 8/Foot Artillery R 1, which set up north of Doncières) and found positions north of Xaffévillers.

At 0900hrs overwhelming artillery fire landed on the 2 ID positions on the ridge south of the Belville stream, which were easily visible, even at great distance. The troops sought to avoid the fire or dig in, but to no avail. The feeling of helplessness spread; nerves were tested by the sight of horrible wounds and the frequent cries of fear and pain. Every calibre of shell landed, from light to 28cm. The bombardment lasted hour after hour. It was no wonder that the lines began to crumble, or that leaders used any opportunity to reduce casualties and pull their troops out of this hell. The artillery could not suppress the French fire. The French infantry, on the other hand, remained quietly at Roville and the Mortagne Valley.

In the 3 Bde sector, shell after shell landed in Doncières, which was burning, and on the bridge over the Belville stream east of the town. At noon the Household IR began to leave the Bois du Jard, and IR 20, in the fields west of Doncières, gave way. The IR 3 commander felt justified, indeed obligated, to pull his battalions out of the artillery fire; the regiment had reached the valley both sides of Doncières when the brigade commander ordered it to reoccupy the positions. The French had taken the high ground south-west of Doncières and I/IR 3 had to fight for it. 5 and 6/FAR 9 left their forward positions south-east of Doncières. The 3 ID commander turned them around and sent them back. Perhaps they arrived just in time to prevent a strong attack against the 3 Bde flank, for they took rifle fire from the Bois de la Grande Coinche, and their return fire into the treeline cut down rows of French troops who had obviously been surprised in their assembly area.

The 4 Bde commander reported to 2 ID early and often that occupying the high ground south of the Belville stream was causing heavy and unnecessary casualties. The same grounds motivated the II/FAR 7 commander to displace his guns from behind the Menu Bois, where he was taking artillery fire from three sides, to the south side of the Bois de la Horne at 0730hrs. 4 Bde and the rest of 4 FA Bde hung on in their positions the entire morning, under continual bombardment. The woods at Menu Bois and Grande Pucelle offered the French an easily visible target. Heavy shells turned the strongest trees into matchsticks. IR 1 and IR 12 had to withstand the severest test and the most serious casualties. The trenches were on the forward slope, only knee-deep and strongly held – man next to man. It was understandable that the troops began to fall back at noon. IR 15 got off easiest – it concealed itself well on the slopes north-west of Xaffévillers. The artillery forward observers on the high ground and the batteries both suffered severely from the artillery fire, to which they could not reply because they could not locate the French guns. Far and wide, there was hardly a target visible.

At noon 9/IR 1 on the regiment left flank took a direct hit, which blew the company commander and a number of other men to pieces. The cry went up: 'The captain is dead! It's all over!' and the company disintegrated. The companies of I/IR 1 in the Menu Bois sought to escape the murderous enemy fire by continually changing position. At the request of the regimental commander, the 1 ID commander permitted a withdrawal to the Bois de la Horne at 1400hrs. I/IR 1 immediately began to pull back in open-order waves. II/IR 1 (except 8/IR 1) and the MGK/IR 1, which did not receive the order, followed. III/IR 1 also did not receive the order and stayed between the Menu Bois and Grande Pucelle wood, except for the remnants of 9/IR 1, which followed the other two battalions. By 1530hrs IR 1, except for III and 8/IR 1, was assembled in the Bois de la Horne.

I/FAR 4 was now unprotected. At 1500hrs the enemy artillery fire was increasing in intensity and there were still no targets; some of the gunners of 1 and 2/FAR 4 were pulled back to Xaffévillers, carrying the breech blocks and sights. After a short time the commander of 2 FA Bde ordered them back to the guns.

At noon the ranks of IR 12 began to crumble into the Belville Valley. Most of II/IR 12 had withdrawn on orders of the regimental commander to the midpoint of the Xaffévillers–Doncières road, hile I and MGK/IR 12 had moved to the south-east side of Xaffévillers. The commander of II/FAR 4 objected that this left his guns without protection, so 1, 2 and 3/IR 12 reoccupied the Grande Pucelle wood. The MGK, which had fired off all of its ammunition, moved to the reverse slope. The commander of III/IR 3 also moved his companies up to the Grande Pucelle wood.

Before 1500hrs the 2 ID commander, who was at Ménarmont, permitted 4 Bde to move the supply units farther to the rear, if necessary. At 1550hrs he allowed all units to withdraw to the old positions on the north side of the Belville stream, so long as strong security detachments remained on the south side. I and MGK/IR 12 were withdrawn to the orchards on the north-east side of Xaffévillers. In the Bois de la Horne, IR 15 relieved IR 1, which pulled back to Fontenoy. In the Menu Bois and Grande Pucelle wood, the commander of III/IR 1 brusquely denied the company commanders' requests to withdraw. At 1700hrs 12 and 11/IR 1 retreated down the slope to Xaffévillers; the III/IR 1 commander hauled 12/IR 1 back, but was unable to stop 11/IR 1, so 10/IR 1 was moved from reserve into its place.

By means that are not clear, an order reached FAR 4 to abandon the guns and recover them after dark. The limbers moved off, and the breech blocks and sights were removed. Some of the guns were rendered long-term unserviceable by hammering on the elevating screws. Loyalty to the guns soon asserted itself, beginning with the adjutant of 2 FA Bde, who encountered the limbers of 1 and 2/FAR 4 on the bridge at Xaffévillers and turned them around. He also met the commander of 8/IR 1, who had already offered his help to the commander of I/FAR 4, and who agreed to try to save the guns. It became a regular competition, actually encouraged by the continuing enemy artillery fire. Two platoons of 8/IR 1 dragged the guns out of their dug-in positions and rolled them to the limbers, while the third platoon provided protection. The guns were moved off at a gallop through a French artillery barrage behind the position. Officers helped limber up the guns, and drivers dismounted from their horses to assist. All the guns of 1 and 2/FAR 4 were moved, as well as the equipment lying near the gun positions. 3/FAR 4, 400m away, was brought off by its commander. I/FAR 4 only left some shot-up caissons and suffered few losses. Wounded infantrymen were carried off on the limbers and caissons.

The commander of FAR 4 had accompanied the limbers of II/FAR 4 back to the Bois de la Horne. When I/FAR 4 arrived at 1800hrs with its guns, the order was immediately issued to II/FAR 4 to retrieve its guns also. Two lieutenants of the light munitions column of II/FAR 7 at Bois de la Horne had already offered their assistance and apparently had already set to work; all the II/FAR 4 guns were saved.

10 and 12/IR 1 and the III/IR 1 still held out on the high ground between Menu Bois and the Grande Pucelle wood. The artillery fire was practically insupportable: the commander of 12/IR 1 kept his men together by leading them in prayer. At 1800hrs French infantry approached, opened fire at 700m and continued to advance. The III/IR 1 commander did not let his men open fire until the French were at close range (400m) and the French attack was repulsed. When the battalion took what they supposed to be friendly artillery fire at 1910hrs, the III/IR 1 commander ordered a withdrawal, which was conducted in perfect order, carrying the non-ambulatory wounded. The commander of 12/IR 1 was killed and command was assumed by a corporal.

The commander of 10/IR 1 formed the rearguard with a handful of men and held off the advancing French. In Ménarmont III/IR 1 assembled – all 100 men.

After dark IR 12 (minus III/IR 12) moved from the Xaffévillers–Doncières road to the Bois de la Haie la Rousse. III/IR 12 and III/IR 3 remained with the numerous wounded that had assembled on the road. III/IR 12 was ordered to outpost the high ground west of Xaffévillers, but it ran into enemy troops on the bridge in the town, and at midnight a bitter close-range fight developed, with neither side being able to cross the stream.

3 Bde pulled its troops back over the Belville stream at 1930hrs, IR 20 (minus II/IR 20) to the wood west of Bazien and IR 3 (minus III/IR 3) to Château de Villers. II/IR 20 held the south treeline of the Bois de la Haie la Rousse to both sides of the Doncières–Ménarmont road, while III/IR 3 was positioned at the fork in the road north-east of Doncières. The wounded in Doncières, which was burning, were successfully brought away. Enemy artillery fire accompanied the march to the old positions north of the Belville stream. Towards evening two mortar battalions, which had been at Manonviller, were attached to I b. AK. The day ended with a tremendous thunderstorm at 2200hrs. The troops spent the night in the open: wet, freezing, exhausted, hungry and shocked by the day's combat.

I b. AK had obviously moved into an area which the heavy batteries of Épinal had used as firing areas and therefore knew every corner and range. I b. AK and 29 ID had been opposed on 27 and 28 August by the French XIII Corps and XXI Corps, reinforced by 44 ID. On 27 August they had attacked what they thought were withdrawing German troops. XII Corps had moved from Roville in the direction of Ménarmont, initially committing 25 ID. Only after they had lost Xaffévillers and Doncières was 26 ID committed to the right of 25 ID. XXI Corps, which urgently required rest, also only committed 44 ID, but supported it with the artillery of 13 and 43 ID, to attack on both sides of the Ménil road. When I b. AK withdrew, XII AK remained on the battlefield, while 44 ID fell back to rejoin XIII Corps east of Rambervillers.

In the following days strong French forces were detected north of Rambervillers. The enemy did not budge in front of I b. AK, but held a strongly fortified position on the west side of the Mortagne. The high ground between the Mortagne and Belville was sometimes occupied, sometimes not.

On 29 August trench warfare began for I b. AK. There were periods of heavy French artillery fire. The Château de Villers, in which lay 150 wounded under protection of the Red Cross, was ruthlessly bombarded and burst into flames at 1600hrs. Volunteers from I and III/IR 2 rescued the severely wounded, including twenty French, by lifting them through the windows. Ménarmont in particular was often and severely shelled. The troops gradually constructed better cover and learned by being careful, changing positions and using dummy positions to avoid or misdirect French fire. Nevertheless, random direct hits caused painful casualties. The German artillery got revenge with the surprise shelling of trenches and visible troops. Aviators sought out the well-concealed French batteries, which frequently changed locations, but the results of aerial reconnaissance were too general and too slow in reaching the firing batteries to form a basis for the artillery duel. The French exploited the greater range of their guns to fire at long range, so that they could only be reached by the German heavy artillery, which had to move far forward to be effective, and which wasted their precious shells for lack of good observation of the targets. It was soon necessary to conserve shells.

On 29 August XIV AK extended its right to the low ground 800m east of Nossoncourt, so that I b. AK had a sector only 5km wide. This, and the relatively quiet tactical situation, allowed the rotation of major units (regiments, brigades and artillery sections) and a thinning-out of the front line. The construction of trenches and the marching through the bottomless mud of the Bois de Glonville still cost a great deal of energy. The engineers corduroyed the muddy stretches and built entirely new roads. Due to false alarms, the resting troops were frequently alerted and moved forward. Nevertheless, the troops got some rest for the first time since the beginning of the campaign. Combat readiness rose and discipline firmed up through training. Replacement troops arrived, but there was a shortage of experienced leaders, many of whom were dead or wounded. The troops' health suffered from intestinal disorders, one source of which was the poorly buried bodies; the air at Nossoncourt, Bazien and Château de Villers was foul.

On 1 September I b. AK returned to Sixth Army. On 2 September XIV AK on the left extended its flank to the high ground west of Nossoncourt, so that I b. AK could hold its sector with a single regiment.

Continuation of the Battles at St Dié, 28 August (sketch 20)

Seventh Army intended to pull XV AK out of the line and assemble it at Raon l'Étape. To do so, it was necessary to push the enemy away from the Meurthe north and south of St Dié. XIV RK needed to firmly hold the important Raon l'Étape–St Dié road and cross the Meurthe. On 28 August XIV RK gave 30 RD and the Bavarian ED an absolutely necessary rest day. This order never reached 30 RD, and the troops were held in readiness to march. The troops were packed into the villages and, in the rainy weather, many could not put a roof over their heads. I and II/RIR 14 and Fortress MG Sec. 2 marched to St Dié south of the Meurthe to provide security, and found large quantities of rations in the French barracks there. Towards evening heavy enemy fire made it appear that the

enemy was going to attack, so the two battalions pulled back to the north side of the river; when nothing happened by dusk, they reoccupied the south side.

(Sketch 27) By 0600hrs the corps order had not reached the Bavarian ED, so the commander decided to advance on St Dié on both sides of the Meurthe, since the town was the objective of the previous day. The left flank seemed to have been secured by 9 *Ersatz* Bde at the pass west of Azonel, and reports from Mandray in the south were reassuring. As soon as the division order was issued, the corps order telling it to rest at Entre-deux-Eaux arrived. 1 *Ersatz* Bde was now ordered to hold the high ground east of Saulcy and south of Entre-deux-Eaux. RIR 15 was attached and ordered to march in this direction. 9 *Ersatz* Bde was to defend Saulcy and the pass west of Azonel. The artillery occupied positions east of Saulcy. The heavy morning fog led to errors in land navigation and subsequent corrective marches.

In Mandray the chief surgeon received permission from the commander of the French Alpine infantry to recover the wounded. In Basse Mandray the officers of the ambushed munitions column had assembled their troops during the night and, at dawn, cut the dead and wounded horses from the traces, and oriented the vehicles towards Saulcy, aided by the dense fog. However, shots were fired as they began to move.

Due to various difficulties the order to move to Mandray only reached *Ersatz* Bn IV at the battalion position west of Claingoutte at 0300hrs. As it approached the west side of Basse Mandray at 0600hrs, along the road from Saulcy, it deployed 3/*Ersatz* Bn IV, with 2 and 4/*Ersatz* Bn IV in the second line and 1/*Ersatz* Bn IV in the third, and encountered stragglers from the munitions column, which, if armed, were ordered to accompany the *Ersatz* men. The battalion passed quickly through Basse Mandray, but took murderous fire from Mandray. 2 and 4/*Ersatz* Bn IV were immediately deployed on both sides of 3/*Ersatz* Bn IV and bitter house-to-house fighting began. The French Alpine troops hid themselves masterfully and shot down the Bavarian troops advancing in the open. The fight was particularly hot around the church, whose tower was strongly held, as was the churchyard. The first assault on both failed, even though 1/*Ersatz* Bn IV was committed. Then the back door to the church was broken open and the steps to the tower were set on fire. The windows to the nave were broken and the church was stormed; some of the French fled at the last minute, but those in the tower burned to death. Soon the town was cleared; the French withdrew east, south-east and south to the nearby wooded high ground. The French had moved the prisoners out of the town at the beginning of the fight. *Ersatz* Bn IV had taken eighty casualties. It occupied the south side of Mandray, partly along a favourable steep slope, partly along a ridge 100m in front. But the enemy had also recovered and prepared to attack.

RIR 15 marched from Saulcy and arrived at Hill 514, south-east of Entre-deux-Eaux, at 0800hrs. On their own initiative, elements of the regiment had answered calls for help from Mandray. The RIR 15 commander ordered III/RIR 15 to march to Basse Mandray, and I/RIR 15 to Mandray itself. 1 *Ersatz*/FAR 4 set up on Hill 514. III and I/RIR 15 reached their objectives unopposed, crossed the valley and, as the fog began to lift, ascended the south side and engaged the French Alpine troops who left their trenches halfway up the slope and retreated to the north treeline of the Bois de Mandray, with RIR 15 pursuing. With the arrival of RIR 15, *Ersatz* Bn IV withdrew to the north side of the road and cooked breakfast, fortified by supplies of wine they discovered. The munitions column marched to Saulcy.

The Alpine troops were reinforced by MG and artillery, and were well hidden in the broom bushes which hindered German artillery support. It is possible that this is why the order was given for RIR 15 to fall back; perhaps the enemy reinforcements were making themselves felt. In any case, at 1500hrs the regiment moved in good order back into the valley; I/RIR 15 moved directly to Hill 514, probably thinking its left flank was threatened. The regimental commander stopped III/RIR 15 halfway down the hill and it was reinforced by *Ersatz* Bn IV. But the enemy was gaining the upper hand. He engaged 1 *Ersatz*/FAR 4 in its open position on Hill 514 with artillery and MG fire, and began to put pressure on III/RIR 15 and *Ersatz* Bn IV, especially against the open left flank. In the evening, 1 *Ersatz* Bn IV moved to the high ground north of Mandray, followed by III/RIR 15. Mandray fell back into enemy hands, including six vehicles from staff wagons of the Bavarian ED and 1 *Ersatz* Bde, which contained valuable documents.

9 *Ersatz* Bde and LIR 71 prepared Saulcy for defence, which was wrecked and otherwise abandoned. *Ersatz* Bn XI and 2 and 3/LIR 71, which were on outpost duty near Azonel, were withdrawn in the morning as the enemy appeared. From 1 *Ersatz* Bde, *Ersatz* Bn I and II moved early in the morning east from Saulcy to the west and south sides of Hill 450. *Ersatz* Bn III at St Léonard did not receive any orders, but it became aware of the situation as it moved east to Hill 510. RIR 4 left the high ground at Mangoutte and, with *Ersatz* MGK 1, moved south and south-west of Entre-deux-Eaux.

When the fog lifted at Saulcy, the 9 *Ersatz* Bde situation became lively. *Ersatz* FA Sec. I, II and III, and 2 *Ersatz*/FAR 51, shelled infantry visible at Anozel and Moncel-les-Cours. Early in the afternoon invisible enemy artillery west of Anozel and at les Censes covered the Bavarian ED artillery with overwhelming fire, particularly 15cm howitsers. The *Ersatz* artillery took up the unequal battle, supported by 3/Res. Foot Artillery R 14 (10cm cannons) attached to 30 RD north-west of Coinches. *Ersatz* FA Sec. I (minus 1 *Ersatz*/FAR 4), which had insufficient cover, took serious casualties. 2 *Ersatz*/FAR 1, which had fired off its ammunition, was pulled out of the position; 1 *Ersatz*/FAR 1 remained under fire for four hours. At 1600hrs in the *Ersatz* FA Sec. III area, 2 *Ersatz*/FAR 12 was able to engage strong enemy cavalry leaving St Léonard and scare it off. A French battery, obviously from this cavalry unit, went into position between St Léonard and Mandray and attempted to take *Ersatz* FA Sec. III in the flank, but was held in check by 2 *Ersatz*/FAR 12. Saulcy was also shelled by these enemy batteries, and RIR 4, south-west of Entre-deux-Eaux, was forced to change position several times; *Ersatz* Bn II had to seek concealment in a small wood.

When the commander of the Bavarian ED learned of the fighting at Mandray and of enemy patrols at La Croix, he moved RIR 4 and 2 *Ersatz*/Eng. Bn 1 east to the dominating hill, the Tête de Behouille. *Ersatz* Bn VI was moved to Omégoutte–Algouette, 1 *Ersatz*/FAR 2 to La Behouille, and *Ersatz* Bn VIII assumed the security of Laveline.

29 August (map 22)

On 29 August, in order to disengage XV AK, Seventh Army ordered XV RK to cross the Meurthe and hold the high ground on the west bank of the Meurthe at St Michel and Étival (off map, 5 and 10km north of St Dié), which took the entire strength of 28 RD, 19 ED and 26 RD. XIV AK was to hold the east bank of the Meurthe. However, the commander of XIV RK also believed that he had to throw the enemy back across the Meurthe between St Léonard and Anould. He gave this mission to the Bavarian ED, to which he attached 30 RD. The Bavarian ED was to attack at 0600hrs between Saulcy and Entre-deux-Eaux, while 30 RD was to remain available at Coinches. The XIV RK order did not reach the Bavarian ED until 0600hrs. It was scattered over a 6km front and to bring it into position to attack involved long and dangerous flank marches in the face of the enemy. 30 RD was oriented to attack St Dié and north of the Bavarian ED. To bring it into position to attack to the south, either east or west of the Bavarian ED, required considerable difficult and time-consuming marching. The Bavarian ED commander therefore decided to intermix the two divisions. 10 Res. Bde would attack from Entre-deux-Eaux to St Léonard, 1 *Ersatz* Bde and RIR 15 through Mandray, and 5 *Ersatz* Bde and RIR 4 over the high ground south-west of La Croix towards Anould. 10 Res. Bde and 1 *Ersatz* Bde would be under the operational control of the 30 RD commander.

9 *Ersatz* Bde was already engaged at Saulcy. *Ersatz* Bn II pushed 1 and 2/*Ersatz* Bn II to the Meurthe, south of the town, with 3 and 4/*Ersatz* Bn II echeloned left in a wood on the west slope of Hill 450. To the left, *Ersatz* Bn I had all four companies on line. Under cover of fog the enemy attacked, but was repulsed; 250 POWs were taken. A second attack at noon was beaten off. *Ersatz* Bn XII and IX, and *Ersatz* MGK 9, occupied the fortifications built the previous day; *Ersatz* Bn XI was behind the town on the right, with *Ersatz* Bn X and 1 *Ersatz*/Eng. Bn 3 on the left. When the fog lifted at about 0900hrs the French shelled Saulcy.

The Bavarian ED artillery was not immediately able to respond; *Ersatz* FA Sec. II and III were moving to Hill 520, west of Fouchifol, to support the attack on St Léonard and arrived there at 0900hrs. *Ersatz* FA Sec. II was called back to its position 700m north-west of La Planchette; as it moved, it offered the enemy batteries on the far side of the Meurthe a wonderful target, but returned their fire in kind. Of *Ersatz* FA Sec. I, 2 *Ersatz*/FAR 1 was at La Planchette, and the other two batteries were in Coinches, where they had bivouacked.

During the course of the day the enemy artillery fire at Saulcy caused serious casualties, but it did not seem prudent to pull the troops back from the west side of the village to the cellars and other better-protected areas in the village, because the field of fire to the bushes in the Meurthe Valley was only 300m. It was a severe test of the troops' nerves, holding out under artillery fire without being able to fire at the enemy. The castle of Saulcy, which served as the aid station and was clearly marked by the Red Cross, was shelled; the surviving wounded could only be rescued with difficulty. The worst hit was *Ersatz* Bn IX, especially 4 *Ersatz* Bn IX on the southern bridge over the Meurthe; elements of X and 1 *Ersatz*/ Eng. Bn 3 were sent as reinforcements. Between 1000hrs and 1100hrs the brigade commander ordered *Ersatz* Bn XII to send a company across the Meurthe Valley to attack the French artillery at Les Cesnes. 4/*Ersatz* Bn XII slipped across the valley in small groups and assembled on the north side of Les Cours. Just before reaching their objective they were met by overwhelming rifle and MG fire and forced to turn back. In Saulcy the artillery fire finally caused the defence to crumble; individuals and squads snuck away, especially where supervision broke down in the large demolished village. The companies were also intermixed, which reduced cohesion. 2/*Ersatz* Bn IX had lost all its officers. Nevertheless, *Ersatz* Bn IX, X and XII continued to hold Saulcy. LIR 71 also had to hold its positions north-east of Saulcy under artillery fire.

At 1000hrs in the 10 Res. Bde sector, RIR 11 at and south-east of Entre-deux-Eaux deployed to attack in the direction of Benifosse with II/RIR 11 on the right and I/RIR 11 on the left. Of RIR 14, only III/RIR 14 had arrived; 12/ RIR 14 guarded 3/Res. Foot Artillery R 14 (10cm cannons) on the west side of Remomeix; the rest of III/RIR 14 went into reserve east of Entre-deux-Eaux, along with *Ersatz* Bn VII. I and II/RIR 14 left Coinches at 0900hrs. It did not appear prudent to begin the attack, since 1 *Ersatz* Bde, which was to attack on the left, was just arriving. *Ersatz* Sec./FAR 80 and 2 *Ersatz*/FAR 51 (with only three guns) had gone into position behind Hill 520, west of Fouchifol, but appear to have fired against enemy artillery at Anozel and Les Censes.

At noon, when the 1 *Ersatz* Bde attack still had not taken plane, the 10 Res. Bde commander decided that he could not wait any longer and ordered RIR 11 to attack. II/RIR 11 deployed 8 and 6/RIR 11 in the first line, and I/RIR 11 deployed 1 and 3/RIR 11. As the skirmisher line left the woods on the ridge south and south-west of Entre-deux-Eaux, it took heavy fire; the enemy was defending the hilltop south-west of Benifosse, with his artillery behind it, as well as with infantry and MGs on the wooded north-east slope, in Benifosse, and along the road north of the town. Nevertheless, by 1400hrs RIR 11 advanced to the Mandray stream valley and threw back the enemy along the road. At the crossroads halfway to Saulcy, a few men took 200 POWs. 5/RIR 11 seems to have turned in this direction. Now overwhelming fire, principally from MGs on the left flank, brought the attack to a halt. Two officers of II/RIR 11 tried to carry the skirmisher line forward and paid with their lives. At 1300hrs *Ersatz* FA Sec. IV brought 2 *Ersatz*/FAR 2 into position east of La Cuche, and 1 *Ersatz*/FAR 12 at 1500hrs west of Fouchifol, but there was still no sign of 1 *Ersatz* Bde. Nevertheless, at 1625hrs the 10 Res. Bde commander ordered a continuation of the attack. I/RIR 11 committed 4/RIR 11 to the fight on the left flank. Between 1700hrs and 1800hrs the brigade commander sent III/RIR 14 there, too, with 10 and 11/RIR 14 in the lead, which managed, in spite of heavy fire, to reach the Mandray stream just west of Basse Mandray. 9/RIR 14 initially provided support from Hill 514, then at 1800hrs was sent to the skirmisher line, and *Ersatz* Bn VII moved onto Hill 514. The enemy at Benifosse defended himself desperately. The Bavarian battalions were involved in a hot firefight, took painful losses and only gained ground step by step. When dark came the Bavarian troops went over to the assault. Enemy troops hanging onto individual houses and woods were overwhelmed. Often the French fled before the Bavarians could close. RIR 11 took Benifosse; III/RIR 14, which had swung to the left, pushed through the forest south-west of the town. I and II/RIR 14 arrived at Entre-deux-Eaux between 1500hrs and 1600hrs, while Fortress MG Sec. 2 and Res. MG Sec. 3 moved forward from Coinches, but were not engaged.

That evening 1 *Ersatz* Bde arrived, but since *Ersatz* Bn I and II were fixed in their positions south and south-east of Saulcy, this meant that only *Ersatz* Bn III and IV, reinforced by RIR 15, arrived. That morning the troops had been on the high ground north of Mandray, but were forced by French artillery fire from the south and south-east to shift position. Misunderstandings and erroneous reports led to all kinds of marching to and fro. At noon the brigade deployed to attack, but the enemy artillery had the upper hand, causing 2 *Ersatz*/FAR 2 serious casualties; the brigade commander was unwilling to send his troops into the Mandray valley until this fire was suppressed, so it was 1800hrs before they began to advance. The 10 Res. Bde attack had by this time severely shaken the enemy resistance. Fire from *Ersatz* MGK 1 on the high ground north of Mandray cleared the way for the brigade. 3 and 4/RIR 15 and *Ersatz* Bn IV took the middle portion of Mandray against weak resistance. 2 and 3/*Ersatz* Bn III bounded quickly in thin skirmisher lines from one firing position to the next to Haute Mandray and, in thirty minutes, the enemy retreated. Although it was dark, *Ersatz* Bn III and IV conducted a hasty reorganisation and then pursued the enemy. *Ersatz* Bn IV reached the wooded hilltop south-west of Benifosse and linked up with III/RIR 14; 2, 3, and half of 1/*Ersatz* Bn III pushed on to Mangoutte, where it arrived at 2145 hrs, having lost contact with both the enemy and German troops.

Ersatz Bn VII and V, along with *Ersatz* MGK 5, had become 30 RD reserve. The commander of 5 *Ersatz* Bde had only RIR 4 immediately available on Tête de Behouille, with *Ersatz* Bn VI and VIII to the north. Early in the morning RIR 4 had occupied the treeline on the south slope of the hill with all three battalions on line. Between 0700 hrs and 0800 hrs an advance by French Alpine troops from the valley at Haute Mandray was turned back. Concentrating to attack, as ordered by the Bavarian ED, required troop movements which, given the dispersal of the troops and the terrain, required time. RIR 4 left a few companies in loose skirmisher lines on the treeline on the west slope of the Tête de Behouille and moved to the east slope and deployed, with I and II/RIR 4 in the first line, III/RIR 4 following behind the left, and *Ersatz* Bn VI and VIII in the rear as brigade reserve. The intent was to reach Hill 704, south-west of La Croix, and then to envelop the enemy right flank, pushing through the Bois de Mandray to Anould. The brigade moved out between 1300 hrs and 1400 hrs. The skirmishers had just reached the open ground in front of the south slope of the Tête de Behouille when they took fire from Hill 704. Enemy artillery there and east of the La Croix road swept the field from the front and left flank. 1 *Ersatz*/FAR 2 lost its commander and, when it had shot off its ammunition, was forced to retire. By 1600 hrs the RIR 4 attack had come to a halt 500m in front of the enemy position, although III/RIR 4 had been committed on the left. *Ersatz* Bn VIII and VI, which were following, came under a crossfire; *Ersatz* Bn VI, on the left, took considerable losses. After dark *Ersatz* Bn VIII relieved RIR 4, which had not been adequately fed for two days, and which was pulled back behind the Tête de Behouille.

The attacks of the Bavarian ED and 30 RD moved in diverging directions, and large uncovered gaps appeared between the brigades. The flanks of 10 Res. Bde, which had pushed far forward, were unprotected. 9 *Ersatz* Bde could only maintain itself in Saulcy with difficulty. Nevertheless, at 1930 hrs the Bavarian ED commander ordered all units to defend that night in place. He intended to determine the situation in Saulcy for himself, but at dusk came into swampy terrain and ended up in Coinches. There he heard (erroneously) that 9 *Ersatz* Bde had left Saulcy and fallen back 2.5km to the east. He decided to assemble the scattered troops of both divisions, which were also tired and at reduced strength, on the ridge that ran from south-east of Coinches to west of La Croix. The requisite orders were issued at 2100 hrs; transmitting them sometimes required considerable time. 10 Res. Bde pulled back from Benifosse after the wounded had been moved, and 1 *Ersatz* Bde left Mandray.

30 August (sketch 28)

XIV RK ordered 30 RD and the Bavarian ED to defend in place on 30 August. 26 RD would attack towards Anozel to relieve the pressure on them. The Bavarian ED commander ordered 9 *Ersatz* Bde to defend along the ridge 2km to the west and south-west of Coinches, with 30 RD to its left as far as the hilltop north-west of La Croix, and 1 *Ersatz* Bde and RIR 15 in reserve.

However, 9 *Ersatz* Bde still held Saulcy, and the Bavarian ED commander did not know this until 0800–0900hrs. The commander of XIV AK, who happened to be present at division HQ, told him to order the commander of 30 RD, who was also present, to reoccupy Mandray and the ground to the south-east, while 9 *Ersatz* Bde, *Ersatz* Bn I and II were to hold Saulcy and Hill 450 to the south-east. This order could not be executed, however, for in the meantime 9 *Ersatz* Bde had carried out the orders of the previous night and evacuated Saulcy, taking up the position 2km west of Coinches and beginning to dig in. When the fog lifted at 1000hrs the French artillery laid massive fire everywhere.

This fire disrupted the entrenching work of 9 *Ersatz* Bde. The units were intermixed, the companies shrunken. *Ersatz* FA Sec. II set up behind the brigade, but was silenced for the entire day by enemy artillery fire. The duel with the enemy artillery west of Anozel was taken up by *Ersatz* FA Sec. I, 3/Res. Foot Artillery R 14 (10cm cannons) and 2 *Ersatz*/FAR 8. The other two batteries of *Ersatz* FA Sec. III were kept in reserve south-west of Coinches. The enemy occupied Saulcy, but only pushed patrols beyond it.

1 *Ersatz* Bde assembled 1.5km south-west of Coinches, with only *Ersatz* Bn IV (now shrunk to company strength), *Ersatz* MGK 1, 2 *Ersatz*/Eng. Bn 1 and RIR 15. *Ersatz* Bn III, which had pushed forward to Mangoutte the night before, had lost contact with the brigade. On the morning of 30 August it moved to the high ground 800m south-west of Mangoutte and observed a French battalion assembling halfway between St Léonard and Anould, as well as three squadrons riding towards St Léonard. As the French battalion began to attack, *Ersatz* Bn III withdrew towards Mandray. On the way a half-platoon of French hussars appeared on the flank at a distance of 250m and was shot to pieces; in turn *Ersatz* Bn III was taken under fire by the pursuing French infantry, which had climbed the Mangoutte hill. The battalion passed through Mandray without incident, but while climbing the slope on the north side of the town the battalion took artillery fire from all sides and dispersed, the fragments later making contact with other units. I and II/LIR 71 linked up with 26 RD and was employed as the garrison of St Dié; *Ersatz* Bn III moved to the Col de St Marie.

In the 30 RD sector 10 Res. Bde began digging in on the high ground south of Coinches, with *Ersatz* Bn VII and Fortress MG Sec. 2 in the village of Fouchifol, RIR 11 to the west and RIR 14 to the south-east; II/RIR 14 and Res. MG

Sec. 3 were held in reserve 500m behind 10 Res. Bde. The trenches were located on the reverse slope directly behind the crest, so that an attacking enemy would immediately become engaged in close combat. Four artillery batteries set up behind the infantry. Except for security outposts, RIR 11 and 14 were withdrawn from the trenches, which were either ready or half ready, to assembly areas in the rear. This proved to be wise, for when the German artillery opened fire on St Léonard and the Bois de Mandray, the French opened a massive bombardment on this area, which lasted all day. Only when enemy infantry appeared near evening were the trenches partially or completely manned. There was no attack. 5 *Ersatz* Bde held the south slope of the high ground north-west of La Croix with *Ersatz* Bn VIII and VI; RIR 4 was on the reverse slope behind them. The 30 RD commander designated *Ersatz* Bn VII and V division reserve 1km south of Coinches. 1 *Ersatz*/FAR 2 attempted to resume its old position on the high ground behind 5 *Ersatz* Bde, but took effective enemy artillery fire and suffered considerable damage. It moved to Hill 577, north-east of Coinches, and began a duel with French artillery. At 1500hrs the French shelled and attacked *Ersatz* Bn VIII and VI, particularly the left flank of *Ersatz* Bn VI, which began to weaken. Both battalions had to withdraw uphill, except for 4/*Ersatz* Bn VIII, which held out in its trenches for two hours, beating off three attacks and only withdrawing uphill when threatened in the flanks and rear, taking considerable losses. I and II/ RIR 4 had had been moved to Hill 577 to the north-east of Coinchimont, III/ RIR 4 to the south-west, but at 1800hrs moved back about 500m behind *Ersatz* Bn VIII and VI, which were again forced to withdraw at 1900hrs. 11/RIR 4 was committed to the fight, with 7/RIR 4 covering the left flank, and at 2200hrs beat back an attack. The two batteries of *Ersatz* FA Sec. IV took fire in the left flank and 1 *Ersatz*/FAR 12 on the hilltop had to withdraw.

In the meantime, the commander of 30 RD had received an order from XIV RK releasing the Bavarian ED from his operational control and directing several days of defence in place. He decided to hold the ridge south of Coinches with outposts from II/RIR 11 and *Ersatz* Bn VIII and VI, while the rest of the division would be dispersed in a zone 4km to the north-east of Coinches to rest. An enemy attack would be met on the high ground to both sides of Coinches and north of Coinchimont. The orders were issued that evening, but arrived in the course of the night and were executed the next morning.

31 August (sketch 29)

30 RD did not get its rest day. The outposts on the ridge were too close to the enemy and too weak. In the 5 *Ersatz* Bde sector on the left, they consisted of the remnants of *Ersatz* Bn VIII and VI (which had been reduced to company strength and attached to *Ersatz* Bn VIII) on the high ground south of Coinchimont;

Tête de Behouille 30. 8.   Textskizze 28.

1 : 75000

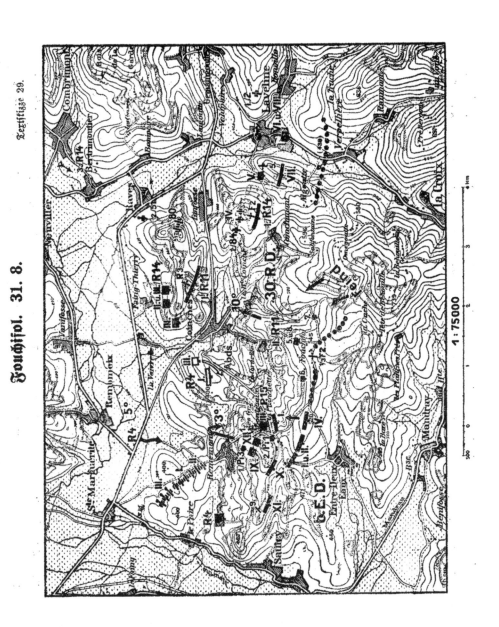

RIR 4 had moved to rejoin the Bavarian ED. 10 Res. Bde had only II/RIR 11 (reinforced by a platoon of Fortress MG Sec. 2) south of Coinches. There was a wide gap between them. The fog lifted early and, at 0600hrs, 6/RIR 11 on the right flank was under serious attack, which was beaten off with the assistance of *Ersatz* Bn IV on Hill 520 to the right. 7/RIR 11 on the left was attacked by French Alpine troops, which infiltrated through the wood and turned the open company left flank. The threat was only stopped because 8 and 5/RIR 11, which were the outpost reserve, were committed one after the other by 0930hrs, and because the attached MG platoon fired superbly. At 1000hrs II/RIR 11 had to break contact and withdraw to Coinches. The enemy did not immediately pursue.

30 RD had hardly reached their bivouac areas when the division commander was forced to roust the division out to occupy assembly areas between Coinches and Laveline. At 1600hrs the enemy appeared out of the woods south of Coinches, but was pushed back by fire from I/RIR 11 and Res. MG Sec. 3. The 30 RD troops came under periodic artillery fire.

In the early morning the enemy moved closer to the Bavarian ED, especially against *Ersatz* Bn I and II to the right of *Ersatz* Bn IV on Hill 520; they were attacked between 0500 and 0600hrs from Entre-deux-Eaux by perhaps a battalion reinforced with MGs, which they threw back. The French approached carefully from Saulcy against *Ersatz* Bn XI and X. French detachments also moved from between Saulcy and La Paire towards Remémont, meeting no opposition and apparently gaining the rear of *Ersatz* Bn XI. While returning from inspecting the troops, the Bavarian ED commander came under fire north of Remémont. The only German troops in this area were *Ersatz* FA Sec. III, I and II, which had moved during the night to the high ground to the north-west of the town, and indeed *Ersatz* FA Sec. II had fired on approaching French infantry at 0600hrs. RIR 4, which had arrived early in the morning south of Remomeix, was sent by the division commander to the north of Remémont. II/RIR 4, in the lead, immediately deployed against the woods north of Remémont, from which it took weak fire, and quickly disappeared into it. I and III/RIR 4 swung right to Hill 467 between Saulcy and La Paire without making contact; the French in this area consisted of isolated detachments. The enemy artillery resumed firing, principally against *Ersatz* Bn X, and during the morning more and more troops left for the rear. Even the troops in reserve positions (*Ersatz* Bn IX and XI, I and III/RIR 15, an MG and two engineer companies) took casualties. Once again the Bavarian ED artillery was unable to locate the French guns.

The position of the Bavarian ED only became serious around noon when the 30 RD outposts withdrew under pressure on the left. Initially, only *Ersatz* Bn IV (now reduced to company strength) withdrew from Hill 520 to La Planchette in the valley behind it, where I/RIR 15 had already set up. At 1500hrs, due to the withdrawal of 30 RD, or an incorrect order, the Bavarian

ED troops, already shaken by continual artillery fire, withdrew in the direction of Remomeix.

With the first reports of the situation in 30 RD, the commander of the Bavarian ED recalled RIR 4 (minus II/RIR 4, consisting of 6 and 7/RIR 4) to the area west of Coinches and himself moved to a good observation point on the high ground north of Remomeix. At 1500hrs he could see groups of his troops leaving the woods at Remémont and moving north; he moved towards them and ordered them back to their positions, which they quickly and willingly did, as did other officers, in particular the commanders of 1 and 9 *Ersatz* Bde. *Ersatz* Bn XI did not leave its position at all. The commander of III/RIR 15 turned his unit around in Grands Gonteaux and occupied the south side of the village at the run, just in time to stop pursuing French troops. This allowed the other troops the course of the afternoon to reoccupy the abandoned positions, generally without meeting enemy resistance. Of course, once in the old positions they were greeted with heavy artillery fire. *Ersatz* Bn XII occupied the trenches of *Ersatz* Bn X; due to privations, exertions and effects of combat, *Ersatz* Bn X was nearly wrecked and the remnants were assembled west of Remémont. Everywhere the units were mixed together. La Planchette was no longer occupied. III/RIR 4 (minus 11/RIR 4, but including 5/RIR 4) was sent back to Hill 467, south-west of Remémont, and repulsed a weak enemy attack at 1900hrs. *Ersatz* Bn III, now the strength of two companies, pulled itself together and assembled behind the high ground north of Coinches on the right flank of I/RIR 11.

During the afternoon and evening the enemy had approached to within 500m and that night began to dig in. The Bavarian troops also resumed digging, which had been continually disrupted during the day. Since the reserve and *Ersatz* regiments did not have pioneer tool wagons, there were no large shovels or picks. Requisitions in the surrounding villages and St Dié were insufficient and the work proceeded slowly.

A detachment led by Brigadier General Rasch, composed of troops from Strasbourg (LIR 81, II/LIR 120, 1 *Ersatz*/FAR 15 with two batteries, a platoon of 1 *Ersatz*/FAR 51), as well as II/RIR 15, IV/RIR 4, II/RIR 60, Fortress MG Sec. 1, 2 *Ersatz*/FAR 15, *Ersatz* Sec./FAR 84 (2 *Ersatz*/FAR 84, 1 *Ersatz*/FAR 51), 2 *Ersatz*/FAR 13, 5/Res. Foot Artillery R 10 (sFH), were moved from Markirch to 30 RD on 31 August.

The German XIV RK positions on the west side of the Meurthe did not materially change. It was opposed by the badly shaken French XIV Corps. In front of 30 RD and the Bavarian ED, a brigade of the French 58 RD had established itself on the high ground west of the Meurthe between St Léonard and Anould. The French Dragoon R 8, reinforced by Light Infantry Bn 13 and 30, were operating between St Léonard and La Croix. On 29 August the dragoons left to rejoin 8 Cavalry Div. On 30 August a fresh brigade of the French 41 ID appeared here and pushed in the outposts of 30 RD and the Bavarian ED. The brigade of 58 RD was moved 6km to the south to rest, the gap being filled by XIV Corps and the brigade of 41 ID.

1 September

The commander of 30 RD was determined to retake the high ground south of Coinches. The commander of XIV RK approved and instructed the Bavarian ED to cooperate with the 30 RD attack, but initially to hold its positions. The 30 RD order was issued at 1830hrs on 31 August, in order to make allowance for the time that experience had shown was required to transmit orders in such a newly formed unit; nevertheless, there were friction and delays. According to the order, at 0500hrs 10 Res. Bde was to attack from Coinches and Ginfosse against Hill 520 and Fouchifol, while 5 *Ersatz* Bde attacked on its left to Tête de Behouille and 59 Bde paralleling the road to Hill 704, south-west of La Croix. The morning fog quickly gave way to scorching heat.

The Rasch Detachment marched from Gemaingoutte at 0315hrs and reached Laveline at 0630hrs. 1 *Ersatz*/FAR 15 and 2 *Ersatz*/FAR 84 went into position north-east of the town, protected by II/LIR 120, and opened fire on infantry and guns on Hill 704. 59 Bde took fire from an invisible enemy hidden in the trees and bushes of the woods south of Coinchimont. 2 *Ersatz*/FAR 15 unlimbered south-east of Coinchimont. LIR 81, supported by Fortress MG Sec. 3, II/RIR 15 and II/RIR 60 deployed south of Coinchimont and became involved in a hot and costly firefight with French Alpine troops, which mainly took place in the woods and resulted in intermixing of units; the enemy was driven back and pursued to the south slope of the Tête de Behouille.

5 *Ersatz* Bde assembled early in the morning on the Laveline–Coinchimont road, moved out at 0500hrs and also reached the Tête de Behouille. The advance guard, *Ersatz* Bn VIII, took fire from the wood on the hilltop and first committed 1/*Ersatz* Bn VIII, then the consolidated 3 and 4/*Ersatz* Bn VIII; attacked from two sides, the enemy fled. In the middle of the wood, *Ersatz* Bn VIII and LIR 81 had a blue–on–blue firefight. When this was over, at about 0900hrs or 1000hrs, the brigade assembled at the south-west corner of the wood. Two companies of French Alpine infantry, which had been bypassed 1km east of the hilltop, were detected by 2/*Ersatz* Bn VIII, attacked and annihilated, even though the Alpine troops were supported by artillery fire from the south of Mandray. French infantry approached from Mandray, but were forced to stop at 900m range.

East of the Tête de Behouille, 59 Bde was attacked at noon, but with the help of I/LIR 80, which arrived on the left flank of LIR 81, the French were driven back. 59 Bde assembled north of the Tête de Behouille.

The commander of 10 Res. Bde moved RIR 14 (minus I/RIR 14) to Coinches and ordered it to attack Hill 520, while the commander of RIR 11 ordered I/RIR 11, I/RIR 14 and Fortress MG Sec. 2 to attack from the south-east end of Coinches to Fouchifol, east of Hill 520. II/RIR 11 and Res. MG Sec. 3 were in reserve at Coinches. The RIR 11 group moved off at 0500hrs and were able to approach in march column to within 50m of the east side of Fouchifol by 0600hrs, when 1/RIR 11, the advance guard, took rifle and MG fire from the town and the high ground to the east. Bitter house-to-house fighting developed, but by 0900hrs the French Alpine infantry had fled and the town was in flames.

RIR 14 deployed III/RIR 14 on the right, with 9 and 11/RIR 14 leading, II/RIR 14 on the left, 6 and 8/RIR 14 forward; the attack began at 0630hrs. It soon became clear that the French Alpine troops were going to give a hard-necked defence of their trenches; nevertheless, the Bavarian attack gained ground. The two battalions clawed their way to the north slope of the hilltop, when heavy artillery fire stopped them and forced a partial withdrawal, then they resumed the attack, which cost considerable time; it was nearly noon before the enemy was forced away and the ridge taken.

Of the 30 RD artillery, only 1 *Ersatz*/FAR 12 made itself felt, unlimbering south of Coinches and supporting RIR 14 as it climbed Hill 520. The other two batteries of *Ersatz* FA Sec. IV remained in assembly areas. *Ersatz* Sec./FAR 80 and 2 *Ersatz*/FAR 51 were on Hill 571, north of Ginfosse, but fired to the west against Le Paire and Claingoutte. 3/Res. Foot Artillery R 14 (10cm cannons), on the south-west side of Combrimont, fired on Mandray. Once 10 Res. Bde had taken the ridge, *Ersatz*/FAR 80, all of *Ersatz* FA Sec. IV, 1 *Ersatz*/FAR 84 and 2 *Ersatz*/FAR 51 did not hesitate to come forward, mainly firing on enemy batteries at St Léonard and behind the Bois de Mandray.

Such quick success led the 30 RD commander to continue the attack; at 1030hrs he ordered 10 Res. Bde to take Entre-deux-Eaux and Hill 514, south-east of the town, with the rest of the division orienting on it. Between 1300hrs and 1400hrs 10 Res. Bde moved down the slope in loose lines of skirmishers, taking artillery fire from St Léonard, Mandray and guns 1km to the south of La Croix, but meeting no resistance. III and II/RIR 14 passed through Entre-deux-Eaux at 1530hrs, picking up a number of French stragglers. I/RIR 11, I/RIR 14 and Fortress MG Sec. 2 followed in the second wave.

5 *Ersatz* Bde had moved before 1300hrs west from Tête de Behouille to Hill 514, south-east of Entre-deux-Eaux, with *Ersatz* Bn VII on the right, *Ersatz* Bn VIII (including the attached *Ersatz* Bn VI of company strength) on the left, *Ersatz* Bn V behind VIII, and *Ersatz* MGK 5 following. As it left the woods it took enemy artillery fire from the south-west in the flank and rear, which caused few casualties, and the attack continued. Hill 514 was held by the enemy, and the firefight was taken up from woods about 500m from the hill. *Ersatz* Bn VIII

began the fight with only 2/*Ersatz* Bn VIII and a company from *Ersatz* Bn VI, but soon committed 3 and 4/*Ersatz* Bn VIII on the left. At 1500hrs *Ersatz* Bn V was committed on the left, but took fire in the flank and rear from Mandray. On the right flank *Ersatz* Bn VII, which had only 3 and 4/*Ersatz* Bn VIII on line, made rapid progress; at 1500hrs 3/*Ersatz* Bn VIII stormed a trench on Hill 514. Soon after 1600hrs 5 *Ersatz* Bde stood on the hill; it had pushed in front of 10 Res. Bde and surely aided their attack. II and II/RIR 14 moved onto Hills 509 and 514 after 1700hrs; II/RIR 11 and Res. MG Sec. 3 moved up to Fouchifol. Rasch Detachment seems to have received the attack order late and made little contact.

The left flank of the Bavarian ED attacked to the right of 30 RD, principally RIR 15 at Grands Gonteaux to the south of Remémont, which committed III/RIR 15 at 1000hrs. It deployed 11, 10 and 12/RIR 15, with 9/RIR 15 and the attached 2 *Ersatz*/Eng. Bn 1 following. To the left German skirmishers were visible, but there was no real contact with the neighbouring unit. Nevertheless, the battalion went determinedly against the enemy on Hill 520 to the south. It took heavy rifle and MG fire and soon both 9/RIR 15 and the engineers were on the firing line, supported by *Ersatz* MGK 1, which had taken position west of Grands Gonteaux, until it could no longer distinguish friend from enemy. The III/RIR 15 commander, who was on the firing line, ordered the assault and was then severely wounded; his companies took the hill in a single movement. The enemy retreated, but his artillery covered the battalion with more fire than it could stand, and it too withdrew to Grands Gonteaux, perhaps at the same time and for the same reason as RIR 14 to the left. I/RIR 15 was ordered to renew the attack; it was now noon and RIR 14 had taken the ridge west of Fouchifol. I/RIR 15 reached the top almost without casualties by 1400hrs and pushed on, accompanied by heavy enemy artillery fire, to the south-west side of Entre-deux-Eaux, with *Ersatz* Bn XII, which had occupied a position on its right the previous evening, west of La Planchette. From its trenches that morning 3 and 4/*Ersatz* Bn XII had engaged enemy detachments moving from Entre-deux-Eaux to the ridge west of Fouchifol and caused them heavy casualties. Now 1 and 2, in reserve, moved on their own initiative with I/RIR 15 to the high ground, accompanied by 3/*Ersatz* Bn IX, which had filled a gap on the left of *Ersatz* Bn XII the previous day. III/RIR 15 later moved to Entre-deux-Eaux.

The battalions of 1 *Ersatz* Bde proper attacked at noon from La Planchette towards Hill 450, south-east of Saulcy, from right to left: *Ersatz* Bn II, I and IV (IV was in company strength, reinforced by 4/*Ersatz* Bn III and half of 3/*Ersatz* Bn III). Two batteries of *Ersatz* FA Sec. III only found inadequate positions in clearings in the wood south-east of Remémont; the third battery, 2 *Ersatz*/FAR 12, went into position south-east of La Paire. *Ersatz* FA Sec. I appeared at Grands Gonteaux. As the infantry came into the open in front of Hill 541, it took murderous artillery fire. It reached the houses on the south side of La Planchette, whose walls were splattered with body parts. 3/*Ersatz* Bn XII was pulled forward. But then the attack stalled; casualties were heavy. Several companies remained in the woods north of La Planchette, while some units that reached the south side of La Planchette went back to the woods. There was a wide gap in the 1 *Ersatz* Bde position between Grands Gonteaux and Entre-deux-Eaux, which was filled by six companies of RIR 4 (1, 8 and 11).

Near Remémont 9 *Ersatz* Bde did not participate in the attack. Enemy troops from Saulcy approached, but were easily driven off. The brigade was in poor condition. 2/*Ersatz* Bn IX only consisted of fragments which were attached to *Ersatz* Bn IV. *Ersatz* Bn X had 200 men divided into two companies. Enemy artillery fire fell all day and caused painful casualties.

2 September

XIV RK planned to finally give the troops a rest day and ordered that strong outposts be established while the mass of the troops bivouacked. The Bavarian ED was to be disengaged completely; security between Saulcy and Tête de Behouille was the responsibility of 30 RD. Although these orders were issued on the preceding evening and night, friction and delays occurred due to the general exhaustion of the troops and the intermixed units. The terrain was hilly and wooded, there was a lack of maps and communication equipment, and the units had been formed during mobilisation, which caused poor reporting: the senior leaders lacked reliable information concerning the troop's locations, the tactical situation or the enemy.

The commander of 30 RD did not think that he could relieve the Bavarian ED in place and redeploy his troops in depth until he had attacked to break contact with the enemy, which meant attacking in the Rasch Detachment sector, south of the Tête de Behouille. 5 *Ersatz* Bde and 10 Res. Bde were instructed to join the 59 Bde attack in a timely manner. From early morning onwards, the good sunny weather facilitated the enemy artillery fire. In particular, I and II/RIR 14 and *Ersatz* Bn V took serious losses, and the fire caused confusion and casualties in the supply units and artillery battery vehicles at Fouchifol.

Elements of the Bavarian ED (RIR 15, I, 8 and 11/RIR 4, 1 *Ersatz* Bde and *Ersatz* Bn XII) did not wait to be relieved by 30 RD before marching off to their bivouac areas at Neuviller–Raves, maintaining that they could see 30 RD units to the south of them, or knew that they were there. *Ersatz* FA Sec. I and III also left their positions. On the other hand, 9 *Ersatz* Bde (with the exception of *Ersatz* Bn XII), II and III/RIR 4 (except 5, 8, and 11/RIR 4) and *Ersatz* FA Sec. II held their positions under artillery fire until relieved. The diary of *Ersatz* Bn IX, in reserve on the steep slope west of Remémont, was frank:

> The battalion waited for the announced relief or a cancellation of the last order.
> Troop morale was extremely low; the French artillery fire was very effective.

It was possible to escape it only to a limited degree by digging small holes. The repeated waves of French shells resulted in many men leaving to help evacuate the wounded, sometimes at night, and never returning. In addition, rations were completely inadequate; above all, there was no bread. The ration vehicles never came close enough to the troops, but unloaded someplace or another that was inadequately guarded. By the time the ration carriers arrived, the greater part of the food had been stolen by the masses of stragglers wandering around in the rear area. Men sent to the rear often never came back. Cooking was not possible, because the rising smoke attracted artillery fire. Depression and unreliability were rampant. Many men reported sick for trifling reasons; others were so deadened as to be completely indifferent. The reason was not only the daily heavy casualties caused by artillery fire, against which they were helpless, and the inadequate rations and daily battles, but also sentry duty and combat readiness in the open; the rucksacks [which had been taken off and lost on 21 August] with the coats and ponchos had for the most part not been replaced. Not enough was done to round up stragglers in the rear areas and return them to their units. These circumstances show that effective artillery fire, especially in woods, has an extraordinarily negative effect on morale, especially on units that lack cohesion and combat experience.

It was probably the same in the other 30 RD and Bavarian ED units, which had been created at mobilisation, even sometimes on the battlefield, from older year groups, and were inadequately equipped. They were then given combat tasks that were not reasonable. The weak *Ersatz* cavalry sections attached to the *Ersatz* brigades were not even adequate to provide the HQ with mounted messengers. Day after day small numbers of riders were sent into the mountains on reconnaissance; they produced exceptional results, but eventually the horses were completely worn out. 30 RD and the Bavarian ED had more difficult missions and time in combat than the regular divisions in Lorraine. The responsibility for this state of affairs rested not with the Army or with the troop leaders, who were forced to use such units so ruthlessly, but with the false economy of the people's representatives in the Reichstag, which forced the Army to make do with such inadequate equipment and military readiness.

The position that 30 RD and the Bavarian ED took up on 2 September was a half-circle, on all sides of which, at St Léonard, in or behind the woods south of Mandray or south of La Croix, were enemy batteries that brought death and destruction anywhere they detected life or movement, and it was not possible to find or suppress them. Fortunately, on 2 September Airship Troop 14 (from Strasbourg) arrived and its captive balloons ascended at Benifosse; even though it was forced in the next few days by enemy artillery fire to continually shift its position, it provided the artillery, especially

3/Foot Artillery R 14 (10cm cannons) with target locations, which relieved the situation somewhat.

It was noon and 9 *Ersatz* Bde waited in vain for relief from 30 RD, which was not even able to disengage from the enemy on its own front, much less relieve its neighbour on the right.

The Rasch Detachment commander of 59 Bde had decided to avoid the open slopes by La Behouille, north of La Croix, which the painful experience of the previous day had shown to be dominated by the French artillery, and move the troops assembled at Coinchimont–Fouchifol over the Tête de Behouille. During the morning the woods on the hilltop were swept out and troops deployed on the south treeline. On the far left flank, II/RIR 15, with 8, 5 and 7/RIR 15 on line, had advanced by noon, partly in the wood, partly in the open, through La Behouille. As 2 *Ersatz*/FAR 15 and 1 *Ersatz*/FAR 51 moved into Les Planches Prés, they were shelled and suppressed. The troops in the wood on the Tête de Behouille and at Les Planches Prés suffered from the artillery fire so severely that the order was given to withdraw to Coinchimont after noon. It is possible that the *Landwehr* units did not execute this movement with the desired calm and discipline, especially in the woods. Fortress MG Sec. 3 drove immediately all the way back east to Col de St Marie. But determined and ruthless leaders prevented more serious damage. The battalions that had not held their ground were brought back to the south side of the woods on the Tête de Behouille. The brigade commander appeared in the skirmisher line. The Governor of Strasbourg had come to the battlefield and intervened several times. 2 *Ersatz*/FAR 15 moved to the high ground south-east of Fouchifol; 1 *Ersatz*/FAR 51 had to leave the guns in place, while, due to a misunderstanding, the limbers and vehicles moved to Markirch. They were recovered by 2/RIR 11. II/RIR 15 pushed halfway to Hill 631, south of Tête de Behouille, and resumed the attack at 1500hrs and took it. But the rifle ammunition began to run low, the intensity of the artillery fire increased and the battalion was completely isolated; at 1530hrs it withdrew to the east slope of the Tête de Behouille. II/RIR 60 did not budge from Les Planches Prés and towards evening beat back a serious French attack. After dark it was pulled back to Laveline for redeployment elsewhere. The situation in the 59 Bde sector caused 1 *Ersatz* Bde to move during the night to the south of Coinchimont. The Governor of Strasbourg took command of the Bavarian ED, 30 RD and the troops of the Strasbourg garrison. The attack by the brigade from the French 41 ID had caused 30 RD and the Bavarian ED great difficulties, but they had fended off a dangerous thrust against their open left flank.

Advance into the Vosges West of Colmar and into the Upper Alsace (map g, sketch 16)

To 26 August the enemy did not budge from the east side of the Vosges south of Colmar and at Mühlhausen; indeed, he seemed to have moved troops away.

On 27 August the deputy commander of XIV AK saw an opportunity to retake the east side of the Vosges and the Upper Alsace. The French held the foothills west of Colmar. At 0500hrs on 28 August, 1 *Landwehr* Bde at Colmar was to attack Ingersheim, 3.5km to the north-west, while, 8km to the north at Ostheim, 2 *Landwehr* Bde would attack at 0430hrs. The two brigades were subordinate to the 1 *Landwehr* commander. At Bergheim, 5km north of Ostheim, a detachment would advance from Rappoltsweiler on Urbach, 10km north of Munster, which had been taken by the Rasch Detachment on 27 August. On the left, 51 *Landwehr* Bde would attack towards Egisheim, about 3km south of Colmar.

Between 0500hrs and 0600hrs, 1 *Landwehr* Bde deployed LIR 1 on the garrison training area north of Colmar, and LIR 2, with *Landsturm* Bty 1 and *Landsturm* Eng. Co. 1 on the west side of the town. 1 and 2/*Landwehr* Foot Artillery Bn 20 (sFH) went into battery on the south side of the training area and opened fire at 0815hrs. The 1 *Landwehr* Bde attack was dependent on the progress made by the Rappoltsweiler detachment to the north. Reconnaissance established that the French in front of 1 *Landwehr* Bde were in the meadows east of the Fecht. Noon arrived, and nothing was known of either the Rappoltsweiler detachment or 2 *Landwehr* Bde. 51 *Landwehr* Bde reported that it had taken Winzenheim, 3km south of Ingersheim.

The 1 *Landwehr* Bde commander could delay his attack no longer; he committed I/LIR 2 on the right of the Ingersheim road, and III/LIR 2 on the left. *Landsturm* Bty 1 joined the fire preparation from Logelsheim. LIR 1 sent III/LIR 1 directly west towards Ingersheim, while II/LIR 1 swung to the right and I/LIR 1 was in reserve at Colmar. The enemy quickly withdrew. At 1730hrs the Germans entered Ingersheim, which was prepared for defence but showed the effect of the German artillery fire. The bodies of *Landwehr* men who had died on 22 August were found in the vineyards north of Logelbach. The regiment bivouacked in Colmar and Logelbach, with security at Ingersheim.

On the right, 2 *Landwehr* Bde and the Rappoltsweiler detachment advanced carefully behind a thorough artillery preparation. However, the French had already been driven off by the Rasch Detachment attacking out of Urbeis. 51 *Landwehr* Bde, south of Colmar, took the strongly held village of Wettolsheim by 1200hrs (off Sketch 16 to the south) and Winzenheim by 1300hrs – the enemy had fled – and bivouacked at Winzenheim and Egisheim (off sketch to the south).

The *Landwehr* attack had driven the French back into the Vosges with little trouble; it was tempting to consider continuing the attack, but Crown Prince Rupprecht had decided to rest the troops in Lorraine and the Vosges, which is what, only interrupted by some marches, the *Landwehr* men did from 29–31 August. The enemy did not disturb them, but held the east side of the Vosges, with a strong group of forces at Zell (La Chapelle) and Drei Ähren (Les Trois Epis), 8km north-west of Colmar.

On 1 September the *Landwehr* troops were to renew their advance into the Vosges to relieve the pressure on 30 RD and the Bavarian ED. 1 and 2 *Landwehr* Bde were to attack towards the Col de Bonhomme (Diedolshausen), and 51 *Landwehr* Bde down the Munster Valley and over the Schlucht Pass to Gérardmer. On their right, the Rappoltsweiler detachment (two battalions of RIR 70, plus a *Landwehr* cavalry squadron and two artillery batteries) would move west. But completing and transmitting the orders took so much time that it was not possible to move far on 1 September. 2 *Landwehr* Bde received the order at 1445hrs, but the troops could not begin movement until after dark. III/LIR 12 was moved by rail to Urbach. The lead element of the main body, LIR 12, reached Kaysersberg (8km north-west of Colmar) between 2100hrs and 2200hrs.

1 *Landwehr* Bde required the entire afternoon to assemble at Ingersheim. An all-arms battle group built around LIR 2 began the climb into the mountains at 1730hrs, gaining 450m elevation and moving 7km by 2000hrs, when it bivouacked. Neither brigade made contact.

Eschelmer–Zell–Drei Ähren, 2 September (sketch 30)

The commander of 1 *Landwehr* Bde intended to attack the high ground west of Zell at 0800hrs from the east and north simultaneously. The two heavy howitzer batteries (half of *Landwehr* Foot Artillery Bn 20) were ordered to start the artillery preparation at dawn. Since midnight, II/LIR 2 had outposts on the high ground at Évaux, from which they could see that there was a strong enemy position from Kapelle to the Klein-Hohnack. I/LIR 2 was to deploy at Meyerhof, south of the road, while III/LIR 2 was in reserve west of Drei Ähren. The howitzers were marching to their positions west and south of Évaux. Before the German troops had arrived at their assigned places, II/LIR 2 moved prematurely onto the hill at Évaux and immediately became involved in a firefight. Soon enemy artillery began falling and the battalion took heavy casualties; entire squads were cut down, especially in 6/LIR 2, and the line began to waver. Then an enemy attack from Zell hit the open right flank; 6/LIR 2 was enveloped and partly encircled, its leaders captured. Its remnants and 7/LIR 2 fled. 8/LIR 2 withdrew south over the road, pursued by enemy fire, and stopped 800m west of Drei Ähren. 5/LIR 2 on the far left also had to withdraw. The enemy occupied the Évaux hill with MGs and mountain artillery. This defeat completely upset the attack plan. It seemed initially advisable to hold the treeline 800m west of Drei Ähren, where I and 5/LIR 2 deployed to the left of the remnants of II/LIR 2, with III/ LIR 2 (minus 10/LIR 2) on the Frauen-Kopf hill to the right. 11/LIR 2 was held in reserve, while 10/LIR 2 reinforced II/LIR 2. The units were thoroughly intermixed. The howitzer batteries had to turn around on the narrow road west of Drei Ähren and set up in the village. They fired using the map against enemy artillery assumed to be at Place, as well as on the high ground at Zell, and later found a good spot for forward observers on the Frauen-Kopf. The officers and some NCOs of the *Landsturm* Eng. Co. 1, charged with protecting the guns, made useful fire direction observations from the roofs of Drei Ähren. *Landsturm* Bty 1 set up on the road east of the village and fired on Gross-Hohnack.

The remains of II/LIR 2, supported by 10/LIR 2, made several attempts to take the hill back, but were stopped by the fire of several heavy batteries there. At 1100hrs II/LIR 1 arrived and moved between II and III/LIR 2. Around noon there were indications that 2 *Landwehr* Bde was approaching north of Zell, and the commander of LIR 2 gave the order to attack the hill, but the enemy had established himself so well that he could not be driven out. In particular, it was not possible to suppress the enemy MG or the mountain guns, which continually changed position. An order from the 1 *Landwehr* Bde commander to renew the attack at dark changed nothing. LIR 2 had taken serious casualties.

The commander of 2 *Landwehr* Bde planned to attack the enemy forces on Hill 885, north-west of Zell, with LIR 3, reinforced by *Landsturm* Bty 2 and *Landsturm* Eng. Co. 2 (minus 3 Platoon) coming from the east, and LIR 12, reinforced by 3 Platoon/*Landsturm* Eng. Co. 2, simultaneously from the north. LIR 3 moved out at 0500hrs; since the morning was unusually hot, the packs were carried on carts. III/LIR 3, which consisted of only 9 and 12/LIR 3, with the artillery battery and engineer company, moved up the Wal-Bach and then climbed the stony, often heavily forested slope to the top of Hill 676, east of Zell. Since the north-west slope was under artillery fire, the battalion deployed behind the hilltop. On the northeast slope of the hill beyond Zell, terraces of occupied trenches were visible; *Landsturm* Bty 2 had set up three guns where the two streams came together and shelled the trenches, as well as Zell, as probably did the two howitzer batteries at Drei Ähren.

I and II/LIR 3 moved through the wood and hills, led by local guides, getting shot at by Alpine snipers, to reach Hill 885 at 0900hrs, where it deployed to attack Kapelle. II/LIR 3 on the right had 6 and 8/LIR 3 on the front line, with 7/LIR 3 behind the centre and 5/LIR 3 behind the right flank; I/LIR 3 on the left had 4/LIR 3 on the right and 2/LIR 3 on the left, 1/LIR 3 behind the left (3/LIR 3 was still coming up, because there were not enough vehicles to carry its packs). II/LIR 3 moved out first; it had hardly left the woods when it took murderous fire from the trenches, and French artillery fire swept the open slope and treeline. 6 and 8/LIr 3 took up the firefight with the invisible enemy, and were soon reinforced by 5 and 7/LIR 3, but the artillery fire caused heavy casualties and forced the battalion back into the wood. II/LIR 3 took cover behind rocks and dug in. The enemy also took casualties from German rifle and artillery fire. At 1400hrs the two platoons of *Landsturm* Eng. Co. 2 advanced to the north of Zell after an hour-long firefight, followed by a platoon of *Landsturm* Bty 2, which pushed forward to conduct direct fire. By evening, I and II/LIR 3 had expended their basic load of ammunition. II/LIR 3 had 30 KIA and 100 WIA. III/LIR 3 left its position after 1800hrs to rejoin the regiment, but following an incorrect order moved to Drei Ähren, it arrived there at 2200hrs.

Landwehr IR 12 moved out at 0700hrs, with III/LIR 12 moving fully deployed, as patrols had already taken fire. Eschelmer was reported as occupied and the battalion moved to attack it at 0930hrs, with 11/LIR 12 in the centre; 12/LIR 12 forded the stream to attack on the right flank, but took such heavy fire that it took cover in the woods on the north side of the valley. 9 and 10/LIR 12 remained at the fork in the road, while I and II/LIR 12 turned left. II/LIR 12 soon stopped to serve as regimental reserve, but I/LIR 12 climbed Hill 573. The attack on Eschelmer gained ground; 12/LIR 12 slowly advanced on the wooded slopes north of the road in a continual firefight. At 1100hrs 9/LIR 12 deployed on the left of 11/LIR 12. Between 1300hrs and 1400hrs the skirmisher lines approached Eschelmer; 4/LIR 12 attacked on the left, with 1/LIR 12 avoiding the flat tableland, using the woods as concealment and then moving up from the south. Half of 1/LIR 12 and a platoon of 4/LIR 12 went further west to drive off snipers firing into the left flank. By 1400hrs 11, 9 and the remaining platoon of 1 and 4/LIR 12 swept through Eschelmer; the enemy had abandoned the town, but when the west side was occupied a firefight developed that lasted until 1600hrs. III/LIR 12 held the town while I and II/LIR 12 resumed the march to the south. II/LIR 12 was surprised in a clearing in the woods by mountain gun fire, but was able to run to cover. The two battalions took position behind I and II/LIR 3 on Hill 885. 2 *Landwehr* Bde bivouacked on the battlefield. The terrain made it extremely difficult to bring up rifle ammunition, rations and water, especially since the cooking gear was in the rear with the packs and the proximity to the enemy made it imprudent to light fires. Fortunately the weather was dry and warm, because the troops had neither coats nor ponchos. *Landsturm* Bty 2 and *Landsturm* Eng. Co. 2 returned to Ammerschweier (off map to the east).

51 *Landwehr* Bde made no progress in the Munster Valley due to enemy artillery fire. It appears that, on 28 August, the *Landwehr* troops in Alsace were opposed by a few Alpine battalions, plus later a regiment and an artillery section from 41 ID. On 30 August the *Landwehr* troops at Neuenburg–Mühlheim re-entered Mühlhausen: the French had left.

In order to strengthen the French–British left wing, on 1 September Joffre decided to take troops from the First and Second Armies in Lorraine. It appeared that the Germans had, to a considerable degree, replaced their active army units in Lorraine with reserve and *Landwehr*. Between 31 August and 2 September, 5, 8 and 10 Cavalry Div. and a brigade of 2 Cavalry Div. were sent from Épinal and Nancy to Châlons-sur-Marne and Épernay. First Army gave up XXI Corps, which on the night of 2/3 September pulled out of its position north of Rambervillers and began rail movement at Épinal. A day later Second Army set XV Corps, south of Lunéville, in march west, while the rest of IX Corps (18 ID) loaded trains at Nancy on the morning of 4 September. The French First and Second Armies were now on the defensive.

Renewing the Offensive, 3–8 September (sketch h)

The French Second Army commander might have at least withdrawn to the Moselle had not the firmness of the First Army commander prevented him from doing so. The German Sixth and Seventh Armies would therefore have to attack, but before they did so, the hopes maintained by OHL for a breakthrough at the gap at Charmes began to fade, particularly since the progress of the right flank in Northern France made it likely that the gap would be opened from the rear. Nevertheless, it was necessary to fix in place the enemy forces in Lorraine, which was the concept of the 2 September order issued by Crown Prince Rupprecht. In view of the strength of the enemy position, reinforced with numerous heavy artillery, the necessity of advancing carefully, step by step, allowing the German artillery to do its work, was impressed on the troops. Seventh Army would attack on 3 September; Sixth Army would complete its preparations.

On 2 September the commander of Seventh Army thought that the situation in the Vosges was so uncertain that only XIV RK, reinforced by 39 ID, would attack on a line from St Dié to Étival, 10km to the north. The progress made here would determine the nature of the XV and XIV AK attacks. The *Landwehr* troops in the Upper Alsace were to attack to take the French opposing XIV RK in the flank and rear.

Upper Alsace and the Vosges, 3–8 August (map 24)

Since the French units east of the border at Belfort did not budge from their positions, the Bodungen detachment moved forward to the Ill River at Altkirch. On 5 September the Mathy detachment moved west against weak resistance until it reached Sennheim on 8 September.

The commander of 1 *Landwehr* Bde ordered 2 *Landwehr* Bde to renew the attack at 0600hrs on 3 September. 2 *Landwehr* Bde deployed and moved out at 0900hrs against the high ground at Kapelle, but the enemy was gone. The signs of combat were easy to see, and the troops could admire the clever positioning of the enemy trenches, while the French dead paid testimony to the accuracy of German fire. The French had clearly left in haste, with all sorts of equipment still in the bivouac areas, including two wagons full of rucksacks. The French rations were more than welcome.

LIR 2 deployed between Frauen-Kopf and Meyerhof to attack at 0600hrs on 3 September. In the course of the morning, LIR 2 took Évaux and both

Blatt 5 Vorderseite

24. **Urbeis – Wetzstein – 4.9. – 1. u. 2. b. gem. L. Br.**

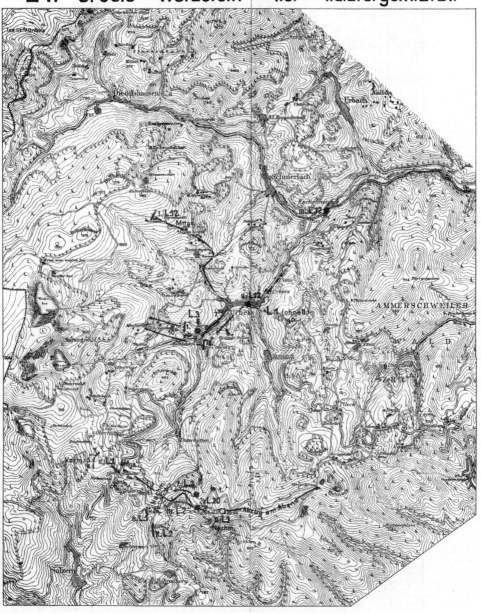

Eſchelmer—Zell—Drei Ähren. 2. 9.   Textſkizze 39.

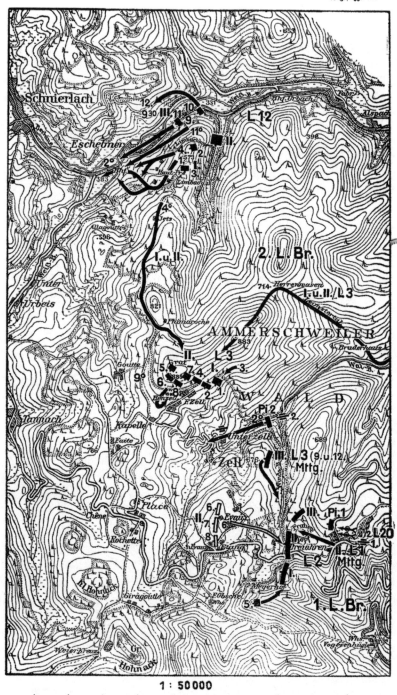

1 : 50 000

Klein-Hohnack and Gross-Hohnack without a shot being fired. *Landsturm* Eng. Co. 1 buried eighty dead on the Évaux battlefield. At 1430hrs II/LIR 1, the advance guard, reached the Hörnles-Kopf (Hill 1000).

At 0900hrs the commander of 1 *Landwehr* Bde ordered the continuation of the attack to the border. LIR 2 advanced on two trails in the woods, on each side of the ridge from Gross-Hohnack to the west. The mass of the regiment used the northern path, while I/LIR 2 took the southern. The march was slow, as the ground was soft and hilly. By dark the columns were 3km west of Gross-Hohnack. On the left, the Germans occupied Münster without opposition. In front of 2 *Landwehr* Bde the enemy was thought to be west of Urbeis and Tannach, so that afternoon the brigade only advanced to the high ground to the south-west.

Unsuccessful Attack on the Crest of the Vosges

On 3 September the deputy commander of XIV RK ordered the 1 *Landwehr* Bde commander to energetically pursue the enemy in the Vosges. The 1 *Landwehr* Bde commander therefore directed 2 *Landwehr* Bde on 4 September to cross the crest of the Vosges at the saddle south-west of the Immerlinskopf (Hill 1215) at 1000hrs and take the Col du Bonhomme (off map, south-west) from the rear. It would be assisted by LIR 2 attacking from the south-west of Urbeis at 1300hrs. The enemy appeared to have withdrawn over the crest of the Vosges. It was thought to be important to relieve the pressure on 30 RD and the Bavarian ED by advancing on the roads running north of Gérardmer.

On the morning of 4 September, II/LIR 1 was the advance guard at the Hörnles-Kopf with the main body 2.5km to the south-east. Even before the main body began to move, II/LIR 1 had sent two platoons of 7/LIR 1 1km to the high ground at Hill 970 to get a better field of fire, and at 0730hrs 7/LIR 1 was attacked from the north-west and west by superior forces. The II/LIR 1 commander reinforced 7/LIR 1 with 5 and 6/LIR 1, while 8/LIR 1 remained on the Combe-Kopf (Hill 966) to the south-east. As they moved on the road to Hill 970, casualties were taken from artillery fire from half-left. They deployed left of 7/LIR 1 and engaged three companies of French infantry due west descending the hill at 1.2km range. 7/LIR 1 had stopped the attack from the north-west at 700m with well-directed fire. The slope was now covered with irregular clumps of French infantry, which fired ineffectually.

At 0800hrs the two heavy howitzer batteries began to go into position 2.5km to the southeast, assisted by *Landsturm* Eng. Co. 1, which helped level out firing positions on the hillsides and felled trees to clear fields of fire. The guns could only unlimber and open fire one after the other. *Landsturm* Bty 1 found a hairpin turn in the trail 750m to the north-east, which offered observation to the west, and brought two platoons into firing position, which were able to engage both the stationary French infantry, as well as more arriving from the north-west, so effectively that they were scattered in all directions or retreated. The enemy attack had been defeated.

II/LIR 1, which had fired off all of its rifle ammunition, would have been able to breathe easy had it not been for the continual enemy artillery fire, which constantly caused casualties. French batteries appeared near the Vosges crest to the north-west and west. It was not possible to suppress this crossfire, which came from positions that could not be detected. At 1000hrs an enemy attempt to turn the right flank forced the commitment of all available troops.

At noon II/LIR 1 was no longer engaged in a firefight and the battalion commander seized the opportunity this freedom of manoeuvre provided to pull his troops back at twenty-minute intervals out of the enemy artillery fire and into the woods on the south-west slope of the Hörnles-Kopf. III/LIR 2 had arrived on the north slope and sent several platoons to reinforce II/LIR 1; 10/LIR 1 occupied the Klein-Hörnles-Kopf (Hill 941) to the north-west. The brigade commander ordered that the hill be held under all circumstances and sent I/LIR 2 forward as reinforcements. But the enemy artillery made this position untenable as well; covered by a rearguard on the south slope, made up of 5 and 6/LIR 2 and a platoon of 7/LIR 2, the main body marched east 1km to the next line of hills (III/LIR 2 on Schratzmännele in the middle, with I/LIR 2 on the Ligne-Kopf in the north, II/LIR 2 Barren-Kopf in the south), followed by the enemy shells, which did no damage, and the enemy did not pursue.

At 1800hrs successive rows of skirmishers were seen approaching from Oberhütten to the north-west, as well as two companies from Buchteren in the south, and a third enemy force was reported moving east from Sulzern to Hohrodberg. At the same time, the enemy artillery resumed firing. The German artillery conducted counter-battery fire, but was now almost out of shells, and given the terrain and lack of transport, replenishment was not to be expected until the next morning. The French Alpine troops were capable of moving in the woods at night around both flanks and into the *Landwehr* rear to cut off the line of supply.

The LIR 2 commander therefore reluctantly decided to withdraw before dark. *Landsturm* Bty 1 laid a barrage on the French infantry advancing from Oberhütten, then withdrew on the northern ridge trail along with the heavy howitzers; the infantry moved on the trail on the ridge crest. *Landsturm* Eng. Co. 1 occupied a delay position on the Kuh-Berg. The enemy infantry did not hinder the movement, as his artillery fired on the northern trail after the artillery had already passed by. The LIR 2 task force reached Klein- and Gross-Hohenack at 2000hrs and went into defensive positions. Losses were relatively light: II/LIR 1 had 14 KIA, 84 WIA and 16 MIA.

The detachment on the left had a bloody battle west of Munster, but with the withdrawal of LIR 2 the enemy dominated the Munster Valley, so the detachment withdrew to Weier and Sulzbach.

The commander of 2 *Landwehr* Bde ordered LIR 12 (minus III/LIR 12 at Eschelmer) to enter Urbeis at 0600hrs on 4 September and leave a battalion of II/LIR 12 as a reserve, while I/LIR 12 would move as a security detachment below Hill 1145. LIR 3, reinforced by *Landsturm* Bty 2 and *Landsturm* Eng. Co. 2, were to advance on the pass south-west of the Immerlinskopf (Hill 1215).

I/LIR 12 had moved halfway up the hill to the crest by 1145hrs, where it took an hour's rest. As it moved out again, it took heavy fire and was forced to deploy. The enemy also had two MGs, whose position could not be determined. The battalion became involved in a standing firefight. The fieldstone walls on the bare hillside offered some cover against the enemy on the higher ground.

LIR 3 had moved out of jam-packed Urbeis in march column at 0730hrs as it received a report that the enemy was moving east on the road in their direction. I/LIR 3 in advance guard had just begun the ascent of the mountain to the pass when it encountered French infantry in woods near Les Machielles and deployed, while III/LIR 3 deployed facing west on the road and II/LIR 3 was held in reserve. Protected by *Landsturm* Eng. Co. 2, *Landsturm* Bty 2 put a platoon into position behind a hill at the south-west side of Urbeis, which shelled the wood at Les Machielles; the other two platoons were oriented down the road. When LIR 3 began the attack, it met no resistance, but took artillery fire, particularly into the left flank of III/LIR 3. The woods at Les Machielles were taken, but it did not seem prudent to cross the open hillside under artillery fire. The platoon of *Landsturm* Bty 2 attempted to suppress the French guns on the crest, but soon the tables were turned and the two guns took a rain of shells, which forced the gunners to take cover. *Landsturm* Bty 2 bivouacked on the battlefield, although some troops were still without packs, ponchos or coats. LIR 1 (minus II/LIR 1) moved from Colmar and arrived in Urbeis at 2100hrs. III/LIR 12, positioned near Schnierlach, did not feel strong enough to attack Diedolshausen.

The commander of 1 *Landwehr* Bde was now convinced that it was impossible to cross the steep and largely open hillside to the pass with the troops at his disposal. He therefore decided to attack through Diedolshausen, even though the terrain there was also unfavourable. At 0600hrs on 5 September LIR 1 (minus II/LIR 1) moved from Urbeis to Schnierlach, reinforced by *Landsturm* Bty 1, the two howitzer batteries and *Landsturm* Eng. Co. 1, to conduct the assault. I/LIR 2 was to support by attacking the Buchen-Kopf (Hill 1219), but the rest of LIR 2 was to hold its positions.

On 5 September LIR 2 dug in on Klein- and Gross-Hohnack. The French advanced as far as the line of hills 4km to the west. Trench warfare set in here, too. The considerable distance to the enemy positions permitted active patrolling, which speaks highly of the *Landwehr* men, given the terrain and their advanced age. These forces, as well as the troops defending Urbeis, were subordinated to 2 *Landwehr* Bde.

The commander of 2 *Landwehr* Bde pulled his men back early that morning from the woods at Les Machielles. LIR 3 and II/LIR 12 dug in on the hills south of Urbeis with the help of *Landsturm* Eng. Co. 2. I/LIR 12 held the south-east slope of the Buchen-Kopf (Hill 1219) and 4/LIR 12 on the right flank on the Rabenfelsen (Hill 1145), with only grass and juniper bushes for concealment. 4/LIR 12 exchanged fire with French Alpine troops at the top of the hill, and at noon took such serious artillery fire that it was dispersed. Towards evening French infantry approached from the woods at the Immerlinskopf, but they were chased off by fire.

LIR 1 moved out from Schnierlach at 1000hrs to Langenwasen, with a company point element at Diedolshausen, without encountering the enemy. The Ferling detachment – RIR 70, III/RIR 12, 1 *Ersatz*/FAR 13 and 4/Res. Foot Artillery R 14 (10cm cannons) – was to the north at Embets. In the afternoon the 1 *Landwehr* Bde commander ordered 2 *Landwehr* Bde to leave a battalion at Urbeis and send the rest of the brigade to Eschelmer. By evening II/LIR 3 had reached Schnierlach, and III/LIR 3 Unter-Urbeis, when 4/LIR 3 became involved in a firefight west of Urbeis at Geishof, lost forty men and had to return to Urbeis. 3/LIR 3, which had climbed the Schwarz-Berg south of the town, was forced to give it up as its left flank was being turned by Alpine troops. The commander of LIR 3 called his troops back to the positions that they had just vacated; II/LIR 12 held Urbeis. During the night of 5/6 September, II/LIR 12 reoccupied the Grand-Faudé (Hill 713, north of Urbeis) with great difficulty.

The *Landwehr* mission on 6 September was to take the Col du Bonhomme (off map, on road south-west of Diedolshausen). Strong French forces were reported at the pass, as well as the Buchen-Kopf (Hill 1219, south of Diedolshausen) and the Ross-Berg (Hill 1126, north-west of Diedolshausen); it had to be assumed the enemy had artillery. It appeared absolutely necessary to take the Ross-Berg first. Since early morning Bavarian ED troops (half of II/RIR 60 and I/LIR 120) were moving south along the Vosges crest towards Les Grands Ordons, while RIR 70 from the Ferling detachment moved from the north of Diedolshausen to Tournées, and the artillery batteries and III/RIR 12 moved to Diedolshausen.

In the early morning *Landsturm* Bty 1, accompanied by a platoon of engineers, climbed the road north of Diedolshausen to the saddle east of Hill 922; the engineers cleared trees felled as obstacles by the French. The artillery was awaiting orders to go into position when at noon, with suspicious precision, shells landed directly on the battery. The horse teams of two guns and a caisson were cut down by direct hits; the remaining teams bolted downhill, the guns and wagons overturned on the steep slope and rolled into the valley. The battery was not combat-ready again for four days.

This may have discouraged preparations for the attack on the Ross-Berg, which seem to have taken a great deal of time. It was not possible to establish reliable contact with the Bavarian ED troops, which took Les Grands Ordons but did not attack the strongly held Ross-Berg. Except for a platoon north of Diedolshausen, I *Ersatz*/FAR 13 stayed on the road in Diedolshausen until dark, while 4/Res. Foot Artillery R 14 (10cm cannons) and 1 and 2/*Landwehr* Foot Artillery Bty 20 (sFH) did not open fire from Schnierlach until evening. I/LIR 12, on the east side of the Buchen-Kopf, took rifle and MG fire throughout the day.

On the morning of 7 September 4/Res. Foot Artillery R 14 (10cm cannons) began to shell the Ross-Berg. I *Ersatz*/FAR 13 hauled its guns to the high ground north of Diedolshausen and then, at 1000hrs, moved a platoon to the Markircher Höhe (Hill 1037), from where it could also shell the Ross-Berg. At 0800hrs III/LIR 12 deployed half of 12/LIR 12 and all of 10/LIR 12 in the woods close to the crest. The troops were able to approach through the thick undergrowth, but took fire in the left flank. Nevertheless, in the course of the morning they were able to approach to within 200m of the French position. At noon I/LIR 120 risked an attack on the bare top of the Ross-Berg, with half of II/RIR 60 (6 and 7/RIR 60) on the right. In the afternoon 9/RIR 60 was committed on the left flank, while I/LIR 20 and half of II/RIR 60 advanced on the open plateau of the Ross-Berg. But then the enemy on the treeline south of the open hilltop gained fire superiority, the fight had to be broken off and the Germans withdrew to the east.

I and II/LIR 12, II/LIR 1 and a platoon of *Landsturm* Eng. Co. 1 assembled that morning at Merelles, 2km west of Schnierlach, and moved through the woods to attack the Buchen-Kopf (Hill 1219). II/LIR 3 at Grand-Faudé (Hill 773, north of Urbeis) attacked with 7 and 8/LIR 3. Moving deployed, they reached Hexenweiher and the Rabenfelsen (Hill 1145). The heavy artillery (half of *Landsturm* Foot Artillery Bty 20 and 4/Res. Foot Artillery R 14) set up on the road 2km east of Diedolshausen and hammered the Buchen-Kopf and Immerlinskopf, but also prevented the Bavarian infantry from attacking and, due to lack of communication equipment, their fire could not be stopped; the infantry had to return to Schnierlach.

On 8 September the 1 *Landwehr* Bde commander anticipated an enemy attack and instructed his troops to defend in place, but the day passed quietly. I/RIR 12 reoccupied the Rabenfelsen and, since the enemy had left the Buchen-Kopf, put a security detachment there. The artillery shelled the Ross-Berg and the Col du Bonhomme.

30 RD, Bavarian ED, 3–8 September (map 25)

3 September

In the western Vosges three groups were formed for the attack on 3 September. On the right, north of St Dié, 39 ID, 28 RD and 19 ED; and in the centre at

St Dié, 26 RD. These divisions were stopped by the terrain and enemy resistance 4km west of the Meurthe

On the left, under the Governor of Strasbourg, 30 RD was to defend between Saulcy and the Tête de Behouille, while the Bavarian ED was to attack at 0600hrs from Algoutte–Verpellière to the south. On 2 September these units, which had barely reorganised, were mixed together, along with the troops from Strasbourg. Command and control and logistics, particularly rations, again suffered. The troops were exhausted, but it was impossible to rest them because the enemy was too close and aggressive. To untangle this situation, 30 RD and the Bavarian ED were given control of all the troops in their sectors; nevertheless, the chain of command remained unclear.

Good weather returned on 3 September and the French artillery again shelled 30 RD, but by now the troops had constructed some cover. Between 0900hrs and 1000hrs the enemy attacked the prominent Tête de Behouille, again accompanied by almost unendurable artillery fire; one battery was apparently firing straight down the flank. Nevertheless, the first attack, begun at 1100hrs and directed principally at Les Planches Prés, was beaten back. But in the woods on the Tête de Behouille the artillery fire and attacks shook the Prussian *Landwehr* battalions somewhat; here and there the French were able to penetrate the position, and the hilltop fell into enemy hands. But help was at hand in the form of the 1 *Ersatz* Bde, which during the night had arrived 500m–1,000m north of the hill. The 30 RD commander had probably intended to use the brigade in an attack, but now they appeared on the Tête de Behouille just in time to stabilise the situation. Right to left deployed I and II/RIR 4 (minus 5, 8, 11/RIR 4) then *Ersatz* Bn I, II and III. The companies of LIR 80 and 81 were absorbed by the Bavarian battalions. Soon a wild fight was in progress; everywhere French infantry fired from the trees or other well-concealed places. All order was lost. Leaders, above all the commander of RIR 4, pulled their anxious men together as far as possible in the thick underbrush and spurred them on. By the afternoon the skilled and crafty Alpine troops had been thrown back and the Tête de Behouille cleared, although at the price of heavy casualties. All attempts to continue the attack onto the open ground to the south failed in the face of overwhelming enemy fire. 2 *Ersatz*/Eng. Bn 1 was brought forward to help digging in. RIR 4 had taken heavy casualties, including the majority of the officers. The Tête de Behouille was covered with bodies. II/RIR 15 had been forced by artillery fire to evacuate its position and had dispersed; that evening the battalion had only seventy men, had not received regular rations in four days and had not had a night's rest for a considerable period. 1 *Ersatz* Bde took control of all units on the Tête de Behouille.

On the morning of 3 September the commander of the Bavarian ED put his remaining units – *Ersatz* Bn IV and XII, RIR 15 (minus II/RIR 15), *Ersatz*

MGK 9, 1 *Ersatz*/Eng. Bn 3, *Ersatz* FA Sec. II and III – on the road through Betrimoutier to St Croix. The infantry was put under 9 *Ersatz* Bde. The march began late because the transmission of orders in the pitch-dark took an unusually long time. At Bonipaire supply vehicles blocked the road. At the crossroads south of Laigoutte the Governor of Strasbourg ordered the Bavarian ED commander to advance east of the road instead of astride it. II/LIR 120, which was south-east of Lavaeline, was attached to the Bavarian ED.

Since the enemy artillery was at Le Chipal, at the hairpin turn in the road 1.5km south of St Croix, the Bavarian ED artillery advanced by bounds: the horses of *Ersatz* FA Sec. II were exhausted and pulled slowly. *Ersatz* Bn XII, with *Ersatz* MGK 9, formed the advance guard. Elements of *Ersatz* Bn IX, which had scattered, were also attached. As it left Lavaline at 0900hrs, *Ersatz* Bn XII took artillery fire, sought cover in the houses, then deployed and advanced. The fight at Tête de Behouille had begun again, and *Ersatz* FA Sec. II was firing in that direction. At 0830hrs RIR 15 (minus II/RIR 15) deployed behind the high ground south of Gemaingoutte: III/RIR 15 on the right, I/RIR 15 on the left. *Ersatz* Bn IV moved forward to make contact with RIR 15, took artillery fire at Laveline and swung east to Québrux, which it reached at 1100hrs. En route it encountered an ad hoc group of *Ersatz* Bn X men in company strength and incorporated them. Between 1000hrs and 1100hrs RIR 15 began moving south and reached Hill 636, east of Verpellière, at noon without difficulty, with *Ersatz* Bn IV and IV/RIR 4 following echeloned left. The cross-country march over hilly, sometimes swampy, land covered with vegetation cost a great deal of time and effort. Two batteries of *Ersatz* FA Sec. II remained in Honville because their horses could not climb the hill.

Since morning, II/LIR 120 was on Hill 697 east of La Croix, supported by 1 *Ersatz*/FAR 15. It was quiet until the afternoon, when enemy infantry attacked from the treeline against the left flank; 1 *Ersatz*/FAR 15 was forced to change position. But towards evening the Bavarian troops began to arrive. I/RIR 15 attacked over Pré Bergon, while IV/RIR 4 swung over Lauterupt from the east, uphill and down, over fallen trees and steep slopes. Finally, all the Bavarian battalions were on Hill 697: left RIR 15 and IV/RIR 4, right *Ersatz* Bn XII, with *Ersatz* Bn IV in reserve. 1 *Ersatz*/Eng. Bn 3 corduroyed the path south of Hill 697, which took until midnight.

4 September (map 25)

The XIV RK commander ordered 39 ID, 28 RD, 19 ED and 26 RD to continue the attack. They made some gains after heavy fighting. 30 RD and the Bavarian ED were to defend in place; it seemed prudent to await the arrival of the *Landwehr* units from the east on the road to Diedolshausen. In addition, the enemy between

St Léonard–Mandray–Le Chipal had obviously been reinforced from Gérardmer. For this reason, on 4 September Seventh Army sent 61 Bde (IR 132 and II/IR 126, plus the MGK/IR 126) from Raon l'Étape to Bertrimoutier.

On a fine fall day 30 RD improved its positions, organised and prepared for an extensive stay. Construction of huts began, latrines were dug, the dead and the horse cadavers buried, the weapons and equipment lying around collected. The 1 *Ersatz*/FAR 51 horse teams, wagons and gunners returned from Markirch that morning, recovered the guns they had left the previous day and occupied a position south-east of Fouchifol.

The Bavarian ED redeployed to assume a defensive posture. II/LIR 120 maintained its forward position on Hill 697, once again supported by 1 *Ersatz*/FAR 15, with III/RIR 15 on the treeline further to the south. The rest of the division dug in behind this screen on both sides of Hill 636, east of Verpellière, assisted by the newly arrived 2 Res./Eng. Bn 15. The two batteries of *Ersatz* FA Sec. II in Honville pulled their guns to the high ground east of Laveline, in part by using ten teams of horses. Several horses broke down completely and had to be shot.

Thirteen companies under Brigadier General Rekowski had arrived at La Truche, south of Honville, the previous day. In order to be secure against surprise from the large forest to the south, they marched up difficult paths to the south of Hill 1022, drove off weak enemy outposts and returned to La Truche that evening, leaving II/LIR 60 at Les Gelles.

The enemy hardly disturbed the work or movements. His infantry held Saulcy, Mandray and the high ground south-west and south of La Croix and also dug in. His artillery was less active and only did serious damage to *Ersatz* Bn II and III on the Tête de Behouille. The German artillery returned the favour in kind and caught careless French infantry in movement several times. 1 *Ersatz*/FAR 15 was surprised by French infantry and attempted to move off, but in the dark the guns overturned on the steep slope. The horses fell and became tangled in the harness, so that they had to be completely cut away. The battery was withdrawn to Wisembach and was not combat-ready until 9 September. 61 Bde and FAR 80 arrived at Bertimoutier, and IR 126 HQ with III/IR 126 at Gemaingoutte. In the night of 4/5 September 61 Bde moved to Tête de Behouille, while FAR 80 took up a position west and north of Hill 545, south of Coinches. In general, 4 September had been quiet.

5 September (map 26)

With the arrival of these reinforcements, on 5 September the commander of XIV RK wanted to conduct a general attack south on both sides of the Meurthe. But 39 ID, 28 RD, 19 ED and 26 RD were unable to gain any ground west and south of St Dié.

The Governor of Strasbourg ordered 30 RD, reinforced by 61 Bde and FAR 80, to attack between Saulcy and Tête de Behouille on the Meurthe at St Léonard–Anould–Fraize, while the Bavarian ED, with the forces east of the La Croix road, would attack south of La Croix against the enemy right flank. The attack would be preceded by a thirty-minute artillery preparation on the Bois de Mandray and the woods and high ground 1.5km south of La Croix. The troops were to be assembled by 0515hrs.

30 RD was for the most part in suitable attack positions. LIR 80 and 81, which had been on the Tête de Behouille, had been replaced by 61 Bde and were now behind the hill in division reserve. 2 *Ersatz*/FAR 2 and 1 *Ersatz*/FAR 51 were attached to the Bavarian ED. The bombardment of the Bois de Mandray and the towns of Mandray and Benifosse was assigned to FAR 80 and 1 *Ersatz*/FAR 2 and began at 0615hrs; at 0645hrs the infantry jumped off.

On the right, III/RIR 4 (minus 11/RIR 4) attacked from Hill 467, north-east of Saulcy, with *Ersatz* Bn XI on the left and *Ersatz* Bn IX (which had absorbed *Ersatz* Bn X, yet still only had the strength of two weak companies) on the right; echeloned right followed half of II/RIR 4 (6 and 7/RIR 4). As the troops began to descend the hill to Saulcy they took weak rifle fire from the town, and a little artillery fire. The advance was made by bounds, with a few losses, and between 0800hrs and 0900hrs Saulcy was taken. *Ersatz* Bn IX, which entered the northern part, took thirty POWs.

10 Res. Bde attacked with only two battalions. On the left, on Hill 509 south of Entre-deux-Eaux, the I/RIR 14 commander had control over 1/RIR 14, 3/RIR 11 and 1 Platoon/Fortress MG Sec. 2, and behind them 3/RIR 14 and 4/RIR 11. As they left the wood at 0700hrs to advance on the valley west of Mandray, they took heavy rifle fire from the town into their left flank, which, together with artillery fire, froze them in place. A platoon of 1/RIR 14 was destroyed. On the brigade right, III/RIR 14 deployed 9 and 10/RIR 14 in the first line and sent them in loose waves towards Benifosse. The two companies had been hit in their assembly areas by French artillery fire from the other side of the Meurthe. More artillery fire on the Mandray streambed, in addition to small arms fire from Mandray and Benifosse, stopped the skirmisher lines on the Mandray–Saulcy road.

5 *Ersatz* Bde deployed behind the ridge south-east of Entre-deux-Eaux. On the right was *Ersatz* Bn VI, now down to company strength, *Ersatz* Bn VIII in the middle, *Ersatz* Bn V on the left, *Ersatz* Bn VII and *Ersatz* MGK 5 in reserve east of Entre-deux-Eaux. *Ersatz* Bn VIII deployed 1 and 3/*Ersatz* Bn VIII, which were merged into one company, with 2 and 4/*Ersatz* Bn VIII, in the same condition, following. *Ersatz* Bn V deployed 2, 4 and 1/*Ersatz* Bn V, with 3/*Ersatz* Bn V behind the centre. In spite of their low strength, *Ersatz* Bn VI and VIII had a 700–800m sector. At 0700hrs the brigade left the protection of the reverse

slope of the hill. It seemed prudent to wait until the neighbours on the left and right had come up, and the French artillery fire also called for caution, so the troops occupied the trenches dug the previous days on the forward slopes and conducted a slow firefight with the French in Mandray. But the French were too well protected behind the cover of walls and rooftops and could not be driven out by rifle fire. The attack only got moving after I/FAR 80 went into position at La Cuche and began to shell the town, and the units on the left arrived. Between 1400hrs and 1500hrs Mandray and Haute Mandray were taken. Once again it was necessary to wait for the neighbouring units to come up before wooded hills south of the town could be attacked. The units were so reduced in strength and in such wooded and compartmented terrain that it was difficult for them to maintain contact with each other. The commander of *Ersatz* Bn V was killed and the battalion was merged with *Ersatz* Bn VIII.

On the Tête de Behouille, 1 *Ersatz* Bde deployed I/RIR 4 on the right, half of II/RIR 4 (5, 8, 11/RIR 4) on its left, then *Ersatz* Bn III and II, while *Ersatz* Bn I, 2 *Ersatz*/Eng. Bn 1 and *Ersatz* MGK 1 were in reserve. 61 Bde was between the Tête de Behouille and La Croix, including 300 stragglers from II/RIR 15. A firefight developed between the German troops and the French in Haute Mandray. Here the attack got rolling at noon, after the artillery had softened up the French infantry in Mandray. *Ersatz* FA Sec. I had initially deployed 2 *Ersatz*/FAR 1 on Hill 580, south of Omégoutte, and then the entire section went into battery south-east of the Tête de Behouille, from where it suppressed two French batteries, set Mandray on fire and engaged French infantry south of the town. I/RIR 4 quickly took Haute Mandray and half of II/RIR 4 took the high ground south of the town. *Ersatz* MGK 1 set up on the slope north-east of the town and engaged the French troops heading for the woods with pursuit fire. Further advance was not possible because the French held the north edge of the Bois de Mandray and the French artillery was quite active. In the early afternoon *Ersatz* Bn I and II gained the north slope of Hill 704, close to the south-east side of Haute Mandray, but encountered unshaken enemy infantry who were not thinking about retreat. Between 0900hrs and 1000hrs 61 Bde took Hill 704, south-west of La Croix, chasing off the French Alpine troops there.

In the Bavarian ED sector, 9 *Ersatz* Bde, with RIR 15, IV/RIR 4, *Ersatz* Bn IV and XII, II/LIR 120, and Fortress MG Sec. 1 and 3, had the mission of taking the high ground north-west and south of the hairpin turn in the road south of La Croix. The Rekowski detachment was to move far to the left to turn the enemy right flank. The artillery occupied the same positions as the previous day, and between 0600hrs and 0700hrs conducted a thirty-minute preparatory bombardment.

9 *Ersatz* Bde moved forward as far as possible during the night. On the right flank, *Ersatz* Bn XII (with *Ersatz* Bn IX attached) was in an assembly area south

of La Croix at 0300hrs. At 0700hrs the first line, composed of 1 and 3/*Ersatz* Bn XII, moved out, covered by Fortress MG Sec. 3 on the high ground east of St Jean. Two hours later they climbed Hill 704, apparently at the same time as 61 Bde, against weak enemy resistance, but taking artillery fire. Before dawn the other troops of the brigade moved behind Hill 910 to attack the enemy on Hill 704 in the flank; there was a large gap to *Ersatz* Bn XII on the right. I/RIR 15 deployed 1 and 3/RIR 15 in the first line. Echeloned behind the left flank were III/RIR 15, *Ersatz* Bn IV, IV/RIR 4, 1 *Ersatz*/Eng. Bn 3 and II/LIR 120. Fortress MG Sec. 1 took up a firing position just north of the hairpin turn.

The Rekowski detachment had moved out at midnight, without any sleep, and at 0600hrs once again climbed the steep and difficult path through the hills and woods to Hill 1022; at 0615hrs, 6 and 7/RIR 60 remained on the hill to guard the flank and rear. The advance guard, III/LIR 71, turned west, quickly made contact with the enemy and deployed, with half of RIR 60 (5 and 8/RIR 60) moving up on the left.

Shortly before 0800hrs RIR 15, supported by Fortress MG Sec. 1, attacked at the hairpin turn. I/RIR 15, on the right flank, moved straight west. When 1 and 2/RIR 15 left the woods they immediately took lively small arms fire in the left flank from the treelines and high ground to the south-west. They were forced to turn left, passed through the village of Le Chipal and climbed 200m up the steep slope. 3/RIR 15 filled a gap in the line, while 4/RIR 15 guarded the left flank. The attack stalled in the face of strong enemy opposition. At 0845hrs III/RIR 15 came up on the left. Nevertheless, progress was slow due to the lack of officers and the necessity of waiting for the artillery support to be effective. 12 joined 4/RIR 15, and *Ersatz* Bn IV, now reduced to two companies, moved 1/*Ersatz* Bn IV between I and III/RIR 15. II/LIR 120 climbed the steep west slope of Le Grand Rien and chased off the enemy detachments there, and then climbed the opposite hillside. At noon the Rekowski detachment appeared, but the enemy, who was very proficient in forest warfare, did not retreat.

Between 0700hrs and 0845hrs *Ersatz* FA Sec. III set up near Verpellière. At noon 2 *Ersatz*/FAR 8 moved to the south of La Croix; the other two batteries followed at 1400hrs, but without going into firing position. *Ersatz* FA Sec. II set up near the church at La Croix before 1300hrs, but by 1415hrs two batteries moved into an assembly area on the road leading down from the town. 2 *Ersatz*/FAR 13 went into battery at 1000hrs east of St Jean. The German artillery fire increased in power and accuracy, but the enemy artillery could not be found and was very active: at noon IV/RIR 4 and 1 *Ersatz*/Eng. Bn 3 were caught in an assembly area on the west slope of Hill 910 and dispersed.

During the afternoon there was a confusing back-and-forth fight in the woods on the ridge top against French troops in trees, on steep slopes and other hiding places. Brigadier General Rekowski committed all or part of I and III/LIR 80. III/RIR 15, whose right flank had pushed far forward while the left was under severe pressure, was forced, along with *Ersatz* Bn IV, to fall back to the high ground east of the road. II/LIR 120 pulled all the way back to Gemaingoutte; III/RIR 15, now with only seventy men, withdrew to Laveline, where it was joined after dark by IV/RIR 4 and 1 *Ersatz*/Eng. Bn 3, which had reassembled. IV/RIR 4 was sent to La Croix. A few companies of the Rekowski detachment withdrew to Le Grand Rien, while the rest were scattered or had become lost in the dark woods: III/LIR 71 ended up at Laveline, III/LIR 80 at La Croix. *Ersatz* Bn XII and *Ersatz* MGK 9 held Hill 643 south of the road, and at noon I/RIR 15 had occupied some houses at the hairpin turn, as did the right flank of III/RIR 15.

At 1500hrs the Governor of Strasbourg personally informed the commander of the Bavarian ED at La Croix that, according to aerial reconnaissance, the enemy was in full retreat over the Meurthe; the Bavarian ED commander then ordered pursuit in the direction of Fraize and Plainfaing. On the left flank this order had been overtaken by events. At 1800hrs I/RIR 15 threw the French off the high ground south of the hairpin turn. 1/*Ersatz* Bn XII pushed south on its left at 2000hrs, but took heavy fire and turned back. In any case, pursuit was not possible due to heavy enemy artillery fire on the road from south of La Croix to the hairpin turn; the Bavarian ED staff and the Governor of Strasbourg were caught in this fire. While leaving its firing position 2 *Ersatz*/FAR 84 came under artillery fire, took considerable damage and moved to Gemaingoutte.

At noon the commander of 30 RD also ordered his troops forward. On the left flank, 61 Bde pushed into the Bois de Mandray along the road to La Cosette, cleared out the French Alpine troops in a tough fight and reached the south treeline by midnight. II/RIR 15 attached themselves to the brigade right; 6 and 7/RIR 15 took the high ground at 1930hrs and were thrown back. 5, 6 and 7/RIR 15 then made another attempt and took the enemy position. On their right, *Ersatz* Bn I and II advanced into the Bois de Mandray at dark. The companies became intermixed, but pushed the enemy back and pursued him during the night. Elements of *Ersatz* Bn II threw back an attack by Alpine troops at 2300hrs. *Ersatz* Bn III appears to have only reached the road south-west of Haute Mandray. Half of II/RIR 4 therefore remained on the high ground south of the village. I/RIR 4, in Haute Mandray, renewed the attack at 1800hrs, but was stopped by flanking fire after an advance of only 200m. The enemy troops south of the Mandray stream were kept down by the fire of 1 *Ersatz*/FAR 4, which set up, oblivious to the enemy artillery fire all around, at the saddle between Hill 631 and 704, west of La Croix, and was joined by a platoon of 1 *Ersatz*/FAR 1.

Two battalions of 5 *Ersatz* Bde (*Ersatz* Bn VIII and V) attacked from Mandray at 1800hrs and took the high ground south of the town, but the enemy would not give up the north treeline of the Bois de Mandray. *Ersatz* Bn VII was ordered to relieve the two forward battalions and push a company to Le Faubourg. In the dark it approached Miromay Farm in march column when the advance guard, 4/*Ersatz* Bn VII, became involved in a firefight at point-blank range (20m); the rest of the battalion took cover behind a house and in a sunken road. Since the intensity of the enemy fire signalled strong resistance, the battalion was withdrawn to the valley south of Mandray. *Ersatz* Bn V and VIII, and *Ersatz* MGK 5, bivouacked in Mandray, and 1 Res./Eng. Bn 15 collected pioneer tools lying about and bivouacked in Entre-deux-Eaux.

10 Res. Bde also resumed the attack. On the right flank III/RIR 14 crossed the road west of Basse Mandray in loose waves of skirmishers at 1800hrs and had taken Benifosse by 1930hrs. Outposts were put on the wooded hilltops south-west of the village and 7/RIR 11 occupied Contremoulin. On the left flank I/RIR 14 reached Basse Mandray at 2000hrs; 3 and 4/RIR 11 marched to Benifosse. There was no enemy resistance.

The far right flank of 30 RD in Saulcy was under fire the entire afternoon from French snipers in trees, houses and bushes. The commander of III/RIR 4, who was responsible for this sector, evacuated Saulcy to allow the artillery to shell the French; after an hour the town was reoccupied, although it was in flames and for the most part burned to the ground during the night.

In the morning III/LIR 120, 10/LIR 71 and 6 and 7/LIR 81, under the LIR 120 commander, were in reserve on Hill 636, east of Verpellière, and moved forward to the high ground south-east of La Croix at 1500hrs, where their blue peacetime uniforms occasionally drew the attention of the French artillery.

I/LIR 120, at the Col de St Marie, was ordered to guard the far left flank, and that morning moved south on the crest of the Vosges along footpaths through the immense pine forests until it reached Hill 950, north of Diedolshausen.

On 5 September 30 RD and the Bavarian ED made a modest advance, but this put the exhausted troops at the end of their tether. Bringing rations to the forward positions on the night of 5/6 September was especially difficult, and only part of the field kitchens and ration vehicles were able to do so. Half of II/RIR 4 in Mandray collected rations from the abandoned Bavarian ED supply vehicles left there.

On the right of XIV RK, XV and XIV AK made no progress at all, even though the French XXI Corps had been withdrawn. In particular, the enemy heavy artillery could not be suppressed. Seventh Army was unable to take its objective, the enemy position at Rambervillers.

OHL had become concerned that the British and French could penetrate from Belgium into the open rear area of the German right wing. It therefore planned to establish a German army there. During the afternoon of 5 September, OHL asked Crown Prince Rupprecht if it was possible to detach a corps from Sixth and Seventh Armies each for this purpose. Rupprecht did not believe this to be possible, unless the attack which had just begun was broken off and both armies withdrew. Only when there was some success at Rambervillers, the most important point on the front, could a corps be transferred. Rupprecht offered OHL 7 KD. Seventh Army, on the other hand, said that XV AK was available. That evening OHL decided to assemble the Seventh Army HQ and 7 KD at Saarburg on 8 September, and XV AK on the Franco–German border south-west of Saarburg on 9 September, for transport to Belgium. A corps of Sixth Army was to follow two days later. HKK 3 was to be transferred to East Prussia. The remaining Seventh Army units would be subordinated to Sixth Army.

Even though he had lost a considerable number of manoeuvre units, Rupprecht felt it was still his mission to attack. He was reinforced in this belief by the OHL general order of 5 September, which said that the German right wing had advanced until it was east and south-east of Paris, but was itself seriously threatened from Paris. It could be assumed that the enemy had assembled strong forces in Paris, drawn from the Belfort–Toul front. OHL did not think it was still possible to envelop the French left or push the entire French army into Switzerland. It was necessary for the First and Second Armies to assume a defence position opposite Paris, on both sides of the Marne, to stop a French attack on the German flank. Fourth and Fifth Armies were to advance west of Verdun and open a corridor across the Upper Moselle for Sixth and Seventh Armies. OHL had considered switching the *Schwerpunkt* to the left wing for some time, and this concept was the basis of the original order to Rupprecht to break through between Toul and Verdun, but it was only now presented with full clarity. The Sixth and Seventh Army missions were unchanged: they would fix the enemy to their front in place and attack between Toul and Belfort as soon as possible. But their forces were weakening, and the French began to gain the upper hand.

Defence against French Attacks, 6–8 September (map 26)

In the Seventh Army sector, XV AK began to pull out of line on 5 September, marched to the railheads at Saarburg and to the south-west, and began rail movement on 8 September. On 6 September XIV RK was to defend in place. XIV AK, with 60 *Landsturm* Bde attached, was to attack, but this did not take place on 6 September or even on the following two days, as XIV AK had to occupy XV AK positions.

On 6 September in the 30 RD sector it was mostly quiet, which did the troops good. There was an occasional artillery duel. FAR 80 was detached and marched off. On the right flank there were exchanges of small arms fire in Saulcy; I and II/ RIR 14 relieved the battalions of the Bavarian ED and RIR 4. RIR 11 reunited in Basse Mandray and occupied Mangoutte. 10 Res. Bde thereby assumed control of the right half of the 30 RD sector. The French had pulled out of the Bois de Mandray in front of 5 *Ersatz* Bde; *Ersatz* Bn VII was able to occupy Le Faubourg at 0900hrs. The rest of the brigade spent the day in Mandray. In the 1 *Ersatz* Bde sector, RIR 4 was reunited in Haute Mandray and pushed security elements into the Bois de Mandray. *Ersatz* Bn I and II probably occupied the south treeline of the Bois de Mandray, near Breheuille, with II/RIR 15 (200 men) digging in on their left.

The woods to the east were occupied by 61 Bde of XV AK, which 30 RD was ordered to relieve in place at noon. The enemy had withdrawn over the Meurthe at Anould, Fraize and Plainfaing, but in the afternoon a French bicycle messenger was captured by a security detachment of 12/RIR 14 at Belle Goutte (east of St Léonard) with an order for an attack by two battalions on Mangoutte and five battalions on La Folie, north-east of Fraize. This prevented 61 Bde from moving off. There was no activity at Mangoutte, but a strong enemy attack took place at La Folie.

It was also quiet on the morning of 6 September in the Bavarian ED sector. North of the Meuse, the French only had a weak detachment on Hill 628, south-west of La Folie. The division commander had received no instructions, but since the south slopes of the hills were sure to be shelled by enemy artillery, he ordered them to only be weakly held by artillery FOs and infantry security; it was evening before this order reached the units. The Governor of Strasbourg ordered the French positions at Fraize to be shelled by *Ersatz* FA Sec. II and III, and 5/Res. Foot Artillery R 10 (sFH), which opened fire at 1100hrs.

Early in the afternoon in the 9 *Ersatz* Bde sector, outposts from RIR 15 east of La Folie observed French infantry in lines and columns, accompanied by heavily loaded pack animals, assemble behind the high ground east of Plainfaing and then move through the low ground to the east of Scarupt; it was soon clear that the enemy was preparing to attack. 3/RIR 15 was moved 200m in front of the forested ridge and instructed to defend there to the last man, with 1/RIR 15 (which had a platoon at La Folie) on the right, 4/RIR 15 echeloned left on the wooded ridge, and 2 behind 4/RIR 15. On the left III/RIR 15 occupied a position 20–50m in front of the south-west edge of the wood, with *Ersatz* Bn IV covering the treeline itself. The enemy attacked at 1800hrs, hitting I/RIR 15 frontally and accompanied by murderous artillery fire. 4/RIR 15, with no field of fire, moved forward in skirmisher line 200m and lay down, probably left of 3/RIR 15. 2/RIR 15 moved into this long skirmisher line on its own initiative. The platoon of 1/RIR 15 at La Folie had a good field of fire, but was forced to withdraw by flanking fire. III/RIR 15 and 2/*Ersatz* Bn IV were also soon threatened by French Alpine infantry which had approached to within 600m of the left flank. The German artillery was not able to give fire support; *Ersatz* FA Sec. III was displacing forward, but was stopped at 1700hrs by the Governor of Strasbourg and returned to its previous positions. It was delayed by enemy artillery fire and blocked roads, only arrived at 1830hrs and then shelled Fraize.

5/Res. Foot Artillery 10 was also moving, as was 2 *Ersatz* FAR 13, which was halted in Verpellière. When 2/*Ersatz* Bn IV received a report that the French Alpine infantry had reached the undefended crest on their left flank and had turned towards them, it broke contact to occupy a position that could not be outflanked. RIR 15, whose left flank was now exposed, held out for a short while, supported by Fortress MG Sec. 1, and then withdrew. At this time a division order, issued at 1145hrs, arrived directing a withdrawal from the woods south of the hairpin turn; the scene was now set for all sorts of misunderstandings. From 1900hrs onwards the firing line crumbled more and more to the rear. Nevertheless, isolated groups held out around their officers until dark, then withdrew, carrying the wounded with them. RIR 15 more or less assembled at the hairpin turn and then marched to La Croix. 2/*Ersatz* Bn IV occupied the high ground east of St Jean. The right-hand neighbour of RIR 15, *Ersatz* Bn XII, was not affected by the enemy attack, but withdrew at 1900hrs to Hill 704 after receiving heavy artillery fire, while *Ersatz* MGK 9 pulled back to the south-east of Haute Mandray.

The Rekowski detachment was able to dig in undisturbed. 61 Bde, on the high ground north of Bon Repos, beat back an attack that evening, but the relief in place could only be partially completed. The brigade had not received rations for two days. At 2100hrs IV/RIR 4 arrived in La Croix, but during the morning it had marched from Hill 910 south of the town and became lost in the woods. It then marched in the direction of gunfire near Hill 1022.

On Hill 1022, half of II/RIR 60 had linked up with I/LIR 120 in order to march south along the crest of the Vosges to the Col du Bonhomme (off map 26 to south-east; upper left corner of map 24). Between 1000hrs and 1100hrs they made contact with the enemy on the north slope of Les Grands Ordons. IV/RIR 4 now appeared as an unexpected but welcome reinforcement; it deployed 16 and 14/RIR 4 on the first line, 15 and 13/RIR 4 behind the centre and right to turn the French left flank. The French were soon driven back and Les Grands Ordons stormed before noon. The battalion commander now felt he was required to return to 9 *Ersatz* Bde, but did not dare to move directly west through the broad and insecure forest. The battalion therefore swung north through La Truche and Honville, and by this detour arrived at La Croix. Half of II/RIR 60 and I/LIR 120 reached the treeline on the north slope of the open high plateau of the Ross-Berg. Since prisoner statements gave the defensive force on the hill at as many as twelve Alpine companies and two mountain batteries, more than twice the German strength, the II/RIR 60 units returned to Hill 1022 and I/LIR 120 to Les Grands Ordons.

For 7 September the Governor of Strasbourg ordered 30 RD and the Bavarian ED to dig in on the south treeline of the Bois de Mandray. If the Bavarian ED had lost portions of the south treeline, it was to retake them as soon as possible. In addition, 30 RD was to finally release 61 Bde, but the situation still seemed too serious to do so. In particular, since *Ersatz* Bn XII and RIR 15 had left the woods south of the hairpin turn, the 30 RD left flank was exposed. In front of the 10 Res. Bde, two enemy regiments were observed during the morning moving from the south towards La Croix and then deploying towards Benifosse and Mandray against the positions of III/RIR 14 and RIR 11. The platoons of 9 and 12/RIR 14 on the wooded hilltop south-west of Benifosse, with the help of Fortress MG Sec. 2, easily drove the enemy off before 1300hrs. The position of RIR 11 at Mangoutte was more serious. II/RIR 11 had deployed only 6/RIR 11 on the treeline east of Mangoutte, and was forced to commit 5 and 8/RIR 11 on the right, and 7/RIR 11 on the left, between 1600hrs and 1700hrs. I/RIR 11 moved by stages forward from Basse Mandray to Benifosse and sent 3/RIR 11 to assist the left flank of II/RIR 11. Two platoons of Fortress MG Sec. 2 entered the fight and the French infantry was stopped. But II/RIR 11 could not hold out under the continual and murderous French artillery fire, and began to slip back into the woods at 1800hrs. The battalion was assembled and moved forward, and once again pulled back, but at 2300hrs the treeline west of Mangoutte was again securely in German hands. The 30 RD artillery supported 10 Res. Bde as much as possible. At Saulcy, where I and II/RIR 14, and the remnants of *Ersatz* Bn IX and X were located, the day was quiet.

5 *Ersatz* Bde had only *Ersatz* Bn VII at Le Faubourg (south of Hill 744) on the south treeline of the Bois de Mandray; the rest of the brigade was resting in Mandray. Shortly after noon they were alerted and moved to the high ground south of the town, in order to support the outposts of RIR 4, which were supposedly withdrawing, and to attack the enemy in the left flank.

The XV AK commanding general had insisted on the return of 61 Bde. During the morning *Ersatz* Bn I, II and III moved left of II/RIR 15 at Les Séches and into the positions of the Prussian battalions on the south treeline of the Bois de Mandray, west of La Folie. The difficult relief in place certainly did not proceed without friction in the heavy woods and, at the very least, took considerable time. The departure of 61 Bde had perhaps generated the impression among the exhausted Bavarian *Ersatz* troops of being abandoned. At the same time, about noon, the French attacked, accompanied by hellish artillery fire that swept through the Bois de Mandray as far as Haute Mandray, where RIR 4 was located; the 1 *Ersatz* Bde commander, also at Haute Mandray, was wounded. The *Ersatz* battalions on the south treeline, and probably elements of 61 Bde, were under severe pressure and threatened in the left flank. They retreated across the low ground south-east of Mandray and towards the Tête de Behouille, pursued by artillery fire, which caused casualties and disorganisation; *Ersatz* Bn III broke up. *Ersatz* MGK 1 was only able to bring its ungainly wagons up the steep ridge west of the Tête de Behouille with the help of the artillery battery teams. RIR 4, positioned in and near Haute Mandray, was ordered to withdraw north to the high ground; its outposts stayed on the south treeline of the Bois de Mandray and were not attacked. There might have been considerable concern on the Tête de Behouille, but this lessened when the enemy did not pursue. In the course of the afternoon RIR 4 and *Ersatz* Bn I returned to Haute Mandray, while *Ersatz* Bn II and III, and II/RIR 15, went back to the area of Behouille at dusk. There were no enemy troops in the Bois de Mandray and the outposts took up positions on the south treeline. *Ersatz* Bn I, II and III, and II/RIR 15, were in bad shape, and they were consolidated into one unit the next day. 5 *Ersatz* Bde, which was in a sunken road near Mandray, was also engaged by French artillery fire into the German rear areas. The Rasch detachment (II/LIR 80 and LIR 81) were in an assembly area near Entre-deux-Eaux, with *Ersatz* Bn XI and Res. MGK 3 at Fouchifol, where they were joined by *Ersatz* Bn IX and X from Saulcy in the late afternoon.

The commander of the Bavarian ED had ordered the advance to the south treeline at La Folie and La Malfille to begin at 0600hrs, but the reports from the unit commanders convinced him that this was not possible. In particular, RIR 15 at St Croix had the strength of two weak companies due to numerous stragglers, and the morning was spent reorganising the units. There were only weak enemy outposts on the treeline south of the hairpin turn, but behind these there might be stronger forces, as the attack on the 30 RD made likely. At noon the Governor of Strasbourg attached 61 Bde, which had already begun its march back to XV AK, to the Bavarian ED. The Bavarian ED commander set the attack time at 1400hrs, to be conducted by IV/RIR 4, which had made strenuous marches from La Croix against Hill 782, north of La Folie, the previous day, but had not been engaged. *Ersatz* Bn XII would follow on the right, with *Ersatz* Bn IV on the left. The Rekowski detachment, which now included II/LIR 120 and the Breyer detachment (III/LIR 120, 10/LIR 71 and 6 and 7/LIR 81) were to support by fire and cover the left flank, if necessary offensively. 61 Bde, at least part of which was in the Bois de Mandray and west of La Folie, was to envelop the enemy left. RIR 15 was to continue assembling at La Croix, where Fortress MG Sec. 1 was also located. Some of the Bavarian ED artillery had opened fire on enemy positions and guns at Fraize. *Ersatz* FA Sec. I was again at positions on Hill 631, south of the Tête de Behouille. Near the attack time the artillery fire was concentrated on the treelines south of the hairpin curve.

RIR 4 moved out at 1400hrs with 13 and 14 on each side of the road that led south from Hill 643 to La Folie, with 15/RIR 4 following 13/RIR 4. 16/RIR 4 moved from the hairpin turn and took fire from the houses and the treeline to the south. By dark the battalion had taken the ridge north of La Folie and dug in while being shelled. *Ersatz* Bn XII and IV were at the north treeline behind the left and right flanks. *Ersatz* MGK 9, which required rest for man and horse, was left in La Croix.

To the right, 61 Bde had stormed the ridge and rocks to both sides of the road to La Folie, taking heavy losses, and elements pushed on through thorn bushes and creepers to the south treeline. Some elements, however, returned to Hill 704. On the left, the Rekowski detachment took up position just north of Hill 1022. Towards evening the RIR 4 attack seemed to stall, so III/LIR 120 and the two attached companies of LIR 81 attacked west. At dusk they encountered French Alpine troops and mountain guns in the wood and were held up, but finally fought through to the south treeline east of La Folie. III/LIR 71 and II/LIR 120 were also ordered to attack, but were prevented from doing so by artillery fire and the approach of night.

On 8 September 30 RD and the Bavarian ED mission was to defend in place, but the troops still did not get a thorough rest, although nothing of note happened except indecisive artillery duels; enemy artillery fire on the infantry positions caused several casualties. 10 Res. Bde was at and south of Saulcy, 5 *Ersatz* Bde in Mandray with *Ersatz* Bn VIII forward at Le Faubourg, 1 *Ersatz* Bde was in Haute Mandray, and the combined 'regiment' composed of II/RIR 15 and the remnants of *Ersatz* Bn I, II and III was at Behouille. *Ersatz* Bn IX, X and XI were in an assembly area 500m east of Haute Mandray. 1 Res./Eng. Bn 15 was divided into platoons to assist preparing fortifications. The Rasch detachment was initially at Entre-deux-Eaux, but elements relieved RIR 14 in place at Saulcy.

Three guns of 5/Res. Foot Artillery R 10 (sFH) were hauled individually, with enormous difficulty and with the help of sixty infantrymen, up the wooded ridge south of the hairpin turn, which was covered with fallen trees, to set up directly behind the trenches. Between 0700hrs and 0800hrs enemy infantry moved from Sarupt against the Rekowski detachment east of La Folie, but were stopped by fire at long range. IV/RIR 4 and 2 *Ersatz*/Eng. Bn 15, north of La Folie, were not attacked, but were hard hit by artillery fire. 61 Bde, in the woods between La Folie and Les Seches, had already taken casualties from enemy artillery fire when the right flank was threatened, and withdrew to Hill 704. The Bavarian ED commander ordered them to reoccupy their positions at 0840hrs. At the same time, 9 *Ersatz* Bde was to attack from La Folie into the enemy right flank with *Ersatz* Bn XII, reinforced by RIR 15 and Fortress MGK 1, which moved from St Croix, as well as *Ersatz* MGK 9.

61 Bde reported that the troops were completely exhausted, had not received rations for hours, that the units were at much reduced strength, had lost nearly all of their officers, and were in no condition to attack. The Bavarian ED commander insisted that the attack be made; the troops deployed, but barely moved forward. The 9 *Ersatz* Bde attack also did not take place. IV/RIR 4 was unable to hold its ground in the face of the French artillery fire and the battalion commander withdrew it at noon to the high ground east of the hairpin turn. The three howitzers that had been hauled up the ridge, which had in any case been smothered by counter-battery fire, were lost. The enemy took the narrow woods on the ridge north-east of La Folie and, at 1500hrs, put rifle fire on RIR 15, which held the south slope of Hill 704. I/RIR 15, on the left, took up the firefight, and

III/RIR 15, on the right, first pushed 11/RIR 15 into the Bois de Mandray, then 10/RIR 15; they encountered enemy troops well hidden in the undergrowth and bracken, suffered severe casualties and withdrew. A platoon of 2 *Ersatz*/FAR 13 fired from a position 800m south-west of La Croix against the Bois de Mandray, west of the road to Fraize. Fortress MGK 1 also added fire support.

Both flanks of II/LIR 120, 6 and 7/LIR 81, I/LIR 80 at La Malfille were now unprotected. When they began receiving artillery fire, they withdrew to the south-west slope of Le Grand Rien. Brigadier General Rekowski sent III/LIR 71 and half of II/LIR 120 as reinforcements, but these came too late and were also forced to withdraw by artillery fire.

During the afternoon, streams of stragglers entered La Croix. The Governor of Strasbourg was in the town and decided he could not continue to expose his troops to the enemy artillery fire. The Bavarian ED commander, also at La Croix, was told to give up the Bois de Mandray and hold the high ground to the north. 61 Bde was to suspend its attack; it had taken the north treeline from weak enemy forces, but now fell back to Hill 704. 9 *Ersatz* Bde moved to the Tête de Behouille and relieved 61 Bde the next day. The Rekowski detachment was told to hold the ridge east of St Jean, echeloned left. The situation in the 30 RD and Bavarian ED caused concern at XIV AK and Sixth Army HQ, and led to the transfer of 55 *Ersatz* Bde from Lorraine to XIV RK; it would initially move by rail to Markirch.

Between Lunéville and the West Slope of the Vosges, 3–8 September

(Map 21) Since the right wing of Seventh Army made no progress after 3 September, neither could the left wing of Sixth Army. I b. AK defended in place from 3–7 September: 6 and 7 September were completely quiet. On the evening of 7 September OHL ordered Sixth Army to move a corps at the railheads at Mörchingen and Bensdorf by 10 September for deployment to Belgium: Rupprecht chose I b. AK. On the night of 7–8 September both divisions set combined-arms advance guards in motion. The period between 3–8 September was also quiet in the XXI AK sector.

(Map 27) It was quite different in the II b. AK sector south of Lunéville. On 4 September Sixth Army had received reports that the French had moved two corps away from the Belfort–Toul front. At 1600hrs 4 ID reported that it had the impression the enemy to the front had disappeared. At 1750hrs II b. AK HQ ordered 4 ID to conduct reconnaissance in force, sending a battalion that evening to Rehainviller; at 0430hrs on the following morning 4 ID was to take the Bois St Mansuy and Bois de Bareth, and 3 ID the Bois de Coyard and the Bois de la Reine. This was reported to Sixth Army, which ordered the corps to advance immediately to the Mortagne. An aerial reconnaissance report that arrived at corps HQ at 1920hrs said that there were no enemy troops between the Mortagne and Moselle, not even vehicle parks

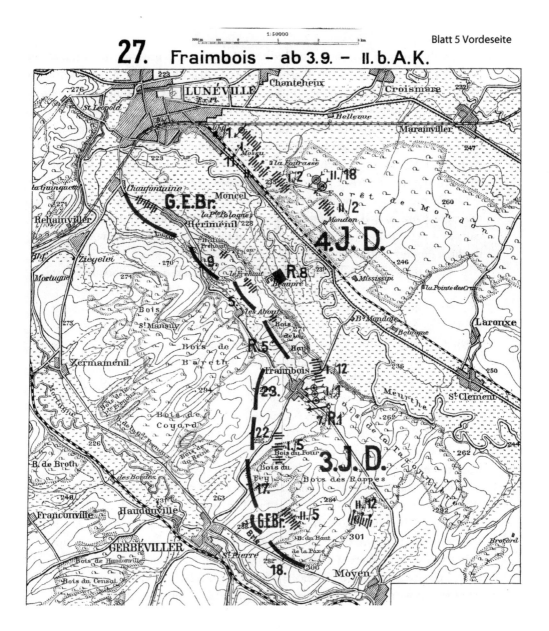

27.   Fraimbois – ab 3.9. – II. b.A.K.

Blatt 5 Vordeseite

and supply dumps. In the meantime, 4 ID reported enemy forces in the Bois de St Mansuy and Bois de Bareth, and 3 ID reported strong enemy forces in general, so II b. AK kept the 1750hrs corps order in force, with the attacks to begin at 0430hrs the next morning.

Only the Guard *Ersatz* Bde, attached to 4 ID, had an offensive mission on the evening of 4 September, to take Rehainviller. The Guard *Ersatz* Bde succeeded in doing so, at a high price, against enemy forces twice as strong (eight companies). The next morning overpowering enemy artillery fire forced the evacuation of the village.

In order to better support the attack, I/FAR 11 was brought back over the Meurthe to its old position on both sides of Hériménil, II/FAR 2 to Fréhaut, while II/FAR 11 overwatched from the Forêt de Vitrimont, north-east of Moncel. At noon II/FAR 2 pulled back to the east of Mondon.

On the morning of 5 September the Guard ED was brought forward to guard the right flank of 4 ID at Hériménil. The Guard *Ersatz* Bde (minus the two battalions detached to 3 ID) attacked again in the direction of Rehainviller and the high ground south of the town, taking heavy casualties.

In the 4 ID sector, 7 Bde, with RIR 5 attached, attacked at 0400hrs. The first line was formed, right to left, by I and III/IR 9, III and I/IR 5 and II/RIR 5. In spite of heavy defensive fire, IR 9 stormed the trenches on the treeline of the Bois de St Mansuy, but then took heavy flanking fire. IR 5, with II/RIR 5, pushed 800m into the Bois de Bareth, where they became entangled in thick undergrowth and encountered all manner of abbatis, barbed wire and tough resistance. There were heavy casualties, the units became intermixed and lost contact with each other; wild rumors spread. Some of the IR 5 and IR 9 reserves were committed early. At 0900hrs both regiments had to return to their defensive positions. Only elements of III/IR 9 maintained their hold on enemy trenches 200m from the edge of the woods and later were able, under cover of fire support from the mortars of II/Foot Artillery R 18, to recover MGs whose crews had been wiped out. The 7 Bde commander ordered RIR 5 to pull out of the Bois de Bareth in order to allow the artillery to fire. But since the right flank of 3 ID was deep into the Bois de Coyard, he ordered it to renew the attack at 0915hrs, which was to be conducted from the left in echelon. It was noon before the advance got going. Once again, there was tough enemy resistance, and once again IR 5 and RIR 5 pushed into the wood (since 4 September, I/RIR 5 was commanded by a first lieutenant); this time they were able to maintain themselves there. IR 9 was so disorganised that it was not able to attack again.

In the 3 ID sector, only two battalions of 5 Bde attacked: by 0700hrs, and in spite of heavy defensive fire, III/IR 23 reached the Bois de Coyard, and a battalion formed from half III/IR 22 and half of II/IR 23 entered the Bois de la Reine, supported by I/FAR 12 on Hill 284, west of Fraimbois. In the woods they took fire from invisible enemies in trees and fortified hideouts, as well as artillery fire, which caused such severe losses that they returned to Fraimbois at noon. II/IR 23 was badly dispersed, but quickly reassembled around the unfurled standard. In the 6 Bde sector, a weak enemy attack at 0200hrs against I/IR 18 in the south-west corner of the Bois du Haut de la Paxe was easily driven off, and the counter-attack at dawn against the French trenches on Hill 282 just in front of the treeline captured several abandoned French guns; the enemy retreated in masses to Gerbéviller. At 0800hrs several battalions of 31 ID on the left joined the advance, and III/IR 18, on the left of I/IR 18 at the south edge of the Bois du Haut de la Paxe (II/IR 18 still had not been reconstituted), sent a few platoons to the Mortagne Valley, which had been evacuated by the enemy, and a platoon of 12/IR 18 captured seven abandoned MGs on bicycles. Right of IR 18 the two attached Guard *Ersatz* battalions and IR 17 moved on Gerbéviller around noon; the Guard was stopped and IR 17 fully disorganised by artillery fire. Nevertheless, by 1300hrs II and III/IR 17 were firmly established in the town, which also had been abandoned by the enemy. I/IR 17, following behind the right flank, was drawn by flanking fire north into the Bois de la Reine. IR 22 (I/IR 22 also had not been reconstituted) was sent towards the same wood around noon and took such heavy artillery fire that some companies were dispersed. II/IR 22 succeeded in clearing out the wood, which was only weakly held, and by 1500hrs had advanced to the south treeline. III/IR 22 followed. In order to support the IR 17 and IR 22 attack, I/FAR 12 and 1/FAR 5 set up on Hill 295, west of the Bois du Four; the rest of I/FAR 5 remained limbered up and ready to move if necessary to Gerbéviller. IR 23 moved out of its positions west of Fraimbois to a position south of the town behind Hill 295 in order to attack south; this movement was disrupted by enemy artillery fire, which caused casualties, and the regiment was not committed.

The enemy had clearly not given up the area between the Moselle and the Mortagne; in the 4 ID sector they were east of the Mortagne in good positions between Xermaménil and Rehainviller. In view of its apparently reduced strength, the French infantry no longer intended to attack, but protected the artillery.

The reconnaissance in force had clarified the situation. It is true that the II b. AK HQ had ordered the troops to take and hold the south-west sides of the wooded zone between the Meurthe and Mortagne, but that evening ordered a return to the old positions, undoubtedly because the construction of new positions, under enemy shellfire, would have brought losses without significantly improving the situation. XXI AK had also withdrawn its troops, which had advanced over the Mortagne, in order to reduce the effect of the enemy artillery. The withdrawal of both II b. AK divisions was conducted undisturbed under cover of darkness. The order never reached II/RIR 5 in the Bois de Bareth, and it advanced during the night as far as the south-west side of the woods without encountering enemy forces. It was contacted around noon on 6 September and returned without difficulty. The action on 5 September caused the II b. AK severe casualties, and to a degree eliminated the gain in strength produced by the arrival of replacements. However, it helped the troops recover from the effect of the recent reverses.

The situation in the II b. AK sector remained tense. Since an enemy withdrawal was possible, patrols, sometimes reinforced with engineers equipped with hand grenades, were continually entering the forests to the front. On 7 September I/RIR 5, with two platoons of I/IR 5 on the right, pushed 600m into the Bois de Bareth and overran French trenches; 4/IR 5 even reached Hill 294. At the same time, 3 and 4/RIR 8 moved 1km along the south edge of the Bois de Bareth, suffering some casualties; they were only withdrawn on 8 September. That morning half of III/IR 23 pushed into the Bois de Coyard, but immediately made contact. Here and there French troop concentrations were detected, which might have indicated an impending attack; reserves were moved to the threatened sector. The elements of the Guard *Ersatz* Bde on the front line were relieved in place by 5 *Ersatz* Bde on 5 September. The mass of the Guard ED was in II b. AK reserve.

The enemy also sent out patrols; the approach of small groups of the enemy, especially at low-light periods, was often transformed by overstrained nerves into attacks, which led to mass, uncontrolled firing. The French did attack, in five waves, at 1700hrs on 8 September against the left flank of 3 ID, which in places seemed to be another false alarm, as the French remained at a harmless distance, firing ineffectively. Perhaps they wanted the German infantry to occupy its positions in order to create a target for their artillery. In the II b. AK sector the French XV Corps had moved off on 3 September and been replaced by 74 RD.

The Attack on the Nancy Position, 3–8 September (map 28, sketch 31)

Preparations

The core of the defensive position at Nancy was built around permanent and field fortifications constructed in the Forêt de Haye, west of Nancy, which covered the angle between the Meurthe and Moselle. East of Nancy there were, in peacetime, only a few weak battery positions and trenches on a plateau barely 3km from the city. But a well-developed road system forward and to the flanks of the plateau indicated that the French intended to push the defence of Nancy further to the east in wartime; the watershed between the Meurthe and Selle invited such a measure. This ridge, between Pont-à-Mousson and Nancy, which followed the east bank of the Meurthe and Moselle, falls to the east quickly and steeply by 150–200m. Reports reaching Germany shortly before the outbreak of war said that work on this ridge had begun in the spring of 1914. Land had been

Night Battle at Hoéville and Ste. Libaire 2/3 September

Nachtgefecht bei Hoéville und Ste. Libaire 2./3. 9.

Textskizze 31.

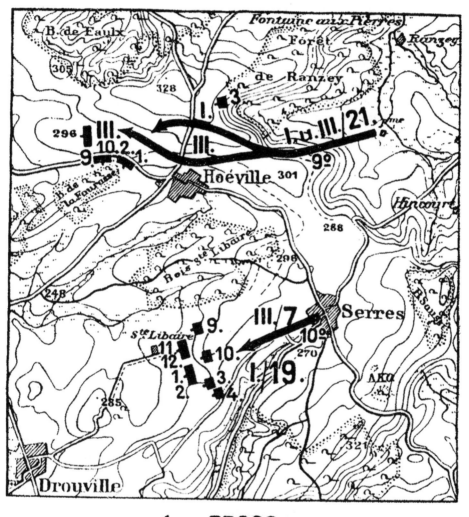

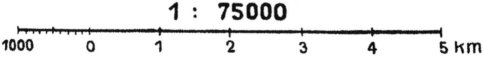

1 : 75000

purchased, roads and light rail lines built, woods cleared for fields of fire, building material brought up and the construction of various works were clear indicators. South of the road from Nancy to Château-Salins, the land flattens out and the position reached the Meurthe at Fort Varengeville, on the high ground halfway between Nancy and Lunéville

On 26 August OHL directed Sixth Army to bombard the fortified position at Nancy. On 30 August it issued a formal order to do so. Preparations began immediately. The experience of 25 August showed that the attack had to proceed according to siege warfare doctrine. Above all, the infantry had to be protected by the suppression of the enemy artillery. The construction of the necessary infrastructure – an extensive telephone net, reconnaissance, briefing aviators and assembling ammunition – would require considerable time. From the very beginning, OHL's demand for immediate action hindered these preparations.

On 31 August, Crown Prince Rupprecht issued the order governing the attack by the *Ersatz* Corps, III b. AK and I b. RK (reinforced by the *Landwehr* Div. Wening) on Nancy, and for the remainder of Sixth and Seventh Armies for the breakthrough between Toul and Épinal. The group under the commander of III b. AK was dissolved; Sixth Army would control the attack on Nancy. The first objective for the *Ersatz* Corps and III b. AK was the forward position north-east and east of Nancy; I b. AK was to throw the enemy south of Dombasle back over the Meurthe. The right flank would be covered by 55 *Ersatz* Bde and HKK 3, under the operational control of the commander, *Ersatz* Corps. Some corps boundaries were shifted, particularly between III b. AK and I b. RK, which was difficult due to the proximity to the enemy, and which delayed the attack.

Forces and equipment had to be brought forward from the fortresses of Metz, Strasbourg, Germersheim and Mainz, in particular the heavy artillery. The work crews 'arming' the fortresses (digging field fortifications between the permanent forts) would assist with ammunition resupply. The artillery was placed under the commander of the Bavarian Foot Artillery Bde. Beginning movement on 31 August, the artillery would mass on an arc about 11 km from the eastern edge of the city, from south of the road from Nancy–Château-Salins to the Meurthe, 5 km north-west of Lunéville. The guns, munitions and equipment were moved up with the greatest possible speed and immediately as they were available, which led to congestion on the roads and at the railheads. Nevertheless, the artillery commander and rail officials succeeded in conducting the rail move in the proper order and bringing the guns into position with adequate ammunition in four days. The batteries with horse teams were unloaded at Mörchingen, while those without horse teams were brought forward by rail to the north and south of Duß. The artillery in each corps area was formed into a 'brigade'. The corps were reinforced as follows:

Ersatz **Corps**

HQ 3 Foot Artillery Bde with vehicle park
HQ b. Foot Artillery R 2, b. Res. Foot Artillery R 3, b. *Landwehr* Foot Artillery R 3

7/Foot Artillery R 13 (10cm cannon 04)	4 guns
I/Res. Foot Artillery R 3 (10cm cannon 04)	16
II/Foot Artillery R 8 (15cm howitzer, vehicle-drawn)	8
II/b. Foot Artillery R 2 (fortress sFH)	24
I/b. Res. Foot Artillery R 3 (sFH 02)	16
Half of II/Res. Foot Artillery R 3 (sFH 02) 8	
I/b. Foot Artillery R 2 (21cm mortar)	16
I/Res. Foot Artillery R 12 (21cm mortar)	16
II/b. Res. Foot Artillery R 3 (21cm mortar)	16
28cm Mortar Bty Essen (vehicle-drawn)	1
42cm Mortar Bty 1 (vehicle-drawn)	2
Total 127	

Bavarian Eng. R
Fortress Airship Sec. Metz and Strasbourg
Bavarian Land Survey Sec.

III b. AK

HQ 2 b. Foot Artillery Bde with vehicle park
HQ Foot Artillery R 14, 8

II/Res. Foot Artillery R 10 (13cm cannon) 8	
II/Res. Foot Artillery R 13 (fortress sFH)	24
I/b. Res. Foot Artillery R 1 (sFH 02)	16
I/Foot Artillery R 12 (21cm mortar)	16
II/Res. Foot Artillery R 18 (21cm mortar)	16
Total 80	

II/Eng. Bn 15, II/Eng. Bn 16
Fortress Airship Sec. Germersheim
Fortress Airship Troop Metz
Fortress Searchlight Troop Germersheim
Land Survey Sec. Metz

I b. RK

HQ 4 Foot Artillery Bde and vehicle park
HQ b. Res. Foot Artillery R 1, Res. Foot Artillery R 10, Res. Foot Artillery R 13

Half of II/b. Res. Foot Artillery R 1 (10cm cannon 04)	8
I/Res. Foot Artillery R 10 (13cm cannon)	8

I/b. Foot Artillery R 3 (sFH 02)	16
II/Res. Foot Artillery R 14 (sFH 02)	16
8/Foot Artillery R 13 (21cm mortar)	4
I/Foot Artillery R 14 (21cm mortar)	16
30.5cm Mortar Bty 2 (steam tractor)	2
Total 70	

Eng. R 19
Bavarian Field Airship Sec.
Fortress Airship Troop Germersheim
Land Survey Sec. Strasbourg

Munitions

10cm cannon	1¾ day's supply
13cm cannon	1½
15cm fortress sFH	1
sFH 02	8¾
21cm mortar	10
28cm mortar	1
30.5cm mortar (β)	1
42cm mortar (γ)	1

OHL had assigned Sixth Army twenty-six munitions trains with heavy shells. This was an imposing mass of heavy artillery and ammunition, which was surely capable of smashing the enemy position and clearing the way for the infantry, given adequate time.

The positions of the *Ersatz* Corps and III b. AK were so far from the French fortified zone that even the heavy artillery did not have enough range to reach it. It was necessary to push the German front line forward to Mazerulles, Erbéviller, Réméréville, Drouville and Crévic. To prepare, III b. AK would attack on the night of 2/3 September to drive in the enemy outposts, which had become steadily stronger and more intrusive.

At 1600hrs on 2 September 5 ID ordered 9 Bde to attack at 2100hrs through Hoéville to Hill 296, and 10 Bde through Serres and the St Libaire Farm to Hill 285; each brigade would employ only two battalions, which would return before dawn. From 2000hrs to 2100hrs 5 FA Bde and the heavy artillery which was already in position (fifty-four 7.7cm, eight 15cm and eight 13cm guns) put massive preparatory fire on Hoéville and the woods to the west, the Bois St Libaire and the St Libaire Farm.

In the 9 Bde sector, IR 21 would attack with I and III/IR 21 and attached engineers. The troops dropped their packs and ammunition pouches and moved out at 2030hrs with fixed bayonets and unloaded weapons, with III/IR 21 in the lead and I/IR 21 echeloned right, in squad column across terrain illuminated by moonlight, preceded by a thin skirmisher line to guard against surprise. 3/IR 21, which had been on the treeline east of Hill 328 since 1 September, guarded the right flank. The high ground east of Hoéville was crossed on schedule at 2100hrs. The left flank of III/IR 21 guided on the north side of Hoéville and reached the road leading north from Hoéville with 9 and 10/IR 21 leading, 11 and 12 echeloned right and left, without encountering the enemy, and stopped there. In order to stay on the high ground, I/IR 21 swung in an arc in front of III/IR 21, and at 2145hrs took heavy fire at a range of 500m from the north end of the woods, west of Hoéville, and the high ground to the north. 2 and 1/IR 21 deployed into skirmisher line and bounded across the Hoéville–Réméréville road, with 4/IR 21 echeloned right. 9/IR 21, a platoon from 10/IR 21, and probably 12/IR 21, joined 2 and 1/IR 21, while the rest of III/IR 21 headed for enemy infantry on Hill 296, and a heavy firefight became general. They took fire on the right flank from the north side of Hill 296, and on the left from the bushes west of Hoéville. The elements of III/IR 21 engaged with Hill 296 pulled back to the road leading north from Hoéville. 10/IR 21 later went to assist 3/IR 21. The Bavarians lay in front of the woods west of Hoéville illuminated by moonlight, while 50m to their front the French were on a 600m-long line hidden in the shadow of the trees; success was out of the question, the more so because the troops only had the ammunition they could carry in their pockets and that was being used up quickly, while losses mounted. At midnight the commander of 9/IR 21 led his surviving troops back to Hoéville, and in order to reach German lines before dawn, the regimental commander ordered the battle broken off at 0200hrs, and the battalions moved back in groups. They had suffered serious casualties and the regimental commander was killed.

It went no better with the two battalions of 10 Bde, I/IR 19 and III/IR 7. Under the IR 19 commander and accompanied by a MG platoon and engineers, they reached Serres at 2200hrs and deployed at the bend in the road west of the village; III/IR 7 put 11 and 1/IR 7 in the first line, 9 and 10/IR 7 behind the open right flank, while I/IR 19 had 1 and 2/IR 19 in the front, with 3 and 4/IR 19 echeloned left. 8/IR 19 and 4/IR 7 covered the flanks at a considerable distance. At around midnight III/IR 7 approached St Libaire Farm, from which it took fire. The battalion went to ground, then assaulted, and took a hail of fire from buildings to the front and trees on the left flank; a wild, uncontrolled firefight developed. The Bavarian officers soon re-established calm, and the French fire was reduced as engineers threw hand grenades into the buildings; 11/IR 7 pushed through the farmyard to the far side. The III/IR 7 commander began to move 12/IR 7 to the left of St Libaire, and the French fire resumed, causing confusion. The battalion commander rallied the troops around him, and they stood fast without returning the fire. I/IR 19 now came up and also suffered some uncertainty and disorder, which was quickly brought under control. The fight swayed back and forth for an hour. Finally, the engineers set the farm on fire. In view of the enemy resistance, further progress was impossible, and at 0100hrs the IR 19 commander ordered a withdrawal, which was made in good order. It was possible to recover some of the wounded, but others had to be left behind, along with the dead, whose number was not inconsiderable.

In the 6 ID sector only two companies of IR 13, accompanied by engineers, attempted to conduct a reconnaissance in force from the regiment's position west of the Einville–Valhey road into the Bois d'Einville, and if possible chase away or capture enemy artillery on the west side of the wood. II/FAR 8 conducted a preparatory bombardment against the east side of the wood from 2030hrs to 2130hrs. At 2130hrs 8/IR 13 pushed from the south-east to the north edge of the wood, but took converging fire and was threatened with encirclement. It broke through and tried to push forward again, only to have the same experience. At the same time, 2/IR 13 moved from Einville to the west and was able to overrun French security outposts on the treeline. As it pushed north-west on a cut in the woods bordered by impenetrable undergrowth, it encountered a cleverly placed abbatis, and it was thanks only to the enemy's inactivity that it was not shot down on the narrow clearing. Both companies returned during the night.

The Bois d'Einville was only 600–700m in front of the IR 13 position and a source of continual problems, in particular providing enemy FOs with concealed positions. On the afternoon of 3 September II and I/IR 13 again attacked the east treeline in order to clear it out, with FAR 3 firing a preparation from 1300hrs to 1400hrs. The battalions quickly crossed the open low ground, entered the woods without meeting much resistance, and by 1600hrs reached their objective, the first cut in the forest, running south-west–north-east. The main body returned, leaving security detachments until dark, then listening posts at night.

These attacks did not always reach their objectives, but they accomplished their missions. The enemy outposts were driven back and they largely abandoned the terrain that the attack on the evening of 4 September initially had to cross. On 3 and 4 September III b. AK was able to advance the front line, both in order to move the artillery forward and to establish the conditions for the main attack.

For the same reasons, on 3 September the *Ersatz* Corps pushed 10 ED forward on both sides of Moncel, with 8 ED keeping pace 3km to the north. The heavy artillery arrived between 31 August and 2 September, but only I/b. Res. Foot Artillery R 3 (sFH 02) could go into position because the infantry had not gained enough ground, in particular on the west side of the Selle. 5 ID relieved 4 ED in place; 4 ED became *Ersatz* Corps reserve. At about 1300hrs on 4 September 5 ID was instructed to mass its forces forward as far as the outpost line; since the division was deployed in depth, this took hours.

On 3 September 6 ID gave up Einville and its positions to the south to 1 RD. On the morning of 4 September 6 ID pushed its outposts forward level with Serres. After noon the infantry brigades were ordered to move forward to the level of the Bois St Libaire. They were greeted by heavy artillery fire as they left the protective ridge at the Bois Saussi and moved downhill. Nevertheless, II/IR 6 on the right of 12 Bde reached the west side of the Bois St Libaire at 1500hrs, but the increasing enemy artillery fire brought it to a halt there. For the same reason, II/IR 11, moving from Serres, was only able to advance as far as the south-east side of the Bois St Libaire by dark. In the 11 Bde sector, III/IR 10, which took St Libaire Farm at 1600hrs, remained in the fields of grain to both sides. As III/IR 13 climbed the slope on the north-west corner of the Bois d'Einville, it took such effective fire from the enemy heavy artillery that it only reached its objective, the hairpin turn east of Drouville, at dusk. The remaining battalions of both divisions were deployed in depth on the high ground behind Serres. To support the infantry, the cannon batteries of 6 FA Bde were displaced forward in the early afternoon. Withdrawing enemy infantry and batteries west of Réméréville provided worthwhile targets. II/FAR 8 supported IR 6, and II/FAR 3 supported IR 10. All attempts to find and engage the enemy artillery were fruitless. FAR 3 drew heavy enemy artillery fire, as well as the attention of enemy aviators, who dropped bombs and sharpened steel darts. The heavy artillery that did not have organic horse teams, and their ammunition, were brought forward from the railheads by horses of other units during the evening of 4 September, often at the wrong time and place, which led to considerable unnecessary movement. The last unit, II/Res. Foot Artillery R 18 (21cm mortars), arrived on the night of 4/5 September. On the night of 2/3 September in the I b. RK sector, 5 RD shifted right and 1 RD went into the line to its right.

The fighting on the night of 2/3 September had shown that a renewed attack on the night of 3/4 September required more thorough preparation, and it was postponed. But reports received on 4 September in turn made it appear that further delay was not justified. That morning Erbéviller was reported free of enemy troops, and the order went out to closely observe the enemy. At noon reliable agent reports said that the French had withdrawn two corps from the Nancy–Belfort front. An aviator reported that the area between the Moselle and Mortagne was free of enemy troops. Crown Prince Rupprecht ordered that the three corps north of Lunéville occupy the terrain necessary for the employment of the heavy artillery, while II b. AK was to take the Mortagne Valley from Gerbéviller to its junction with the Meurthe, just south-west of Lunéville. XXI AK and I b. AK were to be prepared to attack west on 5 September. The Metz reserve, 33 RD, received orders from OHL to support Sixth Army with an attack from the north. Sixth Army also intended to advance west of the Moselle towards Pont-à-Mousson.

The First Step, 4–5 September

On the night of 4/5 September the *Ersatz* Corps was able to advance without particular difficulty to the area south-west of Brin–Mazerulles.

III b. AK HQ ordered its units, which were already in movement, to advance again at 2100hrs to take the line Bois Morel–Erbéviller–Réméréville–Courbesseaux–Drouville. However, the order arrived so late that not all of the units could meet the attack time. It was not possible to make any preparations for the attack, the approaching dark prohibited reconnaissance and the artillery could only fire a few rounds against the objectives.

In 5 ID the forward movement to the former outpost line was far from being completed, and the artillery had just begun to move. There was considerable moonlight, which facilitated movement without giving the enemy artillery enough light for observed fire, but removed the possibility of surprise. IR 19 on the right flank had the easiest time. It moved out at 2100hrs with I/IR 19 on the left and II/IR 19 on the right, quickly reached the west side of the Bois Morel and dug in, with III/IR 19 and the MGK in reserve near the Erbéviller–Mazerulles road.

The IR 7 objective was the high ground immediately west of Erbéviller. Although I/IR 7 and the MGK had not arrived, II and III/IR 7 advanced from the woods east of the village at 2100hrs. Soon after they entered open country they took rifle fire from Erbéviller, mixed with high-explosive and shrapnel shells. An attached platoon of 4/FAR 6 unlimbered, shot Erbéviller in flames and swept the trenches south of the town clean. The moonlight made it possible to conduct the fight like a daylight attack. The two battalions steadily gained ground, especially after 2300hrs when I/IR 7 came up to the left of II/IR 7. Both flanks were still unsupported and knowledge of this engendered rumours and reduced the troops' aggressiveness; it not until 0200hrs that I and II/IR 7 took the empty French trenches on the ridge west and south of Erbéviller without firing a shot. The commander of I/IR 7 led 4/IR 7 1km further west without encountering the enemy. The platoon of 4/FAR 6 unlimbered on the high ground occupied by II/IR 7 and fired its last shells down the road to Réméréville. At 0500hrs 3/FAR 6 arrived on the south edge of the Bois Morel and shelled Erbéviller, which allowed III/IR 7 to take the village and the high ground to the north. At 0600hrs 3/FAR 6 moved to the high ground south of Erbéviller to fire on the area near Réméréville.

In the 9 Bde sector, I/FAR 10 was able to take Réméréville under continual fire. The 9 Bde commander moved the attack time back to 2130hrs in order to give his units a little time to prepare. IR 21 was ordered to move 200m past the Erbéviller–Réméréville road and dig in. I, II and 11/IR 21 moved out on time, but they were stopped by heavy fire into the flank and possibly friendly artillery fire 500m short of the road. Only near dawn did they reach the road and the high ground south of Erbéviller, where I/IR 7 was already located. III/IR 21, which began the attack far to the rear, moved during the night, frequently harassed by enemy artillery fire, to Hill 305. At 0700hrs it reached a rise 200m north-west of Réméréville and fired into the flank of enemy trenches west of the town, forcing the French out of them. The brigade commander held the MGK back at Hoéville.

The IR 14 mission was to take Réméréville and the high ground to the west. It did not move out until 2230hrs, with I/IR 14 north of the road and II/IR 14 to the south, in march column behind a skirmisher screen, with III/IR 14, the MGK and the attached 4/Eng. Bn 15 following on the road 300m behind. There were numerous halts to insure control. At 2300hrs, 500m east of Réméréville, the lead units took what they thought to be friendly rifle fire, and called out 'Cease fire!' and 'Germans!' while continuing forward movement. It soon became clear that it was fire from enemy rifles and MGs in front of Réméréville and in the woods 1km south-east of the village. The lead units quickly deployed skirmishers, which at the beginning were very thick, one man next to the other. They took up the firefight and approached by bounds to within 300m from Réméréville; 2 and 4/IR 14 reached the road to Erbéviller. Initially, III/IR 14 took cover in shallow ditches along the road to Réméréville, but was soon committed, along with an MG platoon, to suppress enemy holding the woods on the left flank. At 2300hrs 2 and 3/FAR 10 moved to Hill 296, north-west of Hoéville, but were forced by rifle fire to pull back to the west slope of Hill 328. The men of IR 14 were slowly worn down by the night battle, particularly flanking fire from the right, which forced II/IR 14 to reorient in that direction. Casualties were more severe due to the dense formation. The officers were for the most part dead or wounded, and the men had no leadership. A cry of 'Withdraw!' was repeated and led to a few men dropping to the rear, which grew by 0330hrs to a general retreat. The brigade, regimental and battalion commanders, their staffs and other officers used signals, whistles, shouts and singing 'The Watch on the Rhine' to stop the regiment halfway to Hoéville. Many troops got past the officers; 300 were collected in Hoéville and brought back forward. Artillery support had been requested and, at 0430hrs, two guns from 3/FAR 10 appeared, unlimbered among the infantry and strengthened their self-confidence by immediately firing on Réméréville. In part under the leadership of officers from the brigade staff, IR 14 once again gained ground towards Réméréville. Several lucky hits from the guns destroyed a long stone wall on the north side of the town and put the French to flight; German pursuit fire paid the French back in kind. Elements of IR 14 stormed through the north side of the town behind the French as far as the Erbéviller road. The brigade commander asked for Res. *Jäger* Bn 2 from the division reserve and it arrived at 0700hrs, along with a company from II/Eng. Bn 15. They deployed on both sides of the Réméréville road, pushed into the disorganised IR 14 skirmisher line and pulled the attack forwards again, but on order stopped at 0900hrs, 2km from the town, to allow the artillery to soften it up. The attack was not renewed: IR 14 had suffered severe casualties, with eleven officers killed, including the commanders of I and III/IR 14. The regiment dug in 800m east of Réméréville. Reserve *Jäger* 2 moved right to fill the gap with IR 21.

On 5 September 5 ID dug in and reorganised, at times shelled by enemy artillery. III/IR 19 was moved to Hill 296 to support IR 14. After dark III/IR 21 was pulled back to the regimental left flank. During the morning I/b. Foot Artillery R 1 (sFH) occupied a position behind Hill 328 and, in conjunction with II/Res. Foot Artillery R 18 (21cm mortars), successfully engaged enemy artillery south-west and west of Réméréville.

During the afternoon of 4 September 6 ID was ordered to advance that night over the Réméréville–Courbesseaux–Drouville road. On the right flank, II/IR 6 left the north-west side of the Bois St Libaire and moved west at 2130hrs. It took fire from the south-east side of the woods, north-east of Courbesseaux, at 2230hrs, but did not return the fire and, instead, assaulted and overran three successive and weakly held trench lines in a single rush. By 2300hrs the battalion was on the slope north-east of Courbesseaux, but had lost contact with IR 14 on the right and never even established contact with IR 11 on the left, while taking fire from both flanks as well as to the front. IR 6 was now commanded by a captain, who permitted the battalion to withdraw to the Bois de St Libaire before dawn. III/IR 6 and MGK/IR 6 were brought forward to Hoéville and the west side of the Bois de St Libaire in support; I/IR 6 was brigade reserve in Serres.

I/IR 11 advanced from the north-east corner of the Bois de St Libaire, on the trail from Serres to Courbesseaux, and II/IR 11 moved through the south side of the wood (III/IR 11 was division reserve at Foucray la Basse). As soon as they were west of the wood they suddenly took intense artillery fire, which brought such heavy casualties that they retreated back to the trenches. The officers succeeded in preventing a greater misfortune and re-established order. A renewal of the attack was out of the question.

While III/IR 10 assembled east of St Libaire Farm, I/IR 10 left its bivouac area 400m south-west of Serres at 2130hrs and advanced through the Bois de St Libaire to Hill 285, 800m north-east of Drouville. To the south, II/IR 13 moved towards the hairpin turn in the road east of Drouville and approached Hill 285 by midnight. After a short firefight it drove the enemy out of a small wood there. I/IR 10 came up and a blue-on-blue firefight began, which lasted until daylight, when enemy artillery fire began to fall, with some of the troops seeking cover in the captured enemy trenches. The artillery fire grew more accurate and effective, and squads, platoons and, finally, entire companies began to withdraw; I/IR 10 was pulled back to Serres, and in the afternoon II/IR 13 withdrew to the north side of the Bois d'Einville. During the night I/IR 6 collected stragglers and returned them to their units.

6 FA Bde was not in position to support the attack at 2100hrs. During the night, FAR 8 was in march column on the road east of Hoéville and prepared to follow the infantry. On the morning of 5 September I/FAR 8 was able to set up west and north of the town; II/FAR 8 had to turn around to unlimber north-east of Serres, and only between 1100hrs and 1500hrs were the three batteries moved in succession to the south side of the Bois de St Libaire. FAR 3 was moved on the evening of 4 September to the area on both sides of Valhey, but shortly after midnight I/FAR 3 moved forward positions west and south-east of Serres, and fired on enemy batteries and trenches in the area of Courbesseaux–Drouville–Bois de Crévic, while taking counter-battery fire. II/Res. Foot Artillery R 13 (sFH) moved during the morning to the east of the Bois de St Libaire, and I/Foot Artillery R 12 advanced to a position 200m north-west of Serres.

During the night of 4/5 September, 6 ID was unable to take its objectives and was considerably behind the left flank of 5 ID. The attack was therefore not resumed that evening, as originally planned, but at 1530hrs. The troops, who were already worn out by the previous night's combat, were given only a few hours' rest. The 5 ID artillery was to support with flanking fire, but had great difficulty conducting the artillery duel with the French guns to its front, which even if they could be found could often only be reached by the mortars. On the other hand, the artillery of both divisions could effectively engage the enemy infantry, and the towns of Courbesseaux, Gellenoncourt and Drouville were set on fire.

Perhaps for this reason, the attack by 6 ID at 1530hrs met little resistance. 12 Bde left the cover of the Bois de St Libaire with III/IR 6 on the right, which moved to the woods north-east of Courbesseaux. II/IR 6 took enemy trenches south of the Courbesseaux–Hoéville road and, by dark, was east of the village, which was only entered by patrols. I/IR 6 and the MGK were in Hoéville and the woods to the south-west. The enemy occupied terraced trenches on the high ground west of Courbesseaux and brought artillery fire down on any movement by III/IR 6. When IR 11 left the west side of the Bois de St Libaire, it was also greeted by artillery fire, but by dark I/IR 11 and II/IR 6 had driven the enemy from his trenches on the ridge east of Courbesseaux–Drouville. They were relieved in place by III/IR 6 and withdrew to the Bois de St Libaire.

In the 11 Bde sector, IR 10 crossed the high ground to both sides of St Libaire Farm, with II/IR 10 on the right, III/IR 10 on the left, I and MGK/IR 10 following. They bounded forward against lively enemy fire to take the ridge north of Drouville by dark (committing I/IR 10 to the attack) and for a time even crossed over the road. The IR 13 attack was somewhat delayed, with III/IR 13 departing from the hairpin turn east of Drouville, covered by the fire of the MGK. III/IR 13 attempted to bypass Drouville to the left as ordered, but received such heavy fire from there that it had to turn in that direction and swept through the town, which stood in flames. At 1700hrs I/IR 13 was committed south of Drouville. Supported by the MGK and artillery, it succeeded in climbing the weakly held high ground south-west of Drouville, although it drew flanking fire from the Bois de Crévic. II/IR 13 was not yet combat-ready and bivouacked in Serres.

The batteries of 6 FA Bde quickly followed the infantry. I/FAR 8 supported IR 6 from the south edge of the woods north-east of Courbesseaux. From 1730hrs onwards II/FAR 8 sent forward individual platoons, which were followed an hour later by the complete batteries: 5 and 6/FAR 8 on the south-west side of the Bois de St Libaire, and 4/FAR 8 from Hill 285, north-east of Drouville. As of 1700hrs FAR 3 came forward, first by platoon, then by batteries: 6/FAR 3, two platoons of 4 and 5/FAR 3 and one of 3/FAR 3 to Hill 285; a platoon of 5/FAR 3 on the ridge south-east of Courbesseaux; two platoons of 3/FAR 3, one of 4/FAR 3 and then 2/FAR 3 to the hairpin turn. The guns on Hill 285 took heavy casualties from direct hits. But the arrival of artillery, which suppressed or drove off the enemy in the trenches in the ridge west of Courbesseaux–Drouville, massively increased the infantry's confidence.

On the night of 4/5 September the I b. RK mission was to take Drouville–Bois de Crévic–Flainval–Anthelupt–Vitrimont. The corps had been strongly reinforced with heavy artillery: II/Res. Foot Artillery R 14 (sFH) was brought far forward during the night to 1km east of Deuxville, and I/Foot Artillery 14 (21cm mortars) to Le Charmois. Out of concern for the effectiveness of the enemy artillery, the I b. RK commander decided to conduct a night attack; only on the far right flank would the attack be conducted by day, to support 6 ID.

1 Res. Bde therefore was ordered to attack on the afternoon of 4 September to take the west side of the Bois d'Einville and hold it until 2 Res. Bde, which was to attack at 2100hrs, came up to the south of Maixe on its left. 1 Res. Bde received the attachment of 2/RFAR 1 and three engineer companies: 1 Res./b. Eng Bn 1, 4/Eng. Bn 19 and 2 Res./Eng. Bn 19. It moved out from the bivouac areas east of Crion at 1400hrs through Hénaménil and Bauzemont behind IR 13, which was holding the high ground between Valhey and Einville, and deployed with RIR 1 right and RIR 2 left. The approach march in the heat caused many casualties. The east side of the Bois d'Einville was reported free of the enemy, and at 1800hrs the brigade commander ordered the regiments to advance. RIR 1, with 1 Res./b. Eng. Bn 1, moved through the north side of the woods, where the undergrowth was so thick that the companies sometimes had to move in single file, and it reached the west side at dusk, without making enemy contact. RIR 2, with the two Eng. R 19 companies, moved south into the woods in a column, drove off French stragglers and reached the south-west end at 1945hrs. The regiments lost contact with each other. When it became dark, 2/RFAR 1 was released. Acting

on a request from the RIR 2 commander, the brigade commander ordered RIR 2 to attack at 2100hrs to take Hill 316, north-west of Maixe, while RIR 1 took the northern spur; the order did not reach RIR 1 until 2300hrs. RIR 2 attacked Hill 316, infamous from the combat of 25 August, with III and half of II/RIR 2 (6 and 7/RIR 2) and took salvoes of fire in front from rifles and MGs on the hilltop, as well as fire from Maixe on the left flank. 4/RIR 2 was deployed against Maixe, while 2/RIR 2 lengthened the III/RIR 2 left flank. 1 and 3/RIR 2, and the two engineer companies, remained in the Etang streambed. Around midnight the platoons of the MGK were divided amongst the battalion and returned the enemy fire as best they could in the dark. RIR 1 took artillery fire when it reached the west side of the Bois d'Einville, deploying II/RIR 1, half of III/RIR 1 (9 and 10/RIR 1) and I/RIR 1 in the first line, with 11 and 12/RIR 1 behind the middle and the MGK/RIR 1 on the north-west corner of the Bois d'Einville. It was not possible to make reconnaissance and the other preparations necessary for an orderly night attack: it is no wonder that the skirmisher lines broke apart, got lost and interfered with each other. The objective was occupied by the enemy, who gave off heavy defensive fire. Nevertheless, 600–800m was gained in the first push, and the regiment dug in generally along the line of the path from Serres to Crévic, with the right flank pulled back 150m due to flanking fire.

In the meantime, 1 Res. Bde and RIR 2 waited for 2 Res. Bde to come up and relieve the pressure on the left flank. It was not possible to establish communication between the two brigades because the Sanon Valley between Maixe and Einville was controlled by French patrols. Shortly after 0100hrs, a report arrived that 2 Res. Bde had overrun the first enemy position, but this had no effect on the RIR 2 situation. At 2300hrs a LNO from 6 ID had reported that the west side of the Bois de St Libaire and the hairpin turn to the east of Drouville had been taken without a shot fired. At 0310hrs the 1 Res. Bde commander decided he could wait no longer and gave the order to attack. The initial objective for RIR 1 was the Maixe–Drouville road, while RIR 2 would only move out when the situation on its left flank permitted. When there was still no sign of 2 Res. Bde by 0420hrs, the 1 Res. Bde commander asked the RIR 2 commander if he could attack nevertheless, and at 0445hrs RIR 2 moved out. A few minutes later, 1 Res. Bde received a message from 1 RD saying that 2 Res. Bde had taken the high ground south of Maixe and that 1 Res. Bde should not advance beyond Hill 316. Nevertheless, the 1 Res. Bde commander decided to allow the attack to continue, and asked 1 RD to ensure adequate artillery support at daylight to avoid a repetition of 25 August.

In RIR 2, a number of stragglers from the approach march on 4 September rejoined the unit, and 5 and 8/RIR 2, which had found no support on the west side of the Bois d'Einville, rejoined the regiment on the south side. 1/RIR 2, reinforced by stragglers and a platoon of 8/RIR 2, was ordered to clear out

Maixe. Initially, the troops took such heavy fire that they were forced back to the woods, which were being held by 5/RIR 2. But through a skilful and surprise advance they forced the enemy out of the town. The mass of the regiment – 2, 6, 7 and III/RIR 2, with 4/RIR 2 on the left flank, and supported by the MGK – attacked Hill 316 at 0500hrs. In spite of heavy rifle fire, the trenches were quickly stormed and the regiment descended the west side of the hill. They now took small arms and MG fire from the Bois de Crévic and the Crévic–Maixe road, as well as artillery fire, especially in the flank from guns at Flainval: the advance stalled. The enemy seemed to counter-attack from the Bois de Crévic, and strong enemy detachments on the road, which had been in full retreat, turned around and advanced against the RIR 2 left flank, forcing the I/RIR 2 commander to commit 3/RIR 2, his last reserve. A furious firefight developed, but the enemy, heavily supported by artillery, was superior, and the skirmisher line began to crumble. However, Captain Ditteberger, the I/RIR 2 commander, in spite of numerous wounds, walked the firing line upright and his men held their positions. In III/RIR 2 the MG platoon was the backbone of the defence, both due to its effective fire and the determination of the platoon leader, who dealt ruthlessly with any weakness. In spite of heavy casualties, RIR 2 held Hill 316. It even appears that the right wing (6, 7, 9 and 11/RIR 2) pushed into the north end of the Bois de Crévic and linked up there with RIR 1, but enemy artillery fire prevented further advance. The French trenches on the north spur of Hill 316 were taken, but in general the advance was stopped after 300m. I/RIR 1 and II and III/RIR 2, which had entered the Bois de Crévic, turned back at 0800hrs.

On the afternoon of 4 September in the 2 Res. Bde sector, RIR 12 held the line from Einville to La Rochelle while RIR 3 moved forward from Hénaménil, assembled behind it and conducted a forward passage of lines at 2100hrs, with I and II/RIR 3 in the first line, each in a diamond formation, and III/RIR 3 in marching column to the rear. The MGK and the attached 3/Eng. Bn 19 were divided up. To ensure control, there were halts at four phase lines. The first enemy trenches, which were probably only weakly held, were easily overrun, but as the regiment descended towards the streambed, it took fire from the woods to the front, which it had planned to bypass to the north and south. II/RIR 3 turned in this direction, engaged its attached MG and stormed the wood. But fire from Maixe led the battalion to swing that way and prevented movement in the direction of attack. I/RIR 3 was scattered by enemy artillery fire and had to reassemble, which cost considerable time. After the wood had been taken, I/RIR 3 was able to continue the advance and climb the north spur of Hill 291. III/RIR 3 was also disorganised by enemy artillery fire. 11/RIR 3 continued the advance, while 10/RIR 3 moved to clear out the woods, which was its mission according to the attack order. Instead of following 11/RIR 3, during the night 9 and 12/RIR 3 followed 10/RIR 3: the battalion could not be reassembled until 0200hrs. Towards morning I/RIR 3 began to dig in south of Maixe, with III/RIR 3 behind it. II/RIR 3 did not arrive to the right of I/RIR 3 until the evening of 5 September. 3/RIR 3 was given the mission of clearing out the valley between Einville and Maixe. It left Raville at 0500hrs, but 600m from Maixe took fire from the houses and church tower. It drove the enemy off, probably in conjunction with 1/RIR 2, but did not enter the town, which was set on fire by the German artillery.

Between 0800hrs and 0900hrs RIR 2 had been forced to evacuate Hill 316, in part because it had run out of ammunition; it moved, in reduced strength but in good order, covered by 1 and 8/RIR 2 at the west side of the Bois d'Einville, 1.5km north of Maixe. Outposts stayed on Hill 316 and were joined by troops who had pushed farther west. The commander of 1 RD sent RIR 12 (minus III/RIR 12) to assist 1 Res. Bde. I/RIR 12 arrived at 0900hrs and relieved RIR 2 in place; it moved to Einville. 1 *Landwehr* Eng. Co./I b. AK assembled material in Einville to build footbridges and assisted with evacuating the wounded and collecting stragglers.

1/RFAR 1 moved forward at 0800hrs, with considerable difficulty, to the high ground north-east of Maixe to support 1 Res. Bde, followed ninety minutes later by 3/RFAR. An officer of the division staff moved 2/RFAR 1 to Hill 247, south-east of Maixe. During the early morning 1 and 2/Foot Artillery R 3 (sFH) displaced forward to the north edge of the Bois d'Einville, with 3/Foot Artillery R 3 (sFH) following that evening; I/Res. Foot Artillery R 10 (13cm cannons) moved to the area north of Crion.

For the attack on the night of 4/5 September, the commander of 5 RD gave 9 Res. Bde the high ground north-west of Deuxville as the initial objective, and the high ground to both sides of Léomont as the 11 Res. Bde objective, to be followed by an advance to the east side of Athelupt. The positions of RFAR 5 had not changed in the last several days. At 2000hrs the artillery conducted preparatory fire on the terrain leading to the initial objectives; the infantry advanced at 2100hrs, with unloaded weapons and fixed bayonets, and instructions to advance quietly and only yell 'Hurrah!' when they broke into the enemy position.

In the 9 Res. Bde sector, RIR 6, with 1/Eng. Bn 19 attached, advanced from an assembly area on Hill 276, south-east of Bonviller, with I and II/RIR 6 in the first line. RIR 7, with 1 Res./Eng. Bn 19, was to its left, with II and III/RIR 7 forward. III/RIR 6, I/RIR 7 and the two MGKs were to follow 50–100m behind and carry pioneer tools in order to quickly dig in on the objective. Wagons of building material also followed. A skirmisher screen would protect the battalions, which advanced in close formation. RIR 7 guided its left flank on the north end of Deuxville, while RIR 6 advanced on both sides of Hill 276. Initially, the movement proceeded undisturbed and in good order, with enemy outposts withdrawing. Serious resistance was encountered on the ridge north-east of

Deuxville, but was swept away by II and III/RIR 7. However, this misled RIR 6 to swing left and caused confusion east of Deuxville, which was further increased when the enemy was again encountered in the orchards and vineyards north and east of the town. I/RIR 7 dropped the pioneer tools and entered the fight. There were incidents of friendly fire. Nevertheless, the enemy was overrun or forced to retreat. The commander of RIR 7 assembled about six thoroughly intermixed companies in the Deuxville churchyard and led them north of the town to Hill 285 at midnight. Elements of RIR 6, which had been gathered up by their leaders, seem to have joined them, and they covered I/RIR 7 as it eventually recovered the pioneer tools and began to dig in north-east of Deuxville, albeit disturbed by enemy fire. III/RIR 6 was the only unit to maintain the correct direction of march. 10/RIR 6, the lead unit, took heavy fire at 2130hrs and was supported by 9/RIR 6, but encountered a water-filled streambed lined with barbed wire. They took serious casualties and 11 and 12/RIR 6, and the engineer company, were committed; the enemy did not retreat until a MG platoon opened fire at 0200hrs. The battalion set up on the south-west side of the streambed and dug in, established contact with RIR 3, and was joined later by elements of II/RIR 6.

11 Res. Bde advanced with RIR 10 on the right and RIR 13 on the left, while Res. *Jäger* Bn 1 closed up on RIR 13. The last battalions, I/RIR 10 and III/RIR 13, were carrying pioneer tools, although 2/Eng. Bn 19 was attached to RIR 10 and 1 Res./b. Eng. Bn 2 to RIR 13. Soon after dark, 1 and 4/RIR 13 fought bloody battles on Hill 347, with 1/RIR 10 to the north of it, to secure these excellent battery positions for the artillery, which also led to enemy artillery fire on RIR 13.

The attack order does not seem to have reached all units on time. RIR 10 did not move out until 2145hrs, led by III/RIR 10 in a square formation, followed at a 50–100m interval by II/RIR 10 with four companies on line, the MGK 100m behind them, then I/RIR 10 and the engineers in marching column. Enemy artillery fire flew harmlessly overhead. Companies and battalions lost contact with each other and some pushed forward, so that the units became intermixed. The first enemy resistance was met on the high ground south of Deuxville and broken by II and III/RIR 10 with cold steel, not firing a shot. I/RIR 10 had left 3/RIR 10 near the line of departure and picked up 1/RIR 10 north of Hill 347, took flanking fire from the south side of Deuxville but evaded it moving by bounds. The regiment intended to make a temporary halt on the Deuxville–Vitrimont road, but was detected and fired on by enemy infantry and MGs located on the slope to the front. II and III/RIR 10, joined by 1 and 4/RIR 10, returned the fire and stormed the ridge. On the far right flank, 9/RIR 10, with elements from II/RIR 10, were about to overrun a French battery 400m to the front when they were forced back by supposedly friendly artillery fire, which also hit the rest of RIR 10. The regiment also took rifle and MG fire from the front and on both flanks. A panic threatened to break out, but was suppressed with iron firmness. I/RIR 10 began to dig in 50m down the reverse slope; the units were reorganised and, towards morning, III/RIR 10 occupied the position I/RIR 10 had dug. The MG teams carrying their heavy guns had fallen behind and, with the exception of one gun, drifted off to the right.

When RIR 13 moved out to the north of Lunéville towards Hill 347 at 2130hrs, with II/RIR 13 in front, followed by I and III/RIR 13, it was greeted by heavy fire from all kinds of weapons. The enemy, located in copses and foxholes, was overrun with the bayonet. II/RIR 13 ran into overwhelming French fire north of Vitrimont, took serious casualties and was stopped cold. I/RIR 13 came up and established itself at the crossroads on the left. III/RIR 13 reached Hill 347 and took fire on the left flank, but was able to reach the crossroads and dig in as ordered. The regiment was then ordered to advance on both sides of the road to Hudiviller; the entrenching tools were put aside and the advance resumed. Fire from the front, and especially from Vitrimont, soon forced a halt; a part of the regiment turned to take cover on the road embankment, facing south. The mass of the regiment was withdrawn to the start line, while II/RIR 13 remained to finish digging the strongpoint at the crossroads.

Reserve *Jäger* Bn 1 (minus 1 and the MGK/Res. *Jäger* Bn 1, which were left at the start line) was charged with protecting the left flank, and moved on the south side of Hill 347. The enemy abandoned his trenches there without firing a shot; the battalion only met resistance at the crossroads north of Vitrimont, taking heavy casualties. 3/Res. *Jäger* Bn 1, with 4/Res. *Jäger* Bn 1 to the left and 2/Res. *Jäger* Bn 1 to the right, stormed trenches held by two French companies. They advanced at a run down the road to Dombasle and threw back more enemy forces, in spite of fire from all directions. A Jäger platoon took a farm at the foot of Hill 337, shot down most of the French troops there and captured the rest, around thirty men, and three MGs; by this time it was 0300hrs. The *Jäger* were then sent to the area west of Vitrimont, to take up flank security to the south. In order to find cover from the enemy fire sweeping the fields, the battalion crept along the roadside ditches. As it was assembling in an orchard on the north-west side of Vitrimont, it received heavy fire from the town, which had been reported free of the enemy. Now under fire from all sides, the *Jäger* had to retreat north so quickly that only a part of the wounded could be brought off. As it approached RIR 13 near the crossroads, it was mistaken by the two attached engineer companies for the enemy and they launched a bayonet charge; the *Jäger* battalion commander ordered his men to lie down, advanced alone towards the oncoming engineers and clarified the situation.

Soon after midnight, I b. RK HQ at Crion recognised that the troops were not going to be able to take the second, final, objective early enough to be able to prepare cover against the enemy artillery fire. They were therefore ordered to stop on the first objective. At dawn 1 RD was still deployed as it had been during the night. 5 RD was able, as ordered, to leave only four battalions at dug-in strongpoints from the crossroads north of Deuxville to the crossroads north of Vitrimont, and withdraw the remaining battalions at 0400hrs behind the start line from the Einville road, west of Bonviller, to Lunéville. To support the infantry, RFAR 5 moved I/RFAR 5 forward to the high ground north-east of Deuxville, 4 and 5/RFAR 5 north of Hill 347, with 6/RFAR 5 to the east; they all immediately drew heavy French artillery fire and 3/RFAR 5, which had pushed 500m forward, was hard hit and had to evacuate its position.

6/RIR 13, reinforced by two MGs and two artillery pieces, advanced on the afternoon of 5 September to secure the farm on Hill 337, but took such heavy artillery fire that it suffered numerous casualties and was forced to turn back. Both the infantry company commander and the commander of II/Res. Foot Artillery R 14 were killed.

Otherwise, 5 September in the I b. RK sector was quiet. The troops dug in and the intermixed units sorted themselves out. RIR 2 had 50 per cent casualties, and many of the companies had lost all of their officers. Fortress Aviation Sec. Germersheim, at an airstrip near Saarburg, was attached to the I. b. RK. On the night of 4/5 September 6/LIR 10, with 7 and 10/LIR 10, moved halfway down the Lunéville–Vitrimont road to guard the corps left flank.

On 5 September there had been advances, and some setbacks, along the entire line in front of Nancy. The Kaiser appeared at Sixth Army HQ in Duß, bringing instructions from Moltke to attack primarily with heavy artillery and spare the infantry for the next two or three days, when the approach of Fifth Army would make itself felt. The OHL chief of ammunition, on the other hand, demanded strict economy with shells for heavy guns, particularly the 21cm mortars. Nevertheless, Rupprecht was determined to continue the attack, although the prospects of success seemed less promising. On 6 September the three corps in front of Nancy would consolidate their gains. The Seventh Army mission was still to take Rambervillers in order to clear the Sixth Army left flank and set the stage for the breakthrough between Toul and Épinal.

The *Ersatz* Corps continued to defend in place, with 8 and 10 ED on the first line, 55 *Ersatz* Bde behind the right wing, and 4 ED in reserve behind the centre. On 5 September I/b. Res. Foot Artillery R 3 (sFH) had been moved forward to 1km north of Mazerulles, and 6 and 7/b. Res. Foot Artillery R 3 (21cm mortars) were brought into position in the wood (La Grande Goutte) south-west of Moncel. During the night II/b. Foot Artillery R 2 (sFH) was moved close behind the forward 8 ED infantry on the treeline west of Brin. I/b. Foot Artillery R 2 (21cm mortars) still did not have any ammunition. The artillery duel against French guns on Hill 408 (Grand Mont) began on 5 September. Any French guns detected on the east slope were quickly destroyed, forced to move, or silenced. When the German shells landed, the French infantry fled from their trenches in panic. The hilltops and reverse slopes could only be engaged with the help of observation balloons, but their effective utilisation was restricted by the insufficient and overloaded telephone network, which forced the German guns to resort to unobserved area fire, which in turn suffered from a lack of accurate maps and adequately surveyed positions.

III b. AK re-established the occupation of the position in shifts; each regiment had a battalion in the trenches, one behind it in support and the third further to the rear in reserve. Since the mission was to protect the artillery, the front-line positions were placed on reverse slopes or hidden in folds in the terrain. On 6 September there was a continual artillery duel: both sides shelled the opposing infantry. The III b. AK artillery was unable to suppress the cleverly hidden French guns, but the aerial and balloon observers, and the surveyors, were clearly making progress in identifying and reporting the enemy gun positions.

I b. RK also organised its position, while the enemy artillery fire decreased considerably. RIR 2 enjoyed some badly needed rest. In the 5 RD sector, the farm on Hill 337 was occupied in turns by French and German patrols and was shelled by the opposing artillery. 6/RFAR 5 on the east slope of Hill 347 was able to put flanking fire on a French attack on Lunéville on the night of 6/7 September. On 9 September it was joined by 5/RFAR 5.

LIR 8 and 10 improved their positions in Lunéville and were reinforced on 6 September by LIR 122 and 1 *Landwehr* Eng. Co./I b. AK. Sweeping measures were taken to combat the appearance of intestinal diseases, including repairing the damaged water pipes. The woods on the east side of Lunéville were a constant problem, but it proved impossible to burn them down; a fortress searchlight platoon was brought up to illuminate them at night, but nevertheless every night there were continual false alarms, as well as exchanges of gunfire and actual attacks.

The Second Step, 7–8 September

On 6 September Rupprecht came to the conclusion that the enemy was attempting to hold firm between Nancy and Épinal. Therefore it seemed important to reduce the outer works of the Nancy Position, particularly the southern cornerstone at Varengeville, for this significantly narrowed the avenue of approach to the Moselle. I b. RK was given the mission of taking it, with the assistance of III b. AK, while the *Ersatz* Corps would support III b. AK by suppressing the enemy artillery near Hill 408 and taking the hill itself. The orders issued by these three corps stipulated attacks at widely varying times. II b. AK, XXI AK and I b. AK would observe the enemy and follow him if he withdrew. Captured enemy documents pointed to a French attack on 7 September. The uncertain situation led the corps to assume a more defensive rather than offensive posture and to conduct much back-and-forth movement.

On the evening of 6 September Sixth Army assumed command over the Seventh Army units, so that its area of operations extended to the Swiss border. XIV RK, 30 RD and the Bavarian ED were put under the operational control of the XIV RK commander (Corps Schubert), while 19 ED and the 60 *Landwehr* Bde were subordinated to XIV AK. There were no changes to the overall mission.

On the evening of 6 September the OHL chief of ammunition appeared personally at Sixth Army HQ and requested the release of the heavy artillery with ammunition along with the suspension of the attack on the Nancy Position, in favour of attacking Antwerp, Paris and the intermediate forts between Toul and Verdun. Rupprecht and his chief of staff objected strongly; it seemed senseless to break of an operation that had just commenced and had already cost serious casualties, which in turn would have a strong negative effect on troop morale and their confidence in the leadership. Rupprecht was determined to discuss the matter at OHL, and let the attack order for 7 September stand. The OHL chief of ammunition restricted the expenditure of shells for the 13cm guns and 21cm mortars to exceptionally high-value targets, severely limiting the most long-range and effective artillery. However, the general of foot artillery at Sixth Army HQ released the necessary shells for heavy artillery for the duration of the attack on the Nancy Position.

The *Ersatz* Corps attacked at 0230hrs and reached the west side of the woods north of Champenoux without particular difficulty, with the artillery effectively clearing the way. 5 and 8/b. Res. Foot Artillery R 3 (21cm mortars) joined 6 and 7/b. Res. Foot Artillery R 3 in the Grande Goutte, west of Moncel, while 8/b. Res. Foot Artillery 2 (sFH) displaced forward to the woods north of Champenoux. During the afternoon 10 ED was pushed back to the level of Champenoux by a French counter-attack. 55 *Ersatz* Bde, guarding the *Ersatz* Corps right, was ordered to board trains for transport to Markirch on the Sixth Army left; its place was taken by 4 ED, which moved up from reserve. On the night of 7/8 September, 3 and 4/b. Foot Artillery R 2 were finally brought into action in the 8 ED sector. On the night of 8/9 September, 1 and 2/Foot Artillery R 2 moved into the 10 ED sector. 8 September was quiet in the *Ersatz* Corps sector.

III b. AK HQ set the time of attack on 7 September at 1700hrs, because the preceding three days' experience showed that it was best to conclude combat before dark, giving the troops the entire night to construct defensive positions. Around noon rumours were circulating in the Sixth Army HQ that the attack on the Nancy Position was to be broken off, apart from, at the most, taking Hill 408 in the north and Varengeville in the south. III b. AK told Sixth Army that, in its opinion, the attack only made sense if the intention was to take the Nancy Position, even if the heavy artillery were withdrawn. At the same time III b. AK learned that I b. RK was not going to attack until the night of 8/9 September; III b. AK also delayed its attack by twenty-four hours. Then a request for support arrived from the *Ersatz* Corps: the left flank of 10 ED in the woods north of Champenoux was hanging in the air and in trouble. The III b. AK attack was reset for the original time, and a request sent to I b. RK to attack then as well. The III b. AK objectives were the east side of the woods south of Champenoux, the Bois de Haraucourt and the high ground west and south-west of Gellenoncourt. The artillery would conduct preparatory fire. During the night of 7/8 September the heavy artillery was to be pushed far enough forward that it could support the attack on Fort Varengeville.

In order to support the left wing of the *Ersatz* Corps on the morning of 7 September, which had pushed forward of the III b. AK right, 4 and 5/FAR 6 were moved forward to the protruding woods and low ground west and south-west of St Jean, and, before dawn, 5/FAR 10 advanced to Hill 305 on the treeline south-east of Erbéviller. From 1600hrs to 1700hrs 5 FA Bde and the heavy artillery shelled the infantry objectives, the treeline and trenches west of the Champenoux–Erbéviller–Réméréville road, and then shifted their fire into the French rear areas. In the 10 Bde sector on the corps right, the artillery preparation was so effective that it chased the enemy out of his positions entirely. IR 19 deployed from Point 260 at the bend in the road north-east of Champenoux to the south-west end of the Bois Morel, with II, I and III/IR 19 on line. As they advanced at 1700hrs they took heavy artillery fire, but no serious resistance from infantry. At 1730hrs II/IR 19, accompanied by the MGK, entered the burning Champenoux; numerous dead French soldiers and horses littered the roads, and there was some fire from the houses. With the help of 3/b. Eng. Bn 3 the battalion set to work fortifying the town. At 1930hrs I and III/IR 19 had reached the treeline south of Champenoux at and south of the road to Velaine. Outposts were pushed forward to the north–south cuts in the southern part of the Forêt de Champenoux.

The colonel commanding IR 7 became ill and was replaced by a major, who let the artillery preparation continue until 1800hrs before attacking from positions close to the west side of Erbéviller, with II/IR 7 right, I/IR 7 left, III/IR 7 in reserve, and one MG platoon per battalion. The regiment took weak fire from the treelines west of Erbéviller, which was soon suppressed by MG fire. II/IR 7 did not make any contact, linked up with IR 19 on the east side of the Bois de Champenoux at 1930hrs and sent patrols to the west side. When the enemy advanced the next morning, it fell back 300m to the east to gain a clear field of fire. I/IR 7, with 1/b. Eng. Bn 3 reached the edge of the treeline south-west of Erbéviller at 1800hrs and, in the next three hours, bored its way through the nearly impenetrable underbrush, probably reaching the north–south cut in the woods. 3 and 4/IR 7 became detached and joined the neighbouring units. A regimental order the next morning recalled the battalion from the woods, which was swarming with isolated French troops, to the same level as II/IR 7, where the bulge in the wood facing Erbéviller joined the main forest. There, 1/b. Eng. Bn 3 bloodily repulsed a French attack. During the night, companies from I and II/IR 7 moved back to the north–south cut, and patrols went to the west side of the forest. III/IR 7 moved to the south-west side of the Bois Morel. To support IR 7, 2/FAR 6 moved to the south side of Erbéviller on the early morning of 8 September.

IR 21 was now also commanded by a major. It crossed the line of departure, the Erbéviller–Réméréville road, at 1700hrs, right to left I, II and III/IR 21, with a MG platoon attached to each. I/IR 21 penetrated about 1km into the wood north-west of Réméréville, just north of the treeline, without any opposition, but taking many prisoners. In the open country to the south, II and III/IR 21 took small arms fire from the Forêt de St Paul in front and artillery fire from the left flank. After some back-and-forth movement they took up a position in front of the wood. III/IR 21 was reduced to company strength, but nevertheless threw back an enemy attack at midnight. At the same time, II/IR 21 tried to advance again, but was quickly forced back by fire into the flank. Only in the afternoon of 8 September did II/IR 21, and then III/IR 21, succeed in establishing themselves in the north-west corner of the Forêt de St Paul and push detachments after the retreating enemy to the west treeline.

IR 14 continued to take fire from Réméréville. On the night of 6–7 September the town was burned to the ground and no longer an obstacle. As the unit rose out of its trenches east of Réméréville at 1700hrs, it took heavy artillery fire, but swept through the ruins of the town without difficulty. The enemy trenches on the high ground to the west were weakly defended and quickly taken. The artillery fire prevented further advance and forced some of the troops to take cover on the west side of Réméréville. I, 7, 8 and 10/IR 14 were north of the road to Cerceuil, with III/IR 14 to the south. The rest of II/IR 14 and the MGK were in reserve. At dawn on 8 September 4/FAR 10 moved to the high ground north-east of Réméréville, followed by 2 and 6/FAR 10 at 1000hrs. With their fire support, IR 14 attacked during the afternoon. With I/IR 14 also providing fire support, II/IR 14, which had been reunited on the regimental right flank, advanced by bounds north of the road to Cerceuil against enemy trenches at Hill 246, east of the Forêt de St Paul, taking considerable casualties. Before II/IR 14 could assault, the enemy sought the protection of the woods, with severe casualties to German pursuit fire. Numerous prisoners were taken in the trenches. III/IR 14 (minus 10/IR 14) took the trenches on Hill 246, south of the road, although what it thought was friendly artillery fire caused casualties and confusion. The battalion advanced to the woodline, but at dark returned to defend Hill 246, with patrols combing the woods. 9/IR 14, which pushed into the wood as far as the north–south cut, was surprised by the enemy and almost destroyed. IR 14 had shrunk to the strength of four companies and was therefore relieved on the evening of 9 September by Res. *Jäger* Bn 2.

5 ID had reached its objectives, but now stood in front of a heavily fortified position on the ridge to both sides of Velaine.

Between 1530hrs and 1630hrs in the 6 ID sector, 6 FA Bde and the heavy artillery did their best to suppress the French artillery, but were not successful; the enemy artillery replied with full force, and where the fire from the German batteries threw up dust and betrayed their positions, they suffered serious losses. As of 1630hrs the German guns shifted fire to the enemy trenches on the ridge west of the Courbesseaux–Drouville road.

At 1700hrs 12 Bde attacked with IR 6 right and IR 11 left of the Hoéville road. They had hardly left their positions on the slopes east of Courbesseaux when elements of FAR 8 limbered up to follow. A platoon of 1/FAR 8 moved to the treeline 800m north of Courbesseaux at 1710hrs, and a platoon from 2/FAR 8 moved to the angle of the wood 900m east of Réméréville at 1730hrs, then to the high ground 800m south-east of the town at 1800hrs, while 4/FAR 8 and a platoon from 6/FAR 8 moved onto the ridge south-east of Courbesseaux.

IR 6 attacked with I and III/IR 6 in the first line. They took artillery fire while still in their attack position in the trenches on the treeline 800m north of Courbesseaux and the slope to the south, which increased when the dense skirmisher lines moved out at 1700hrs. Nevertheless, some troops reached the Réméréville–Courbesseaux road in one continual movement. The French infantry on the high ground west of Courbesseaux left their positions, generally in haste, and were pursued by fire from FAR 8. But the enemy artillery fire forced IR 6 to be cautious, and it took renewed rifle fire from the woods to the front. Until dark III/IR 6 held the low spur between Courbesseaux and Réméréville, with I/IR 6 north of Point 244 in abandoned French trenches on the road to Haraucourt. 2/FAR 8 moved at 1800hrs to a position 800m south-east of Réméréville. The two rearmost platoons of 1/FAR 8 were brought forward and united with the third at 2000hrs.

IR 11 advanced, with III, 3 and 4/IR 11 under Major Mexel, from an attack position in trenches south-east of Courbesseaux, with 1, 2 and MGK/IR 11 in regimental reserve, and II/IR 11 in brigade reserve. The advancing troops drew heavy artillery fire, but the firefight with French troops dug in on the ridge south-west of Courbesseaux and south of the Haraucourt road was conducted with exemplary order and steadily gained ground; the enemy position was stormed at 2000hrs, and the defenders killed or captured. IR 11 losses were also heavy. In the course of the night 1 and 2/IR 11 came forward, while the MGK and II/IR 11 occupied the old positions on the slope south-east of Courbesseaux; II/FAR 8 moved up after dark.

In spite of all their courage, IR 6 had not taken its objective, the high ground north-west of Gellenoncourt, nor had IR 11 taken the Bois de Haraucourt. The regimental commanders therefore agreed to continue the attack at 0130hrs. IR 14 was also ordered to attack. Since I and III/IR 6 were badly intermixed, II/IR 6 conducted a forward passage of lines to continue the attack. It immediately took heavy rifle fire and sought cover in the bushes on the meadow of the Etang streambed, lying half in water, 300m from the edge of the wood. 12/IR 6 was committed to protect the right flank against the northern point of the wood and overran a French trench, but since II/IR 6 did not follow it pulled back. In IR 11, Major Mexel's group reorganised rather quickly, ate a meal and moved out at 0130hrs. 3 and 4/IR 11 ran hard into the enemy in the south part of the Bois de Haraucourt under crossfire and returned thoroughly disorganised. III/IR 11 met little resistance and soon took the high ground west of Gellenoncourt, with the burning village illuminating the terrain far and wide.

On the morning of 8 September French heavy and light artillery shells began to hit the battalions of 12 Bde, in part from the flank. The troops hardly had time to dig into the stony soil of Lorraine, hardened by the sun. Since the division once again ordered that the Bois de Haraucourt be taken, the commanders of IR 6 and IR 11 decided to attack again at 1700hrs, together with IR 14. To support the attack, I/FAR 8 (minus 2/FAR 8) was moved to the high ground west of Courbesseaux and north of the Haraucourt road around noon. 2 and 3/b. Res. Foot Artillery R 1 (sFH) had moved during the night to the east end of Courbesseaux in order to be able to shell Fort Varengeville, while 1 and 4/b. Res. Foot Artillery R 1 (sFH) assembled in the wood west of Hoéville, but took heavy artillery fire during the afternoon and moved back behind Hill 328.

At 1700hrs IR 6 once again attacked the north part of the wood, with II and half of I/IR 6 in the front, III/IR 6 echeloned right, the other half of I/IR 6 left, and 2, 12 and MGK/IR 6 in reserve behind the right wing. To the left, 6 and 7/IR 11 attacked the south part of the wood. The French infantry in the wood and on the Haraucourt road quickly retreated, but this allowed the French artillery, directed by aircraft, to increase their fire. To avoid it, not only did the skirmishers of IR 6 and IR 11 push into the woods, but sometimes, and contrary to the intentions of the leaders, so did the reserves. The effect on morale of the bursting shells, coming mostly from the left flank, was increased by isolation in the thick underbrush, which also made command and control more difficult, and together with the approach of darkness led to disorder and confusion. Nevertheless, every battalion pushed through the woods to reach the west side at 1900hrs. Now the troops took overwhelming rifle and MG fire from the fortified position between Romémont and the high ground north-east of Buissoncourt, and the Germans returned the fire. It quickly became evident that the wood could not be held, and, in addition, 6 and 7/IR 11 were being threatened on the left flank by an attack out of Buissoncourt; before midnight the commander of IR 6 ordered a withdrawal. III and I/IR 6 occupied their old positions west of Courbesseaux. 6 and 7/IR 11 moved back to the high ground west of Gellenoncourt, where they were relieved in place by 8, 9 and III/IR 11. 5/FAR 8 moved to the high ground south-west of Courbesseaux, south of the Haraucourt road, before dawn.

To the south, IR 10 was deployed in depth, with the first wave composed of III/IR 10 and an attached MG platoon, which occupied the position east of the Courbesseaux–Drouville road. It was followed by I/IR 10 and the rest of the MGK positioned 1.2km to the east, while II/IR 10 was in brigade reserve east of St Libaire. The troops had hardly risen from their trenches at 1500hrs when they took murderous, and supposedly friendly, artillery fire, which forced some into the low ground behind the position. But 4/IR 10, the lead company of I/IR 10, soon came up and not only stabilised the dangerous situation, but brought the attack back in movement. The Courbesseaux–Drouville road was crossed and a firefight begun with French troops on terraced positions on a low ridge 400m to the front. This position was taken at 1930hrs; the enemy fled. There could be no thought of taking the village until the intermixed units were reorganised. The regimental commander, Colonel Weiss, had been killed.

IR 13 attacked in a broad and deep formation, with III and I/IR 13 on line in Drouville and on the slopes to the north-west, and II/IR 13 positioned 3.5km to the rear on the north-west corner of the Bois d'Einville. In spite of the enemy artillery fire, which increased considerably at 1700hrs, the attack moved forwards quickly. The MGK had taken up position on Hill 285, north-east of Drouville, and provided III/IR 13 with excellent support as it moved north of Drouville, threw back the enemy west of the town, and, accompanied by 4/IR 13, moved north of the road to Haraucourt to the trail from Gellenoncourt. I/IR 13, charged with the protection of the left flank, reached the high ground south-west of Drouville by 1900hrs. II/IR 13 and the MGK were brought forward.

A platoon of 4/FAR 3 had already appeared at 1800hrs on Hill 285, and the other two platoons, plus 6/FAR 3, arrived somewhat later on the ridge 800m north of Drouville. Lack of intelligence concerning the enemy restricted the activities of the batteries. The II/FAR 3 adjutant rode forward on reconnaissance and later brought a platoon of 4/FAR 3 forward to III/IR 10 on the high ground 400m east of Gellenoncourt, and then, under cover of darkness, into the skirmisher line, and opened fire against the town at 2230hrs. The infantry fire, which had mostly died down, resumed. The French defenders of the town, probably one or two battalions, were surprised by the shelling and fled. When III/IR 10 and 4/IR 10 attacked at 0200hrs, they found nothing but the remnants of interrupted meals, abandoned vehicles and other signs of a hasty withdrawal. I/IR 10 occupied the old positions on the high ground 500m south-west of the burning town.

The progress made on 7 September by 6 ID allowed I/Foot Artillery R 12 (21cm mortars) to move to the middle of the west side of the Bois d'Einville in the late afternoon. During the night of 8/9 September II/Res. Foot Artillery R 13 (sFH) was brought behind Hill 285, north-east of Drouville.

I b. RK had decided to advance on the night of 7/8 September. When III b. AK reported at 1515hrs on 7 September that, out of consideration for the *Ersatz* Corps situation, it would attack at 1700hrs, the I b. RK commander decided to attack then too, beginning with his right flank.

At 1850hrs 1 RD received a report that 6 ID had taken Drouville. 1 Res. Bde, which had already received the corresponding warning order, was now ordered to attack immediately. A fragmentary order an hour latter instructed the brigade to make contact with the 6 ID left wing north of the Bois de Crévic, but without entering the wood. The mission was to occupy the west slope of Hill 316, north-west of Maixe, and the east slope of the high ground north-east of Crévic. Then 2 Res. Bde would take the high ground 1km to the south-east. During the afternoon the artillery was to shell the Bois de Crévic.

It was already dusk as RIR 1 advanced out of its trenches. On the right flank II/RIR 1 moved across the open ground north of the Bois de Crévic, with 7, 5 and 6/RIR 1 in the first line, followed by the attached 9 and 10/RIR 1 and 1 Res./Eng. Bn 1. To the left, I/RIR 1, reinforced by an MG platoon, attacked with 1 and 4/RIR 1 forward in the direction of the east side of the Bois de Crévic. Behind the gap that immediately began to open between the two forward battalions, the regimental commander positioned the rest of III/RIR 1 (11 and 12/RIR 1), 8/RIR 1 and the other two MG platoons. As the regiment approached the Bois de Crévic it took increasing rifle fire. Nevertheless, I/RIR 1 took the west slope of Hill 316 and extended the right flank with 3/RIR 1, in order to suppress fire coming from the eastern extension of the Bois de Crévic, and then began to dig in. II/RIR 1 had also taken up the firefight; its left flank, 6/RIR 1, was on the north-east corner of the Bois de Crévic, while the right flank had already begun to envelop the north side. 9 and 10/RIR 1 were committed left of 6/RIR 1. The battalion commander did not believe that he could bypass the wood and, at midnight, ordered an attack. 7, 5 and 6/RIR 1 assaulted the north-east side, but received overwhelming fire from enemy infantry and MG; the battalion commander and the commanders of 6 and 7/RIR 1 were killed directly in front of the enemy position. The troops who did reach the treeline were stopped by abattis and barbed wire and forced to turn back. 1 Res./Eng. Bn 1 was committed on the right flank, first 8 and later 12/RIR 1 on the left, as well as the four MG, but with no success. Towards morning the regiment returned to its old positions on the north side of Hill 316, in good order and undisturbed by the enemy.

II/RIR 12 held the regimental position on the west side of the Bois d'Einville, north of Maixe, while I/RIR 12 had been pulled back to Einville; on the afternoon of 7 September I/RIR 12 was ordered to attack. It was 2100hrs before it, with the attached 2 Res./Eng. Bn 19, reached the west treeline and deployed – in no way prepared for its mission. The first wave, 2 and 1/RIR 12, and the engineer company, in very open order, reached the area between Maixe and the vineyards north-west of the town by midnight, after overcoming all sorts of friction and incidents. It was met with overwhelming small arms and MG fire from the high ground north-west of Crévic and began to dig into the hard, stony ground. 3/RIR 12 was committed between 2 and 1/RIR 12, while 4/RIR 12 was still in reserve. On 8 September the attack still made no progress, even though the enemy was no longer on the high ground north-east of Crévic, because the enemy artillery swept the area north-west of Maixe, the half-completed trenches and the valley of the Etang Valley so thoroughly that, towards evening, I/RIR 12 had to be pulled back to the west side of the Bois d'Einville. In view of the unproductive course of events on the night of 7/8 September in the 1 Res. Bde sector, the 2 Res. Bde attack was cancelled.

5 RD had originally planned to attack on the night of 8/9 September against the high ground east of Anthelupt and south-west of Vitrimont, but at 2300hrs on 7 September the attack time was changed to 0600hrs on 7 September; the preparations and assembly of the troops had to be made in haste. At 0500hrs the corps HQ ordered the resumption of the previous deployment in depth and set the attack time back to 0900hrs. Then the attack was cancelled.

On 7 and 8 September the enemy may have launched serious attacks against the *Landwehr* troops in Lunéville, or perhaps only have made feints, but in any case he had no success. He was particularly active in the LIR 8 sector on the night of 8/9 September, which may have been attacked twice; 1 *Landsturm* Bty/ II b. AK fired 600 rounds. 12/LIR 8, which was committed to maintain contact with II b. AK at Chaudfontaine, threw back a French attack on the morning of 8 September.

After the withdrawal of the second division of the French IX Corps, the *Ersatz* Corps, III b. AK and I b. RK had been opposed by the French 68 and 70 RD. The German attacks had forced the commander of the French Second Army to consider withdrawal over the Moselle, and was prevented from doing so only by the objections of the First Army commander.

In the HKK 3 sector on the Sixth Army right, 7 KD defended in place on the Delm Ridge. The Bavarian KD defended to the left of Delm on 3, 4 and 5 September, with 55 *Ersatz* Bde to its right. On 3 September II/Foot Artillery Regiment 8 (15cm cannons with gun shields) arrived to engage the high ground east of the Moselle, covered by LIR 17. Since the enemy was completely inactive, OHL ordered a reconnaissance in force, which the Bavarian KD conducted on 4 September with *Jäger* Bn 2, 3/*Uhlan* R 2, a platoon from Bavarian MG Sec. 1 and a platoon of 2 Horse Artillery/FAR 5. *Jäger* Bn 2 drew heavy artillery fire, but came close enough to its objectives, at the cost of forty casualties, and was then withdrawn. The cavalry also drew artillery fire. HKK 3 had recommended its own dissolution on 29 August for lack of an appropriate mission, and on 3 September

HKK 3 and 7 KD were sent to East Prussia. On 6, 7 and 8 September the Bavarian KD, reinforced by *Jäger* Bn 1, defended the Delm Ridge with a cavalry brigade and the horse artillery on line; the remainder of the division remained in bivouac.

Right of HKK 3, on 5 September a task force composed of troops from the southern perimeter of Metz – I/LIR 25, LIR 30 (six companies), LIR 68 (nine companies), four batteries and two engineer companies – moved east of the Moselle towards Pont-à-Mousson. The batteries shelled the French 59 RD there, and in the afternoon the infantry climbed the Mousson Hill under heavy artillery fire, were ambushed in the town at the top, became involved in furious house-to-house fighting and were thrown back, but reoccupied the hill that evening. During the late evening of 6 September, the task force attacked St Geneviève Hill and succeeded in the dark in breaking through the nearly undamaged obstacles protecting the position, followed by back-and-forth combat that ended when the German troops withdrew to the Mousson Hill.

On 5 September the Metz reserve, 33 RD, advanced west of the Moselle to Thiaucourt–Pont-à-Mousson against weak resistance. When it continued the advance the next day it met stronger forces, presumably from Toul. It reached the northern works of Toul and Nancy, where it was forced to halt.

Until 8 September the attack on the Nancy Position had made progress, in spite of all the obstacles and difficulties; success was not out of the question. The troops of the Sixth Army had done their duty and not shied away from taking casualties. Although the battle had just begun, OHL was to put an end to it.

Breaking Off the Battle and Withdrawal, 9–15 September (map i)

The first sign of this fateful change in strategy came in the form of another directive on 8 September from the chief of ammunition, who demanded the actual transfer of the heavy artillery shells for other purposes. Sixth Army had just conducted an advance at the cost of serious casualties, and Rupprecht was even less willing to comply. Withdrawing the shells was tantamount to the termination of the attack on the Nancy Position and an admission of failure. Rupprecht demanded a formal decision from OHL, and personally went to OHL that afternoon to press his case.

By 8 September the French and British had stopped their withdrawal in front of the German right-wing First, Second, Third, Fourth and Fifth Armies, and were attacking all along their front. The situation had become so serious that the need for reinforcements was imperative; OHL finally acknowledged the necessity of transferring the corps in Lorraine. It was becoming clearer from day to day that Sixth Army could not break through between Toul and Épinal; indeed that it had not even been able to fix strong French forces in Lorraine. The hope that the French fortress line could be broken by attacking it from the rear was disappearing, as the Fourth and Fifth Armies were stuck fast between the Marne and Verdun.

Moltke therefore decided on the afternoon of 8 September to break off the unpromising attack in Lorraine and reinforce the right wing. This meant a return to the Schlieffen Plan, but it occurred too late and was made under duress; the enemy now had the initiative. The OHL order said:

> Since it cannot be expected that Fourth and Fifth Armies will soon reach Neufchâteau–Mirecourt [west of Épinal], nor that Sixth Army can cross the Moselle unassisted, it is intended to withdraw further strong forces from Sixth Army; preparations are to begin immediately. The additional heavy artillery, especially that drawn from Metz, is to be made available for employment elsewhere.

The OHL LNO who brought this order arrived at Sixth Army HQ after Rupprecht had gone to OHL. He reported that OHL intended to bring the German defensive line back to Metz–Saarburg. The Sixth Army chief of staff emphasised the effect this would have on morale, and the problems associated with it: the movement of ammunition and supply dumps, the fact that the heavy artillery did not have horse teams, as well as transferring the wounded. Nevertheless, in the absence of the Army commander, he issued orders to cease all attacks. At 1740hrs the Bavarian KD was ordered to move north to protect the right flank of the 33 RD at Thiaucourt; it began movement at 2300hrs, accompanied by *Jäger* Bn 1 and 2.

Rupprecht's arrival at OHL naturally occasioned a review of the overall situation. But whereas Moltke was pessimistic, Rupprecht made no secret of his optimistic appraisal. He expected that, in four or five days at most, Fifth Army would advance to the west of Toul. He did not credit the enemy with much aggressiveness and thought their offensive would soon burn itself out. During the entire discussion, the fact that the OHL LNO had already left for Sixth Army HQ with a direct order to stop the attack was never mentioned, nor even that such an order existed; Moltke apparently assumed Rupprecht already knew of it. Nevertheless, Rupprecht was able to wring permission from Moltke to continue the attack on the Nancy Position. When Rupprecht returned to Sixth Army HQ on the morning of 9 September and learned of the OHL order that had arrived the previous day, he was amazed and confused. A request for clarification to OHL did not help: the order that the OHL LNO had brought to Sixth Army was confirmed, but at the same time the concessions made to Rupprecht were acknowledged, with the caveat that Sixth Army use ammunition sparingly. Rupprecht decided to end all uncertainty. With the concurrence of his chief of staff, he concluded that the Nancy Position was not going to be taken quickly and ended the operation for good; preparations were immediately set in motion for a withdrawal. At 1330hrs a telephonic message arrived from OHL at Sixth Army HQ:

> His Majesty orders: attack against Nancy Position is not to be conducted. It is essential that as soon as possible all elements of Sixth Army that can be spared be made available for employment elsewhere. Preparations for the occupation of a rearward defensive position are to be taken at once.

OHL now saw dangers everywhere. It feared an enemy breakthrough between Verdun and Metz, and on the evening of 9 September instructed Sixth Army to send all possible units to Metz as quickly as possible, if necessary by night march. I b. AK was ordered to break off its rail move and assemble south-west of the city. The *Landwehr* detachment that had advanced on Pont-à-Mousson was withdrawn to the fortress, and 33 RD moved to Thiaucourt (23km south-west of Metz). II and III b. AK and XXI AK were to pull out of the front line and assemble around Metz, while the remaining units held a defensive position along the Franco–German border. The idea of holding on the Meurthe was rejected: the army would be too close to the French fortresses and their heavy artillery. In the Vosges, the valleys were to be held as long as possible, with the final line on the Breusch Position and the Rhine. From 10 September onwards the heavy artillery and its shells would be moved; this rail movement was also not without friction and delays.

The concept of the Sixth Army order on 10 September was to withdraw, beginning that day with the left flank, 30 RD, the Bavarian ED and XIV AK, while on 11 and 12 September the centre corps would join in; the *Ersatz* Corps on the right would serve as a pivot. In order to avoid crossing march columns, II and III b. AK and XXI AK were instructed to initially withdraw north and only swing towards Metz when they had passed through the defensive position on the Franco–German border. The new defensive position consisted of:

Delm to Château Salins (excluded): *Ersatz* Corps, with Bavarian Eng. R attached
Château Salins (included) to 5km south-east of Marsal: I b. RK, *Landwehr* Div. and Eng. R 19
I b. RK left flank to 10km north-east Elfringen: XIV AK with Guard ED and 60 *Landwehr* Bde
Elfringen to Cirey: XIV RK, with 19 ED attached
The Vosges from the Donon to the Breusch Valley: 30 RD, Bavarian ED, 55 *Ersatz* Bde, troops from Strasbourg
Upper Alsace: *Landwehr* troops under the deputy commander XIV AK
5 *Landwehr* Bde was Sixth Army reserve at Duß

The Meurthe bridges were to be destroyed; demolitions on the Rhine–Marne Canal were forbidden. The troops were to be told of the withdrawal at the last possible moment and the enemy was to be deceived by heavy artillery fire. The organisation of the withdrawal, including measures to defend the withdrawal roads and the conduct of the rearguards, required careful planning, in particular because the enemy might pursue, in which case Sixth Army HQ planned to conduct a counter-attack when the enemy had moved beyond the protection of his fortresses.

On 10 September wide areas of Lorraine, which had cost streams of blood to take and hold, were given back to the enemy, at the same time as the withdrawal of the German right and centre. In many areas the withdrawal was preceded by defence against enemy attacks, as here and there French units obeyed Joffre's order for a general offensive.

(Map 21) In the last few days the sky had become increasingly cloudy and, on 9 September, it began to rain heavily, which favoured the withdrawal. On the night of 8/9 September XXI AK and XIV AK extended to relieve I b. AK in place, with the exception of 4 Bde, which held a rearguard position north of the Belville stream, with III/IR 12 at the Bois de la Horne, I/IR 12 on the ridge east of Xaffévillers, II and III/Household R on the slope from the north of Doncières to Château de Villers, supported by II/FAR 9 on the high ground north of Ménarmont and I/FAR 7 on the high ground north of Bazien. The heavy artillery attached to I b. AK was still in place, with the exception of II/b. Foot Artillery R 1 (sFH), which had left with I b. AK. On the morning of 9 September the rearguard was hit by a powerful bombardment, and soon enemy infantry attacked between Xaffévillers and Doncières, which, along with the following waves, were met by overwhelming fire from II/FAR 9 and the heavy artillery, then from IR 12. The enemy infantry was able to cross the Belville stream in places, and even approached to within 500m of the Bois de la Horne in an attempt to turn the right flank of III/IR 12 defending there, but they were thrown back and pinned down. Only 11/Household on the battalion right was engaged, and the enemy was stopped at 800m. In an hour-long firefight the Bavarian infantry, supported by its artillery, maintained the upper hand. The French infantry suffered heavy losses and withdrew at 1000hrs. The French artillery attempted to make good the defeat with furious fire. I/FAR 7 quickly drove back French infantry that attempted to attack from the woods south of Anglemont. On the night of 9/10 September 4 Bde was relieved by XXI and XIV AK.

I b. AK moved in marching column to load at railheads between Bensdorf and Mörchingen. Some of the movement was conducted at night to conceal it from enemy air observation, and the exertions of night movement was increased by pouring rain. The first trains left the rail stations on the afternoon of 10 September. On the evening of 9 September the corps was ordered to break off the rail move to Belgium, detrain in Metz and assemble south of the town, to prevent an enemy breakthrough between the Meuse and Moselle. The troops were worried that they would never get away from the Lorraine and the French fortress line. At 1900hrs on 12 September, before the corps had completely assembled, it was clear that the French were not going to attack at St Mihiel and the corps was ordered by OHL to reboard the trains and continue the rail-march to Belgium: there was general rejoicing, muted by the news that the German right wing had been forced to withdraw. The rail movement resumed on 14 September. The rearguard, 4 Bde, which had boarded the trains at Bensdorf–Mörchingen on 13 September, had not disembarked at Metz and now became the advance guard.

(Map 24) On 9 September 2 *Landwehr* Bde made another attempt to take the Ross-Berg (Hill 1126), west of Diedolshausen. RIR 70 was to attack from the east. Half of II/RIR 60 (6 and 7/RIR 60) and I/LIR 120 were held in reserve on the Markircher Höhe (Hill 1037). III/LIR 3 was north-west of the Markircher Höhe, west of the ridge on the border, with III/LIR 12 east of the ridge. They carefully moved out at 1000hrs through an eerie mountain forest, led by thin skirmisher lines, followed by company columns and then teams whose mission was to engage snipers in trees. They passed many abandoned but well-sited positions and numerous bodies, mostly French Alpine troops, which was evidence of the effectiveness of the German artillery. There were, however, still French troops on the bare top of the Ross-Berg, nearly invisible, in terraced fortifications, with overhead cover and protected by obstacles. The fight began at 1500hrs; III/LIR 3 deployed 9, 10, and 11/LIR 3, and III/LIR 12 deployed 9 and 12/LIR 12, supported by fire from half of *Landwehr* Foot Artillery Bn 20 (sFH). But it was not possible to gain ground on the bare top, and on the wooded flanks the attack stalled 80m from the French trenches. Elements of II/RIR 60 reinforced the right flank, while III/LIR 3 attempted unsuccessfully to turn the enemy left, itself taking fire in the right flank. II/LIR 70, near the top of the Ross-Berg, took fire in the left flank from the Col du Bonhomme. Towards evening the French artillery entered the fight, and the last hope for success disappeared. Elements of III/LIR 12 retreated in disorder. The commander of III/LIR 3, who was in charge of this sector, decided to break off the attack and renew it the next morning. The troops spent the night immediately in front of the enemy position (III/LIR 3 and III/LIR 12) or on the Markircher Höhe (half of II/RIR 60 and I/LIR 120). A thunderstorm burst over the troops, soaking them through. The attack the next morning was called off by higher headquarters; III/LIR 3 and III/LIR 12 withdrew north of the Markircher Höhe.

1 and 2 *Landwehr* Bde had not succeeded in retaking the ridge on the Franco–German border. The troops cannot be blamed, as they certainly did not lack courage. But it was a gamble to send units created during mobilisation and lacking unit cohesion into the mountains in the first place. In addition, these

units were made up of the oldest and least physically fit year-groups, lacking training and equipment (field kitchens, communications, supply) and, above all, with insufficient artillery. To top it off, they were opposed by French Alpine troops: fit, trained and equipped for mountain warfare.

Of all the German troops in the west, only the *Landwehr* troops in the Vosges were not affected by the OHL decision to conduct a general withdrawal: they held their positions and defended in place. 1 and 2 *Landwehr* Bde had a 15km-wide sector – far too broad – and creating a defensive line was extremely difficult. Until that could be accomplished, the best that could be done was to hold key strongpoints behind security outposts, which left avenues of approach through valleys and forests that favoured enemy infiltration. Continual vigilance was necessary, and required considerable manpower. Patrolling was constant, and in such terrain dangerous and difficult. *Landwehr* Sqn 1 and 2 also patrolled on foot. After 10 September the *Landwehr* men dug in with vigour. The engineers built and improved roads, helped construct defensive positions and lay telephone lines. Rain and stormy winds at high elevations made the work a trial and disturbed rest. Intestinal sickness rose. The enemy maintained a respectful distance, but also occupied commanding positions on the border ridge, with good observation.

On 12 September the right flank was extended as LIR 12 occupied the Markircher Höhe. III/LIR 12, reinforced by 7 and 8/LIR 12, occupied the treeline east of the hill and the ridge to the south towards Diedolshausen, while I and the other half of II/LIR 12 took quarters in Schnierlach and Eschelmer. III/LIR 12 and its reinforcements had hardly occupied the position that afternoon when they were hit by artillery and MG fire, causing a panic in which several companies, platoons and squads fled into the valley that ran from the east end of Diedolshausen. Once the initial shock had passed, they returned to their positions. *Landsturm* Bty 1 was displacing to the Markircher Höhe and had reached Hill 950 south of it when the panic set in, and tried to turn around. One gun rolled downhill, and to make room two caissons were pushed downhill and the observation wagon got stuck. The battery returned to Schnierlach, where all manner of alarming rumours concerning the panic were circulating. I/LIR 1 west and south of Diedolshausen, and II/LIR 1 on the Rabenfelsen (Hill 1145, 2km south), were shelled on 12 September and engaged by enemy patrols. It was quiet at the LIR 3 positions in Urbeis and Hill 773 to the north.

II/LIR 12 held the treeline east of the Markircher Höhe and Hill 950 to the south on the morning of 14 September with 11 and 9/LIR 12, while 12 and 10/LIR 12 were echeloned behind the flanks, with II/LIR 12 on Hill 922 to the left. French artillery fire began to fall at 0630hrs. The stony ground had made digging the trenches difficult, and they were not deep enough, provided no overhead cover and were also possibly to heavily occupied; the troops took casualties. At 0700hrs small groups of French infantry appeared, moving expertly and engaging III/LIR 12 from the flanks. At 0830hrs 11 and 12/LIR 12 on the right flank broke and fled; 11/LIR 12 quickly rallied, but 12/LIR 12 moved at once to Eschelmer. The hole in the line at Markirch was filled by 10 and 5/LIR 12, which was attached, 8/LIR 12 was moved behind the right wing, and it was possible to block the French attack on the right and push them back. Since morning *Landsturm* Bty 1 was north-east of Hexenweiher (1km south of the east end of Diedolshausen) and attempted to suppress the French guns on and north-east of the Ross-Berg, while 2/*Landsturm* Foot Artillery Bn 20 fired on French artillery on the Col du Bonhomme.

During the morning II and III/LIR 1 at Schnierlach were brought forward to Diedolshausen. III/LIR 1 (minus 9/LIR 1) went behind the right flank, east of the Markircher Höhe. II/LIR 1 sent two companies to fill a gap west and north-west of the church at the crossroads in Diedolshausen and pushed back weak French feelers. At 1400hrs French artillery took 3 and 4/LIR 1 under fire; the shells splintered the rocks, which added to their effectiveness. Two platoons of 3/LIR 1, taking fire from both flanks, fled to Diedolshausen and were reassembled there. Later the town was also shelled. By evening the fire on III/LIR 12 had ceased and the battalion took quarters for the night in the farms to the south. III/LIR 1 got lost in the woods and spent the night on Hill 1229 to the east.

On 14 September LIR 1 was also forced by artillery fire to leave its positions. It was never possible to locate the enemy guns due to the commanding positions they occupied on the ridge, the vast forest and their frequent change of position. The *Landwehr* Bde's artillery did not have the number of guns, equipment or training necessary for such counter-battery fire.

On the morning of 15 September II and III/LIR 12, and 10/LIR 1, reoccupied the Markirch position. Near noon III/LIR 3 moved between them. That morning the enemy artillery resumed the game from the previous day, but this time with no success: the *Landwehr* battalions had learned to adopt open formations, move carefully and use all available cover. South and south-west of Diedolshausen, I/LIR 1 put only 1/LIR 1 in the front line, upon which fell the entire weight of French artillery. Enemy infantry established themselves 700m west of the church in Diedolshausen. The battalion was forced to fall back to a position south of the road about 500m east of Diedolshausen.

The enemy was held in check by the few batteries of *Landsturm* artillery. *Landsturm* Bty 1 suppressed French artillery on Hill 780, west of Diedolshausen. By evening it appeared that the French had withdrawn to the border ridge. The *Landwehr* men were exhausted and badly needed a rest. The first replacement troops arrived.

(Map 26) The French detachment defended the Munster Valley and, as of 13 September, the Gebweiler valley. The Mathy detachment attacked the French in the Thann Valley several times; the French withdrew into the mountains. Mathy continued to defend Mühlhausen, with the Bodungen detachment from there to the Swiss border.

In the corps of the Governor of Strasbourg (30 RD and Bavarian ED), the situation on 9 and 10 September was unchanged. The mass of the enemy troops were being held behind the Meurthe and Morte, and the French only sent patrols forward. The outposts of 30 RD on the south side of the Bois de Mandray were shelled continually, sometimes massively, with minimal effect, as the troops dug ever better cover. A forward detachment of RIR 4 on the south treeline south of Haute Mandray was forced by the shelling on the morning of 9 September to seek cover by withdrawing to the ridge in the centre of the woods. Enemy infantry exploited the gap this created and threatened the left flank of *Ersatz* Bn VIII at Le Faubourg, but were thrown back with the assistance of a MG from *Ersatz* MGK 5. When *Ersatz* Bn V appeared between 1700hrs and 1800hrs, the position was secure. RIR 14 also sent several companies to clear the enemy out of the Bois de Mandray. In order to better support the outposts on the south woodline of the Bois de Mandray, on the early morning of 10 September *Ersatz* Sec./FAR 51 moved to Mandray and pushed 2 *Ersatz*/FAR 51 to a position on the road to Benifosse. The enemy artillery shelled Mandray and the troops trying to rest there. Several units received personnel replacements.

Artillery FOs from the Bavarian ED, accompanied by infantry patrols, attempted to set up on the south treeline of the woods south of the hairpin turn in the road south of La Croix, but were driven back by French artillery fire and infantry; the French were also unable to establish themselves there. It became a no-man's land, shelled all day, and again on 10 September by both sides, and also became the scene of continual combat between patrols. On 9 September 61 Bde was finally relieved in place by the units subordinate to 9 *Ersatz* Bde. 2 *Ersatz*/FAR 13 was sent back to Markirch for rest and recuperation. 55 *Ersatz* Bde arrived in Markirch and marched towards Gemaingoutte.

(Map 30) On the morning of 10 September 30 RD and the Bavarian ED made preparations to withdraw that night; the wounded were evacuated and the stockpiles of ammunition, food, equipment, weapons and supply units were moved to the rear. So far as possible the local livestock was also driven off. 30 RD, with 55 *Ersatz* Bde, would march to the south of Saal, while the Bavarian ED would move to Coinches. Rearguards would remain until 0530hrs on 11 September, 30 RD on the high ground north-east and east of Coinches, and the Bavarian ED south of Laigoutte and Gemaingoutte. The Rekowski detachment would move to the Col de St Marie. The withdrawal allowed the Bavarian ED to recall its detached units, particularly RIR 4, II/RIR 15 and 1 and 9 *Ersatz* Bde.

Movement began at 2000hrs on 10 September, artillery first, then infantry; the last infantry began moving at midnight. The night was rainy and pitch black, the ground was wet and soft, the movement went by stops and starts, held up by wagons, cattle and all sorts of traffic jams. The Bavarian ED was so split up that it was not possible to prescribe an order of march, which was created on an ad hoc basis.

The Bicycle Co./RIR 60 and the newly arrived personnel replacements protected the right flank at La Paire (north of Saulcy). The Bavarian ED artillery covered the movement by one last shelling of the woods south of the hairpin turn. The ED outpost line on the south treeline of the Bois de Saulcy, north of Fraize, composed of 6/RIR 4 and platoons from 3, 10, 11 and 12/RIR 4, was attacked at dusk by French Alpine troops advancing in close column and had its left flank turned; the French advanced to close range, but were thrown back by well-aimed rifle fire. The Bavarian ED rearguard was made up of a replacement detachment of 800 men that did not even belong to the division, plus 3/Res. Hussar R 9 and *Ersatz* FA Sec. I (minus 2/*Ersatz* FA Sec. I) from south of Laigoutte and Gemaingoutte. As rearguard, 30 RD placed RIR 11, Res. MG Sec. 3, *Ersatz* FA Sec. IV and *Ersatz* Sec./FAR 80 on Hills 517 and 577, north and south of Ginfosse.

By early morning on 11 September the mass of 30 RD was south of Sall, with a few battalions at Provenchères. The rearguard had moved at 0500hrs and took up position at Beulay; the Bicycle Co./RIR 60 moved last. The mass of the Bavarian ED reached Colroy le Grande, with battalions at Lusse, Lesseux and Combrimont. The rearguard pulled out of the Bois de Mandray at 0900hrs, when it appeared that it would be flanked, though it retreated undisturbed.

The corps commander issued orders at 2200hrs on 10 September to occupy a defensive position on 11 September along the line Chatas–Saal–Lubine, with 30 RD on the right and Bavarian ED on the left; the troops, tired from the night march, would get no rest, and the climb into the mountains on the soft ground cost more energy. The normal chain of command in the Bavarian ED could be re-established, and enough personnel replacements arrived to fill up many of the units that had been amalgamated or dissolved. 1 *Ersatz* Bde was reorganised as a regiment. By noon the troops were digging in; evening brought a downpour and high winds, everyone was soaked and freezing, and there were rain showers throughout 12 September.

The weather also seems to have prevented enemy pursuit; on 11 September the French approached the empty positions tentatively. Only on 12 September did stronger forces reach the 30 RD and Bavarian ED outposts. IV/RIR 4 was forced to retreat from Provenchères to Colroy. 7/RIR 11, on outpost at La Petite-Fosse, was surprised while issuing lunch and dispersed. Several companies of 55 *Ersatz* Bde, to the east of Chatas, were forced by artillery fire to temporarily evacuate their positions; enemy infantry continually crept closer.

To the right, 26 RD withdrew to Senones on 11 September and would continue to withdraw on 12 September; the right flank of 30 RD was exposed. On 12 September Res. Hussar R 9 and Res. MG Sec. 3 were sent to Ménil, *Ersatz*

Bn 58 and 82 and 1 *Ersatz*/FAR 31 moved to St Maurice that afternoon, and II/ LIR 80 and III/LIR 81 were attached to 55 *Ersatz* Bde. The enemy occupied Ménil; a counter-attack was impossible due to a howling storm, which brought total darkness, heavy rains and winds that uprooted trees.

30 RD and Bavarian ED at Senones–Saal, 13–14 September (map 30)

Since the French had closed on 55 *Ersatz* Bde on 12 September, the 30 RD commander proposed to break contact by attacking the next day, which was approved by the Governor of Strasbourg, who saw a favourable opportunity to hit the enemy in the flank. Both divisions were ordered to attack west on 13 September, crossing the line of departure La Grand Fosse–Brafosse– Provenchères at 0500hrs. The Bavarian ED was also ordered to cover the left flank at the high ground north of Lusse.

On the 30 RD right, the 55 Bde mission was to take Senones, which *Ersatz* Bn 82 and 58 quickly accomplished, supported by fire from 1 *Ersatz*/FAR 31. *Ersatz* Bn 84, 55 and 57, with the right wing on Chatas, supported by their MG, began a firefight with enemy infantry. *Ersatz* Bn 56 was in reserve. 2 *Ersatz*/FAR 31 and *Ersatz* Sec./FAR 80 were on the ridge north-east of Chatas. Under Brigadier General Rasch, II/LIR 80 moved to Senones and defended the south-west corner of the town, while III/LIR 81 came up on its left during the afternoon. 1 *Ersatz*/FAR 13 unlimbered to the north.

5 *Ersatz* Bde moved out from Saal at 0400hrs in pouring rain, followed by *Ersatz* FA Sec. IV at dawn. When it had advanced west 3.5km, between 0700hrs and 0800hrs, it deployed with *Ersatz* Bn V and VIII in the first line, *Ersatz* Bn VII and *Ersatz* MG Sec. 5 in the second. The continual rain, fog and soft ground hindered movement. 2 and 4/*Ersatz* Bn V lost contact with the main body and drifted left. Finally the ridge west of Le Rouaux was reached, where 55 *Ersatz* Bde had established itself. The enemy on the high ground at Laitre could not be attacked as ordered because enemy artillery fire, which had been landing for some time on the 55 *Ersatz* trenches, appeared so overwhelming that *Ersatz* Bn V and VIII restricted themselves to reinforcing the Prussian battalions. By 1415hrs they had succeeded in occupying the treeline south-east of Le Rouaux.

When 10 Res. Bde moved out from the area of La Grande Fosse at 0500hrs, it had no idea where the enemy was located, and was forced to partially deploy and advance carefully. RIR 14 moved with considerable difficulty to both sides of the La Grande Fosse–Nayemont road, over soft ground and through thick forests, with II/RIR 14 on the right, to which *Ersatz* Bn 57 attached itself, and I/ RIR 14 on the left, with III/RIR 14 behind the left flank. RIR 11 swung north of Brafosse and deployed in the direction of Gemainfaing. 1 *Ersatz*/FAR 51 and

2 *Ersatz*/FAR 15 unlimbered on the high ground east of La Grande Fosse to provide support.

The brigade did not make contact with the enemy until 0900hrs when RIR 14 reached the treeline 1km east of Nayemont and Le Fraiteux, taking heavy rifle and MG fire from these towns and Hill 620 between them. For the rest of the day II/RIR 14, north of the road, was hardly able to make any progress, and some troops moved back into the woods. A standing firefight developed south of the road, in which I/RIR 14 made slow forward progress. Two companies of III/RIR 14 and the attached Fortress MG Sec. 2 were committed on the left.

RIR 11 also moved cross-country from Benifosse. I/RIR 11 reached the treeline south of La Fraiture at 0900hrs, and was engaged at close range in the thick underbrush by enemy patrols that caused several casualties before being chased off, then attacked the enemy position south of La Fraiture, but could get no closer than 400m. Between 0800hrs and 0900hrs, II/RIR 11, on the left, was on the high ground north of La Petite-Fosse when it took fire from infantry in and behind the town; to avoid it the battalion moved north, and lost both considerable time and contact with the regiment, which was only re-established at 1400hrs when II/RIR 11 moved behind the I/RIR 11 left flank in the woods south-east of La Fraiture. At 1000hrs 1/*Ersatz* FAR 51 moved a platoon to the pass 1km west of La Grande Fosse and, at 1500hrs, the entire battery moved to the treeline 500m west of there, with 2 /*Ersatz* FA Sec. 51 moving forward to the pass.

I/LIR 81 moved north very early to act as security at Le Puid. In the afternoon II/LIR 81 deployed between 5 *Ersatz* Bde and 10 Res. Bde, but was stopped by enemy fire 1.2km in front of Nayemont. Fortress MG Sec. 3 followed, but was unable to climb the steep slope 2.5km west of Saal.

The Bavarian ED moved to the assembly in pitch darkness, storm winds and pouring rain; under such circumstances, delays were inevitable, with 1 *Ersatz* Bde and RIR 4 on the north side of Colroy la Grande, the artillery and behind it, and 9 *Ersatz* Bde and RIR 15 on the road from Lubine to Colroy. *Ersatz* Bn IX would guard the left flank on the ridge south-east of Colroy. The artillery in particular had great difficulty pulling the guns out of position in the soft ground and then moving up the steep slopes; the batteries arrived individually, further disturbing the march of the infantry. Hardly organised, the artillery was sent to the high ground north of Colroy at dawn to cover the division approach march, since it was unknown if the enemy was on the high ground west of Provenchères. The Fave Valley on the left flank also merited mistrust and sharp observation. Therefore, while 1 *Ersatz* Bde and RIR 4 were to advance through La Petite-Fosse to Gemainfaing, 9 *Ersatz* Bde would hold the high ground west of Provenchères.

9 *Ersatz* Bde advanced at about 0700hrs from Colroy and deployed 1km south of the town with the advance guard, *Ersatz* Bn XII. It found Provenchères weakly

held by the enemy, and the brigade assumed defensive positions facing the Fave Valley. The enemy sent reconnaissance patrols, but did not attack.

1 *Ersatz* Bde marched at 0400hrs towards Brafosse, led by RIR 4, minus III/RIR 4 (division reserve at Burg-Breusch) and 5 and 8/RIR 4, which had not arrived. From there it turned south-west, moved with considerable difficulty through woods, up hill and down dale, to reach the treelines south of La Petite-Fosse at 1000hrs. In the town, enemy detachments that had been chased off by II/RIR 4 attempted to make a stand, while trenches were visible on the high ground to the west. I/RIR 4 immediately took up the firefight, supported by 15/RIR 4. *Ersatz* FA Sec. II had reached Brafosse, but due to unfavourable terrain, by 1100hrs could only get a platoon of 1 *Ersatz*/FAR 8 in position on the bend in the road 1km east of La Petite-Fosse. These two guns, however, were liberally supplied with ammunition and fired 325 shells into the village and the positions near it; the French retreated. Around noon *Ersatz* Bn I, reinforced by 2 *Ersatz*/Eng. Bn 1 and elements of *Ersatz* Bn IV entered La Petite-Fosse without difficulty and hauled 300 POWs out of the houses. At 1400hrs the brigade resumed the advance. *Ersatz* Bn I and IV and the engineers remained to finish clearing the town and guard the prisoners. *Ersatz* FA Sec. II and *Ersatz* MGK 1 could not advance past the town because artillery fire blocked the narrow road to Gemainfaing. *Ersatz* Bn II, with *Ersatz* Bn III following, reached the treeline at Hermanpère, but were hit with overwhelming fire from nearly invisible troops in Gemainfaing and could advance no farther than the high ground to the north. Both battalions took fire from enemy artillery located west of Gemainfaing. At 1630hrs 6 and 7/RIR 4, moving down the road to Gemainfaing, left the cover of the woods by Hermanpère and were immediately engaged by artillery and pinned down. I and IV/RIR 4 used the Bois d'Ormont as a concealed avenue of approach and turned the flank of the enemy at Gemainfaing. As they advanced against the French guns, they encountered the troops protecting them and 1, 3 and 15/RIR 4 became involved in an indecisive fight.

On the left flank of 10 Res. Bde, south of the road to Nayemont, the firefight between I and III/RIR 14 and I/RIR 11 against the French in La Fraiture lasted all day. Towards evening I/RIR 14 was hit hard by French artillery. Just before dark the commander of III/RIR 14 decided to risk an assault. 10 and 12/RIR 14 deployed thick skirmisher swarms, followed by 9 and 11/RIR 14 at a 150m interval. I/RIR 14 formed on the right, with I/RIR 11 on the left. With cries of 'Hurrah!' the Bavarian battalions closed with cold steel against the visibly shocked French, and in bitter hand-to-hand and house-to-house fighting took La Fraiture.

Since the French had clearly withdrawn, after dark 1 *Ersatz* Bde returned to Brafosse and La Petite-Fosse and made contact with the right wing of 9 *Ersatz* Bde, re-establishing a continuous Bavarian ED front. In the 30 RD sector, 10 Res.

Bde retained possession of La Fraiture. The French artillery fire died down after dark. Le Rouaux was finally occupied. *Ersatz* Bn V advanced as far as Laitre by 2230hrs, without making contact. 55 *Ersatz* Bde, Res. Hussar R 9, Res. MG Sec. 3 and the Bicycle Co./RIR 60 all marched to Senones.

The right wing of 30 RD and the left of the Bavarian ED were completely unprotected. It had poured with rain all day and the troops were wet and freezing. Many had not found shelter for days. The Governor of Strasbourg ordered the troops to defend in place on 14 September. But since the objectives of 13 September had not all been taken, the battle resumed on 14 September, once again in rain that lasted the entire day.

On the right wing of 30 RD it was quiet, aside from artillery fire. 55 *Ersatz* Bde dug in at and to both sides of Senones. 2/Res. Hussar R 9, Res. MG Sec. 3, 1 *Ersatz*/FAR 13 and Bicycle Co./RIR 60 marched north-east to Schirmeck at noon to guard the open right flank; a force was also being assembled at the Donon, which included III/RIR 4 and RIR 70. For the immediate protection of the 30 RD right, that evening II/LIR 80 moved to Moussey (off map, 5km north-east of Senones), with III/LIR 81 2km to the south.

5 *Ersatz* Bde had no reason to renew the battle. At 1000hrs *Ersatz* FA Sec. IV and *Ersatz* Sec./FAR 15 set up on Hill 696, east of Ménil, and shelled French positions at La Fontenelle, Ban de Sapt (Hill 627) and Nayemont, while 5/Res. Foot Artillery 10 (sFH) went into action west of Grandrupt.

The enemy was determined to defend Nayemont and Hill 620 to the south. LIR 81 (minus III/LIR 81) attacked on the morning of 14 September and was gradually able to approach to within 600m. Rainy mist struck the troops in the face, low clouds restricted visibility and the ground was soft. II/RIR 14 attacked Nayemont, while I and III/RIR 14 attacked Hill 620, supported by Fortress MG Sec. 2 in La Fraiture, but were soon pinned down by heavy fire, especially from the left flank. Nevertheless, III/RIR 14 committed all its companies and pushed to 200m south of the hilltop. The enemy was invisible. 5 and 8/RIR 11 attacked from La Fraiture against La Faite, with Launois as the objective. Although the troops used all available cover and moved from house to house in La Faite, they gained no ground towards Launois, while taking serious casualties. Even I/RIR 11, moving to its reserve position in low ground 800m south of La Fraiture, took rifle fire from an invisible enemy. Only *Ersatz* Sec./FAR 51 was available to provide fire support.

The 10 Res. Bde commander soon asked 5 *Ersatz* Bde to assist the attack on Nayemont. At 1000hrs *Ersatz* Bn VIII, on the south side of Le Rouaux, took up the fight with French troops on the high ground north of Nayemont. *Ersatz* Bn VII deployed to its right and, supported by *Ersatz* MGK 5, drove the enemy out of his first positions on the slopes south-west of Le Rouaux. While 2 and 3/*Ersatz* Bn V held Laitre, 1 and 4/*Ersatz* Bn V attacked south. They took flanking fire from La Fontenelle; several platoons and a replacement detachment with 90 men were turned in this direction. The enemy gained fire superiority and the attack stalled. However, *Ersatz* Bn VIII, in spite of occasional fire from the left, and with help from RIR 14 and LIR 81, took Nayemont at 1700, and Hill 620 south of the village an hour later. *Ersatz* Bn VII took the high ground northeast of Launois at 1600 and near evening the town itself. 8/RIR 11 took 74 POW. The enemy withdrew. *Ersatz* Bn V was concerned for the troops holding Laitre, so *Ersatz* FA Sec. IV was deployed north and east of the town, 2 *Ersatz*/FAR 15 in Laitre; they engaged the enemy infantry at La Fontenelle.

The Bavarian ED commander thought that 30 RD held Gemainfaing and instructed the division to defend in place. At 0830hrs the corps commander ordered him to take Gemainfaing, which 1 *Ersatz* Bde set out to accomplish at 1100hrs. II and IV/RIR 4 were corps reserve at Saal. Three reserve lieutenants were the only officers left in I/RIR 4. It deployed in the woods to the left of the road south of Gemainfaing. 2 *Ersatz*/FAR 10 brought several guns into position 700m to the rear, and 2 *Ersatz*/Eng. Bn 1 cleared fields of fire for them; for the rest of the day they shelled enemy infantry in and around Launois and Gemainfaing. 1 *Ersatz* Bde moved slowly west along the north slopes of Hills 874 and 880 in the Bois d'Ormont, across soft ground and over felled trees, until it was 1km south of Gemaifaing, where it deployed. At 1600hrs *Ersatz* Bn II attacked, supported by a platoon of *Ersatz* MGK 1. As it crossed the low ground and began the climb to the village, it took rifle fire in the left flank until the enemy was driven off by *Ersatz* Bn IV. *Ersatz* Bn I advanced on the high ground west of Gemainfaing, while *Ersatz* Bn III was ordered to take the wooded hill east of St Jean d'Ormont. The enemy fled before 1 *Ersatz* Bde could close. At 1900hrs *Ersatz* Bn II and IV took Gemainfaing, while *Ersatz* Bn I and III climbed the hills west of the village.

At noon reports reached the Bavarian ED that a French infantry regiment had been seen on the Wein-Berg (Hill 966 north-west of Urbeis), which threatened the division left flank and lines of communication. At 1400hrs I and III/RIR 15 were sent from Lusse and Colroy la Grande in that direction, and IV/RIR 4 was sent to Burg-Breusch, with two batteries of *Ersatz* FA Sec. I to the west. The three infantry battalions combed the hill without finding anything. In the 9 *Ersatz* Bde area there were only occasional artillery duels.

After 14 September the positions occupied by 30 RD and the Bavarian ED hardened into trench warfare, but only after there was considerable fighting for local advantage.

On the night of 10/11 September XIV RK (19 ED, 28 RD, 26 RD) began to withdraw. It crossed the Vezouse on 12 September and dug in between Elfringen and Cirey. On 12 September XIV AK withdrew through Baccarat north to the Rhine–Marne Canal, was reinforced by the Guard ED and dug in north of Elfringen, while XXI AK forced marched out of the front line to Duß. On 13 September it moved to Bensdorf and on 15 September, after a rest day, to the area south-west of Metz.

(Map 27) After 8 September the situation in the II b. AK sector remained tense; at midnight on 13 September, during a thunderstorm, there was heavy and lengthy firing in 3 ID and on the right flank of 4 ID, apparently only in part caused by an actual enemy attack, which in any case quickly failed. The enemy did not risk holding the woods in front of 4 ID and the right flank of 3 ID, while on the left flank of 3 ID he did try to hold the high ground on the north side of the Mortagne, east of Gerbéviller. IR 18 disrupted the French at every opportunity and pushed them back when they got too close. The artillery duel continued, and the artillery also fired on real or imagined enemy infantry attacks. The French artillery had fire superiority because they had more shells, during rapid fire the French guns did not throw up dust, and the French changed their gun positions and used dummy positions to avoid air reconnaissance and counter-battery fire.

The II b. AK withdrawal was particularly difficult. The troops were in close contact with the enemy and had the Meurthe and its broad valley to the rear; it was necessary to form march columns quickly, and they would have to concentrate at a few bridges. They then had to traverse an extensive forest and, after a short march, cross the Vezouse. In addition to the permanent Meurthe bridges, the engineers built six pontoon bridges across the breadth of the corps sector, plus a number of footbridges behind the centre.

An attack at 1930hrs against IR 17 and IR 18 on the 3 ID left, which was easily thrown back, did not disturb the withdrawal. Rainy weather, which brought pitch darkness, concealed all movement from the enemy, but the rain-softened ground meant that the artillerymen had great difficulty pulling the guns out of their positions; horses broke down and guns and wagons sank in the mud or overturned. Obstacles, especially in the woods, could be only cleared with the help of the infantry, preventing serious loss of equipment.

The Guard ED, in close contact with the enemy, moved first at noon on 11 September. 3 and 4 ID began moving their main bodies at 1800hrs to bivouac areas north-east and east of Lunéville, which were often reached deep into the night or early the next morning. The rearguards, in the old positions, began to withdraw at 2000hrs, beginning with 3 ID. Once north of the Meurthe they destroyed the bridges.

After a short rest the main bodies began movement at 0430hrs, with 4 ID to the north half of the area between Duß and Château Salins, and 3 ID the south. The march was stop-and-go; frequently there were two and even three march columns on the road, which blocked it up. It was not possible to avoid march columns crossing each other. The 3 ID route led through the Forêt de Parroy, and although it had been reconnoitred, it was so rain-softened that 3 ID had to put some of its vehicles on 4 ID's roads. Where the road crossed the border, it was so soft and torn up that the guns and wagons had to be brought forward individually, with great exertions and loss of time. The rearguard moved out of their positions north of the Meurthe at 0530hrs, the same time that I b. RK left Lunéville, and set up again near the border south of Duß. The Guard ED was detached and put under the operational control of XIV AK. On 12 September the enemy artillery shelled the empty positions south of the Meurthe, but either did not follow or did so carefully and at a great distance.

On 13 September 4 ID conducted a generally comfortable route march to Han, with 3 ID behind it bivouacking to the south-east, though forming a single column led to conflicting routes of march and more friction. The 3 ID rearguard passed through I b. RK near the border and rejoined their parent units; the 4 ID rearguard did not get the withdrawal order and remained in place until 1700hrs, forcing it to march until midnight just to reach the previous day's bivouac area. In spite of the long marches, morale was good. Nevertheless, the recently joined replacement personnel fell out of the march in large numbers. A part of 3 ID marched past the King of Bavaria. 14 September was a well-earned rest day. On 15 September the corps reached the area east of Metz.

(Maps 28, 29) I b. RK spent 9–11 September preparing for the withdrawal, moving back supply dumps and wounded and taking down telephone lines. The most painful task was leaving a number of non-transportable wounded in Lunéville. The combat and field trains were moving on the same roads as the combat troops of III b. AK, so that it was not always possible, in the rainy weather, to bivouac under a roof. Work in the front-line positions was reduced as much as possible. The enemy artillery remained alert and active, but casualties were reduced to the degree that the troops learned to protect themselves. The Bavarian artillery returned the French fire. The wet weather damaged the trenches and caused intestinal problems. On 10 September the first personnel replacements arrived, and the heavy artillery began to move off.

On 11 September officers from I b. RK and Eng. R 19 began to reconnoitre the new defensive positions from Château Salins to the south-east of Marsal. The withdrawal began that afternoon, beginning with the battalions in reserve at Crion, Sionviller and north of Chanteheux, their place being taken by 4 ID units. The 5 RD battalions in reserve moved to Bauzemont–Bathelémont, under the 9 Res. Bde commander; that afternoon and evening the battalions in support, plus RFAR 5, occupied an assembly area from Bonviller to Jolivet, where they would become rearguard on 12 September. I b. RD released RIR 12 at noon on 11 September to Valhey. During the night II/RIR 2 dug in a delaying position at the south end of the Bois d'Einville, while I and III/RIR 2 occupied the old trenches on the Einville–La Rochelle road. RFAR 1 pulled back to Bauzemont and Valhey that evening. RIR 1 was attached to 6 ID and moved back to the bend in the road 1.5km east of Drouville, where it dug in, in the dark and rain and at the wrong place. The *Landwehr* Div., except Brigade Reichlin in Lunéville, pulled back to a position 5km north of Parroy on 11 September. The continual rain and the softened, heavy loam of Lorraine made all these movements slow and difficult.

The forward positions were held unchanged, and the withdrawal from them began on 12 September, at 0430hrs in the 5 RD sector, and in 1 RD an hour later. Brigade Reichlin, with the two attached engineer companies, left Lunéville at 0400hrs. To guard against sniping by the inhabitants, III/LIR 8 lined both sides of the road, so that the buildings on the opposite side were under continual observation; hostages were taken and released after the brigade had cleared the city. The engineers blew the remaining bridges over the Meurthe and Vezouse. The four battalions of 5 RD at Deuxville and to the south moved at this time and reached Crion at 0600hrs without difficulty, where they were released to their parent regiments. The units under the 9 Res. Bde commander held their rearguard position until 1000hrs at Valhey and formed march column on the road to Wich, with the other 5 RD units. The march was stop-and-go in streaming rain, but at 1800hrs they reached Wich. I and II/RIR 6 and I/RIR 7 received the order late, remained at Bathelémont and did not arrive at Wich until late at night. A new rearguard, under the 11 Res. Bde commander and consisting of RIR 10, Res. *Jäger* Bn 1, 3/RFAR 5 (plus 5/RFAR 5) and half of II/Res. Foot Artillery R 1 (10cm cannons) remained on the high ground south of Arracourt and began to dig in during the storm and rain. During the night an endless stream of troops moved through the narrow and crooked streets of Wich.

In the 1 RD sector the front-line battalions of RIR 2 and 3 moved out at 0530hrs and passed through the delaying position at Einville. At 1000hrs another delaying force was formed around RIR 12, reinforced by II/RFAR 1 and 3/Res. Cavalry R 5 at the high ground north and west of Bezange la Grande. RIR 2 and RIR 3 passed through at 1100hrs, with II/RIR 2 and I/RFAR 1 as rearguard moving out at 1300hrs. By 1800hrs the main body of 1 RD, with the exception of II/RIR 2, had reached the area south of Château Salins and bivouacked under the protection of the delay position at Bezange. This did not proceed without all sorts of friction and conflicting routes of march with the *Ersatz* Corps and III b. AK; the march through Valhey in particular was a problem. The enemy did not disturb the withdrawal of I b. RK and, on the morning of 12 September, shelled the empty positions.

RIR 1 was released from attachment to 6 ID at 1700hrs and marched, without having been fed, from its position 1.5km east of Drouville. The movement was detected by the French and the regiment was shelled. It arrived at Château Salins to find that the houses it had been assigned as quarters were already occupied.

On 13 September I b. RK began preparing its defensive positions, with 1 RD south of Château Salins, 5 RD at Wich and the *Landwehr* Div. to its left. During the evening the rearguards became outposts and were considerably thinned out.

(Map 29) On 8 September III b. AK had instructed its divisions to go over to a strict defensive stance. The troops were in desperate need of a rest. They had been worn down by nearly continuous combat for weeks, in which they had been exposed to artillery fire, with little rest or shelter, and irregular rations. Even the outward appearance of the troops suffered. Average rifle company strength was 100 men and most of the leaders were casualties.

But the newly won positions had to be improved, trenches deepened, dugouts and approach trenches constructed and obstacles erected. The enemy artillery fired on any movement, sometimes reaching overwhelming intensity. The enemy guns avoided counter-battery fire by using skilfully chosen and dispersed positions, changing positions frequently and firing beyond the range of the German artillery. Local French attacks kept the German support and reserve units alert and prevented them from getting any rest. It was not always possible to conduct regular reliefs. Positions in proximity to woods were particularly insecure. Firefights between outposts were continual. Warm food could only be brought up at night. Masses of dead bodies made the air foul. On 10 September the beautiful, dry autumn weather was replaced by rain, turning the clay of Lorraine into heavy mud, which stuck to everything, hindering movement and the functioning of weapons.

Every enemy attack failed in the face of alert III b. AK infantry. Artillery pieces were brought directly behind the trenches, but drew counter-fire that landed on both, and the infantry often asked the guns to cease fire. On the night of 10/11 September the forward guns of I and 5/FAR 8 were returned to their previous positions in the rear.

It was not clear to 5 ID that higher HQ intended to withdraw, and on 9 September it conducted a reconnaissance in force, with half of II/IR 19 (5 and 7/IR 19) reinforced by two MG platoons attacking the Forester's House (M. F. on the map, 700m west of Champenoux) from the west, while 10 and 11/IR 19, with a MG platoon, would attack from the south. 5 and 7/IR 19 succeeded in taking the Forester's House, but took overwhelming rifle fire from French infantry in trees, behind impenetrable undergrowth and abbatis on the other side of the forest road. When artillery fire began to fall at 1400hrs, they were forced to retreat. The operation had cost IR 19 extraordinarily heavy casualties.

The 6 ID far left flank, west of Drouville, was the target of French attacks. At noon on 11 September II and III/IR 13, in trenches west and south-west of the town, bloodily repulsed two strong French attacks, with the help of the MGK and a counter-attack on the left flank by I/IR 13, which in turn took casualties from flanking fire from the Bois de Crévic. Enemy artillery fire landed on IR 13 the entire day and brought heavy casualties. The day proceeded similarly for IR 10. III/IR 10, in positions south-west of Gellenoncourt, and supported by II/IR 10, successfully threw back an enemy attack. On 10 September French infantry established themselves a short distance in front of the II/IR 10 trench on the high ground north-west of Gellenoncourt, but the next night II/IR 10 drove most of them out, with the rest eliminated by MG fire the following morning.

A platoon of 13cm guns from 4/Res. Foot Artillery R 10 moved on the night of 9/10 September to positions close to the north-west side of Rémeréville to shell Nancy, in order to make the French believe the attack was to continue.

In the 5 ID sector, Res. *Jäger* Bn 2, on the east side of the Forêt de St Paul, with two platoons from 1/FAR 10 directly to the rear, were the object of French fire and small attacks. The guns were engaged on 11 September by a French battery moved into close range in the Bois de Haraucourt and were shot to pieces. The same fate met 6/FAR 10 and the last platoon of 1/FAR 10 on the high ground north-west of Rémeréville. Right of Res. *Jäger* Bn 2, in or near the Bois de Champenoux, IR 21, 7 and 19 received continual French attention. At noon on 11 September II/IR 19 in Champenoux village threw back a French attack with unusually heavy casualties.

The enemy attacks were probably made to feign a threat or gather intelligence. The impression the troops gained after 8 September was that the enemy was employing second-rate troops at Nancy and had already transferred strong forces from this front.

On the night of 9/10 September the artillery without organic horses teams was pulled out of position and transported to Wich, then Château Salins, where they were loaded on trains, overtaxing the rail system and causing friction and delays.

At 2200hrs on 11 September III b. AK pulled out of its positions, bought with rivers of blood, and withdrew to a line from both sides of Erbéviller—Bois St Libaire—high ground south of St Libaire. The dark, rainy night concealed the movement, but the softened, torn-up ground caused problems, especially for the artillery. Since the movement had been kept secret until the last minute, masses of munitions, equipment, dead and wounded had to be left behind and provided the enemy with 'proof' of a great a victory. 1/FAR 10 had to leave behind two shot-up guns and several vehicles. The enemy hardly noticed the withdrawal.

Early on 12 September the main body moved in the direction of Château Salins. At 1630hrs the rearguards left the previous day's positions, sometimes earlier than the planned time set at 2100hrs. Until the I b. RK defensive positions were reached, the movement was cross-country and deployed. Beyond I b. RK, the divisions each formed a march column. Stops and starts were caused by other units on the march route, and by insufficient numbers of Selle bridges, steep hills and last-minute decisions by unit leaders. Château Salins was jammed. The troops reached their bivouac areas (5 ID 6km north-east of Château Salins, 6 ID 3-4km north) late at night or near morning, wet and cold. The enemy followed the rearguard on 12 September too late and carefully.

On 13 September 5 ID moved to 5km of the south-east side of the Metz fortress line. The units marched with their combat trains, but had to move on a single road. This combination was slower and less fluid than collecting the trains together, and once again the troops bivouacked late and exhausted. On 14 September the corps entered Metz behind the unit bands; the population showered the troops with gifts. The corps bivouacked on the old St Privat battlefield, west of Metz, for several days' rest. The march had been a trial for the troops; lassitude and indifference had risen to an alarming degree, while clothing and equipment had suffered from the wet and dirt.

The *Ersatz* Corps had the last and shortest movement to make; on the night of 11/12 September it pulled back to Delm–Château Salins. On 12 September Fort Manonviller was blown up.

5 *Landwehr* Bde arrived at Zweibrücken on 13 August and preformed rear-area security duties, principally guarding the railways, especially the Zabern–Saarburg line. It also conducted training, helped bring in the harvest, guarded prisoners, transported wounded and policed up battlefields, burying hundreds of decomposing bodies, mostly French, near Duß, backhauling ammunition from Manonviller and then pulling anything useful out of the fort before it was blown up. After 14 September it was put in the line.

Between 9 and 11 September the French attacked in conformity with Joffre's order for a general offensive. The French recognised early that the Germans were withdrawing, and intended to vigorously pursue, but their caution prevented them from doing so. The enemy also thinned out his front at Nancy. On 11 September XIII Corps was sent north of Paris and replaced by the Épinal reserve (71 RD). The French put their *Schwerpunkt* in Lorraine between Toul and Verdun, where they feared the Germans might try to break through, which is the same thing the Germans feared that the French would do.

Crown Prince Rupprecht moved his HQ to Metz on 14 September. Subsequently, orders were received to transfer II b. and XXI AK, then XIV RK and XIV AK. III b. AK, the Bavarian KD, V AK and 33 RD were formed into an army with the mission of breaking through between Verdun and Toul. Command of the troops between Metz and the Vosges was given to General Freiherr von Falkenhausen; Sixth Army HQ was available for reassignment.

The Sixth Army troops did not feel that they had been defeated. They had beaten the French in the open field and thrown them back to their fortress line. That they had not broken through this line was not their doing; they had not been given the means to do so. They were, however, happy to leave Lorraine, the French fortress line and its heavy artillery.

Casualties

It is difficult to establish Bavarian losses in Lorraine. The first casualty reports were incomplete, and often lacked an accurate date. Some casualties were reported months after they occurred, and this was especially the case for the wounded. Assigning numbers of casualties to each battle or unit is therefore a questionable undertaking. The best approach is to list the number of dead for the time frame from the commencement of hostilities to 15 September for representative units, chosen because their level of combat and losses could be assumed to reflect the average for that type of unit. Those still missing were counted as dead. This would allow, by extension, an estimate of total Bavarian casualties. Experience showed that there were three times as many wounded as dead. The data was provided by the Bavarian branch of Central Office for Casualties and War Graves.

	Dead				Total estimated casualties including wounded rounded off
	Officers	NCOs	Enlisted	Total	
3 ID					
IR 17	12	37	412	461	1,800
IR 18	11	46	379	436	1,700
IR 22	14	39	455	508	2,000
IR 23	14	42	378	434	1,700
Chevauleger R 3	–	2	9	11	40
FAR 5	3	8	44	55	200
FAR 12	1	4	43	48	200
1 + 3/Eng. Bn	2	5	10	17	60
Total	57	183	1,730	1,970	7,700
1 RD					
RIR 1	6	32	205	243	1,000
RIR 2	10	34	231	275	1,100
RIR 3	4	16	167	187	750
RIR 4	5	32	228	265	1,100
RFAR 1	–	2	12	14	50
Total	25	116	843	984	4,000

Table continued on next page.

	Dead				Total estimated casualties including wounded rounded off
	Officers	NCOs	Enlisted	Total	
1 *Landwehr* Bde					
LIR 1	1	13	102	116	450
LIR 2	5	15	203	223	900
Total	6	28	305	339	1,350
1 *Ersatz* Bde					
Ersatz Bn I	3	10	85	98	400
Ersatz Bn II	2	11	144	157	600
Ersatz Bn III	5	7	64	76	300
Ersatz Bn IV	1	8	42	51	200
Total	11	36	335	382	1,500

The Bavarian Army in Alsace-Lorraine had six infantry and three reserve division equivalents, three *Landwehr* brigades and three *Ersatz* brigades, so that total casualties can be estimated at 17,000 dead and 66,000 wounded. Roughly 300,000 Bavarians fought in Alsace and Lorraine in the autumn of 1914; they suffered 20–25 per cent casualties. Naturally, this rate was higher among combat troops. The infantry regiments lost 15 per cent killed (officers, 20 per cent) and 60 per cent total casualties. This high rate exceeded all peacetime calculations. The battles in front of the French fortress line (and its heavy artillery) in Lorraine and in the mountains of the Vosges cost far more casualties than in the open terrain of Northern France and Belgium. This raises the question as to whether the mission in Alsace-Lorraine justified such a sacrifice.

Analysis

Two questions surround the battle in Lorraine. First, Crown Prince Rupprecht's attack has been criticised as premature and poorly executed. The correct course of action would have been to have drawn the enemy into the sack between the Nied and the Saar and destroyed him there. Howevever, this overlooks several factors. OHL had ordered Rupprecht to fix the enemy in place, which meant that it recognizsd that he would attack at the proper time. If OHL did not want him to attack, it had to issue appropriate orders or reduce the forces at his disposal; the forces Rupprecht commanded were too powerful to permit him to turn his back on the enemy. No one could criticise the Bavarian troops' eagerness to attack the enemy, or their desire to show the rest of Germany what Bavarian troops could accomplish on the field of battle, and what they had learned since 1870/71. It was generally assumed that the war would be decided in weeks; the Bavarian troops wanted to return home with a victory to their credit, not with a successful withdrawal. OHL had to anticipate that, given Rupprecht's sense of responsibility and recognition of the superiority of his troops, he would be disposed to take the offensive. It was a sin against the spirit of Count Schlieffen's brilliant plan to employ such a strong army, and the army of the second largest German state, in Lorraine, a secondary theatre of operations.

Second, Rupprecht has been criticised because he failed to conduct the breakthrough between Toul and Épinal, and instead persevered in the attack on the Nancy Position. But the responsibility for conducting the campaign and coordinating the actions of all the armies lay with OHL. Rupprecht had argued in vain on 22 August that the mass of Sixth and Seventh Armies be employed elsewhere. He knew the situation in Lorraine, but he could not pass judgement on the overall situation as a basis for objecting to the breakthrough between Toul and Épinal. The situation on the right wing changed so quickly from day to day that Rupprecht could hardly be kept informed. His opposition to breaking off the attack on the Nancy Position, which had been ordered by OHL and cost streams of blood, was based on its effect on troop morale. If OHL had even the slightest inkling that it would pull Sixth and Seventh Armies out of Lorraine, it had no business ordering such an attack.

The responsibility for deciding both questions lay with OHL. It had the duty of issuing clear orders if the army commander was going down a false path. In neither case did it do so.

Crown Prince Rupprecht and the Bavarian Army were only responsible for the manner in which they executed their orders; in this regard they are beyond reproach. Their mission was far more difficult than those of the right-wing armies, and cost more casualties. There were occasional setbacks, which also occurred elsewhere and are understandable at the beginning of a war; the stress of the first battle is immense, even for the bravest. They do not besmirch the honour of the Bavarian Army, and it would be wrong to conceal them, for they serve as lessons for the future. They are vastly outweighed by the innumerable deeds of courage performed each day by the Bavarian troops in Alsace and Lorraine.

Rupprecht accomplished his mission. He protected the left flank of the German Army; he fixed strong French forces in place in the open field in Lorraine; when the French withdrew to their fortress line, it was impossible for him to do so.

The Bavarian Army had the good fortune to begin the Great War unified, with an independent mission. Rupprecht showed himself to be a sober and resolute leader, and the Bavarian Army to be a sharp sword. But it was employed at the wrong place; its mission and the area of operations were too limited. We will never know what such an army, under such a leader, could have accomplished on the right flank in Belgium and Northern France.

The Bavarian Army won the first battle of the Great War. This honour is incontestable.

Order of Battle

Battalions were numbered with Roman numerals I, II, III, and referred to as I/IR 2 (1st Battalion, Infantry Regiment 2). Companies were numbered consecutively within the battalions: the 1st, 2nd, 3rd and 4th companies always belonged to the I Battalion, 5th, 6th, 7th and 8th to the II Battalion, 9th, 10th, 11th and 12th to the III Battalion. 3rd Company, 1st Battalion, Infantry Regiment 2 was abbreviated 3/I/IR 2, or 3/IR 2. The same system applied to cavalry, artillery and engineers.

The Bavarians had only twenty-four infantry, twelve cavalry and twelve artillery regiments, so low-number units are generally Bavarian. Generally the 'b.' (Bavarian) designation has been dropped. Corps are designated with 'b.' (i.e., I b. AK) to maintain consistency with the maps.

★ Denotes non-Bavarian units

Sixth Army

Staff, Foot Artillery R 1: II/Foot Artillery R 3 (21cm mortars)
Staff, Foot Artillery R 18: II and III Mortar Bn (2 batteries each)★
Heavy Coastal Mortar Bty 2 (30.5cm mortars)★
Short Marine Cannon Bty 1 (42cm mortars)★
b. Eng. R
Eng. R 19★

I Bavarian Army Corps (I b. AK)
25 battalions, 8 squadrons, 24 light batteries, 4 heavy batteries,
3 engineer companies

II/Foot Artillery R 1 (sFH)

1 Bavarian Infantry Div. (1 ID)
1 Bavarian Infantry Bde (1 Bde): Household R, IR 1
2 Bde: IR 2, IR 16, *Jäger* Bn 1
1 Field Artillery (FA) Bde: FAR 1, FAR 7
Chevauleger R 8
1 and 3/Eng. Bn 14

2 ID
3 Bde: IR 3, IR 20, *Chevauleger* R 1
4 Bde: IR 12, IR 15
2 FA Bde: FAR 4, FAR 9
Chevauleger R 4
2/Eng. Bn 1

II b. AK

I/Foot Artillery R 1

3 ID
5 Bde: IR 22, IR 23
6 Bde: IR 17, IR 18,
Chevauleger R 3
3 FA Bde: FAR 5, FAR 12
1 and 3/Eng. Bn 2

7 ID
7 Bde: IR 5, IR 9, *Jäger* Bn 2
5 Res. Bde: RIR 5, RIR 8
Chevauleger R 5
4 FA Bde: FAR 2, FAR 11
2/Eng. Bn 2

III b. AK

I/Foot Artillery R 3

5 ID
9 Bde: IR 14, IR 21
10 Bde: IR 7, IR 19
Chevauleger R 7

5 FA Bde: FAR 6, FAR 10
1 and 3/Eng. Bn 3

6 ID
11 Bde: IR 10, IR 13
12 Bde: IR 6, IR 11
Chevauleger R 2
6 FA Bde: FAR 3, FAR 8
2/Eng. Bn 3

XXI (Pr.) AK★

II/Foot Artillery R 3

31 ID
32 Bde: IR 70, IR 174
62 Bde: IR 60, IR 137, IR 166
Uhlan R 7
31 FA Bde: FAR 31, FAR 67

42 ID
59 Bde: IR 97, IR 138
65 Bde: IR 17, IR 131
Dragoon R 7
42 FA Bde: FAR 8, FAR 15

I b. Reserve Corps (I b. RK)
25 battalions, 6 squadrons, 12 light batteries, 3 engineer companies

1 Res. Div. (1 RD)
1 Res. Bde: RIR 1, RIR 2
2 Res. Bde: RIR 3, RIR 12
Res. Cavalry R 1
RFAR 1
1 Res./Eng. Bn 1

2 RD
9 Res. Bde: RIR 6, RIR 7
11 Res. Bde: RIR 10, RIR 13, Res. *Jäger* Bn 1
Res. Cav 5
RFAR 5

4 and 1 Res./Eng. Bn 2

5 (b.) *Landwehr* Bde: LIR 4, LIR 5

Bavarian *Landwehr* Division
(as of 21 August 1914)

Landwehr Bde Reichlin (later 13): LIR 8 (2 battalions), LIR 10 (4 battalions)
Landwehr Bde Glück (later 14): LIR Schmauß (later 15) (3 battalions, 30 August),
 LIR 122 (Wü)★ (3 battalions)
Fortress MG Sec. (Germersheim) 4 and 5 (6 guns each with wagons)
Landwehr Sqn/II b. AK

4 *Ersatz* Division★ (4 ED)
13 battalions, 1 squadron, 13 light batteries, 3 engineer companies

Ersatz Bde 3: *Ersatz* Bn 9, 10, 11, 12; *Ersatz* Sec./FAR 18 and 39 (2 batteries each)
 (Each *Ersatz* Bde included 1/3 squadron of *Ersatz* cavalry and an *Ersatz* engi-
 neer company)
Ersatz Bde 13: *Ersatz* Bn 13, 14, 15, 16; *Ersatz* Sec./FAR 40 and 75
Ersatz Bde 33: *Ersatz* Bn 33, 34, 35, 36, 81; *Ersatz* Sec./FAR 45 and 60

8 *Ersatz* Division★ (8 ED)

Ersatz Bde 29: *Ersatz* Bn 29, 30, 31, 32, 80, 86; *Ersatz* Sec./FAR 23 and 44
Ersatz Bde 41: *Ersatz* Bn 41, 42, 49, 50; *Ersatz* Sec./FAR 25 and 27
Ersatz Bde (Wü) 51: *Ersatz* Bn 51, 52, 53, 54; *Ersatz* Sec./FAR 29 and 65

10 *Ersatz* Division★ (10 ED)

Ersatz Bde 25: *Ersatz* Bn 25, 26, 27, 28, 79; *Ersatz* Sec./FAR 22 and 43
Ersatz Bde 37: *Ersatz* Bn 37, 38, 39, 40; *Ersatz* Sec./FAR 46 and 62
Ersatz Bde 43: *Ersatz* Bn 43, 44, 76, 83; *Ersatz* Sec./FAR 47 and 55

Seventh Army★

XIV AK★

II/Foot Artillery R 14

28 ID

55 Bde: IR 109, IR 110
56 Bde: IR 40, IR 111
Jäger zu Pferde R 5
FA Bde 28:FAR 14, FAR 50
2 and 3/Eng. Bn 14

29 ID
57 Bde: IR 113, 114
58 Bde: IR 112, 142
84 Bde: IR 169, IR 170
Dragoon R 22
FA Bde 29: FAR 30, FAR 76
1/Eng. Bn 14

XV AK★

30 ID
60 Bde: IR 99, IR 143
85 Bde: IR 105, IR 136
Jäger zu Pferde 3
FA Bde 30: FAR 51, FAR 84

39 ID
61 Bde: IR 126, IR 132, *Jäger* Bn 8
82 Bde: IR 171, IR 172, *Jäger* Bn 14
Dragoon R 14
FA Bde 39: FAR 66, FAR 80
2 and 3/Eng. Bn 15

XIV RK★

26 (Wü) RD
Res. Bde 51: RIR 180, RIR 121
Res. Bde 52: RIR 119, RIR 120
Württemberg Res. Dragoon R
RFAR 26 (9 batteries)
4/Eng. Bn 13

28 RD
55 Res. Bde: RIR 40, RIR 109, Res. *Jäger* Bn 8
56 Res. Bde: RIR 110, RIR 111, Res. *Jäger* Bn 14

Res. Dragoon R 8
RFAR 29
1 and 2/Eng Bn 13

30 RD
(as of mid-September)

Res. Bde 3: RIR 4, RIR 15
Ersatz Bde 5: *Ersatz* Bn V, VI, VII, VIII; *Ersatz* MGK 5
Res. Bde 10: RIR 11, RIR 14
Bicycle Co./RIR 60★
Reserve MG Sec. 3★
Fortress MG Sec. (Strasbourg) 2★
Res. Hussar R 9★
Ersatz FA Sec. IV: 1 and 2 *Ersatz*/FAR 2, 1 *Ersatz* FAR 12
Ersatz Sec./FAR 15, 51, 80, 84 (2 batteries each)★
3/Foot Artillery R 14 (10cm cannons)★
1 and 2 Res./Eng. Bn 15★

Landwehr

Landwehr Bde 1: LIR 1 and 2, *Landsturm* Sqn 1/I b. AK, *Landsturm* Bty 1/I b. AK, *Landsturm* Eng. Co./I b. AK

b. *Landwehr* Bde 2: LIR 3 and 12, *Landsturm* Sqn 2/I b. AK, *Landsturm* Eng. Co. 2/I b. AK

60 *Landwehr* Bde★: LIR 60 (2 battalions) LIR 99 (3 battalions), *Landwehr* Sqn/ XIV AK

55 *Landwehr* Bde★: LIR 40 and 109 (3 battalions each)

LIR 110 (3 battalions), *Landwehr* Sqn 2/XIV AK, Wü *Landwehr* Bty/XIII AK, *Ersatz* Sec./FAR 31 (2 batteries)

Bavarian *Ersatz* Division
8 battalions, 2/3 squadron, 9 light batteries, 2 engineer companies

b. *Ersatz* FA Sec. I, II (3 7.7cm batteries each) III (3 10.5cm howitzer batteries)
2 *Ersatz* engineer companies
b. *Ersatz* Bde 1: b. *Ersatz* Bn I, II, III, IV, b. MGK 1, *Ersatz* Cavalry Sec./I b. AK

(1/3 squadron)

b. *Ersatz* Bde 9: b. *Ersatz* Bn IX, X, XI, XII, *Ersatz* MGK 9, *Ersatz* Cavalry Sec./ III b. AK (1/3 squadron)

Guard *Ersatz* Division★
15 battalions, 1 squadron, 12 light batteries, 2 engineer companies

Guard *Ersatz* Bde 1: Guard *Ersatz* Bn 1, 2, 3, 4, 5, 6

Ersatz Bde 5: *Ersatz* Bn 5, 6, 7, 8

Ersatz Bde 17: *Ersatz* Bn 17, 18, 19, 20, 77

Each brigade included 1/3 *Ersatz* cavalry squadron and 2 *Ersatz* artillery sections with 2 batteries each. The Guard *Ersatz* Bde and 5 *Ersatz* Bde included an *Ersatz* engineer company

19 *Ersatz* Division★

Ersatz Bde 21: *Ersatz* Bn 21, 22, 23, 24, 78

(Saxon) *Ersatz* Bde 45: *Ersatz* Bn 45, 46, 63, 64

(Saxon) *Ersatz* Bde 47: *Ersatz* Bn 47, 48, 88, 89

Each brigade included 1/3 *Ersatz* cavalry squadron and 2 *Ersatz* artillery sections with 2 batteries each. 45 and 47 *Ersatz* Bde included an *Ersatz* engineer company

55 *Ersatz* Bde★: *Ersatz* Bn 55, 56, 57, 58, 82, 84, two MG platoons, 1/3 *Ersatz* cavalry squadron, two *Ersatz* batteries

On 18 August reinforced by LIR 119, *Ersatz* Sec./FAR 31 and 2 *Landwehr* batteries. When unit was transferred to Lorraine on 27 August LIR 119 and the *Landwehr* batteries were detached

HKK 3★

Jäger Bn 1 and 2

Bavarian Cavalry Division
24 squadrons, 3 horse artillery batteries,

Cavalry Bde 1: Heavy Cavalry R 1, Heavy Cavalry R 2

Cavalry Bde 4: *Uhlan* R 1; *Uhlan* R 2

Cavalry Bde 5: *Chevauleger* R 1, *Chevauleger* R 6

MG Sec. 1

Horse Artillery Sec./FAR 5

7 KD★

(Wü) Cavalry Bde 26: Dragoon R 25, Dragoon R 26
Cavalry Bde 30: Dragoon R 15, Dragoon R 9
Cavalry Bde 42: *Uhlan R 11, Uhlan R 15*
MG Sec. 3
Horse Artillery Sec./FAR 15

(Saxon) 8 KD★

(Saxon) Cavalry Bde 23: Saxon Guard Cavalry R, *Uhlan R 17*
Cavalry Bde 38: *Jäger zu Pferde 2, Jäger zu Pferde 6*
(Saxon) Cavalry Bde 40: *Carabiner R, Uhlan R 21*
MG Sec. 8
Horse Artillery Sec./FAR 12

33 RD
(Metz mobile reserve)

8 Bde: IR 4, IR 8, Res. MG Sec. 2
66 Res. Bde★: RIR 67, RIR 130 (4 battalions), Fortress MG Sec. (Metz) 12 and 14
Res. Hussar R 2 (2 squadrons)★
Ersatz Sec./FAR 33, 34, 69, 70 (2 batteries each)★
Res. Foot Artillery R 2 (sFH) (8 batteries)
4/Eng. Bn 22★

Notes

1 See Translator/Editor Preface.
2 *Reichsarchiv, Der Weltkrieg, Band I, Die Grenzschlachten im Westen* (Berlin, 1925); *Band III, Der Marnefeldzug. Von Der Sambre bis zur Marne* (Berlin, 1926); *Band IV, Der Marnefeldzug. Die Schlacht* (Berlin, 1926).
3 Ministère de la Guerre, *Les Armées Françaises dans la Grande Guerre*, tome I, vols 1 and 2 and *Annexes* (Paris, 1923−5).
4 Dubois, *Deux ans de Commandemment sur le Front de France. I Le 9e Corps.* Palat *La Grande Guerre sur la Front Occidental.*
5 German place names are used in Alsace-Lorraine in order to correspond to the Bavarian maps. Locations not on Bavarian maps use French place names to allow them to be found on modern maps.
6 Each infantry regiment had three battalions (with four companies) and an MGK.
7 Most cavalry regiments had five squadrons; *Cheveauleger* R 2, 4 and 7 had only four squadrons.
8 Each artillery regiment had two field artillery sections (*Abteilung*). Each section had three batteries, each battery had six guns. Most batteries were equipped with the M 96 n/A 7.7cm cannon, but in each corps there was one section equipped with the M 98 10.5cm light howitzer, for a total of eighteen light howitzer batteries.
9 Excepting the Prussian system of one-year volunteer officer candidates.
10 Army Inspectorates became Army Headquarters in wartime, but their armies in wartime did not necessarily include the corps they inspected in peacetime. The Fourth Army Inspectorate was the Bavarian Army (plus III

AK) in peacetime and became the Sixth Army in wartime, including all four Bavarian corps and XXI AK. The Second Army Inspectorate in Berlin was similar, including the Guard and both Saxon corps in peacetime and, as Third Army, all three Saxon corps in wartime.

11 Bavaria adopted universal conscription in 1868.

12 Conscripts had an initial eight-year obligation with the active army, generally from the completion of their 20th year to the completion of the 28th year. As of 1905 this meant infantrymen served two years with the active army, and were 'on leave' from the army for the next six years as reservists. Cavalrymen served three years in the active army. For the next five years they were assigned to the *Landwehr* I Class, which had a drill requirement, then to the *Landwehr* II Class, which had no drill requirement, until they reached the end of their 39th year. They then joined the *Landsturm* until the end of their 45th year.

13 German peacetime infantry companies had a present-for-duty strength of around 100–150.

14 Each *Ersatz* brigade was composed of four *Ersatz* infantry battalions, a cavalry section and four artillery batteries. There were also two engineer squadrons. There were no division troops whatsoever (no ammunition, medical, ration, signal or supply units) and the infantry did not have field kitchens.

15 Each Replacement Battalion consisted of four companies, two of which were used to form the brigade *Ersatz* battalions.

16 *schwere Artillerie des Feldheeres* – Army Heavy Artillery. Three battalions of sFH 02 (15cm howitzers) each with four batteries (of four howitzers) and a light munitions column, one battalion of 21cm mortars with two batteries (two mortars each) and a light munitions column.

17 Two Engineer Replacement Battalions with two companies and a recruit depot, two with three companies and two recruit depots.

18 Sec. 1 with Otto biplanes, Sec. 2 and 3 with L. B. G. biplanes, ceiling only 1,200m.

19 Intended to motorise the *Jäger* battalions, but rarely used in that capacity, but rather employed as supply vehicles.

20 No field fortifications were dug between the permanent masonry fortresses.

21 Ulm is closer to Munich (125km to the east) than it is to the Rhine (165km to the west). The fact that the Germans would put it in a state of defence would be a strong indicator that the Germans thought things could go badly wrong. The fortifications around Cologne, which is east of Belgium, were also put in a state of defence.

22 Also explosives, gas for non-rigid airships, fortress tramways, field railways, bridging and the equipment of the Bavarian Volunteer Nursing

Organisation. Further, a list of which rear-area bureaus continued to function (garrison administration and offices dealing with replacements), which were dissolved (mostly military schools, which was accounted to have been a mistake) and which were created (new headquarters).

23 The army also included 128 judge advocate personnel, 81 apothecaries and 18 chaplains.

24 Including field *Ersatz* units.

25 Including two Bavarian infantry regiments and three reserve artillery regiments that were part of the Metz reserve, four reserve infantry regiments that were part of the Strasbourg reserve, and were soon deployed with the field army, and a *Landwehr* infantry regiment that became part of the Bavarian *Landwehr* Division. See Order of Battle.

26 The fortresses also included ten 10cm canons.

27 Plus eighty-four army railroad trains.

28 Deuringer regretted the breakup of the Bavarian Army, which he said would have been more effective if employed as a unit, both for reasons of Bavarian national patriotism and administrative efficiency.

29 It had originally been planned that Schmidt von Knobelsdorf, a Prussian officer, would have been the chief of staff for the Bavarian Sixth Army and Krafft von Dellmensingen for the Prussian Fifth Army, but the designated commander of Fifth Army could not assume his post, and was replaced by the Prussian Crown Prince, who asked for Knobelsdorf as his chief of staff. This may have had unfortunate consequences, as it appears that the decision by both Dellmensingen and Knobelsdorf to attack as early as possible was influenced at least in part by their desire that their own royal army commanders win quick victories. In the event, both attacks were premature. Had the Bavarian been paired with the Prussian and vice versa, purely military considerations would probably have taken precedence.

30 108 battalions, 28 squadrons, 81 batteries (9 heavy) with 468 guns (36 heavy), 11 engineer companies.

31 Both of these units were stationed in peacetime in south-west Germany.

32 2 *Landwehr* Bde at Rheinau, 1 *Landwehr* Bde at Markolsheim (as of 12 August), *Landwehr* IR (Wü) 110 at Neuenburg and Istein, 55 (Pr.) *Landwehr* Bde at Hüningen, 60 (Pr.) *Landwehr* Bde rear-area security.

33 This battle is described in more detail in the German official history: *Reichsarchiv, Der Weltkrieg* I, pp. 159–68.

34 Gerden (Lagarde) is on the Rhine–Marne Canal about 17km south-east of Château Salins, south of the D 953.

35 This is the first specific mention made of Bavarian air reconnaissance.

36 The memorandum was actually written by Krafft von Dellmensingen, the Sixth Army chief of staff, and can be found at the Bavarian Army Archive

Nachlass Dellmensingen 145. A translation is available in Zuber, *German War Planning, 1891–1914. Sources and Interpretations* (Boydell and Brewer, 2004), pp. 231–9.

37 In Alsace-Lorraine on 13 August, twenty-six French active and reserve divisions against eighteen German.

38 It was actually in the middle of Fifth Army, north of Metz.

39 Sketch 4 was not used in the original.

40 This is incorrect – it had originally been intended to send them to East Prussia.

41 A 'division slice' of the support units in a reserve corps was a medical company, three field hospitals, two infantry and two and a half artillery munitions columns, three and a half supply columns, a field bakery, a bridge unit and two engineer companies.

42 Half Prussian, half Bavarian: see Annex for Order of Battle.

43 12 Co. was attached to an armoured train.

44 That the French artillery had a longer range than the German artillery was a common German complaint in 1914. While it was possible that the French were employing long-range siege guns from Nancy, since the great mass of the French artillery was made up of 75mm field guns, it is much more likely that those guns were simply well hidden.

45 21cm mortars firing in close support from open positions – Napoleonic tactics with monster artillery!

46 2 ID (actually, 4 Bde) advanced 14km from Oberstizel to Gunderchingen – a remarkable accomplishment.

47 This was later the cause of considerable negative comment; allegedly, on the day after a great victory the cavalry did not pursue because it was too tired.

48 The troops would have had to detrain at Aachen, as the Belgians had destroyed their rail lines. The right wing was already on the Sambre–Meuse, six days from Aachen. Add to that three days for the rail move itself, and the right wing would have been nine days ahead. The only possible way for the forces in Lorraine to join the right wing was to march through Metz, which, as Deuringer later makes clear, is what Rupprecht and Krafft actually expected to do.

49 Map 13.

Index

UNITS
All units Bavarian unless designated
pr. (Prussian) or wü (Württemberg)

b. - *bayerisch* (Bavarian) retained
when commonly used

Units listed Bavarian first, then
Prussian, in German-army order:
active army, reserve, *Landwehr*,
Landsturm, Ersatz

within those categories infantry,
artillery, cavalry, engineers, others

REGIMENTS

If you enjoyed this book, you may also be interested in …

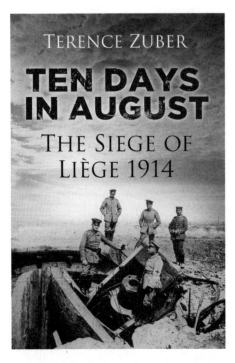

Ten Days in August: The Siege of Liège 1914

TERENCE ZUBER

978 0 7524 9144 8

In August 1914 the German main attack was conducted by the 2nd Army. It had the missions of taking the vital fortresses of Liège and Namur, and then defeating the Anglo-French-Belgian forces in the open plains of northern Belgium. The German attack on the Belgian fortress at Liège from 5 to 16 August 1914 had tremendous political and military importance. Nevertheless, there has never been a complete account of the siege of Liège. The German and Belgian sources are fragmentary and biased. The short descriptions in English are general, use a few Belgian sources, and are filled with inaccuracies. Making professional military use of both German and Belgian sources, this book for the first time describes and evaluates the construction of the fortress, its military purpose, the German plan, and the conduct of the German attack on the night of 5-6 August. Previous accounts emphasize the importance of the huge German 'Big Bertha' cannon, to the virtual exclusion of everything else: the Siege of Liège shows that the effect of this gun was a myth, and shows how the Germans really took the fortress. This is how the whole bloody mess started.